ADOLESCENTS
Behavior
and Development

Boyd R. McCandless
Emory University

THE DRYDEN PRESS Inc., Hinsdale, Illinois

Copyright © 1970 by The Dryden Press Inc.

Some of the ideas appearing in this book were previously published in *CHILDREN AND ADOLESCENTS* by Boyd R. McCandless, copyright © 1961 by Holt, Rinehart and Winston, Inc.

All rights reserved

Library of Congress Catalog Card Number: 78-113496

ISBN: 0-03-089014-4

Printed in the United States of America

3456 038 9876

Preface

Why should there be a psychology of adolescence? Adolescents are partially mature intellectually, physically, socially, and emotionally. Cannot they simply be subsumed under the heading of "general psychology of human beings," rather than form the topic of still one more specialized treatise?

This was the author's point of view until a few years ago. He thought of adolescents simply as a category of young adults. They were worthy of some special mention as one dealt with general psychology, but not enough to justify writing a book about them.

Time and events change one's mind. The author's own children and their friends entered adolescence, both they and he changed, and he watched them face many psychobiological and social conditions that differed dramatically from those with which they had to deal as children, and which were equally different from those which face adults.

At the same time, the author taught courses on adolescence to Pakistani graduate students in Lahore, West Pakistan. He observed that styles of handling adolescence differed markedly there from the patterns in the United States. Later work brought him for the first time into continuous daily contact with Pakistani and United States junior and senior high school students, teachers, and administrators. It became vividly apparent that the secondary school is a world of its own, seemingly even more remote from the "real world" than elementary school or college.

Some years ago, Ausubel (1954), in justifying his own book on adolescence, put the case this way: "The laws of behavior that apply with equal validity at *all* age levels apply at such a high degree of abstraction that they are woefully inadequate in illuminating behavior at any given age level" (p. 4).

Adolescents are no longer children, nor are they adults. A psychology of adolescence must be partly a motivational psychology and partly a psychology of change. It is a motivational psychology because a new drive—the reproduction, or sex, drive—has emerged in mature form, and it is the first new drive which the average individual has had to socialize since his preschool years. This motivation has been explicitly recognized since the time of Freud, and was of course implicitly considered long before Freud. Ausubel (1954) documents this socialization process more systematically than most people who have written in the field.

A psychology of adolescence is a psychology of change because the individual is moving from childhood to his adult role in society. He is not really *anywhere* that he particularly wants to be; he is only in transition. Adolescence is startling because the adolescent must adjust to striking changes in his own body, in his social role, and in society's attitudes toward him and strictures and expectations about him.

This book is about the specific biological, personal, and social changes that affect adolescents, but that are different from those which characterize either children or adults.

The author is mostly concerned with young people from the ages of about 13 to about 18 or 19, by which time most youth have either graduated from or dropped out of high school. By this time, some 30 or 40 percent of them have at least tried college, but most are living without further recourse to the adult dominated and structured world of the school. The author has drawn somewhat but not very heavily on research material about college students.

However, the chances are that most consumers of this book will be college students, and therefore the material in it should be relevant to them. This book should help them adjust to their own past and present biographical status. It should enable them to understand and put into focus the experiences they have recently been through and to which they are still being exposed. Hopefully, those readers who plan to work with adolescents will be more knowledgeable and understanding of their charges and the system within which they will be working than they were before they read the book.

The behavior of human beings under conditions of high drive in circumstances of ambiguity and rapid change is well worth studying in and of itself, so a psychology of adolescence stands some chance of making a contribution to general psychology, and is more than a dependent subsection of the body of general psychology.

The author has had the good fortune to know many disadvantaged adolescents. Whenever something contributive can appear, he has devoted attention to their particular circumstances.

While an author assumes full responsibility for what he writes and publishes, he always owes much to many people. Each of the many referenced authors of research and theoretical papers has, in essence, been a contributor. The author used Ausubel's 1954 volume, *Theories and Problems of Adolescent Development*, as a text for some years, since it was one of the few books available that offered a theoretical treatment of the phenomena of adolescence. Much is owed to the many students who have taken the author's classes, and who have discussed, reacted, criticized, and evaluated. Some 300 of them wrote papers discussing their own adolescence, the content of which has shaped much of the material included in this book. These papers were all coded, and the names of those who wrote them are now all lost.

The author's own children and their friends appear in these pages, well disguised. Young people from many countries have provided insights that have shaped the form of much of the following material. The author has known a rather large number of these young people through counseling situations. Some of them have been constructively planning extension of already good lives; others of them have been and are still in deep trouble.

While the material in this book has been presented in some form to many students, seven Emory graduate students deserve special thanks for toiling through the first draft of the manuscript: Joseph Doster, Kathleen Drasky, Randall Edwards, Lance Hart, Kristine Ludwigsen, William Martin, and David Waters.

Ellis Evans and Roger Williams, the University of Washington and the Dryden Press, respectively, have consistently given constructive support and criticism.

Four colleagues in the field have provided valuable critical opinions and suggestions for organization and revision, addition, and deletion after having read through the entire manuscript: Richard Coop, Elizabeth Douvan, Dale B. Harris, and John P. Hill have all been exceptionally helpful and the author owes them real gratitude. Many others—too numerous to mention—have reacted usefully to sections of the manuscript. The author owes particular appreciation to Elinore O. McCandless, a front line educator, for her help with all sections dealing with school operations and strategies, as well as her work with the manuscript as a whole.

For an intelligent copy editing of the manuscript, the author is grateful to Susan Robbins.

Atlanta, Georgia
March 1970

B. R. McC.

Contents

Preface v

1   A Conceptual Framework for Adolescence 1

Introduction 1
Definitions of Puberty and Adolescence 1
A Drive Theory Applied to Adolescence 7
The Major Functions of Drive 11
Biological Drives 14
Frustration, Aggression, Anxiety, Curiosity, and Dependency 17
Need Systems and Social Learning Continuity 22
Adolescence: A Theory of Change 28
Sex-Specific Social Goals and the Double Code 32
The Major Areas of Adolescent Adjustment 34
Summary 35

2   Methods and Problems in the Study of Adolescents 37

Introduction 37
Dimensions of Research in Adolescent Development 38
Methodological Problems 45
Statistical and Measurement Considerations 58
Reading Primary Sources 64
Summary 67

3   Physical Growth 69

Introduction 69
The Sexual Dichotomy 70

The Body, Social Context, and Self Concept 72
Characteristics of Physical Growth 74
Summary 92

4 Changes in Function and Sexual Socialization 95

Introduction 95
Changes in Genital Function 96
Socializing Sexual Behavior 106
Components of Male Sexuality 112
Goals of Adolescent Sexual Socialization 115
The Course of Male Sexual Socialization 116
General Discussion 119
Summary 124

5 Physical Factors and Personality 127

Introduction 127
Physical Maturity and Personality 128
Body Build and Personality 143
Six Life Stories 155
Motor Development and Physical Fitness 167
Summary 175

6 The Community, Adolescents, and Deviant Behavior 177

Introduction 177
What Is a Community? 178
Community and Opportunity Hypothesis Studies 182
Summary 200

7 Intelligence and Intellectual Growth 203

Introduction 203
Definitions of Intelligence 204
Approaches to Measurement 212
Growth of Intelligence 219
Factors That Affect Cognitive Development 226
Summary 233

8 Cognitive Function: Determinants, Development, Applications 235

Introduction 235
The Nature-Nurture Controversy 236
Cognitive Growth in Adolescence 244
Educational Practices and Intellectual Level 250
Summary 257

9 Youth and the Schools 259

Introduction 259
The Functions of a School 260
How Successful Are Schools? 269
Factors Contributing to School Success 273
The School as a Social System 279

10 School and Church Influences on Youth 285

Introduction 285
Schools, Boys, and Girls 286
Sexuality and the School System 294
Schools, the Advantaged, and the Disadvantaged 295
Toward More Positive Interactions between Youth and Social Institutions 304
The Church and Youth 310
Summary 316

11 Adolescents and Work 319

Introduction 319
Work Patterns of Four Young People 320
Results of Adolescent Work Experiences 327
The Nonconformers 329
The Meaning of Work 332
Theories about Career Development 336
Determinants of Vocational Choice 339
Theories of Vocational Behavior 345
Summary 348

12 Social and Emotional Development 351

Introduction 351
Dimensions of Socialization 352
Cultural Impacts on Socialization 362
Socialization and Theories of Learning 365
Stage Theories of Socialization 372
Summary 376

13 Sex and Moral Identification: Modeling and the Role of Power 379

Introduction 379
Power 380
Mediation of Power in the Modeling Process 387
Relationships between Modeling and Identification 397
Conclusion 410

14 Sex and Moral Identification: Development and Problems 413

Introduction 413
Illustrative Research about Identification 414
Cross-Sex Identification 420
Role of the Peer Group 424
Common Problems of Adolescent Adjustment 426
Summary 434

15 The Self Concept 437

Introduction 437
Definitions 439
An Illustration of the Development of the Self Concept 441
Critique of the Self Concept 445

Measurement of the Self Concept 452
The Self Concept and Personal Adjustment 456
Future Time Orientation 464
Changes in Self Concept 466
Goals for Self Concept Development 473
Summary 477

References 479

Index 501

1

A Conceptual Framework for Adolescence

INTRODUCTION

An adolescent is different from a child because he is sexually mature, or at least he has passed the hurdle of puberty and is headed for full physical maturity. He is psychologically different for the same reason. In large part because he is sexually mature, society changes its attitudes toward him and its rules for him, so that he moves onto new social ground, both in and out of school. He is different, at least until he reaches legal age, because he is not granted adult status.

Adolescence is a bridge period, a time of shifting from one stage to another.

As will be seen throughout this book, many facts about adolescents have been gathered. The author believes it is important to try to order them systematically. Thus, in this chapter, he tries to provide a conceptual framework for viewing adolescence. It would be pretentious to call this framework a theory, as it is loosely knit and is not rigorous. A conceptual framework does, however, draw on many theories, as will be seen. It is useful for organizing facts, and has certain advantages over simply cataloguing them.

First, it helps us remember the facts by providing a useful retrieval system—a guide or index for grouping and recalling facts. Even the telephone directory demands a certain basic conceptual organization: The telephones in the residential directory are alphabetized; in the yellow pages, the conceptual framework is a combination of service, location, and alphabet.

Second, when facts are grouped according to some general concept that fits them together, it can become clear that some facts are missing *or* that apparent inconsistencies must be reconciled by further research *or* that the logical structure of the facts suggests or demands further research *or*, finally, that the theory or concept itself should be revised or abandoned. Any conceptual framework, then, is a way of regarding the completeness and logical coherence of data.

Conceptual frameworks have a third, often risky, use, which is somewhat more of an implication than the previous advantages: They suggest applications and practices for modifying or coping with behavior. Many such applications emerge in the following pages.

The overriding behavioral assumption in the present conceptual framework is that drive provides energy that instigates (motivates, or moves) organisms to respond. A new drive added to an organism increases energy supply, intensifies all behavior potentials that already exist, and introduces new capacities for behavior change and modification that were not present before the drive existed. These changes, depending on the situation and the history of the organism, range from malignant to benign behavior modifications.

The new drive that signifies the change from childhood to adolescence is the reproductive capacity. It demands many behavior changes, some of them sexual in nature, but yet many of them nonsexual.

The new drive demands enormous change in the adolescent individual: He must socialize it and live with it; *he must change*. The reproductive drive is reacted to socially in ways very different from any of the drives that the individual has socialized before. When a child becomes sexually mature, society regards him differently and he must adapt to their expectations.

Adapting is a process of seeking both to learn about and live with the new drive so as to enjoy it while, at the same time, not running into disaster because of it. Adaptation brings four major domains of human motivation into play: *frustration and aggression, anxiety, curiosity,* and *dependency*. There are others, of course, but these areas seem to be the principal motivational domains of the adolescent. As new sexuality interacts with previous learning, and as his social world changes accordingly, an adolescent is bound to encounter frequent and basic frustration, which often leads to aggression. Sexuality *and* frustration *and* aggression are likely to produce anxiety. Sexual maturity, though, is a strong factor in altering the way an individual handles his dependency, and a male's behavior patterns will differ from a female's.

Eventually, young people incorporate their sexual drive, and most

Figure 1.1

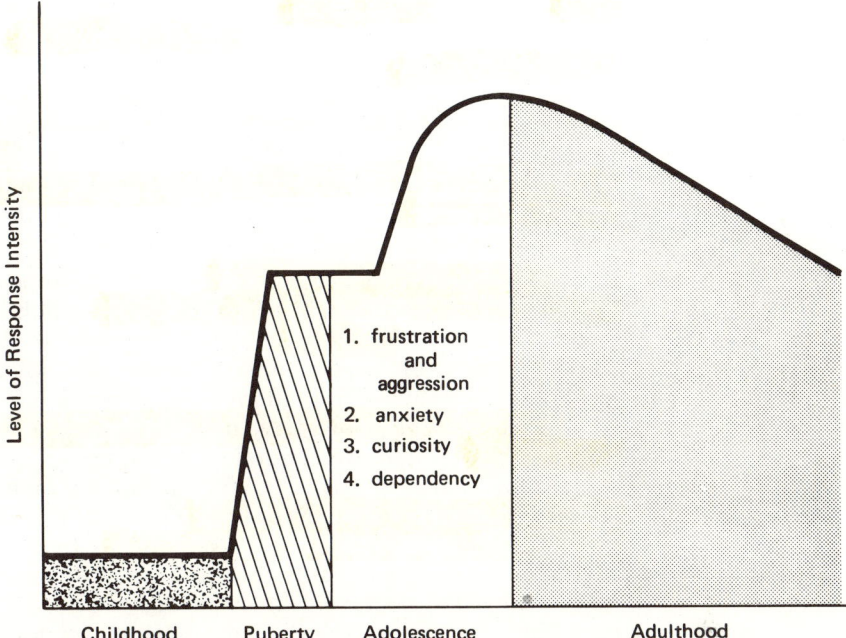

A graph of the reproductive drive of an individual during his lifetime. Note the level of behavior intensity during the period of adolescence. The social-personal changes related to the mature reproductive capacity result in the four drives shown, and discussed in the text.

of them socialize it moderately well. By the time they have done so, almost all will have moved out into the world on their own and assumed responsibility for their own behavior. At that time, they become adults. A psychology of adolescence treats this process of moving from childhood to adulthood and thus must be considered a psychology of change. Figure 1-1 illustrates the initial great change in behavior intensity due directly to the new reproductive drive as well as to its interaction with social changes adolescents ordinarily experience. As the adolescent adapts, the effects of frustration and aggression, anxiety, curiosity, and dependency typically abate, and the behavior intensity curve drops.

Thus, both directly (sexually) and indirectly (psychosocially) adolescence is a time of heightened drive and heightened response. Most of the rest of this chapter is devoted to the implications that follow from such a state of affairs.

DEFINITIONS OF PUBERTY AND ADOLESCENCE

Puberty is the time of the change from childhood to adolescence. The definition of puberty adopted here differs for boys and girls. For each sex, the definition has been chosen for psychological reasons, although for both sexes physiological events provide the basis.

Puberty

Data provided by approximately 300 of the author's students,[1] half of them women, half of them men, clearly indicate that for this well-educated sample, the event that signified the change to manhood for

[1] See the Preface to this volume.

boys was their first orgasm that they clearly related to adult biological sexual function. Menarche—the first menstruation—was the corresponding event for girls. These definitions have been found equally suitable among other populations, for example among Pakistani whom the author knows, and among a wide variety of nonstudent youth with whom he has had occasion to discuss the matter. Thus, while arbitrary, these psychobiological events seem preferable to any other single criterion for defining puberty; moreover, they are as satisfactory as other often-used multiple criteria.

Other landmarks of puberty have been proposed: first occurrence of coarse, kinky pubic hair, breast budding, which has a special significance for girls, or shaving, which has a similar significance for boys. However, none of these events so affects the individual's reproductive drive as the correlated definitions of puberty that have been selected.

Psychosocial factors have little effect on the time of first menstruation for girls, although nutrition, physical health, heredity, and possibly geographical area influence it. While hormonal factors are preponderant in determining maturation for boys even as they are for girls, psychosocial factors do enter into the first orgasm. In the completely natural course of events, it is likely that formation of the first viable sperm is soon followed by nocturnal emission (the wet dream). Evidence suggests that many boys speed the time of puberty by masturbation or other sexual behavior. In *Manchild in the Promised Land*, for example, Claude Brown (1965) recounts how he masturbated to climax at a very early age (apparently at about eleven). His avowed intent was to become a man as soon as his boy's body could possibly manage the event. One can assume that he anticipated his first wet dream by a considerable amount of time, and that this experience is not unique to him.

The average time of puberty for boys is between 13½ and 14 years, and for girls from about 12 or 12½ to 13 years. The variability is great, with many 10-year-old girls and 11-year-old boys having experienced puberty, while many 14-year-old girls and 15-year-old boys have not. As will be seen later, there are apparently many other important correlates with early and late pubescence. Girls who mature exceptionally early seem to be disturbed by it for a time, but there are no clear long-term social and personal effects. Early pubescence seems to be an advantage for boys, at least during their youth and young manhood. Finally, the time of puberty seems to be moving earlier for United States boys and girls, and is estimated currently to be a good two-and-one-half years earlier than it was at the turn of the century.

Before and after puberty there are dramatic changes both in primary and secondary sex characteristics, which are of great importance to the individuals concerned. Primary sex characteristics include the genitals: penis, testicles, scrotum for boys; vulva and supporting structures for girls. There is no obvious overlap of primary sex characteristics between the sexes, although there are many organic similarities. From the social point of view, secondary sex characteristics are more important than primary sex characteristics, since it is they that signify the youth's changing status to observers. There is some overlap between the sexes in secondary sex characteristics, such as breasts, face and body hair, hip-shoulder ratio, musculature, deepening of the voice, and so on.

Adolescence Unlike puberty, adolescence for both boys and girls is *a psychosocially defined period of time following puberty and extending to the time of reaching "executive independence."*

Executive independence is a term used by Ausubel (1954) to suggest that one does things for himself. Ausubel employs "volitional independence" to suggest that one makes his own decisions without depending on others. Ideally, some entirely new term should be coined for the context of this book. The term chosen is *self-governance*. As used throughout the volume, "self-governance" means essentially complete personal autonomy, both subjective and objective in nature. In males, the youth no longer depends on his elders, most particularly his parents, for major decision making. He may consult them, but he is his own man and lives his own life. For girls, the time of self-governance is often the date of marriage, which may also be true for boys. For some boys, self-governance begins when they leave school and take their first jobs. For others, it is the time of entering military service. For boys more than girls in United States culture, it is likely to be the time when they become economically independent. More and more the same criteria as used for boys and men apply to girls and women. Of course, some men and women never achieve self-governance: They remain forever mommy's and/or daddy's boy or girl.

In American society, there is no single formal event that testifies that the stage of self-governance has been reached. Many societies have such an event, as in the *rites de passage* (the ceremony of passing into adulthood, more common for males than females). The formal signal of adulthood is often helpful to the society and its relationship to youth.

No arbitrary average can be set for the time of attaining self-governance. The upper chronological age limit of 24 is set by some as the end of adolescence. Legal authorities in the United States typically consider that adulthood begins at age 21. Still others use the single criterion of financial independence. Vague though the term may be, self-governance seems to be the most psychologically meaningful definition of the end of adolescence, or the condition of adulthood.

Social Class, Sex, and Self-Governance Achieving self-governance is so much affected by "social class" that it is necessary at this point to describe the term and discuss how social class affects the psychosocial period we have called adolescence. Since the effects of social class differ for boys and girls, the interaction of sex and social class on self-governance must also be discussed.

Social class refers to the position of status an individual holds in United States society. An adolescent's social class is usually determined by some index of his parents' status (usually his father's occupation). In turn, a father's occupation is closely related to parental education and income.

The simplest division of social class is into the two categories of white- and blue-collar workers. More elaborate descriptions consider fathers' education, place of residence, source of income (whether inherited or earned), and the prestige level of his occupation. Warner, Meeker, and Eels (1949) use these classifications in their classical treatment of status characteristics. The author uses the following definition of social class, and interchanges the terms socioeconomic status, social class, and social status:

Upper class is reserved for those who have inherited wealth and enjoy the highest social position in their reference community. Upper-middle class refers to professional and managerial families. In such families, the father and often the mother are highly educated (college plus), the social position ranges from being secure to being prestigious, and the family income is high enough that it imposes no serious limits on the security of the family. Some successful fathers who are not highly educated must be classified as upper-middle class; and some fathers with high-prestige occupations (such as ministers in churches that require a high level of education for their pastors) are not well-enough paid that one can say they are economically secure.

The term middle-middle class refers to the great body of respectable, relatively secure business or lower level professional families. The term lower-middle class (often called the *petit bourgeoisie*) includes white-collar people who are "respectable but just getting by." Upper-lower class includes skilled workers. Lower-lower class refers to semi- and unskilled workers and their families. Usually parents in such families have less than twelfth grade education.[2]

There is no clearly agreed upon set of percentages to express how many youth come from each of these social-class categories. But any worker with adolescents will come into contact with youth from each of the social-class levels, with the possible exception of young people from the upper class as judged according to national population norms. It is important for youth workers to know—*without prejudice*—what the social-class background is for the youth with whom they work. Many attitudinal and behavioral variables are associated with social class for *groups* of young people, but not necessarily for *individual* adolescents.

One encounters few upper-class adolescents in public settings. They do not typically attend public schools. Neither are they easily or frequently available as research subjects. Thus, data are sparse concerning whatever characteristics differentiate them from youth in other social classes.

Psychosocially disadvantaged young people are of particular importance to workers with adolescents. They are usually but not necessarily the sons and daughters of lower-lower class parents. The circumstances of their lives and development are unusually difficult from any point of view, and it is inevitable that they have more (and more difficult) educational and behavior problems than youth from other social classes. They spring with disproportionate frequency from prejudiced-against minority groups in the United States culture, although

[2]McCandless (1967) includes a more detailed account of methods of indexing social class.

they include many from Appalachia. Thus, they are likely to differ from the core majority in skin color and/or language.

Approximately one-fourth of the adolescent population of the United States must be considered psychosocially disadvantaged. This is the bottom fourth in terms of privilege and available opportunity. They may be found in urban or rural slums. Their frequency is disproportionately high in the rural South and Appalachia. The largest number of disadvantaged youth is white but, of the copopulations, the highest percentages come from such discriminated-against minority groups as the Afro-American, the American Indian, and the Puerto Rican and Mexican American (Hispano youth). Other often discriminated-against cocultures such as Jewish or Oriental include proportions of psychosocially disadvantaged young people no higher and perhaps lower than the general United States population.[3]

Disadvantaged youth probably achieve self-governance earlier than young people from higher social-class groups. Their families cannot afford to keep them in school. Their family ties are typically weaker than among middle-class youth. As a general rule, the longer the "apprenticeship for life," the later a youth achieves executive independence. Apprenticeship for life can be roughly equated with time spent for education and training. This is shortest for lower-lower, next for upper-lower, next for lower-middle, and longest for upper-middle-class youth. One may conjecture that apprenticeship training becomes shorter as one moves into the upper social class than for upper-middle class. However, a strong sense of family unity and continuity in upper-class families may prolong adolescence for a long time. In general, the more money a parent invests in his child and the longer the period of time over which he invests it (as in continuing education), the longer executive independence is postponed.

Marriage commonly signifies the beginning of self-governance, and girls marry, on the average, earlier than boys. Thus, adolescence is typically shorter for girls than for boys. However, the picture is confused by the male-dominant nature of our culture: Girls, upon marriage, may only be transferring dependence for major life decisions from parents to husbands. However, since the typical United States marriage is relatively democratic, it is likely that a wife has more to say than has a daughter about major life decisions that affect her. Bowerman and Elder (1964) report judgments made by 19,200 white Ohio and North Carolina seventh through twelfth graders about their parents' marriages. Forty-six percent of them considered their homes to be equalitarian; about one-third reported that their fathers were clearly dominant; and one-fifth believed that their mothers were dominant.

A DRIVE THEORY APPLIED TO ADOLESCENCE

The most basic of the present conceptions that make up the framework for viewing adolescence is drive or motivational theory. A new drive—the reproductive drive—has emerged, and it is the first since early childhood that must be socialized by each individual in the culture.

Drive theories are imbedded in learning. Any good elementary psy-

---

[3]This is the author's educated guess. He has no solid data about the matter.

chology text can be used to review the principles of learning. These principles are reviewed in some detail in McCandless (1967, Chapters 4 and 5), and a clear and more detailed presentation is given by Mednick (1964), for example. A brief review of learning principles follows.

Learning A good practical definition of learning is *a change in behavior as a result of practice*. However, since not all learning results in *observable* behavior change, then, for practical purposes, we may say that we *observe* performance and we *infer* learning. The practical importance of this distinction is illustrated below.

It is common for youth (particularly boys) to obtain Cs and Ds in their schoolwork. These grades represent the teachers' judgments of the learning progress of each pupil, and are usually based on performance on classroom-administered tests. Yet, when a standardized test covering the same subject matter is administered to them, many of these young people will score at the 80th or 90th percentile.[4] The teachers' tests are generally less well constructed than the standardized test, and grading and evaluation are likely to be affected by whether a student is paying attention in class, is behaving himself, is studying consistently, likes the teacher, and many other things. From performance in class, in other words, the teacher infers less learning than is inferred by the standardized test. For well-behaved and well-scrubbed children, particularly girls, teachers are likely to infer more knowledge than the standardized test will infer. The chances are very great that the inference about the student's knowledge gained from the standardized test is more accurate than the estimates made by teachers.

An estimate of learning, in other words, is always arrived at by inference from behavior of some sort. This estimate may be based on recorded or unrecorded observation, something written (as a classroom test), or a person's report.

Inferences of learning cannot always be made by a teacher. Since adolescents are reticent and there are sanctions against asking, it is difficult to make sound inferences about sexual learning. Likewise, the average American classroom is a "tight ship" where, for necessary reasons, aggressive and rowdy behavior (and unfortunately very often spontaneous, free, creative behavior) is forbidden. The average teacher is therefore able to make few sound inferences about how students learn to handle anger, or of how well they know how to behave in a free democratic situation.

Habits Habits are established or customary ways of behaving. They may be quite simple and automatic, as in tying one's shoelaces or following a certain order of getting dressed in the morning. They may be very com-

---

[4] A percentile names the mark below which a given percentage of a similar United States population falls. For example, if a girl scores at the 90th percentile on a well-standardized test of physics (that is, one that was standardized by giving it to a large sample of United States boys and girls to find out how well they know the subject, and who are themselves of about the same age and grade as the student in question), it means that 10 percent know more physics than she does, 90 percent know less.

plex, such as how to go about establishing a courting relationship, or the procedure to follow when beginning a new job or moving into a new community, or the approach to a major term project for a class, or studying to pass examinations.

Like learning, habits appear from "inside." They must be inferred by others from behavior or responses. When an individual consistently behaves in a given way, others assume it is habitual. Habits are learned linkages between stimuli and responses, some of which are so well established that they are literally unconscious (the way in which one walks, for example). Other habits are new, or weakly established, and may be quite variable.

The stimuli that set off a habitual or characteristic response may be either inside or outside the person. The mother of teenagers usually has well-established verbal habits, such as saying, "Chew with your mouth closed," "Don't slouch," or "You are wearing too much eye shadow" when her son or daughter presents her with the appropriate stimuli. Her children often say she has a habit of nagging: Her predictable tendency is to make a reproving response to a wide range of behaviors to which she objects. Most adolescents seem to think of most of their caretakers (parents, teachers, custodians, police, bosses, and so on) as nags.

Internal, private stimuli also trigger responses. Every person can recognize the stimuli associated with the drive state of hunger, and, when strong enough and circumstances permit, the stimuli lead not only to thinking about but to obtaining food.

Drive In its most basic sense, drive is the "mover," the energy that initiates and maintains behavior. As will be seen, it also plays an important role in shaping behavior, and the nature of a given drive at a given time determines which of a variety of possible behaviors will occur.

Like learning and habit, drive is a hypothetical construct. It cannot be directly observed, but it can be logically inferred from behavior or circumstances. If inferences about drive are correct, behavior prediction is more accurate. Knowing that an individual has been without food for twelve hours, for example, makes a prediction about his behavior in a bakery more accurate.

In most cases, a response that reduces a drive is more likely to be learned (that is, repeated again in similar circumstances) than a response that does not reduce the drive. However, many activities that increase excitement are also pleasant, and the increase in excitement—adding *more* drive rather than reducing drive—results in learning. A moderate level of arousal (such as tension or involvement) seems to be pleasing to human beings, whereas too little arousal or not enough stimulation seems to produce boredom. Doing something "for kicks" seems to be designed not to reduce but to increase drive (or at least amount of stimulation and excitement). Adolescent boys are likely deliberately to seek sexual stimulation through discussion, voyeurism, and fantasy. Their state of arousal appears to be pleasing, as they repeat the behavior often, yet do not necessarily always follow up arousal by finding a sexual outlet.

Stimulus, Drive, and Habit Interaction

The likelihood that a certain behavior will occur is a combined and multiplicative function of an individual's drive and the degree to which he has learned the behavior as a habit (that is, how much practice he has had in exercising the behavior, how well and consistently it has been rewarded or punished, or how important the reward or punishment is to him). With technical exceptions, a habit develops more quickly and possibly more strongly when the behavior is quickly, consistently, and generously rewarded or reinforced.

Rewards may be tangible or psychological. The most effective rewards for adolescents (that is, in shaping their behavior in constructive ways) are usually social and psychological. However, the adolescent's intense physical pleasure resulting from consummatory sexual behavior (when an orgasm or some way station toward it is reached) cannot be overlooked.

Punishments are negative reinforcements that often but not always operate in reverse fashion to rewards. There is considerable evidence suggesting that punishment may fixate (consolidate, or set) behavior. Certainly, much of the punishment administered to adolescents defeats the purposes it was designed to accomplish. For example, in situations where there is conflict between the peer group and the caretaker, things that the adult considers to be punishment may actually be a complex psychological-social reward. To the degree that adolescents rebel against authorities, this is often likely to occur. The adult's reproof or physical punishment signifies to the peer group that the culprit has "got to" the enemy-caretaker. He has him on the run. This situation adds to the youngster's standing in the group, and, for almost anyone, this is indeed a potent reward. Caretaker-administered reward, conversely, often acts as punishment: In a setting where good grades are not only unimportant but may signify to the group that the recipient is dull or boring, an A for a course may actually constitute a punishment. Coleman (1961) suggests that this attitude is common, perhaps even typical, in the Midwestern high schools he studied. In delinquent and lower-lower class youth societies, approval, particularly from the caretaker, actually punishes the child who receives it. It renders him suspect by his group and he loses status.

The stronger the drive and the better learned the habit, the more likely it is that a given type of behavior will occur. All adolescents have learned aggressive and hostile ways of responding: name calling, biting, kicking, and hitting. However, by the time of adolescence or adulthood, individuals have also built up elaborate sets of counteractive habits and drives, and have also learned (if they were "well brought up") to respond to their own and others' open aggression by anxiety. The stimuli of anger or ideas of open aggression arouse the drive of anxiety, which in turn prevents the actual aggressive behavior, the thought of which aroused anxiety. However, given a powerful enough anger drive, almost everyone can be driven to fight openly or covertly. One may confine his hostility to gossip or criticism, or he may fight for his very life.

There are many theories of learning and considerable disagreement exists about their respective merits. One such theory, the Yale-Iowa theory, has been carefully worked out, applies plausibly to many situations, fits adolescent data reasonably well, and is employed here, although in no doctrinaire fashion. The basic equation in Yale-Iowa learning theory is $E = D \times H$. In this equation, E represents the expectancy or probability that a response will occur, D represents drive, and H, habit. To predict the likelihood that an outburst of physically manifested anger will occur, one needs to know how strong the anger drive is, and how well the organism (an adolescent in this case) has learned the habit of striking out physically against those who frustrate him and toward whom he is angry. One also needs to know how strong are the organism's defenses against physical aggression. How afraid is the organism of retaliation? How anxious do anger and physical aggression make him? Thus, one develops a pair of equations and sets them against each other:

E (striking out angrily) = D (anger) × H (strength of having learned to strike out) [1]

opposed by:

E (withdrawing, for example) = D (fear of retaliation + anxiety about aggression) × H (tendency to make withdrawing responses) [2]

If, in Equation 1, $D = 10$ and $H = 5$, then E (probability of striking out) = 50. Some have called this result the strength of the instigation.

If, in Equation 2, D (fear of retaliation + anxiety) = 5, and H (withdrawal learning strength) = 5, then E (instigation actually to withdraw) = 25. Since the instigation to strike out is stronger than the counteractive behavior, withdrawing, it may be predicted that the angry boy or girl will lash out in physical expression of anger.

The factors that are involved in Equation 1 probably differ little between boys and girls, or from one to another social class. However, there seem to be distinct sex and social-class differences in the factors that make up Equation 2. Lower-lower class youth seem to have fewer inhibitions about open physical aggression than middle-class youth (see Lesser, 1959, and McKee and Leader, 1955, for examples). Inhibitions against physical aggression seem to be greater for girls than boys, although Mallick and McCandless (1966) present evidence for first grade girls that suggests that such inhibitions lessen or disappear when girls know that their physical aggression will not be known to anyone.

When the E, or instigation to physical aggression, is equal to the instigation to withdraw, an individual is placed in conflict. He is immobilized and can do nothing. An additional insult by his opponent may increase his anger and resolve the conflict in the direction of physical combat. His opponent may draw a knife, thereby increasing the instigation to withdraw so that he leaves the situation. He may seek a compromise through displacement, and walk away.

THE MAJOR FUNCTIONS OF DRIVE

Melton (1950) and I. E. Farber (1955) have dealt helpfully with the different functions of drive. According to them, drive has three major functions. (The first is a double function, in the sense that the head and tail sides of a coin are double although part of the same unit.)

1. Energizing and sensitizing.
2. Selective.
3. Directive.

Energizing and Sensitizing Function

The energizing function of drive sets the adolescent into action. The higher the drive, the higher his level of activity. When he knows definitely how to satisfy his drive and methods of satisfying it are available, this heightened activity level (consisting of an increase in both amount and intensity of activity) leads him efficiently and purposefully toward his goal—the direct satisfaction of his drive. In other words, the over-all purpose of an increase in drive is to signify to the boy or girl that he needs something and that he should maximize his effort to obtain it. In a sense, drive is the energy for meeting needs.

There may be interesting personal and possibly social class differences in reaction to increased drive that concerns forbidden areas, such as sex. It may be that inhibited middle-class youngsters who are also relatively rich in verbal behavior resources, under heightened sex drive daydream more; while relatively uninhibited and low verbal lower-class youngsters (more likely boys than girls) become more restless and go on to explore.

The situation is different when an adolescent does not understand his drive very well. In American culture, this is quite true of the sex drive, particularly for middle-class girls. A young person wants to know about sex, but does not know how to begin. And, in addition, the culture officially forbids indulging the sex drive to climax before marriage.[5] The appearance of the sex drive heightens potential for all sorts of responding. Young people, regardless of social class, cannot fit their new sex drive immediately on its arrival into a socially approved framework of regular marriage. Consequently, the level of their restless energy mounts, frustration and aggression are likely to ensue, anxiety is likely to be aroused, curiosity is mobilized, and dependency needs are stirred up and new stances required. All these secondary effects lead to still further heightened drive, often (many say *typically*) expressed as random, excited behavior. Figure 1.1 illustrates such an energizing function of drive.

Too high drive, or too much energizing, leads to another phenomenon that is frequently encountered among adolescents. This is *tunnel vision*, a narrow preoccupation with one's own needs to the exclusion of the interests of others and often to the neglect of valuable developmental tasks. Very high drive may be the source of what many find is the complete egocentrism of adolescents.

High drive often seems to interfere with making discriminations that are necessary for learning and adapting to others in the environment (see Broen, Storms, and Goldberg, 1963, for example). In human life, it is necessary to be task-oriented—to get on with the major business at hand; but it is also necessary to attend to other things, perhaps incidental, that exist in the environment as one is learning. Attention to things outside the immediate task is known as *incidental learning*.

[5] Boys in particular almost universally ignore this sanction.

Such incidental learning may be useful to the adolescent at a later time than when it is learned. It is also known to characterize creative more than noncreative adolescents (Laughlin, Doherty, and Dunn, 1968).

The energizing function of drive is thus adaptive within limits: It gives an adolescent high energy to make the changes he must make if he is to become a constructive adult. But if drive is too high, behavior may become rigid, random and reckless, simplistic, and socially insensitive. The "storm and stress" theory of adolescence—a theory to which all of us must subscribe to some degree—describes such adolescent behavior characteristics.

The sensitizing function of drive is the other side of the coin from the energizing effect. Drive can operate to energize before much learning has taken place (the newborn infant is frantically energized by hunger or pain, but has only the most primitive learning repertoire). For a drive to be sensitized, however, the organism must have learned what stimuli satisfy which drives. Sensitization lowers the threshold for perceiving stimuli: The organism becomes more alert and is more sensitive to stimuli that are the appropriate, already learned satisfiers of the drive that is in the ascendant. The hungry newborn reacts to *anything* that touches his face. The older infant will stop crying and thrashing only when the bottle or nipple is present.

With the advent of the sex drive and the learning connected with it, boys and girls become more aware of the opposite sex. They perceive sexual overtones in conversation and the mass media. Other exacerbations of drive that accompany the new sex drive, such as frustration and anxiety, alert them to hostility and persecution (often where none is intended); they become anxious over nothing, or go to pieces over things they took in their stride as younger children. These outcomes may also be thought of as the result of "too much drive," as indicated above.

Selective Function The selective function of drive is most commonly associated with learning. The type of learning that relates to most of adaptive, problem solving behavior may be thought of as *instrumental learning*. It arises in the first place, and is refined and made more efficient, by the selective function of drive. An adolescent has many roads open to him for passing his examinations, for example. He may cheat; he may prepare for the exam by group study, or by individual study; he may cram; or he may study systematically, reviewing his work daily. He selects the method that works best and most safely for him, and he engages in it whenever possible.

If group study is the method selected, the adolescent may wish to refine his group study techniques. He may discover that friend A is a distractor and he works to eliminate him from the group. Furthermore, he discovers that studying in friend B's house is more efficient than in anyone else's home. He tries always to arrange to hold study sessions in friend B's house. He begins to realize that boredom reduces the efficiency of the group after about an hour of study, and thereafter institutes a 10-minute break every hour.

He may not make these innovations either quickly or insightfully, but may arrive at them slowly and after trial and error. The selective function of drive serves the goal of *parsimony*, or picking the easiest way of obtaining the highest reward. It applies in very simple learning situations as well as in the complex situation described above.

A fully shaped behavior—where the selective function of drive has run its full course—is (ideally) efficient, well-adapted to satisfying the drive to which it relates, minimally tension arousing, and the simplest and easiest of the possible methods of arriving at a goal. Education in the fullest sense of the word is intended to help people achieve socially acceptable and useful behavior in all the important areas of life. Achieving such levels and types of behavior creates personal competence, which is a necessary component of the sort of self concept with which an individual can live comfortably. Competence in their major need areas is probably the highest goal for all normal adolescents.

Directive Function

The directive function of drive is its cue or information-giving function. It tells the organism which of a number of already learned behaviors is most appropriate to use in dealing with a given stimulus or environmental situation. One dominant drive cues different information and different behavior as opposed to another dominant drive. When a particular drive is absent or minimal, stimuli usually related to it will be responded to differently from when the drive is present and strong.

Not thirsty, the adolescent passes by the drinking fountain. He may be so little sensitized to it that he does not even notice it. Thirsty, he notes it and drinks from it, even though he may have to stand in line to do so. Driven by need to pass tomorrow's algebra test, a boy may use his parking time while on a date with the smartest girl in class to prepare himself for the next day's ordeal. If he is himself competent in the field of algebra, he is likely to behave very differently. If he is competitive with the girl for grades and rank in class, his competitive motives may and often do preclude his sex drives from giving him any information about her at all. He may never consider her as a sex object, even though she may be the prettiest girl in the class.

BIOLOGICAL DRIVES

Although, as already discussed, the new sex drive is psychological and social, it is, strictly speaking, a biological phenomenon. As such, it must be defined.

Reproductive

Boys' sexuality, hormonally stimulated, expresses itself hydraulically: Sex pushes them in an involuntary and almost irresistible fashion. The author has heard adolescents (and not only adolescents) refer to their reproductive drive as "the monkey on their backs." The Kinsey (1948) data concerning frequency of sex outlet for boys, briefly, reveal that from pubescence until well into adulthood the average male experiences from two to four sexual outlets per week, married or single. For teenagers, it is certain that this frequency is not high enough to assure freedom from more or less chronic sexual tension. Each ejaculation is by definition an intense physical experience. It is preceded and accompanied by physical excitement and tension. For most boys, the physical excitement (arousal) preceding and accompanying ejaculation is accompanied by considerable emotion, which may range from relatively mild to overwhelming. Sexual arousal may occur in isolation or in social situations, some of them extremely embarrassing. A boy who gets an erection in the group showers, or the boy who is called on to stand to recite in class when he has an erection is usually thoroughly mortified. Sexually aroused, the male of the species is likely to show poor judgment; tunnel vision is likely to accompany intense drive states. Many boys feel guilty and ashamed about being sexually aroused, and many experience intense guilt feelings following sexual release by unapproved means (the only means available in our society to the unmarried male). Fear often follows sexual outlet: fear that masturbation is harmful; or fear of having impregnated the girl; or fear of being caught; or fear of having contracted a venereal disease (not too frequent in this antibiotic age); or fear of the consequences of having exerted undue force on the sexual partner. Shame and guilt are equally frequent accompaniments of sexual outlet, although sexual arousal usually drives out the more subtle emotions.

Many adolescent girls, but probably a minority in our culture (see Kinsey, Pomeroy, and Martin, 1953; and Johnson and Masters, 1966), are as buffeted as boys by the sheer biology of sex. For example, Kinsey reports that by the age of 17 almost 100 percent of boys have experienced orgasm, compared to only about 35 percent of girls. A girl's sexual system seems not to be so easily triggered into readiness for action as a boy's. A normal girl, however, is bombarded by sex stimuli and, at least by the time she begins dating, is subjected to at least some degree of social pressure to behave sexually. Her involvement is social, emotional, and often physical to such a degree that no assumption can be made that the over-all problem presented by the reproductive drive is any less for girls than boys. In many respects, it is less straightforward in its manifestations, and more social-emotional in nature than for boys. Nor do girls have to cope with the problem of "public" evidence of sexual arousal.

Drive and Social Interaction

For purposes of convenience, drives may be classified in two categories: biological (often called unlearned, or physical) and learned (social). In its simplest sense, sex is a biological drive. However, to serve its biological function (reproduction) it must function in a learned, or social, context. Sex drive also plays an important social role, and it is so imbued with much learning and emotion that, for practical purposes, it is impossible to separate its biological from its psychological and social aspects. It is inevitably linked through classical conditioning during the process of childhood socialization (for example, during toilet training) with the inhibited or controlled functions of elimination. Many existing attitudes about elimination generalize to sexual behavior (Sears, Maccoby, and Levin, 1957).

A widely employed list of biological drives includes thirst, air hunger, sleep hunger, food hunger, comfort seeking and pain avoidance, and sex. The ways in which these drives are satisfied are conceded to be important in shaping personality. Where satisfaction or frustration of a drive occurs in social settings, the drive is more likely to be importantly related to personality than where a drive operates in isolation or where no social satisfaction or frustration for it is likely to occur. Obviously, no one interferes with the drive of air hunger. Even the infant takes care of himself or he dies forthwith. Nor is there any general interference with an individual's thirst. Few rules exist regarding thirst other than limiting soft or hard drinks, or fussing with children about their juice and milk intake. Accordingly, air hunger and thirst rarely have much importance in a theory of personality development.

The matter is different for comfort seeking and pain avoidance, hunger, elimination, and sex. These drives are surrounded by social sanctions and reward and punishment contingencies: Children are threatened or praised by parents, who show disapproval, disappointment, or hurt feelings, or provide tangible and intangible rewards.

Satisfying hunger is closely and intimately related to social interactions from birth throughout childhood. The way in which a mother gives her baby the breast or bottle is probably important to the infant's lifelong security (see McCandless, 1967, Chapter 3). Later, parents and children interact constantly within the eating context, sometimes pleasantly, sometimes unpleasantly. Experts (Brody, 1956; Escalona, personal communication) have stated that the best over-all indication of a mother-baby relationship is given by watching how the mother feeds her baby. One of the major complaints of teenagers is that their parents, particularly their mothers, continue to nag at them about their table manners and diet.

Not too much is known about the interrelations of parents and their young children concerning sex training. Most parents seem to disapprove mightily of sexual interest or behavior among their young children. However, they seldom seem to be severe punishers (at least physically). Parents from all social classes attempt to suppress children's expressions of sexual interest and sexual behavior, although middle-class parents may be more effective. By the time a child is 5 or 6, his sex interests and behavior have usually gone underground, except when he is alone or with trusted peers. Boys are probably more open in expressing sex interest and behaving sexually among their peers than girls, although this pattern seems to be changing. However, most children of both sexes in the United States still obtain most of their early sex education (if it may be called that) from their peers.

A visit to the boys' room in any elementary school demonstrates that sex interests do not disappear during preadolescence. Vivid *graphiti* are inscribed in all but the most recently scrubbed and painted restrooms. Apparently girls' rooms do not provide the same eloquent testimony, at least not as frequently and intensely.

In summary, the four major biological drives that involve frequent and prolonged social interaction for their satisfaction undoubtedly play a crucial role in shaping an adolescent's personality. These drives are food hunger, comfort seeking and pain avoidance, elimination, and sex. Of these, only the last is not essential for sustaining life, and is probably more under cortical control than the life-essential drives.

Knowledge of how youth handle these drives is useful in understanding them, although there are cultural sanctions against inquiring about eliminative and particularly sexual habits.

FRUSTRATION, AGGRESSION, ANXIETY, CURIOSITY, AND DEPENDENCY

There is dispute among personality theorists about whether frustration, aggression, anxiety, curiosity, and dependency are learned or innate drives or whether they are drives or strongly overlearned habits. The use of the terms contributes to the confusion. For example, frustration is used both to describe a state of affairs, meaning that the individual is blocked from some goal, and to describe how he feels about this state of affairs (what his emotions are). This latter usage corresponds to drive. Aggression may be used either to describe behavior or an emotion, feeling, or state of mind. The latter use corresponds to the present conception of drive. Anxiety is traditionally used in the drive sense: a strongly aversive state of mind with unclear causes. Curiosity and dependency, like aggression, are both used to betoken either behavior or drive. The latter use is the one employed here.

The author believes there is enough evidence in the research and theoretical literature to justify classifying all five constructs as drives, and will discuss them accordingly. Details of the evidence belong in a more specialized treatise than this book but, briefly, Brown and Farber (1951) present a detailed argument for viewing emotion in general and frustration in particular as a drive. Frustration has been classically and convincingly linked to aggression (Dollard, *et al.*, 1939), and much evidence supports the linkage (Mallick and McCandless, 1966, for children; Pytkowicz, Wagner, and Sarason, 1967, for college males). Usage from at least the time of Freud considers aggression alone (that is, in the absence of frustration) to be a drive, and such detailed treatments as Berkowitz, 1962, 1969; and Buss, 1961, suggest that such usage is legitimate. Anxiety, again since at least the time of Freud, has been considered to possess drive properties; Taylor (1956) gives it drive status within a behaviorist system of psychology; and much experimental evidence supports its use as a drive (Lekarczyk and Hill, 1969). Gewirtz (1969) makes a strong theoretical appeal, well supported by evidence, for viewing dependency as a drive. Among others, Berlyne (1966) and Charlesworth (1965) provide the same reasoning coupled with research results, for curiosity among human subjects.

Whether these drives are learned or innate is a moot question. For practical purposes, since they seem to exist to some degree for all people, the question is not important. Presumably, eventually it will be answered by research.

Frustration and Aggression

The reproductive drive is intensely physically satisfying and, when appropriately socialized, leads to a wide range of other personal and social satisfactions. When adolescents first begin to seek direct expression of their sexuality, typically they find only physical satisfaction. Even this physical pleasure is overlaid with training and sanctions that often lead to fear, anxiety, guilt, and shame. This state of affairs is bound to be intensely frustrating to young people. Because of the greater intensity of their open sexuality, boys usually encounter more frustration on this score than girls, although there are great individual differences. Many girls are undoubtedly conscious of being directly blocked and are severely frustrated thereby.

Adolescents' attempts to seek information and frank guidance in sexual matters are also blocked. Thus, curiosity is frustrated and presumably adds to the total "overdrive" that characterizes adolescents.

It seems clear that frustration is an important instigation to aggression; that, when sufficiently frustrated, almost all people will *feel* aggressive; and that most people, when they feel aggressive enough, will *behave* aggressively. Thus, one can expect adolescents to be more aggressive and hostile than prepubescent children. Open anger and physical aggression are more acceptable in the culture for boys than girls, for, tacitly, such emotion and behavior signify manliness. Thus, a greater increase in open aggressive and antisocial behavior can be predicted for boys than girls; but more increase in verbal aggression (such as gossip and spitefulness) can be predicted among adolescent girls. Over all, aggressiveness may increase more for boys than girls, partly because of their activity level, partly because of cultural sanctions, and partly because the frustrations they meet may be sharper and more dramatic than those that face girls.

Anxiety An adolescent is no more a stranger to anxiety than he is to aggression. It has been with him for a long time and he has usually managed to come to some sort of terms with it. But the new sex drive and the many, complicated, and ambiguous new expectations that society holds for him put new strains on an adolescent's ability to cope with anxiety, if for no other reason than that he suddenly has more anxiety with which to cope.

Given the confusing expectations that society holds for adolescents—and confusion is in and of itself anxiety evoking—it can be predicted that the new sex drive and its attendant social complexities will lead to a sharp increase in anxiety for a time following pubescence. Since the situation is equally complex for boys and girls, no sex difference can be predicted.

There is another complication to be added to the factors discussed above: Adults are afraid of adolescents. Adolescents are bigger and stronger than children. Teachers and parents who earlier relied on physical power to control their charges can do so no longer. This leaves many adults with a feeling of alarmed powerlessness that, when perceived by adolescents, must make the latter uncomfortable and anxious. It is for such reasons that adults should neither abandon control nor overcontrol their adolescents, but rather hold on to clear, firm, and reasonable guidelines and limits.

Adults also are likely to be jealous of adolescents. The latter are so intensely alive, so bursting with energy, and they have so much of their lives still to lead. This jealousy may be particularly intense in United States culture, which is strongly oriented toward worship of youthful beauty and vigorous health. Such jealousy, perceived in those who hitherto have cared for and nurtured young people, will understandably be anxiety evoking for them.

Adolescents also frighten and worry adults. Perceptions of such attitudes are likely to add further to the freight of anxiety carried by youth. Reasons for adults' worry and fear are obvious: Adolescents get into more serious trouble than children. They may fight to the death or may incur serious injury in fights.

Their recklessness, often an outlet for their frustration, anger, and anxiety, often leads to their death in fights, behind the wheel of a car, or while engaged in sports. Adolescent girls become pregnant by adolescent boys with distressing frequency. Adults' worry is often translated into aggression toward the youth who cause it. Aggression notoriously triggers aggression. Thus, a vicious circle of contagious anxiety leading to aggression may be set up between youth and their caretakers.

In addition to their frequent although typically unconscious jealousy and their fear of and worry about youth, adults seem to have an almost institutionalized dislike of adolescents (see, for example, Redl, 1966, pp. 409–417). This dislike leads to restrictive and punitive attitudes and behaviors, and further accelerates the vicious spiral of mutual aggression, distrust, fear, and anxiety in which the adult and juvenile society often seem to be caught—the generation gap, in short.

Finally, at adolescence, children are brought bluntly face to face with the fact that they are soon going to be adults: that they must soon cope with the very real problem of self-governance. They are, for the first time, close to what they will look like and be like as adults. Their attractiveness, their competence, and their personalities are fairly well set. Careers must be chosen. (This is a more serious problem for boys than girls, according to Douvan and Adelson, 1966.) Marriage, with profound implications for the rest of one's life, must be thought about (Douvan and Adelson find that this problem preoccupies girls more than boys), and certainly competence in the courtship area is demanded.

In sum, an upsurge of anxiety at adolescence is clearly understandable and is abundantly *overdetermined*.

Curiosity Curiosity is well organized by adolescence. The emergent sex drive is bound to arouse curiosity that seeks satisfaction through talking with one's peers, poring over pornography, "girl watching," avid reading of sex education and sex how-to-do-it books, and so on. Adolescents also act out their curiosity both in hetero- and homoerotic exploration. Too frequently, these excursions are followed by intense guilt and fear.

The adolescent's other intense needs, such as his search for identity, are also likely to increase curiosity: The adolescent reads and listens to learn about religion, values, ethics, vocational problems, and understanding of self. For many adolescents, the burden of their new drives is so great that they retreat into inertia, as evidenced by withdrawal and underachievement. Underachievement, however, may occur partly because there are so many new interests and opportunities open to adolescents that the old interest (in books and grades or studying diligently) crumbles; it simply may be that there is not enough time or energy to go around.

Or it may be that the upsurge of anxiety associated with adolescence inhibits curiosity. Penney (1965), who worked with fifth and sixth graders, and Mendel (1965), whose research subjects were preschool and kindergarten children, find that the higher a child's anxiety, the lower his curiosity. On the other hand, it is theoretically plausible that children and adolescents may try to allay anxiety by seeking information in the areas about which they are anxious, which is a practical and realistic approach.

In any event, the potential for an upsurge of curiosity is present. It is an asset that can and should be exploited by teachers, parents, and others concerned with youth. Unfortunately, the organization of American society (including junior and senior high schools) is such that the opposite seems more often to occur.

Dependency Techniques to deal with dependency needs have long been known to boys and girls by the time they reach adolescence. However, puberty brings with it a demand for a sharp change in these techniques, particularly for boys. Adolescent girls may continue to be "feminine"—to cling, to confide, to depend on others for decisions. Within reasonable limits, such behavior is approved of for girls in American culture. Such is not so for adolescent boys. To be dependent is to be unmanly. It is not appropriate for an adolescent boy to ask openly for affection signs from adults, no matter how much he may want them. Girls, too, are expected to show increased "maturity" or independence following pubescence, but the change is not so extreme as for boys. Boys and girls are apparently pushed in different directions by adolescence, or at least there is a sex difference in the urgency with which autonomy is sought. Obtaining it seems to be a major goal for boys, and a relatively minor goal for girls (Douvan and Adelson, 1966). This may reflect cultural pressures, as the culture emphasizes self-reliance, independence, and initiative for boys; but obedience, reliability, and nurturance—looking after others—for girls (see Barry, Bacon, and Child, 1957).

There are many speculations about the urgency toward autonomy that characterizes the average United States adolescent boy (perhaps that characterizes adolescents in general). Pressure of the culture is one hypothesis. The male autonomy drive may be partly rooted in biology: strong, action-oriented body build and high metabolic activity level. Or the drive for autonomy may be related to the traditional role of the male in the game of sex: He is supposed to lead in courtship, to mount in copulation.

Regardless of the reasons, American boys seem to have stronger drives toward autonomy and independence than American girls. Thus, an adolescent boy's own developmental course pushes him away from adult comfort and affection (to him they are signs of dependency); the culture moves its adults in the same direction, so they deny him affection and comfort, and the net result may be a lonely boy who at times desperately wants comfort and affection yet for complex reasons can neither ask for nor accept them.

The drive theory espoused in this book postulates that adolescence will bring with it the same *psychological* upsurge in dependency drive as it brings for all the other drives. But society demands that this upsurge be masked. Some of the many reasons for this situation follow. Pubescence is a universal sign of manhood or womanhood, and men and women must learn to stand alone and be strong (be executively independent). Generations of experts have told American parents that they must not overprotect and cling to their children, but must set them free. Conscientious parents, taking this advice to heart, may become so intent on setting their children free that the children see themselves not as free but as rejected. Also, for reasons that are dealt with somewhat convincingly by psychoanalytic theory, parents are rather embarrassed by close contact with their adolescent children, particularly opposite-sexed children. We are likely to assume unhealthy undertones to any but token expressions of physical affection between mothers and adolescent sons or fathers and adolescent daughters. Demonstrations of affection between mothers and daughters are somewhat suspect; between fathers and sons they are considered downright peculiar. Adolescents know that they are not free to seek this type of assurance that they are loved. For developmental reasons of their own, they may need to shun physical contact with their parents and other adults.

Teachers and other caretakers of youth are bound by the same social attitudes and sanctions. It is all right—perhaps desirable—to bestow open affection upon nursery school, kindergarten, and primary grade children. It becomes less acceptable in the intermediate grades, and is all but forbidden from the junior high school ages upward. There are realistic as well as unrealistic reasons for this. The pretty young teacher who rumples the hair of the adolescent boy is likely to be censured. Physical contact with his adolescent girl charges is even more strongly forbidden to the man teacher. To some degree, these social proscriptions have a realistic base: Adolescents are keyed up sexually and hungry for human love, although, because of bravado, need for autonomy, or unreadiness for love relationships, they may deny it. They are eager for sexual tutelage. Their eagerness leads easily to crushes, and crushes may carry both the adolescent and his caretaker further than either of them cares to or can go safely.

Even more suspect than purposeful, tender physical contact with adolescents of the opposite sex is contact with those of the same sex. Any suspicion of homosexuality, particularly between men and boys, throws United States society into panic. There are enough documented instances of heterosexual and homosexual relations between caretakers and charges to provide some foundation for the fears and sanctions of society.

It is essential that teachers and other youth caretakers be, if not sexually well adjusted, at least sexually well behaved. It is possible for an adolescent's first experiences with sex in a social context to define his future sex life. A first affair with a teacher or a caretaker, whether it is heterosexual or homosexual, may be devastating to a vulnerable adolescent *and* to his adult partner. Peters' *Finistère* (1951) is a moving, clinically valid fictional treatment of such a relationship between an adolescent boy and his teacher.

To summarize, American society rather leaves the adolescent, particularly the boy, out in the cold. He has nowhere to turn nor is he free to turn anywhere with his dependency, love, and affection needs. Most adolescents handle this void satisfactorily and eventually find a relationship of intimacy with friends, sweethearts, spouses, and their own children. Intimacy is usually not established until late adolescence, and for many people it is never achieved (see Erikson, 1956). True intimacy is a condition of total trust in another person, coupled with close affection or love for him, and it cannot be attained without surrender of autonomy. Paradoxically, autonomy cannot be soundly maintained without intimacy—but more of this later.

There is a solution to the emotional isolation and lack of tenderness which adolescents find characterize this period. Warmth and love need not be expressed in only a physically intense relationship. Fortunately, human beings possess words and can thus give reassurances. Warmth, support, and friendship can be conveyed covertly and indirectly but clearly by gestures, glances, and words between and among people of both sexes and all ages and types of relationship. During the period when an adolescent cannot openly deal with tenderness, such devices can maintain communication and promote security.

NEED SYSTEMS AND SOCIAL LEARNING CONTINUITY

Biological and social needs often assume particular importance in adolescent adjustment according to the consistency with which a society handles them during the individual's growth. If they are consistently handled from early childhood into adolescence, then they presumably have little *special* significance within a psychology of adolescence. If they are inconsistently handled, and particularly if the inconsistency appears strikingly during adolescence, then the inconsistency contributes to the pattern of change that makes up an essential part of a psychology of adolescence.

Thus, it is well to look again at the needs upon which attention has been centered, and to analyze society's training pattern for each so as to see what special contribution changes in dealing with the need makes to a psychology of adolescence.

From early childhood through adolescence, social training is consistent and predictable for the needs of comfort seeking and pain avoidance, elimination, hunger and feeding, frustration, aggression, and anxiety. American society is remarkably inconsistent in the way it trains for and allows expression of the sex, curiosity, and dependency needs.

Comfort Seeking and Pain Avoidance

Comfort seeking and pain avoidance are constantly manipulated in child training from infancy onward. Rewards consist of giving physical or psychological comfort, or a mixture of the two. For infants and very young children, psychological comfort depends wholly on physical comfort (or gratification). Society steadily and progressively substitutes intangible psychological and social comforts for physical comfort, although provision for the latter must be made at all ages. A 6-week-old baby must have a bottle to be comfortable. A 3 year old will tolerate his hunger for a considerable time when his mother's warmth and affection accompany her assurance that presently he can eat. The most important comforts for adolescents are psychological although, like everyone else, they must eat, be free from pain, obtain enough sleep, and so on. Adolescent boys irregularly but with high frequency (as has been demonstrated) demand sexual comfort, and seek both relaxation of physical sexual tension and the pleasure of orgasm. Sex demands similar relief for many girls. If a boy cannot secure sexual relief and pleasure through other channels, nature takes care of his need by a wet dream. Some girls also find orgasm in dreams, and many report pleasant erotic dreams.

However, most of the adolescent's comforts are psychological and, of them, most are social in nature. An adolescent may be self-rewarding, taking pride in competence and, in effect, saying to himself, "That was a good job." But, even as adults, few can survive comfortably without social, as well as self, recognition. Gewirtz and Stingle (1968) document this position in a detailed learning theory treatment of imitation and identification.

For individuals and within a family, a consistent style for managing children's comfort seeking and pain avoidance needs has been demonstrated repeatedly (see, for example, Bandura and Walters, 1959; McCandless, 1967; and Sears, Maccoby, and Levin, 1957). Adults follow reasonably predictable patterns that range along a punitive (or punishing) to a permissive continuum.[6]

Not only are individual parents and other caretakers rather consistently either high or low in punishment, both over time and for a wide variety of behavior, but they show consistent and thus predictable patterns of warmth at one end of a continuum to emotional coldness at the other. Highly punishing parents are likely to be cold, but there are many exceptions and the relationship is not strong.

Parents also seem to be rather consistently either "thing-" or "love"-oriented in their techniques of child control. The thing-oriented

[6]A continuum refers to a distribution of traits, behavior, or characteristics. In the present case, one extreme of the continuum is high parental or caretaker punishment. The other extreme represents almost complete lack of punishment in child training. The figure below shows a normal distribution of hypothetical punishment behavior.

The curve indicates that almost no caretakers manage children without occasionally employing punishment. An equally small number (represented by the extreme right of the curve) rely almost exclusively on punishment to manage their children.

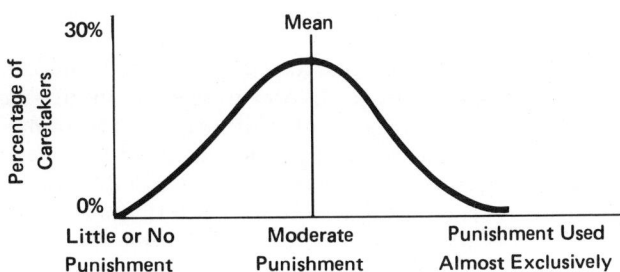

The curve rises steadily from both ends toward the middle, indicating that most caretakers use a moderate amount of punishment, but that punishment for the total population of caretakers ranges from almost none to a very large amount. The average, represented by the line in the middle of the figure, is the mean, or average. Included between the curve and the baseline, called the abscissa, and the vertical, the ordinate, is 100 percent of the hypothetical population of caretakers.

caretaker gives tangible rewards and punishments. He spanks, slaps, offers money for good grades; threatens loss of privileges, isolation, or physical punishment for undesirable behavior. The love- or psychologically-oriented parent uses intangible rewards and punishments, such as gestures of affection, smiles, words of praise, assurances of love and acceptance, disapproval because a behavior is morally or socially wrong, or because a child has behaved in such way as to disappoint, hurt, or fail to live up to the caretaker's expectations, or because of the child's own failure to sense right and wrong.

Of the two extremes, love-oriented techniques seem to be more effective than thing-oriented methods in producing the type of end-product best suited for a democratic society. Of course, few if any caretakers employ exclusively either thing- or psychologically-oriented techniques. Rather than the absolute frequency of one or the other, probably the balance between them is important. Love-oriented techniques (or a high ratio of love- to thing-oriented methods) seem to produce adolescents with more ambition to achieve and more capacity for intimate and healthy interpersonal relationships. Evidence for these conclusions is given later.

Individual caretakers and the society as a whole, then, can be said to be reasonably consistent from early childhood onward in using the comfort seeking and pain avoidance drive to shape children's behavior. Girls at all ages receive less physical punishment than boys, perhaps because they are less active, strive less for autonomy, and, in general, are better behaved. The older a child grows, the less he is the object of physical punishment. This is partly because society does not approve very much of physical punishment at any age; because the older a child grows, the easier it is to reason with him rather than spank him; and the bigger he becomes, the more able he is to retaliate in kind for physical punishment.

Elimination and Hunger

Society is similarly consistent with eliminative and hunger drives: With regard to elimination, continual pressure is early put on the child to be dry and clean. Consequently, almost all children quickly learn continence and almost all have established bowel control by the time they are 3 or 4 years old, and day and night bladder control by 6 or 7 years. Boys as a group are harder to train than girls, particularly in bladder control.

Caretaker manipulation of the hunger drive is more variable than for toilet training, and continues longer. It has already been mentioned that one of the frequent complaints of adolescents of both sexes concerns their mothers nagging them about their table manners. Such nagging is undoubtedly often justified.

Throughout childhood and adolescence, parents and other caretakers also struggle to train their children to eat balanced meals, not to overeat, not to undereat, to take a solid breakfast, and not to eat between meals. This is a serious health problem area for adolescents. Their predilection for French fries and hamburgers, soft drinks, potato chips, sweets, gulped-down glasses of whole milk, and hurried meals is likely to be bad for their general health, their cholesterol level, and their complexions. Ill-adjusted adolescents often overeat (just as they often abuse each of the other basic drives), which obviously compounds their difficulties by obesity. Obesity in this culture is rejected by peers and adults alike (see Staffieri, 1967; and Dwyer and Mayer, 1967, for examples). Other young people—probably more girls than boys—diet unrealistically and even dangerously for fear of obesity, so heavily penalized in our "slim oriented" culture. It is common for young people with already bad complexions to compound their difficulties by eating too many nuts and French fries, too much chocolate, and by drinking too many soft drinks.

Whether or not caretakers are successful in training their children's food taking, they are consistent. The consensus of their training is: Eat properly and according to social dictates, but allow a little leeway.

Frustration and Aggression

Frustration and aggression (and anxiety, discussed in the next section) are also handled with moderate consistency. Parents attempt to train children to tolerate frustration and to hold in violent verbal or physical expressions of aggression. Children are usually encouraged to talk, even though it may be quarrelsomely, rather than to hit, although malicious talk is discouraged—not, however, very effectively. Girls are easier to train in control of aggression than boys, perhaps because of their nature. Mallick and McCandless (1966) found that first grade girls will show as much open aggression as boys if they believe no one will know about it. But most authors (for example, Pauline Sears, 1951, 1953; and McCandless, Bilous, and Bennett, 1960, all working with preschool-aged children) report that girls are more verbally but less physically aggressive than boys. Observation suggests that this is equally true in adolescence. However, anyone who has worked with delinquent and criminal girls and women knows that the female of the species can be exceptionally physically violent as well as verbally abusive.

As a group, lower-lower class boys and girls seem to be more openly aggressive than middle-class children (see, for example, McKee and Leader, 1955; and Lesser, 1959). However, presumably well-brought-up, middle-class young college men report a high incidence (nearly one-fourth) of physical aggression in the form of their having started fist-fights in adolescence (Clark and Tifft, 1966). Although this was a small sample (45 young men in an introductory sociology class), and the authors give evidence that the men rather strikingly overreported the facts, this result lends credence to the idea that fighting is manly and that boys take pride in it, even though they may be slightly ashamed of themselves. These same young men, interestingly, also overreported willful destruction of property and intercourse with women other than their wives (for those who were married). There was even overreporting, however slight, of behavior, usually strongly disapproved of by college-type young men, such as homosexual experiences and masturbation.

Nondelinquent adolescent boys rarely report physical violence when contrasted with well-matched boys who come from the same social status, but who are delinquent (Bandura and Walters, 1959).

However, any morning newspaper will verify the statistically dangerous current violent crime rates. Clearly, aggression-anger training in the United States, consistent and well-articulated though it may be, is not particularly successful for either sex. The senseless murders of John and Robert Kennedy, Medgar Evers, and Martin Luther King, Jr., testify tragically to the "American as cherry-pie" strain of violence[7] that runs through the society.

Anxiety

Anxiety, too, is consistently but ineffectually handled by adolescents. It is expressed more subtly than anger. Universally and consistently parents deplore anxiety in their children and other youth and, when they detect it, they try to comfort them, reassure them, or talk them out of it. These devices work very poorly.

Reproductive Drive and Sex Behavior

There is consistency in handling sexual behavior in childhood: Parents try to ignore it, and, if it comes to their attention, they register disapproval, openly or covertly, and often by evasion. They are consistent in this reaction and are generally effective in channeling sex expression underground. Ostensibly, children and adolescents are not supposed to think about sex, or to know about sex, or to indulge in sex. There are signs—not well documented with evidence, however,—that this pattern is changing. There is a conspiracy about sex of largely silent adult suppression, ignoring, and disapproval. All parents of adolescent children know perfectly well, especially fathers about their sons, that adolescents are curious about sex, seek to satisfy their curiosity, and almost certainly practice consummatory behavior. Both mothers and fathers are often equally suspicious about their adolescent daughters, usually with less cause, as we have seen; and are typically even more worried about their daughters' behavior than about their sons'.

While parents do little about sex education themselves, most of them endorse the schools' teaching it. There is some question about whether schools are any better equipped to handle sex education than parents. Certainly, few schools have been willing to tackle the subject at a level that is genuinely useful and realistic for adolescents.

The most dramatic inconsistency in American society about expressing the sex drive is its shift in expectation following marriage. A youth is expected to change in one night from a sexless individual to a regularly and competently copulating mate. The boy who comes to marriage as a virgin possesses a large range of mostly implicit expectations that he give his bride satisfaction by knowledgeable copulatory techniques and optimally delayed orgasm. The virgin wife has similar expectations that she should respond warmly and lovingly, psychologically and physically, and join her husband in a simultaneous orgasm. Substantially similar expectations commonly accompany physical union outside marriage. As has been stated, boys are more likely than girls to be heterosexually experienced before marriage, and premarital sex experience is more frequent, certainly among males, as one moves down the socioeconomic scale. As is true for all areas of adolescent behavior, we have little information about the upper-class population.

---

[7]An allegation made by Rap Brown, a leader in the Black Power movement.

Curiosity Encouragement and shaping of curiosity vary by social class. Most of our knowledge about curiosity training comes from studies of young children [for example Bernstein, 1960; Deutsch, 1965; Susan Gray and her coworkers (Gray and Klaus), 1965; or Endsley and Kessel, 1969]. Curiosity is least encouraged and shaped constructively in the lower-lower class, and is more likely to be encouraged and followed through the higher up the socioeconomic scale one goes. But it is not consistently treated: Middle-class parents and teachers are pleased when the topic of exploration is socially acceptable ("Who built the pyramids?" "Where does silk come from?"). They are less happy when the topic is socially embarrassing ("Why did Uncle Clyde shoot the lady in the motel?" "Why is Grandma in the State Hospital?" "What does 'rape' mean?").

Dependency Dependency seems to be rather consistently dealt with among girls, but it is treated discontinuously for boys in much the same way as their sex training and sexual expectancies. Girls are progressively and rather gently shaped toward relative independence. Throughout their lives, however, substantial open and obvious dependency and love and affection seeking behavior are not only permitted but encouraged. Boys are likely to experience two sharp breaks in the manner in which response is made to their love and affection demands (the author is again speaking clinically). The first discontinuity, which also characterizes girls, comes at the time of entering formal school. A boy, for example, is suddenly given clearly to understand that he is no longer a baby, but is now a little man. The second, clearly different for boys and girls, comes at puberty. At that time the adolescent boy particularly is given to know that obvious seeking of dependency and love and affection is girlish and, in effect, is not to be tolerated. As has been noted, his own needs for autonomy are likely to keep him from accepting tenderness even when offered, which may hurt the feelings of his well-disposed and affectionate caretakers. This difference between the sexes is demonstrated by Kagan and Moss' (1960) data.

It has been mentioned that adults in general withdraw emotional support from adolescents. The organization of the schools contributes to this. Most elementary school children in America attend self-contained classes: Almost all their schoolwork comes to them from a single teacher during an academic year. (Special teachers, of course, handle such things as art, music, and speech.) United States children enter junior high school at about the time of puberty or somewhat earlier. Most junior high and secondary schools are organized according to the platoon system where a child has one teacher for English, another for mathematics, another for social studies, and so on. With so many children in several classes, teachers of adolescents (for actuarial reasons if nothing else) cannot give the same emotional support that elementary school teachers can.

Such loss of emotional support at home *and* at school is likely to result in considerable adolescent insecurity and possibly feelings of rejection, leading often to exaggerated independence ("I don't care!"), coupled with anxiety and hostility.

Summary of Consistency Patterns

Need systems that have been socially handled reasonably consistently from childhood probably assume no special significance in adolescence. Those that have been handled inconsistently are likely to assume particular importance, most notably when the major inconsistency is encountered during adolescence.

Adolescence offers nothing dramatically new in terms of social regard for comfort giving and pain avoidance, elimination, hunger and feeding, frustration and aggression, and anxiety. However, in the case of pain avoidance, adolescents are less likely to be physically disciplined than younger children but, when they are, the discipline is likely to be more violent. In the instance of comfort giving, physical affection is less likely to be bestowed by adults on adolescents than on younger children.

Sharp changes in regarding and/or dealing with sex, curiosity, and dependency needs occur at adolescence, and these needs thus require attention in the psychology of adolescence. Curiosity about sexuality, for example, is discouraged; and curiosity that is construed as an attack on the status quo for such things as politics and religion is likely to be strongly put down by home and school authorities. Such curiosity is particularly likely to emerge in adolescence, as will be seen later when cognitive development is discussed.

ADOLESCENCE: A THEORY OF CHANGE

Lewin (1935) was one of the first to postulate specific psychological theories for adolescence that refer to the change inherent in this period. Barker (1953) refined Lewin's theory, giving fuller attention to adolescence. Barker conceived of the adolescent as moving from the accustomed structuring of childhood into a new region in which the boundaries were unknown and the rules of conduct and expectations were unclear. New maturity was postulated as the reason.

The new regions entered at puberty were both attractive and frightening. The old ones of childhood held the appeal of familiarity and predictability, but were no longer suitable for one with adolescent developmental status. Consequently, the adolescent vacillated back and forth, retreating toward the old at times, impelled toward and venturing into the new but with hesitation, anxiety, and great uncertainty. The process of changing generated great stress.

Barker's ideas are not too different from the learning-drive theory described briefly earlier in this chapter. The explanatory principles differ, but the phenomena are similar.

Festinger (1957, 1964) has developed a theory of cognitive dissonance that fits well with the idea of adolescence as a theory, perhaps not *of* change, but one which must account for the phenomena of change. Briefly, Festinger thinks that, when inconsistent perceptions are held by a person, either about himself or his environment, he is placed in a state of tension or *dissonance.* This condition is unpleasant and motivates the individual to change and hopefully to eliminate it. This he does by bringing his perceptions, beliefs, and attitudes closer together. In the process, he may (1) change his own perceptions and beliefs, bringing them closer to a reality that will not be changed. Or he may (2) seek to change his environment to bring it in line with what he believes. He may work to do this in reality, or he may simply deny that things are as they are. Finally, he may (3) attempt to combine the two processes.

As an illustration, consider the following case. An adolescent with a strong sense of honesty comes to a new school. He soon sees that cheating is widespread. Following the first alternative above, he changes his own attitudes toward cheating, rationalizing that, after all, it is not so bad. He learns to cheat to protect himself. Under the second alternative, he keeps his own attitudes about the undesirability of cheating, and works within the school for the adoption of an honor system. He refuses to cheat. On the other hand, if cheating by others causes him too much anxiety, he may turn his back on the cheating and even convince himself that it does not go on. The third alternative is more typical: If he wants to get into the social swim, he may devalue cheating in the sense of regarding it as less serious than he had formerly thought it to be, but argue with his friends privately for greater honesty on their part.

Among healthy adolescents, the first and third alternatives are those most frequently chosen. Their new bodies, for example, are with them to stay. The world and its expectations for them are undeniably realities. Thus they alter their perceptions and beliefs to fit things as they are. But healthy adolescents, like healthy adults (and often more so because of their great energy and lack of cynicism and resignation), also seek to change those aspects of the world that they see as pathological. Such changes reflect the selective function of drive.

Some deny reality. The rate of schizophrenia[8] is high among adolescents. Some adolescents are defeated and kill themselves. Suicide is the fourth ranking cause of death among young people between 15 and 19, exceeded only by accidents, cancer, and homicide (Teicher and Jacobs, 1966). Hippies attempt to build a new reality for themselves. Some Black activists are sure they can live outside the white power structure and create a Black world that is better than the world they now live in, although their moderate Black brethren and the white power structure itself believe they are denying reality.

Ausubel (1954) includes two aspects of change in his theory of adolescence, although he also documents changes in society's attitudes and practices toward adolescence. The first factor, like the author's, is biological change: the new drive of sex. Like the author, Ausubel sees a sharp discontinuity between prepubescent and postpubescent sexual drive, response, and attitudes. He notes clearly that this new drive is the first since infancy to demand socialization.

His second major change is psychosocial. Normally developing preadolescents, Ausubel believes, have satellized—have modeled on or identified with and been dependent upon adults, usually their caretakers. But, as a complex function of personal biological and psychological drives and social forces, desatellization must occur. The adolescent must break free, psychologically and socially, from his caretakers and begin the process of becoming his own man. Successful desatellization means

[8] A mental illness whose major symptom is building a personal reality often having no perceptible relationship to things as they actually are.

much the same to Ausubel as self-governance means to the author, and as a successful resolution of the identity crisis means to Erikson (1956).

Ausubel and Erikson both see all the elements of struggle involved in this process of change that have been documented in the preceding pages.

Continuity in Development

The author thinks of human development as essentially continuous; it is a stream flowing from its source to its terminus but differing in its components, rate of flow, and environmental setting from one stage to another. Adolescence differs enough from what has gone before and what follows to deserve, at the least, a separate navigational chart. As has been said, there is plenty of justification for a psychology of adolescence.

Major Changes at Adolescence

A psychology of change is applicable to the following four characteristics of adolescence:

1. The addition of a new drive, sex, in the mature, orgasmic, procreative sense, for which society inexorably demands acceptable socialization.
2. Sharp changes in the social expectations that are held for the adolescent. These changes are parallel to and are triggered by his new biological maturity.
3. Necessary, urgent, and dramatic changes by the adolescent in his self concept. These must be made because of the joint demands of his biological maturity and the changes in social expectations that parallel it.
4. Related to this need to change his self concept, there is an especially urgent need to "find his own identity," much as described by Erikson (1956) in his classic article, *The Problem of Ego Identity*. During adolescence the young person must seek and hopefully find a satisfactory answer to the uniquely human question, "Who am I?"

There are many developmental continuities in drive-related behavior that are not affected specifically by adolescence. However, under the influence of new, added drives, regressive or more vigorous responses may be made to such old drives. Some, like anxiety, may surge because of the confusions and frustrations that accompany adolescence. Adolescents may be inconvenienced because they so rapidly outgrow their clothes, as there is a sharp growth spurt preceding and following puberty for both sexes. Boys' genital and girls' breast growth may cause them a mixture of pride and embarrassment. But the body per se certainly does not grow so rapidly that the adolescent cannot keep up with it perceptually. It is likely that the awkwardness commonly attributed to adolescents is due, if and when it occurs, to the general difficulties of life adjustment rather than to the body and its accelerated growth. The only *new* thing about this body is its mature sexual function and society's reaction to this function. But as far as absolute change is concerned, infants change more in their first year than adolescents do between puberty and the time when they become self-governing. The crucial psychological difference is that infants possess little if any of the self-awareness and cognitive organization possessed by adolescents.

There are certainly special storm-and-stress phenomena associated with adolescence in any culture, although they are maximized in industrialized or industrializing societies.[9] In discussing adolescents, however, one is likely to overstate the storms and stresses and underplay the stabilities. Douvan and Adelson's (1966) data suggest that, for the majority of United States youth, adolescence is a reasonably calm and stable developmental period, and that the crises are more surface than depth phenomena. Offer (1969) reaches similar conclusions. However, in contrast to Douvan and Adelson's large, stratified sample of early teenagers, Offer worked with seventy-three older suburban middle- and upper-middle-class high school boys, all volunteers, and only two of whom were Afro-American. These boys generally accepted their parents', the school's, and society's values, were liberal in sexual attitudes but did not admit to much sex life of their own, and rather derogated their high school teachers (except for their coaches).

In short, striking change during adolescence must be considered in any psychology dealing with the period, but it should be remembered that many and perhaps most adolescents handle it without melodrama.

Adjustment to Change

The difficulties adolescents experience with their new drives, societal discontinuities, needs to adjust to personal and social changes, and struggles toward self-governance should not be taken as so overpowering to the individual that he is unable to adjust to the changes in his life. Adolescence, while certainly fraught with frustrations, anxieties, changes, and new social demands and expectations, is also a period where the youngster is alert to and capable of making major new constructive *or* destructive adaptations. His drive state is high. This implies capacity for dramatic new learning. Old responses, some of which may be regressive but others of which may be useful, are likely to reappear and be met by success or failure. The adolescent thus is given a chance to unlearn permanently old ways of behaving that are socially useless or destructive, or to reincorporate and consolidate old responses that will now be useful.

The modified crisis situation in which many adolescents find themselves calls for new responses. A high motivational state (even though it may produce tunnel vision) also puts the adolescent in a good position for rapid learning: New good responses can be quickly established, since drive is high and reward is consequently great. New useless or harmful responses can be quickly unlearned for the same reason, since, like reward, disappointment (punishment) is more effective when drive is high. This dynamic adjustment may underly what we often think of as the great variability, the impulsiveness, or the changeability of adolescents.

[9]The author does not believe in the conventional term primitive, or simple, culture. No culture is simple. Even the most primitive man (for example, the Australian aborigine untouched by Western society) possesses skills so complex and refined that no Western man can hope to master them without beginning literally as an infant. The converse is equally true. Adolescence seems to be an important function of industrialization, which demands long training before an individual can enter the labor market and its increasingly high level for skills. As Mead (1939) has indicated, adolescence may not be a particularly turbulent phase of development in a nonindustrialized society where, as soon as he is able, the boy follows his father into herding or hunting or farming or fishing, and the girl moves into marriage soon after or even before her first menstruation.

In periods of labor glut, when there are more potential workers than there are jobs, a society may prolong adolescence to keep boys and girls out of the higher competitive job market. At the time of writing, there is no such glut except in the unskilled labor market.

Researchers suspect that many youngsters who enter adolescence with confused sexual identity, if their environment and learning opportunities are benign, can consolidate an appropriate sex identity through the influence of wise teachers and counselors. The opposite can also happen. Psychoanalytic theory treats quite well the potentially optimal fluidity of adolescence. The author has to a degree drawn on psychoanalytic theory for his treatment.

Social psychology includes a notion of crisis and the hypothesis that, during crisis, individuals are particularly susceptible to suggestion and thus to change. Events in history and politics suggest the validity of this theory, and it is also buttressed by research evidence. Samorajczyk (1969) very reasonably believes that first grade is a time of crisis, particularly for children who have not previously had kindergarten or other preschool experience. He compared two well-matched groups of first graders during their first three weeks of first grade. One group had gone to kindergarten, the other had not. The nonkindergarten, unprepared, group was significantly more suggestible than those who had previously experienced schooling. Adolescents, who to some degree are in a state of crisis, may be similarly suggestible. If so, their possibilities for changing are increased even more.

A major prediction of a drive theory of adolescence is that it is a time when great change can be produced in an individual, for better or worse. It is a period of greater flexibility than the individual has known since his preschool years, or that he is likely to know again. It is society's duty to organize itself so that chances of constructive change are maximized.

SEX-SPECIFIC SOCIAL GOALS AND THE DOUBLE CODE

Differences between the sexes exist in expression and association of the reproductive drive, in amount and type of frustration encountered, in aggression, and in dependency. In addition to such drives, there are socially induced goals toward which the members of all cultures are exposed. If individuals socialize according to the customs of the culture, they adopt its goals and are motivated (possess a drive) to reach them. For example, United States culture is highly achievement-oriented and, in different ways, most well-socialized children, youth, and adults come to value achievement, competence, and success for their own sakes, quite in addition to material gains that may be associated with them.

Such socially induced goals may be thought of as developmental tasks. The chief developmental task discussed up to this point has been achieving the stage of self-governance. Evidence suggests that boys and girls in American society differ sharply from each other in how they work toward this goal. An important section of such evidence has been provided by Douvan and Adelson (1966), who report on interviews conducted with a well-defined, representative sample of United States adolescents. Their sample contains 1045 boys aged 14 through 16 years and 2005 girls in grades six through twelve. They conclude that there are different major drive-need systems for boys and girls.

Boys' Major Social Motive

Douvan and Adelson believe that for the average American boy the major developmental task is to achieve personal autonomy. Thus, his behavior is geared toward independence, self-sufficiency, and competence above all else; and his behavior— social and antisocial—can be understood only if it is viewed within such a framework. These conclusions fit well with those drawn from a world sample and reported by, among others, Barry, Bacon, and Child (1957). Hallworth and Waite (1966), using very different methods, find similar results for English adolescents, all of whom were 14 years of age or more.

Girls' Major Social Motive

From their data for girls, Douvan and Adelson conclude that the American girl, in contrast to her male counterpart, strives principally to define herself as a woman and to achieve personal security. This includes finding and maintaining stable and intimate personal interrelations. Douvan and Adelson's boys were intensely vocationally oriented, for example; their girls were remarkably hazy about career plans, even including marriage. But girls were more preoccupied with friendship, social relations, and definition of self.

This sex-differential theory leads us to predict more conflict for boys generally, and particularly with authority figures such as parents and teachers. It can be predicted that girls will value the social returns from their peer group more than boys.

Douvan and Adelson's conclusions fit most of the data known to the author reasonably well. However, Musgrove (1966) reports an interesting and logical exception for English youth aged 14 to 20 years. Both boys and girls and both middle- and lower-class youth are emphatic in their demands that the schools serve them better than at present in preparing them to live competent lives. Girls were as emphatic about this as boys. Like Douvan and Adelson's sample, girls placed more stress than boys on friendship. Also, like Douvan and Adelson's youth, these English young people were on the whole content with their relations with their parents.

The Double Codes

The term double code, or *code duello*, is so familiar when applied to sexual behavior as to need no definition: Boys are expected to sow their wild oats, and to act out and consummate their sexual drive. This behavior may be simply the sign of society's realistic recognition of the urgency of the boy's sexual system. It may be one of many signs suggesting that American society gives greater privilege to males. On the other hand, girls are expected to be sexually discreet, and to come virginal to their marriage beds.

Times seem to have changed this double code remarkably little, although sexual experimentation by girls and women is more acceptable (or at least more openly discussed and less vigorously condemned) than fifty years ago. There is no solid evidence that the sex behavior of either boys or girls, or men or women, has changed much since the time of World War I. "The pill" may make a big difference, but it is too early to know certainly. History suggests that attitudes and behavior change much more slowly than techniques. Today, as in 1900, boys seem to want sex first and love second; girls seem to want love first, with sex a relatively poor second.

As has been implied earlier in this chapter, there is a second double code. It is more subtle and has figured little in the professional and popular literature. But it may be more important in the differential adjustment of the sexes than the double sexual code. It concerns communication of emotions and seeking of intimacy. Girls and women are relatively free to admit and behave as though they were afraid, lonely, anxious, dependent, and insecure. Within sensible limits, they can do these things with little fear of condemnation or rejection, and with no sense of loss of their femininity.

Boys and men cannot make such admissions. To make them is dangerous in even the most intimate relations, and there are few such relations in the average person's life. If boys and men reveal themselves as weak, fearful, or anxious, they are likely both to be labeled and to label themselves unmanly or feminine. Medical men state that such refusal to admit weakness applies even to physical illness. Relative to women, men must almost be convinced that they are *in extremis* before they consult their doctors or take to their beds. Preserving his concept of masculinity, in other words, can prevent the average boy or man from using his simple common sense. He behaves so, it is thought, because of his need for autonomy.

Girls and women can tell others of their sex that they like them very much, even love them. If a man admits to this, he may suspect his own motives and may be suspected by others. This is not to say that men and boys do not have deep friendships, both with their own and the opposite sex. But such friendships seem on the whole to be less well articulated than among females, and less useful as vehicles to express conflicts and tensions.

It cannot be said what price this sex characteristic exacts from men, or what advantage it gives women. It is conceivably related to such factors as differential delinquency and crime rate, and to the male's shorter life expectancy.

THE MAJOR AREAS OF ADOLESCENT ADJUSTMENT

A combination of professional practices, professional reading, and friendship with adolescents from all social classes and many ethnic and national variations leads the author to postulate four major areas of adolescent adjustment. These are areas in which the adolescent should gain not merely *equilibrium* or *homeostasis*, but *competence*.

The four areas are:

1. Status.
2. Sociality (in the ideal sense, intimacy).
3. Sexuality.
4. Values and morality.

There seems to be little difference within United States culture in the relative importance of status and sociality. Status involves achievement-related skills of all sorts, and may be more important for boys than girls; sociality (as in intimacy or friendship) may be more valued by girls. Douvan and Adelson's findings suggest that this is the case.

Sexuality seems, in the long run, clearly to rank last in the importance of its effect on the way adolescents shape their lives. It has been stressed in this chapter because it has been neglected by middle-class society and in most books about adolescents. Of these four major adolescent life goals, society is least equipped to guide adolescents in the sexual and moral and values areas.

Little has been said in this chapter about morality and values. The topic has more often received narrow doctrinaire than thoughtful and rational consideration. There are broad guidelines that can be laid down, and these are developed in Chapter 14. As far as the total life of any human being is concerned, his morality and values are more likely than anything else to be the determinant of whether or not he has lived a happy or an unhappy life or a constructive or destructive life.

Even with all their conflicts and all their crises, most American youth, as has been said of the British, muddle through.

SUMMARY

The conceptual framework for adolescence which has been described in this chapter will help to organize and give meaning to the data throughout the book. Reasons for this conceptual framework are both practical and academic: it helps to organize data, it points out gaps in existing data and suggests new research, and it is useful in suggesting applications to real life which, however, must be done cautiously.

Adolescence is the period of time between puberty (for boys, first ejaculation that they associate with sexual maturity; first menstruation for girls) and a condition of self-governance. An adolescent attains executive independence when he becomes independent from his caretakers in making all his major personal decisions. The length of adolescence varies by social class (longer for middle than lower) and sex (shorter for girls).

Learning is inferred from performance. It is generally faster under conditions where reward and punishment are immediate, consistent, and plentiful. It is defined as a change in behavior following practice. Drive is a fundamental part of learning, and may be thought of as the energy that makes it possible. Drives function in energizing and sensitizing, selective, and directive fashions.

Drive theory is the foundation for a psychology of adolescence, but a theory of change must also be included. Adolescence is both a time of drastic change and a part of the continuous stream of human development. Drive and change theory thus interact with each other.

The most dramatic change in adolescence is the addition of the first new drive to be socialized since infancy. The over-all impact of the sex drive differs little between the sexes, although its direct biological impact is more urgent for boys than girls.

Biological drives that must be satisfied in social settings are the most important in shaping personality. Such drives are comfort seeking and pain avoidance, hunger (for food), elimination, and sex.

Frustration, aggression, anxiety, curiosity, and dependency are also drives. An increase in any drive increases both the strength and likelihood of occurrence of all the other responses a person has learned. Thus, under high drive, old responses may reappear. The regression that is considered characteristic of adolescents is one product of such reappearance. High drive may also result in a "tunnel vision," in which adolescents appear insensitive to their environments. Many aspects of the environment that do not relate directly to the adolescent's needs often go unnoticed.

Puberty alone produces many new pressures, and the attitudes and expectations of society also change sharply at pubescence. Such changes expose the adolescent to many new frustrations and ambiguities that may increase aggression, blunt curiosity, increase anxiety, and frustrate dependency needs. All these things in turn add to total drive state.

Social training is reasonably continuous and consistent from early childhood for needs for comfort seeking and avoidance of pain, hunger, aggression, and anxiety. However, sex, curiosity, and dependency are inconsistently and discontinuously handled in American society. With reference to dependency, boys are caught in a two-way bind: Their drive for autonomy, independence, and initiative prevents them from seeking the dependency they often need; and the expectations held for them by society prevent tenderness being offered and, when offered, from being accepted.

The high drive state of adolescence coupled with the rapid changes in social attitudes and practices and insecurity produced by such changes often intensify an adolescent's search for his own identity to the crisis level.

There are two double codes: sexual, under which boys and men are allowed more freedom than girls and women; and emotional-expressive, under which girls and women are given more latitude.

[Boys' major social-personal goals seem to be for autonomy (competence and independence or self-sufficiency) in achievement-related behavior; while girls seem more to seek a role of well- and comfortably defined femininity and security.]

Major adolescent goals are status (competence in achievement-related skills and respect for possessing them), sociality (possessing friends and intimates), adequate sexual adjustment, and self- and socially fulfilling values and morals. Status may be more highly valued for boys, sociality for girls. Both are probably more important in the long run than sex, although the importance of sexuality is likely to be underplayed within the core, middle-class culture. [While often neglected by scholars, an individual's moral-values development is likely to be more important than anything else in determining the quality of his life.] These four major goals are achieved in all life settings, whether family, school, community groups, or job.

[The point that needs greatest emphasis in a psychology of adolescence is that a drive-change theory predicts that the period is one in which great personal change can occur. Such change can be malign or benign, and it is society's responsibility to maximize the latter while minimizing the former.]

2

Methods and Problems in the Study of Adolescents

INTRODUCTION

This chapter is a logical and necessary follow-up to Chapter 1, for certainly if a theory is to organize the facts within an area, then at the absolute minimum, the *facts must be accurate*. Some of the facts dealing with adolescents are open to question. The collapse of G. Stanley Hall's theory of development, particularly his theory of adolescence (1904), under the impact of Margaret Mead's factual data (for example, 1939) is a case in point. Maslow and Sakoda (1952), among others, present data that raise doubts about Kinsey's (1948, 1953) facts; Maslow and Sakoda show that volunteers are either sexier, or franker, or both, than nonvolunteers.

A theory also must point out factual contradictions and gaps in factual knowledge; but, if the facts in the first place are not accurate, then further research may simply be a wild goose chase.

Finally, if facts are to be applied to real-life guidance of adolescents—which, in the nature of things, must be done—facts must be accurate, or using them for guidance would be irresponsible and dangerous.

For such reasons, before plunging further into research and conclusions about adolescents, one must carefully regard the nature of the study within the field.

DIMENSIONS OF RESEARCH IN ADOLESCENT DEVELOPMENT

Some years ago, Spiker[1] suggested that every research study in human development can be described according to its position on four dimensions. Each of these can be thought of as a continuum ranging between two extremes (see Chapter 1, footnote 6). Although some of these dimensions may vary together, there is no logical necessity for them to do so. The four dimensions are: (1) normative-explanatory; (2) ahistorical-historical; (3) naturalistic-manipulative; and (4) atheoretical-theoretical. Figure 2-1 depicts the four dimensions of research study.

As an interpretive example of Figure 2-1, the third dimension, naturalistic versus manipulative, can be explained on the continuum as follows. In the naturalistic research area the prime examples are the work of cultural anthropologists of the classic stripe: scientists who study their peoples, whether in Samoa or Kansas, in a natural setting, and who do not personally exert any influence on the population; they simply look to see and take notes. Of course, their presence alters the natural setting to some degree but, once the group they are observing is familiar with them, it goes back to behaving naturally.

Observers, for example, have little influence on a class of children accustomed to having teachers-in-training in the room who are sitting in chairs and taking notes. The author was both an observer and a group leader in the famous Lewin, Lippitt, and White study of authoritarian–laissez-faire–democratic group management (1939). This study involved ten intermediate grade level boys at a time, and about twenty observers. The physical circumstances in which the study was conducted were in a large, third floor attic room of an old academic building on the University of Iowa campus. The observers made their notes in moderate twilight concealed from the children only by a waist-high burlap cloth barrier: They could easily be seen by any youngster at any time. During certain phases of the study, it was required that the group leaders leave the boys to see how they behaved when alone. One activity involved making papier-mâché masks, a messy operation which involves soaking newspapers in water. There was no plumbing in the attic so that, to dispose of the water, the boys had to leave the attic and travel some distance to pour it down the custodian's sink. During one such period of leader absence, and with several pails of water to dispose of, the group agreed to dump the water out of the window. Their reason for doing so was expressed by one of them and agreed to by all: "Why go all the way down the hall to pour the water out? Let's just dump it out the window. Nobody's watching." But twenty or so adults were sitting there in plain sight.

Even taboo behavior is likely to appear under strong motivation and in the presence of observers. The author and two graduate students

[1] In informal conversation.

Figure 2.1

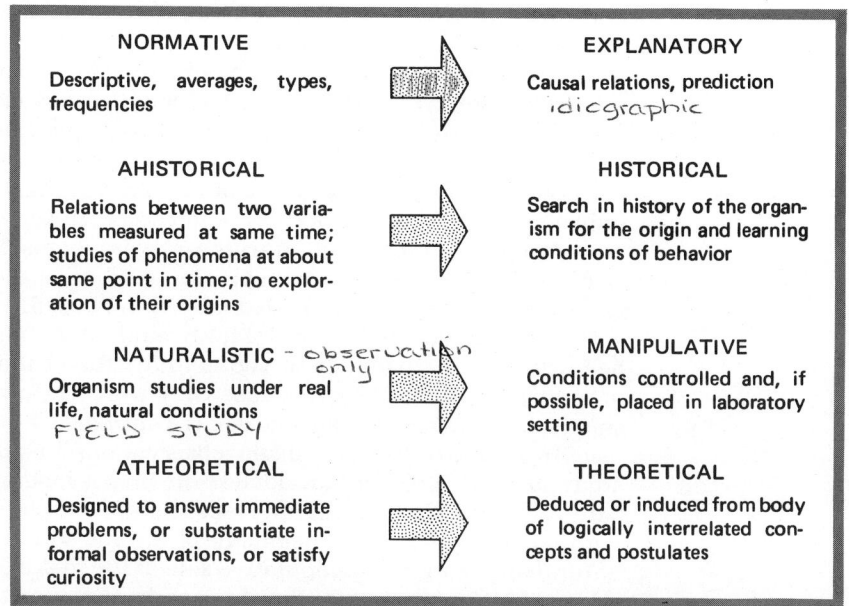

NORMATIVE	→	EXPLANATORY
Descriptive, averages, types, frequencies		Causal relations, prediction *idiographic*
AHISTORICAL	→	**HISTORICAL**
Relations between two variables measured at same time; studies of phenomena at about same point in time; no exploration of their origins		Search in history of the organism for the origin and learning conditions of behavior
NATURALISTIC — *observation only*	→	**MANIPULATIVE**
Organism studies under real life, natural conditions *FIELD STUDY*		Conditions controlled and, if possible, placed in laboratory setting
ATHEORETICAL	→	**THEORETICAL**
Designed to answer immediate problems, or substantiate informal observations, or satisfy curiosity		Deduced or induced from body of logically interrelated concepts and postulates

Study requires interaction

Four dimensions of studies in human development. (From McCandless, 1967.)

were recently conducting physical growth research with adolescent delinquent boys of normal intelligence, who knew them only moderately well. The boys were brought into the private research room in groups of five to ten. To secure the necessary physical measurements, the youngsters (who ranged in age from 15 to 18 years) had to strip to their shorts. On one occasion, a boy developed an erection. He asked to be excused to go to the men's room (immediately adjacent). Permission was given. Another youngster almost immediately also asked to be excused for the same destination. The discreet checking required by the protocol of the institution revealed the boys masturbating each other. The circumstances were such that the youngsters almost certainly knew that this check would be made by one of the three research workers present, but their drive was sufficiently intense that they went ahead to behave to all intents and purposes as though they were alone, using only the flimsy disguise of retreating a few steps to the men's room. This latter, somewhat unusual, episode may, of course, simply illustrate tunnel vision, or an insensitivity to nondrive-related aspects of the environment. However, it appears, regardless, that it *is* possible for a good research worker to observe his subjects with validity in their natural setting if, in a manner of speaking, he makes himself a part of the scenery.

A. J. Reiss (1968) reaches similar conclusions from a study of the controversial topic of police brutality. Under the circumstances of a research study, one would expect the police to go to extremes to conceal from the observer instances of brutality. However, Reiss reports that thirty-six people observed encounters between police and citizens in Boston, Chicago, and Washington, D.C. With police permission, observers spent seven days a week for seven weeks sitting with the police in patrol cars and monitoring booking and lock-up procedures in high-crime precincts.

Reiss reports a startling amount of police brutality, even under such conditions. He believes the incidence observed was minimal, but thinks it represents what was actually going on at the time of the study (the summer of 1966). He believes there are three reasons why police behaved brutally in the presence of observers: (1) each department was enlisted with the cooperation of the top administrators; (2) the observers were trained to fit into a role of trust and were themselves genuine in this role; (3) Reiss states that "people cannot change their behavior in the presence of others as easily as many think" (p. 15), most particularly when they are deeply involved (highly motivated) in the situation. Reiss believes that the police observed actually forgot that an observer was present and often, partly because they were not quite sure what they should do, simply went ahead to behave normally.

In contrast to naturalistic observations, a purely manipulative study involves bringing an adolescent into a laboratory, giving him a carefully defined treatment, and recording his response to the treatment.

Somewhere toward the middle of the continuum — more toward the naturalistic than the manipulative side of the average — is a study by the author (McCandless, 1942) in which an autocratically managed cottage for delinquent adolescent boys was turned over to new cottage parents, who were given a detailed manual for handling the cottage group in a democratic fashion. At the time their regime was established, friendship choices were elicited from the boys to determine who were the leaders and the more popular boys, who were the followers, and who were the isolates. Independently of securing these measures from the boys, the autocratic adults who managed the cottage and knew the boys well were asked to rank them on a continuum from "bully boy or muscle man" to "works toward mature democratic goals for welfare of entire group."

At the beginning of the democratic regime, the bully boys were the leaders and the most popular boys. After some weeks of democracy, the procedures were repeated and it was found that the leadership-popularity hierarchy had changed drastically so that the erstwhile bully boys were now isolates and rejects; the formerly middle-of-the road "good boys" became the leaders.

Validity is lent to the results by the demonstrated disturbance of several of the bully boys who, as they saw themselves losing status and "power," ran away or engaged in such egregious delinquency that they were voted out of the cottage.

A study can also be a mixture of types, as, for instance, in studies of the influence of water fluoridization on dental caries (tooth decay). It is manipulative in the sense that something has been added to the water that people drink. It is normative in the sense that its effectiveness is judged by the number of tooth cavities per person before fluorine was added to the water compared with the number of cavities per person after fluorine was added. Some studies of lung cancer and smoking are further examples of mixtures of continua and types illustrated in Figure 2-1. The resulting norms are assumed by the experts to have some *explanatory* value with reference to lung cancer.

Normative-Explanatory Perhaps the major goal of early workers in human development was to describe the behavior and characteristics of the developing human organism, hopefully from conception onward. Many of the research findings reviewed in the previous chapter are normative (for example, the average United States male reports two to four sexual outlets per week during adolescence; fewer girls than boys have premarital intercourse).

Most of the many studies of adolescents' interests and activities are normative: Who and how many among them like acid rock music? What is the average age at which one begins to date? How much money does the average adolescent spend annually? How much mathematics does he know?

Collection of such norms can be helpful. An adolescent's parents and possibly his physician begin to be concerned if there is no sign of pubescence by the time he is 15 or 16. A teacher, knowing that the average IQ of his class is 85, will pitch his instruction lower than if he knows it is 115. Thus, a majority of the class, although not each individual, may be more effectively taught. If the average American parent allows his daughter to begin car dates at 14½ years, then there may well be some special and meaningful characteristics of parents (and daughters) when the girl is allowed to begin to date at 12, or when she is not allowed to date until age 17.

In an explanatory approach to research, the attempt is made to go beyond compiling frequencies and averages. Such an approach concerns itself less with the average time of girls beginning to date than in documenting why some parents allow early dating, others insist that dating be much delayed, and how both the average and the deviating tendencies affect the girls. One author will simply interview (verbally or by questionnaire) to find out how many high school students cheat. Another will vary factors of risk of detection and amount of public knowledge about performance in an effort to determine the circumstances that produce cheating (see Hill and Kochendorfer, 1969), and thus help to explain and predict it.

Research at the explanatory rather than the normative end of this methodological continuum seems more likely to contribute to an understanding of human development, although the establishing of accurate norms is often the essential first step in explanation. Good, accurate norms help identify the range of the best guesses. The teacher who knows that the average IQ of his class is low is less likely to err in his teaching level than the teacher without such information. The author of a text to be used for eighth grade social studies finds it useful, even necessary, to know how extensive and difficult is the vocabulary that can be understood by the average boy or girl in the eighth grade. It is commonly granted that history textbooks have not provided adequate normative information about the contributions made by Afro-Americans to the history of the United States.

But norms, in the statistical sense, are not explanations. They do not enable prediction of the development of an individual adolescent nor do they truly help adults to guide him. It is reassuring to the parents of an adolescent girl as well as to the girl who has just menstruated at the age of 13 to know that this is about when the average American girl experiences this event, but it is no reassurance to the girl who does not menstruate until three years later.

Norms are frequently taken for explanation, even by those who should know better. Troubled parents ask the school guidance worker about their rebellious 15-year-old son. They are given Douvan and Adelson's (1966) normative results: Boys of this age are almost desperately preoccupied with seeking autonomy. Both the parents and the counselor seem to be relieved once these data are shared, and each apparently believes that something has been explained. However, the fact is not the explanation, which involves much more: an accounting of how or why this circumstance came to be, where it is likely to lead, and how the parents and counselor can employ it most usefully for all concerned.

Norms, while essential and of interest to all, are concerns for the pragmatist. Developmental psychologists (particularly those who are interested in adolescents) are likely to be pragmatists and empiricists. This may be why there are so many facts—and of them there are many about which thoughtful scholars are skeptical—and so few explanations. It is for this reason that in this book an attempt is made to maintain a conceptual orientation. It seems more promising to depend on theory for explanation than on mere collections of facts. Additionally, facts (particularly about adolescents) are likely to go out of date quickly. The rock 'n roll of last week is yesterday's acid rock, and acid rock, in turn, will have a replacement soon after these words are written. It is for somewhat similar reasons that scholars of today are tentative about using Kinsey's figures concerning sexual behavior. It is not at all unlikely that sexual behavior in the late sixties and early seventies is very different from what it was in the late forties and early fifties when Kinsey published his findings about American males and females respectively. As was mentioned in Chapter 1, the advent of "the pill" may produce profound changes, particularly in the sexual behavior of females.

Ahistorical-Historical There are two major types of ahistorical research. The first type poses a question that, illustratively, might be: "Are adolescents less reluctant to have physical check-ups if they must depend on their parents to drive them to the doctor's office or clinic than if the school (for example) provides an impersonal, nonfamily pick-up and delivery service?" In a hypothetical study to answer this question, an investigator might form two groups of boys and girls: an experimental group for which the school provides a pick-up and delivery service, and a control group for which parents provide the transportation. The two groups should be about the same in average age and number, should include equal numbers of boys and girls (boys may react very differently from girls to *mothers* taking them to the doctor), they should include similar numbers of only, first, and second and later-born children. The parents and adolescents should be of about the same educational level and social class, and so on. If there is a greater frequency of going for the physical examination and less resistance to the whole process under the school-related transportation system, the research worker concludes (after he has checked his findings statistically to see that they could not have occurred merely by chance) that health care for adolescents may be better fostered if the school rather than the parent implements it.

In research like this, the investigator does not concern himself with the parent-child history that produces resistance, nor does he necessarily relate it to adolescents' need for autonomy. Neither does he inquire about the behavior of those who do not follow the general trend: for example, those girls who will accompany their mother, but will not take part in the school program for getting them to the doctor.

In the second type of ahistorical research two variables are measured at about the same time and related to each other. For example, a psychologist wishes to determine the relation between siblings' (brothers and sisters) intelligence test quotients. As close together in time as possible, he administers intelligence tests to all the brother-sister pairs (or total families) he can find. He tries to find brother-brother, sister-sister, and brother-sister pairs and, ideally, tries to get a wide selection of subjects corresponding, perhaps, to the United States census of occupational and educational distributions. He may confine himself to a sample made up entirely of white, or Afro-American, or Hispano children between the ages of 15 and 18, all of whom are attending public schools. His results show that brightness clusters together in families: All children in a family tend to be bright or dull. He concludes that there is a statistically significant correlation between the intelligence test scores of siblings. But he does not necessarily (or usually) try to determine why some bright brothers have dull siblings. Did an older, bright brother so overshadow his younger sib that the younger was in some way slowed down in intellectual development? Was the home extremely disorganized when an older, duller sibling was in his most impressionable time of intellectual development while it had stabilized by the time the brighter younger one came along?

As can be seen, the historical approach has much in common with the explanatory approach, and holds that the experiences an individual has had in the past determine the kind of person he is at the moment, how he perceives his current situation and, therefore, what he will do at the present moment in time.

A true historical approach to many of the pressing questions about adolescent development involves longitudinal study (repeated measures of the same subjects) of children as they grow up and move into adolescence. Perhaps much of the current concern about the storm and stress of adolescence is that researchers do not follow adolescents on into maturity when, as many predict and some data show, most of them will "turn out," regardless. Longitudinal studies are exceptionally complex, difficult, and expensive. Thus, almost no individuals and few research centers can undertake them. Not least among the difficulties is maintaining the cooperation of a representative or typical sample of families year after year—or even for a few months. Even when they have been maintained for all the years of their childhood, many adolescents will drop out of a longitudinal study, perhaps because of the autonomy seeking that has been discussed.

Many investigators attempt to reconstruct an individual's history by interviewing his mother or both parents, or by interviewing adults about their own adolescence. Many of Kinsey's data about adolescent sex behavior come from adults looking back in time at themselves, or at what they believe to have been themselves. This approach may be called the semihistorical approach. The classic Sears, Maccoby, and Levin (1957) study is one of the best known examples of this technique. However, Irene Rosenthal (1963), who worked both with longitudinal and semihistorical data, finds that accuracy of retrospect upon one's adolescence leaves much to be desired. Women tend more than men to reflect their present life circumstances into their past, and neither sex is entirely accurate in its retrospection.

Naturalistic Manipulative

The naturalistic-manipulative dimension of research methods has already been discussed in some detail in the introduction to this section. Naturalistic study observes the subject in his natural setting. Manipulative research is more likely to be laboratory research in which the experimenter exerts controls in order to study, in as pure a form as possible, the phenomenon in which he is interested. Astronomy is naturalistic, whereas modern physics is predominantly manipulative. An observational study of an adolescent in his classroom or on the ghetto street corner is naturalistic. A study in which his behavior is observed and contrasted when he is performing a task, first for a man, and second for a woman experimenter, is manipulative.

Historically, developmental research has been entirely or partially naturalistic. An exception is the multitude of experimental studies done with college students. There seems to be greater use of manipulative studies with more representative samples, which is probably good. The manipulative approach is much superior to the naturalistic approach in precision. However, well-done naturalistic studies are always desirable. It is unlikely that researchers can now or in the near future replicate the more dramatic aspects of real life in the laboratory. There are many developmental problems that cannot ethically be taken into the laboratory, such as raw violence and anger, mother fixation, and sexual aberration. These problems will of necessity be dealt with either naturalistically or by interview for a long time.

However, some problems are now being taken into the laboratory, and very constructive answers are emerging concerning topics that, even a few years ago, no one thought could be studied experimentally. Johnson and Masters' (1966) *Human Sexual Response* illustrates such research.

Methodological problems in manipulative research are enormous. For example, Money (1961) addresses himself to sex hormones and human eroticism. He finds it necessary to introduce his chapter by discussing the limitations of such research. Laboratory difficulties exist because of possible and even frequent transformation of androgens (male sex hormones) into estrogens by males; and the opposite by females. The sex hormones in real life are also very unstable compounds. "Determinations of hormone levels in blood and urine are, in general, determinations of derivative forms and metabolic end-products of the actual compounds active in the body, some of them biologically inert" (p. 1385). Further, hormonal assays can only be regarded in the total context of the organism; for example, urinary ketosteroids may have no significance in males, but they may have great significance in tumorous enlargement of the adrenal gland, or when there are signs of precocious puberty. Nor do the sex hormones have consistent effects on secondary sex characteristics. For example, eunuchoid youths who are short in pituitary development may become quite virile except for their beard growth, while artificially castrated boys will grow beards under the same hormonal treatment.

Parenthetically, Money concludes that about all that can be definitely said within his context is that it is clear that androgen specifically arouses males erotically and that, without it, sex fantasy, erections, and ejaculation decline in frequency and effectiveness. On the other hand, estrogens (female sex hormones) do very little for the female except to make her more lubricous (genitally well lubricated) and thus more likely to enjoy sexual activity. Even with these conclusions, Money remarks that there are many reports of continuing cognitional sexuality following castration among males, particularly after an adult sexual pattern has been established.

Atheoretical-Theoretical

In the early days of developmental psychology, research workers were likely to be atheoretical, even antitheoretical. Today few deny the usefulness of psychological theory. Many practical problems, however, remain to be settled in areas (for example, education) where little theory of any rigorous sort has been developed. Such problems continue to demand answers and receive much attention. Eventually, it is almost certain (as has proved to be the case in the relation between physics and engineering) that truly sound (efficient and effective) educational practice will come only when sound, rather abstract, psychological, sociological, and educational theories have been developed and tested.

METHODOLOGICAL PROBLEMS

This section treats the problems that beset the scientific investigation of adolescent development. The following difficulties are among the most frequent in research concerning youth. They are of equal concern for studies of younger children and adults, and are encountered by any who do psychological, psychiatric, educational, and sociological research. The are: (1) contamination; (2) reconstruction through retrospection; (3) faulty logic; (4) poor definition of concepts; (5) direct influence of the investigator; (6) problems of sampling; and (7) unsound generalization.

Contamination

The most frequent type of contamination occurs when the investigator knows the predicted nature of the relation between an independent and a dependent variable and can exert control over the measurement of both. The less objective and quantifiable the measurement of the variables, the more likely it is that contamination will occur. Ratings or judgments made from interviews are notably subjective and difficult to quantify satisfactorily.

A typical piece of research, unless it seeks simply to describe adolescents in terms of some single factor such as height, weight, pubescent progress, intelligence, or reading ability, is designed to test the relation between an independent (or, speaking loosely, causal) variable and a dependent (or effect) variable. For example, in a study of the relationship between maternal employment and a youth's intellectual functioning, the latter may be designated as the dependent variable. But when a study seeks to establish whether (and to what degree) intelligence is related to school work, intellectual functioning becomes the independent variable.

The possibility of contaminating research results always exists when the person collecting the data is aware of the predicted relation between the independent and the dependent variable. For example, consider a young, sophisticated, and eager research worker who wishes to check for himself the Douvan and Adelson (1966) hypothesis that adolescent boys are very strong in autonomy, independence, and initiative seeking, while adolescent girls are weak in this sort of striving behavior, being mainly eager to establish themselves as feminine and socially secure. Further assume that this research worker is emotionally invested in the Douvan-Adelson hypothesis, perhaps because it makes sense to him in terms of his own adolescent development. He believes in it! (Or he may disbelieve it—the contamination effect is equally likely to occur.) Quite unconsciously, the putative scholar may influence his results in the direction he wishes by any one of a number of means, all of which have been depicted in the research literature (see, for example, R. Rosenthal, 1966).

He may slant his questions so as to pull out autonomy directed answers from boys, feminine role seeking answers from girls. If a boy gives an answer that suggests but is not definitive concerning autonomy goals, the interviewer may probe until he comes up with an answer that definitely fits his autonomy category. An identical ambiguous answer from a girl may go unnoticed.[2] Similar errors may creep into the categorization of his responses. In sum, there is (as Rosenthal has demonstrated) much likelihood that research workers, working absolutely honestly as far as they are aware, may come up with data that look just the way they want them to look. This is contamination.

Rosenthal has also demonstrated that expectations of results influence actual results. He finds, for example, that children expected to be bright behave as though they were, and conversely. Some of Rosenthal's work (Rosenthal and Jacobson's 1968 book, *Pygmalion in the Classroom*) has been tellingly criticized (see R. L. Thorndike 1968, for example). However, the position of caution about bias that Rosenthal takes is more than justified. Beez (1968), checking the Rosenthal hypothesis, finds that presumably sophisticated education graduate students at Indiana University, when given children to teach who were labeled as possessing high or low ability completely without regard to their actual tested intelligence, behaved as follows: (1) They tried to teach more symbols to high- than to low-ability children. (2) The "high-ability" children actually learned more items (although not more accurately) than the "low-ability" children, although they did not really differ in intelligence. (3) The "teachers" rated the putative high-ability children more favorably than the putative low-ability children on achievement, social

---

[2]This illustrates the sensitizing effect of drive, as discussed in Chapter 1.

competency, and intellectual ability. (4) The "teachers" cued the children on their expectations, quite unconsciously apparently, by giving the "low-ability" children more explanations of the symbols to be taught, by presenting more examples, and by spending more time on nonteaching activities. (5) Although the "high- and low- ability" groups did not differ in actual intelligence, only one of the "teachers" rated the task to be taught too difficult for a child in the "high-ability group," while 63 percent of the "teachers" considered the task too difficult for the "low-ability" group.

Thus dramatically do expectations work!

Another type of bias is often seen in individual intelligence testing. The implications of this for evaluating disadvantaged youth are horrendous. If a youngster is known or suspected to be of high intelligence, borderline performance on an item is likely to be scored as pass; for a child judged to be of lower intelligence, the same item will likely receive a grade of fail. The same principle applies to young people's classroom examinations, particularly to the relatively formless essay questions where a teacher's judgment of right or wrong is free to operate.

Even in experimental situations with clear-cut categories and mechanical means of recording responses, human subjects are extremely sensitive to variations of expression on the experimenter's face, or to differential systematic cues emanating from the apparatus. *Behavior guided by such cues, then, determines the outcome of the study, not the variable that is being investigated.*

Reconstruction through Restrospection

The technique of reconstruction through retrospection is widely and often necessarily used in studies of the effects of child rearing practices on adolescent adjustment or in reconstruction of adolescent experiences per se. An investigator may be concerned with how the need for achievement in college has been influenced by the way the young people were handled during childhood. The investigator constructs a questionnaire for mothers to fill out, or interviews the mothers about how the experimental subjects were fed as infants: whether or not feeding was scheduled; when and how the subjects were weaned; when and how they were toilet trained; how they were disciplined; and so on. He relates these reported practices to the characteristics of the young people he has studied and concludes that such-and-such a practice has so-and-so effect on personality.

Many factors, among them forgetting, force us to regard such retrospective data with skepticism. For parents who have had several children, memories about the development of any given child blend with memories of the growth of others.

A lack of frankness often accompanies reports of child rearing and experiences during earlier periods of one's life. Most parents have been exposed to people who have told them how their children should be reared, and all individuals have clear perceptions of what is and what is not socially desirable. No parent, on the other hand, has dealt entirely according to the book with his children, and few people conform in all aspects of their lives to the social desirability norms. Hence, reports are likely to be slanted in the direction that the interviewee or questionnaire answerer thinks is correct or respectable; or in the direction he thinks fit the opinions of the research worker. Since the research worker is most likely to be middle class, white, and Anglo-Saxon Protestant, this is likely to produce massive bias in research results. Anyone wishing to use this method should study Robbins (1963) and I. Rosenthal (1963), for example, carefully and thoughtfully. Retrospection perhaps points in the correct direction, but it is likely to be rather wide of the precise mark.

Faulty Logic

The most frequent example of faulty logic in this area, one that is made even by sophisticated scholars in the field, is that since two things are related to each other, then one *causes* the other. A classical finding in the research literature is that the number of frying pans in the home correlates positively with the intelligence test quotients of the children. Thus, "Frying pans cause intelligence." There is an obvious intervening link here: Better educated parents are more prosperous as a group; people with more money have more frying pans; and better educated parents have brighter children. Thus, for reasons—but not *causes*—that are perfectly sensible, there is a positive correlation between incidence of frying pans and level of IQ.

A more subtle illustration was discussed earlier: Adolescence causes awkwardness because of rapid growth. A more plausible speculation is that the awkwardness is simply one more expression of the high drive level that characterizes adolescence and includes embarrassed self-awareness and heightened anxiety. Not only does exceptionally high drive seem to produce the tunnel vision phenomenon but it also seems to interfere with both the speed of learning and the efficiency of performing complex acts. (See DiBartolo and Vinacke, 1969, for one of many examples of this phenomenon.) In other words, all that a relationship tells us is that one thing goes together with, or is concomitant with, or covaries, with another, *not* that one causes another. *Cause cannot be inferred from correlation.*

Another example, as applicable to the psychology of adolescents as to the younger children whom it concerned, is a classic study of toilet training practices (Holway, 1949). From rather full information gained from mothers of children attending a child development center's nursery school, certain mothers were rated as strict, others as permissive. The children's behavior in a fantasy play situation was then studied. It was concluded that the play of strictly toilet trained children indicated that they were more disturbed and less happy than the permissively trained children. This difference was related to the differential toilet training in a causative fashion. The possibility was ignored that strict toilet training may be associated with other restrictive child rearing practices (as is suggested by Sears, Maccoby, and Levin, 1957), and that it may have been the other practices, singly or together with toilet training, that produced the fantasy differences. Furthermore, it is possible that neither strict toilet training nor general restrictiveness was associated with disturbed fantasy play, but that the children with disturbed fantasy were harder to handle than other children, so that the mothers were driven to restrictiveness by the characteristics of children. Human relations is a two-way street. Delinquents are said to come from broken homes. But has anyone ever checked to see how many broken homes are due to the fact that the behavior of the delinquent child so disturbed the parents that they separated?

Poor Definition of Concepts

The results of scientific study are dependable to the degree that an investigator has spelled out what he means and what he has done. Both the specification of a concept and its measurement determine the clarity and ultimate usefulness of a scientific definition.

Every scientific study must make use of concepts that are abstractions from observed events. Some concepts are quite close to the phenomena they represent (for example, concepts such as house and car). Most of the concepts used in developmental studies (particularly in the personality and social areas) are abstractions at a higher level and are much less easily related to events in the concrete world. Examples of such concepts are maladjustment, dependency, aggression, overprotection, and even drive.

The concepts used by an investigator must be defined both in abstract terms that mean the same thing to the reader or listener and to the originator and in terms of the operations (measurements or methods) used for a particular study. Operational or experimental definitions are adequate to the extent that they are satisfactory behavioral indicators of the concepts they are intended to represent. Without a clear conceptual definition, an adequate and useful operational definition is impossible.

The Clark and Tifft (1966) study referred to earlier represents an attempt to relate two operational definitions of the same thing to each other. Clark and Tifft were interested in behavior that differed from the norm of social acceptability. As will be remembered, they used as their research subjects forty-five college males who were enrolled in an introductory sociology class. First, they administered an anonymous questionnaire asking the young men to report about whether they had engaged in each of a number of deviant behaviors. The questionnaire was coded so that identities could be determined, and the subjects were brought in again for a polygraph interview session dealing with the same offenses (this is the modified lie-detector technique). Clark and Tifft assumed that the latter was the more accurate measure of what these college boys had actually done.

For example, 22.5 percent of them admitted to starting fistfights since they began high school, but this was originally overreported by 17.5 percent. And 22.5 percent admitted to homosexual relations, but 15 percent of the boys originally overreported, 5 percent underreported. Fifty-five percent had willfully destroyed the property of others, but 12.5 percent of them originally underreported. Sixty-two and one-half percent had driven an auto without a license or permit, but 12.5 percent originally underreported this delinquency. Ninety-five percent of them had drunk liquor illegally; 55 percent had had intercourse with girls or women other than their wives; 85 percent had speeded excessively (but 40 percent underreported); 95 percent admitted to masturbation, but 30 percent originally underreported and 5 percent overreported; and so on.

In other words, one's results are likely to vary greatly according to the clarity and adequacy of the measure he uses; and two measures of the same thing, as in the Clark and Tifft study, do not necessarily give the same results.

The research literature for adolescence abounds with poor definition. Few authors have been so ingenious or careful as Clark and Tifft. To repeat, Clark and Tifft's abstraction deals with delinquency; their methods are (1) questionnaire and (2) polygraph interview.

Direct Influence of the Investigator upon His Research Results

Another problem frequently encountered in research dealing with adolescents is that the investigator himself affects the results of the study he is conducting. Illustrations of this have already been given for contamination and, to some extent, this topic is a special case of contamination of results. One of the potentially most profitable methods of studying human development is to make repeated or continuing studies of the same person over time. Such studies have furnished valuable information about the development of intelligence and the rate and pattern of physical growth. These are examples of topics where the influence of the investigator is relatively slight, and for which there are valid and reliable techniques of measurement. But longitudinal studies have thrown little light on the effects of child rearing practices or on the question of how personality develops. There are two major reasons for this. First, it is difficult to ask meaningful (conceptually clear) questions about personality development. What, for example, is meant by adjustment? dependency? maternal rejection? Second, the investigator and the things he stands for influence the very child rearing practices that are being studied, or impinge on the unfolding personality dimension in which the research worker is interested.

The average person who conducts research with children, youth, and their parents has a real and special regard for them. If he sees them developing in a fashion that he knows is likely to lead to maladjustment, it is almost impossible for him to behave in a coldly dispassionate, purely scientific fashion. He must do something to help. But his behavior, although well intentioned, distorts his results. The study becomes one not of personal development but, in a longitudinal study, of parents and children *and* investigator and their relations with each other. Someone has facetiously defined the typical Eskimo family as one father, one mother, one child, and a cultural anthropologist and his wife. Whenever the research worker, for extrascientific motives—no matter how well intended—directly affects the relations he is studying, the study he produces becomes different from what he originally intended.

The phenomenon of experimenter influence has been clearly demonstrated in the Hawthorne studies of the effects of different kinds of working conditions on the productivity of factory workers (see Homans, 1958). Regardless of the kinds of change introduced and regardless of whether the changes were in the direction of better or poorer physical working conditions (in this case, lighting), the productivity of the experimental group increased. The effect of physical working conditions was overshadowed by the effect of other changes: the workers' awareness of taking part in a study; their being set apart as a special small group; their altered relations with supervisory personnel; perhaps merely the fact that they believed that someone was genuinely interested in them.

Such social and attitudinal variables are indirectly related to the experiment itself and actually work against the investigators' purpose. Thus, they obscure the effects of the factors the study was initially designed to explore. Something similar seems likely to occur in longitudinal studies of personality where, over the years, an investigator has maintained an intimate interaction with the parents and children who form the core of the study. In view of Beez' results (the influence of expectancy on children's learning, 1968), one wonders what was the effect on the subjects of the Terman studies of genius (see, for example, Terman and Oden, 1947). These youngsters and their parents knew that they were very bright indeed, even brilliant. May this not have produced something like the self-fulfilling prophecy? ("I *am* brilliant. Thus I must behave brilliantly!"), Terman's subjects *did* indeed behave intelligently and were successful as a group.

As has been inferred, research workers may have not only direct but indirect influence on the populations they study. The author once conducted a study that remains unpublished for reasons that will become clear as it is described. His purpose was to check the influence of psychotherapy on delinquent 15- to 17-year-old borderline retarded boys of two types: One group was made up of boys whose verbal IQs were much higher than their performance IQs, and the second group was made up of boys with the opposite pattern. Total IQ was the same for each boy in a group and his matched pair in the other group. Each boy in the experimental group (receiving psychotherapy) was matched closely for verbal, performance, and total IQ with a control boy of the same age and general social background.

Parenthetically, the verbal IQ is inferred from items like a vocabulary test, ability to reason verbally, and comprehension of common-sense situations and their explanations or outcomes. A performance IQ is made up by the results on speed and accuracy of completing things like jigsaw puzzles, constructing designs from multicolored blocks, and mastering and executing a coding task. The total IQ falls somewhere between the verbal and performance IQs.

The majority of the high V(erbal)-low P(erformance) boys, for reasons that it is not necessary to go into here, were more severe behavior problems to their teachers, cottage parents, and job supervisors than the high P-low V boys, and this was true for both the control and experimental boys.

Since a residential treatment center is like a small town, word soon gets around concerning anything that is going on. Within a week or two of beginning the psychotherapy with the experimental boys, everyone in the institution knew that "Doc" McCandless was doing something special with the eighteen boys, and that this involved seeing them for rather long periods of time, regularly, in his office. One could almost perceive the teachers, supervisors, and cottage parents saying, "Oh, oh. Anything I do with these kids is going to get back to Doc. I'd better be careful." There is a paranoia that exists between professional and nonprofessional personnel in the institutions the author knows about that creates such an atmosphere. The author soon became aware of the fact that the caretakers were changing their behavior toward the experimental boys, and that this change was greater for the high V-low P than for the high P-low V boys. This was true because the former were more severe behavior problems and thus had been treated more punitively before the experiment began. An effort to reassure the boys' caretakers was fruitless and, while the experiment was continued because almost all the boys seemed to be benefiting from it and enjoying it, the results were scientifically worthless.

Experiments in social and community action are almost impossible to carry on in an acceptable scientific fashion: If it seems that they are working, those responsible for or involved with the control groups (for example, adjacent matched communities, or neighborhoods, or schools) begin to adopt the procedures and thus change the behavior of the controls in the same direction as the experimentals. This dilutes the statistical significance of the results. The author has worked with a compensatory education program for disadvantaged youngsters in Jamaica, a small island with a high gossip rate, where this phenomenon occurs. While this is probably good because more children are benefiting from the procedures, it leaves everything to be desired from the viewpoint of scientific procedures.

For those with special interests in research concerning social action, it will be useful and interesting to read Campbell (1969), who discusses the problems, liabilities, and benefits in depth and with sophistication.

Problems of Sampling The problems of sampling range from the practical difficulties of obtaining human subjects for study to the question of making generalizations from the population studied to other populations.

Practical difficulties in obtaining subjects have limited the knowledge about the relations between lower-lower-class and upper-class adolescents and their parents. Lower-class parents usually do not understand, or they are suspicious, or they are not interested in research. Many have been so much studied during the years of studying poverty and race, and so little has happened to benefit them, that they are understandably hostile. The blame for this state of affairs often lies more at the door of the research worker than with the disadvantaged research subjects. If the research worker approaches parents (for example) sincerely, if he communicates clearly, and if he is able to convince his subjects that he is neither untrustworthy nor patronizing, lower-class parents and others will go along with research efforts just as do most of those in the middle class. But it takes more time to recruit them and keep them involved. We know literally nothing about upper-class adolescents and their parents; they are essentially unavailable for research purposes.

On the other hand, because of the accessibility of students in college psychology and sociology classes, much of our knowledge about adolescent development is based on the study of such young men and women (very shakily based, since they are not typical). The author includes relatively few college student studies in this book, because he is skeptical about whether they form an adequate sample of adolescents from which generalizations can be made to adolescents in general.

The nature of the population on which a study is based determines how well one can generalize from it. Biased samples limit generalization. A biased sample is one in which the measured sample fails to represent and thus to predict the sample it was originally supposed to predict. Bias is essentially a matter of *systematic* variation as opposed to *random*, or chance, variation.

Since it is almost impossible to work with a total population (or universe, as it is often called), a subsection of the population (a sample) must be selected with which to do research. In a random sample, each member of the total population being considered has an equal chance of being selected as a member of the sample, or of being assigned to some particular method of study or experimental treatment within the total research program. The reason for randomizing selection is that *if and only if* a sample is random can the laws of mathematical probability be applied to findings based on that sample, and any sort of confident generalization applied to the total population from which it is drawn.

The problem of biased samples is serious for all research, but particularly so for normative studies. Questions have been raised, for example, about the adequacy of our norms for toilet training. In normative research, it is almost impossible, speaking practically, to avoid biased samples. For example, in studying or comparing the height and weight of 16-year-old white or Afro-American adolescents, a typical procedure is to enlist the cooperation of the public schools of a city or several cities so that all, or a random, or a representative sample of 16 year olds can be measured during the shortest possible period of time. But such an apparently comprehensive sample is biased because some 16 year olds will be absent from school during the time of the study and, in states where 16 is the legal age at which a youngster can leave school, many will have dropped out. The chances are that there will be a higher proportion of Afro-American than of white drop-outs. Over-all, the 16 year olds who are ill on a given day are likely to be those with poorer health, and the drop-outs will come disproportionately from the ranks of the disadvantaged. The drop-out rate will also vary by sex: More 16-year-old boys than girls will usually have dropped out, so that one's sample of girls will be less biased than his sample of boys.

Since chronically ill children are likely to be shorter and lighter than chronically well children, and since disadvantaged youth are likely to have suffered more from poor nutrition and disease than middle-class youth, the population actually going to school will *overrepresent* the height, weight, or almost any other desirable characteristic of United States 16 year olds.

Further, there will be some severely handicapped 16 year olds who never attend school, and their absence will also affect the norms. Finally, there will be some young people who will refuse to cooperate in the study and others whose parents forbid their taking part in research. One can only speculate on how such adolescents differ from the general population. All one knows is that, since most adolescents and their parents are cooperative about such practical matters as research on height and weight, these nonparticipating children differ from the average or normal. It is not known whether their psychological-social differences (their refusal to cooperate) are related to their height and weight.

If this hypothetical research was conducted in St. Louis or Detroit, one cannot say that the results hold for St. Louis and Detroit 16 year olds, but only for "cooperative St. Louis and Detroit 16 year olds who attended public school during the time the study of height and weight was being conducted." Nor does one know whether the results would be the same for Los Angeles or New York 16 year olds.

Occassionally, another type of bias is introduced by an investigator. He formulates a hypothesis, designs a method to test it, secures the cooperation of subjects, and collects his data. The results fall in the direction of his prediction, but are not dramatic enough to reach statistical significance. He looks at his individual cases and sees that most of them have behaved as he predicted they would. A minority has not, and this reduces the over-all effect he had hoped to find. He checks with this minority and finds that each one had "seen through" his research plan—the purpose of his investigation. He concludes that this seeing-through prevented such subjects from behaving according to prediction, and discards their results. The behavior of the remaining subjects is striking enough to support his hypothesis statistically. But he has not checked to see whether, among those who remain, there are also some who had seen through the experiment and, as it were, gone along with him. In other words, he has systematically altered his final sample from the one he originally studied. He would not have been in error if he had included in his original research plan a check for "seeing through," and declared in advance his intention of discarding results obtained from all such insightful or suspicious subjects.

Still another type of bias results from substituting volunteers for persons originally scheduled to take part in a study or experiment. Consider a hypothetical evaluation study being made by a large urban educational system whose administrators are trying to find out why so many 16 year olds leave school. The research worker obtains a census tract of several different areas of the city and matches the names of high school drop-outs in each census tract to the over-all characteristics of the census tract. Thus he presumably constructs a representative sample of all drop-out youth for the city. The number is so large that he cannot study all the youth, so he selects them, much in the manner of the public opinion polls, so as to represent all city drop-outs.

He makes contact with his preselected sample. Most are willing to serve as subjects for study, but some are not. He then looks for volunteers, selecting from among them boys and girls who match the characteristics of those who have refused: for example, so many 17 year olds from college educated families, so many boys, so many girls, so many American Indian youngsters, and so on. He continues to go through his files until he has rounded out a sample that fits his original specifications. In so doing, he has biased his sample. The volunteers differ from the refusers on the very important dimension of cooperativeness. It may be that cooperators in contrast to refusers are more sympathetic toward the school's practices toward them when they were students. Thus, they will give an unduly rosy report of what the system had been like for them. In this fashion, the results may hinder reform of poor school practices or fail to reveal practices that may have been responsible for their dropping out of school, particularly if the practices reflect on the school or their former teachers. Obviously, such a bias influences the conclusions about the universe (here, the total population of high school dropouts). Kinsey (1948, 1953) has often been criticized because of volunteer bias.

Biased samples, then, are those that do not predict the sample they were originally intended to predict. Stratified samples help to overcome bias. A stratified sample is a population like that discussed immediately above. It is based on the known characteristics of the total population. Bias most frequently results from one of the three processes: failure to measure all of the intended sample; elimination of subjects without previous specification of the conditions under which this is to occur; and substitution of one type of subject, most frequently a volunteer, for another.

Unsound Generalization

The three most common types of unsound generalization are:

1. Writing or speaking as though findings were more significant statistically, or more clear cut, than they actually are.
2. Applying findings gathered in one situation to circumstances different in essential characteristics.
3. Applying findings from one population to another population that differs in one or more important dimensions.

Hypothetical examples of these are, for (1), using the well-established, moderately high correlation between the intelligence of brothers and sisters as though it indicated that every child in a given family was himself bright, or dull. Many youngsters have been victimized by this. There is the almost classic example of the teacher who has hurt an academically mediocre younger sib by saying when she first meets him: "Oh yes, I have had Betty in class. I expect you to do as excellently as *she* did for me." Equally frequent are teachers' expectations that each of a series of Jukes brothers and sisters will be as stupid and disturbing as the ones who went before. Since there is reason to believe children tend to live up to what is expected of them, even though Jukes number 4 is a fine boy, he is likely to go to pieces under the impact of his teachers' implicit and frequently *explicit* expectations that he will be stupid, lazy, mean, dishonest, sexy, and vulgar.

The following real-life example of (2) is worth including: Mrs. Johnson, an intelligent lady of 50, is a career high school English teacher in a medium sized town with only one high school. She is known for her tough-mindedness. She cannot be got around; she is a firm taskmistress, and is known as a good teacher. When possible, the high school juniors in whose education she specializes try to get into an English section taught by one of the other teachers. A given number of them, obviously, fail to secure another teacher and are faced with at least a semester of toeing the line with Mrs. Johnson.

Mary Epworth and Joe Dillinger were among those who failed to escape Mrs. Johnson one late summer as they preregistered. Both Mary and Joe are "bright kids," testing above 130 IQ; and both are approaching 16. Mary comes from one of the town's best families, is a school cheerleader, has perhaps more interest in extracurricular activities than in academic curricular activities, but is bound for one of the "better colleges" and must keep up her grade point. Joe's father is a top mechanic and holds a job consistently, although he is known to drink on the job and sometimes makes mistakes on those mornings while he is still nursing his hangover from the day before. Joe's mother left for parts unknown, taking his younger sister with her, when Joe was 8. Neither she nor the sister has been heard from since. Joe and his dad keep a bachelor household in which ladies come and go and parties often last until dawn. Joe is an early maturing boy, tall and muscular, a brunet who has a fairly heavy beard growth. He is by no means naïve in the ways of the world, and makes no secret of the fact that he drinks. He carries his cigarettes conspicuously in his shirt pocket, and dresses "tough." Although he has never been in serious trouble, he is the type of boy on whom school authorities keep a watchful eye. He has a C+ average and is realistically considered to be an underachiever. He has no D grades, however. He disdains sports, although the coaches have long been interested in recruiting him.

Mrs. Johnson conscientiously makes a point of meeting each student during the week before classes begin and goes to great trouble to make appointments. These are closely scheduled. Her appointments with Mary and Joe follow each other.

Mary, a socially adroit girl, has familiarized herself with the situation before coming into it. She has unerringly spotted Mrs. Johnson's Achilles' heel: a love for potted plants such that the classroom resembles a greenhouse. On arriving a minute early for her appointment, she exclaims, without being unduly exuberant, about the lovely plants. She says she knows that Mrs. Johnson would *never* let anyone else fool around with them, they are simply too *precious* and too *lovely*. But she knows they are a lot of work and if ever—after Mrs. Johnson comes to know that she can be trusted—if *ever* she can help, she will be glad to. They must be *such* a lot of work.

Mrs. Johnson is hooked, and Mary is off to a rousing start. By doing enough to get by, she enjoys her extracurricular activities of the semester, but also comes with the B that she needs, rather than the C she has earned. The B is as much for social skill and conscientious watering as it is for performance in English.

Joe is late for his appointment. He comes in, unshaven and bristly, an extinguished but half-smoked most recent cigarette tucked behind his ear. He grunts responses to Mrs. Johnson's conversational gambits; says, before she is quite finished with him, "Well, I guess you don't need me any more," and leaves. Joe is off to a bad start before a week of classes is finished and receives his first school mark of D. Mrs. Johnson, even though she cannot stomach Joe, is too honest to fail him even as she was too honest to give Mary an A. Joe is tired of school anyway and the D is the last straw. He sticks out the semester but, since he is past 16 at its end, drops out of school and goes out into the world.

To summarize, Mrs. Johnson predicted both Mary Epworth and Joe Dillinger from the wrong set of norms. She did them different but perhaps equal injustices.

Another example of this type of unsound generalization is the assumption that, because a young person behaves inflexibly in an experimental situation (for example, fails to change his approach as the type of arithmetic problem presented to him changes), he will act rigidly in a wide variety of real life situations. Mrs. Johnson made this sort of error with Joe Dillinger: Because he was socially uncouth, she judged him to be equally uncouth in English.

An illustration of the third type of unsound generalization is the assumption that the height and weight of the aforementioned "cooperative Detroit and St. Louis 16 year olds attending public school" provide an adequate basis for judging height and weight of 16 year olds in Tahiti or New Orleans.

Generalizations, then, should be made according to the scientific certainty of the original findings, to situations having as much as possible in common with the original research setting, and to populations as similar as possible to the research population from which the findings were obtained. The more closely these conditions are met, the sounder the generalization.

Increasing confidence can be placed in a finding if it has been replicated. If a relation between a certain type of reward pattern and speed of learning has been demonstrated for white rats, rhesus monkeys, 3 year olds in Arizona and New York, Minnesota eighth graders, and college sophomores in California, one can be more confident in saying that it is a general truth or law than if the relation had been demonstrated for only one of these populations. However, one would still hesitate to say that it held for *kooris* (Australian aborigines).

Research workers in developmental psychology frequently overgeneralize or generalize imprecisely, and advisers of parents and teachers err in this direction even more than research workers themselves. For example, it is generally held that praise is better than punishment as a method of motivating learning. Strictly speaking, this generalization is imprecise, because praise and punishment can seldom be compared for their effect on precisely the same behavior. In teaching a learning driver parallel parking, for example, one does not compare the results (1) of praising him for coming to rest exactly two inches from the curb and (2) of punishing him for the same result. A test in this situation is to compare the speed with which he learns this complex skill under conditions (1) of praise for each correct thing he does while parking and (2) of punishment or criticism for each wrong move made with the car. Still a third test, making for more precise generalization, would be (3) to train a group of children by praise for correct responses and criticism for mistakes. With such evidence, it could be said that praise was preferable to punishment, or that a combination of both was better than either alone.

The logical consequences of reward or punishment alone, or a combination of the two, are often not recognized: Reward often tells a person only what he can do; punishment often tells him only what he cannot do; but a combination of the two (used almost automatically as a common-sense technique by most parents, teachers, and others who deal with adolescents) tells young people both what can and cannot be done. The prediction follows that an adolescent handled with a combination of reward and punishment will learn faster and perhaps more flexibly (or at least across a broader range of possibilities) than a child trained entirely by either.

However, in nonemotional, task-oriented situations, the verbal negative (particularly when it is informative and allows for alternative solutions) is one of the most effective learning motivators (H. H. Marshall, 1965). It may be that it is the one most familiar to American children, a conclusion that fits research reported by Ostfeld and Katz (1969). These authors find that young middle-class children respond best to mild threat (their criterion was resistance to the temptation to play with an attractive but forbidden toy and later devaluation of the toy by rejecting it). Lower-class children responded best to harsh threats but did not translate their response into actual devaluation of the toy.

It is easy to make overgeneralizations for data concerning the effects of early physical maturity upon boys: Generally, these effects are benign, at least into middle age (see, for example, M. C. Jones, 1965). These studies will be reviewed extensively in the next two chapters but, for present purposes, the data suggest that one can predict that early maturing middle-class white boys will be relatively more personally and socially mature than late maturing boys. It is easy, then, to expect a given early maturer (for instance, Joe Dillinger in the preceding example) to act in accordance with his developmental age. If his social age and emotional maturity have not kept pace with his physical being, however, we may put him under undue strain and disadvantage him seriously. Early maturity and strong body builds may have different effects in different environments. For white middle-class boys in the suburbs, early maturity and a strong mesomorphic body may simply put a youngster in an even stronger position to shake his own particular apple tree and obtain more goodies than his later maturing peers. But for a Black ghetto boy, the same early maturity and strong physique may lead him to the mastery of the only environment known to him: an asphalt jungle, manipulation of which depends on his being successfully delinquent.

STATISTICAL AND MEASUREMENT CONSIDERATIONS

Without some grasp of measurement and statistical concepts and with no appreciation of common research faults such as those discussed in the preceding section (particularly *unsound generalization*), a reader is lost if he ventures into primary sources—original research articles—or tries intelligently to follow the research summarized and discussed in the rest of the book. He may have been lost at times as he has read to this point. Conversely, this section will be unnecessary review for others.

Correlation

A correlation is an expression of the relation between one thing and another: the degree to which two things vary together, or covary. The correlation between height and weight in the hypothetical sample of Detroit and St. Louis 16 year olds can be illustrated as follows. Assume a random sample of 100 of the boys in the total sample. First, they are arrayed in order of their height with the shortest boy at the left, the tallest at the right. Observation alone will show that there is a tendency for the shorter boys to be lighter, the taller ones heavier. But there will be a number of boys who are heavier than some who are taller than they, and vice versa. For the group as a whole, however, height and weight will covary — will be positively correlated with each other.

Correlation coefficients can theoretically range from perfect positive (+1.00) to perfect negative (−1.00). The condition of a perfect positive correlation is met if, in the above illustration, the tallest youth is the heaviest, the next tallest the next heavy, and so on down the line to the 100th boy, who is both the shortest and the lightest. The more interchange in weight status between boys of different heights (for example, the third from the shortest boy is also the third from the heaviest), the lower the correlation will be. If there is no covariance between height and weight, but simply a chance relation, the correlation is zero. If the shortest boy should be the heaviest, the next shortest the next heavy, and so on, until the tallest was revealed to be the lightest, the condition for a perfect negative correlation would be fulfilled.

Nature includes few perfect correlations, although there are some: Blackness, by definition, is perfectly negatively correlated with whiteness.

Prediction through Correlation

The principal reason to calculate a correlation[3] is to predict one variable from another. By so doing, one must first compute the strength and direction of their relation to each other. Knowledge of a boy's height is more useful if it also gives knowledge about his weight than if it gives no information about him other than how tall he is. Correlations, as has been mentioned, are likely to lead to deceptive inferences about causality. When two things are closely related, people are likely to act as though one caused another. Correctly, one can only assume that they are related. However, in looking for the reasons for the relationship, the search often leads to explanation. In general, tall boys are heavier than short boys for the elementary reason that they have more bone formation to cover and coordinate with muscle and fat. There is simply more to them. But their height does not cause their weight.

A simple calculation is useful in estimating the predictive value of a correlation coefficient. It is easy (but incorrect) to assume that the rather high correlation of .70 (the +, or positive, direction is assumed if the sign is omitted) between a test of reading comprehension and intelligence for tenth graders means that all the high IQ children read better than all the lower IQ youngsters. This correlation indicates that there is a substantial relation between reading and intelligence, at least for the population from which the coefficient has been derived. Hence, knowledge of this group's intelligence helps to predict their standing in reading ability among other children of their age and class level. But the relation is by no means perfect. To determine how much of the total variance of reading (all the factors that influence, or determine, reading skill) is accounted for by intelligence, one multiplies the correlation between the

---

[3] r is the common indication or symbol for the commonly used Pearsonian correlation coefficient.

two variables by itself: .70 × .70 = .49. Translated, this means that 49 percent of the variance of reading in the sample of tenth graders is accounted for by the children's intelligence. In other words, the .70 correlation between intelligence and reading accounts for 49 percent of the possible range of factors that enters into making a perfect prediction of where a child stands in his reading group. But 51 percent of the variance remains unaccounted for when only the intelligence test scores of a group of students are known. Much of this remaining unexplained variance may remain forever a mystery, since it is due to such factors as unreliability or other sorts of error in the tests used to measure intelligence and reading comprehension (or anything else).[4] At a practical level, at least for individual children, it is well to continue to search for reasons why bright youngsters do not read well and for methods to improve the reading of all children.

The average correlation of about .50 that has been found between the intelligence of parents and children indicates that only 25 percent of the variance of their children's intelligence can be accounted for by the brightness of their parents. A correlation of .20 between adolescents' strength and their speed of response means that only 4 percent of the variance of speed of response is accounted for by strength. This leaves 96 percent to be accounted for by unreliability or other measurement error, and by other factors.

In sum, much faulty generalization results from failure to calculate how much of the variance of one variable is due to another with which it is correlated. Educators, registrars, and those utilizing screening procedures for special training positions (or for employment) are egregious offenders in overgeneralizing from correlation coefficients. It is now legend that Einstein failed algebra and thus would have been denied admission today to many graduate schools of physics because of the rather high correlation between proficiency in mathematics and success in such quantitative sciences as physics.

The correlation of about .50 that is usually found between the intelligence of children and their parents is often used in ways that are detrimental to both children and their parents: A teacher assumes that because father is a doctor and mother is a lawyer, then Junior is bound to be bright. It is not necessarily so, and the teacher's overexpectations for Junior may do him real damage. The point has been mentioned repeatedly, but is so important that it is worth belaboring it, that children, young people, and old people for that matter, behave as others expect them to behave. Claude Brown (1965) describes his elementary and secondary school days in his autobiography, *Manchild in the Promised Land*. As most readers know, he was a poor Black from the ghetto. Academically, he performed wretchedly (nor was his social behavior impeccable) in his elementary school years. Eventually, teachers, their eyes unclouded by knowledge of or prejudice about relations between intelligence or behav-

---

[4] Professor William Asher, in a personal communication, points out: "Thus a person who looks at a correlation of .70 between intelligence and reading and says that 51 percent of the variance is still unexplained *and then* proceeds to attempt to explain it in terms of motivation, study efficiency, books in his home library, acuity of vision, etc., usually is kidding himself since generally *all* the explainable variance has already been explained."

ior and family status, perceived that Claude Brown was bright and potentially "good" (in the sense of his eventually becoming a good citizen). He satisfied both types of caretakers: For those who expected him to behave stupidly and undesirably, he behaved stupidly and also became a proficient delinquent. Later, as an adolescent, but gradually and with many temporary slips backward, he was equally obliging to those who expected him to behave intelligently scholastically and constructively as a citizen. At the time he wrote his book, he was a college graduate with further educational ambitions and, even by stringent criteria, he was a good citizen.

Some General Measurement Concepts

A *concept* is the general term for the class of behavior read about or which the author of a research paper has studied. Illustrative concepts have been given in the section immediately preceding this. Others are frustration, regression, anxiety, curiosity, and so on.

As has been stated, a *population* is the group the author of a study has worked with and on which he reports: It may consist of twenty-seven hooded rats, eight babies 4 days old, 10,000 Detroit and St. Louis 16 year olds, or 100 unmarried pregnant girls in their teens.

A *normal distribution* is one that lies between the ends of a continuum, and is shaped somewhat like a bell (indeed, it is often called the bell curve). It was diagrammed and discussed on page 23. Many human characteristics such as height and weight or, as in Figure 1.1, parental techniques of child control, are distributed normally and, when graphed, fall into a bell-shaped curve. For such a normal curve, the *mean* or average, and the *median* or midpoint, are the same. By median is meant that point in the distribution above and below which exactly one-half of the population falls. Means and medians are different from each other when a distribution is *skewed* or abnormal. If we compute the average annual income of five men picked at random from the street, we may obtain figures as follows: $3000, $7000, $8000, $9000, and $1,000,000. Our *mean*, in this case, is $205,400. To say the least, it is unlikely that the average American male earns more than $200,000 per year. By chance, we have secured an extremely biased sample.

In this case, the median or midpoint gives a more accurate, or at least a more meaningful, picture of the true state of affairs in the United States. The median for this population is $8000 and the sample includes two men who earn more and two who earn less than this. Income and education figures for industrializing nations are often more meaningfully represented by medians than means: In such countries, there are typically a few very wealthy and a few very highly educated men and women, but a great mass that is desperately poor and/or illiterate. The weight (envision a balance bar as the abscissa of the continuum) that is exerted by the few at the very end of the continuum produces a deceptively high mean, as in the case of the income of the five men selected at random from the street.

Another illustration of misleading means is provided by boys' athletic participation in large high schools where the emphasis is predominantly on spectator sports, an all too frequent condition in United States secondary schools. The *average* boy, as represented by adding in those select boys who spend most of their waking and nonclass hours in football or basketball practice, can be portrayed as having a rather meaningful physical education experience. But the *median* boy presents a very different picture. In the high schools the author knows best, this median boy is far down toward the lower end of the scale, participating passively (often as an onlooker only) in physical education periods in which attention is given mainly to the school stars.

Authors frequently speak of *homogeneous* and *heterogeneous* populations. By homogeneous, they mean that the members of the population are reasonably similar to each other, that the ends of the continuum are close together. By heterogeneous, they mean that the population represents great differences among its various components. A population that includes children from ages 3 to 18, both boys and girls, Afro-American, Hispaño, and Applachian people, individuals who come both from great poverty and great wealth, is more heterogeneous with reference to almost any conceivable research dimension than a population of white Methodist girls from a rural junior high school in Cleothia, New York.

When authors speak of the results of their studies as having high *variance*, they mean that some children changed not at all as a result of their treatment, other youngsters changed only a little or changed in a direction opposite to prediction, while still others changed a great deal. When changes are similar in amount and uniform in direction, the results of a study are said to have low variance. A standard method of expressing variance (actually, its square root) is the *standard deviation* (S.D., or sigma). This is a statistical term, a figure that is used to indicate how variable a population or set of results is. About two-thirds of a population is included in the range of scores on a test from 1 S.D. below to 1 S.D. above the mean.

Many intelligence tests are constructed such that their S.D. is 15 quotient points, and their mean is 100. This means that about two-thirds of the population can be expected to fall between 85 and 115 IQ.

When the reader moves to primary sources, he encounters a number of technical statistical terms, such as Type 1 analyses of variance, F ratios, chi-squares, taus, W's, and a host of others. Without having studied statistics, it is impossible for him to make sense of such terms. He must simply take the author on faith.[5] But, as has been pointed out, the reader should—indeed he must—know at least in an elementary sort of way what levels of statistical significance, or confidence, mean.

Levels of Statistical Confidence   The central task of science is to discover lawfulness in its subject matter. Developmental psychology seeks to determine lawfulness in human structure, growth, and function. Statistics are among the tools used to demonstrate lawfulness. Among other tasks, statistics is used to provide an estimate of the confidence one can place in his findings. One is particularly interested in whether he can assume that they occurred for reasons other than chance.

[5]Most but not all editors of research journals check to see that the authors' statistical procedures are appropriate.

Ordinarily, experimenters speak with "confidence" of results that are statistically significant. In this book, statistical significance refers to any result at or below the .05 (or 5 percent) level of confidence. Such a figure (which may also be referred as to p, for probability, $p = .05$) indicates that the results to which it refers are of such magnitude that they are expected to occur by chance only 5 times in 100 times. The .01 ($p = .01$) level of confidence means that results would be expected through chance alone once in 100 times; the .001 level of confidence refers to once in 1000 times.

Earlier, a correlation of .70 was postulated between intelligence and reading comprehension for tenth graders. To establish the significance or level of confidence for this correlation, one can consult a table or go through certain computations. A standard table for this purpose shows that, if a relationship of this strength exists in a tested population no larger than 12 tenth graders, it is significant at less than the .01 level. In other words, one can reject the null hypothesis (that there is no real relationship) with considerable confidence, inferring that the result would have happened by chance in less than 1 case in 100. The common-sense next step is assuming the positive hypothesis: Something caused this relationship, it is an other-than-chance relationship. For purely logical reasons, this step must not be made, for reasons that have been explained. In real life, however, people often take action based on it, sometimes without due safeguard.

As another illustration, suppose the research worker's purpose is to test the effectiveness of a special diagnostic remedial program that is intended to help a group of overage sixth graders become more self-sufficient in reading so they can move on into the junior high school platoon system without difficulty. All sixth graders in the twenty elementary schools in a sizable city who are two or more years overage for grade are located through the school files. The schools and the classes within each school are randomly assigned to a treatment (or experimental) and a control group. Some safeguard must be introduced, however, so it can be said that any superiority shown by the experimental group is due to the diagnostic remedial program, not to the Hawthorne effect (improvement in performance as a result of taking part in an experiment). This safeguard is introduced by giving the control children an amount of attention equal to that given the experimental youngsters, but social rather than instructional in nature; supplying them with attractive materials that differ in content from those regularly used but are at the same level of difficulty; and representing the program in which they are enrolled to their classroom teachers as an experiment on the effects of social interaction, with individual attention given to academic progress. Other than for these safety provisions, the experiences of the experimental and control groups are the same.

This plan verges on being unethical, in the sense that the program is being misrepresented to the teachers. But the teachers are as likely to be victims of the Hawthorne effect as the children, as has been seen in earlier sections of this chapter, and some method must be provided to control for it: thus, the borderline ethic of seeking to delude them. But such are the difficulties of research in real-life situations.

A true, or leave-things-as-they-were, control group is not necessary, as it is simple to look back through the school records to see that overage sixth graders like the ones in the proposed study have been accomplishing little or nothing in their regular sixth grade work for many years, have been falling by the wayside in seventh grade, and have very high drop-out records on reaching age 16.

The youngsters are tested for reading achievement before and after the treatment. The experimental group does not differ from the control group at the beginning of the study, but has gained a full grade level at its end, while the control group has gained only one-half year. Statistical computations relating to this differential gain result in a numerical expression of sufficient size to have occurred by chance only once in 100 times. As has been indicated, in practice one proceeds from this indication of lawfulness to the conclusion that the special reading program was responsible for the difference in experimental and control group gains. If one wishes to be very careful, he goes to testing records for the previous academic year, matches his research subjects from both groups (or takes all overage sixth graders in the previous year's classes), and compares their gains (he already knows they were negligible, which is the reason he started the study in the first place) with those of the experimental and control groups.

Faulty generalization often results from overconfidence in expressions of statistical significance, such as placing too much faith in a single experiment or study that shows significance at the .05 or .01 level. The significant result may, for example, have happened because of the characteristics of a given population, the personalities involved in the study or, for all we know, sun spots. This is one of the reasons it is desirable to replicate studies when possible.

Less often, insufficient generalization is made because of skepticism about the level of confidence of a finding. This, too, is faulty scientific procedure. Many developmental psychologists, for example, are entirely unwilling to consider that results from studies of animals are applicable in any way to human beings. Others go a bit wild in the opposite direction, reasoning about the human species as though there were no question that it follows the same behavior and motivational patterns as for monkeys, or white rats, or geese. It can be useful (and is interesting) to reason about humans by analogues from animals. But before clear conclusions can be reached, data *for* human subjects are essential.

READING PRIMARY SOURCES

The process of reading original research articles can be very tricky. Although it pertains to infants, a research study by Dennis and Sayegh (1965) illustrates some of the reading problems a student is likely to encounter. Since one can know his field *only* by reading original or primary sources, it is well to be aware of some of the ground rules. Dennis and Sayegh worked with five experimental babies who were resident in an institution. They gave them, to oversimplify, an hour's extra individual attention daily for fifteen days. Control infants did not receive this extra experience.

Dennis and Sayegh's experimental subjects gained significantly in developmental age (at the .03 level). Presumably, the only variation in their lives was the extra daily hour of experience, and their change—rate of growth—was such that it could have occurred by chance only 3 times in 100. This is a respectable level of significance, and the gain had to be exceptionally large or consistent, or both—thus of practical as well as statistical significance—to reach significance for so small a population. For obvious reasons, the larger one's research population, the more likely are his results to be statistically significant if for no other reason than that he will get more "average" subjects who will balance out atypical ones (such as the man with $1,000,000 a year income in the earlier discussion of means and medians).

But Dennis and Sayegh's control group also increased more rapidly in developmental age than would have been expected during the experiment. The authors are vague about the exact level of significance of the control babies' gain. They say only that "the gains of the control group were smaller.... By the sign test, which was used in the case of the experimental group, the change in rate of gain of the control group has a very low level of significance" (p. 88). One is left with the understanding that the experimental group improved significantly more than the control group (which included eight rather than five babies). But there is not given data sufficient for one to decide for himself. It should be added that the author is sympathetic to the Dennis and Sayegh point of view. But he still does not know whether or not there was *really* a statistically significant difference between the babies given the extra hour of experience each day for fifteen days and those who did not have this experience.[6]

It is for reasons like this that the topic of how to read a primary source is included here.

Procedure A primary source is an article that reports original data, talks about them, analyses them, formulates results, arrives at conclusions, and sometimes makes recommendations for action based on them. The following method of reading articles is one the author has found useful and which he applies to references that are germane to his professional activities at any given time. Life, of course, is too short to follow this procedure for everything one reads.

    1. One reads the article either because it interests him or it is something he must read for professional or scholarly reasons. The reading procedure does not differ for the two cases.

    2. Read the summary. What does the author say he has said? In at least half the summaries of primary sources, the reader probably cannot tell, either because the author has not bothered to prepare an adequate summary or perhaps because he wants to make the summary ambiguous and unrevealing so that the whole article must be read to find out what it is about. Some articles are sufficiently complex that a summary cannot do them justice, even in the sense of partially reflecting their content.

    3. Read the hypotheses. What is the author investigating? What questions is he trying to answer? Often, the author's hypotheses are

---

[6]Professor Thomas Ryan, in personal communication, reanalyzed the data in question, and finds that the differences are not clearly different statistically.

backed by considerable theory. When they are, read backward to see what the theory is, because an author has often repeated his hypotheses one or more times as he discussed the theory that led up to them. If the article has scientific merit, its author has also provided the reader with the logic that led to his hypotheses.

4. Move to the method. Psychology includes many general concepts, such as dependency or aggression or underachievement. By this stage in your reading, you will have discovered what general concept it is the author has in mind. As has also been pointed out, any concept, any general term, must be "brought down to earth." If an author is talking about underachievement in eleventh grade, exactly how does he bring this general concept down to earth? To him, is an underachiever a youth who is at the bottom one-fifth of the class, or below the average according to teachers' marks or according to nationally standardized tests? The author's definition can make a great difference in the nature and use of his results. Since teachers assign higher marks to girls than to boys, according to teacher's marks there will be more boys than girls in the bottom one-fifth of the class. But on standardized tests, there will be little difference between the sexes. Actually, since low-achieving boys almost certainly drop out of school earlier than low-achieving girls, by the time students come to the eleventh grade, there may actually be more girls (according to results of standardized tests) than boys in the bottom one-fifth of a class.

Thus, the author who uses standardized tests as his measure of underachievement has performed a more scientifically acceptable job of anchoring the general concept of underachievement than has the research worker who uses teachers' marks. Which is a better definition of underachievement: the bottom one-fifth of a class, or all children who fall below the average of the class? The question is not easily answered.

Academic aptitude or intelligence must also be taken into consideration, since it is related both to teachers' marks and to performance on achievement tests. Many youngsters in the bottom one-fifth of the class academically are often also low in intelligence. Thus they may be achieving up to their ability. Some who are above the average of the class in marks or achievement-test ranking may be so exceptionally bright that they are actually achieving far less than they are able to, even though their objective achievement is high. Hence, an author who uses correlation techniques to predict the subject's actual achievement standing in relation to possible achievement standing approaches underachievement on a more meaningful basis than one who considers only class standing.

5. The reader should note the nature of the population the research worker has studied. Is it European, Australian, French, United States? If the last named, is it from a lower-class area in New York City, or an upper-middle-class suburb of Albuquerque, or rural? What is the ethnic nature of the sample? If the author has not said these things, then he has not given the reader enough information to make an adequate judgment about his study. Is the population one of boys or girls; or is it made up equally of both? If of both, do sex differences exist for the principal variables being studied?

Such factors make great differences and knowledge about them is necessary if one is to evaluate and use research results profitably.

6. Move to the author's results section. Look first at the tables to see what the author has found out. Only later go on to see what he *says* about his tables. Sometimes the text and tables disagree. If they do, the author has been somewhat less than completely honest. One also often finds out things of interest and use that the author has not stressed, perhaps because he was not interested in them, perhaps because he overlooked them.

7. Read the author's discussion section if he includes one. Today, with an increase in theory and an interest in speculation and extension and application of knowledge, most articles include a discussion. Here, an author is free to speculate about what his results mean, and he is not completely bound by his data. He can ponder about why they do not fit his hypotheses, or why they do. He can consider where his results may possibly lead, what relation they bear to other research, where he made his mistakes if he made any, what were the most interesting and useful aspects of his findings; and he can propose new research ideas for himself and his readers. The discussion is often the most interesting and challenging part of a primary source.

8. Look back over what you have read so as to think about it as a whole. The ideal way to read an article is with a pen or pencil in hand, underlining and making marginal notes, if this is your own property. A review of these jottings is an ideal integrating and critical device, enabling you to formulate your over-all impression of the study, to make a judgment of its worth, to check the author's consistencies and inconsistencies.

SUMMARY

The purpose of this chapter on methodology is to make students in the field more critically alert. The chapter contains material designed to improve observations and research about developmental psychology, and it pertains as much to the study of young children and their families as to adolescents. It is equally appropriate for research dealing with older subjects or animals.

Research in the field of adolescent development can be schematized as varying along four dimensions: (1) normative-explanatory; (2) ahistorical-historical; (3) naturalistic-manipulative; and (4) atheoretical-theoretical. Although these dimensions are logically independent, they often vary together, and each forms a continuum.

Seven major (and all too frequent) defects of research in developmental psychology are: contamination; reconstruction through retrospection; faulty logic; poor definition of concepts; direct influence of the investigator upon his results; sampling deficiencies; and unsound generalization.

Unsound generalization is often related to uninformed use of statistical concepts. Among the more basic statistical concepts or processes are correlation (a measure of relatedness not implying causation), prediction through correlation, and level of confidence. Some familiarity with these concepts is necessary to understand the research summaries that occur later in the book.

A recommended pattern for reading a primary source—an original research article—is presented. Proceed (taking notes on the pages of the article itself, if possible) from the summary to the hypotheses, then the theory, the method, the nature of the population, the tables and their discussion in the results section, the author's discussion and, finally, an overview of the article in its entirety, including your notations about it.

3

Physical Growth

INTRODUCTION

In the study of adolescent psychology and development, it is useful to distinguish between the *psychobiological* and *psychosocial* changes that take place during this period. Ausubel (1954) provides an unusually clear discussion of this distinction and its implications.

The psychobiological aspects of adolescence refer to the psychological consequences of biological change. Pubescence is common both to humans and infrahuman species, but the psychological reactions to it are much more complex and, presumably, more developmentally important for humans than for nonhumans.

However, anyone who has observed group behavior of the higher mammals has noted that their pubescence is by no means totally free from "psychological" and social consequences. The young stallion and mare, ram and ewe, bull and heifer, and male and female primate almost immediately assume very different group roles from what they occupied prior to puberty. These roles involve not only sexual behavior, but social behavior such as aggression and dominance. It is as easy to read stress into some of these new roles among infrahuman as it is for human beings.

The psychobiological aspects of adolescence refer to those factors that are universal (see Ausubel, 1954, pp. xiii–xiv), and independent of the culture in which an adolescent develops, such as sexual maturity, increases in height, weight, and strength, development of secondary sex characteristics, and alteration of self concept and social status. These factors demand personal and social changes, regardless of whether one lives in America, Pakistan, or Dahomey. Becoming tall and strong, like one's father or mother, necessitates making changes in one's way of life in all societies, and change of a personal and social nature demands of the adolescent new ways of adaptation, or socialization. Culturally differential ways of adapting to universal factors in adolescence constitute the psychosocial aspects of adolescence.

Reaching mature or nearly mature height and strength *psychobiologically* means that one now does things for himself that formerly were often done for him. But the specific things he does are *psychosocial* in nature, and culturally determined.

While there is some necessary overlap between this chapter and Chapters 4 and 5, the author attempts to emphasize biological changes of puberty and adolescence in this chapter, and devotes the next two to psychological and social consequences that accompany and are necessitated by physical changes.

Ausubel points out three similarities in adolescence regardless of culture. One thread of this common core, clearly recognized in this book, is the universality of the laws of change, as treated in Chapter 1. The second commonality is the universality of the laws of human motivation; the motivational change that introduces adolescence — mature reproductive drive — increases strength of all responses, and interacts complexly with social changes precipitated by pubescence (see Figure 1.1). The third commonality is anatomical change: Whether one is white Caucasian, Oriental, or Afro-American and whether he lives in Kansas or Tahiti, during adolescence he experiences primary and secondary sex changes, rapid growth, and strong sex pressures (universally so for boys, more variably from culture to culture for girls).

There will be ethnic and regional differences in rate of growth, maximum height, body build, and in distribution of body hair; but the commonalities are greater than the variations. Meredith (1968) provides a dramatic illustration of how great some of these variations actually are, as he documents differences in average bodily measurements taken at similar ages in different parts of the world and among different national and racial groups.

THE SEXUAL DICHOTOMY For all the higher species, little sex variability is genetically provided. There is the *male* of the species, and there is the *female* of the species. The directional influence of these genetic factors is so potent as to be virtually unmodifiable so long as the life course is normal. While the *chro-*

nology, or timing, or maturation *is modifiable* to a largely unknown degree by such factors as nutrition, individual health histories, and perhaps climate as well as other factors, the *sequence is invariant.*

Ausubel's description of the sequence of glandular changes resulting in sexual maturity is an excellent place to begin a discussion of the sexual dichotomy. The gonadotropic and coricotropic hormones of the pituitary begin to influence the gonads; these in turn further stir up the adrenal cortex in a complex interaction sequence; growth of the primary and secondary sex characteristics then begins to occur, after a long phase of almost total absence of growth (see Figure 3-2). There are also dramatic changes in nonsexual physical functions, such as sweating, metabolism, vital capacity (amount of air that can be gulped in and utilized), as well as marked changes in rate and type of growth, strength, and coordination.

Triggered by the endocrine glands, these changes result in a much clearer distinction between the sexes than existed before puberty, although most societies have groomed their boy and girl children for differential roles almost since birth. Pubescence speeds up, indeed necessitates, the final casting of boys into the male role, and girls into the female role.

Sexual changes bring about ultimate role fulfillment in several ways. First, as was discussed in Chapter 1, the new sex drive is both a hormonal energizer and sensitizer. In boys, the androgens bring about masculine sexuality, stimulate sexual fantasy and organ arousal, and increase the frequency of orgasms. In girls, the estrogens produce female sexuality, increase receptivity although more indirectly through lubricity, thus making sexual stimulation more enjoyable.

Second, the diffuse new sex drive (through the selective and directive processes discussed in Chapter 1) demands modification of behavior so as to result in specific satisfaction, which may range from fantasy and masturbation to heterosexual coitus. A galaxy of personal–social behaviors comes into play: courtship, grooming, flirtation, seduction.

Third, the individual observes his own bodily and motivational changes and those of his peers. In turn, his peers and the adults in his world observe him and reflect back to him his new image and the changes in behavioral expectancies it entails.

Finally, probably much in the manner in which Festinger (1957, 1964) describes adjusting to cognitive dissonance (see Chapter 1), changes occur in the individual's self concept. Boys adjust to being baritones rather than sopranos, girls adopt women's ways in personal hygiene, and adolescents begin to protect children and no longer seek protection for themselves.

Ausubel (1954) believes that a youth must be capable of adult sexuality and receive recognition for "being ready" before he can adopt the adult sex role or participate in adult sexuality. However, there is much prerehearsal, at least in United States culture: for example, girls wear training bras, and girl friends and boy friends are sought well before pubescence as a step toward later formal dating.

Assignment of sex, in the overwhelming majority of cases, is made at birth, appropriately for the external genitalia. However, as Hampson and Hampson (1961) point out, the true sex of a person depends on more than genitalia. There are at least six components involved in being male or female. If any of them deviates, the accomplishment of appropriate sexuality may be rendered more difficult.

These sexual components are: (1) chromosomal sex; (2) gonadal sex; (3) hormonal sex; (4) internal accessory reproductive structure; (5) external genital morphology; and (6) sex assignment and rearing. For the relatively small group of hermaphrodites, a seventh factor of gender role or psychological sex must be considered.

For hermaphrodites, Hampson and Hampson present evidence to indicate that this seventh factor is crucial. By implication, it is equally crucial although less ambiguous for normals. The Hampsons subscribe to a position that sex is not a biological entity but a name for the biological, social, and psychological contrasts that characterize any given species, male or female. Total sexuality, Hampson and Hampson seem to believe, is established by interaction of biological structure and psychological and social factors that start as early as age 6 weeks to age 24 weeks, and the critical period[1] extends from then for about two years or somewhat longer (p. 1404).

Mead (1961) subscribes to a point of view not unlike that of the Hampsons. The hormones certainly initially organize sex prior to birth and for some time thereafter but, shortly after birth "gonadal hormones cease to be organizational and become purely activational" (p. 1433). This position coincides with the point of view taken in the present book to the effect that sexuality is most usefully considered as a drive, of which one biochemical part is hormonal secretions. Their activational (or drive) function is important primarily as it affects an individual psychologically and socially.[2]

THE BODY, SOCIAL CONTEXT, AND SELF CONCEPT

The major purpose of the following sections dealing with physical growth and motor development is to relate these biological and skills characteristics meaningfully to the psychological and social dimensions that constitute the principal thrust of the present volume.

[1] A critical period is that developmental span during which an organism must develop a trait or quality, or else it will never develop.

[2] To anticipate some of the later material in this chapter, but to speak directly to the point of endocrinology and sexual development, it is necessary to say that this area of study is confusing. Even a casual reader can find studies that provide data about maturation, secondary and primary sexual development, and height and weight different from those listed in this chapter (see Meredith, 1967, for a synopsis of puberal changes).

The field of adolescent endocrinology, including hormonal sequencing, is too new and complex to be treated in any meaningful way here. Tanner (1962), in his definitive volume on physical growth, discusses it in detail, but comes to no clear conclusions. In the face of the confusion in the field, the author has chosen to limit his discussion to the generalities that have been given up to this point in the chapter.

As medical laymen, such people as the author and most readers of this book can do little about endocrinological function. Even the experts to a considerable degree work blind, as they are the first to admit. Those responsible for adolescents should keep a thoughtful eye on their physical development, and refer those who seem to deviate conspicuously and "undesirably" from the norm to relevant medical specialists. Even such specialists are often helpless (for example, there seems to be all too little that can be done about the adolescent nightmare, acne). As has been mentioned, adolescents are very sensitive about exposing their biological development to the eye of even the most competent and sympathetic specialist. When they can be persuaded to do so, however, the benefits are often great, as Schonfeld (1950) convincingly documents.

Readers need only to examine their present self concepts, no matter what their ages may be, to verify the statement that at this cross-sectional moment in time and certainly as they retrospect about their own adolescence, the characteristics of their bodies are important in what they do, how they view themselves, and how they have developed.

Adolescents' bodies are exceptionally important to them in shaping their self concepts, and in facilitating or retarding their attainments of status and adequate social relations.

The advantages to boys and girls of strong, attractive, well-coordinated bodies are so obvious as to need no special mention. A good body and an attractive appearance usually do much to reduce the frustration and ambiguity that surround the adolescent and add to his upsurge of general drive level. The theoretical context in which this occurs was discussed in Chapter 1: To the degree that a healthy, well-proportioned, strong, and graceful body and attractive face reduce the exigencies of change and help to achieve major life goals, to that degree do they reduce the tensions of transition and the conflicts of adolescence. The converse is equally true.

There are social hazards to being too beautiful or too handsome, or to achieving social adulation and status easily through athletics, as some boys do. Beautiful girls or athletes, and probably less often handsome boys, may, because of their easy success as adolescents, neglect other developmental tasks that they must master to manage the long haul of life. Athletic skill benefits few men at 50. Beauty is not the major virtue in a good mother-in-law, an effective community worker, or a successful woman business executive.

In the author's sample of adolescent autobiographies, there are, however, a number written by young men who came from severely disadvantaged social backgrounds, but who, at the time they wrote their autobiographies, were successful and rising young professional men in the welfare fields. In every such case, athletics had been the means by which the young man had moved (or more accurately, had *been* moved) from his social class upward through society. As an athlete, he had received acceptance in high school by the "better set." He had been forced to learn to study to stay in athletics. He had discovered that he had a good mind, and that academic competence was rewarding. He had been able to go on to college because of an athletic scholarship and had found this preprofessional life so attractive he had moved to full professional status. In most cases, such young men had married upward socioeconomically and, also in every case, had begun in high school, or earlier, to be alienated from the friends of their childhood. This alienation was usually accompanied by considerable conflict.

The role of the body in social and personality development has been conspicuously neglected by psychologists and sociologists. It is not easy to understand why this is so since, as has been said, anyone who stops for a moment to think knows that his body is exceptionally important to him. The body is the capsule in which one is permanently enclosed and through which one moves to interact with the world. One's body and face have important effects on the way the world responds to him, at least initially. Doors seem to open easily to attractive people.

Psychologists and sociologists as a group are likely to be optimists, and may often be naïvely optimistic about what environment and the socialization process can do for human development under ideal circumstances. Historically, research about body build and physical and facial characteristics has been geared to heredity and constitutional determinism (for example, see Kretschmer, 1925; Lombroso, 1891; and Sheldon and his colleagues, 1940, 1942, and 1949). A confirmed hereditarian and constitutionalist, it is interesting to note, would recommend to society selective breeding and sterilization of the unfit as measures to bring about betterment of the population. Most psychologists and sociologists reject such measures, for obvious reasons.

The research methods of such men as Kretschmer, Lombroso, and Sheldon did not hold up well under careful scientific scrutiny. Perhaps a combination of their social points of view, their loose research methods, and their sometimes reckless social recommendations (see, for example, Sheldon, Hartl, and McDermott, 1949), has turned modern research workers away from research in the field. Modern researchers may believe (as naïvely as the pure hereditarian-constitutionalist) that studies of such variables are, to put it mildly, unrespectable.

However, the topic of the interrelation of body build, rate of maturation, and personal-social development has recently stirred the interest of a number of sophisticated research people, as will be seen in Chapter 5. Research methods have also been improved.

CHARACTERISTICS OF PHYSICAL GROWTH

Meredith (1959) has provided one of the most useful classifications available for discussing physical and biological growth, not only for adolescents but for individuals of any age. The author follows his classification; and draws heavily from his work and the excellent summary of the literature provided by Tanner (1962).

Physical Growth Norms

A first step in the scientific study of any area is to describe and classify its major dimensions. Such descriptions and classifications precede more sophisticated explanatory and theoretical work. Norms do not explain anything. They simply help to place an individual into the framework of his reference group—the people with whom he primarily interacts and who are most meaningful to him: for example, he is larger than they, smaller than they, earlier or later maturing than most in the reference group, and so on. His placement against the background of his group often leads to legitimate and accurate predictions about his behavior, but locating him on a developmental normative curve does not explain such behavior. Norms simply help in most cases to narrow the range of best guesses.

If, in his role as a psychologist, someone refers a 15-year-old girl to the author for problems of personal and social adjustment, it is useful to know her height, and her weight and its distribution. If she is 5 feet 10 inches tall and weighs 104 pounds, it is clear that her place on a height curve for United States girls is at the extreme right (high, or tall, end of the continuum); and that her weight is well toward the left (thin, or light) end of the distribution for girls of this height. Without seeing her, the author immediately knows that she is a very tall, thin girl. This leads him to postulate that her realistic perception of her deviant body structure may be one factor in her personal and social problems. Mead (1961), for example, advances the position that tall girls are regarded in United States culture as being masculine and have to struggle more than shorter girls to define for themselves an appropriate feminine role and self concept. It is known that this girl will find few boys of her own age who are brave enough to date her, since she is half a head or more taller than they.

This girl may, then, perceive herself as scrawny, unfeminine, and unattractive to the opposite sex. Such debased self-perceptions may generalize to other aspects of her life, thus contributing substantially to her generally poor social and personal adjustment. Her own behavior, from what is known about the self-fulfilling prophecy, may further consolidate her poor self concept. Being convinced of her unattractiveness, she may withdraw from boys, acting cold and aloof so as to avoid the risk of being snubbed or otherwise rejected. Her aloofness understandably results in the boys—and perhaps the girls in her peer group—leaving her strictly alone. She takes this as further proof that she is indeed an unworthy person, withdraws even more, and becomes still worse-adjusted. Such a downward spiral is not infrequent during adolescence, or at other developmental periods.[3]

As a group, it is likely that any set of boys or girls at the extremes of a distribution have certain common characteristics. The author is sure that tall, very thin 15-year-old girls tend as a group to be less well adjusted than girls of the same age who are of about average height, weight, and weight distribution. However, his evidence is clinical rather than strictly scientific. Of course, there are many very tall, thin girls who make excellent personal-social adjustments, and, likewise, among any group of attractive, well-formed, and graceful girls or boys, some will be severely maladjusted. On the average, the group of attractive youths is likely to be better adjusted than the norm, and these socially positively valued traits are statistically clustered together. Socially negatively valued traits of groups tend to cluster together to form the "loser" syndrome.

It is well at this time to refer back to Chapter 1 to tie in the variable of deviance from the norm to the theory of drive: Those who deviate undesirably from the norm on any characteristic that is positively esteemed by society or, more specifically, their reference group, are likely to encounter developmental problems that produce more than average frustration and anxiety, and this increases their total drive level, and thus produces predictable consequences along such dimensions as flexibility, great behavioral variability, high tension and, often, problem behaviors. Adolescence, in other words, may be predicted to be more difficult for the undesirable deviates than for the average. As has been said, the converse (adolescence is easier) is likely to be true for the well endowed.

Extreme deviations at the positive end may also produce problems. Some of the possible difficulties for beautiful girls, handsome boys, and

---

[3]The case history of Cheri, given in Chapter 5, concerns a girl much like the one described above.

Figure 3.1

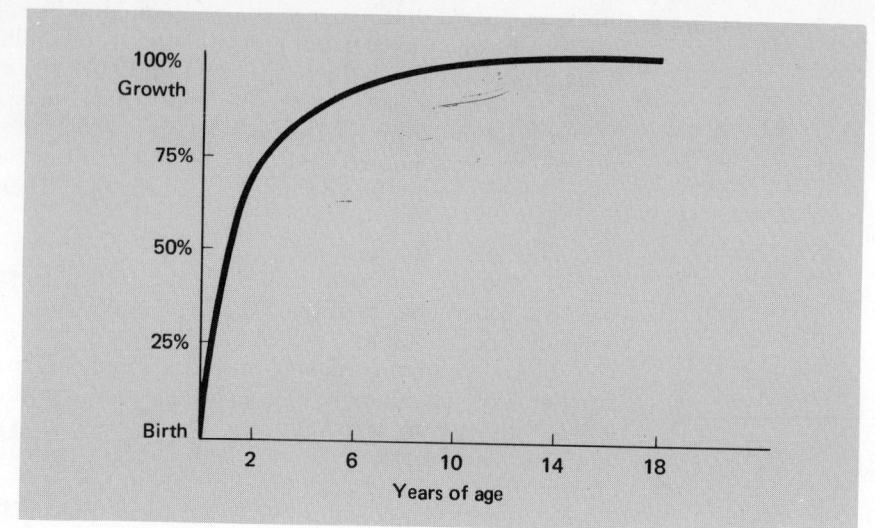

Neural growth pattern. (From McCandless, 1967.)

star athletes have been discussed above. Hollingworth (1942) was a pioneer in documenting the problems that accompany having an IQ of 180 or more. Hollingworth's children demonstrate the problems of socialization that are bound to occur when a child is infinitely more intelligent than his reference group: Such a child might be said to suffer from cognitive dissonance so great that it is almost impossible to resolve.

The preceding paragraphs illustrate the context within which the normative material presented in the following pages should be viewed. In dealing with individual adolescents, one should first emphasize each as a unique individual, and then proceed with the best guesses provided by normative information. This technique usually improves professional efficiency, but the unsophisticated researcher must not be blinded by norms. It is relatively simple to fall into the trap of overgeneralizing from norms, as saying that "All lower socioeconomic status children have low IQs," which would be a gross inaccuracy.

The word normal comes from "norm." Thus, normal means "approximately average." It is often used interchangeably, however, with "free from pathology or defect," and with "good or desirable." Readers and listeners should be alert to the sense in which authors and speakers are using "normal" or "at the norm." Otherwise, there is likely to be, and there often is, miscommunication. *"Normal" by no means implies optimal or ideal.*

Patterns of Physical Growth

Three general patterns of postnatal physical growth have been identified. The first is often called the *neural* pattern. It includes growth of the head, brain, spinal cord, and eye, as illustrated in Figure 3.1.

Inspection of Figure 3.1 shows that neural growth is very rapid in infancy, but changes quite abruptly during childhood to a much slower rate of growth. Essential maturity of neural function has been achieved long before the onset of adolescence, an illustration of the fact that not

Figure 3.2

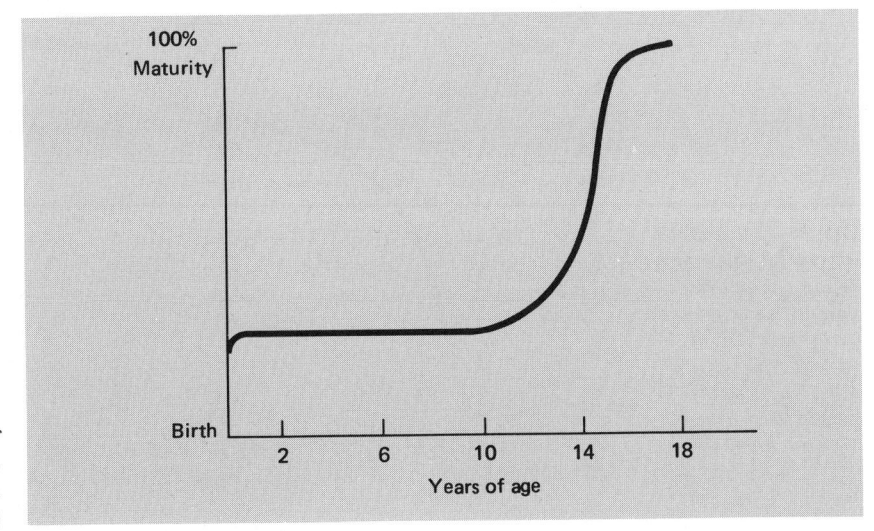

The development of primary sex characteristics. (From McCandless, 1967.)

all things change rapidly around and following puberty. An exception of considerable importance is the course of growth of the eyes, which grow faster in depth than in height. This progressive egg shape may result in myopia (nearsightedness) for adolescents who as children had normal vision and whose vision will later return to normal.

A second growth pattern characterizes the primary and secondary sex characteristics. It may be called the *reproductive pattern*, and is diagrammed in Figure 3.2. It is obvious that the reproductive growth pattern is strikingly different from the neural pattern. There is no dramatic change in the latter, but for reproduction-associated characteristics the child at adolescence "bursts out all over." Changes between the ages of 10 and 15 years are indeed dramatic. Their extent and general sequencing are similar for boys and girls, but the timing differs sharply. On the average, girls are more advanced than boys by one to two years.

Children on the average have been more or less dormant sexually from infancy until about 10½ years, but growth spurts suddenly for all physical characteristics associated with reproduction. Detailed information about these changes is provided later in the chapter, but in Figure 3.2 a vivid general illustration of the changes is provided, and some of the foundation for a psychology of change during adolescence is clearly documented.

The third pattern of growth is less dramatic than the reproductive curve, when viewed over the entire course of development (contrast Figures 3.2 and 3.3), but it is the one to which most overt social attention is drawn preceding and during adolescence. It can be called the *somatic* pattern, and includes such easily observable characteristics as length of arms and legs, girth of chest and abdomen, weight and height, the surface area of the body, and width of shoulders and hips. Some of the internal organs, such as the liver and kidneys, also grow according to this general pattern. It should be repeated that different timing characterizes

Figure 3.3

The general growth curve for the more obvious body dimensions of some of the major internal organs. From point A, the solid line represents girls' growth; the dotted line, boys'. (From McCandless, 1967.)

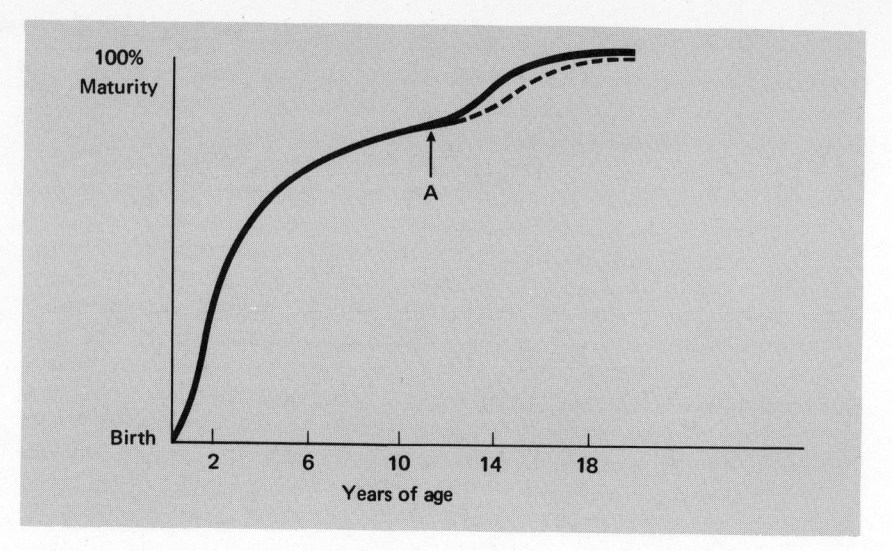

not only the two sexes, but individual organs and dimensions within the sexes.

It can be seen in Figure 3.3 that the rate of growth is rapid during infancy (although there is a brief postnatal decline). During childhood the rate of growth is slow. At around pubescence—girls begin this spurt a year and a half or so before their first menstruation—there is rapid gain, followed by slow year-by-year increase during later adolescence.

It is obvious that society uses its observation of general bodily growth as the basis for communicating to young people its perception that they have become adolescent. These general body changes, of course, are less spectacular, even though more public, than changes in primary and secondary sex characteristics.

Maturity—the end of increase in growth—varies greatly according to the characteristic being considered. The average adolescent girl reaches mature height by about 16 years of age; the average boy by about 17½ years. Increase in musculature and weight, however, continues after full height has been gained. Boys do not reach maximum strength until their mid-20s or later, and their full vital capacity may not be reached until the 30s. Boys reach maturity as judged by length of penis some time earlier (one to two years) than when judged by size of testicles. Body hair often increases until the mid-20s or later, while many boys begin to lose the hair on their heads in their late teens. Girls' breast structure is greatly affected by child bearing and nursing. Diet and exercise play important roles in weight gain and distribution, and in fat-muscle ratio.

In other words, maturity cannot be expressed in terms of a single given physical or psychological characteristic. The whole pattern of physical growth in adolescence is exceedingly complex. Interactions with self concepts are equally complicated. In one autobiography that the author has been given, a young man, 25 years old when he wrote it, reported suffering acutely because he had been a late maturer and was much shorter and thinner than any of his classmates when he was graduated from high school. His growth pattern had been unusual: He kept growing until he was in his early 20s. When the author knew him, he was a strongly muscled, well-proportioned man of 6 feet 2 inches who weighed 190 pounds. But his report of himself at age 25 indicates that he still holds a most unrealistic self concept of a slight, asthenic (thin, weak) male. Many young women, conversely trimmed down from their adolescent plumpness, similarly experience difficulty in changing their self concepts to fit their new figures.

These physical growth data anticipate later material, but some of the implications for self concept will be discussed at this time. A person's self concept is his method of coming to terms with himself, and often the self concept may be very unrealistic. If a girl possesses a good figure and clear complexion at age 19, her conception of herself may not fit with her public appearance, for it may have been set when she was a pimply, overweight, nearsighted 14 year old. Her behavior may, as an attractive 19 year old, still smack of negative self-fulfilling prophecy, and she may be miserably adjusted and unhappy. In such cases, individuals may need professional help to revise their self concepts in the direction of reality.

One's self concept represents *his* most efficient way of coming to terms with himself in his social group. Even though a self concept may be objectively poor or maladaptive, it is likely to be resistant to change. Change is in itself uncomfortable and stress producing. It may also be that the upsurge of drive in early adolescence helps to form remarkably durable but not necessarily accurate self concepts. As has been pointed out, learning under high drive is likely to be rapid, narrowly and inflexibly related to the goal in the context of which it occurs (see, for example, Spence, 1958), and quite unsuitable for the maturity of the later teens, the 20s, or full adulthood.

Primary and secondary sex characteristics have a great deal to do with determining self concept. A boy is likely to judge his masculinity *for himself* as much or more according to the size of his penis and the extent of his pubic and body hair as he is by somatic changes such as height or weight. Self concept is a very personal identity, and as such it is generally based on very personal, or private, judgments.

In United States culture virility is commonly equated both with early maturity and size of genitals. Among Caucasians, amount of bodily hair is also commonly considered to be an index of masculinity. A boy makes his judgment about his own penis from covert (or overt) comparison with other boys' and men's. His intense curiosity may lead him into relations that can be labeled homosexual. If a boy is an early maturer, he may acquire an exaggerated notion of his "manliness"; if a late maturer, he may form a concept of masculine inadequacy that can be difficult to change. The same is true for girls.

Irregularities in growth sequences often put many youngsters, mostly boys, into lively, albeit usually temporary, conflict. A substantial proportion of boys experience rapid penis and testicle growth, typically accompanied by abundant pubic hair, before they enter their somatic growth spurt phase. They know, from their own personal inspection and experience that they are, indeed, men! But to the world at large (which does not see them stripped) they remain boys for a considerable period of time, as long as it takes their bodies and whiskers to catch up with their genitals and pubic hair.

The discrepancy between their private images of themselves as men and society's "belittling" — and infuriating — continuing perception of them as boys may lead to seemingly incongruous behavior, designed on their part to assert their manhood but often socially disruptive.

Other boys' private manhood lags considerably behind their physical growth spurt, and these boys may encounter societal expectancies that they secretly consider themselves unable to live up to.

Boys and girls want to dress modishly. In the modern era, for Western society clothes have accentuated girls' breast development and hourglass figures, although popular cycles of shapeless clothes have occurred. Episodically during history, dress for men and boys emphasizes shoulder width and hip narrowness. The current vogue for men's tight hip-cinched trousers seems designed to emphasize the genital region. Popular women's fashions in the United States today seem designed to display the female's mammary nature as realistically and advantageously as possible: Small breasts are enlarged, sagging breasts are bolstered, and unduly exuberant breasts are restrained.

Boys in all cultures, as far as is known, esteem large genitalia. For white Caucasian or white culture-identified boys, it is desirable to be rather hairy except for the back. Sexual awareness and mass media have exalted large breasts, so that they are desired by most girls. Boys and men hope to be 6 feet tall or more, and to be broad shouldered, narrow hipped, and well muscled. Girls fear becoming much more than average height and they too wish to be relatively broad shouldered and narrow hipped. The thick and heavy endomorph is at a real disadvantage at all ages in Western cultures; and the long, lean ectomorph falls intermediate in society's esteem between the endomorph and the "triangular ideal" mesomorph. Research literature concerning this is discussed in the next chapter.

Anatomical Changes The classification of anatomical changes employed in this book is modified from Meredith (1959). The author finds it a useful way to view physical development.

Changes in Kind Life starts with change in *kind*. The union between sperm and ovum produces a new entity, the zygote. This simple structure is modified during prenatal life to include blood cells and bone cells, muscle tissue and adipose (fat) tissue, nervous system and skeletal system, and limb segments. In the second month of prenatal life, an external tail begins to grow, which disappears a few weeks later. Most of the cartilaginous portions of the skeleton of the baby and preschool child change to bone in the older child and adult. One of the most accurate assessments of physiological maturity is provided by X rays that reveal the degree of ossification of the wrist and hand (change from the many bits of bone interspersed with cartilage of the child to the solid bone and joint structure of the later adolescent and adult).

An adolescent's bones are both harder and more brittle than a child's, and bones grow still more brittle with advancing age. Following puberty, the ratio of fat to muscle changes rapidly and differentially for boys and girls; it is much smaller for boys. The skin texture of preadolescent boys and girls is similar, but it changes rapidly during adolescence, so the well-developed girl is cuddlesome, the well-developed boy, firm and hard muscled. "Hard as a rock" is considered a delightful muscular attribute by adolescent boys.

Changes in Number During adolescence the number of bone masses drops from around 350 to fewer than 220, principally because of epiphyseal (loosely, "joint") union. The head of the average 5 year old contains from forty-eight to fifty-two teeth in one or another stage of development. By the time he is 15, an adolescent has ordinarily lost twenty deciduous (baby) teeth. With increasing age, more teeth are likely to be lost. The wisdom teeth typically are lost first either because of decay or because the jaws cannot accommodate them.

Hair Changes Because hair changes signal adolescence and also play an important role in the developing self concept of masculinity and femininity, this topic is discussed in considerable detail. The words puberty and pubescence actually come from the Latin words, *pubes* and *pubescens*. The former refers either to the lower abdomen (in its singular form, *pubis*) or the hair of the groin; the word *pubescens* means "becoming hairy or downy."

Hair has been associated with masculinity from very early times: Samson lost his strength—his masculinity, the Freudians would say—when Delilah cut off his hair. The current furor about the length of boys' hair is intimately related to conflicting value judgments. The historical attribution of masculinity to long hair has given way to considering that long hair for boys is effeminate. The fact that so very many adolescent males in today's societies have cultivated long hair, and even looked upon it as a symbol of group membership, provides extremely interesting speculation for psychologists. Also, it may be necessary to add that adolescent girls seem to be thoroughly infatuated with boys' long hair. In white-dominated cultures, body hairiness is generally considered desirable for males, undesirable for females (except for appropriate pubic hair and reasonably abundant tresses on the head).

For both males and females, the values attached to long or short hair vary by cultures and periods of time. Nuns presumably shed their femininity in a symbolic sense when they cut their hair and don the coif. Monks' tonsures perhaps relate to a similar renunciation of the male sex role. Older boys and men in the United States consider it inappropriate to shave under their arms, while in middle-class white American society it is thought to be antisocial if girls and women do not have shaved armpits. Underarm shaving has positive religious significance for good Muslims. Beards, once a symbol of masculinity and wisdom, tend now to be associated in the United States with social nonconformity, although this association appears to be weaker now than a few years ago. Women who develop stubbly chins following the menopause deplore the failure of their femininity. The adolescent boy can hardly wait to shave, and may suffer damage to his masculine self concept if his beard develops late or is very scanty.

Regardless, then, of the meaning given to the crewcut or the long locks of popular male musical groups, hair plays a prominent role in society's, and thus the individual's, concept of his own masculinity and femininity.

There are striking developmental, sex, and ethnic differences in hairiness. Among males, the hair around the genitals proliferates, darkens, and changes in texture following puberty, starting usually some time between 10 and 15 years of age. By their middle or late teens, most boys possess the adult type of relatively thick, coarse, and curly pubic hair around their genitals and much of their groin region. The average girl of 14 has also reached such an adult status (see Tanner, 1962). Individual variations are great: For example, some boys achieve the landmark of full adult pubic hair by age 14, others only by age 18 or later (see Figures 5.1 and 5.2, which illustrate pubic hair development for early and late maturing boys and girls).

The modal distribution of pubic hair among boys is triangular, with the apex of the triangle extending upward toward the navel. Adult-type axillary (armpit) hair usually follows the appearance of pubic hair, but occasionally accompanies it or follows it only after a long time. Next comes thickening of facial hair for boys. This growth is usually noticeable first on the upper lip, and, in time, it extends outward and upward and downward, until by his middle 20s the average male is bearded over his lower and lateral face and the upper portion of his throat. Last in the maturational sequence is mature-type hair distribution on the extremities. First thicker, longer, and coarser hair appears on the lower legs. With time, it extends upward toward the crotch and buttocks. Hair also appears on the lower arm, developing progressively toward the elbow in one direction and the back of the hand and finger joints in the other. For a substantial proportion of the male population, particularly Caucasoids, coarse hair also begins to develop around the nipples, extending in area until, by their middle 20s, many men have hairy chests, which they consider desirable. The less frequent growth of hair on the upper back and shoulders is considered less desirable. Many males develop little chest hair. The whole matter of hairiness, including baldness, seems to be genetically determined.

The child's "widow's peak" disappears following puberty, and is replaced by a relatively circular hairline. Adolescent boys' hairlines are higher at the upper sides than at the middle. Receding hairlines are common. The process typically begins at the temples and extends to the mid-forehead. By 30, many men are balding and are likely to continue to lose hair.

Ethnic differences in hairiness are more conspicuous for men than women. For the three major ethnic groups, Caucasoids are hairiest, Negroids intermediate, and Mongoloids least hairy.[4] The adult Mongoloid

---

[4]The three terms used here, Caucasoid, Mongoloid, and Negroid, have clear physical anthropology referents, and are used entirely in the physical anthropology context. However,

male is lightly bearded, has relatively circumscribed pubic hair, an essentially hairless chest, and little hair on his lower arms and legs. He seems to differ less from the other ethnic groups in axillary hair, although it may be less curly than among Caucasoid or Negroid males.

One can only speculate on ethnic variations in the value placed by males on bodily hair, as the topic, to the author's knowledge, has not been studied. It is plausible that Mongoloid males value bodily hairiness to the degree that they identify with the white culture. If he makes a clear *ethnic* identification, one may predict that an Afro-American or Mongoloid youth will attach no great value to body hairiness. Since hairiness is distinctly *not* one of his ethnic characteristics, a boy of Oriental ancestry may actually deplore being hairy. The matter should be studied, as it is of some importance. Afro-Americans, if ethnically anchored, should place a value on body hair between the white values (which have been stressed in this section) and the Mongoloid or Oriental or American Indian values.

Informal data gathered by the author from young West Pakistani men and older boys (who are Caucasoid) indicate that they value bodily hair in about the same way as do white United States males.

So far as is known, there is no evidence linking body hairiness in males with virility-masculinity for any ethnic group. But insofar as cultural stereotypes are incorporated within and shape self concepts—and self concepts affect behavior—one can predict mild facilitation of masculine self concept for hairy Caucasoid males. As hypothesized, the converse may be true for Mongoloid males. Factors of identification with United States white culture may complicate this picture for boys of Oriental and African descents.

Parents and counselors of adolescent boys should be aware of the importance of this aspect of masculine development. Schonfeld (1950) provides evidence about the usefulness of counseling for boys who actually or self-perceptually are deficient in masculine development. Deviations in hair pattern almost certainly bother boys less than deviations in other sex characteristics, such as body build, strength, and genitalia. It may be that a boy who is gravely concerned over a deviant body hair pattern is simply using the concern to mask deeper problems.

Ethnic differences among females are less marked than among males. The differences are similar in direction to those for male populations. The United States culture includes sharp differences between sexes in the values attached to body hair. The manufacture and distribution of depilatories is big business. Not only chemical hair removers but ladies' razors are much a part of the mass media.

For girls, just as for boys, longer and coarser hair that becomes

---

for those sophisticated in the history of mental retardation, *Mongoloid* carries with it the association of a diagnostic classification of mental retardation, which is not the case here.

Negroid is considered by many to be "the white man's word," and is resented whether in this form or rendered as the noun or adjective, *Negro*. Usually throughout the book, the terms, Black or Afro-American, are employed when relevant.

The less pretentious and less controversial term, white, is used throughout except when, to be technically correct, it is essential to speak of *Caucasoid* or *Caucasian*. By no means are all Caucasoids white or any approximation thereof, any more than all Blacks are black.

curly appears around the genitals. It extends laterally and upward, and eventually assumes the distribution of an inverted triangle. The triangular area is confined to the gential region rather than extending upward toward the navel, as for males.

This "sex-typical" pubic hair distribution characterizes only a majority, however. Many boys have so-called feminine pubic hair distribution, and "masculine" distribution is not uncommon for girls.

As with boys, girls develop axillary hair soon after their pubic hair begins to appear. Some girls also have noticeable facial hair that follows the same pattern as for boys, but is far less thick. The hair of the lower legs and arms becomes thicker, longer, and coarser, and the hairier girls in the normal range have more body hair than the less hairy boys at the hairless end of the normal male distribution. The same is true for the other secondary sex characteristics.

In the United States, girls with noticeable or heavy facial, arm, and leg hair are typically ashamed, embarrassed, and anxious about it. A common reason for battle between white middle-class adolescent girls and their mothers concerns the day when the girl may begin to shave her legs. Mothers want to delay it, girls, to hasten it. Many mothers believe that shaving legs coarsens and speeds hair growth, a belief that is without foundation as far as the author knows. The author knows a few mothers, whom he has casually pegged as "overaccelerators," who encourage their daughters in depilatory behavior before there is any apparent necessity.

Women's hair also thins with age, but not as often or as much as men's. Baldness in women is rare, but many older ladies are thin on top. Following menopause, as has been noted, women are likely to be troubled and embarrassed by increasing whiskeriness.

Hair is every bit as important to women as to men, but women are freer to admit it. They spend even more time fussing with the hair on their heads than they do in removing it from their armpits and legs. Any white middle-class husband and any father of adolescent daughters is accustomed to the horrendous sight of the beloved females in his family reeking with chemicals and "wired" in their efforts to strengthen, straighten, or curl, or whatever is appropriate at a particular time or place. In the current battle for a proud self concept, African, or natural, hair styles are making a long overdue comeback among Afro-Americans, male and female. Regardless of social class or race, girls and women and many boys and men fuss endlessly with their hair.

For some reason, perhaps simply because it is attractive just the way it is, girls of Oriental descent seem more content to leave their hair the way nature made it.

Changes in Size In considering physical growth, people typically think mostly of changes in size, particularly in height and weight. Such changes may be the most publicly conspicuous, but, as has been said, they are less dramatic than the changes in primary and secondary sex characteristics.

As a general rule, the size of everything increases during adolescence. Maximum penis growth is reached at the average age of about 15, and occurs for almost all boys somewhere between 13½ and 17 years. However, the mature penis (Tanner, 1962) is likely to be somewhat smaller than the maximum size attained in adolescence. Testes reach their maximum size about age 16, although there is relatively little research on the matter and there is disagreement in the literature, with some placing the age of mature size much later. The normal age range for reaching maximum testicle size, according to Tanner, is between 14½ and 18 years.

The thymus gland is an exception to the general tendency for everything to grow larger in adolescence. It is presumably a regulator of growth and increases in size almost until the time of puberty, then declines strikingly in size. Both boys' and girls' genitals remain, relatively speaking, at infant size until shortly before puberty. At age 11 to 12 for the average girl, a year and a half or two years later for the average boy, the physical growth spurt begins. Tanner estimates that the growth spurt is at its peak for boys at age 14 and for girls at age 12.

Tanner observes that girls' breasts reach mature contour at 13½ to 14 years of age, although they will probably continue to increase in size for another two or three years.

Data, most of which come from United States Army measurements, are available for height for western European men from 1850. Correcting for the present-day tendency to reach puberty early (this is discussed later in this chapter), Tanner estimates that the increase in adult height for western European males has been about 1 centimeter per decade from 1850 to 1962. This represents an average increase in height in less than 120 years of almost 4 inches. The tendency has presumably been the same for girls and women.

Mature height is a matter of serious concern for boys and girls. Estimating the average age of reaching mature height is subject to the hazards that have been described earlier (e.g., prediction is uncertain, generations grow at different rates). However, making such an estimate is useful from a practical point of view. Tanner, rather reluctantly, selects an age at which "one may say that growth in stature virtually ceases, that is, after which only some 2% is added." These ages (Tanner, 1962, p. 27) are 16¼ years for English private school girls and 17¾ years for boys. The data to which he refers were published in 1954. Thus, granting the validity of the secular trend, one can risk saying that today's adolescents for all practical purposes, and on the average, reach mature height at about age 16 for girls and age 17½ for boys.

It is equally difficult to say what the average height of mature white males and females is: Figures of about 5 feet 4 inches or a bit more for girls-women and 5 feet 10 inches or a bit more for boys-men are reasonably accurate estimates. However, there are ethnic differences (apparently no important ones between Black and white) and social class differences. Thus, a figure that expresses the average height of the United States male or female is not very useful in working with a given adolescent. As has been previously pointed out, extreme deviations from the norm may present problems of adjustment to both boys and girls.

Whiting, Landauer, and Jones (1968) summarize considerable evidence on the influence of stress in infancy and early childhood on later growth in height. By one means or another, including cross-cultural studies of diet, they have exercised rough controls to make sure their adult height status differentials are due to stress rather than to diet, race, geography, including sunlight and rain, height of parents, illness and selective death rates, self-selection of treatment (such as immunizations) by parents, and the direct benign effects of such treatment as immunization.

Their cross-cultural data (Landauer and Whiting, 1964) show that, for five societies that systematically inoculated children before the age of 2 years, average adult male height was 66.8 inches compared to 63 inches for societies in which no preage 2 stress was reported. For two samples of California and Ohio children, differences as a function of immunization prior to age 2, with appropriate corrections made for height of parents, were statistically significant at the .02 level, with the early inoculated children, both boys and girls, being taller at age 18. Only for one group, Ohio boys, was the difference significant in a striking sense. For them the average additional height for the early inoculated was 1 inch (the difference between slightly more than 5 feet 10 inches and slightly more than 5 feet 9 inches for the young men who were not inoculated early). The early inoculated California boys (adjusted height) were about ½ inch taller than those inoculated later. The differences for the Ohio and California girls were intermediate, from about ½ to about ⅔ inches taller for the early inoculated girls.

The growth curve for weight is about the same shape as the one for height. The fat-rumped, relatively narrow-shouldered boy of 11 to 13 years of age may take some comfort from the fact that boys' shoulder width increases more rapidly than hip width. Thus, the chances are that his adult proportions will be closer to the adult ideal than are his prepubescent dimensions.

The weight curve does not reach an asymptote in the late teens. Typically, weight increase continues into and frequently beyond the "sagging 40s." As one passes middle age, this trend is usually reversed, so that the elderly are relatively thin. Overweight is a serious problem in many societies where the food supply is abundant. In the United States, it is one of the most serious health problems. Chronic obesity based on overeating seems to have its roots in emotional maladjustment. Clinical reports suggest that compulsive eating is as hard to remedy as alcoholism. Indeed, weight watching clubs have been organized on a large scale.

Many children seek security in eating, and food-based obesity is considered a symptom of serious emotional difficulty when found in children and adolescents. Since eating is one of the earliest, infantile methods of gratification and since exceptionally high drive coupled with frustration with present circumstances may lead to regression, troubled adolescents may take an infantile, eating route to relieve their anxiety. Thus, they compound their over-all problem, but reduce their painful anxiety for the moment. Such regressive behavior is likely to occur only when an adolescent has no effective techniques for solving his current problems in an objectively more adaptive way. He must then resort to old ways, ill-suited to his present chronological age. Since eating is "overdetermined" (that is, is pleasurable, keeps one alive, is tied to infantile security), it is a difficult symptom to eliminate when it is adopted as a method of reducing anxiety.

Under constant environmental conditions, weight and height are both determined principally by heredity. Of course, such findings as those reported by Landauer and Whiting (1964) and Whiting, Landauer, and Jones (1968) introduce the question of important environmental influences even on height. Regardless, weight is more subject than height to environmental manipulation. A regime of proper nutrition and appropriate exercise keeps most adolescents and adults reasonably trim. But equivalent amounts of food affect different individuals differently. One may burst at the seams with steadily increasing avoirdupois, while another, eating exactly the same amount and type of food, maintains a constant weight. Exercise may subtly make a difference: Two apparently sedentary people actually may exercise very differently on their desk jobs, one twitching, twittering, getting up and down from his chair, and pacing around the office, while the other simply sits. It seems that nervous, high activity level people burn up calories that would otherwise go into waistlines.

There is currently some thought that babies who are allowed to grow very fat may have a propensity to be overweight for the rest of their lives.[5] One outstanding pediatrician known to the author puts all his bottle-fed babies, particularly boy babies, on skim milk from birth, partly for purposes of weight control, partly to keep the cholesterol level down.

Adolescents desperately need good physical fitness programs. Such programs in almost all junior and senior high schools the author knows fall far short of their goals. For many nonathletic boys and girls, the outcome of physical fitness training, including college training, is that the students develop a distaste for athletics and exercise. This is even more unfortunate in that coaches and physical education teachers, by the nature of their duties and their charges' relative freedom while under their tutelage, are ideally in a good spot to serve as models and exemplars for youth.[6]

Changes in Shape The baby and runabout child are head and trunk dominated. With childhood, there begins the approximation to adult proportions. Such proportions are approached with great rapidity before and following puberty. Male shoulder width increases much more rapidly than hip width. The result is the characteristic male dominance of back and shoulders over hips and buttocks. Such dominance in the male may be biologically related to the mating act, or to hunting, or to driving off aggressors. In any event, it is characteristically male and represents an ideal configuration to adolescent boys.

[5]The author knows this only through personal communication.

[6]Often, even though he may emerge from his college training possessed with an ideal program of physical fitness *for all,* the average coach in the average junior and senior high school is forced by the community to put principal emphasis on team athletics (public relations) in the interest of his own survival. The effects of the late President Kennedy's physical fitness emphasis are still being felt and it may be that today's schools are providing increasingly better physical fitness programs for the average student. But, in the face of community demand for competitive, public relations athletics, progress is bound to be slow.

Such predominance of shoulder width growth compared to hip width growth is absent in girls. Girls' hips widen markedly before and after puberty, and the resulting hourglass approximation of the female figure is a configuration which may be biologically related to ease in childbearing.

Both boy and girl preschool children are potbellied as well as head and torso dominated. During the first few years after puberty, the typical boy has a concave abdomen. In his early 20s, the concavity fills out. From 30 on, he is likely to be fighting to keep his girth restrained or passively surrendering to it. His feminine counterpart will have been more curvilinear than he since puberty. She, too, will have problems of sagging and bulging where she does not want to. Childbearing often renders her problems more acute than those of the male, although it is the author's impression that women watch their figures more closely than men.

Around puberty, sex differences in proportion become more marked. The winged shoulder blades of childhood pull in so that backs become flatter transversely. The sex differential rates of growth for shoulders and hips have already been noted.

The lower part of the face spurts in growth more than the upper part, so that jaws become more prominent and less childlike. The nose comes into better proportion with the rest of the face and the forehead. The hairline also changes, as has been mentioned.

For boys, not only does the penis increase in length and diameter, but the glans (head) enlarges greatly, and even more conspicuously during erection. This presumably serves the biological function of presenting a greater sensitive surface area so as maximally to stimulate ejaculation and procreation. Some (for example, Hampson and Hampson, 1961, advance the postulate) propose that the exquisite sensitivity of the erogenous receptors for male and female, of which the male glans is a conspicuous illustration, can be substituted for the concept of drive. The erotically sensitive parts of the human body, as used and stimulated by oneself or another person, give rise and are inextricably linked to positive experiences (such as orgasm and its pleasurable physical-psychological-social associations). Thus "during the process of psychologic growth and development erotic sensations become firmly associated with and inextricably a part of adult gender role," (pp. 1413–1414). The Hampsons are inclined to endorse an imprinting theory of sexuality, and reason along such lines in looking for a possible explanation of psychological (or "true") homosexuality.

The increased size and weight of the testicles make the scrotum more conspicuously pendulous as well as larger. The lower hanging of the left testicle becomes more conspicuous under conditions of relaxation and normal temperature. The scrotum contracts during cold so as to conserve heat and maintain constant testicular temperature, both by presenting less surface and drawing the testicles closer to the body. The nonerect penis is similarly affected by cold. The scrotum also contracts during the peak of sexual excitement, as an aspect of the contracting and pumping process immediately preceding and accompanying ejaculation. Usually, immediately following ejaculation, both the scrotum and the penis rapidly assume their relaxed contours and dimensions, although multiple ejaculation in rather quick sequence is not infrequent for teenage boys and young men (see Kinsey, Pomeroy, and Martin, 1948).

For girls and women, the loss of the blood suffusion that results in tumescence and accompanies sexual excitement and orgasm is considerably slower than for boys and men (see Masters and Johnson, 1966, 1968). Multiple, rapid, sequential orgasm is not uncommon for girls and women; and they seem not to lose the capacity for such orgasms with age, as appears to be true for men.

The girl's vulva and clitoris show the same growth process as for boys' genitalia. Her ovaries increase in size according to about the same pattern as the boy's testicles. Her clitoris and vulvular lips have tumescent properties similar to the boy's penis. In sexual excitement and with stimulation, tumescence occurs and lubrication of the vulvular lips and passage takes place. Girls with large clitorises may actually extrude the clitoris in sexual excitement, a condition that is likely to result in anxiety and conflict of the sort that characterizes males with unusually small primary organ development. Hampson and Hampson (1961) report that clitorectomies have been used to advantage in extreme cases, in that the operation made the subject feel more normal, more feminine.

Feminine lubricity and tumescence accompany and facilitate sexual interaction. Lubricity of the glans for the male is also frequent and serves the same facilitative purpose. Apparently, tumescence and lubricity for females more often follows direct physical stimulation and less often occurs as a result of fantasy and visual stimulation than is true for males. Girls and women seem less easily and frequently aroused than boys and men (although Masters and Johnson, 1968, believe this difference is heavily psychosocially determined). Once aroused, girls are as urgently sex-driven as boys. If girls wish to avoid intercourse, the advice of not letting boys go "too far" is sound, since most girls are not as avidly anticipatory and triggered by ideas of sex as boys.

As adolescence progresses, increasingly heavy musculature also results in changes in shape: The neck, trunk, buttocks, arms, and legs all become thicker and stronger. This increased musculature is more obvious for boys than girls, and is a source of great pride to the male in most cultures. Girls' relatively high tissue-fat component masks the pure musculature that is the male ideal. Girls, perhaps to some degree because of cultural expectations, do not increase in strength nearly as much as boys. Goss (1968) provides recent data that document this point.

Biologically, however, girls may be more durable than boys, despite less strength and fleetness.

Changes in Position The most striking position changes in postnatal life involve the teeth. At age 5 years, the child has between forty-eight and fifty-two teeth at one or another stage of development. In the child's acquiring of his permanent teeth, two separate sets—the deciduous and the permanent teeth—have moved upward or downward, depending on whether they were in the upper or the lower jaw, and have otherwise extensively changed their position.

As has been mentioned in the preceding sections on changes in number and shape, the deciduous teeth have been lost by adolescence; and the winged shoulder blades of the child have been pulled in to form the relatively flat back of the adolescent or adult.

Changes in Pigmentation With age, the hair and skin progressively darken for most whites. Less evidence is available for more heavily pigmented groups. The iris of the eye, particularly in the blue and gray range, becomes lighter because of resorption of pigment granules. Hair seldom becomes gray during adolescence. Graying is probably genetically determined, and is subject to great interindividual variation ranging from people who are gray in their teens to raven haired octogenarians. The process is more obvious for brunettes than for blondes.

Among light skinned people, the darkening of the nipples around the time of puberty is notable for both sexes. The change is from pink to pinkish brown or brown. The darker the pigmentation, for obvious reasons, the less noticeable is this adolescent pigmentation change in nipples, male genitals and scrotum, and body hair. For light skinned whites, darkening of the skin of the scrotum and, to a lesser degree, the penis is conspicuous, as is the contrast between the body hair, or "down," of the pre- and postpubescent youngster. This darkening among lightly pigmented people obscures the contrast between the genitals and the pubic hair and may conceivably have some protective biological utility. Conceivably, in man's history, it may have been protection against sunburn of the sensitive and vulnerable male genitals and the almost equally sensitive nipples of both sexes.

In sexual excitation the glans penis and vulvular lips suffuse with blood. Their somewhat purplish red color when so stimulated is intense to a degree unknown in childhood. This phenomenon, like blushing, occurs but is less noticeable for darkly pigmented people. As has been mentioned, among light haired people the new pubic and other body hair of the adolescent presents a sharp contrast to the skin not presented by childhood hair, or down. Texturally, the new body hair is thicker, longer, and coarser than prepubescent down. Among straight haired people, the new body hair is curlier and kinkier than any textures they have known before. There is less contrast for groups like Afro-Americans, whose prepubescent hair on the head is quite curly. Adolescent body hair may actually be less curly.

Of the body hair, the pubic hair is usually curliest. However, many straight haired men have curly beards and curly chest and limb hair.

Changes in Texture Most of the changes in texture have been mentioned earlier in the chapter where they were relevant in other contexts. To recapitulate briefly: Changes in texture throughout the developmental process, and conspicuously at adolescence, are striking and easily observable. The older preschool child has lost his body fat and no longer has the sponge rubber feel of the 6-month-old infant, whose fatty tissue is easily compressible. The postadolescent girl "feels" different from the preadolescent, since she has a higher fat-muscle ratio than earlier.

The postadolescent boy, on the other hand, has more muscle and less tissue fat than before adolescence. His muscles are thus harder to the touch and resist pressure. Adolescents' bones are brittler than children's, and become harder and more brittle with age.

From the time of early maturity, the skin progressively and noticeably loses elasticity, and crows' feet and wrinkles develop. Facial skin becomes coarser and more porous. As their beards become heavier and stiffer, males with heavy, coarse facial hair have sandpapery chins and jaws except for a short time after shaving. The pubic, axillary, and body hair of adolescents is very different from the down it replaces, and usually grows even coarser with age. Textural changes in the nipples and genitals are obvious. For example, the skin in the scrotum sac not only darkens, but thickens and coarsens. In cold and sexual excitation, it thickens still further and is deeply and coarsely wrinkled.

Changes in Timing: The Secular Trend The average girl today menstruates first at about age 13. As was discussed in Chapter 1, it is more difficult to set so clear, if overly simple, a time for sexual maturity for boys. For the landmark employed in this book, the first ejaculation, the average age for first occurrence is 13 to 14 years.[7]

Almost all girls are sterile for a year or longer following their menarche. Maximum fertility seems not to be reached until the early 20s. Girls' breasts reach bud stage at about 11 years. The typical girl is likely to be embarrassed about her new dimensions, just as the typical boy is about his newly large penis. Both sexes worry about their sex revealing itself through their clothing but, on the other hand, are proud of their development. The frequent unpredictable erections to which boys are prone often prove embarrassing, as does the occurrence of menstrual flow on a day when the often irregularly menstruating adolescent girl does not expect it.

For a long time now, puberty has been coming increasingly earlier. Tanner (1962) estimates that the age of menarche has become less by some four to five months per decade in western Europe over the period from 1830 to 1960. The average western European girl, he says, is thus mature some four and one-third years earlier than was true less than a century and a half ago. Apparently, United States girls have followed this pattern, and there is no reason to believe that the trend is different for boys. Parallel changes in height were summarized in the section "Changes in Size."

This so-called secular trend may be exaggerated by the method of reporting. Poppleton and Brown (1966), working with British samples,

---

[7]Time of physical maturation varies widely from country to country. The determining factors are not clearly established. Perhaps the best generalization is that it is later for the lower socioeconomic classes, most probably because of less adequate nutrition and health care. Many of the national and climatic differences that have been reported are likely a function of income level and nutrition rather than ethnicity or climate.

The figures given as typical or average in this section represent approximate medians for United States white children. There are no convincing data to demonstrate that nonwhite children in the United States differ from these averages in any way other than directions that can be attributed to social class-nutritional-medical care variables.

find that retrospective (backward looking) reports of menarche consistently move the event forward in time to an earlier age. An on-the-spot check from school records made by school nurses results in an average menarcheal time during the 1960s, when their data were gathered, that was some four months later than the averages commonly reported in the literature.

Similar factors may operate for boys' and men's reports of first ejaculation. In fact, since ejaculation is typically more a prideful event for boys than menarche is for girls, males may move it earlier by an even greater interval. To repeat, data about the time of physical maturity, defined in this manner, are not firm, and less so for males than females.

SUMMARY

The concept of his body is central to one's concept of himself. One lives with his body twenty-four hours a day from birth until death. Its characteristics such as strength, proportion, and attractiveness are intimately related to how society responds to a person. Since social feedback shapes the self concept, it is easily seen that the interaction of body and self concept is inevitable and important.

The study of physical growth is worthwhile as a field of scientific endeavor. Such study at adolescence is particularly interesting and important, since adolescents' rapidly changing bodies and society's changing reactions to them are central both to drive and change theory as applied to adolescence.

Concentration in this chapter has been on the conventional data of physical growth. In the next chapter functional change (which is profound as mature sexual development enters the picture) and motor development is dealt with; while the chapter after that is concerned with the body and personality-social relations.

Thus, the main thrust of this chapter has been physical or biological; Chapter 4 is bio-personal-social; and Chapter 5 is principally psychosocial.

To understand youth, it is important to know the norms—the group averages—for physical growth. As a general rule, youngsters who cluster together at the socially evaluated negative part of the normal curve in important physical characteristics (boys who are too short, girls who are too tall) may need help to understand themselves. The opposite is usually true for those who cluster together at the socially positive end of the normative continuum, although there are dangers there too, as with the beautiful girl who becomes too narcissistic. But physically well-endowed youngsters typically find the frustrations and anxieties of adolescence eased.

The three major patterns of physical growth are neural, reproductive, and somatic. The neural curve is very steep in childhood. It reflects little of the parapuberty growth spurt. Eyes grow in such a manner that many become temporarily nearsighted in adolescence.

Reproductive growth is intense immediately before and after puberty, having been near dormant since birth. The suddenness and great extent of growth of primary and secondary sex characteristics are often embarrassing and troublesome to adolescents. Some who experience marked deviations become seriously disturbed. Counseling has been demonstrated to be useful in such cases.

The third pattern of growth is somatic. Society cloaks its reactions to the emergence of children into sexually mature men and women within references to the public dimensions of physical growth, such as height, weight, and musculature. However, somatic changes are less sudden and sharply accelerated than reproductive changes.

Physical growth may be fitted into seven classifications for convenience in study and description. The first of these is changes in kind. Such changes include a decreasing muscle-fat ratio for girls, but an increasing one for boys. Pubic and other body hair represent conspicuous changes in kind, with postpubescent hair (pubic hair comes earliest of the adult-type body hair) being longer, coarser and, at least for relatively straight haired people, curlier than the down it replaces. For lightly pigmented and light haired groups, this new hair contrasts much more sharply with the body than had been true for the child hair.

A second type of change is in number; for example, with the calcification of the joints, the number of separate bone masses decreases by more than one-third. Because it is important in this culture to the self concept, changes in amount, distribution, and kind of body hair were discussed in detail.

The third classification of growth concerns changes in size. The adolescent changes dramatically in size, almost all over. Most such changes are increases, although the thymus gland decreases greatly. Some evidence exists suggesting that environment (stress in infancy and early childhood) may significantly increase adult height, as much as 1 inch among some groups.

A fourth classification of growth is shape change. Around puberty, youngsters move rapidly toward adult configuration: relatively small headed and long legged, and toward an elongated inverted triangular shape for males, and a modified hourglass shape for females. The lower jaw experiences a growth spurt that brings about a fuller lower face and puts the nose into proportion.

Relatively few changes in position—the fifth classification—that are entirely independent of changes in size occur during adolescence. There continues to be change in tooth position, and the pulling in of the winged shoulder blades of childhood to the relatively flat transverse back of adulthood occurs.

The sixth classification of growth is pigmentation change. For the light skinned, nipples and genitals darken conspicuously.

The seventh type of change is texture. It is most conspicuous for pubic, axillary, and other body hair. The changes in fat-muscle ratio increase the difference in "pinching" texture between boys and girls following puberty.

Puberty seems to be growing earlier with each succeeding generation, and this secular trend seems to have been going on for the past 150 years. Puberty apparently occurs today about four years earlier than it did one and one-half centuries ago. There is little proof that social and intellectual maturity have grown correspondingly earlier, although evidence is inconclusive. As puberty has moved earlier in time, people have grown taller, perhaps by as much as 4 inches on the average in the last century.

4

Changes in Function and Sexual Socialization

INTRODUCTION

The emphasis in the preceding chapter was on anatomical changes and certain of their accompaniments. Selected changes in function were discussed when relevant, since structural changes invariably result in functional changes. From a social and psychological point of view, changes of function that accompany or result from changes of status are more interesting than the changes of status themselves. For example, the structural changes in amount, type, and distribution of hair was analyzed in such great detail in Chapter 3 to highlight the relationship of these changes to the functioning of adolescents in society.

A seldom discussed but important sex-related change in function is mouth and tongue changes. Long before adolescence, the mouth and tongue have mastered their adult functions of eating, drinking, talking, gesturing (as in smiling, registering disapproval). After adolescence, in many cultures the mouth becomes at times a sexual auxiliary, not just used for kissing but often for active tongue involvement, as in "French kissing." The mouth's tactile sensitivity makes it a useful instrument for sexual stimulation, facilitation, and often consummation.

Somatic-type functional changes in posture, locomotion, and establishment of laterality (hand-foot dominance) have occurred and for the most part been consolidated long before adolescence. The increased bodily strength and speed that follow pubescence make possible facilitation of new skills and greater mastery of older ones, particularly in boys.

Parenthetically, it may be noted that there are areas of development where function can lag behind structure. There is evidence that vital capacity (amount of air per unit of time that can be taken in and used) increases *more slowly* than body size. In junior and senior high school, this may lead to overexpectations in rough sports and activities involving endurance for mature seeming boys. The risk is less for girls (see, for example, McCandless and Ali, 1966). This matter is serious enough to deserve more research attention than it has received. If the tenuous evidence is correct (Stolz and Stolz, 1951), this developmental fact should be carefully considered by coaches and those who hire adolescents for hard physical labor. Shortage of vital capacity may put an impossible physical strain on a boy who is going all out in a physical activity, and this may in turn result in psychosocial problems.

In United States society, as has been made clear in earlier chapters, actual adult genital functioning is expected to be delayed long after structural and "mechanical" readiness has been achieved. Therein lies much of the stress to which adolescents are subject. To understand some of the frustrations and facilitations of adolescence, it is useful to discuss functional changes in detail.

CHANGES IN GENITAL FUNCTION

Ausubel (1954) postulates a clear and sharp break between pre- and postadolescent sexuality (a "stage" theory). While stage theorists are likely to neglect bridge or transitional behaviors, the case for sharp pre- and postpuberal stages in sexual behavior is better than for most age or stage classifications. Although by no means certain, it appears that boys may experience the change more keenly than girls.

Adolescents themselves almost always perceive sharp (stage) transitions: One day girls are premenstrual, and the next day they are menstruating. One day—literally, one minute—boys have not experienced orgasm-ejaculation, and at the next minute this profound psychobiological experience has happened, they have recognized its meaning, and they will never be the same again.

Even from what little has been said about the protracted glandular and growth processes and interactions that have preceded these events, it is obvious that much has led up to the climactic moment of menstruation or ejaculation. Preliminary sexual sensations approaching those of maturity are likely to have been experienced by normal adolescents with increasing urgency prior to puberty. But even so, the break is sharp, both psychologically and physically.

The discontinuous method of handling the sex drive within United States culture was discussed in Chapter 1. Ostensibly (but not *really*), it is expected within this society that sex should be repressed, or kept from consciousness. Failing that, as must be the case for all normal boys and almost certainly almost all normal girls, suppression is the goal of society's sex "education." Clearly this subject can not be ignored.

Adult genital functioning, if one follows the official social ethic, is supposed to emerge full blown on the night of the honeymoon. Most people are more realistic than to believe such things, but still the myth exists. Cultural unrealism, regardless of social class, is the rationale for presenting this topic as extensively as it is treated in this chapter.

Unrealism, incidentally, is as flagrant in one as another social class, despite the "freedom" that research among lower-socioeconomic-class people has shown. Their supposed greater freedom is likely to be gained at the cost of what Ausubel calls the psychoaffectional (tender, interpersonal) aspects of sex. Certainly, neither the affectional nor the biological faces of sex should be neglected or underplayed. Existing data about the right mix of the two are few and often suspect. Does the middle-class ethic of sexual restraint enhance the psychoaffectional aspects of one's sexual relations? If so, is this at the expense of purely sensuous enjoyment of sexual relations? If one is very free sexually, does the physical emphasis in sexuality attenuate psychoaffectional relationships? Are purely physical gratifications on the one hand and interpersonal respect and intimate communication on the other incompatible?

There are no clear answers about the right mix between physical and psychoaffectional sex. The most satisfactory mix undoubtedly differs greatly among individuals, depending upon one's background and physical make-up, and the data available suggest that the "ideal interaction" differs for the two sexes. Achieving an ideal interaction should be an important goal within a happy marriage; most probably the appointment calendars of marriage counselors and the letter boxes of lovelorn columnists certify to the great number of couples who have not achieved it.

Sexual behavior is related in very complex ways to common sense, ethics, and morality. At the common-sense level, it is obvious that sexual relations between people will be more rewarding and enduring if both psychoaffectional and physical satisfaction are achieved. Ethically, it is equally clear that sexual behavior that gratifies one partner while the other is exploited is undesirable. The morality of sexuality is a very touchy matter. Moral sanctions about sex are laid down within almost all the religions of mankind, as well as within the social class structure. Politically, it is considered so important that there is an elaborate, confusing, and in some cases totally unrealistic web of legal prescriptions and proscriptions about sex. In the United States, for example, some states forbid—under penalty of law—certain sexual acts. On the whole, sexual behavior seems to be more closely linked to morality among girls and women than among boys and men, with the possible exception of the male who deviates from conventional heterosexual behavior.

This discussion of sexual behavior anticipates a later discussion of the total process of socialization. Life styles may be broadly classified into Apollonian (cool, restrained, intellectually directed) and Dionysian (sensuous, self-expressive, free). These traditions are discussed more fully in Chapter 9 and later. It is sufficient to say here that such life styles are as relevant to sexual as to broader interpersonal socialization. Only a cursory reading of history will point out that human sexuality does not fit easily into the Apollonian life style. Apollonian handling of sex is undoubtedly far more difficult for adolescents than for older people, and the daily newspaper headlines proclaim that perhaps society's elders cannot be classified uniformly as Apollonian in this part of their lives. Certainly, a major developmental task in adolescence is to strike the right balance of affectional–physical, Apollonian–Dionysian, in sexual attitudes and behavior.

Organization of Genital Function

Genital function among United States adolescents is best appreciated in a broader cultural context. Mead (1961) provides such a framework in her excellent chapter "Cultural Determinants of Sexual Behavior." She outlines the eleven commonest cross-cultural sexual careers, and her discussion is worth summarizing. It sets the stage, outlining the roles from which adolescents must choose and to which they must eventually accommodate.

1. Wife and motherhood is the commonest sexual role in United States culture. Indeed, it is the "normal" function. Douvan and Adelson (1966) show clearly that preparing for and achieving this role is the major preoccupation of adolescent girls of all social classes and ethnic backgrounds in the United States. It is the career of the married female who will bear and care for children. Though normal and desired, it is viewed with mixed emotions by many women as indicated by the frequent response to a question about occupation: a sigh and, "I'm just a housewife."

2. The role of the adult male who will beget and provide for his children is modal for males but, Douvan and Adelson believe, less a preoccupation among adolescent boys than wife and motherhood among girls.[1]

3. The third role is that of the adult male who will not marry or beget children, but who will exercise some sort of prescribed social function. Across cultures, such functions may be celibacy with or without religious connotation, sexual abstinence, renunciation of procreation, specialized forms of ceremonial sexual license (such as have been described in tribal life, most particularly for religious leaders such as witch doctors), or exemption from social restrictions placed on other men.

4. Many adult females neither marry nor produce children, but are accorded status in a religious context, as nuns. Other roles may be ceremonial prostitution. The spinster, or bachelor girl, or old maid is a recognized minority in our culture.

5. In some cultures, adult males assume institutionalized female roles, including transvestism, where such an adult sexual career is open only to males. This role was not uncommon for actors in early Grecian society.

6. In some societies, females assume male roles, including transvestism, where such a career is open only to females.

7. In other cultures, nonprocreative ceremonial roles are important. These may involve transvestism and adoption of the behavior of the op-

---

[1] With reference to roles 1 and 2, there is a percentage of women and men who marry but voluntarily refrain from having children. However, they clearly prefer the married state to single and unmarried living.

posite sex; in such cases, genital construction is ignored or denied. Mead gives interesting accounts of selecting shamans or *berdache* among the American Indians and training them for their roles.

8. There are some sexually mutilated persons. The mutilation may be congenital or socially created, as it has been through the centuries for eunuchs and at times in history for boy sopranos. In such cases, society clearly expects nonmarriage, nonparenthood, and allows a relaxation of the ordinary relations between the sexes.

9. Professional or commercial prostitution is recognized in a very large number of societies. In the United States, this more frequently involves women than men, but either may be included. Cases of boy prostitutes are by no means uncommon in this country, and are frequent in others.

10. A role that is presumably rare in the United States is zoolagnia, or sexual preference for an animal. Pornographic movies frequently are concerned with such sexual interactions.

11. In most cultures, chronological age is differentially related to expectations for sexual behavior. Homoerotic behavior of adolescents is forbidden in this culture, but it is openly expected in other cultures. Elderly heads of households may be expected to withdraw entirely from an active sexual role. In many societies (rather openly for males in this culture, increasingly openly perhaps for females) a period of license is allowed before marriage, but chastity after marriage is expected. The reverse may be true in other cultures. In some cultures, widows are not expected to remarry or to indulge in further sex relationships of any type.

Within United States culture, freedom of choice among these sex careers is rather severely limited. A clear premium is put on role 1 for females (married woman who bears and rears children) and role 2 for males (married man who begets and provides for children). The religious are accorded respect. Spinsters are accepted but rather pitied. In most cases, those seeking any of the other roles described by Mead are driven underground; some of the roles are not even recognized to exist in this culture.

It is obvious that anyone seeking a sex career outside social sanctions will suffer acute problems as he attempts to adjust to society. Mead points out that other societies often provide for much more complex sex role assignment than is allowed in United States society (p. 1453); and she worries a bit about the determined modern attempt "to induct every child into an active and exclusively heterosexual role within the bonds of legal monogamous unions."

Mead also believes that the organization of genital function must follow two general principles: First, sex behavior must be disciplined so that it does not disturb orderly social function to the point of social disruption. Panic about such disruption may underlie the rigid proscriptions on social interactions of Afro-American males and white females so common in the United States. The elaborate mythology of the Afro-American male's sexual prowess will be discussed later in this chapter.

Second, female sexual activity must be disciplined in such a way that the male is put into a situation where he assumes responsibility for the family. Male sexuality must be expressed along socially accepted lines *but at the same time* males must be given enough freedom that their continued potency is guaranteed. Lack of such discipline is commonly attributed to the lower social classes, and particularly to lower-class Afro-American males. It is possible that the modern concern about the increased feminization of the American male may be based on fears about his adequacy to assume the roles of husband and father, which are essential if society is to survive.

Mead points out still another factor in human sexuality that serves to make it uniquely important in human socialization: "the capacity of some human females to attain orgasmic sexual pleasure, a manifestation which is absent, as far as observation can tell, from most other species" (p. 1465). She believes this is a late evolutionary development, present in only some women, and that it varies greatly from society to society and from one woman to another. Mead also points out that menopause is another uniquely human occurrence. Thus, for the human female, aging presents a psychosocial situation for which there is no model in other species.

In the summary to her excellent chapter on "Cultural Determinants of Sexual Behavior," Mead includes a number of other points that are worth mentioning and discussing (pp. 1475–1476).

She thinks the double standard has almost disappeared, and believes that the earlier view of lower-class girls as being fair game has also almost gone. It is also possible that middle-class boys are beginning to approach the freedom in sexual behavior previously attributed more to lower-class youth.

Mead postulates a new double standard under which boys are protective and given to postponing sexual relations with girls they plan to marry. Kirkendall (1961) presents evidence supporting this point. On the other hand, girls are less self-protective and less rejecting of boys whom they plan to marry.

In today's society, Mead believes that uncommitted people over about age 25 are expected to meet each other's sexual needs or encounter marked hostility. The *Playboy* way of life may be an expression of Mead's hypothesis. Certainly open sexuality is not uncommon among middle-class urban young people.

Mead points out that the American stress on early and clear-cut heterosexuality puts adolescents under much strain. Boys in particular are expected to be heterosexually active early, exclusively and vigorously interested in girls, are suspect if they have too close male friends, are expected to marry at least by 30, and so on. Offer (1969) presents evidence about middle- and upper-middle-class boys that supports Mead's conclusions.

Mead says that the tomboy was disapproved of a generation ago, but today even prepubertal girls are more likely to be criticized for lack of feminine charms rather than for virility. Mead views all this as part of the American pressure to conform: "Not only this pressure to seem to conform, but the burden of nonconformity with the attendant sense of sin, or guilt, puts a heavy pressure on the very large proportion of Americans who deviate from the recognized patterns of temperament and behavior" (p. 1476).

Social Sanctions about Genital Function

From this discussion of sexual careers, it is obvious that society has much to say about *when*, with *whom*, and *how* genital function should take place. To live with minimal social frustration, the adolescent's initially diffused sex drive must be channeled and, when at all possible, directed along socially approved lines. Its first appearance is likely to flood the adolescent with undirected or inappropriately directed energy, as well as with a confused and wide ranging set of sexually related sensitivities. His drive activates him, but his responses are not yet efficient and well directed.[2] The selective and directive functions of drive have not yet operated to shape his reproductive and reproduction-associated behavior along mature lines. If he is lucky, this shaping will come with time and practice.

The selective and directive functions of drive eventually lead the adolescent to distinguish between psychoaffectional and psychobiological sex drives (Ausubel, 1954, p. 397). For those emotionally mature men and women in this culture, the two aspects of sexuality are well blended, ideally within the framework of marriage. But the adolescent still has a long way to go.

The problems of psychobiological and psychoaffectional merging are equally severe for boys and girls, although very different in nature. Boys usually approach the ultimate psychobiological–psychoaffectional blend from a pronounced initial psychobiological stance, while girls typically move from a psychoaffectional orientation toward psychobiological adjustment. Therein lies much of the communication problem between the sexes, as will be seen.

Ausubel discusses four more role differentiations that must be made: type of activity or erogenous zone implicated, sex object desired, degree of passivity or activity in sexual behavior, and appropriateness of adopted sex role.

Type of Activity and Erogenous Zone Implicated The only fully approved way for genital function in United States society is coitus between male and female that involves the genitals of each. Even for this, approval is awarded only within the context of matrimony.

Casual reading of the police reports, "arrest and arraignment for unnatural sexual act," suggests both that society imposes strict sanctions against other types of sexual activity and that these sanctions are frequently violated. Kinsey's data substantiate this point if one has residual doubt remaining after his own reading, observation, and experience. Of the unsanctioned sexual activities, it is apparent that those involving the mouth and the anus are most common, with relations with animals being not infrequent, particularly among rural youth.

Style of Genital Function The next major social sanction concerns being passive or initiatory, and the styles thereof. In United States society, the male is expected to take the initiative both in courting and copulatory behavior. This varies greatly among cultures (see Ford and Beach, 1951, for examples). It is also in sharp contrast to the behavior

---

[2]See the discussion of energizing and sensitizing functions of drive in Chapter 1.

of many other species, where the female (as in the higher apes) "presents" aggressively, although the male still does the mounting. If there is no male available, many female mammals go to great lengths to find a sexual partner.

While to the author's knowledge the matter of initiative has not been studied in great detail in relations between the sexes, Bieber, *et al.* (1962) report styles within a population of male homosexuals whom they studied intensively. While most men are mixed in their preferences for style of sexual relations, one group clearly prefers to do the inserting and another group clearly prefers to do the receiving. The former have no particular preference in partners, although they incline somewhat to passive and effeminate males. The latter, on the other hand, want hairy, muscular, large penis partners: the prototype of the virile, American man. This matter should be studied for more conventional populations.

Parenthetically, Masters and Johnson (1968) point out that size of the male penis has no relation to the satisfaction his female partner receives. Female genitalia are obviously capable of an enormous range of expansibility and contractibility, ranging from insertion of small objects to accommodating the birth of a baby. In an enjoyable relationship and within normal limits, female genital equipment simply adjusts to the structure of the partner's sexual equipment. Masters and Johnson also dismiss as unfounded in fact the conventional distinction between clitoral (relatively superficial) and vaginal (profound) orgasms in females.

Kinsey, Pomeroy, and Martin (1948, 1953) add the information that depth penetration brings little stimulation to females, since the vagina is short on sensory receptors. If this is correct, the length of the male penis is irrelevant. The genital sources of erotic arousal for females "result from the contact of the external areas of the vulva, of the areas immediately inside the outer edges of the labia, and of the clitoris" (1948, p. 576). This means that only the diameter of the male penis plays a part in providing satisfaction to one's partner in intercourse. Furthermore, because of the range of contractability of female genitals, it is doubtful if even this dimension has any importance other than as it affects its possessor's self-evaluation.

There are great variations in the degree of initiative taken by United States males in courting behavior, ranging from the youth or man who commits rape and sexual murder to the "nice boy" who is frightened to give his date a peck on the cheek as he says good night at her front door. Aggressiveness in sexual advances among males seems to be greater among the lower socioeconomic classes, and the male usually clearly dominates sexually. Ford and Beach (1951) believe that sexual behavior is more amenable to learning among males than among females.

Regardless of her social class, the average attractive girl who does considerable dating has had to put up at least some degree of physical defense on behalf of her virtue. Groups of boys sometimes force sexual attentions on a single girl. This may be a group rape, or it may occur in a situation where the girl was initially receptive but, as the group became aroused, objected, and was then forced to submit. There ought to be some way to make adolescent females understand that seductive behavior on their part can lead to aggressive male responses.

While the matter of initiative among conventional male-female pairs has been little explored, Kinsey and his colleagues (1948, 1953) devote considerable space to variations in technique. There are enormous differences from one couple to another, and among social classes. About 70 percent of the population however, confines itself to the conventional face-to-face, male-on-top position. However, women seem most often to achieve orgasm when they are on top, and this position is assumed much more frequently in better educated couples.

When compared with the poorly educated, the better educated receive more outlet from masturbation, both preceding and following marriage; less from intercourse before marriage; less from homosexual relations; and more frequently prefer sex while nude and in the light. Males, because of their wider receptivity to sexual stimulation and, probably, with less emphasis on modesty training, like sex in the light better than females. As has been said, males may be more amenable to learning in this area. Middle-class people do considerable kissing, including deep kissing; they are more likely to fondle their partners' breasts and genitals, including mouth–genital contact; they are less likely to have intercourse while standing up or sitting down, but more likely to have it while lying down beside or with the female on top. There seems to be relatively little anal sex play at any social level, although of course it is more frequent in homosexual relations between men than in other types of coupling. Kinsey reports that anal sex seldom results in orgasm for the receiver (1948, p. 579). Lest these variations be considered perverse, the reader should think of the variety of sexual styles that have been documented or that he has observed in the nonhuman species. Man, in short, denies himself sexual stimulation in a number of ways that are biologically common at other phylogenetic levels.

Sex Object Desired. The third area of social sexual sanction concerns the sex object desired. Society says firmly that it is "normal" only when boys and girls or men and women of about the same age participate together sexually, and even then only in marriage. Conventionally, the wife should be the same age or a year or so younger than the husband. More mature men are given considerable leeway in all types of sexual approach, including marriage, as long as the women are *not too young*. Nabokov's *Lolita* is considered by many to be a *dirty* book, and Nabokov is said to have written it to shock and thus force thought. Child molestors whether within or between sexes provoke extreme outrage, despite the fact that sexual induction of very young females is not at all uncommon in other cultures, even ritualized in some, and that the adult male's boy lover was commonplace in classic Greek society and is not uncommon today in some cultures.

The woman who shows an interest in a man much younger than she is criticized and regarded with some contempt, whether or not she marries him.

Women are given more latitude for homosexual attractions than men. Among men, male homosexuality produces panic despite the fact that, according to Kinsey (1948), about 50 percent of his sample was "homosexual" at least to the degree that they had had and were willing to admit to sexual fantasies about homosexual relations, and 37 percent had taken part in homosexual activities that led to orgasm. The figures are much lower for females: 28 and 13 percent for the cumulative incidence of homosexual responses during the lives of the individuals responding, with 13 percent having had orgasm in a homosexual context (Kinsey, Pomeroy, and Martin, 1953, pp. 474-475).

It is interesting to speculate about the reasons for the sex differences in society's reactions to homosexuality. Mead, as reported earlier in this section, may have provided the answer in her assumption that sexuality among males must be permitted, as a man needs freedom which will enable him eventually to procreate and preserve the species.

The great difference in incidence of male and female homosexual consummatory activity (37 and 13 percent, according to Kinsey) may be accounted for by the higher drive of the male, his greater social freedom, generally less aggressive sexual pursuit by females (although there are many exceptions to this), and the fact that the concentration of unmarried females (those most likely to undertake homosexual relations) is in the rather inhibited middle and upper-middle social classes. Although homosexuality is generally disapproved of for either sex, society's differential attitudes may be due to the fact that folklore has described the homosexual male as uninterested or unable to procreate, hence avoiding his primary sexual role of father, whereas a woman can receive the male and become impregnated with no effort on her part. Thus, the homosexual female is less a threat to the preservation of the species than the homosexual male.

Mead (1961) makes an interesting, rather controversial point in this connection: She documents the fact of much casual homoerotic behavior between adolescent boys, recognizes that it is rather frequent among sailors and most other isolated groups of males and females, as well as among illiterates and "those who share a meager tradition." As is well known, homoerotic behavior increases greatly in prisons, boys' and girls' reform schools, probably in sex-segregated schools, particularly those that are residential, and in the armed services. However, Mead believes that "*genuine* role inversion, where ideas of love and passion and problems of identity enter in, seems to be characteristic of high levels of civilization" (1954). She considers it possible that such things as body type, height, preference for art, music, and so on, may well influence this state of affairs. Historically, inversion of sex role among the great Greek actors seemed to be almost as frequent as their playing all dramatic roles, whether male or female. They probably also played both roles in the sexual act (see Bieber, *et al.*, 1962).

Kinsey's data also indicate that the better one's education, the more likely he is to experiment with a wide variety of sexual and sex-related behaviors.

The timing of sexual maturity, at least for boys, may affect the direction of sexual behavior. Levitt and Brady (1965) suggest that early maturing boys show a wider range of sexual response than those who mature later. They respond to many things that are not considered respectable sex objects by society. This may be due to the interaction of high drive, most notably its sensitizing function; little legitimate opportunity; and immature value-moral organization. The sample of young men whom Levitt and Brady studied was very special. All subjects were volunteer graduate students. The investigators checked only on the range of stimuli that elicited sexual arousal but, even so, it is likely that in our culture sexual responses to deviant or abnormal stimuli arouse considerable conflict.

Appropriateness of Adopted Sex Role The fourth of society's demands about genital function concerns the appropriateness of the adopted sex role. This category clearly overlaps with the discussion above. In later chapters on imitation and identification, this matter will be dealt with in much more detail. Obviously, to return to Chapter 1, adoption of a socially inappropriate role adds to frustration, potential aggression, and anxiety—thus to increased total drive.

Developmental Trends in Genital Function

To conclude this long section on changes in genital function, it is well to look at the dimensions of the over-all adaptation that must be made by each adolescent. Ausubel (1954) provides a useful breakdown of this topic, and the analysis below is adapted from him. Ausubel sees four dimensions to the problem that must be resolved:

1. Whether male or female, Maori or WASP, each adolescent must adjust to a certain amount of perplexity and uneasiness that is necessarily produced by a strange and powerful new drive. This adjustment, obviously, relates to the psychology of change introduced in Chapter 1.

2. This drive comes on him suddenly, and it is powerful, perhaps particularly for boys. Thus, usually in our culture without adequate preparation, he faces an urgent demand for *initial* control and direction in line with social sanctions. As has been pointed out, these are complex, often arbitrary, not well adapted to human *biology*, and exceedingly ill-suited to youngsters who differ from the social norm, either biologically or psychologically.

Levitt and Brady (1965) suggest to the author that at least for early maturing boys, greater deviation and thus possibly greater conflict occur, perhaps because of a combination of their high drive and psychological-"moral" immaturity.

3. Each adolescent individual must adjust to the cultural pressures to assume an appropriate biological role. The literature suggests that, for young men who deviate, such an adjustment is impossible among late teenagers and early 20 year olds (Doidge and Holtzman, 1960); while it may be worked out in the context of good general personal adjustment by somewhat older, well-educated males (Chang and Block, 1960).

4. Finally, there is a general and necessary trend for the style of sexual gratification to become increasingly more specific and clearly differentiated as young people move through adolescence. Such specificity and probably greater efficiency result from learning and, presumably, from a

reduction of interfering drives, such as anxiety, in sexual situations—roles where sex-related behavior is called for.

SOCIALIZING SEXUAL BEHAVIOR This section foreshadows material on sexual identification and moral development that is treated in Chapter 14. Since such socialization is triggered by the new sex drive, it is necessary to begin discussion of the topic here, and to fit it into the broader context of values and moral development later. Readers will do well to check forward to Chapters 13 and 14 at this time, and later to check back from them to the present section.

There is much hue and cry at present about decadent sexual morality and a sexual revolution. Gagnon (1967), at the time a research worker in the Indiana University Institute for Sex Research (founded by Kinsey), lists four criteria to describe a sexual revolution. His criteria are:

1. More premarital intercourse at all levels of society.
2. Couples having premarital sexual intercourse more often.
3. More sexual promiscuity (sex relations with many different people).
4. More frequent intercourse with people outside a love relation.

Citing data already published as well as those to which he had access but which at that time were unpublished, Gagnon interpreted his four criteria with the following results. The percentage of people engaging in premarital intercourse has not changed in more than forty years; about half the women born after 1900 have intercourse before marriage but of them half have relations only with the person they intend to marry. Only about 5 to 7 percent of women have intercourse with five or more men before they marry and they, Gagnon believes, are the sexual targets for men, and are exploited. Of men who go to college, 70 percent have premarital intercourse; 80 percent of those with only a high school education have premarital intercourse; while 90 percent of those with an eighth grade education have premarital intercourse. College men still have intercourse disproportionately with noncollege, and often socially disadvantaged, women. Postmaritally, about one-half of the married men and one-fourth of the married women have a single extramarital sexual experience. Morton Hunt's estimate that these percentages have moved to 60 percent of married men and 35 to 40 percent of married women appeared in the September 1969 *Ladies' Home Journal.* The most frequent reason given for such affairs was boredom. Affairs were undertaken to bolster self-esteem in large part. Church attenders have both less intra- and extramarital sex than nonattenders.

On the basis of such data, Gagnon concludes firmly that there is no sexual revolution. The recent report of increase in percentages would be considered simply that—not a revolution.

A fifth criterion of a sexual revolution can be added: people having first sexual relations earlier. However, the author knows of no data bearing on this criterion.

Clearly, more data about the situation are needed. It is doubtful that there is indeed a *behavioral* sexual revolution; certainly, sex education in the public schools, churches, and the information media is fuller, franker, and more frequent than it has ever been, but is still the subject of often violent controversy; treatment of sex in all media is franker and probably more frequent than it has been for at least 150 years, and hitherto taboo topics such as homosexuality are now rather freely treated in public forums, especially in movies and the theater. Thus, there may be a sexual revolution of ideas and information, which may be followed by a behavioral revolution. Since ideas have tended to strike the middle classes first (this is less true now that we possess mass media such as television), one may predict that *if* sexual behavior liberalizes markedly, the first manifestations will be among the intellectuals, then the simply well-informed, then the "run of the mill" middle class.

What the results will be is anyone's guess. Since "sex is surfacing" and old ways are changing, it is likely that adolescent conflicts about sex may also become more open and, quite likely, stronger.

Special Problems of Middle-Class Youth

As noted in Chapter 1, middle-class youngsters are considerably more hemmed in by internally and externally imposed sexual restrictions than lower-class youth. It may be that white youth are less free sexually than Afro-American youth (e.g., I. L. Reiss, 1968), but to the author's knowledge this point is not conclusively documented. Psychological and sociological data suggest that social class differences are of much more practical guidance value than ethnic differences.

Ausubel (1954, p. 400) discusses the topic of sexual behavior for middle-class boys. His analysis is modified here, and the author has extended it to apply to girls.

Parenthetically, there is a widely but perhaps not accurately held notion that, because of boys' hydraulic sexual system, they suffer more acutely from society's restrictive sexual sanctions than girls. Kinsey's (1953) data support this view. Masters and Johnson (1966, 1968), studying the actual physical responses in sexual behavior, adduce evidence that, once aroused, the human female is as breathlessly rushed along by sex as her masculine counterpart. Certainly, many girls and women, perhaps particularly after they have become sexually experienced, are subject to as urgent demands for sexual outlet as males, and are as disturbed by nonconsummation as males. Generally, females seem not to have, or few of them have, or they less frequently have, available to them the masculine equivalent of the nocturnal emission. As has been mentioned, it is also indicated by research that fewer females masturbate, and that they masturbate less frequently.

Ausubel argues that girls in some cultures do not develop sexual urges, so that many of them are placed in no sexual conflict. Conventional psychoanalytic theory also includes this idea. But the coeducational life and dating career of the average American girl, the almost inevitable very explicit sexual advances that occur in dating or in other contexts, the constant barrage of the mass media, and the almost universal availability of pornography, with its emphasis on sexual acrobatics, make it almost impossible for girls in industrialized cultures to avoid sexual stimulation. The only advantage they have over males appears to be that they do not become aroused unless they are "touched and handled," whereas males are more likely to be triggered sexually by almost anything. In the institutional settings where the author has worked, the girls give evidence of being just as sexy as the boys. It thus seems artificial to separate middle-class boys from girls in discussing the special sexual problems of the middle-class youngster.

United States society stresses sexual repression, then suppression, as the two basic methods by which adolescents should handle their sexual interests and urges. Neither of these methods works well!

Problems faced by middle-class children as a special group emerge from a sharp discongruity and resulting conflict between what they have been taught by their caretakers and what their own bodies, peer group experiences, and the mass media tell them to do (or suggest is permissible) and what they observe among their elders. Actually, caretakers to lower-class children seem to tell the children little that is different, but middle-class parents seem to get it across more effectively. Thus sex urges become a part of the middle-class adolescent's value system, as they frequently do not with lower-class children, and produce sharper conflicts than are typical for lower-class children. Hoffman and Saltzstein (1967) present evidence that middle-class youngsters identify more with their parents' moral standards than lower-class children do. In identification of this sort, the standards of another are incorporated as one's own.

First, the culture produces discongruity by telling children that sex urges are natural, necessary, and nothing to be ashamed of; and in the next breath a clear indication is given that sex urges should be repressed or suppressed. This must be remarkably puzzling to bright and thoughtful young people, and they must be at least as frustrated and potentially anxious over the matter as youngsters who do not cognize the contradiction but who also must live with it. The whole matter is one of acute cognitive dissonance, to relate it to Festinger's theory.

Second, society is faced with the fact that youngsters can not repress or even in most instances suppress what they honestly believe should be repressed simply because they have been told to do so by people they trust. Adolescents simply are not that socially sophisticated.

Third, this state of affairs may lead to excessive frustration and overpreoccupation with sex. Since frustration only adds to an already excessively high drive level, interference with all sorts of necessary complex learning, including academic learning, is likely to occur.

Fourth, it is possible that sex urges may blunt personality maturation, since they are major sources of hedonistic satisfaction. (This may be thought of as a conflict between the Apollonian and Dionysian life styles. It is also a hypothesis derived from the Calvinist middle-class ethic.) This last point is of major importance. Few will argue against the statement that the middle class is often too rigid for its own good. The price for middle-class "uptightness" is paid daily in psychiatrists' bills, ulcer treatments, cardiac ills, projected hostilities, and a host of other painful and expensive symptoms. There are many who argue that sexual freedom (for example, the well-known Dionysian *Playboy* philosophy) will remedy or at least alleviate such rigidity.

Others sincerely believe that relaxation in sexual behavior is a major symptom of decay of "the Protestant ethic." The Protestant ethic differs little from the core ethic of a good Catholic, Jew, or Muslim (all are monotheistic religions). The term can be considered as simply shorthand for a whole set of values that seems to be essential if a democratic society is to operate: honesty, responsibility, regard for the rights of others, reasonable orderliness and predictability, sacrifice of considerable momentary pleasure either for the sake of others, for the sake of future gain, or for both, and renunciation of violence as a method of problem solution, among other things. The fact that these qualities are in short supply in society may be a more potent source of conflict, frustration, anxiety, and anger among thinking adolescents than any of the frustrations they encounter sexually.

There is considerable evidence suggesting that moral development more or less in line with the Apollonian rational aspects of the Protestant ethic is useful in our society. This evidence will be reviewed in the sections on modeling and identification (Chapters 13 and 14). There is no evidence to suggest that a fulfilling *psychoaffectionally oriented* sex life runs counter to the Protestant ethic. The effects of hedonism *qua* hedonism in our society have not been documented scientifically. As things now stand, the effects would likely be disruptive. At the very least, the matter most urgently deserves, even demands, dispassionate attention of research workers and educators.

Ausubel (1954, p. 402) makes another good point that is frequently overlooked: There is no simple relation between the severity of sex restriction and the amount of conflict a youngster experiences. Conflict occurs only when an adolescent has internalized the values of his elders. If Hoffman and Saltzstein are correct, lower-class children as a group thus suffer from less conflict than middle-class youngsters, despite the strong evidence that lower-class children are more severely disciplined (receive more physical punishment, and are handled more autocratically). Bowerman and Elder (1964), among many others, document this point. Their data concern adolescents' perceptions rather than observation; but there is generally a strong relation between such reports and the actual state of affairs, as Clark and Tifft (1966) demonstrate.

If middle-class adolescents are more frustrated sexually, their advantages in other areas go a long way to compensate: For example, they are more equably and democratically disciplined; as Erikson suggests, they enjoy a prolonged period of psychosocial moratorium (protection by their parents and the authorities from the disastrous, long term consequences of their adolescent mistakes); they are given parental support and active assistance in developing competencies of value in an industrial society.

There is still an amazing amount of misinformation about the area of masturbation, which is the principal sexual outlet for middle-class adolescents. There are no known physical ill effects that result from masturbation. Masturbating youngsters suffer because of their feelings of guilt and impaired self-esteem, because of their fear which arises from the common folklore that masturbation results in physical, mental, and moral deterioration, and because it may interfere with later adequate heterosexual relations.

Special Problems of Lower-Class Youth

This topic has not been well studied in the literature, but reasons for this have been given implicitly earlier: Research workers are almost invariably middle class, and lower-class adolescents and adults, for good reason, are suspicious of people who inquire into their affairs. Lower-class people as a group are not particularly verbal. Middle-class research workers often bring with them values that, regardless of their skill at hiding them, signal clearly to the lower-class research subject that he is being disapproved of, or that he is likely to incur disapproval if he is frank.

Kinsey and his colleagues (1948, 1953) provide the best set of information available, and enough of this has been reported that the pattern is clear: Lower-class youth engage more in premarital intercourse, less in masturbation, have more total sexual outlets, and are more likely than middle-class youth to have been involved in homosexual interactions. Variations by social class are greater for males than females, however. Variation in female sexual behavior is at least as great and perhaps greater along religious than social class lines, while religiosity makes less difference for males. Speculatively, any greater sexual activity that may exist for lower-class girls is due, not to their values, but to the aggressiveness and lack of inhibition of their suitors. As was mentioned, I. L. Reiss (1968) has gathered data that suggest ethnic differences, with Afro-American youth being somewhat more permissive about sex than white youth.

Reiss' data also indicate a strong relation between the beliefs of late adolescents and their parents' beliefs. Children from more liberal and permissive families are themselves both more liberal and permissive than the average in attitudes and behavior. Youth tend to seek out as their best friends others who hold attitudes and beliefs similar to their own, but who are seen by them as being more permissive than they themselves are. However, youth report themselves as being somewhat more similar to their best friends than to their parents. On the whole, youth seem to pick their friends so as to ameliorate or cushion the generation gap.

The remainder of this subsection on problems of lower-class youth is speculation, suggested by personal communication with colleagues and friends who are or have been members of the staff of Indiana University's Institute for Sex Research and Department of Sociology. It is presented more for its heuristic value than for its basis in fact: That is, it may help to stimulate much needed thinking and research.[3]

The material that follows is particularly related to people who are severely disadvantaged economically. Some of the author's thinking results from his work with disadvantaged children and their families who live in the inner city (or urban ghetto, as it is frequently called).

The excessively disorganized (or at least, nonmiddle-class) family structure of the poor has been documented again and again, both among Afro-American and white populations (see, for example, Glazer and Moynihan, 1963; Harrington, 1962; Hodges, McCandless, and Spicker, 1969; Pettigrew, 1964; and Silberman, 1964). The incidence of so-called matrifocal or matrilinear families is very high, particularly among the Afro-American poor. For example, 43 percent of the Black children in an inner city population with which the author is now working come from fatherless homes. Since the situation is so common, it cannot be considered pathological. But its existence is bound to result in very real prob-

---

[3]The author especially appreciates his interactions with William Simon (now at the Institute for Juvenile Research, Chicago) and John H. Gagnon (now at the State University of New York, Stonybrook).

lems for children and adolescents who aspire to success in middle-class terms, since they will have learned an entirely different set of ground rules.

Not only are the families of the poor disorganized, by middle-class standards, but they are singularly lacking in all sorts of tangible and clearly predictable rewards. This deprivation ranges from basic diet, shelter, and clothing to lack of esthetic satisfaction in the inner city or the rural slum. It is thus no wonder that the disadvantaged seek out one of the few satisfactions available: sex. The body may be the currency with which one can purchase personal gratification, and also gain social acceptance. In the author's experience, the disadvantaged are just plain lonely, despite the common middle-class notion of the "happy poor." This stereotype may be based on middle-class guilt or on an uptight Apollonian envy of a presumed gratifying Dionysian way of life among the disadvantaged, or both.

Among the middle class, it seems that sex serves either as a very binding or a very disruptive factor in marriages and other enduring relationships between the sexes. Sex seems to serve an enduring function less among the extremely poor, because marriages among the poor only rarely break up over sex. Also, there seems to be less reciprocity between the sexes about either sexual activity or sex-related communication. The lower-class male is *clearly* the initiator, and girls or women who initiate sexual advances are perceived as rather threatening.

As has been stated, on the average the very poor boy starts premarital heterosexual activity early and intensively. This same boy has grown up in a social structure where men and women and boys and girls are much more separated in social interactions than among the stable working and middle class. Hence, the boy refers his behavior not toward a new phase of expanding his skills in dealing with women but backward to his homoerotic society. He commonly uses his sexual prowess to establish himself as a man among his peers. He takes unto himself *machismo*,[4] which is highly esteemed and much sought after in Latin American society. The same phenomenon (in practice, if not in principle) can be observed in the middle class as well as among the poor. It is illustrated by Ted's history in Chapter 5. In other words, a promiscuously fornicating boy is validating his *maleness*, not his *heterosociality* (social group including both sexes). Nor do poor boys seem to build up romanticized fantasy about sex as do middle-class boys, partly because they receive immediate gratification, partly because they are short of language and fantasy. Lower-class boys, in other words, *publicly* act out heterosexuality in a homosocial (one-sex social group) context; middle-class boys *privately* work out a heterosexual commitment that they will eventually consolidate with girls and women. As has been indicated, boys from among the very poor (Kinsey's sample with education below eighth grade) spill their sexual behavior over into homosexuality more often than better educated boys.

It simply may be that the lower-class boy's early involvement in heterosexuality in his homosocial setting forestalls the socially desirable

---

[4]This term comes from the Spanish and refers specifically to manliness in the sense of impregnating many women.

goal of integrating sex and love. Since girls vary in sexual behavior less along social class lines than boys, girls often disastrously read love into a relation that is entirely biological for boys. This state of affairs in by no means confined to poor youth.

Speculatively, the idea may be advanced that the masculine self concept of very poor boys from disorganized families, a disproportionate number of which are woman dominated, is weak. Thus the masculine self concept must be constantly reconfirmed: In marriage, this may be done by keeping the wife constantly pregnant, thus publicly proving again and again that the husband is a *man*. It may also be confirmed by fighting. It may be that such insecurity of masculine self concept relates to ineffectiveness in family planning, since wives sense that they serve some strong need of their husbands by bearing many children. Poor girls and women also have poor self concepts. For many, a baby is the only technically perfect thing they can create. However, the baby gives the mother love, and she is likely to remove herself affectionally from the father and perhaps from her male children.

If the world of the very poor remains homosocial, as it does for many, then sons who model on their fathers follow the same old pattern and they in turn move too early into a self- and family-defeating heterosexual role. Thus, the sexual family dilemma of the poor is perpetuated. Of course, if poverty sets up the situation so that family life can not provide satisfactions that compensate for the responsibilities thereof, then self-preservation, in the broadest sense, dictates living outside conventional family structure. Since men can more easily escape the home and children, it is not surprising that more men than women choose such a life pattern.

COMPONENTS OF MALE SEXUALITY

Thorne (1966) has made an effort to isolate the factors that enter into male sexuality. Although less than one-fifth of his sample is adolescent, and even though they are University of Miami college students, it is worthwhile to look at the components of masculine sexuality that Thorne has revealed. Like Mead's social sexual roles, they provide a framework within which boys particularly, but also girls, can view the development of their sexual selves. Thorne applied the statistics of factor analysis to responses to psychological tests. He reports the sexuality factors, while Haupt and Allen (1966) report the results for separate groups of men who were studied. The author knows of no similar study of feminine sexuality.

Thorne studied 101 male college students, 41 addicts confined in a rehabilitation center in California, 246 convicted felons from North Carolina, and 157 convicted sex offenders in Michigan. His sample ranged in age from 15 to 65 years, the average being $30^{1}/_{10}$ years. Education averaged a little less than eleventh grade, almost half were unmarried, and the majority was Protestant.

Using such statistical techniques, Thorne separated eight factors in male sexuality:

1. The first factor concerned the *intensity of sex drive and interest*. His college group ranked highest on this factor.

2. Thorne's second factor was *sexual frustration and maladjustment*. Forty percent of his sample admitted to serious problems in outlets for and expression of sex, with 36 percent wishing to see a psychiatrist, their problems were so troublesome to them. At first, this seems understandable, since more than four-fifths of Thorne's sample consist of incarcerated males. However, the normal college sample reported the second highest incidence of problems related to this factor. College youth were exceeded in frequency of frustrations and maladjustments only by the group of convicted sex offenders! In interpreting the result, however, it should be remembered that a college sample is inclined to be sophisticated about sex and cooperative with research workers. Thus, as Thorne, Haupt, and Allen recognize, college men may have overreported or perhaps were the most honest group. However, the sex offenders could afford to be honest, since their problems were already public knowledge by virtue of their convictions.

3. Thorne's third factor was *generalized anxiety and neurotic conflict associated with sex*. This differs from the second factor in representing more repression and openness. Normal college youth scored next lowest on this factor, with only the addict group being lower. This lends support to the notion that college young men know what their problems are and are willing to admit them.

4. The fourth factor was *sexual fixations and cathexes*. Here again the college group scored next to highest, with more than one-third of them having "perversions." They admitted to a very wide range of sex interests, "normal" and "not so normal."

5. Thorne's next factor was *repression of sexuality*. As might have been predicted from what has been said earlier about male sexuality, this factor plays a minor role in male sexuality. It accounts for only about 1 percent of the total variance. The college group scored far, far below any other group for this factor, as could have been predicted from their frank and open behavior.

6. The sixth factor that makes up Thorne's picture of male sexuality was *loss of sex controls*. Here, the college group scored high; college men ranked below only the group of sex offenders. The authors point out that the frankness of the college sample should be remembered in reporting the results. On the other hand, this may reflect the conflict between Apollonian and Dionysian life styles that seems to have surfaced in American life.

7. Thorne's seventh factor was *homosexuality*. The college group was at the median in its concern about this component of male sexuality.

8. The eighth factor was *sex role confidence*. Despite all the concerns shown by this group in their results for the previous factors, their scoring for *sex role confidence* was the highest of any of the groups studied.

9. The ninth and final factor was called *promiscuity and sociopathy*. The college group scored next high for this factor, falling only .2 percent lower than the highest scoring group, drug addicts undergoing rehabilitation.

Thorne's and Haupt and Allen's research is useful in throwing light on a problem that typically generates more heat than light. The results can not be applied directly to male adolescents taken as a whole, since as a group they are less experienced than the young and not-so-young men who provided the factor analytic data that have been reported above. College youth are probably more articulate, and franker, than adolescents in general; and groups of addicts, felons, and sex offenders may also be expected to be atypical in their sexuality.

On the other hand, these nine factors applied to the sexuality of all the groups investigated. Thus, it is likely that they also apply to the sexuality of the "mainstream American adolescent."

Since more is known about college men than about any other group of male adolescents, there is a better chance of generalizing from them to typical adolescents. Thus, it is well to review their standing for the nine factors of male sexuality. They were found to be high in the factors of intensity of sex drive and interest, sexual frustration and maladjustment, sexual fixations and cathexes, loss of sex controls, sex role confidence, and promiscuity and sociopathy. In other words, as might be expected, college men's sexual adjustment as they perceive it is a "mixed bag." They are reasonably confident about their masculinity and are high in drive and interest, but are frustrated and possess a good many maladjustments, as maladjustments are defined by society.

On the other hand, normal college youth as a group score low for generalized anxiety and neurotic conflict and repression of sexuality. These results suggest that normal, bright, and well-educated young men are not immobilized by their sexual problems, and that they bring them out into the open to consider them. Given frustrations and maladjustments, this seems a healthy way to handle sexual problems.

College youth stand at about the median of the four groups investigated for the *homosexuality* factor. There seems no reason to be surprised by this result.

Male Anatomy and Sexuality

The American way of life dictates that the male sexual role in copulation is initiatory, assertive, and insertive. His social role is expected to be similarly initiatory and assertive. But Mead (1961) points out: "The anatomic complexity of the male body, with the analogy between anus and vagina, makes the problem of activity-passivity a recurrent one and one which may be intrinsically antithetical to a procreative heterosexual role" (p. 1471). By this she means that young males may be confused about whether they are supposed to receive passively through the anus as females do through the vagina, or whether they are supposed to confine themselves to that portion of their body designed for assertive-insertive behavior, the penis. Mead notes that female anatomy is more harmonized, in that it includes only orifices, and that neither the vagina nor the female anus is structurally out of line with the feminine sexual role of passively receiving and gestating. Bieber, *et al.*, (1962) have been quoted as presenting data that support Mead's hypotheses to some degree. From a structural point of view, it should be easier and less confusing for girls to adopt the female sex role than for males to adopt the male role.

As we have seen (for example, Money, 1961), male sex hormones are specifically erotically arousing. They stimulate fantasy, erections, and ejaculations, and affect ejaculations in both frequency and intensity. But these male sex hormones – androgens – do not have a direct effect on the *direction* or *content* of erotic inclination. Nor do female hormones – estrogens – affect direction or content of female sexual goals. Money and many others believe that the direction and content of sexual behavior may well be imprinted, and that imprinting may occur before the age of 3 years. *If* the young male can be imprinted *and* if he is confused about active and passive sex roles and the analogy between the anus and the vagina, it is possible that he is a logical candidate for imprinting as a homosexual. The potential fluidity of behavior under high drive, as at adolescence, may make the adolescent singularly vulnerable in this area. As Ford and Beach (1951) point out, the human male's sexuality seems to be more modifiable by learning than the female's.

If males are more given than females to sex role confusion, this may account for the fact that proscriptions or other institutionalized methods of dealing with male instead of female homosexuality are more often built into formal social codes. Mead describes two general methods of handling the situation. In the first, and the one used in American society, focus is almost exclusively placed on heterosexual relations. Any other type of sexual relationship is officially treated as being so peripheral that it is hardly worth bothering about. When and if homosexuality does occur, particularly among males, strict legal sanctions against it are provided.

Alternatively, (Mead, 1961) homosexuality may be recognized and provided for by official and socially sanctioned institutions, such as permissiveness among men when on war duty, accepting adolescent but not adult homosexuality, creating a modified priesthood, as for the American Indian shaman, or institutionalizing boy lovers and prostitutes.

Society pays two types of prices for sweeping this problem under the rug. First, boys and men are often exploited, frequently with serious psychic consequences. The underground homosexual society is characterized by competition for partners, infidelity, mutual suspicion, and a host of other conditions that make life for the homosexual difficult, dangerous, and often unrewarding except in a superficial, immediate sensory gratification sense.

In turn, much is lost to society. Many homosexuals are exceptionally creative. Since persecution is likely to add to drive in such a way as to reduce efficiency, society cheats itself of many of the real contributions that homosexuals would make if they were treated more equably.

GOALS OF ADOLESCENT SEXUAL SOCIALIZATION

It seems very unlikely that sex can be healthily socialized so long as people are not fully and accurately informed about it. No one would presume to train an electrician without giving him full, objective data about the phenomena of electricity and its channeling and control. The analogy between electricity and sex is apt: Both can be constructive or destructive forces, both are powerful, both must be channeled and controlled for an orderly industrial society to exist.

With ignorance, misinformation, and myth dispelled, the next step toward frank interpersonal communication can be made. Intercommunication should stress the physical, personal, and interpersonal aspects of sex, as these are its enduring and potentially constructive-destructive components.

The previous two steps taken, the way is clear to proceed with sexual socialization within a context of ethics, values, and total family living.

Finally, sexuality among human beings should emphasize psychoaffectional sex.

What are the differences between males and females in attaining these four general goals? From the autobiographies of adolescents in the author's possession, it seems that at all social class levels girls are given a better education in sex than boys, but that the education is subminimal. The nature of menstruation and the risk of pregnancy almost demand that mothers supply their daughters with a little information about personal hygiene, and that they warn them about the results of copulation. These minima are much less often supplied by their fathers to boys. Except for this subminimum, there seems to be little advantage held by one sex over the other in the range and accuracy of sexual information possessed.

There is probably little difference between boys and girls in interpersonal communication about sex: Girls do not treat the topic as frankly as boys, but boys are probably more dishonest about it. This conclusion, however, is impressionistic.

It is probably easier for girls than boys to incorporate sex in a context of ethics, values, and total family living. This conclusion, too, is clinical and impressionistic. However, it follows logically from the difference in child rearing practices and goals for boys and girls; and fits with the fact that the girl who becomes pregnant needs family shelter in a very direct way, while fatherhood for a boy is a seemingly more casual matter.

The goal of emphasis on psychoaffectional sex seems much easier to attain for girls than boys. Girls' psychoaffectional attitude toward sex perhaps springs partly from their own biology and their nonhydraulic sex system, but it seems likely that is a spin-off from the other personal–social attributes of their sex. Femaleness is characterized by nurturance, responsibility, and obedience (see Barry, Bacon, and Child, 1957; Douvan and Adelson, 1966).

THE COURSE OF MALE SEXUAL SOCIALIZATION

Kephart and Ainsworth (1938) and Bijou, Ainsworth, and Stockey (1943) suggest that the sexual careers and, to a major extent, the life adjustment of girls, are determined by the type of marital career they finally select, and their good or bad fortune in selecting a marital partner. Within these data, this is less true for boys, who are more autonomous. For such reasons it is useful to explore the course of male sexual socialization, since light is thrown on the destinies of both the male and female.

Although his subjects are college males, it is worth looking in some detail at Kirkendall's (1961) findings. He interviewed 200 college men who gave case histories that covered their experiences in premarital intercourse with 668 partners. His subjects ranged in age from 17 to 28 and, at the time he gathered his data, the young men averaged 20$\frac{3}{5}$ years old. Their ages at the time of their first premarital intercourse ranged from 9 to 26 years, the average young man having had his first premarital intercourse at the age of 17 years. From Kirkendall's valid seeming data, he classifies premarital intercourse into six plausibly defined levels. These levels range from exclusively psychobiological to primarily psychoaffectional. The latter seemed to be the most mature and is marked by the most genuine solicitation for the integrity of the partner as a worthwhile human being. It is also the most rewarding in that the young men saw it as leading to marriage. As will be seen in Chapter 14, it accords best with the highest level of moral development.

Kirkendall's first stage of premarital intercourse is intercourse with prostitutes. The young men who had experiences in this category, as well as in the next two "developmental" categories, stressed the psychobiological, physical satisfaction aspect of the sexual relationship almost exclusively. They expressed little or no concern for the partner. They talked with other boys and men about the experience, thus, perhaps, acting like their counterparts among the disadvantaged who were discussed earlier: They were enhancing their status in their masculine peer group in a possibly homoerotic or at least homosocial fashion. Their relations in this and in Kirkendall's second category were also frequently homoerotic, in that they visited prostitutes or copulated with casual pick-ups in groups. The financial transaction with prostitutes seemed to serve to strip from the relationship any "human" overtones.

The second stage is intercourse with pick-ups. The casual pick-up was held in little if any higher regard than the prostitute. In some ways (the author is now speaking from his clinical experience, rather than drawing upon Kirkendall), the prostitute may be more highly regarded by middle-class boys than the casual pick-up. The prostitute is often thought by the middle-class people to be the victim of circumstance (which, of course, she often is), driven by adversity into selling her body and thus more to be pitied than despised. Middle-class people often show an almost morbid interest in the case histories of prostitutes; and women of that calling often complain about their more sophisticated clientele probing into their backgrounds. The casual pick-up, on the other hand, is seen as cheap. The average boy will use her if she is available, and leave her with some distaste and contempt for her. If his contacts have been in a homoerotic setting, the middle-class boy is likely to have added to his distaste and contempt considerable anxiety of whose source he is typically not aware. Later, he is likely to inform his peers of how she can be found, so that the peers may avail themselves of the same opportunity he has had.

The third stage of premarital intercourse is that which is held with casual acquaintances, or the one-night stand. Such girls may be held in higher esteem than prostitutes or casual pick-ups, but they are no safer from gossip. Many a girl, departing from her usual standards of conduct while intoxicated or under specially provocative circumstances, learns within the week that she has been fitted into a new category in her high school or college crowd, her companion having talked to his male friends and the girls in the crowd having picked up the information.

The fourth type of premarital intercourse is held with dating partners for whom no affection is held, although affection sometimes develops if the relationship persists. Such girls are known not as the "easy lay" of the second and third categories above but as "available." Boys are quite willing to spend money and time on a reasonably attractive girl with whom it is not a disgrace to be seen *if* the odds are good that the relationship will move to full sexuality. Boys are less likely to gossip about such girls than those in the first three categories, although often, after the relationship has ended, the male partner tells his best friends so that they can take up where he left off. Such relationships are not common among younger adolescents, but are frequent among moderately sophisticated unmarried or divorced persons in their 20s and older. They are more common among educated middle-class than among lower-class people. The male is not likely to keep his relationship with such girls secret from his friends, but, on the other hand, he seems less likely to use it purely to enhance his status as a virile male than is the case with his more casual relations. He "admits frankly" but does not brag.

Kirkendall's fifth stage is intercourse with dating partners for whom there was much affection. These relations are mutually rewarding, the former partners are spoken of with respect and affection; gossip about the girls had not occurred while the relation was in effect nor usually after it ended. Among close friends who also double dated, it was taken for granted that the relationship between the pairs was sexual, but this was as often implicit as explicit. Marriage had often, perhaps usually, been a probable goal for the couple until they broke up. Sometimes, when the relation has broken in such a way as to anger the boy or young man, he will discuss it in order to take revenge on the girl; but his talking is of quite a different type than that which characterizes the first through fourth stages (this conclusion is the author's, not Kirkendall's).

The sixth stage is intercourse with fiancées. It differs little from the fifth category above, except that it had most frequently resulted in marriage and, in most cases, the marriages still existed at the time Kirkendall gathered his data. Boys and young men will seldom talk about such relations, even though they may have broken up short of marriage, unless the break-up has been particularly damaging to the male's ego and the motive for getting even or hurting back is very strong.

In looking at Kirkendall's data for his 200 young men and at his own collection of adolescent autobiographies, it seems to the author that some men function within several of Kirkendall's categories simultaneously. Others have progressed from level one and/or two through to a stable adjustment within level six (fiancées and marriage). Still others are fixated at various places within the range from levels one or two through level four—at the psychobiological or perhaps almost purely biological level—and never achieve the psychoaffectional relationship characteristic of categories five and six. Other, and particularly middle-class, youth never indulge in premarital intercourse at all or, if they do, only at levels five and six.

For United States society, the only fully approved adjustment for young people is marriage. But if, as many females and apparently most males do, youth is to indulge in premarital intercourse, it seems consensual that it should be psychoaffectional in nature (Kirkendall's levels five and six). It seems likely that more middle-class than lower-class males are category five and six types, although the exceptions among the middle class are many.

GENERAL DISCUSSION

In terms of the biology and often the psychology of sex, the male is a hit-and-run participant. The problem of socializing him—moving him toward a responsible and psychoaffectional role in copulation and reproduction—is definitely real, even at this point in the twentieth century. The "rogue male" is as frequent today as he has ever been, although his psychological immaturity and incompleteness are now better understood.

In many cultures and in some United States cocultures,[5] the biological irresponsibility of the male has been semi- or fully institutionalized, such as in the case of the Latin *machismo* or the "now and then" role many lower-class Afro-American males play in family life (for example, Glazer and Moynihan, 1963). Such men's precarious and often irresponsible seeming role in the family can not be fully explained. Since this group, although perhaps not greatly different from other poor men, has been much studied and discussed, it seems well to talk specifically of them at this time. A number of factors probably play a part in their family adjustment, of which the important role of poverty as it prohibits compensating satisfactions for family responsibilities has been mentioned.

Inferior status is also afforded by contemporary society to the lower-class Black man, both in the United States and the Indies. The blacker he is, the less worthwhile he is, the less likely he is to have been allowed a stable family upbringing, and thus the less competent he is to compete for power and money in an industrial society. (For example, Errol Miller, in personal communication, reports a correlation approximating .70 between skin color and socioeconomic status, education, and social group prestige among Jamaican youth, where skin color is judged on a continuum: white, clear, light, brown, dark, and black.) This relation is probably stronger in the Indies than in the United States. Regardless of the degree of his pigment, the Afro-American male is still "black" and discriminated against.

The result is to deprive the lower-class Black male of the competencies necessary if one is to be a stable and effective head of the household: He is ill-equipped to earn the money to support his family; and the social-personal treatment that has been meted out to him often undermines his sense of masculinity. A man needs to be certain of his maleness to be a good husband and father.

The Black man's historical status as a slave is inextricably mixed with the deprived status society accords the Black man in the West. Any account in this book of the dynamics of this condition would be specula-

---

[5] The term coculture is used here rather than the more familiar "subculture" because the latter implies a certain patronizing, condescending attitude. By coculture is meant any definable set of people with behaviors and mores that differ from the majority of white Anglo-Saxon Protestant (WASP) culture. WASPs make up about 116 million of the 200-plus million citizens of the United States. It seems evident to the author, who himself is WASP, that WASPs have as much to learn from other groups as the other groups have to learn from them, thus, the term coculture, which implies equality in value if not in number.

tive, but the history of slavery is unquestionably important. The slave was inferior, and United States society seems determined to keep the descendants of its slaves in the same inferior status. Historically, the slave family was matriarchal, headed by the woman. Throughout the Indies and in many places in the United States, the Afro-American male served two and only two functions: laborer and stud. It is considered likely by many that, intermixed with the slave stud role, there was the tribal heritage in which the male had many wives. His role was defined as warrior and hunter and, if he performed these functions well, his status was secure. But he "worked" only episodically to execute these functions. The Western Hemisphere denied him his status but, because procreation was necessary, preserved his mating function. It is unlikely (see Whitten and Szwed, 1968) that this "Africanism" has persisted in the continental United States, but it may have, as in such islands as Haiti and Jamaica (where runaway slaves in the mountainous interior kept much of African custom alive), and in parts of northern South America. However, Whitten and Szwed, rather than attributing lower-class Black social organization to Africanism, consider it as a logical adaptation to exclusion from access to capital resources and resultant economic marginality. This is the sociological as opposed to the psychological theory of "the culture of poverty."

The Afro-American male is given much credit for sexual prowess. Speculatively, this relates to his slave culture function as a stud and to his historic and often contemporary relegation to "less than human" status. If less than human, then he was animal, and the animal male makes a redoubtable stallion or bull or ram. Possibly for such reasons, lynchings were often preceded, accompanied, or followed by castration. It is not at all unlikely that the Black man's superior sexual prowess is as much a myth as is the "constitutional intellectual inferiority" often attributed to him (see Tulkin, 1968, for example, for data concerning, and a sophisticated analysis of, the latter myth).

The really poor man, Black or white, meets little encouragement by contemporary society for his efforts to head and support his typically large and growing family. One side effect of conventional Aid to Family and Dependent Children (AFDC) is to drive the able-bodied poor man out of his house. If he is there but not working, welfare is cut off. It is not often he has the skills either to obtain or to keep a job that includes any factor of interest or dignity, or consists of other than relentless, sweaty toil. In an increasingly mechanized industrial society, even such honest (but grim) jobs are increasingly scarce. Unemployment among Black male youth often runs to 50 percent or higher.

It is for reasons like these, and the speculations advanced in the earlier section on "Special Problems of Lower-Class Youth," that it is more difficult to socialize lower-class males sexually than middle-class males. It has been seen that the cycle is endless: Sons growing up have as their models fathers who themselves have socialized poorly as a group. Nor does poverty decrease among the acutely disadvantaged.

The drives of adolescence are not going to go away. It has been seen that they can neither be denied, suppressed, nor repressed. Lower-class society, since it offers less possibility for rewarding, long-time psychoaffectional relationships, must provide for immediate gratifications or something will explode. It may well be that the availability of immediate gratifications is self-defeating and thus adds to the vicious circle in which poor people are caught. This is to say that it may detract from psychoaffectional relationships.

Promiscuity seems to be a sign of more serious maladjustment among girls than boys; but even among boys, it seems to accompany personality incompleteness and impoverishment (for example, Bandura and Walters, 1959). Many young and old Don Juans seem to be insecure in their masculine self concept, and seek to bolster this psychological portion of themselves by copious copulation, as though to prove that they are ultramale in character. In clinical practice it is axiomatic that Don Juanism is rare at any age among well-adjusted males. Such youth and men seek out their sex in more intimate relations and as one aspect of their total psychoaffectional relation with their partners. Promiscuous women, with suspicious frequency, present a picture of "punishing their own mothers," and frequently report that they do not even receive sexual gratification from their sexual behavior. However, today there are women and men who are simply testing out their bodies sexually preparatory to entering love relations.

As has been mentioned, relatively few male homosexuals achieve psychologically intimate relations with their partners, and both male and female homosexuals are likely to drift randomly and exploitively from one basically physical relationship to another. However, there are frequent "good marriages" among homosexuals of both sexes, probably more among females.

Ausubel (1954, pp. 29–30), drawing on the writing of Rank, makes an interesting and plausible point about adolescent promiscuity: If indeed, as has been seen to be likely, adolescents are striving for independence, then promiscuity may serve a useful (although unconscious) purpose for a youth in that it isolates him from any genuine, intimate sort of emotional attachment that would require him to subordinate himself to another person. Asceticism, the other side of the coin from promiscuity, serves the same purpose. Since it appears likely that boys have more drive toward independence and autonomy than girls, it can be predicted (and seems to be the case) that there will be more boys than girls who are either promiscuous or ascetic.

Most junior and senior high schools include some promiscuous girls whose well-publicized behavior is extremely disturbing emotionally to a whole class or school. They find multiple male partners easily and "pulling a train"—semipublic intercourse with two or three or more boys—is not uncommon. The attendant voyeurism sometimes leads to photography. The lurid descriptions including pictures can and often do send a whole school into near hysteria, since the boys are sexually hypersensitive and alert, and the "good girls" are equally alert, but self-conscious and threatened.

The only corrective for such not-infrequent situations has been implied earlier: full and frank discussion, open to both sexes, of the place of sexual behavior in psychosocial relations. School personnel are typically ill-prepared for and frightened of such group counseling and instruction. Many communities would accept it reluctantly if at all. However, this is a moot question: Surveys indicate that two-thirds or more of the parents in average United States communities want the schools to take on the task of sex education. Whether these communities will permit education of the necessary honesty and practicality is another question.

Impulsivity, loss of control, and incomplete and inaccurate information lead to many illegitimate pregnancies. However, an amazing number of youngsters as well as those not so young engage in sex relations with appalling casualness and lack of information and as though they have no idea that they are playing with dangerous "fun." A very frequent male attitude reported often among middle-class male youth by Kirkendall (1961), and equally often encountered by the author among adolescents of all social classes, is: "She is letting me do it. Let her take care of the consequences." This casualness is understandable in terms of the theoretical context of drive: When drive is high enough, the sole object of the organism is to gratify the drive directly and immediately. If this is accurate, then the safeguards become irrelevant for both the boy and the girl in the relationship *at that moment.*

The young male who becomes an unwed father has received little attention. The difficult and often tragic case of the unwed mother has been more fully documented. Vincent (1960) is one of the few to look carefully at the case of the unwed father. He located a population of 201 unwed white mothers from Alameda County, California. He excluded from his sample those who were divorced, separated, or married to a man other than the unmarried father; those who did not report the unmarried father's identity; those who had had previous babies out of wedlock; those whose pregnancies were due to rape or incest; and those who were pregnant by other than white fathers.

One-sixth of the fathers were 18 years of age or younger; and almost another one-fourth were 19 to 22 years of age. Nearly two-thirds of them had high school or less education. The biggest percentage (21 percent) were students; 14 percent were semi- or unskilled laborers, but almost as many came from professional and technical occupations. The relationship between the girls' educational levels and the educational levels of the fathers of their babies was very high: Of the fathers who were college graduates, 70 percent had fathered their babies by young women who were also college graduates; of the fathers who had not themselves completed high school, almost 80 percent fathered their babies with girls who also had less than high school education. Twenty-three fathers were included in the former, fifty-eight in the latter, group.

Age differences between the unwed fathers and mothers also approximated those of United States marriages. For the 94 percent of the fathers for whom age data were available, fewer than one-fifth were seven or more years older than the mothers, somewhat more than one-fifth were four to six years older than the mothers, and considerably more than half (approximately 57 percent) were within three years of the same age.

Vincent believes that the term sexual exploiter is actually an ex post facto term—"a label that is affixed *after* the female has become pregnant" (p. 44). The term, Vincent believes, is less a censuring of males' *sexual misbehavior* (society expects females to avoid illicit sexual unions) than it is a blame for his *role misbehavior*: He is not man enough to assume the appropriate and traditional role of protecting his woman.

Vincent also points out explicitly what is implicit in Kirkendall's (1961) interview data: male-female exploitation in courting is a two-way street. The female uses sex or, in a larger sense, sexual enticement as her means to obtain dates, companionship, recreational expense, upward social mobility, and perhaps marriage. The male is willing to provide each of these things, including often quite false expressions of love "*as a means to sex*" (Vincent, 1960, p. 45).

Clinical data suggest that the unwed father suffers considerably from knowing his status, although he suffers more privately than the unwed mother. The grief and guilt of the latter, often lifelong, over her baby lost to her by adoption, or the defensive posture society forces her to take if she keeps her baby, have been well documented. Less well known is the similar guilt, regret, and often grief of the unwed father who will never know his child, and who will never have a hand in the rearing of his son or daughter. He, too, often sees himself as society sees him: as not man enough to stand up to his own responsibilities as husband and father.

There are few good data about the personal meaning of premarital intercourse to young people. It is probable that when there is love between them and they plan marriage, neither suffers particularly from guilt and that very often both are quite willing to move along into marriage "if something happens." The effect of the pill on premarital relations has not been well documented, but it seems likely that the pill would reduce the tension level for such couples. Many couples report that their physical intimacy simply extends and deepens their psychological intimacy.

The psychological problems seem to lie within more casual relations. United States culture is such that it is probable that most girls who take part in casual sex incorporate into their own self concepts society's evaluation of them: They are cheap and no good. Such girls can hardly avoid knowing that the protestations of love they receive in return for or as the condition of sexual intercourse are counterfeit, and that their search for true psychological intimacy—being loved, valued, and understood—has taken a wrong turn. They must almost always be aware that their conduct is well publicized, and that among their peer group, boys value them as receptacles rather than human beings, while "good" girls typically reject them.

Nor can the often completely cynical lying (the protestations of love) that the casually sexing male makes sit well with his conscience: Both his sexual act and his deceit run counter to that portion of the Protestant ethic he may have incorporated into his conscience. However, the rewards to the male are great: physical pleasure, dominance in a heterosexual situation, enhancement of his status in his peer group.[6]

[6] A well-educated and sophisticated young woman who has read this chapter in manuscript form comments that "I find some of your ideas about girls and women '*derrière garde*.'

SUMMARY

Changes in organic function are most interesting to the developmental psychologist when they accompany or result in changes in the personal-social organization of the individual. Changes in genital function at puberty necessitate major changes in the adolescent's relation to himself and society, and in society's regard for and accommodation to him.

Genital function must be channeled along some socially prescribed pathway. Most common in United States culture are wife-motherhood for girls and husband-fatherhood for boys. Sexual careers such as religious or lay single person or homosexual are the most frequent alternatives in United States society. Sex behavior must be disciplined so it does not disrupt social organization; yet it must be free enough that racial propagation is ensured. Sanctions against sexual deviance are strong, perhaps less rigid for females than males.

Genital function meets social approval or disapproval along four dimensions: (1) type of activity and erogenous zone implicated; (2) degree to which it is passive or initiatory; (3) type of sex object desired (in United States culture, desire for the opposite sex only is permitted); and (4) appropriateness of the sex role adopted. Clearly defined stereotypes for males are dictated by society; more latitude, but still with rather clear boundaries, exists for females.

Postpubescent genital function is bound to produce perplexity and uneasiness in the adolescent. The drive is urgent, new, and comes on suddenly. Adjustment must be made to cultural pressures for channeling genital behavior; and this adjustment must move in the direction of becoming steadily more specific and clearly differentiated.

One clear finding emerges about sexual behavior: Despite confusion in data concerning other aspects, there is no question but that youth want more and more accurate information and education than they now obtain from their parents or other formal aspects of the society.

The sexual urge is strong for both boys and girls. Middle-class youth's problems seem more likely to involve accommodating their sex drive to their consciences, while lower-class youth must struggle more to realize ultimate psychoaffectional relations between the sexes. Actual intrapersonal conflict about sexuality is probably greater for the former as a group, while psychoaffectional frustration is likely to be greater for lower-class youth.

Since female sexuality both seems to depend on males and is also

---

However, female psychology is in need of much study and clarification." She goes on to say that copious and discriminating copulation among women may be adaptive and a good way for an individual to find out who will be a good sexual-marital partner. Such girls may also be out to prove themselves "ultrafemales," not frigid or hung up about sex, capable of obtaining orgasm. They may represent a new wave of anti-Victorianism that arose from the acceptance of Freud's ideas with the concomitant rise of such semimyths as the simultaneous orgasm and the vaginal orgasm as far superior to the "infantile" clitoral orgasm.

Among girls over 18, this young woman reader believes one not uncommonly finds girls who wish to find out what they are capable of sexually and biologically before they settle down to the commitment involved in the love relationship. Such girls are those to whom no male needs to lie cynically: They are after the same thing the male is and there is no conflict.

more socially oriented (fits more easily into an acceptable social structure than male sexuality), more consideration has been given to problems of socializing males than females. Factors in male sexuality have been portrayed by factor analysis of male responses to psychological tests. Nine factors emerged: (1) intensity of sex drive and interest; (2) sexual frustration and maladjustment; (3) generalized anxiety and neurotic conflict associated with sex; (4) sexual fixations and cathexes; (5) repression of sexuality (a minute factor for males, as might have been predicted); (6) loss of sex controls; (7) homosexuality; (8) sex role confidence; and (9) promiscuity and sociopathy. A normal (but apparently very frank and honest) college group scored highest on factors 1 and 8 and lowest on factor 5.

Goals of adolescent sexual socialization are: imparting of full, factual information about the area; promoting frank interpersonal communication about sex and its psychosocial aspects; incorporating sexual behavior harmoniously within a framework of ethics, values, and total family living; and stressing the psychoaffectional aspects of sex as a natural way of life without neglecting the psychobiological.

Premarital intercourse for males seems to range from almost purely biological (intercourse with prostitutes and casual pick-ups), where there is little personal regard for the worth of the sexual partner as a human being, through to mature, confidential, psychoaffectional relations with girls to whom marriage is planned.

Lower-class males, and particularly Afro-American males, encounter striking problems in sexual socialization: They are denied training in economic and personal-social competencies that permit them securely to head a household and support their wives and children; economic marginality plus discrimination combine so that the satisfactions of family life do not compensate for its responsibilities and often relegate the poor male's family role to that of hit-and-run, biological procreator; and current welfare laws seem almost to discourage the man without a job from remaining legally and stably in his home with his wife and children. All of this operates to produce a disproportionate share of matrifocal and matriarchal homes that are incomplete and somewhat distorting for fathers, mothers, and children of both sexes. It is commonly thought that male children suffer most in the sense that they have not been trained to live according to middle-class standards.

Promiscuity seems to be associated with other characteristics of inadequate social adjustment for both boys and girls, but in our society it seems to be a more serious symptom for girls than for boys. Substantial evidence exists indicating that pregnancies outside marriage are not largely the function of exploitive males, but occur as a result of intercourse between partners remarkably similar in educational background and age. Both boys and girls in such situations suffer, although the case has been less documented for boys. Being an unwed father means that a boy has failed in the man's role of protecting women and children; being an unwed mother is, most often, a matter of considerable shame and disgrace.

5

Physical Factors and Personality

INTRODUCTION

During adolescence the body is probably more important to a boy or a girl than it has been before, or may ever be again during the course of development, except perhaps at the time when the body begins to fail. The adolescent's body is beginning to be experienced in several ways: the new sex drive is focused in his body; he must accommodate himself to a rapidly changing body; and society paces its changed perceptions and expectancies for him according to his body.

To a considerable degree, a youngster *is* his body and his body is *he*. Speaking of adolescents with deviant growth patterns, Ausubel (1954, p. 161) says that "any condition which cuts across vital urges or endangers their fulfillment becomes a hazard for an individual and a potential source of basic frustration." Conversely, any aspect about his development that reduces frustration and anxiety is likely to make adolescence easier. As stated earlier, a youth with a well formed, strong, graceful body, attractive face, and clear skin experiences relatively few frustrations when compared with his awkward, ill-built, or homely age mate.

PHYSICAL MATURITY AND PERSONALITY

Between the ages of 11 and 13, the average girl is taller than the average boy. Even at 14 and 15, many girls in a given class are as much as a head taller than many boys. The social problems posed by such differential growth rates are obvious, especially since, at these ages, social events such as school dances require a pairing-off of boys and girls. The average and presumably superior male is hopelessly outclassed by the average girl, except for the few early maturing boys in seventh and eighth grades, and a somewhat greater proportion in ninth grade. Many girls are interested in dating and dancing, but their male classmates seem uninterested in things heterosexual.

Junior high and early high school girls are thus reduced to competing vigorously for the few boys who are physically their equals, or to going out with boys who are much older and often much more sophisticated. When social pairings within the grade are forced, as they often are at school functions, most boys face the choice of withdrawal or conspicuous physical disadvantage.

Maturational differences between the sexes have brought about the proposal that girls should start school earlier than boys. There is some merit to the suggestion, but it is not practical since, except for differences in time of puberty and growth spurt, boys as a group differ little from girls in intellectual, social, or personal maturity. However, boys are more variable in many characteristics.

In many schools, particularly urban schools, most eleventh and twelfth grade girls refuse to date high school youth. Out-of-school or college boys possess some combination of greater sophistication and more free time and money, are more likely to own and/or be legally allowed to drive cars, and hold more prestige as dates. The junior and senior boys must, perforce, turn to ninth and tenth grade girls who are available and delighted to have the opportunity to date older boys, but who are often not sufficiently experienced and psychologically mature to cope with the older boys. Exploitation of the "naïve little freshman" is not at all infrequent. Pressure to date older boys is greater for very early than for later maturing girls. Early maturing boys may, if presentable in appearance, pretty much have their pick of their classmates, and often can compete to advantage for girls in classes above them. The author's file of adolescent autobiographies includes several where extremely early maturing boys found many advantages in dating older girls.

A modest amount of research has centered on this important developmental characteristic. Most of it comes from longitudinal growth studies conducted at the University of California at Berkeley (the California Growth Studies). A typical design for this research is to choose a criterion group, all of the same age but composed of extremely early and extremely late maturers and compare them according to available criteria of social-emotional-intellectual adjustment. These studies tell little about average children or those who are only a little ahead of or behind their age group, but they throw light on extreme deviates from the developmental norm.

It has been pointed out earlier that extreme deviates are likely to have special group characteristics that may illumine more usual patterns of development. It is thus of interest to look at such selected groups of girls and boys, and it is of particular interest here to study the differences associated with physical maturity. It must be cautioned that the number of cases in these particular California Growth Studies is small, that the middle class is overrepresented (because of differential lower-class drop-outs that have been discussed), and that the outcomes may well have been influenced by prolonged interaction of investigators and research subjects. It may be that there are special characteristics of adolescents who consent to remain for many years as subjects in a research study. It is not known, however, what these characteristics (if any) are. It has been conjectured that adolescent boys with strong autonomy and independence drives are particularly likely to drop out of such studies.

Deviant Time of Physical Maturity and Male Development

Research workers associated with the University of California (Ames, 1957; M. C. Jones, 1957 and 1965; M. C. Jones and Bayley, 1950; and Mussen and M. C. Jones, 1957) have investigated the correlates of early and late physical maturing for boys. H. E. Jones (1949) and M. C. Jones and Mussen (1958) have reported results for early and late maturing girls.

The Jones and Bayley study employs skeletal age, judged from X-rays of the long bones of the hand and knee, as its criterion of physical maturity. This measure is perhaps the best of all available measures, and correlates well with the reproductive indexes of physical maturity used heretofore in this book. Today, there is more reluctance to use X ray than in the thirties when the California Growth Study subjects were children and adolescents. Thus, the measure is less often used now. While exact and satisfactory from a scientific point of view, it is expensive and requires X-ray technicians to act as judges. Therefore, most workers in this field use the cruder indexes that have been discussed.

From a group of ninety boys who were studied for an average of about four and one-half years, the sixteen most consistently accelerated and the sixteen most consistently retarded were studied intensively by means of observations and rating made by both adult research workers and the boys' buddies.

Figure 5.1 includes illustrations of a very early and a very late maturing boy. The growth trends that were described in Chapter 3 can be reviewed by glancing at these pictures. Hip-shoulder comparison, differential pubic hair and genital maturity, and relative muscularity are particularly striking. It is difficult to hold in mind, even in photographs, that these boys are actually of the same chronological age. In real life, the difficulty is even greater.

At the age of 14, ratings of physical maturity made from nude photographs of the two boys showed almost no overlap between them. The illustrations of the pairs of boys at ages 13½, 14½, and 15½ (the third, fourth, and fifth from the left pairing in Figure 5.1) clearly demonstrates this lack of overlap. The physically accelerated boy in each case was taller, heavier, showed more advanced public hair, and had larger genitals.

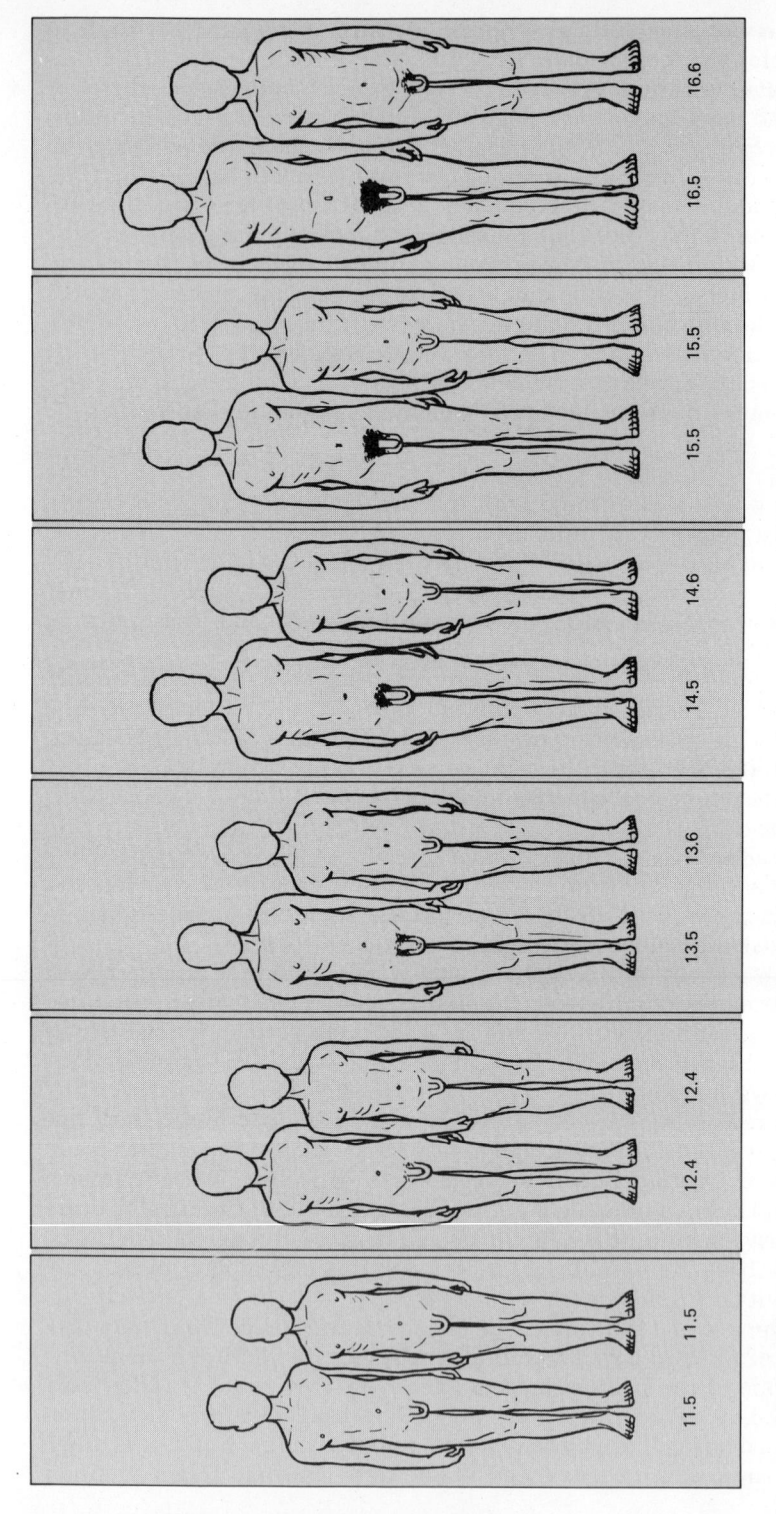

Figure 5.1 *Contrasts between an early and a late maturing boy, ages 11½ to 16⅗ years.* (Drawing based on photograph in F. H. Shuttleworth *The adolescent period: A pictorial atlas. Monograph of the Society for Research in Child Development*, 1951, **14**, Serial No. 50, 1949, p. 24.)

130 PHYSICAL FACTORS AND PERSONALITY

This difference was already somewhat apparent at age 12⅖ years, and was still clear at the age of 16½.

From 13 to 15 years of age, the physically retarded boys were relatively long legged, were of slender build, and were weak during the period when they lagged most markedly behind in size. This is not entirely the case for the boys in Figure 5.1, who are thus not entirely typical. The physically retarded boys were rated by adults as less physically attractive, less masculine, less well groomed, and more animated and eager.[1] They sought attention more, were more affected and less matter of fact, and were tenser. However, they equaled the more accelerated boys in ratings of popularity, leadership, prestige, poise, assurance, cheerfulness, and social effect on the group. They were, understandably, considered to be less mature in a heterosexual relationship.

Ratings by their buddies generally showed fewer large differences between the early and late maturers, and were less complimentary to the late maturers even than the adult raters had been: The retarded boys were considered to be more restless, talkative, and bossy. Their buddies thought them more attention seeking, and less inclined to be self-assured in class. They also believed they were less popular (this means they were *actually* less popular, since popularity is based on peer judgment), and less likely to be leaders. Again, this means they were actually less frequently leaders. They were also rated as less likely to have older friends, more likely to lack a sense of humor about themselves, and less attractive in appearance.

To the degree, then, that youngsters perceive and incorporate the reactions of their society into their own self-images and behaviors, early maturers possess significantly more advantages than do late maturers. These advantages are all in areas of great personal and social importance.

The Mussen and Jones (1957) study includes data from the Thematic Apperception Test (TAT) for seventeen late and sixteen early maturers. As most readers know, the TAT requires the test-taker to tell a story in response to a picture. Scoring the story involves the assumption that the "hero" or central figure is really the person telling the story. From his behavior, the characteristics and life style of the test-taker are inferred. The test has been proved to be a useful research tool and is often useful in the hands of expert clinicians in the understanding of individuals.

Accepting the TAT assumptions (this must be done *most* cautiously), more of the late than the early maturers saw the hero (themselves, inferentially) as being an imbecile, a weakling, or a fanatic. More of them also saw him as being scorned or disapproved of by parents or authorities. This may be a sign that the rather denigrating regard of adult raters and peers (the Jones and Bayley, 1950, study) had been incorporated into the self concept.

Late maturers' heroes also more often left home and/or defied their parents. The interpretation is that they may blame their parents for their condition, or possibly that they feel unappreciated at home because of

---

[1] By "eager," the author thinks perhaps the adults meant "childish."

inferior physical status. They were also more likely to fall in love or have a romance. This can tentatively be interpreted as a yearning for the heterosexual status denied to them by their later maturity. It could also relate back to the discussion of "Special Problems of Middle-Class Youth" in Chapter 4, where it was hypothesized that such boys delay gratification of sexual desires and thus build up and rehearse by means of fantasy an eventual sexual life that will adjust them to a heterosocial world. Such a tendency could be particularly likely to characterize very late maturing middle-class youngsters who are denied direct heterosexual outlet both by upbringing and physical maturity. Direct outlet is presumably easier for earlier maturing boys (as we have seen, they avail themselves more of such outlets than late maturing boys), and thus it may be that they build up less heterosexual fantasy. As will be seen, later studies of these boys suggest that the late maturers, on the whole, manage marriage better than the early maturers. Thus one can conjecture that they are more heterosocial, perhaps because they were older at puberty and had thus been able to consolidate interpersonal relations with girls before the insistent sex drive took over. Peskin's (1967) analyses of the California data suggest that such a hypothesis is plausible, although he does advance it specifically.

Late maturers saw their heroes as being helped, encouraged, or given something by persons other than parents more often than early maturers. This extends the theme of parental rejection by the early maturers, but also suggests that they want help and need praise from others. It may be that their sense of autonomy and independence is weaker than for the early maturing boys. This is borne out by one other theme that approached significance in distinguishing between the two groups: Late maturers more often described the hero of a story as feeling helpless and seeking aid or sympathy.

These patterns cluster sensibly together, fit well with the conceptual framework for adolescence that was developed in Chapter 1, and allow tentative inferences to be made that possess some practical guidance value. Late maturers are more likely than early maturers to hold negative or derogatory self concepts. After all, a prime value for males is to be potent, strong, and big. Late maturers are none of these, and the frustrations at the time must be great. The late maturers seem to blame their parents for their status, although probably not consciously. They seem to feel relatively weak, alone, and helpless and (perhaps unconsciously) are seeking assistance and affiliation. Being male, it is probable that they must deny this vigorously, perhaps even to themselves. If this is true, it may help to account for the rebellious, mischievous, adult-rejectant clown behavior so often seen clinically among very late maturing boys. Late maturers seem to fantasy more about idealized romance. In middle-class life, this may be adaptive in the long run, although it is a quite unsatisfactory adjustment at any given moment.

The physically advanced group more frequently told stories in which the hero was aggressive in a physical and asocial fashion. This may reflect their perception of society's regard for them, as discussed in Chapter 1 (the big, newly potent male is a threat to his culture; it punishes him), and these boys may be fighting back, at least in fantasy.

Fighting back for them is an act that would not characterize the later maturing boys, as the early maturers *are* big, muscular, and strong as a group. They are also men, with men's needs, and society denies them socially acceptable direct outlet for their masculine needs. This immediate frustration of urgent biological and social needs is almost bound to result in frustration and aggression, as predicted from theoretical assumptions advanced in Chapter 1. Since early maturers are in the vanguard of their age group, the frustrations and aggressions society seems to direct toward all adolescent males will be even more sharply (almost defensively) focused on them. Perhaps because of fear of their impulses, however, early maturers seem almost to overcontrol their emotions, and to be almost overconforming (Peskin, 1967).

Early maturing boys, more than late maturers, were likely to say that they had no thoughts or feelings about the TAT pictures. Here, perhaps, is an indication of self-confidence, an assurance that they can get away with aggressive behavior if they feel that way. It also suggests a factual, unimaginative, nonfantasy approach to life—an approach which is reflected in the earlier ratings of the early maturing boys reported by Jones and Bayley (1950). These youngsters, even though relatively frustrated and perhaps angry, know from experience that they can handle their objective environment through direct action: Thus they need less to think and fantasize about it. Such an approach has both advantages and disadvantages (see the discussion of Ted's life later in this chapter. M. C. Jones' mature adult follow-up of these boys also suggests that they may have neglected some of their inner resources of thoughtfulness, imagination, and self-insight. Peskin's analysis supports this conclusion).

There were no differences between the two groups of boys in the number who told stories in which the hero is prevented by his parents from doing something he wants to do, or establishes good relations with his parents, or attempts to gain a high goal or do something creditable, or seeks fame and/or high status and prestige. Thus, one can infer tentatively that, although the late maturers bear somewhat more hostility toward their parents, they have as much positive parental feeling as the early maturers. Since the parents are so close and dependable, they may be the only ones the boys dare to feel aggressive toward. The two groups seem to subscribe equally to the cultural stereotype of the successful, occupationally bold man. Late maturers may have less hope, secretly, of becoming such men.

Mussen and Bouterline-Young (1964) present evidence that suggests that the dramatic effects of early maturity shown among the California Growth Study boys is related to the nature of United States culture. Like early maturing American boys, early maturing Italian boys feel warm and affectionate toward their parents. But unlike the American boys, the Italian boys do not have very positive self concepts. This may be due to a more authoritarian culture in the Italian family: Early maturity does not, as in the United States, automatically bring with it opportunities for leadership and emancipation. In fact, it may be perceived by fathers as threatening so that they become more restrictive with precociously mature boys.

Italian-American early maturers resemble the California boys in self-confidence, but they view their parents as unduly restrictive, controlling, and lacking in nurturance. It may be that, in the school and community, their mature bodies give them status. This is denied them in their traditional homes, and they fight back, at least in fantasy.

The Mussen and Bouterline-Young study lends perspective in interpreting the more elaborate California Growth Studies.

What are these early maturing California boys like at maturity? Ames (1957) reported on a total group of forty early and late maturers. Ames' findings are dramatic, and argue for physical factors overriding purely psychological-social behaviors in the sense that they predict later adjustment better.

The boys had become men who averaged 33 years of age at the time Ames studied them. The index of skeletal age predicted age 33 social and vocational behavior better than *any* social measure obtained for the boys during their earlier life spans from about 11 to about 18 years of age. Ames' data were obtained from interviews. Often the interview is the only possible technique for "real life" research but, as has been suggested in Chapter 2, it often leads to dubious conclusions.

The correlation between the men's adolescent skeletal maturity (this corresponds closely, it will be remembered, to other, more obvious, but cruder indexes of physical maturity) and 33-year-old occupational status was a statistically *and* practically significant .47: The more mature men were significantly more successful. As far as is known, there were no intellectual or social class differences between the early and late maturing groups that might account for this differential success pattern.

Early maturers were likely to go out on the town to have a good time, in that they reported much more informal social participation. The correlation between skeletal index and amount of informal social activity was .48. Formal social participation (lodges, clubs, church affairs, and the like) correlated .44 with the X-ray index. Amount of business-related social life correlated .35.

Fifteen of these forty young men held positions in which they supervised or directed the work of subordinates. Of this group, only three were late maturers. Eight of the men held some type of office in a club, lodge, or civic group, and of these, none was a late maturer.

The best single prediction of adult social behavior resulting from social behavior data gathered when these men were boys was obtained from a measure of clubhouse popularity, based on watching the boys in a number of social situations when they were interacting with both boys and girls. This measure correlated .39 with adult informal social participation measures and adult status and social behavior. It reached statistical significance only at the .05 level.

The single blot on these successes reported by Ames was a tendency, not strong, for the earlier maturers to report less happiness in their marriages. One wonders if perhaps the unimaginativeness and matter of factness reported as characterizing these boys-men may be related to this. It may be that they were simply too busy courting success to spend enough time on their marriages. Peskin's (1967) conclusions of more rigidity, less intellectual curiosity, more need for external control, and more "primitive aggression," which were compensated for by overconformity among the early maturers, could lead to the conclusion that marriages would be less happy, particularly if early maturers are deficient in ability to make intimate affectional social alliances.

It is worth relating this tenuous result to a review of the Kinsey (Kinsey, Pomeroy, and Martin, 1948) data about the sex behavior of early as compared with late maturers. Kinsey defined physical maturity as the time of first ejaculation.[2] Kinsey estimated the time of first ejaculation from his subjects' interviews, which often were held many years after the actual event.

Kinsey's early maturers are described as "the more alert, energetic, vivacious, spontaneous, physically active, socially extrovert, and/or aggressive individuals in the population" (p. 325). In contrast, late maturers tend to be "slow, quiet, mild in manner, without force, reserved, timid, taciturn, introvert, and/or socially inept" (pp. 325-326). These descriptions mesh well with the more quantitative evidence presented by the California workers.

Kinsey, as has been reported, found that early sexual maturity is associated with almost immediate adoption of a pattern of regular consummatory sexual activity, while late maturers delay adopting such a pattern. Early maturers report consistently higher levels of sexual activity from adolescence on until their 50s, although the differences between them and late maturers become less extreme with age. However, over the years, early maturers average about one-fifth more sexual outlets, most of them in intercourse, than late maturers. Early maturers are more likely than late maturers to induce their first ejaculation, late maturers to wait for it.

The sexual needs of the human male and female do not match up particularly well, Kinsey's data (1948, 1953) indicate. The man begins to taper off by the time he is the age of Ames' subjects, while the woman is only reaching her peak sexual appetite. This tapering-off seems to be minimal for early, maximal for late, maturers. Ames' early maturers, then, on the psychobiological side of marriage, should be better husbands than his late maturers. The difference in happiness in the other direction, it seems safe to assume, is more related to psychoaffectional than to psychobiological aspects of the marriages.

However, the pitfalls of comparing Kinsey's large group data, gathered by different techniques from Ames' and Peskin's, and from different populations, are so great that one can consider any conclusions merely as suggestions for further research, not as facts. Perhaps "plausible speculation" is the best term to use for the preceding paragraph.

To return to the California Growth Study male group: M. C. Jones (1965) reports still further on them, this time when they are in their 40s. While they are still well off, their conspicuous superiority to the late maturing boys has largely disappeared. Jones' interpretation of her data, in the author's judgment, leads to a somewhat brighter picture of the superiority of the early maturing boys than the data themselves justify.

The late maturing boys seem at long last to be finding some payoff from their hard-earned lessons in being affable, lively, and self-exam-

---

[2] No clear data exist relating this event to such indexes as skeletal maturity and mature pubic hair, although it is probable that there is a close relation.

ining. Their necessary scrupulous attention to the nuances of interpersonal relations (because, at adolescence, their immature bodies made social acceptance so difficult a problem to solve) probably contributes to the fact that they are finally catching up. There are some indications that for the group as a whole and perhaps particularly for the early maturers, the bodies that have served so well are beginning to betray them. Peskin's (1967) analysis of parapubescent data suggests that this "catching up" could have been predicted.

To summarize, the picture of greater ease and success in adjustment, at least up to middle age, is very clear for the early maturing boy. This may to some degree be a function of the "Kiwanis Club" orientation of United States society, which rewards the conforming, well-controlled energetic, outgoing, vigorous male more than his more thoughtful and withdrawn counterpart. At middle age, the advantage has begun to blur, although it is still present. Whatever the eventual outcome for these early maturing men, they have had some thirty years of clear advantage over the late maturers in reaping society's goodies.

Hopefully, further follow-ups will be done, as the obviously very cooperative group still has many years of life at the time this is written.

Caution should again be stated about the California Growth Study data and conclusions reached from them. First, group tendencies must not obscure attention to the individual. Even the highest of the correlations reported by Ames, for example, accounts for less than 25 percent of the variance of the criterion he is predicting (for example, occupational status and amount of informal social participation at average age 33). Overlap between the groups of early and late maturers is almost certainly great. Early maturing boys (as will be seen later) often fall by the wayside. As has been mentioned, Stolz and Stolz (1951) give a vivid and touching picture of one such early maturing boy. Furthermore, the California sample is small, mostly if not entirely middle and upper-middle class, white, and affected to an unknown degree by its long interaction with research workers. This interaction started at birth.

On the other hand, although one should be cautious, he would be foolish to overlook these data. They contain many plausible suggestions both for adolescent guidance and for further research in what is obviously an important area.

Douglas and Ross (1964) provide further evidence about the relations between early physical maturity and educational attainment, educational ability (roughly, intelligence), and persistence in school up to age 16½ years. The British National Survey of Health and Development is a longitudinal study of 5000 boys and girls born in the first week of March 1946. Douglas and Ross had available to them puberty ratings and tests of ability and achievement at the ages of 8, 11, and 15 years for 1695 boys and 1590 girls. Information about leaving or staying in school was available to age 16½.

At age 15 years, doctors inquired of the girls or their mothers if and when they had had their first menstrual period, and reported on presence of pigmented pubic hair and breast development. Boys' physical maturity was judged by physicians' descriptions of genitalia, presence of pubic hair, and whether or not the voice had broken. Boys were classified at age 15 into infantile, early stages, advanced, or mature sexual status. Percentages at each of these classifications were 10, 35, 30, and 25, respectively.

Average ability scores, based on a mean of 50, were 48.3 for the boys whose genitalia and pubic hair development were still infantile, 50.1 for those with early sign, 51.7 for those of advanced status, and 52.3 for those classified as mature. While not large, the differences in favor of those of more advanced physical status are significant statistically. Similar results for reading skill and school persistence were found.

Douglas and Ross do not find relations between maturity status and social class for their population, although there is a nonsignificant tendency for higher social status to accompany earlier physical maturity. However, the late date (age 15) at which indices of sexual maturity were obtained may have obscured social class differences.

Not all the data bearing on early physical maturity for boys are as clear as the California and British data. More (1953) conducted a six-year longitudinal study of sixteen boys and seventeen girls, all of whom were white.[3] Physical maturity was correlated with such variables as warmth, social participation, dominance, activity, and emotional stability. For all but the last, correlations between these factors and physical maturity ranged from .33 to .39. Because of the small number of boys involved, these correlations do not reach statistical significance.

However, More selected his subjects not because of extremes in time of physical maturation (very early or very late), but by teacher nominations for "adjusted" and "unadjusted" boys and girls. There were more girls in the former, more boys in the latter group. His method of selection is so different from that of the California and British studies that it could not be expected that his differences would be as marked.

Deviant Time of Physical Maturity and Female Development

Figure 5.2 is a companion for Figure 5.1. It shows a pair of very early and very late maturing girls from pre- until postpubescence. The characteristic physical growth patterns (hip-shoulder ratio, increasing roundness, breast and primary sex characteristics) are as striking for girls as for boys.

The data about this subject are less clear for girls than boys. Studies parallel to the early personal–social data and the TAT data for girls up to 17 years of age have been published. Follow-ups into later maturity and the middle years, to the author's knowledge, have not been published.

H. E. Jones (1949a) reports several provocative relations between early and late maturity for girls. He judged physical maturity by the same X-ray indexes of skeletal development that were used for boys. From this data it seems that early development is disadvantageous for girls, while late development is an advantage; this pattern is opposite to that consistently revealed for boys, at least up until middle age. However, the social dynamics behind these opposite results are the same.

At full maturity, early maturing girls (as a group) are stockier than their late maturing sisters. Chubby figures are not fashionable in United

[3]The author assumes they were white. More did not report race.

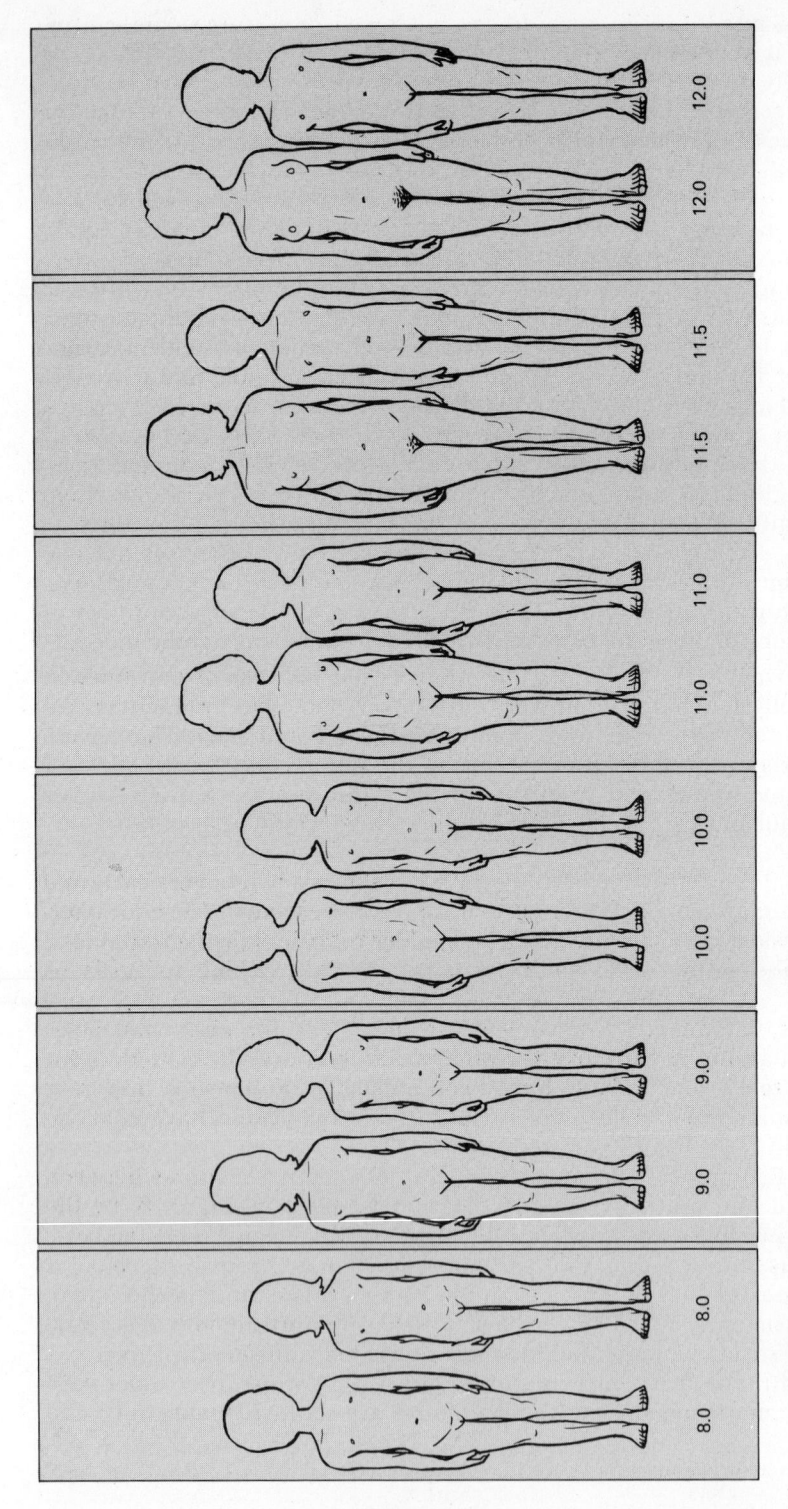

Figure 5.2 *Contrasts between an early and a late maturing girl,* (left-hand page) *ages 8 to 12 years, and* (right-hand page) *ages 12½ to 14½ years.* (Drawings based on photographs in Shuttleworth, pp. 13–14. [See page 130 for complete source].)

138   PHYSICAL FACTORS AND PERSONALITY

PHYSICAL MATURITY AND PERSONALITY

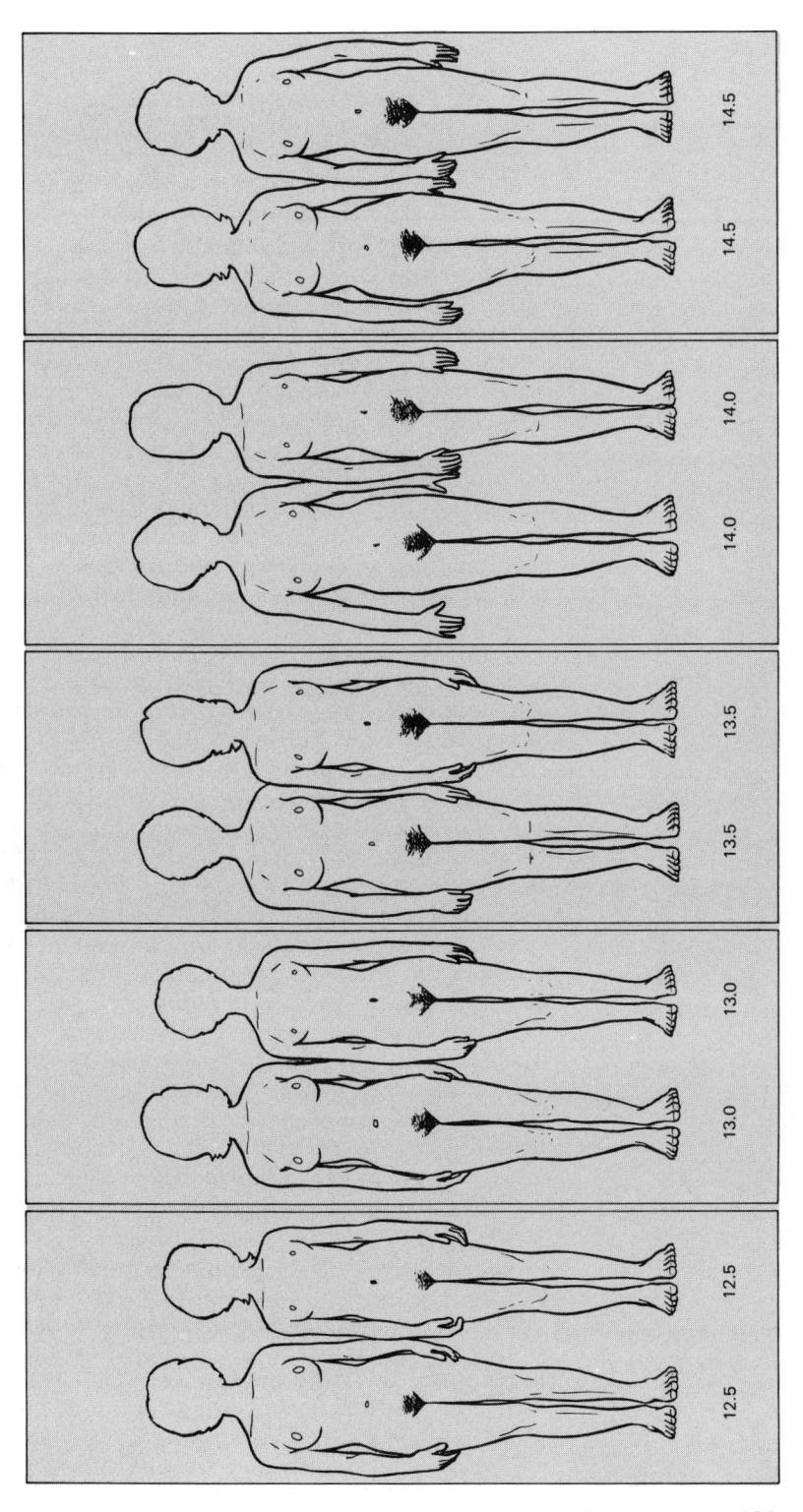

States culture, and the adolescent girl does not like this aspect of her development. The social gap between early maturing girls and all or almost all boys in her class is striking, as has been pointed out. A span of several important developmental years must go by before many boys of her age will be tall enough for her to date without feeling conspicuous and unfeminine. Also, women who are tall are likely to have attributed to them traits of masculinity (Mead, 1961, and clinical data).

Sexual maturity attained while still psychosocially immature may engender confusion, conflict, and uncertainty. This is revealed in the description of the life course of Marilee that is given later in this chapter. As with Marilee, many early maturing girls are driven beyond their depth in dating boys who are older and more sophisticated, which may result in irresistible sexual temptations and pressures, as well as other social-sexual complications.

Girls who menstruate very early often undergo rejection by their feminine peers.[4] Perhaps their exceptional early maturity is a threat to peers who are reminded of their own impending womanhood before they are ready to face the prospect emotionally. Menstruation is the target of much unfavorable folklore in our society. The author has known cases of girls, mature in the fourth and early fifth grades, who are called dirty and generally derogated by both the girls and boys in their classes. In line with this, H. E. Jones observed that early maturing girls were judged by adult observers to have higher prestige and show more leadership than late maturers. Late maturers were also rated as having greater social stimulus value.

There seems to have been less stigma attached to early maturing by the girls themselves, however.

The effects of very early maturing seem to have been transitory for this population. M. C. Jones and Mussen (1958) reported TAT data for the girls when they were 17, an age by which all (or almost all) girls have reached maturity, and found no real differences at that later time between the early and the late maturers. Only two of twenty differences between the groups were statistically significant. One (at the .05 level) could have been expected by chance. When there were differences on the TAT stories, early maturers showed more "favorable" characteristics than late maturers.

Other data concerning relations with physical maturity among girls revealed mixed patterns. The Douglas and Ross (1964) study of British youth and the More (1953) study of adjusted and unadjusted boys and girls have already been described.

Douglas and Ross find early maturing girls as much superior to late maturing girls as early maturing boys were to late maturing boys. Of Douglas and Ross' girls, 29 percent were classified as late maturing, 34 percent as average, 25 percent as early, and 12 percent as very early. Late maturers were those whose menstrual periods started at 14 years or later; average maturers started menstruating between 13 and 13 years 11 months; early maturers between 12 and 12 years 11 months; and very early maturers reached menarche before 12 years of age.

[4]This conclusion has been reached from clinical observation.

Based on an average score of 50 (a T-score, strictly speaking), late maturing girls averaged 47.8, average maturers 49.0, early maturers 50.5, and very early maturers 51.6. Data for reading achievement and school persistence paralleled ability, and for all three indexes, results for boys and girls were almost identical. Douglas and Ross, as has been said, do not believe their results can be due to early maturity being a function of social class. If it were, the results would be vitiated, because it is almost certain that the higher the social class, the higher the ability and educational achievement and the greater the likelihood of school persistence.

Poppleton (1968) reports similar results for 1064 11½ to 15½ British girls. But she found that her early maturers came from smaller families. It may be inferred tentatively that their advantages in intelligence and school achievement were due to family size more than to time of maturity and thus, perhaps, social status is the crucial factor.

More, too, finds striking advantages for early maturity among the seventeen girls he studied, with correlations ranging from .30 for activity to .51 for dominance. His method of selecting his subjects, however (for adjustedness or unadjustedness), raises questions about his results. Teachers may have nominated more early maturing children as adjusted because of the well-known halo effect (see Chapter 2).

Faust (1960), like More, finds certain advantages in prestige accruing to early maturing girls in junior high school. However, if anything, early maturing was a disadvantage to her sixth grade girls. Faust does not report the effects of social class on time of physical maturity for her sample.

Nisbet, *et al.* (1964), who studied Aberdeen, Scotland, children, find that while their early maturing girls were superior to their maturing girls at age 13, the differences had partially disappeared at 16 years of age. Their study, too, has a flaw, however, since they dropped from their sample a large number of low ability and achievement girls as a result of the British 12-plus examinations. Until recently, these examinations were rather rigidly employed to direct children on toward higher education or into vocational training. Such exclusion of subjects may have obscured the sort of results that Douglas and Ross found with British children.

Finally, Shipman (1964) reports results similar to those reported by Jones from the California Growth Studies for 17 year olds. In the Shipman study, age at menarche was unrelated to a measure of timidity or emotional maturity among adult females.

No real conclusion can be made about the effects of early puberty upon girls. Whatever the effects, it seems likely that they disappear by maturity.

It seems unlikely on the face of it that the body and its development is less important to girls than to boys. But a necessary although tentative conclusion must be made that time of physical maturity makes a long term and rather important difference to boys, but that, while it may make a brief difference to girls at about the time they become pubescent, it makes no long term difference. It is plausible to reason the same about this sex difference as it was in the preceding chapter to justify concentrating on socializing males' sex drive while neglecting the topic of girls' sexual socialization. Most girls socialize their reproductive behavior along the lines of the boys they date or the men they marry, while males remain relatively autonomous. In a similar fashion, since the boy must be his own man, his time of maturation and its associated variables may make a real difference to a boy. To a girl, if she marries, such factors recede into the larger picture of her married life. I. Rosenthal's (1963) data should also be remembered: Males reconstruct their earlier lives more accurately than females. Females project backward whatever their current situation. It may be, then, that males are more, females less, affected by history. Girls' maturation time may make a difference to them at the time of menarche. Later, it simply blends with the larger picture, while, among males, it perhaps contributes to shaping the larger picture.

Time of Physical Maturity and Body Build

It is important to link this section dealing with time of reaching physical maturity and personal-social adjustment with the next section of this chapter. The next section concerns the relationships between body build and personal-social development.

The time puberty occurs is associated with body build, this being clearer for boys than girls. Tanner (1962), whose summary was extensively employed in Chapter 3, says, speaking of boys only: "Increasing degrees of mesomorphy are clearly associated with increasing advancement, increasing ectomorphy with increasing retardation, and increasing endomorphy with very slight advancement" (pp. 99-100). By advancement, he refers to the time of reaching pubescence, and the accompanying spurt in physical growth.

Endomorphs are barrel-bellied, large torsoed individuals who are likely to be fat. Ectomorphs are tall, thin, "string bean" persons. Mesomorphs are heavily muscled, not fat, broad shouldered, and relatively narrow hipped. In United States culture, the mesomorphic build is the ideal for both boys and girls (see, for example, Hassan, 1967). Parnell (1964) has developed clear definitions of these body build types, and has simplified the techniques for classifying people as to body type.

Mesomorphs lack only one cultural advantage over the other two body builds: On the average, they are not as tall as ectomorphs. But the ectomorph loses in muscle and proportion what he gains as an advantage in height. Also, in this culture, height is an advantage only for boys and men.

Early maturers are likely to be mesomorphic, while exceptionally late maturers tend to be ectomorphic. Presumably, this is true for girls as well as boys, but definite evidence of this is lacking. There is some conflicting evidence, discounted by Turner, that early maturing mesomorphic boys are relatively broader hipped and narrower shouldered than late maturers. Turner *does* conclude, like H. E. Jones (1949a) above, that early maturing girls are likely to run to fat (that is, to be endomesomorphs) but he definitely states that early maturing boys retain more masculine or mesomorphic physiques than late maturers.

BODY BUILD AND PERSONALITY

For thousands of years, philosophers and physicians and, more recently, anthropologists and other scientists have speculated about relationships between body build, function, constitution, and temperament. More recently, although some have conducted research, psychologists and sociologists have rather neglected this important field of study.

Efforts to classify body type apparently date back at least to Hippocrates (460?-377? B.C.). Three decades ago, Tucker and Lessa's (1940) scholarly review of the topic included a bibliography of 334 items, many of them referring to body build or constitution and temperament. Tucker and Lessa say: "It is a curious and perhaps significant fact that 2500 years ago Hippocrates said that there are two roots of human beings, the long thins and the short thicks. Almost all simple classifications of type since that time have nearly the same basis, despite variety of nomenclature and detail of description" (p. 419).

Kretschmer (1925) used a somewhat similar classification of body type in his controversial but influential hypotheses about the relations of body build to temperament and mental illness. For example, he believed that if long lean people succumb to mental illness they are likely to become schizophrenic, and that short stocky people are likely to become manic-depressive.

Sheldon has received much attention for his work on body build and temperament (1940, 1942). He interested himself in methods of characterizing body build and relating it to personality. In dealing with delinquents, (for example, Sheldon, Hartl, and McDermott, 1949) he takes an extreme position. The statistical and research techniques he employed have been roundly criticized (see, for example, Hammond, 1957; Humphreys, 1957; Meredith, 1940), but he spurred interest in this neglected area, introduced concepts into thinking that have proved heuristic, and certainly can be called a pioneer. It is not necessary to embrace his assumptions of constitutional determinism to use some of his concepts profitably.

Sheldon seems to have believed that constitution *determines* temperament. More recent and careful research workers do not flatly reject his assumption as untenable; they indicate that "he may have had something," although their explanation is not necessarily the one Sheldon would have advanced. The author's point of view is that a person's body has much to do with both the way he approaches his environment and the way people respond to him. Because of such social-psychological interactions, body build has certain perhaps important relationships to temperament, but it does not *cause* temperament.

Much of Sheldon's work was done with college students. He worked from nude photographs, and, probably because of sexual modesty among females, more of his work was done with young men. His initial work involved direct physical measurements, but practical necessity moved him toward a photographic technique, which employs nude front, side, and back photographs from which somatotypic ratings (placing people into the body build categories reviewed above) are made. As has been said, his techniques have incurred severe criticism. Parnell (1958, 1964) has devised more accurate and thus more useful ways of somatotyping.

Sheldon rated each photograph from 1 (having very little of) to 7 (having a maximum of) for each of the components of endomorphy, mesomorphy, and ectomorphy. Figure 5-3 includes photographs similar to those Sheldon and his colleagues used.

In Sheldon's format, a 7-3-1 describes an almost impossibly pure case of endomorphy; a 1-3-7 an equally improbable instance of ectomorphy; a 2-5-2 represents a ruggedly muscular mesomorph, short both on roundedness and linearity. The endomorph in Figure 5.3 is 5½-3½-2; the mesomorph 1½-7-1½; and the ectomorph 1-3½-5½. Sheldon also rated on dysplasia (bodily disharmony), gynandromorphy (bisexuality, possessing the characteristics of both sexes), and hirsutism, or hairiness.

The term somatotype implies a permanence in body appearance and structure that does not necessarily exist. The relatively slender but mesomorphic girl may become fat and resemble an endomorph. Well-nourished and conditioned ectomorphs move toward mesomorphy. Chronically ill or undernourished mesomorphs' ratings skew toward ectomorphy. Changes may be dramatic from pre- to postadolescence, even though there is considerable continuity of body build through life.

For such reasons, the author prefers a more cumbersome term, somatophenotype, which implies a rating or judgment of "how a person's body measures and appears at a given time." The term implies *condition at the time of measurement and judgment* but does not at the same time deny continuity as a population characteristic.

Studies of Preschool Boys and Girls

Walker (1962) worked with preschool-aged boys and girls, and attempted to judge actual behavior of children of different body builds in order to determine body build–behavior relations. His judgments of behavior were taken from nursery school teachers' ratings. Like Sheldon, he used nude photographs as a basis for his body type classifications. He experienced great difficulty in obtaining reliable judgments of body build for these young children. After elaborate statistical treatment, he secured reliabilities in ratings averaging about .75 for his 2-, 3-, and 4-year-old children. As might be expected, he encountered the most difficulty with 2 year olds (reliability of ratings was .71), and higher ratings (up to .81) for 3 year olds. In this study it is interesting to note that boys were more reluctant than girls to be photographed nude.

Walker, more than Sheldon, recognizes the complex interaction of physique and environment and realizes that different learning opportunities are available to children of different physique. He states that "variations in physical energy, in bodily effectiveness for assertive or dominating behavior, and in bodily sensitivity appear as important mediating links between physique structure and general behavior" (p. 79). From such assumptions, he predicts that girls will be steered by mesomorphic body builds into social behavior, boys into physical, gross motor activity.

Walker's girls were higher than boys in rated endomorphy, and the boys were higher in mesomorphy but lower in ectomorphy. As is the case for so many characteristics, boys were more variable than girls. Walker also found support for the original Hippocratic classification of two component physiques: long-lean and short-thick. Walker's correlations between ectomorphy and endomorphy were high and negative in direction

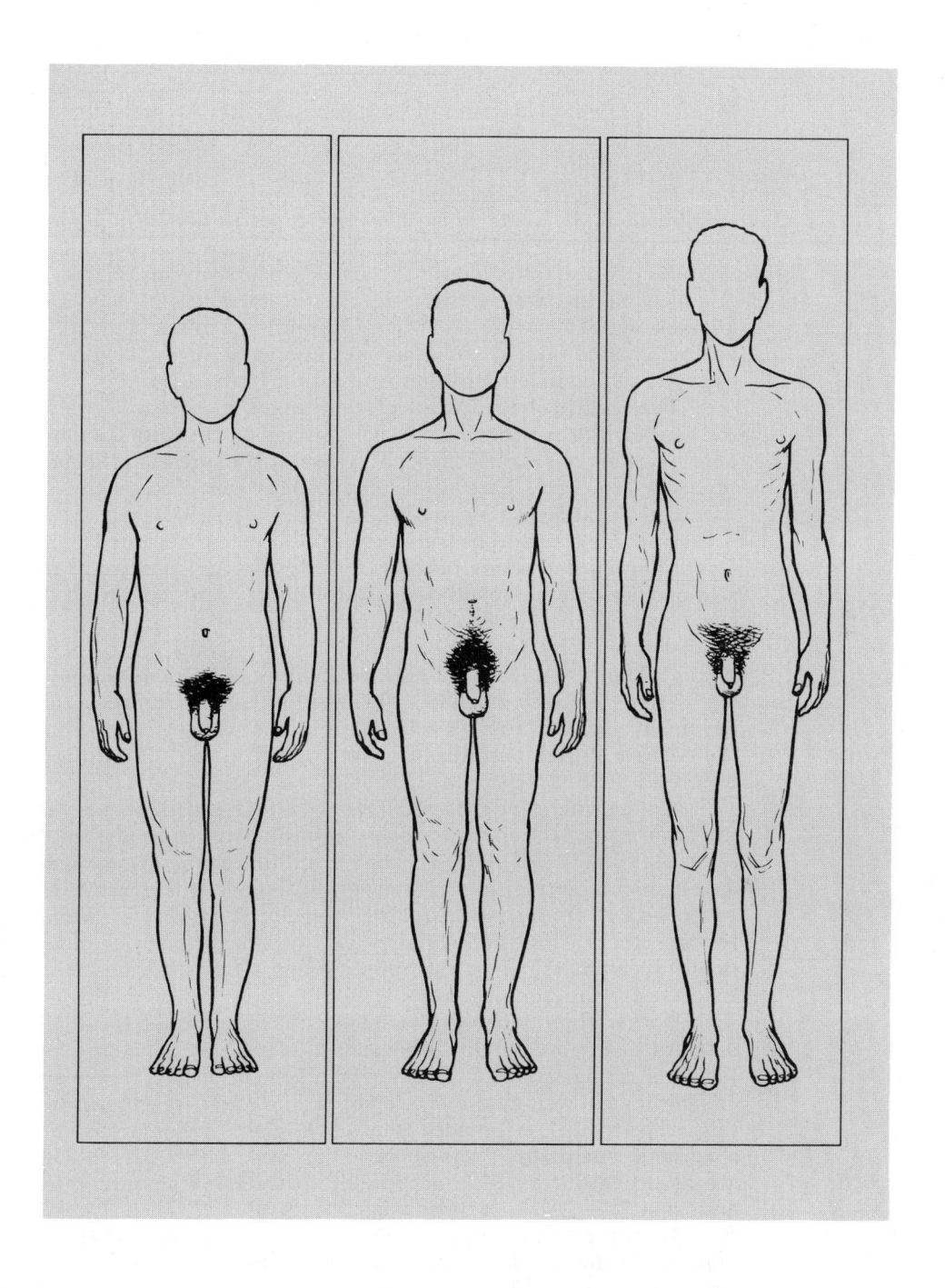

Figure 5.3 *Front view of* (left to right) *endomorph, mesomorph, and ectomorph at age 18 years.* (Drawing based on photograph in Shuttleworth, p. 43. [See page 130 for complate source]).

(−.87 for boys, −.84 for girls). The author has found similar relations for lower-class Afro-American and white 3 and 4 year olds of both sexes, and for 14- to 17-year old males of both races. In fact, he finds no important endomorph component in his data (he uses the Parnell rather than the Sheldon pictorial techniques).

For simplicity's sake, only those of Walker's correlations that are significant at the .01 level or below are reported here. Endomorph boys were self-assertive and revengeful (note the resemblance of this finding to Staffieri's results for older boys discussed later in this chapter). Walker's mesomorphs were easily angered, were leaders in play, and were quarrelsome. They were also rated by their teachers as being ambitious, daring, chance-taking, self-assertive, energetic, noisy, boyish in interests, and self-confident. In other words, they were "all boy."

The preschool-aged traits of easy anger and quarrelsomeness are the ones likely to turn during the socialization process into the more desirable qualities of warmth and naturalness of expression. Socialization probably also takes care of revengefulness, since these boys receive much gratification as they mature.

Walker's ectomorphs were very similar in teacher-rated behavior to older children and young people whose results are reported in the next section. They were not self-assertive or noisy, were not boyish in interests, nor were they daring. They were not very social in their play, were unlikely to attack others, and were neither revengeful, inconsiderate, nor unkind. They dreamed a lot, and were rather dependent and low in energy. They seem very much like the late physical maturers described earlier in this chapter, just as Walker's mesomorphs seem very much like the early maturers described by Kinsey and in the California Growth Studies.

Walker's data for girls revealed little, just as little was revealed by the time of maturation data in the California Growth Study. One begins to suspect that body build is less important in relating to personal–social development among girls. However, Walker's endomorphic girls recovered easily from upsets, and his mesomorphic girls were prone to attacking others. These findings may well have occurred by chance, statistically speaking, since many computations were performed but only a few results were significant.

Walker, thus, uncovers much evidence for personal–social relations associated with body build for boys. As has been mentioned in Chapter 2, teachers' ratings are also always to be taken cautiously. However, Walker's findings fit well with those reported above and, as will be seen, with those reported below for older children. Walker's endomorphs behave in a generally "delinquent" fashion, even as preschoolers. His mesomorphs are assertive but boyishly acceptable. His ectomorphs are withdrawn and "nice."

To reemphasize, it is not children's *behavior*, but teachers' *ratings of behavior* that Walker reports. *If* it is true that society holds firm, consistent, and well-established stereotypes about the traits and behavior of boys and girls (particularly boys) of different body builds, then such representatives of that society as teachers may see what they want to, or what they believe they should see. Research summarized below strongly suggests that there are such stereotypes, and that they already operate in the preschool years. On the other hand, if expectations shape individuals, then the stereotypes may act much like self-fulfilling prophecies: Children and youth actually become what they are expected to become, in terms of the expectations for their particularly bodily configurations.

To interject, the author's results from Parnell's techniques of somatotyping, employed with lower-class Black and white 3 and 4 year olds, reveal almost no interesting relations with behavior and adjustment, other than a tendency for healthier children to be more mesomorphic (hardly a startling finding), and thus more consistent school attenders. Consistent school attendance, in turn, is related to such positive social characteristics as popularity and stable home backgrounds. Even these meager findings suggest advantages for the mesomorph, but do not tell whether the child is mesomorphic because he is healthy, or vice versa. However, the author's population, being lower-class and consisting of two ethnic groups, differs enough from Walker's that comparison is not very useful.

Brodsky's Study of College Men

Walker encountered almost impossible difficulties in using Sheldon's techniques. Other authors, like the writer, have employed Parnell's methods (1958, 1964) or have worked from but not according to the same techniques as Sheldon. Since Brodsky's study anticipates Staffieri's and Hassan's studies of younger children, and Washburn's study of high school youth, it is reviewed here.

Brodsky (1954) assumes that there are differential social reactions to characteristic body builds. Brodsky prepared five 15-inch-high silhouettes of males, representing extreme endomorph, endomesomorph, extreme mesomorph, ectomesomorph, and extreme ectomorph. He also devised a questionnaire containing such items as the following: Which one of this group of five men is most aggressive? Which one of this group of five men is least aggressive?

So that he might generalize his findings more broadly, Brodsky obtained the cooperation of seventy-five medical and dental students from Howard University, all presumably Afro-Americans; and fifty male students from George Washington University, all of whom were probably white. The men answered the questionnaire in groups no larger than five each. There were no important differences in the way the two samples answered, so Brodsky pooled his groups. This homogeneity of response for two demographically quite different samples lends weight to the idea of a United States cultural stereotype, or a characteristic way of regarding body build.

The college students usually assigned the different traits about which they were asked to the "pure" physical-type silhouettes, and neglected the mixed endomesomorphs and ectomesomorphs. Responses given by one-third or more of the respondents are listed below. These responses constitute standard or stereotyped expectancies for this population of research subjects.

The endomorph silhouette was considered to represent a man who eats the most, eats the most often, will make the worst soldier, will make the poorest athlete, will be the poorest professor of philosophy, can endure pain the least, will make the least successful military leader, will be least likely to be chosen leader, will make the poorest university president, will be the least aggressive, will drink the most, will be least preferred as a personal friend (but, ironically and inconsistently, will have many friends), will make the poorest doctor, and will put his own interests before those of others.

This picture is negative and almost completely consistent. It represents an over-all portrait of mild social delinquency. If indeed people become what they are expected to become, a dismal picture of personality growth for endomorphs is presented. Brodsky's results fit well with those of Walker, summarized above, those of studies done with elementary school children, summarized later, and those of Dwyer and Mayer (1967), whose findings about obese girls were reported earlier. All these data suggest that the endomorph in this culture, whether male or female, has brought to bear on himself an important, consistent, and negative set of social expectations.

Brodsky's mesomorph silhouette fares as well as the endomorph fares badly. The respondents said he was potentially the best athlete, the most successful military leader, and the best soldier. They chose him as the man who would assume leadership, and as the man who would be elected as leader. He was predicted not likely to smoke at all, and to be self-sufficient in the sense of needing friends the least among the five silhouettes. However, he was most preferred as a friend, and was judged to have many friends. Respondents also said that he would be the most aggressive, would endure pain the best, would never have a nervous breakdown, and would drink the least.

The stereotype of the ectomorph is much less socially positive than that of the mesomorph, but is noticeably more favorable than that held for the endomorph. The ectomorph silhouetted man was judged to be the most likely to have a nervous breakdown before the age of 30, to eat the least and the least often, to smoke three packs of cigarettes a day, to be least self-sufficient in the sense of needing friends the most (but was judged to have the fewest friends), to hold his liquor least well, to make a poor father and, as a military leader, to be likely to sacrifice his men with the greatest emotional distress. In other words, the ectomorph is a vulnerable, socially acceptable, self-punishing neurotic type.

Brodsky's study illustrates that there are characteristic ways of reacting to different types of male physique, and that the mesomorph physique is much the most favorably viewed. It is worth repeating that the California Growth Study early maturers, perhaps Kinsey's early maturers, and perhaps early maturers in general are more mesomorphic than late maturers.

Studies of Elementary School-aged Children

Staffieri (1967) used an index for linearity (ectomorphy) based on Parnell's (1958) somatophenotyping methods. Staffieri's subjects were 4- through 10-year-old white boys from the midwest, most of whom were middle and upper-middle class. Essentially, his criterion of body build was Hippocrates' long-lean contrasted with short-thick. He was interested in conducting a developmental study of social stereotypes about body build, and his study was partly derived from Brodsky's.

In this context, it is not particularly important psychologically whether body build is a function of two or three components, in the statistical sense. The psychological importance of the body lies in (1) how efficient it is in accomplishing what its possessor wants it to accomplish and (2) the type of social stimulus value it provides. Mesomorphs' bodies seem to be more efficient for gross motor activities, which are socially very important to boys. During the history of the species, mesomorphic bodies may have been more useful biologically than endo- and ectomorphic bodies. Conspicuous exceptions come easily to mind: the Eskimo, who is typically quite endomorphic, and who survived against great odds; the Watusi, who is excessively long and slender and who, as a tribe, also have prospered except until the last decade; or the Australian bushman or *koori* who, while not so tall as the towering Watusi, is typically almost as ectomorphic and who, like the Eskimo, has survived well against tremendous odds.

Concerning social stimulus value, all evidence indicates that in United States culture mesomorphic bodies evoke more positive social reactions from both sexes and a wide variety of research samples than do either ectomorphic or endomorphic bodies. The endomorph elicits the most negative social reaction.

Staffieri asked his subjects to attribute a series of adjectives to three 15-inch-high silhouettes (much like Brodsky's), one set of three representing adult meso-, endo-, and ectomorphic men; and the other, mesomorphic, endomorphic, and ectomorphic boys. Similar tendencies at all age levels were found: Endomorphic silhouettes, whether of men or boys, were described as socially offensive and delinquent. Mesomorphic silhouettes were assigned words indicating that they were boyishly (or mannishly) aggressive, outgoing, active, a leader, and so on. Ectomorphic silhouettes were assigned attributes such as retiring, nervous, and shy—adjectives that, as in Brodsky's study of late adolescents and young adults, betoken an unobjectionable introvert or neurotic.

Staffieri's youngsters were also given the chance to choose which silhouette they would like to look like. Overwhelmingly, they picked the mesomorph as first choice. They were also asked to choose the silhouette that looked most like them and did so with considerable accuracy. This leads to the following conclusions: Boys aged 4 through 10 years of age know what their body builds actually are. They describe endomorphic silhouettes unfavorably and in a socially rejecting way. Ectomorphic silhouettes are seen as social introverts. Mesomorphic silhouettes are perceived as being boyishly desirable, leaders, and so on.

These patterns are already well established by first grade, although they are not as consistent in the preschool years. The boys in Staffieri's study changed little from grade to grade from his first through his fifth grade samples. It must thus be assumed that many boys, probably because of social stereotyping, reject their own body dimensions. Staffieri also found that ectomorphs and mesomorphs were more frequently chosen as friends by the boys in their classes. This leads to the conclusion that endomorphs are less well accepted socially, that they reject their body image, and probably also know that they are not well liked. This finding has important implications for personal adjustment and a genuinely developmental concept of physical fitness, including nutritional control.

A year after this study was completed, Hassan and McCandless located as many of Staffieri's boys as possible in an informal research undertaking,[5] and administered an anxiety scale, which included items to test willingness to admit unfavorable things about oneself. While the mesomorphic boys showed less anxiety than either the ecto- or endomorphic boys, the differences were not statistically significant due to the small number. However, even with the small N, there were significant differences in willingness to admit unfavorable traits or behaviors among the body build groups. The mesomorphs were the most frank, the nine boys in the group admitting to an average of 9.66 negative self-evaluations; the twelve ectomorphic boys were next in "frankness," with an average of 6.8 admissions per boy; and the endomorphs were least frank, the eighteen boys in the group averaging only 3.55 admissions of negative qualities. If freedom from lying, or a somewhat rueful self-honesty, is an index of good adjustment, this minor study suggests that the mesomorphs are indeed better off than the ectomorphs, who in turn rank higher than the endomorphs (only the difference between the meso- and the endomorphs is statistically significant at the .05 level).

This finding led Hassan (1967) to further research on the topic. In her study, she used both boys and girls as subjects. Their ages ranged from 6 to 10 years, and the study was a replication and extension of Staffieri's. Employing an entirely different population of children (although almost all were middle class and white, like Staffieri's), she found social stereotypes to exist that were almost identical with Staffieri's. She supplies much needed data about girls for whom little evidence has been reported. The girls in her study showed the same tendencies as the boys, but were even more pronounced in their stereotypes!

Hassan extended Staffieri's study to include a test of the children's realism in self concept (how accurately they identified their own body types). Evidence is strong (see McCandless, 1967) that realistic self concepts accompany other indexes of good adjustment. Her mesomorphic children of all ages were more realistic on this measure of self concept than were her endomorphs or ectomorphs. Sugarman and Haronian (1964) speak of adolescents' sophistication about their body type, and report results for adolescents quite in line with Hassan's results for younger children. Hassan's older children were more accurate than her younger, and her girls were more accurate than her boys. This latter finding is not surprising, since girls commonly have been found to be earlier and more keenly aware than boys of social-cultural realities.

When asked which stereotype belonged with which body type, all three groups were reasonably accurate, but the mesomorphs of both sexes were most accurate and the girls, particularly the younger girls, were more accurate than the boys.

Staffieri[6] has run one more pilot study using his techniques as adapted from Brodsky. He found that institutionalized, retarded adolescent boys reacted to the major body types in the same fashion his and Hassan's elementary school students and Brodsky's college men reacted.

[5]This study will not be published because of the small number of subjects located.
[6]In personal communication.

In short, the evidence for cultural stereotyping of expectations about body type is strong, and the implications for guidance of children and adolescents are clear. Youngsters and young people must be helped to incorporate realistically into their self concepts what their bodies are like. Endomorphs as a group should be trimmed down; ectomorphs as a group should be helped to build up self-confidence in relations with both things and people. There is no more point in sweeping evidence about body builds under the rug than there is in denying the realities of sexual development and behavior. These extrapolations from the data do not seem too daring.

Body Build, Family Tension, and Self Concept among High School Boys

Washburn (1962) used the same index of linearity (height in inches divided by cube root of weight in pounds) that Staffieri (1967) used. It will be remembered that this is a refinement of Sheldon's somatotyping technique devised by the English physician, Parnell (1958). Thus, Washburn, like Staffieri, compared long-leans with short-thicks.

Washburn worked within the framework of a large California public high school. He had available to him full counseling and personnel records, and the counseling and family and community service personnel in the high school worked closely with him. He was able to obtain two clearly defined groups of boys of forty each, one toward the ectomorphic end of the scale, the other toward the mesoendomorphic.[7] Washburn's subjects were presumably all white. Each of his groups averaged 16½ years of age, and 101 IQ.

Washburn wanted to determine the relationships in family conflict as an environmental or learning variable to body build as a "given" or constitutional-hereditary variable, on the one hand, and to self concept on the other. He devised three different types of measure of the self concept, each of which was moderately valid (that is, the boys' scores for the three different measures correlated between .65 and .68 with counselors' ratings of what the boys' self concepts would actually be).

The first aspect of the self concept Washburn measured he called "inner controlled self versus somatic-primitive self." He believed this measured the degree to which the boy had internalized the social norms functioning to control behavior, on the one end of the continuum, and concern with immediate need gratification, on the other. A sample item was: "I would prefer having parents, teachers, or employers think well of me" versus "I would prefer just taking it easy and enjoying life." For each item like this one, the boy was required to choose one alternative, thereby rejecting the other. This is called the forced choice technique of test response.

Washburn predicted that scores for this aspect of the self concept would not be at all related to body build, but would be clearly related to intrafamily conflict. Boys who had grown up in high conflict, being under constant tension and high drive, would be less likely to internalize—to develop "consciences"—than boys who had grown up in low

---

[7]One finds few pure endomorphs among adolescent boys. Among a population of institutionalized 15- to 18-year-old Afro-American and white boys, all in good physical condition and well nourished, the author and his students have found only one such boy in a population of 180 they have recently measured, using all of Parnell's measurements.

conflict homes. The amount of tension, as it were, would force them out of thoughtful, long range planning and future goals into taking what they could from life when they could get it (this theorizing is the author's, not Washburn's). Such reasoning fits well with predictions from the conceptual framework outlined in Chapter 1.

Washburn's prediction was supported.

The second aspect of his self concept test was "outercontrolling self versus submissive-dependent self." One end of the continuum of response here is that a boy manipulates the external environment to attain approval as symbolized by social status. The other end of the continuum involves avoidance of disapproval by giving in to others. A sample item is: "I like giving directions to others" versus "I prefer following directions given by others."

Washburn predicted that family tension would not affect this aspect of the self concept (and, presumably, actual behavior. The fairly high correlation between counselors' ratings and boys' own private self concepts suggests that boys act overtly to a considerable degree in accordance with their self-perceptions.) However, Washburn believed body build would affect this facet of the self concept. His prediction was partially supported, but only with that 50 percent of the boys who came from low conflict homes. Washburn reasons that, in high tension homes, parents will attempt to curb the boy who is extremely outercontrolling (the mesoendomorphic boy), and push toward a more aggressive stance the boy who is extremely submissive and dependent (the role he predicted would be filled by his ectomorphs). This family pressure counteracts the boys' "constitutional tendencies."

Washburn's third measure of self concept was "integrative-actualizing self versus detached-independent self." An integrative-actualizing adolescent boy will accept his shortcomings (see McCandless and Hassan's informal study, reported earlier), as well as the shortcomings of others; and will be oriented toward self-fulfillment. The boy who scores high on detached-independent self will separate himself from others psychologically and will fear emotional involvement with others. A sample pair of forced choice items is: "One of my best features is that I like people," versus "I don't let feelings influence my judgment." Washburn reasoned that the important determiner of this type of personal-social adjustment would be intrafamily conflict, not body build. His prediction was supported at the .001 level. Again, this finding meshes well with the conceptual framework outlined in Chapter 1.

Washburn's study has important and obvious counseling and guidance implications, and is valuable in that it points out the complexity of the interrelationships between one's body and its function, and differential reactions of those with different body builds to learning opportunities. Where objective physical strength and skill are involved (as in dominance over the people and things in the environment), the nature of one's body seems to influence the life stance one adopts. But in matters of personal control and self–other acceptance, the dynamics of the learning situation (the family, in Washburn's case) seem to exert the major influence.

Washburn's study, incidentally, is one of the best examples the author knows of research that involves variables (such as counselor judgments, school records, and parent interviews) related to the real life of the child, and relates them to quite sophisticated psychological measurements.

Physique and Self-description of Temperament

This heading is a direct quote of the title of an interesting paper by Cortés and Gatti (1965). These authors avoided Sheldon's error (contamination of results; see Chapter 2) of having the somatotyper rate the temperament of those measured. A full set of Parnell (1958) measures was employed to define endomorphs (Cortés and Gatti call them, perhaps more appropriately, "circular types"), mesomorphs (triangular types), and ectomorphs (linear types).

The subjects, independent of any results from their physical measurements and without knowing their own somatophenotypes, took the "temperament test" devised by Cortés and Gatti.

Sheldon (1942) proposed that different types of temperament were associated with different body builds. Endomorphs were "viscerotonic." Working from Sheldon's ideas, Cortés and Gatti constructed a list of descriptions of viscerotonics. It included such items as the following: dependent, calm, love of comfort, extensive rapport, warm, forgiving, lets things happen (p. 433).

Sheldon considered that mesomorphs were "somatotonic." Cortés and Gatti's descriptions of somatotonia included such items as dominant, love of risk, self-assured, active, reckless, makes things happen.

Ectomorphs were thought to be "cerebrotonic." This type of temperament includes such traits as detachment, anxiety, loving privacy, self-centered, cool, inhibited, watches things happen.

A short test asking subjects to describe themselves according to such characteristics was given to a sample of about 100 boys, who were seniors in a Boston high school, and who averaged 17½ years of age. Of this sample, seventy-three were somatophenotyped and included in the analysis of results.

A boy was considered an endomorph *if* his first component was highest of the three possible components, and if it had an endomorphy strength of 4.5 or above. "Thus, a 4.5-3.5-4.0 would be an endomorph, but not the 4.0-3.0-3.5 (does not meet the criterion of 4.5 or more), or the 4.5-4.5-3.5 (a balanced or mid-range somatotype" (p. 434). Since, according to Sheldon (1954) the average United States male somatotype is 3.3-4.1-3.4 and, from the author's data adolescent boys are seldom endomorphic, Cortés and Gatti's endomorphs differ very sharply from the norm, their mesomorphs relatively little, and their ectomorphs substantially. Unfortunately, the authors do not give the average somatyping components for this high school male sample.

When Cortés and Gatti pulled out their very extreme types (fifteen or sixteen boys in each group), viscerotonia and endomorphy correlated .66, somatotonia and mesomorphy .74, and cerebrotonia and ectomorphy .59. For all seventy-three boys, the correlations were much lower, but still statistically significant: .32, .42, and .31 in the same order as that given above.

Thus, among Boston high school senior boys, self-perceptions correlate at well above the chance level with what would be predicted from knowing their body types. The more clearly the boys fall into one or the other physical build category, the better the fit.[8]

Cortés and Gatti were able to secure the cooperation of a sample of 100 Washington, D.C., college girls, who ranged in age from 17 to 28 years, and whose average age was 20. The girls clustered at the endomorphic end of the scale, the average somatotype ratings being 4.0-3.2-3.4. Relations between physique and temperament for the total sample of 100 girls were not much different from those for the boys: The correlation between viscerotonia and endomorphy for girls was .36 and for the younger (and presumably more representative) boys it was .32. For the girls, somatotonia and mesomorphy correlated .47, whereas the correlation was .42 for boys. Cerebrotonia and ectomorphy correlated .49 among the girls, but only .31 for boys. This last pair of correlations may be significantly different one from the other, and suggests that social stereotypes for very thin girls may be significantly stronger than for very thin boys. This would not be surprising. Additionally, it is probable that the very thin girl of this age (20) differs more from the average than does the very thin boy of 17½.

When extreme types of girls are selected from the sample, correlation between viscerotonia and endomorphy was .59 for the forty-one strongly endomorphic girls (it was .66 for boys); for thirty-nine extremely mesomorphic girls, somatotonia and mesomorphy correlated .57 (the figure was .74, substantially higher, for boys); and for fifty-seven extremely ectomorphic girls, cerebrotonia and ectomorphy correlated .60 (the correlation for extreme type boys was essentially identical, .59). This set of findings suggests that social stereotypes favoring mesomorphic boys may be more effective than those favoring mesomorphic girls. Again, this is not surprising. It is risky to speculate, however, as this sample of girls is older, probably better off socioeconomically, and probably brighter than the male sample. All that can be said is that the contrasting findings are interesting and deserve further investigation.

Cortés and Gatti were able to secure the cooperation of a third unrepresentative but interesting sample of twenty adult male prisoners, sixteen of whom were Afro-American. The average age of these men was 33.8, and they ranged in age from 23 to 58 years. Their average somatotype is markedly mesomorphic: 2.8-5.4-3.1. All had committed serious crimes, including five who were murderers, and others who had committed rape, forgery, robbery, aggravated assault, and burglary. For this sample, mesomorphy and somatotonia correlated .47 (contrasted to .42 for high school boys and an identical .47 for college girls). These results suggest considerable generality for a predicted relationship between body build and personality, as reflected in one's self concept. As has been noted, Washburn's results also suggest considerable congruity between self concept and actual behavior. This point is discussed later in the treatment of adolescent self concept.

The question is moot as to whether this relation is determined simplistically by body build or results from an interaction of body build

---

[8]It seems, though, that a paradox is involved in that by the application of social stereotypes of body build to these boys, their "category" response is to some extent predetermined.

and learning opportunity. The author has made it quite clear that he inclines toward an interaction theory. Washburn's results also suggest that simplistic determinism is not indicated as an explanation.

Cortés and Gatti's results are all the more significant because they fit well with other data collected from populations varying in age and that were studied by very different research techniques. Most markedly, for their prisoners, next for their high school senior boys, and least but still significantly for their college girls, the mesomorphs rated themselves more often as confident, energetic, adventurous, enterprising, and so on. Endomorphs regarded themselves as kind, relaxed, warm, and soft-hearted. Is this related to Staffieri's and Hassan's attribution to endomorphs of laziness? Ectomorphs thought of themselves as detached, shy, reserved, and tense. This fits well with Staffieri's and Hassan's results, and correlates equally well with reports by Walker, Washburn, the older and less-directly-to-the-point studies reported from the California Growth Study data, as well as with Kinsey's descriptions of early and late maturers.

It is worth making a final point about the Cortés and Gatti data: Their ruggedly mesomorphic adult males, for the most part ill-educated and Black (thus discriminated against) have by and large committed the types of crime one might expect from confident, energetic, enterprising, *ill-educated and ill-socialized,* and bitterly frustrated males.

SIX LIFE STORIES

The term case history is avoided here because, for each of the six young people whose stories are given, considerable distortion has been introduced so as to prevent identification. These stories, however, concern real people. They have been selected as representatives of "pure cases" of the effects on both boys and girls of time of puberty and/or body build as these interact with real life learning circumstances.

A Very Early Maturing and a Very Late Maturing Boy

This section concerns two boys, similar in age, intelligence, ethnicity, and family background. Both are urban, both come from modest but secure lower-middle socioeconomic status homes, both are bright (IQs are above 120), both are WASP, both have done their best to conform to adult standards, and both did well in school in their early educational careers.

The mothers of both were excessively overprotective, and the fathers of both were inclined to withdraw into the background, permitting their tense and rather dominating wives to dictate the way their sons were reared and the way the household was managed. Both sets of parents were older than the average parents of sons of these boys' ages, although neither set of parents was elderly (each was in the early 30s when the boys were born).

Progress through elementary school was similar for the two boys. They were somewhat withdrawn, attracted little attention to themselves from either their peers or their teachers, although the latter considered them good students and "nice" boys. The neighbors and neighborhood play group also thought of each as a nice boy, although both were regarded as being somewhat "mothers' boys."

Evidence of their overprotection was abundant: Although each lived within walking distance of his elementary school, both were driven to school, picked up to be taken home for a home-cooked lunch (each school had suitable, reasonably priced school cafeterias), brought back again to school, and picked up at the end of the school day. This pattern continued through elementary school. On rainy days, if the storm had come up during the school day, each mother hurried to school with rubbers and a raincoat. The mothers sought constant contact with the teachers about their sons' progress. This is, of course, generally desirable if not overdone.

Jeff: A Very Early Maturer Jeff began to shoot up in height early in junior high school and, by the time he was well into eighth grade, could pass for a young man of 18. He was tall, well built, muscular, very masculine in appearance, and his whiskers showed noticeably if he did not shave daily. As he mushroomed in height, weight, and masculinity of body construction and attributes, his social role changed. Those girls who were mature giggled and fluttered at him. The teachers called on him for chores around the school that demanded height, strength, and (presumably) psychological maturity. Since he was a conforming, obedient boy, he performed in this role maturely and responsibly; and other such roles increasingly came his way.

The athletic coach approached him about taking more part in contact sports. His mother objected, first violently, then tearfully but, for once, the father intervened forcibly, taking the part of the coach and the school. Jeff, always obedient, was content to go along with the coach's wishes, although he did not much like rough sports. At first, he was hesitant and timid in his participation, but his size and good coordination provided him with immediate and easy success experiences. Thus, he blossomed, although not into an outstanding athlete. The coach once reproached him for not having the "spirit" necessary in contact sports. His greatest success was in such things as tennis and swimming.

He freed himself by stages from his mother's overprotection. At first, he found school-related excuses for staying at school for lunch and after school for extracurricular activities. He could "never quite remember" when such after-school activities ended and his mother was thus unable to meet him with any regularity. A high incidence of "lost" raincoats and rubbers finally discouraged his mother from that type of overprotection and, as early as the end of seventh grade, he had effectively and without open rebellion structured his school days so that he was pretty much his own man. His mother did not quite understand how this happened and, the author believes, neither did Jeff.

He began to sneak out on dates as soon as evening activities became an acceptable part of his school life. He had no difficulty finding partners. A little before his 14th birthday, to his startled delight an older married girl cousin provided him a full practicum experience in the facts of life.

In short, by the time he had finished eighth grade and quite painlessly, he had undergone a goodly share of the experiences of a full-fledged young man, and had escaped effectively from the sphere of his mother's dominance. Since his somewhat underhanded rebellion had consistently conformed to the social expectations of school life his mother, obscurely frustrated, had little choice but to go along with him. With increasing masculine self-assurance, he began to cultivate his father. Since his father took great pride in his prowess, particularly in athletics, and gave him back quick responses to his overtures, they became good friends.

The author last knew of Jeff's progress when he was a well-adjusted, B-average college senior, engaged to be married upon graduation and, pending results of the draft, bound either for the Service or a good job that had already been offered him.

Tony: A Very Late Maturer Jeff's peer, Tony, was small, slight, and very late maturing. Not only did he reach puberty late, but it brought with it a flagrant case of adolescent acne that was still noticeably with him in his fifth year of college. His junior and senior high school period was a nightmare for him. His grades fell from their satisfactory elementary school level, chiefly because he was so wretched personally. His grades precipitated a prolonged warfare in the home about academics that went on for years. The author suspects this may have been his socially maladaptive way of rebelling against his mother. However, not until he was well into college did he show any signs of open rebellion.

Because he was so small and thin, he took part in physical activities at only a token level: He attended physical education classes only as required, and physical education teachers often showed open contempt for him. During shower times, he cowered in corners until his body took on some semblance of manhood during his eleventh grade year.

He went through high school without a single date, and dated only occasionally in college. He states that he has masturbated excessively since his first experience at 15.

He was 22 when the author last saw him, and was in his fifth year of college but with graduation still well in the future. His grades were not good enough for graduation, and he had a string of incomplete grades and postponed physical education requirements. He was terrified of being caught by the draft.

At 22, he was innocent heterosexually, and doubted his masculinity seriously. An incomplete sexual relationship with a young male college faculty member had caused him great and persistent anxiety about homosexuality. His doubt is apparently well founded, as he admits to strong homosexual yearnings. He is too timid to do anything about them, and is not attractive enough that he elicits overtures. His physical lack of appeal has also interfered with heterosexual courting success.

He undertook psychological counseling for two years during college, but it seems to have done him little good other than serving to reduce the intensity of his still recurring thoughts about suicide. During counseling, he also brought to the surface, probably openly recognizing what had been true all along, intense hostility toward both his mother and father. At 22, his relation with both parents was as stormy as it had been during high school, the only difference being that at 22 he was usually the attacker rather than the victim. When he was last seen, he was experimenting with both marijuana and the psychedelic drugs, although, even here, his commitment was timid.

In summary, at 22, Tony was a lonely, lost, and ineffective young man with a poor prognosis.

Tony and Jeff are extreme cases but, through their contrast, they represent clearly some of the social-personal interactions mediated by physique and time of sexual maturation.

A Mesomorph and an Ectomorph Boy Tony and Jeff differed sharply both in time of physical maturity and in body build and attractiveness. Ted and Lonnie differ most in body build, and each is rather attractive looking, although neither is handsome. Both Ted and Lonnie come from very large, lower-lower class, inner city, Black slum families. The children in both families are multifathered, although both families are conventional in that there has been a fairly long term, stable father figure in the home.

The mothers of both boys have worked consistently and the streets have been as much their home as their crowded apartments. None of the brothers or sisters in either family has been in "bad trouble," either with the law or in school. Both boys are above average in IQ, testing about 105 on a group test of intelligence. The figure probably underrates their intelligence, as such tests typically penalize lower-class youngsters. Their elementary school progress was similar: passing but mediocre grades.

The boys are not distinguished in their time of puberty: Both "became men" somewhat early, before their 13th birthdays. Nor does color affect them differentially: both are moderately dark.

The striking difference between them is in body build. Ted is a strapping mesomorph, all powerful arms, back, and shoulders; fast, graceful, and very strong. Lonnie is a very tall, thin, straight-standing youngster who is myopic and has worn glasses since he was in early elementary school. Ted's vision is normal.

Ted: A Mesomorph Ted mastered his particular section of the asphalt jungle early. He was fearless, tough, stronger than other boys of his own age, talked a good game, and was well able to compete with most boys who were some years older than he. In several respects, his life is not unlike Claude Brown's in *Manchild in the Promised Land* (1965). Like many boys from very poor families, he escaped early from family control. His mother, the most consistent power figure in the family, had come from the rural part of his southern state, and had little comprehension of the varieties of experience a boy could find in the city. Besides, she was chronically tired and too busy with other children. Ted's own father had left the home when Ted was 4 years old and, while neither of the two subsequent men of the house had showed dislike for or abused Ted, neither had been particularly interested in him.

By the time he was 10, Ted went where he wished, did what he wished, slept where he wished and, unfortunately, stole what he wished. He was popular and respected among his peers, and was the leader of an informal gang before he reached his teens. School bored him, although he seldom got into trouble there. He dropped out at the end of eighth grade, long before he reached legal age. In his southern city, attendance officers did little checking on poor Black boys, so his truancy went unnoticed. It was, however, entered against him in his record when he was eventually and inevitably caught along with some of his friends by the police for aggravated assault and robbery.

At the time of writing, he is 17, and is serving an indefinite sentence as a juvenile in a very inadequate reform school. He is generally bitter with the world. This is understandable although Ted has, in some ways and despite his current incarceration, mastered the world he knows best. His has been a world where illegitimate opportunities far exceed those that are legitimate. His strength and toughness have enabled him to get most of the available goodies: He has been a gang leader and an accomplished delinquent. From his earliest teens, he has enjoyed the spoils of the victor. He has had money, clothes, prestige, friendship, power, and girls. For example, he believes, but emphasizes that he does not know for sure, that he has fathered four children.

It is logical that his powerful mesomorphic body, interacting with a pleasing personality and a rather good mind, has played an important part in his exploitation of the type of opportunities available to him.

Lonnie: An Ectomorph Lonnie could not succeed according to the illegitimate norms of the slum world he and Ted shared. Its most glamorous opportunities were simply not available to a rather weak, thin, myopic boy. Almost for the lack of anything else to do, he persevered in school and was graduated from high school with the reputation of being an above average student and a "good boy."

He says bashfully that he has "known some girls," but his statement has nothing in it of the young stallion's triumph conveyed by Ted's conjectures about his probable paternity. Ted often adds complacently, "I've always had all the girls I want." One suspects Lonnie has had to persevere to get the girls he has had.

Lonnie steadily and reliably holds down a rather menial but respectable job in a middle-class cafeteria, contributes part of his wages to the family, attends college classes at night, and seems to have a good chance for eventual success on society's terms, if he receives even breaks. His story will be resumed later in the section on vocational development. He still has somewhere to go. Ted probably has not. However, one who knows the society in which Lonnie grew up cannot avoid feeling that, if he had had Ted's chances *at the same very early age*, he would have been glad to follow the same route.

In Ted's and Lonnie's society, predominant values seem to include toughness, shrewdness, verbal skills of a "rapping" order, ability to outwit the white society, and total self-sufficiency or autonomy. Lonnie, although he sees his life as being both currently and ultimately superior to Ted's, is a little envious of him about everything except his present reformatory sentence.

Ted and Lonnie are a pair of boys very different from Jeff and Tony but, like them, seem to be playing out roles important aspects of which have been shaped by their bodies. The early maturity and mesomorphy that enabled Jeff, in his middle-class white world, to escape from his overprotective mother and satisfactorily sample and master the opportunities available to normal young males, have been the social ruin of Ted. Ted mastered a delinquent world, the forces of law and order caught up with him, and the odds are that his future will indeed be grim.

Lonnie, despite being poor and Black, has not been as handicapped by his body as Tony. Rather, his body has kept him from the delinquent world and preserved him for what may well become middle-class respectability. At 19 years of age, he seems well on his way toward such status, and now admits to being "hooked" by conventional ambition.

To summarize, factors of physical maturity and body build may exert very different influences on a boy, depending on the opportunities that are open to him. Jeff's body has served him well on all scores. Ted's body made it easy for him to be delinquent: a natural and rewarding way of life in his world *until one is caught*. Tony's body has only exacerbated an already poor psychosocial adjustment. Lonnie's body "kept him on ice" until psychological maturity, facilitated by his personal steadiness, had a chance to take over. He has been helped to maturity through hope engendered by modest vocational and educational progress.

Discussion of the Four Males' Life Stories

As can be seen from the review of these four young men's lives, as well as from the more scholarly data that were presented earlier in the chapter, early maturity and physically strong mesomorphic bodies convey more advantages than disadvantages to boys. Among middle-class boys, the early maturer is likely to meet more direct biologically connected frustration about sex and to meet it earlier. If a boy has legitimate opportunities, his aggressive confidence in his body may lead him to athletics, job mastery, courting skills, and leadership roles with peers and adults, each of which will stand him in good stead the rest of his life. The same aggressive confidence, with illegitimate opportunities predominating, may take the boy along a rebellious and antisocial route.

Early sexual maturity, even though frustrating, is likely to consolidate the young man earlier and more confidently in his appropriate sex role identification (although, as has been seen, this can be treacherous if this consolidation is purely psychobiological and in a homosocial setting, as it often is for disadvantaged youth).

It is relevant here to anticipate a later, fuller treatment of sex role typing. Colley (1959) refers to three dimensions of sex role adoption: the biomode, the sociomode, and the psychomode. The most appropriate biomode for a boy is a clearly masculine physique, for a girl a clearly feminine physique. The sociomode refers to sexually appropriate ways of behaving, including gestures and gait: "He is *all* boy!" "Isn't she a dainty little thing!" The psychomode refers to widely and deeply generalized sex role attitudes. The psychomode may or may not be the same as the bio- and sociomodes. The appropriate, conflict-free psychology of maleness includes easy, unselfconscious masculinity, heterosexual preference and practice, and pride in both one's sex and sexuality.

Appropriate psychomodes in our society seem to set one free to behave naturally (see, for instance, Leventhal, Shemberg, and Van Schoelandt, 1968).

It is logical to expect that, because of their sex-appropriate bodies (their biomode), mesomorphic boys and endomesomorphic girls find it relatively easy, other things being equal, to move into appropriate sociomodes. Attaining an adequate psychomode may also be easier, although there seems to be little if any relationship between body type and appropriate sex identification (psychomode). Bayley (1951) presents data that suggest but do not demonstrate conclusively that an appropriate psychomode is reached with less conflict and more relaxed self-assurance by boys with strongly rather than weakly masculine body builds.

Athletic proficiency is a very important proficiency for a boy (see, for example, Coleman, 1961; Friesen, 1968). Unless it is carried to an extreme, as Coleman but not Friesen suggests it often is, it is likely to be one of the most valuable proficiencies a boy can have in contemporary United States society. This is true, not so much for the sake of athletics alone, but for such side benefits of social acceptance, enhancement of self concept, prestige with adults, and scholarship opportunities. Many poor boys who otherwise would have been school drop-outs and/or non-college attenders have been able to consolidate and continue their educations because of athletic scholarships. The playing field has led them into the academic arena, and, once there, there is a chance for them to become, if not addicted, at least habituated. Thus, socially conventional doors to upward mobility have been opened.[9]

Few lower-class boys have such opportunities. While most of them use their bodies in a less delinquent and dramatic fashion than Ted, they are all too likely to drop out of school early because they are big enough and strong enough to hold down jobs that require muscle. Thus, they follow a dead-end route, using their bodies to gain what they want here and now. Lonnie, by his own statement, delayed his gratification only because he had to, although thereby, hopefully, he can earn his mature living by his head rather than his back.

The author is critical of current physical education programs. All too often (and perhaps because of community pressure rather than physical education teachers' preferences) they seem to waste much of the talent that exists, fail to develop much that might be there, and do little or nothing to remedy such lackluster bodies as Tony's or Lonnie's. The picture is as clear but not as dramatic for girls.

An Early Maturing Mesoendomorphic and a Late Maturing Ectomorphic Girl

It has been said that research dealing with time of puberty and type of body build among girls has not produced as clear results as for boys. Social stereotypes about body build seem to be much the same for girls as boys (Hassan, 1967, finds them, if anything, stronger); self concepts as related to body type follow the same lines as for boys (Cortés and Gatti, 1965); but no important behavior relationships with body build emerge for girls (Walker, 1962). Neither does the date of puberty seem to be of long term significance among girls (the California Growth Study, Shipman, 1964).

There may be several reasons for this. Results from the California Growth Study suggest that adults regard early maturing girls as psy-

---

[9]Parenthetically, a major grievance of "star" Black athletes is that, while their athletic prowess puts them *structurally* into academia, race discrimination does not allow them to become *functionally* a part of it.

chologically mature so that they are often assigned leadership roles. However, in our coeducational society, athletics does not seem to be very important for girls (McCandless and Ali, 1966). Thus, early maturity and the superiority in size and strength attendant convey relatively little prestige to girls. As has been suggested, early maturing girls may be seen as threats by their peers, both male and female (but threats of a different order). If a girl's early maturity is accompanied by corresponding early interest in dating, as is likely, it may lead her into deeper psychological waters than she can manage.

Among the very poor, early maturity and symmetrical bodies are likely to lead girls into trouble rather than keep them out. Early maturing and well shaped, a girl becomes the focus of much aggressive male courting attention. On the other hand, if good looks enhance a girl's self concept, then they often provide her with a wider choice of boys to date and perhaps to marry. Finally, girls adjust if they marry well, boys seem to be more self-determining. Thus, the advantages given to an early maturing, meso- or endomesomorphic girl are often taken away. The net effect is thus likely to be more balanced than for boys.

Even for boys, as has been suggested, there may be disadvantages, appearing in early middle age, because as early maturing mesomorphic white boys they did not learn to look within themselves, perhaps because the good things of the world were always so easily available to them. By their 40s, M. C. Jones' (1965) early maturers were conspicuously characterized by test results showing them to be objective, rational, conventional, and conforming. Peskin's (1967) reanalysis of the California data shows that this could have been predicted. The late maturers seem to have more coping devices such as being able to deal with ambiguity, attending more to things in their environments that are important to them, being more able to laugh at themselves and the world, and more equalitarian in attitudes. Interestingly enough, the late maturers remember much more about their heterosexual and social sexual development than the early maturers. This may be partly due to this development being some years later, but appears to relate more to problems encountered during that period. This differential recall can be related back to an earlier discussion in this and the preceding chapters about values of fantasy rehearsal in preparing for psychoaffectional relations in a heterosocial world, and may also be related to Ames' (1957) tentative finding that marriages of the late maturers were on the whole somewhat happier.

To repeat, as the early maturers' bodies begin to fail them, they may be left without a requisite supply of rich inner resources such as was developed with difficulty by the late maturers. The finding that they pride themselves on being rational and objective relates to this. But this is conjecture: only the small, urban, western United States, middle class, volunteer, white sample reported by M. C. Jones and the other California research workers are the basis for these speculations. More research is clearly needed.

Even though time of maturity and body build show less relation to personal-social adjustment for girls as a group, individuals may be much affected, as Marilee and Cheri demonstrate.

Marilee: An Early Maturing Mesoendomorph Marilee is a strikingly good looking brunette of about 27. She is rather stormily married to her third husband and has three children, one from each of her marriages. Her first marriage took place when she was 17 and two months pregnant. Neither she nor the man she married was sure he was the father of the baby she was carrying.

Marilee's father and mother are prosperous professional people who have been financially comfortable since before her birth. She has one sister who is three years older than she. The sister was a model child and adolescent, performed in a superior way in school all the way through the master's degree, married a solid young professional man, and is currently the successful but tense mother of three children and a doer-of-good and promoter of social reform in her role as upper-middle-class young wife and mother in a prosperous suburb.

Marilee was a headstrong child. She was given severe discipline throughout her childhood and adolescence. She was never the student her sister was, but was extremely popular with both her peers and teachers; she was known as a warm but impulsive child. She first menstruated in fifth grade and by seventh grade was voluptuously mature and approached being beautiful.

Boys swarmed around her, all at least a year older and many as old as college age. With maturity, her warmth, gregariousness, and aura of sexiness seemed seriously to threaten her rather chilly parents and sedate older sister. The sister carried many tales home from school. In the beginning of Marilee's heyday, these tales were seriously exaggerated and, to an impartial observer, clearly motivated by jealousy. Marilee's parents responded by redoubled supervisory measures, and curtailed her freedom in early adolescence much more than they had when she was a younger child. Probing questions about her school and, later, her heterosexual life changed to accusations. At first, the accusations were groundless, but, with time, they became accurate. For the first time since her runabout years, physical discipline, some of it verging on brutality, was inflicted on her.

Just after she turned 14 when she was in the eighth grade, she ran away from home after a particularly violent scene. The author saw her professionally for a time as she was becoming reincorporated into her home after this episode. She was an angry, troubled girl, near despair. Her recurrent theme was, "I've got the name and, damn it, I'm going to have the game!" And have the game she did.

Because of her family's community status, the administration of the excellent suburban college preparatory school she attended never quite got around to expelling her, but they made no secret of their relief when, at the end of ninth grade, her parents decided to place her in an expensive, strict, religious boarding school. (This is an example of the psychosocial moratorium granted to most youngsters from the middle and upper classes.) The nuns in the boarding school were no more successful with Marilee than the public school people had been, and she returned to her old school to begin eleventh grade.

She dropped out of school a few months before graduation, pregnant, and married a young man eight years older than she. As has been mentioned, neither she nor he knew whether he was the baby's father, but he was very much in love and wished to marry her under any circumstances. As he was a "well-situated" college graduate, her parents saw her to the altar with real appreciation of both their luck and their new son-in-law. In the marital storms that followed immediately, they and her sister consistently, unequivocally, and without hesitation took the side of her husband against Marilee. He turned often to them for advice in managing her and, eventually, about what to do with her.

She settled the problem by leaving town in company with a night club entertainer. They were eventually married following a nasty custody fight over the baby of dubious paternity, and lived happily for several years. Then, his attention began to drift (as it happened, in the direction of other young men rather than other young women). Marilee sadly divorced him and returned sedately with her (now) two children to her parents' home. Rather soon thereafter, she married a suitable young man who had been married and divorced. Their marriage, as mentioned, is stormy; and they hurl many and often justifiable accusations at each other.

However, there is a deep core of mutual affection, Marilee's third child is clearly her husband's; and the husband, while his eyes may wander, directs them solely at other women. Marilee understands this type of wandering eye, and copes better with it than with her second husband's susceptibilities. In the words of the marriage counseling columns, "This marriage will probably succeed." Her parents have learned to stay out of her affairs, and her sister is so busy with her own life that she does not interfere. Her parents-in-law give Marilee an easy, unconditional love that she says she has never known before. She, they say, represents the daughter they have always wanted.

Cheri: A Late Maturing Ectomorph Cheri is the improbable name given by a semiliterate rural Appalachian mother to her fourth daughter and seventh child. Perhaps it represents a mother's dream and conveys some sort of special attitude the mother held toward Cheri that has helped her rise out of the misery of her childhood and adolescence.

Cheri is a few years older than Marilee, and is a strikingly handsome but not pretty woman. She is superbly dressed and groomed, is very slender, long legged, sexy, and nearly 6 feet tall. She has recently been appointed by a good university as associate professor of elementary education, and is younger than usual for the relative prestige of her position. Her husband (the second) is a successful businessman who has sufficient talent that his firm transfers him without penalty to whatever area her career has taken her to during the years of their marriage. They have one child, and the husband is a good father both to their child and to the daughter of her first marriage.

The author first knew Cheri as a school referral. Her teachers were concerned because she was so withdrawn that they feared serious emotional disorder. She was a moderately good student, and superior in math and science. During her first several visits to the author's office, Cheri simply sat, looked out the office window, and made monosyllabic comments and even those only in answer to direct questions.

Eventually she volunteered the story of her life. Her parents had come to the city to find a more adequate living than their barren mountain farm had provided. They veered between acute poverty and borderline circumstances, and lived in a really bad white slum. The father had taken to drink and other women, and the mother had retreated into apathetic despair over her problems. By this time, the problem included four children younger than Cheri. Cheri was ignored by her peers. She was plain, very tall and slat thin, "talked hillbilly," and possessed insufficient and unattractive clothing. She despaired of ever attracting either a girl or a boy friend, and was openly and starkly envious of her more popular schoolmates. She went through a series of well-hidden infatuations with the rough, tough, often gang-affiliated boys who were the male leaders of her class. It seemed to her that, if she could change a little, they might be available to her, as many were friends of her brothers. But none ever glanced her way.

Counseling seemed to give her some relief and a little perspective, although it did not help her status with her group. As an indirect result of the counseling, some of the teachers "adopted" her, found her a part-time job, and gave her good advice about posture, physical tonus conditioning, diet, dressing, grooming, hair styling, and etiquette. She adopted all suggestions with pathetic eagerness. Despite much improvement in appearance, she was as alone in her class at high school graduation as she had been three years earlier when she was referred.

She was able to attend a small college on a partial tuition scholarship and the promise of a job that had been elicited by her teachers and school administrators. She majored in elementary and early childhood education, performed competently, and blossomed when she worked directly with young children. Her quantitative skills set her in a position superior to that of other students in her curriculum.

Love came after three lonely college years: a singularly ineffective classmate, as lonely and ill at ease as she, courted her. Since he was her first and, in her judgment likely to be her last, suitor, she married him halfway through her senior year. She blossomed after marriage and was considered to be an exceptionally promising potential teacher by the time she was graduated.

She and her husband secured teaching positions in the same school system. She forged ahead rapidly in the next few years. She attended summer school, worked creatively on a master's degree in the sciences, received rapid promotion, and was delegated considerable responsibility within the system. Her master's thesis was published and received favorable professional attention.

Coincident with her becoming pregnant and dropping temporarily out of the profession, the school administration decided not to renew her husband's contract. If renewed at this time, it would have given him tenure. He blamed her for his predicament, accused her of becoming pregnant to tie him down and ruin his career, tried to persuade her to have an abortion, abused her physically, and in general, behaved so badly that she left him. She had her baby alone in a strange town.

She and her husband were reunited for a time after the baby's birth, but she left him permanently when the baby was 1 year old. She forged ahead relentlessly and moved up rapidly both in professional qualifications and in status.

Soon after she received her doctorate, she married her present husband. He had courted her for more than two years. Since then, she and he have lived happy and successful lives, although their marriage arrangement is by no means conventional nor is her role particularly feminine. She helps her family out when she can, and she has encouraged some of her younger brothers and sisters both professionally and financially to continue their educations. She has by no means martyred herself, however; and she confesses to feeling little affection for any of her family except her mother, who died a little after Cheri's second marriage.

She says she likes every aspect of her present life. She seems to be a good mother and, in a way that would be unacceptable to most United States men, she is a good wife. She admits privately that she would give up her husband before she would surrender her career, and she is exaggeratedly independent. Everything of "his" and "hers" is carefully kept separate, including finances. She goes alone to career-related social and professional events, but accompanies him when she can and when his business and social life require it. They entertain jointly, mostly in connection with their vocations, and well.

Despite her husband's aggressive success in business, the husband appears to be rather passive in his relations with Cheri. He takes as much pride in her success as she does in his. By his statement, he would not alter the conditions of their marriage at all, except to "wish we had more time together."

Cheri now says, "I'm glad for my long lanky body and homely face that kept me out of trouble." She ticks off with a certain malicious satisfaction the darlings of her high school days, and keeps almost morbidly close track of them. "This one had to get married, and she has six children now and her husband cheats and is a drunk." "This one had to marry Sue, and he's never got beyond swinging a pick." "This one is in jail," and so on.

Discussion of Marilee and Cheri

For girls as well as boys, the time of physical maturity and type of body and face can have varied effects. Both Marilee and Cheri have encountered problems resulting from the way nature made them. Marilee's physical characteristics played a major role in pushing her too early into too deep involvements. She is only now beginning to be able to cope with the most basic variables of her life. Cheri, like Lonnie, believes that her lanky body kept preserved until circumstances, maturity, her good mind, and educational competence could operate. But during adolescence, her physique, interacting with her miserable life circumstances, helped plunge her into deep and at times near suicidal depressions.

Neither young woman has made a conventional adjustment, but each is getting along rather well. Cheri is performing superbly professionally, although one has the feeling that there are risky aspects of her current state of affairs.

Other girls like Marilee have stayed in unhappy marriages, have become well-known actresses, or prostitutes, or settled as solid wives and mothers. Some like Cheri have committed suicide, or gone over the brink of depression, or have remained lonely spinsters, or have become model wives and mothers who are humbly and undyingly grateful to the men who rescued them from single blessedness and gave them children. Cheri says that, if she had been given the opportunity, this last role is the one she would gladly have filled for her first husband. Perhaps she is correct, although from knowing both of them, it is hard to believe. Of course, rural and urban Appalachia is full of Cheris who have taken another course through life: married and pregnant early and constantly, prematurely aged, seeming too thin and frail to stand up to the burdens they face but, like Cheri and her mother, often amazingly tough.

MOTOR DEVELOPMENT AND PHYSICAL FITNESS

The United States is increasingly a sedentary culture, although during the early 1960s much needed attention and prestige were brought to physical education in promoting physical fitness. Almost everyone gives the same positive endorsement for a goal of physical fitness and good body condition. Despite episodic waves of enthusiasm such as a vogue for jogging that exists as this is written, deplorably few Americans apply principles of physical fitness to themselves. Any person, by the time he is 45 or so, watches his friends die off from cardiac conditions or hobble around with wretched sacroiliacs. It is probable that appropriate physical fitness programs that include proper diet, abstention from smoking, and so on, could prolong life for years, and prevent a person from a life of nagging or acute pain.

Thus, despite the national admiration of sports, Americans are principally spectators, often not even making the effort to go to the game itself, but content to watch it on television or to read about it.

Horrocks (1969), after summarizing the convincing evidence that adequate to superior motor ability and its presumed accompaniment, physical fitness, are positively related to the general adjustment and popularity of adolescent boys in particular and to some degree of adolescent girls as well, concludes:

> ... a sane, well-rounded program free of exploitation is needed for *everyone* in a reasonably operated school system. Schools might inaugurate athletic programs permitting wide participation for *fun and health* instead of concentrating on a highly specialized program of competitive interscholastic sports oriented firmly toward the Armageddon of a "tough" schedule. A competitive interscholastic program picks boys who are good at sports and may relegate the rest to the spectators' bench.... (pp. 440–441)

Motor Ability

It seems likely that physical proficiency is not a single general ability, but rather breaks down into a number of broad factors that are not highly correlated with each other (Fleishman, 1964). Factor analysis—a statistical device for isolating the components of a trait or function of the type discussed for male sexuality in the preceding chapter—reveals three factors that enter into motor performance (Seashore, 1942): fine motor abilities; dynamic gross motor abilities; and postural steadiness.

The first of these factors may be tested by speed and accuracy, for example, by fitting small pegs into a pegboard or buttoning buttons into a buttonhole, or tapping. Dynamic motor abilities come into play in games and field and track sports. Postural steadiness includes balance, both while standing still (as standing on one foot with the eyes closed) and while moving (as walking on the edge of a 2-by-4-inch board). Such real life skills as carrying a loaded tray or a full glass of water also involve postural steadiness. Strength enters into motor abilities, and it may be separated into dynamic strength of the sort involved in wrestling or throwing a baseball, and static dynamometric strength, as in the strength of one's grip (Horrocks, 1969).

The Oseretsky Tests of Motor Proficiency (Sloan, 1955) are among the more widely used tests of motor proficiency. First published in Russian in 1923, they have been widely employed and much revised in the United States. The current form is called the Lincoln-Oseretsky Motor Development Scale; the tests are given to those ranging in age from 6 to 16 years. The tests purport to measure five functions: general static coordination; dynamic manual coordination; general dynamic coordination; speed; and asynkinesia (precision of movement).

Illustratively, Hartman (1943) finds intercorrelations between .36 and .56 for young children among their performances on the five gross motor tests of hurdle jump, jump and reach, standing broad jump, baseball throw, and the 35-yard dash. Lauten (1968) finds both gross and fine motor skills to be correlated only about .15 with intelligence.

Sloan (1955) has worked with the Lincoln-Oseretsky Motor Development Scale. One item requires the subject to shot-put a ball with his right hand so as to hit a chest-high 10-inch square target 8 feet away from his forward foot. About 10 percent of both boys and girls are able to pass this test at age 6. At age 14, about 70 percent of boys can pass it, and about 62 percent of girls. However, at 14, the percentage of boys passing still shows a rising curve, while percentage of girls passing has begun to drop off at age 13, at which time girls are actually superior to boys.

Another item requires the subject to jump and strike his heels simultaneously with his hands while he is in the air, on the first trial. At age 6, 10 percent of girls pass the item, but about 4 percent of boys. At age 14, about two-thirds of the boys pass it, and about 60 percent of the girls. However, up to age 13, more girls at each year age level pass than boys.

Sloan's results suggest that girls reach maturity in motor abilities earlier than boys. Espenschade's (1940) results support this conclusion: Espenschade used as her tests the 50-yard dash, the jump and reach, target throw, broad jump, distance throw, and the Brace Test. This test is made up of twenty tests that vary greatly in difficulty. Easier items are walking in a straight line, heel to toe, or jumping into the air and slapping both heels with hands behind back. Difficult items are jumping one foot through a loop that is made by grasping the other foot in the opposite hand, or squatting on the left foot with the right foot extended forward, then rising again to an upright position.

For the six criteria employed by Espenschade, girls had reached their peak performance at age 15$\frac{1}{5}$ years for everything but jump and reach and the total number of the Brace Tests passed. In the last, their improvement had essentially peaked, only a tiny average gain being registered at later ages up to past 17 years. Boys, on the other hand, continued to register marked gains up to ages 17-plus in everything but target throw.

For the age ranges she studied (12½ years to 17⅖ years), Espenschade reports essentially zero correlations among girls between age and motor performance. Age actually shows a low negative correlation for dash and broad jump. However, for everything but target throw, motor performance and age are positively correlated among boys, the correlations ranging from −.07 for age and target throw, .27 for number of Brace Tests passed and age, and up to .71 for age and length of broad jump.

As Jersild (1963, pp. 97–98) says, and as is borne out by the figures given above, "Girls 'mature' in this fashion earlier than boys, except, perhaps, in their interest in dancing . . . girls also reach their maximum capacity for physical activity earlier than boys." Implicit in Jersild's summation is the fact adduced by the present author that part of the superiority of boys and men in the motor area is motivational in nature.

The term physical fitness is even more difficult to define than motor ability. To one, it may mean no more than absence of any physical abnormality and debility; another may define it as "within the normal limits of strength, speed, and endurance for one's appropriate age level and sex." Measures of speed of cardiac and respiratory recovery after prescribed periods of exercise comprise another definition. To an Olympic coach, his man or woman is fit only when a record at the mile, or the high hurdles, or the high jump, or 220-meter swim can be approached. Cureton (1964) and Fleishman (1964) have perhaps as much to say on the subject that is constructive as any current authors, and their work should be consulted by readers who wish to check into the matter in depth.

From a practical point of view, physical fitness is a state of good health and reasonable tonus such that the regular duties in one's life can be executed without undue fatigue. Additionally, extra undertakings such as moderate sports activity, a few hours of physical work, and other things that even the most sedentary are occasionally called on to do can be performed without great strain or risk to the health. Physical fitness involves a regime of good health care, sensible diet, and some program of moderate activity designed to keep up muscle tonus in all parts of the body.

Cureton (1964) summarizes the evidence that United States physical education fails dramatically in producing physically fit youth in the sense that between about ages 10 and 17 years boys and girls perform less well than British, East African, and Japanese youth. Some of the measures are pull-ups, sit-ups, and circulatory-respiratory fitness as judged by the 600-yard run-walk.

Cureton concludes his summary by quoting Noguchi (p. 3): "The danger was now in Japanese youth losing their fitness by trying to live like American youth."

During late childhood and adolescence, the pattern for United States children and youth is that gain in muscular strength is greater

Table 5.1 *Increases in strength of grip from third to twelfth grade*

Grade Level	Ethnic Groups			Total
	White	Hispaño	Afro-American	
Three to Six				
Boys	50%	100%	45%	65%
Girls	65%	100%	75%	80%
Six to Nine				
Boys	85%	105%	60%	80%
Girls	55%	55%	35%	50%
Nine to Twelve				
Boys	50%	30%	75%	50%
Girls	5%	5%	40%	15%

(Adapted from Goss, 1968.)

than in physical size. H. E. Jones' (1949b) longitudinal California Growth Study data show that four-fifths of adult strength is gained between the ages of 6 and 18, but only one-third of height.

Illustratively, Goss (1968) measured the hand dynamometer grip (represented to the children as a strength tester) of a total of 192 third, ninth, and twelfth grade students. He had eight students each of boys and girls for each grade level within three groups, white, Hispaño, and Afro-American.

Table 5.1 is adapted from Goss' data and, rounded to the nearest 5 percent in each case, shows the percentage of change in strength of grip for both boys and girls from one of the target grade levels to another for all three groups.

Even from the rough extrapolations made from Goss' data, the trend mentioned by Jones is evident, as is the sex difference pointed out by Jersild. As they moved into adolescence (between sixth and ninth grade), boys almost doubled their gripping strength (an increase of about 80 percent, gaining more than they had between grades three and six (about 65 percent), or more than they did as they were consolidating adolescence (about 50 percent gain between grades nine and twelve).

The picture is very different for girls, who nearly doubled their strength between grades three and six, increased it by only about half between grades six and nine; and by only about 15 percent between grades nine and twelve.

In Table 5.2 (also adapted from Goss) data are shown for strength of boys and girls taking the dynamometer test. Of the forty-eight boys and girls in each grade, sixteen are white, sixteen Hispaño, and sixteen Afro-American. There is little difference between the white and Afro-American subjects except that the grade twelve Afro-American girls are stronger than the grade twelve white girls. At each grade level, both the boys and girls from the Hispaño group are weaker than the white and Afro-American groups. It can be seen that the twelfth grade boys in the

Table 5.2

Dynamometer hand grip
(twenty-four boys, twenty-four girls in each grade)

Grade Level	Mean Grip in Pounds
Three	
Boys	31
Girls	23
Twelve	
Boys	136
Girls	71

(Adapted from Goss, 1968.)

Goss study were almost four and one-half times as strong as the third grade boys; but that the twelfth grade girls were only slightly more than three times as strong as the third grade girls.

In the third grade, boys were about one and one-third times as strong as girls, but twelfth grade boys were nearly twice as strong as twelfth grade girls. Since strength is less highly esteemed by girls, it is possible that some of the sex differences are motivational. At grade six, for example, one may expect from other data that Goss' girls are at least as tall and heavy as, or taller and heavier than, his boys, yet the boys demonstrate greater grip (an average of about 50 pounds for boys and 41 pounds for girls, or a superiority of more than 20 percent for boys over girls). However, Goss' eight randomly selected Afro-American sixth grade girls averaged only 4 pounds less grip strength than the boys from the same ethnic group in the sixth grade (51 pounds for the boys, 47 pounds for the girls, for an advantage of boys over girls of 8½ percent). Since these numbers are small and thus subject to much sampling error, little attention should be paid to the ethnic differences by grade.

Goss' data fit well with Jones' (1939) data. Jones found that boys are about twice as strong at age 11 as at age 6, and that they again double their strength as measured by hand grip between age 11 and age 16 years. The girls in Jones' sample increase in strength by only about 50 percent from age 11 to age 16 years. At 17½ (approximately the same age as Goss' subjects), Jones' boys showed a right-hand grip averaging 123 pounds, and his girls, 79 pounds. All three groups of Goss' twelfth grade boys were as strong as or stronger than Jones' group (white boys averaged 141 pounds; Hispaño boys 123 pounds; Afro-American boys 144 pounds). Two of the three groups of Goss' girls, however, showed less grip strength than Jones' white girls. The white girls in the Goss sample averaged a grip of 66 pounds, the Hispaño girls, 58 pounds, and the Afro-American girls, 89 pounds. The greater strength shown by Goss' boys may be due to sampling difference, or to the earlier maturity shown by youth as a function of the secular trend in which youth matures earlier with each generation. Nearly thirty years elapsed between the Jones and the Goss studies. But Goss' white girls were considerably weaker than Jones' girls.

Espenschade and Meleny (1961) contibute further data about the course of physical fitness from one to another generation. They compared Oakland, California, eight grade 13-year-old boys and girls attending school in 1958–1959 with those attending school in 1934–1935 (a twenty-four-year span). The young people in school in the late 1950s were, as expected, significantly taller and heavier than those in the same schools had been twenty-four years previously. On eight tests of motor proficiency, the girls of the 1950s surpassed those of the 1930s in two, were inferior in three, and were equal in three. Latter-day boys, when compared with boys in the 1930s, excelled in five of the tests, were inferior in two, and were equal in one. Girls, in short, were about holding their own, boys to a modest degree improving in motor performance. The eight tests were: 50-yard dash, standing broad jump, jump and reach, softball throw for distance, Brace Test of stunts, and three dynamometric strength tests (grip, push, and pull).

The Meaning of Physical Skills to Adolescents

To some degree, the importance of physical skills varies with culture. McCandless and Ali (1966) investigated athletic skills and their interrelationships in three populations of ninth grade girls, all of middle or upper-middle class. One group of ninth graders came from a sex-segregated Muslim school in Lahore, West Pakistan; another from a sex-segregated Roman Catholic day and boarding school in the midwestern United States; and the third from a coeducational college preparatory public school in the midwestern United States.

Each girl was rated from 1, a best player or performer, to 5, never plays the game, for skill at volleyball, tennis, broad jump, and sprint. The scores were summed for an over-all index. For the Pakistani girls, it was necessary to substitute netball for volleyball and badminton for tennis. Actual performance for some of the girls in the cooeducational school correlated between .61 and .73 with the buddy ratings. Thus, substantial accuracy may be inferred.

The samples differed significantly from each other in some of the relationships for physical skills: For the coeducational group, physical skills and popularity among girls correlated a barely significant .28, whereas for the Catholic girls the correlation was .66 and for the Pakistani girls, .58. The authors suggest that, in the coeducational school, girls value other girls for their *social* prowess; in sex-segregated schools, the successful competitor for anything is more highly valued by her classmates.

To speculate, it is possible that the importance to the girls in the two unisexual schools of the typically masculine characteristic of high level athletic ability is a function of the homosocial environment: With no boys around, athletic girls take the place in other girls' esteem that is usually held by boys when the setting is coeducational.

Another suggestion emerges from the McCandless and Ali results: In a country where women must fight for their right to emerge from the traditional role of deep inferiority, girls who compete successfully are highly valued, regardless of the nature of competition: For example, popularity and school grades correlate .64 with each other among the Pakistani Muslim girls, but only .40 and .30 respectively for the coeducational and girls' school populations. Intelligence and popularity correlate

.56 among the Pakistani girls, only .04 among the Catholic girls, and intermediately (.39) for the college-bound coeducational girls.

For the two United States samples, correlations between physical skills and academic aptitude (intelligence) were essentially zero, but for the Pakistani girls the correlation was significant at less than the .01 level (.41). For none of the three groups were physical skills and school grades significantly related, although the correlations for the Catholic and Muslim girls were in the .20s. It was expected that anxiety test scores and physical skills would be negatively related to each other, but this did not prove to be the case (none of the correlations was significantly different from zero).

In this connection, it is interesting to compare the results obtained by Coleman (1961), who worked with midwestern United States high school students; and Friesen (1968), who conducted studies similar to Coleman's with large numbers (15,000 from nineteen schools) of Canadian tenth through twelfth grade students. Coleman found that 31 percent of his boys wanted to be remembered as brilliant students, but 45 percent wished to leave a record as athletic stars. Coleman's wording, of course, is unfortunate in the context of United States culture: A brilliant student label, particularly among adolescents, is often equated with being a grind; but an athletic star is *really* a star.

Friesen, not breaking down his sample by sex (in this case, the sample included about 10,000 students from a large western Canadian city), finds that characteristics considered most necessary for membership in a leading crowd ranked in the following order, with the percentages of those responding given in parentheses after each characteristic: friendliness (51.3); good looks (25.4); money (13.8); athletic ability (7.0); and academic excellence (2.5). In other words, for Canadian students, interpersonal relations are clearly most highly valued by more than twice as many students as voted for any other characteristic; and both athletic ability and academic excellence come in a poor fourth and fifth (academic excellence is *fifth*).

When this same sample was asked what were the characteristics most important for success in life, athletics sank to last place, only 0.5 percent choosing it as most important. Personality ranked first (57.4 percent listed it as most important). Friendliness and academic achievement ranked almost together with 17.7 and 15.6 percent of the students respectively listing them as most important. Money was chosen by 8.8 percent.

Items this sample considered most important for popularity showed "athletic star" ranking far higher than "high grades, honor roll," with 19 and 4 percent, respectively, choosing them as most important. "Having a nice car" was chosen by 13 percent.

For their "choice to be remembered by," this sample of about 10,000 western Canadian urban students (not separated according to sex) apparently differed sharply from Coleman's sample: 44 percent of them wished to be remembered as being most popular.

When it comes to choosing characteristics most satisfying in school life, 43 percent of Coleman's boys and girls chose academic achievement. Seventeen percent of the boys but only 8 percent of the girls chose athletics; and 40 percent of the boys and 48 percent of the girls chose popularity. When asked to choose characteristics that were most important for their future, 83 percent of the boys and 80 percent of the girls chose academic achievement; 3 percent of the boys chose athletics and 2 percent of the girls (cheerleading, in the girls' cases). As a future goal, popularity was desired by 14 percent of the boys and 18 percent of the girls.

Jersild (1963) reports data from Tannenbaum's (1959) dissertation, in which more than 300 each of eleventh grade boys and girls were asked to rate hypothetical students on some combination of intellectual brilliance, studiousness, and athleticism. Students who were athletic were ranked higher in all cases than students who were nonathletic. Dramatically in last place (an average ranking of 1.58 of a possible range from +46 to −46) was the "brilliant, studious, nonathletic" youngster. That it is the "grind" rather than the brilliance that is significant is indicated by the fact that top ranking (average rank of 31.36) was held by the "brilliant, *nonstudious*, athletic" youngster (italics are the present author's).

Adams (1964) presents evidence concerning additional student opinions, namely, not what students value most highly but what they worry about the most. It may be guessed that their worries center on those things that they think will be most important in their future lives. He studied 4000 students, about equally divided by sex, from Philadelphia and environs. They ranged in age from 10 to 19 years, and came from thirty different schools. Thirty-five percent of the boys and 23 percent of the girls gave schoolwork as their major problem; but only 4 percent of the boys and 2 percent of the girls listed as a major worry anything to do with sports and recreation.

There were few differences for students from the same age and sex groups, regardless of the type of school they attended. However, as might be expected, the suburbanites (upwardly mobile and ambitious) worried most frequently about academic and school problems.

The tentative conclusion may be drawn that as of the here and now, adolescent high school youth, and particularly boys, place considerable value on skill in athletics. That this value may be superficial and transitory is suggested by Adams' results: If they have it, evidence indicates they like it; if they do not have it, they would like to have it; but, if they do not have it, they do not worry seriously about it. The picture is dramatically different for academic success: It brings little glory on the contemporary scene, particularly if it must be gained by hard and dogged work (Tannenbaum's "studiousness"), but they value it and, if they do not have academic success, it is a major worry.

Both Friesen's Canadian results and Adams' Philadelphia results suggest that youth realistically consider interpersonal relations more important than athletic skills. As noted, Friesen found friendliness listed as most important for membership in the leading crowd by more than twice as many students as listed any other attribute. Adams found three times as many boys worried over interpersonal relations as worry over sports and recreation; and almost ten times as many girls. Girls' greater involvement with popularity and interpersonal relations, when compared with boys', is indicated by the fact that 19 percent of Adams girls worry most about interpersonal relations, compared with 23 percent who worry about school performance. Twelve percent of boys have most serious problems in the interpersonal relations area, but 35 percent of them encounter their most serious problem with academics.

The differences by sex in Adams' sample are probably due to two things: Boys place more emphasis on *doing* (academics) than *being* (relationships of an interpersonal sort); but at the same time, objectively, they more frequently encounter difficulty in their school work than do girls. These differences in emphasis (doing as compared with being) fit well with Douvan and Adelson's results. Differences in academic achievement by sex are a matter of public record in the office of any elementary, junior high, or senior high school.

To summarize, Coleman (1961) is probably correct: The high value placed on athletics, particularly by boys, is a function of the high school social system. This in turn reflects the broader society. The boy who stars on the playing field wins not only personal glory but is publicly acknowledged as having helped his school to be successful. The boy who gets an A receives glory only from his parents, his academic teachers, and perhaps himself.

However, when it comes down to making a hard evaluation of what will be helpful in future life, boys themselves devaluate athletics and upgrade academics. Perhaps, then, society's response to the youth studies should be to consider revising "the system" to fit with the long term reality of academic ability. Certainly long term reality for either a boy or a girl is not particularly well served by two or three athletic or cheerleading letters, but would be better served by a well toned and coordinated body in addition to soundly incorporated habits for keeping it that way.

SUMMARY

Generally, but with allowance for complex interrelations, and with the evidence clearer for boys than girls, it can be concluded that possession of early maturing mesomorphic bodies helps adolescents, particularly males, in resolving the personal-social problems encountered in adolescence.

Well-established stereotypes exist favoring mesomorphic body builds both among boys and girls. These stereotypes undoubtedly ease social-personal problem solving among mesomorphic adolescents, but are particularly inimical for endomorph youth.

The relations between early maturing, mesomorphy, and good personal-social adjustment *may* be unique to United States culture.

Even in United States culture, advantages accruing to early maturing and mesomorphic boys and girls may be confined to middle- and upper-middle-class youth, although the evidence is by no means clear. Strong, early maturing, and well-coordinated bodies *may* make it easier for youth among the very poor to succeed in an environment characterized almost exclusively by illegitimate opportunities, and on a "buy now, pay later" basis that is maladaptive for later life.

The importance of motor skills and athletic prowess varies by culture. The "athletic star" phenomenon seems to be superficial and transitory. Although both young males and females value athletics, youth's deeper concerns seem to be with more durable attributes, such as interpersonal relations and academic ability.

Adolescence, particularly for boys, is a time of rapid acquisition of strength and refined complex motor skills. Girls "mature" earlier than boys in these respects.

There is evidence to suggest that schools do too little to develop or habituate sound habits for preserving physical fitness among either girls or boys. Little improvement over a twenty-four-year period has been demonstrated, particularly among girls.

6

The Community, Adolescents, and Deviant Behavior

INTRODUCTION

Psychology and sociology are the two disciplines that are mainly concerned with the nature and behavior of man. In the preceding chapters, emphasis has been about equally placed on social expectations and rules. Variations of and individual accommodations to these expectations and rules, determined by such factors as sex, social class, and time of reaching adolescence, have introduced the reader to some sociological aspects of adolescence.

The point of view throughout the rest of this book is strongly psychological. Yet no individual (except possibly the hermit or the psychotic) can shape his life independently of the social world in which he lives. Next to his family and his school, the community influences an adolescent the most directly, perhaps even more so than any other factor, since the community's organization, rules, and provisions for growth and development dictate much of the shape and function both of an adolescent's family and of his educational institutions.

In this chapter, then, a rather sociological view of the community and its influence on adolescents is presented. The more psychologically oriented chapters which are presented later can be viewed logically within this sociological framework.

WHAT IS A COMMUNITY? From a number of possibilities, the definition of community that best serves present purposes is simple: It is the answer one gives to a stranger when asked where he comes from. At the time of writing, the author answers this question, "Atlanta, Georgia." Asked, as one often is, "Where did you grow up?" the author answers, "St. John, Kansas." According to the present frame of reference, both Atlanta and St. John are communities, that is, they are circumscribed theaters of operation in which people eat, sleep, seek recreation and socialization, earn a living, suffer, are born, marry, and die. Several of these activities can be performed with more variety and style in one place as opposed to the other, but to its citizens each is a community.

Rural and Urban Communities It seems to make little difference to young children where they live. They take their parents, their homes, and their communities rather for granted, do not question them, and seldom seek to transcend or move beyond them. Their "cognitive organization," according to Piaget, does not include the idea of community. At adolescence, however, the average United States child, particularly the urban majority child, moves from his neighborhood—the narrow segment of his community—to a junior high school for which his neighborhood elementary school is only one of several feeders. Two or three years later, he is likely to encounter an even broader spectrum of his community as he goes on to high school for which, in turn, his junior high school is only one of several feeders.

As he makes these moves, the adolescent is likely (perhaps more likely if he is white) to encounter children who have grown up very differently from him, who are of a different color and religion, whose parents have different educational backgrounds and values or much more or much less money than his parents and other parents in his childhood neighborhood possess. At the same time he begins to make these discoveries, he is more and more often exposed on his own to the different faces of the community. He travels alone or with a few friends. He shops on his own. He begins to act in his own right, and he is reacted to as an individual who is responsible for his own behavior.

People want to perform their major life functions in a setting that provides them with legitimacy, ease, flexibility, individuality and personal safety, challenge, and opportunity for self-improvement; people want a chance to demonstrate that they are competent. Even more so than adults, youth judge their communities by the degree to which these criteria are met. Mature and old people have secured what they wanted or have to some degree become habituated and resigned to not having what they once wanted. They cling to their communities, for the most part, regardless of their frustrations.[1] But youth, if blocked, leave home. St. John, Kansas, and other little towns like it have few young people. Atlanta and most other large cities have more young people than they know what to do with.

In general, communities that offer many legitimate opportunities attract youth, and communities that do not, lose them. Little farming towns all over the nation are dying. St. John, Kansas, retains some vitality because it is a county seat. But as the county system dies or becomes larger and more efficient (it must inevitably do one or the other), St. John, like thousands of other little towns, will also die. Automation of farm labor, and the attendant increase in size and decrease in number of farms, coupled with the farm surplus program have doomed the little farm shopping centers of the United States. In 1900, more than 60 percent of the population lived on farms, and the farming towns thrived on their trade. Now, fewer than 10 percent live on farms, and even they go further on the new roads in their new automobiles to buy where the goods are fresher, more varied, and usually of better quality and cheaper.

Those who are of middle or many years, and many of the young who have always lived in cities, profess a nostalgia for the clean and simple life of the farm. The youth of farms and small towns typically feel differently. Douvan and Adelson (1966) report that their farm sample is one of the least happy and least-able-to-cope-with adolescents of any of the subgroupings of their United States sample. Rhodes (1964) finds that farm youth attending rural schools score highest (percentage above the median) of any of his groups from among a total sample of 960 white Tennessee high school seniors on anomia (alienation). These youth report severe alienation and discouragement because of the great discrepancy between their aspirations and their apparent chances of success.

Movies, radio, and television have placed farms and small towns in poor perspective for youth who live on or in them. Nor do small towns offer youth the adequate opportunities to move ahead that cities seem to offer. There are neither kicks nor opportunities for youth in small towns.

It is a fiction, of course, that cities offer opportunity to all youth. A city may be more merciless to unskilled and uneducated people, particularly if they belong to a disadvantaged minority group, than small towns and rural areas. But small towns and the country can be cruel too: The subjects of the Hodges, McCandless, and Spicker (1969) study were 5-year-old children from the most disadvantaged stratum in several small, central and southern Indiana towns.

These towns are neat looking, dotted with well-painted churches; the streets are paved, the yards on Main Street are green and well tended. Life looks very peaceful and very good. But study of a disadvantaged group involved in this research reveals its cruel isolation and neglect, and the hopelessness of its members' lives. The children's parents who were included in the study were fairly stable people: Their time residing

---

[1] Like all flat statements, this one must be modified: Many old people retire to places that are sunnier or warmer or dryer or wetter than the places where they lived their earlier lives. The average family moves about once every five years (Moore, 1966). Thus, any given person's sense of community is likely to be more fluid than it was a generation ago.

in the house in which they were living when the study began averaged almost four years. However, the project social worker described this average house as a shack. It had four rooms and housed a family of seven. Almost one-fourth of the sample's homes had no running water, more than one-third of the houses lacked indoor plumbing, and nearly half the mothers cooked with coal or wood.

The average father within this sample was 34 years old, the average mother 30. He had married at 21, she at 17½.[2] The average couple had five living children at the time of the study. It could have been confidently predicted that most would have still more children. The parents themselves had come from families that average a fraction more than seven living children. The average father had dropped out of school half way through eighth grade, the average mother had finished only ninth grade, or dropped out in the middle of her ninth grade year. In this area, where the rate of arrest and conviction for crime is very low, 3 percent of the fathers were actually in prison — a rather high percentage.

Occupationally, all were unskilled or semiskilled laborers or were unemployed. Even though this is "Bible Belt" country where family stability is highly valued, about one-fifth of the fathers at one time or another had deserted their families.[3]

All the professional people conducting this study lived in the same towns as the children and their parents. All concur in the following note made by one of the workers:

> These communities are rigidly stereotyped and stratified. These children's older brothers and sisters have had difficulty in school, and they will be expected to have. Their parents have been community problems, and are regarded by the community as without worth. The community makes no bones about wishing it could get rid of the entire family, from the grandparents on down to the youngest children.

The authors of the study, to their surprise, found that there were no community services for these families. No one in an official capacity, public, private, eleemosynary, or other, even knew these disadvantaged families existed! It was necessary to go from door to door to find them, yet there were dozens of them in each of the little towns where the study was carried out. One of the towns, actually, was the home of a major university, but its record was no better than others. These families were not poor and Black: They were poor and of old, white, Anglo-Protestant stock, Appalachian in origin and often in tradition.

Families like this abound both in small towns and in big cities, but the back roads of Appalachia, the rural south, the western deserts, and the northern woods all lead to their homes. Some poor and forgotten families are Appalachian, some "poor white trash," some Afro-American, some Hispano, some Indian.

---

[2]This arithmetic discrepancy results because many mothers had remarried men older than their first husbands.

[3]However, about one-fourth of all United States marriages ends in divorce. It may be that the rural poor cannot afford to leave home.

Criteria of Community Opportunity

Every thoughtful person has at one time or another evaluated his community according to the opportunity it offers him. Long ago the author evaluated the farm and its shopping center, St. John, *for him*. He left it at age 17. He was able to. Many, such as the fathers and mothers described above, and probably their children after them, can not leave; others go in waves. It is estimated that since World War II almost 6½ million Blacks have left the South, most of them seeking opportunity in the big cities of the North.

Cloward and Ohlin (1960) have analyzed communities and opportunity systematically. Basically, they found that a community is successful to the degree that it offers legitimate opportunity to its citizens, unsuccessful to the degree that it offers illegitimate opportunity. Cloward and Ohlin believe that delinquency arises partly from an excess of illegitimate opportunity, but more so because of a lack of legitimate opportunity. Youth will use legitimate opportunities in preference to illegitimate ones when the former are available. They will pursue illegitimate opportunities such as delinquency only when the community provides too few chances to advance themselves (to be competent in a socially desirable sense) legitimately. The life story of Ted in Chapter 5 is an illustration of such a boy and such a community.

Cloward and Ohlin argue that deviant behavior is likely to arise when there is a marked discrepancy between those aspirations which are considered desirable and realistic by a culture and those actual means by which such aspirations can be achieved legitimately. However, the commitment to delinquency, if that is the path chosen, depends on illegitimate opportunities being available to and impinging on the youth.

Durkheim (1897, translated 1951) coined the term *anomie* (roughly, "alienation"). Relative normlessness (lack of clear norms), he believed, was likely to lead to unlimited aspirations, which, if not met, result in alienation. Alienation may take the guise of feelings of formlessness, powerlessness, isolation, or any combination of the three. Under normlessness, goals are no longer clearly regulated, and there results a constant pressure for deviant behavior in pursuit of insatiable and unlegitimized ambition. Such conditions may exist in rapidly industrializing societies, under economic conditions of boom or bust, where vast unexploited markets exist or, possibly, limitless frontiers for expansion and opportunity. To insure its survival, industrial society emphasizes and encourages strong success goals, which in turn lend themselves to developing unquenchable ambition. If blocked, ambition exerts pressure toward social instability and individual deviant behavior. To Durkheim, in short, deviance develops from *anomie* that arises when social controls are ineffective in the face of overweening or unsatisfiable ambition, or both.

Merton (1961) systematized Durkheim's thinking and extended his theory. Merton concentrates on discrepancies between the goals society says an individual *should* have (as in this success- and competence-oriented society) and the structure society provides for individuals and groups so they may realize these goals. A moment's thought is sufficient to realize that youth among the very poor and most particularly among prejudiced-against ethnic minorities are likely to suffer acutely from alienation, and to understand why Rhodes' rural youth scored high in *anomie*.

Merton differs from Durkheim in that he believes youth become alienated because of a breakdown between cultural goals and legitimate ways of reaching them; but he puts little stress on breakdown in control of social goals as such. Since legitimate access to expected goals increases as social class increases, Merton predicts that alienation will be greater the lower the social class.

In short, to refer back to Chapter 1, feelings of alienation are frequent, perhaps inevitable, consequences of unresolvable frustrations. Apathy may result or, if the opportunity is afforded, such accumulated anger may be turned against the social system.

COMMUNITY AND OPPORTUNITY HYPOTHESIS STUDIES

As explained by the discussion in Chapter 1, justification for the special treatment of adolescence comes from demonstrating that the period has unique psychobiological characteristics and that it is sufficiently different psychosocially from other developmental epochs to justify being treated separately from general developmental psychology. Chapters 3, 4, and 5 emphasized psychobiological uniqueness and the adaptations adolescents make to biological changes. This chapter dwells almost exclusively on psychosocial uniqueness. However, it was made clear in the two previous chapters that there is inevitable, necessary, and constant interaction between biological and social-psychological aspects of development. This fact must not be forgotten.

Among the unique aspects of adolescence is the special openness of youth to new learning and to opportunity. In malign settings, this openness to reality becomes vulnerability. In either benevolent or malign settings the community opportunity hypothesis comes into play. For reasons of interest and importance, detailed treatment is given in the rest of this chapter to four representative studies of the community opportunity hypothesis. As the studies are presented, some important special methodological considerations are discussed that were not covered in Chapter 2, because the considerations could better be applied directly here to particular studies.

The first three studies—Landis and Scarpitti; Short, Rivera, and Tennyson; and Tallman—relate directly to the psychology of change and the psychology of self concept development. As the studies are discussed, it will be seen how American society first inculcates in almost all its members "The American Dream" of success, which portrays every boy as a President and each girl as a Cinderella. By adolescence, this dream has been firmly internalized and, while adolescents realize that the world is not entirely at their disposal, almost all of them have exceptionally high hopes for their futures. Such hopes seem to characterize all social classes, races, and ethnic groups. For example, Han and Doby (1966) find in their study of vocational dreams that Black and white high school and college youth all share very high aspirations but are progressively more pessimistic about reaching their goals according to whether they are middle class and white or relatively disadvantaged and Black. Han and Doby actually find some tendency for goals to be higher the less likely their attainment.

During this time of physical and social change, society tells adolescents that it is also time for them to grow up, to focus upon their futures, and to take action to make their futures good. By and large, adolescents accept these goals and tasks. But what if society denies the chance to make good? In the studies that follow, some of the consequences of such social denial are explored.[4]

The studies that follow are within the framework of a psychology of change and frustration. As seen in Chapter 1, change in itself is often alarming and consequently frustrating. It is more comfortable to stay as one is even though the way he is may not be good for him. If one accepts the constructive although not always realistic goals society sets for him—that is, to make people proud of him, to be somebody, to actualize himself, to become competent—and then one is blocked by society, the frustration is acute. Frustration acts as a drive and leads to a wide variety of behaviors—anger and aggression, withdrawal and passivity, reduction of efficiency, fantasy, redoubled efforts to reduce the frustrating condition—as has been shown.

When society provides no legitimate opportunities, youth are likely to take advantage of the illegitimate ones that are available.[5] For some youth, exploiting illegitimate opportunities may be the only solution that is open to them. Exploiting such opportunities at least allows a youth to do *something*; otherwise, total retreat from life and self would be the only solution. The exploitation of illegitimate opportunities not only allows progress of a sort toward a goal, albeit a socially devalued goal, but also allows a youth to strike back and to vent the anger engendered by the blockage and frustration society has imposed on him.

The first two studies that follow represent sociological approaches to the problem of opportunity. The third study is an experimental social-psychological investigation of opportunity and behavior in the laboratory. The fourth study explores personal-social dynamics in cheating and is less directly related to the community than the first three.

[4]In this paragraph, the passive or inanimate noun *society* is linked twice to active verbs—"society tells" and "society . . . denies." This common usage is wrong both grammatically and in the message it may convey to the reader and, more broadly, in the message it may convey to members of a society. The usage is actually a type of shorthand. It is important to be clear about the fact that such terms as community and society are not superorganic. Communities and broader societies are anchored in human interaction. Both the restriction and extension of human opportunity are human enterprises. They are socialized, maintained, strengthened, or weakened by *individuals* during manifold, small, large, simple, and complex interactions with each other. A community is a relatively limited abstraction from such interaction. A society is a broader and larger abstraction.

All the social concepts employed throughout this book should be anchored in human interaction. Forgetting interaction, it would be easy to call upon some amorphous, highly abstract powers, such as "The Establishment," "The System," or, perhaps "The Communists," "The Birchers," "Black Power," or "The White Backlash." These terms possess meaning only in their relationships to people interacting with one another, and usually in situations that demand solutions difficult to find.

Thus, the common reaction people have when faced with "That's the way society is. What can I do about it?" is an evasion. The behavior of the person making such a statement, multiplied by all those who make it, *is* society.

[5]An example of this is the case of Ted, presented in Chapter 5.

The Landis and Scarpitti Study

Landis and Scarpitti (1965) are checking to see if youth who reject middle-class values and who see few legitimate but many illegitimate opportunities open to them are likely to be delinquent or delinquency prone. The authors combine sociological and psychological methods in their research. They secured the cooperation of a large number of children and adolescents (1545 in all), and classified them according to racial group (Black and white) and social class background. They then administered tests and questionnaires.

Landis and Scarpitti employ a social criterion for one of their special subpopulations, *delinquents*. Their 515 delinquents are all boys who have been caught in delinquency, convicted by the courts, and sentenced to a boys' industrial school. Such a population is very mixed, and the only things its members have in common are sex (male) and youth (ages 13 to 18). The crimes committed vary greatly in seriousness, and the boys include a disproportionate number of lower-class and Afro-American youth.

Some Considerations of the Study's Research Techniques The authors assume causality: Membership in one or the other sex or ethnic or social class or delinquency versus nondelinquency group *causes* the result. This is to say that, if middle-class boys, when contrasted to lower-class boys, behave in a certain manner, then factors associated with social class have caused the finding. These factors may include poverty, poor education, more aggressive ways of behaving that are sanctioned by parents, and so on. Social class, like intelligence, is used as a classification concept. It subsumes and, like *community*, is a form of shorthand of the operation of many people, and social and personal forces that affect behavior.

Landis and Scarpitti never actually measure real life behavior. They construct and/or administer tests and questionnaires. Scores from these instruments presumably accurately reflect attitudes held by the youth who respond. It must be further assumed that these attitudes predispose the individual who holds them to behaving in harmony with them. Thus, if a youngster scores high on a delinquency proneness scale, it can be predicted that he will be more likely to behave in a delinquent way than if he scores low. If this prediction is accurate, the test from which it is made is considered to be valid. In the case of the particular scale Landis and Scarpitti used, there is moderately good evidence to support its validity for groups of youth, if not individuals.

In interpreting studies like Landis and Scarpitti's and even before discussing their goals, it is necessary to frame three questions and keep them in mind *before* attempting to apply the results of the study: (1) Is *cause* really being demonstrated, or is it *association*? This point was discussed in some detail in Chapter 2, but is important enough to justify review in this context. Lower-class youth are likely to score higher on delinquency proneness scales than middle-class youth. Is this because of their social class, or may it be due to the part of the city where they live? If the latter, it is not necessarily social class that has caused the delinquency proneness. It may have been learned because delinquent models are present and prestigeful in slum neighborhoods. Social class may have dictated where a boy lives, but it did not cause his delinquency proneness in any direct way. In the case of middle-class Black youth, *de facto* segregation often forces them to live in congested areas where many high prestige delinquency models also live. Thus they are exposed to illegitimate ways of achieving their life goals that white boys of the same social class usually never encounter. Middle-class white people cloister themselves in the suburbs, with miles of insulation between themselves and the Black and white inner slum city.

As was stated emphatically in Chapter 2, when one thing about people in a given setting is correlated with another thing, it is safer to assume an *association* rather than a *cause-and-effect* relationship. For example, boys are more likely to struggle for independence than girls, but "boy-ness" did not cause this directly. The boys' families and their society have taught them that it is essential for males to be independent.

A second question that must always be asked of any study concerns its population. This problem, too, was discussed to some degree in Chapter 2, but deserves more attention. Both educators and theoretical workers with youth must make use of the results other investigators obtain. The author depends on Landis and Scarpitti to help him illustrate a number of points he considers to be very important. Before he uses data from Landis and Scarpitti's population to work, for example, in Atlanta, he must ask how much generalization he dares to make from their to his population. Do Landis and Scarpitti's boys and girls represent boys and girls from all over the United States? from all over the world? Where does their population come from? Is it rural or urban?

Landis and Scarpitti do not say clearly, although they give enough information that one can guess that most of the boys and girls are from urban areas, and probably from Ohio. They specify that their population of delinquents is from the Boys' Industrial School in Lancaster, Ohio. How representative of all delinquents are committed Ohio boys between ages 13 and 18? To answer this, one can make a rough extrapolation from national figures for reform institutions, and make educated guesses that from the point of view of sound rehabilitation practice they are more wisely handled than similar youth from Alabama or Mississippi. But California and New York delinquents are probably better handled.

Since Ohio has many large cities, one can guess that most of the boys are urban, and come from Cincinnati, Cleveland, Dayton, Toledo, and so on. From economic data, one knows that Ohio is highly industrialized but also has considerable agriculture. Politically, it is Midwestern and rather conservative. It has received many Deep South Afro-Americans in the migrations of the 1940s to the present, and many immigrants have come from Europe. It is, then, something of a melting pot state. But it does not represent Nevada or Kansas or Alabama.

Thus, in selecting a single population to work from, on the basis of which to make generalizations for the United States, an Ohio population is a pretty good one. Ohio is a fair cross-section. But one cannot be *sure* that Ohio findings will hold for youth in other parts of the country.

The third question deals with the validity or usefulness of the instruments Landis and Scarpitti employ. Only one of them has been used by other investigators, as far as the author knows. This one, the Gough

Socialization Scale, is designed to measure proneness toward delinquency, and is taken from the California Personality Inventory. Delinquents have been found to score higher on it than nondelinquents. This means that it is embedded in something of a *nomothetic network*. This simply means that other research workers have determined its relationships with still other instruments or behaviors. If one group of newly tested youngsters scores high, another low, one can have some faith that more of the former actually are or will become delinquent.

The intelligence quotient (IQ), for example, resides within an extensive nomothetic network. It is known that high IQ children make better grades in school, come from higher socioeconomic-level homes, are less frequently delinquent (or less likely to be caught), are more likely to attend college, have better educated parents, are healthier, and so on. The reasons for a high IQ may not be brightness at all, for the brightness may have been inherited or learned because the parents were well educated, prosperous, and spent much time playing with and stimulating the child. Some combination or all of these factors may have produced the high IQ *and* the things with which it is associated. What caused it is irrelevant for present purposes. The point is that the IQ as a score means a good bit: It ties into an extensive nomothetic or predictive network.

In the absence of all other information about a child, knowing his IQ helps to predict many other things about him better than if his IQ were not known. The same is true for any other test with a nomothetic network. It is more useful than one with no nomothetic network, although the latter may be promising and may be found to be useful in practical prediction after further research.

Landis and Scarpitti use two other instruments, awareness of limited opportunities (ALO) and value orientation (VO). Both tests *look* as if they should measure what Landis and Scarpitti want them to (real life behavior). Whether they actually measure it is not known to either Landis and Scarpitti or to their readers.

This is a good reason why it is often better to employ a somewhat faulty instrument within a nomothetic network than it is for each research worker to devise a new instrument that *seems* to meet his purposes, but has not had its usefulness demonstrated.

American psychologists and sociologists seem to have a strong need to be original. Thus, they frequently make up new instruments of their own rather than use old ones. This makes it difficult to compare the results of one study with another. Anyone who tries to pull together results in a certain field, as the author tries to do here, is forced to employ findings obtained from several different instruments, some of which possess an unknown degree of usefulness. It is often true that no one knows how the results from one technique compare with the results from another. An author must put them together as best he can, since he often has no other data available to him.

Thus, if Landis and Scarpitti's ALO and VO scales measure what they think they do, and if the scores from the instruments actually predict what it seems logical that they do, then the author of this book and his readers are on reasonably safe ground. So are Landis and Scarpitti.

But if the instruments are unreliable and without validity, then their study has nothing to say.

In short, results of the Landis and Scarpitti study are convincing because they fit with theoretical predictions, and because the tests the authors use seem to be promising. But, lacking much information about the reliability and validity of the scales, one can accept and apply conclusions only cautiously. Parenthetically, a fault of scales such as Landis and Scarpitti use is that brighter youngsters are likely to see the purposes of it. Thus, if they think it to their advantage, they may mislead the investigators. Girls, being conservative, obedient, and responsible, are more likely than boys to mislead research workers by answering items in socially desirable directions. So are middle-class people. (See, for example Hollander and Willis, 1967.) Tendencies like this complicate research.

Conclusions This long introduction is not intended as negative criticism of Landis and Scarpitti. They have reported a provocative study honestly and fully.

Landis and Scarpitti begin honestly by the title they have given the study: *Perceptions Regarding Value Orientation and Legitimate Opportunity.* This title makes no claim to studying "real life behavior." Actually, *all* behavior is real life, whether it is taking a questionnaire administered by a psychologist or sociologist, or robbing a bakery. The distinction between laboratory, or test taking, behavior and real life behavior is somewhat arbitrary and misleading. Two distinctions are actually involved: playing for no important consequences, such as participating in a research study, and playing for keeps, as robbing a bakery; and expressing attitudes that might lead an investigator to think that, given appropriate circumstances, one would be the bakery robbing type and actually robbing the bakery.

Landis and Scarpitti, then, honestly admit that they are not studying the real life of their subjects but the subjects' reports of their perceptions of it. Honesty of these reports must be assumed, however; and this assumption is not always safe.

Their basic hypothesis, as has been said, is that youngsters who reject middle-class values and who also see few legitimate opportunities for themselves in the larger community are likely to be either *prone* to delinquency, *actually* delinquent, or both.

Landis and Scarpitti constructed a scale to measure middle-class values, with items stressing ambition, worldly asceticism, individual responsibility, rationality, cultivation of manners and personality, control of physical aggression and violence, and respect for property. A sample item is, "Good manners are for sissies." Such items make up their VO scale.

Their ALO scale is intended to determine how the subjects perceive their world: Does it or does it not offer them a chance to get ahead? A sample item is, "I'll never have enough money to go to college."

The authors' next step was to find an appropriate population to respond to their scales. They used the "contrast population" technique.

Presumably, lower-class children perceive fewer available opportunities than their economically better buttressed middle-class agemates; and Black youngsters perceive fewer legitimate opportunities for themselves than do white youngsters. To check on sex differences (they do not predict what they might be), they included both boys and girls in their noninstitutional population.

Finally, they reasoned that a delinquent population will be likely to reject both middle-class values and to perceive sharp curtailment of opportunity. Thus, they tested a large sample (515) of institutionalized boys, both Afro-American and white. Altogether, their study reports results from 1030 sixth and ninth grade public school Black and white subjects, and 515 institutionalized delinquent boys from 13 to 18 years old.

As predicted by Cloward and Ohlin, Durkheim, and Merton, the best predictor of delinquency, delinquency proneness, and low morale is the young person's perception of the opportunities open to him. If he perceives opportunities in the world, he is less likely either to be a delinquent or to score as prone to delinquency on the test than if he considers his chances in the world to be quite limited.

Landis and Scarpitti's subjects were rather realistic about their perception of opportunities. Lower-class children were more pessimistic than middle-class children and older children were more pessimistic than younger children. However, older middle-class girls saw more opportunities open to them than sixth grade middle-class girls. This may be realistic for girls of these ages. As predicted, Afro-American youngsters perceived fewer opportunities open to them than did white youths. As could be expected, the delinquent boys were most pessimistic of all in their perceptions of their world.

There were no Black–white and no older–younger differences in delinquency proneness. However, the girls (always conservative and obedient) admitted less to delinquency proneness than the boys; and middle-class children to less than lower-class youngsters.

For the group as a whole, young people who saw the world offering them few opportunities for success and status also rejected middle-class values. They were likely to report, and thus presumably actually possess, rebellious and destructive attitudes about their society.

Caution about causation should be reasserted here. These results do not say that awareness of limited opportunities leads to rebellion. The converse may be true: A delinquency prone child may conceivably reject middle-class values because he is rebellious. In turn, society may deny him opportunities because of his attitudes; and he may perceive this denial quite accurately and report it realistically.

The Short, Rivera, and Tennyson Study

In their *Perceived Opportunities, Gang Membership, and Delinquency*, Short, Rivera, and Tennyson (1965) study phenomena similar to those studied by Landis and Scarpitti. Their methods are very different, however, which makes it difficult to compare the studies, although the results of both come out in directions predicted by the Cloward and Ohlin, Durkheim, and Merton theories.

To measure middle-class values, Short, Rivera, and Tennyson used a semantic differential rather than the "yes and no" structure employed by Landis and Scarpitti. This technique provides a person a statement relating to the concept he wants to measure. For both these studies (*adherence to middle-class values* was measured) Short, Rivera, and Tennyson plausibly judged that "someone who works for good grades in school" possessed middle-class values. Thus they administered this and similar statements to their subjects. Each subject marked along a line from one end to the other to indicate how much like "someone who works for good grades . . ." he believes he is. If he marks at the extreme left, it means he considers himself totally unlike this hypothetical grade getter. If he marks at the extreme right, he believes he and the grade getter are almost exactly alike. The sum of the distances marked is the score for all the items on the test: the lower the score, the more middle class, in the case of this test.

The semantic differential technique has been much used, and has often been shown to be useful. But it cannot be directly compared with Landis and Scarpitti's technique.

The authors of the second study were also interested in obtaining a measure of awareness of limited opportunities. Their measure of this also differed from Landis and Scarpitti's. They simply asked a number of questions about specific opportunities to determine what was characteristic of "the area where your group hangs out."

Like Landis and Scarpitti, Short, Rivera, and Tennyson selected groups that differed sharply in the factors (perception of legitimate and illegitimate opportunities, and acceptance or rejection of middle-class values) that interested the authors. They, too, predicted that middle-class youth would differ from lower-class youth, that Black youth would differ from white youth, and that gang and nongang members would differ from each other. They studied only boys of high school age. They equated gang membership with delinquency, while Landis and Scarpitti equated residence in a boys' industrial school with delinquency. In other words, the concepts in the two studies are almost identical, but the techniques for measuring them are very different.

Short, Rivera, and Tennyson, unlike Landis and Scarpitti, found that all their groups, Black and white, middle and lower class, and gang and nongang, gave about equal lip service to middle-class values, which is not an unusual finding, and fits with Han and Doby (1966), who were briefly summarized earlier. This is part of internalizing the American dream.

Differences began to show up, however, when the semantic differential was applied to such clauses as "someone who is a good fighter with a tough reputation." To the authors, endorsing this statement means that one identifies with conflict. Or one who endorsed "someone who knows where to sell what he steals" was considered to be a boy who held a criminal set of values. Or one who was like "someone who makes easy money by pimping and other illegal hustles" or "someone who gets his kicks by using drugs" was assumed to be a retreatist. Middle-class boys in both races differed in the degree to which they valued and endorsed such behaviors as well as in how legitimate they believed they were. Lower-class boys valued them more highly and believed they were more legitimate than middle-class boys. The gang members of both races valued such statements most highly and considered them most legitimate.

As might be expected, the highest conflict orientation existed among Afro-American gang members. These youngsters are both the most frustrated group and the group that has learned most to handle its frustration by open defiance.

The authors collected data from a sizable sample. Each of their subgroups contained more than fifty boys, except for Black middle class, where there were only twenty-six subjects. The largest group was made up of Black gang members, and included 206 youths. As has been said, as a general rule, the larger the sample, the more the confidence that can be placed in the results.

Judging from the boys' answers, Afro-American boys, regardless of their social class or gang status, perceive more illegitimate opportunities as being open to them than white boys. This difference between the races was greater than the difference within each race between the most delinquent (gang member) and least delinquent (middle-class group). This undoubtedly relates to the *de facto* segregation factor mentioned earlier. It may also relate to greater acceptance by middle-class Black society of persons with unsavory reputations. The author and his students have not found this to be true with institutionalized Georgia delinquent boys: There is no difference between Black and white boys in the number of tough criminals known, for example.

There was more difference in perception of legitimate opportunities within than between the races. Middle-class white and middle-class Afro-American boys were more like each other in this respect than they were like the gang members in their respective ethnic groups.

An actual presentation in tabular form of some of the results brings this study to life. Table 6.1 includes tabulation of the percentages of boys in the indicated subgroups of the study who answer "True" to the two questions given.

To the author, the most striking things about Table 6.1 are (1) the tremendous differences within each race as one moves from the disadvantaged lower-class gang member to the advantaged middle-class boys, and (2) the even more striking and tragic difference between Black and white boys in optimism about legitimate job opportunities.

Table 6.2 summarizes other data from the Short, Rivera, and Tennyson study. The number of adolescents responding is the same in each case as the numbers shown in Table 6.1. Table 6.2 speaks clearly for itself. Neither white nor Black gang members see many legitimate opportunities open to them. There is little difference between Afro-American and white lower-class and Black middle-class boys for this variable. Comparatively speaking, the world is the white middle-class boy's oyster, at least as he sees it. Black boys in every group perceive more illegitimate educational and occupational opportunities than white boys do. This difference, as predicted in previous paragraphs, is most striking for the two middle-class ethnic groups, where Afro-American to white ratio is nearly 2 to 1 (an average of 6.7 illegitimate opportunity perceptions reported by Black middle-class boys, but only 3.5 for middle-class white boys). As has been said, *de facto* segregation forces most middle-class

Table 6.1

Percent of Afro-American and white high school aged boys answering "true" to two questions about opportunity condition in their communities

"In our area it's hard for a young guy to stay in school."

	N	Percent Answering "True"
Afro-American		
Lower-class gang	206	48.5
Lower-class nongang	89	28.1
Middle class	26	7.1
White		
Lower-class gang	90	52.2
Lower-class nongang	79	21.5
Middle class	53	0.0

"It's hard for a young guy in our area to get a good paying honest job."

Afro-American		
Lower-class gang	206	72.2
Lower-class nongang	89	62.9
Middle class	26	46.2
White		
Lower-class gang	90	56.7
Lower-class nongang	79	31.6
Middle class	53	9.4

(Adapted from Short, Rivera, and Tennyson, 1965.)

Afro-American boys to live in areas that are shunned by the residentially freer white middle class.

About as many Afro-American as white boys in each social class group believe it is possible to stay in school and get an education. But only half as many Black boys believe it is possible to *use* the education so gained to get a good paying, honest job. This is a grim, realistic perception that lurks behind the Bedford-Stuyvesants of 1964, the Wattses of 1965, the Detroits and Newarks of 1967, the Baltimores and Chicagos and Clevelands of 1968. Data about the Watts riots suggest that the rioters were not necessarily semiliterate recent immigrants from the South, but that many of them were long time Los Angeles residents, relatively (but not absolutely) well educated, and "within sight of the goal."[6] Other informally reported data from other riot areas since that time are similar.

This fits with such different psychological theories as Hull-Spence (for example, Spence, 1958; and Lewin, 1935): Once one is near his goal and begins to think he will truly achieve success and is blocked, then frustration is most acute. He is more likely to burst out than if he had never envisioned reaching the goal. Blocked hope is more likely to produce violence than blocked resignation.

[6]This was reported in the *Detroit News*, July 28, 1967, perhaps to help Detroit, which was stricken at that time by riots, understand its plight.

Table 6.2

Perceptions of legitimate and illegitimate opportunities, perceptions of adult helpfulness, and delinquency known to police per boy

	Legitimate N Opportunities	Illegitimate N Opportunities	Rating, Adult Power, Helpfulness (8 Highest)	Average N Offenses Known to Police per Boy
Afro-American gang	9.0	11.4	4.5	3.1
White gang	9.3	9.5	4.7	2.7
Afro-American lower class	11.0	9.0	5.6	0.5
White lower class	13.7	8.2	5.6	0.3
Afro-American middle class	15.6	6.7	6.2	0.1
White middle class	20.2	3.5	7.4	0.02

(Adapted from Short, Rivera, and Tennyson, 1965.)

Data for Black Alienation Today's Black teenager is too young to appreciate the significance of the Supreme Court's decision about school segregation in 1954. He does not share his elders' remembered joy as shackle after shackle were struck from the Black man after World War II. He only knows that, despite all the new laws, he is not getting *his*! His piece of the American dream has not yet been given him. He does not like it. He is quite ready to fight (often senselessly, brutally, and perhaps self-destructively) to get it. His elders know that they are relatively well off compared with their former circumstances. The adolescent knows that, *absolutely*, he is badly off *now* when compared with his white peers. Perhaps, if there is a generation gap, it is more acute in Afro-American than in white families in this latter part of the twentieth century.

The story of Black alienation is graphically told by the Louis Harris Poll,[7] which was taken just before the assassination of Dr. Martin Luther King, Jr. Despite the picture of alienation, 73 percent of Harris' sample of Afro-Americans believed that, compared with a few years ago, more progress in racial relations was being made, and 52 percent of whites believed this. Only 5 percent of Afro-Americans thought conditions had worsened, while 16 percent of whites thought so.

But the Blacks were deeply alienated, much more so in 1968 than in 1966. For example, in 1968 the feeling that few understand how it is to live as they live had gone from 32 percent in 1966 to 66 percent. In 1968, only 25 percent of whites felt this way.

In 1968, Harris' Black Americans, 52 percent strong, believed the leaders of the country were indifferent to them. Only 32 percent thought so in 1966. Thirty-nine percent of Harris' 1968 sample of whites believed the country's leaders cared little about what happened to them. It might be added that this last figure is hardly reassuring.

In 1968, 56 percent of Afro-Americans believed they had much less chance than other people to get ahead. This figure was up by two-thirds from the 1966 figure. In 1968, only 17 percent of whites felt this way.

[7] From the *Atlanta Constitution*, April 15, 1968.

Black and White Opportunity Hypothesis Such figures as Harris' suggest that, if Short, Rivera, and Tennyson had conducted their study even three or four years later, their results would have been even more striking — and disturbing — than they were when published in 1965.

Perceptions versus Reality How do reported perceptions correspond with reality? It is interesting but not cheering to compare figures for percentages about perceptions and reports with figures that express the harsh realities of life. The United States Census Bureau released figures for 1967 incomes on August 8, 1968. The median income of white American families was $8300; for nonwhites in general, it was $5200; for Afro-American families, it was only $4900. According to this yardstick, the ratio of Black to white legitimate opportunities in real life is thus .59. It is gaining slowly: In 1966 it had been .58, and in 1965, .54. But it is far too low in general.

Reworking the figures in Tables 6.1 and 6.2, the Black to white ratio of *perception* of legitimate opportunities is .75. Short, Rivera, and Tennyson reported their results in 1965 (the data were probably collected before then, however). Thus, for the time they reported, their sample of Afro-American youth was overreporting — had an overoptimism index — by almost 40 percent.

In short, if the theories of Durkheim, Cloward and Ohlin, and Merton are correct, whites provide ample ground for alienation among Black youth.

To return to Table 6.2, the third column indicates that there is a slow increase of youth's perception of adult power and helpfulness moving from the Afro-American gang boys' perceptions through the groups to the Afro-American middle-class boys. Average frequency of this perception jumps sharply for middle-class white boys. The last column in Table 6.2 simply provides evidence that Short, Rivera, and Tennyson were correct when they assumed that their groups would vary in delinquency.

Police Records versus Reality Police records show that white middle-class boys are almost delinquency free. While the figure is low for Black middle-class boys, it is still five times as high for them as for the middle-class white boys. In turn, white lower-class boys have three times as many police entries as Black middle-class boys; and Black lower-class boys have about five and one-half times as many entries as white lower-class boys.

It has been suggested that police blotters are poor indicators of the true state of affairs, because middle-class youth enjoy a psychosocial moratorium provided for them by their influential and usually fairly stable families. Empey and Erickson (1966) provide some evidence to this effect, in a 180-sample depth study of 15- to 17-year-old white boys from Utah, who came from all social class levels. Nine of ten of the offenses these boys reported they had committed had gone undetected. Almost every boy, regardless of his social class level, reported one or a variety of offenses against the law.

Empey and Erickson's middle-class sample (sons of skilled tradesmen, white-collar workers, and small business men) made up 55 percent of their sample; but had committed two-thirds of all the serious violations. Their lower-class boys (sons of semi- and unskilled workers) constituted 17 percent of the sample, and committed 24 percent of the serious crimes. Boys from this lowest social class specialized in auto theft, alcohol, narcotics, defying their parents, skipping school, and fighting and assault. These seem for the most part to be dramatic and the types of crime that come most forcefully to the attention of the police.

However, many more middle-class boys than the authors expected went in for such crimes as traffic offenses, theft, defying people other than their parents, property violations, destroying property, arson, and armed robbery. Some of these crimes are also undeniably dramatic in nature, but different in type from the lower-class boys' crimes.

Empey and Erickson checked police blotters insofar as possible about the honesty of their 180 youthful subjects, and found them to be remarkably honest. Although Empey and Erickson do not present their data in this fashion, reworking their figures indicates that their social class I boys admitted to an average of 2.8 offenses against the law. These youngsters were the sons of parents in the professions, upper business, and sciences and art.

Their class II boys (middle class) averaged 10.8 admitted crimes each. However, the authors point out that this group included a disproportionate number of what they call hard core extremists (youngsters committed to delinquency by repeated crimes that had been detected and punished).

The class III boys (from families where the occupation was semi- or unskilled labor) admitted to an average of 9.5 crimes.

These findings, even though the crime average may be inflated for the middle-class youngsters by Empey and Erickson's method of selecting subjects, suggest that in today's affluent society, the sons of skilled tradesmen, white-collar workers, and small business men may not see the pathway to life success as being profusely strewn with legitimate opportunities. Optimistic perceptions, in the world of 1966, when Empey and Erickson published, may be confined to the sons of the very well educated and affluent. The forms of alienation for middle-class youth, subjectively speaking, may be isolation or formlessness rather than powerlessness, which may be more likely to characterize disadvantaged youth.

Conclusions To conclude the discussion of the Short, Rivera, and Tennyson paper, their most important single finding is that perception of legitimate opportunities is more closely related to delinquency than perception of illegitimate opportunities. Their data suggest that if a boy has reason to be optimistic about his future, he resists delinquency. If he sees no legitimate opportunities, then and only then does he take advantage of his available illegitimate opportunities. Of course, in light of Empey and Erickson's results, this conclusion must be rephrased to read "then and only then does he *get caught* as he avails himself of his illegitimate opportunities."

The Tallman Experiment   Tallman's (1966) research puts the legitimate-illegitimate opportunity perception hypothesis to experimental test. Tallman's results fit well with both Landis and Scarpitti's and Short, Rivera, and Tennyson's findings.

Experiments versus Studies   When possible, a scientist prefers to test a hypothesis by an experiment rather than a study. In an experiment, as discussed in Chapter 2, he controls as many relevant variables as possible. He puts something into a situation, manipulates the situation according to clear rules, and measures the outcome. Thus, a good experiment is more precise than a study.

In a study, one takes conditions as best he can find them in a real life situation and measures differences between subjects in these different conditions. Short, Rivera, and Tennyson selected race, gang and nongang membership, and social class as their conditions, for instance. They did not manipulate the boys, but only "measured" them (gave them tests). The boys were little affected, as far as can be told, by the study.

Unknown factors are more likely to influence a study than an experiment, because the research worker has little control over the environment. For example, Kenneth Clark's *Dark Ghetto* (1965) is considered a classic, although informal, study of a large, urban, Black slum. Generalizations from it have been made to all Black slums. In it were found hopelessness, apathy, estrangement and isolation, filth, and despair. However, R. J. Hill and Larson (1966, 1967), studied another Black urban slum where the formal characteristics were similar to Clark's Harlem: broken families, unemployment, poor education, matriarchal families, and so on. They found that morale in their slum was as different from that in Clark's slum as the white middle-class boys in Short, Rivera, and Tennyson's study differed from their Afro-American gang boys. For reasons not uncovered by Hill and Larson, their slum dwellers belonged to organizations, visited relatives, and had feelings of intimacy with them and their neighbors, were independent, wished to solve their own problems, and possessed personal resources for solving them.

Such sample fluctuations are never accidental, but the reasons that account for them are often so obscure they cannot be accounted for. Certainly, they greatly affect the results of a study. It has been pointed out in Chapter 2 that, as a research population, volunteers are more likely than nonvolunteers to tell an investigator what they think he wants to know or to possess or be willing to admit more of the behavior he is studying. They are more motivated and eager to be subjects: *They cooperate*. The influence of experimenter expectancies on results was also documented in detail in Chapter 2.

Tallman administered his procedures to groups as uniformly and mechanically as possible. There seems little chance for experimenter bias to have operated, although it can never be totally ruled out. His basic hypothesis was that human beings will exhaust their legitimate opportunities (cheating, in Tallman's experiment) before resorting to illegitimate opportunities. It requires a large inductive leap to generalize from Tallman's findings to the applied world of education and jobs but, on a tentative basis, this inductive leap is possible if for no other reason than that it provides a plan for action that makes good common sense.

Procedures and Results Tallman's subjects were junior college students (young men and young women). He manipulated their working situations, frustrated them, provided them with both legitimate and illegitimate ways of solving their problem, and measured the outcome. For Tallman to execute his research, it was necessary for him to accomplish four things, then to measure the results or outcome: (1) to establish a valued goal within the minds of his subjects; (2) to provide them a legitimate means to achieve it; (3) to block this method of achieving it; and (4) to make sure that they knew there was also an illegitimate way (cheating) to achieve it. Tallman took the following steps to meet his four requirements.

He promised his subjects a letter certifying to the president of the four year college the students wanted to attend after junior college that the student was of good college calibre, and had a good chance of graduating from college. This letter would be issued *if* the student passed the two tests the experimenter administered. This method was to establish a highly valued goal for the students.[8] The first of the two tasks Tallman's students were asked to perform was an exceptionally difficult jigsaw puzzle. Only 15 of the 163 subjects were able to complete it. This was the legitimate but inordinately difficult path to the goal.

The second of the two tasks Tallman assigned to his subjects and by which they might redeem themselves was impossible. They listened to a garbled tape of ten nonsense syllables, and then were asked to pick from a list of printed English words those which were similar to the nonsense syllables. In truth, none of the words was like the nonsense syllables, so that the task could not conceivably be honestly performed. Tallman provided a blatant opportunity for each subject to cheat: The students could either peek under the carbon inserted between the list of English words and the answer key or they could turn over the test packet and see the key through the thin second sheet. They could also do both. "DO NOT TURN" was prominently printed on the face sheet of the test package. For most people, this is an invitation to do what they are supposed not to do. Once the packet was turned over, the possibility of cheating was immediately obvious. As has been said, success was impossible, so that any solution of the task necessarily involved cheating.

In such devious ways, Tallman blocked legitimate opportunities to solve the highly valued task, and at the same time provided awareness of the fact that an illegitimate opportunity was available.

Strange as it may seem, of the 148 students who did not solve the jigsaw puzzle, only 49 (about one-third) cheated on the second task. Of the 99 noncheaters, about half admitted that they knew they could have cheated if they had chosen to. However, only 24 percent of the noncheaters both perceived that they could cheat and also thought they had done poorly. Most of those who were aware of the possibility of cheating

---

[8] Such deception of research subjects, even for scientifically legitimate goals, is questioned by many. It may be that the frequency with which it is employed has something to do with why psychologists and sociologists are often distrusted by the public (see Stricker, 1967).

but who did not cheat, thought they had done well on the task. Thus, their motivation to cheat was low: They did not perceive the legitimate path to the goal as being blocked.

Everyone used all his available time trying to solve the problem legitimately. Tallman believes this certifies to his subjects' desire to exhaust every legitimate opportunity before resorting to illegitimate opportunity. Hill and Kochendorfer (1969) report similar results for sixth grade boys who, in a situation where they could save face by cheating, and for those who cheated, did not cheat until all possibility of obtaining a face saving score legitimately had been exhausted.

Tallman's noncheaters who thought they were doing poorly lowered their evaluation of the goal, which, it will be recalled, was to obtain a letter certifying to their aptitude for four year college. This is the familiar sour grapes defense: If I can't get it, then it is not worth getting. While this is not the most mature possible way of handling conflicts, it is quite effective. This tendency was particularly strong when the noncheating subjects knew they could cheat if they cared to.

This point is exceptionally interesting and potentially important. It provides possible insight into the behavior of many sensitive, highly moral, but disillusioned adolescents. As they become aware of the realities of much within the American way of life—class and racial injustice, political favoritism, influence peddling, hypocrisy among the showily religious—they often conclude that they must cheat or otherwise cheapen themselves if they are to succeed. In refusing to follow what they perceive to be the necessary pattern, it becomes essential for them for their own self-protection to renounce the goals of society. When carried to its extreme, this way of thinking may help to explain the hippie's "doing his own thing," or "dropping out of the rat race." In more conventional forms, this thinking may lie behind choosing the cloistered, religious way of life.

Tallman concludes from his data that cheaters valued the goal more than noncheaters. As a group, his junior college students for the most part resisted an illegitimate pathway to the goal. They took it only when they saw the legitimate goal as firmly blocked. Even then, they cheated only after they had tried their best to solve the problem legitimately. It seems that one is most likely to cheat to reach goals he values highly. The implications of this finding for the practice of placing very high premiums on grades as opposed to learning for the pleasure in learning are obvious.

The results of Landis and Scarpitti, Short, Rivera, and Tennyson, and Tallman all fit well together. This is true although they used very different methods, very different populations of youth, and worked within both natural and experimental (or artificial) settings. Their results testify to the power of the legitimate–illegitimate opportunity hypothesis.

The Shelton and Hill Study

Even with all legitimate opportunities blocked and while working for a highly valued goal, not all people will employ illegitimate methods to reach the goal. This finding emerges clearly from Tallman's results. What are some of the characteristics of those who cheat and those who do not? What circumstances maximize the likelihood of cheating?

Shelton and J. P. Hill (1969) attempted an answer to these questions. Their subjects were forty-nine high school boys and sixty-two high school girls. Most were from the middle class. There were no differences in percentages of boys and girls who cheated, so the results are discussed for the total population of 111 high school youth.

In the first task, creativity was stressed. The students were assured that this was the purpose of their being asked to construct as many English words as possible in 8 minutes, using the letters in the word "generation." After that, it was explained that how people performed on a creativity test was often related to how they feel about taking tests. Within this framework, the young people were given a test designed to measure anxiety about achievement. They then took another test, which was timed so they could not complete it in the available time they had free from classes. This provided an excuse for bringing them back next day.

When they returned, each was assigned to a "success," a "failure," and a "control" condition. "Success" subjects were told that they had produced five to seven words more than another sample of "good students from a good high school," and that anyone who did this well or better had a good chance of succeeding in college. "Failure" subjects received similar information, but were told that their scores were five to seven words lower than the hypothetical reference group. No reference group information was given to the "control" subjects.

The original papers on which words had been constructed from the letters in "generation," ostensibly undisturbed and ungraded, were returned to each student. He was told he could keep his paper. Additionally, copies of a master list of all possible English words that could be constructed from "generation" were passed out, and the students were asked to encircle all words on the list that they had constructed. The cheating score was the difference in number of words between what they encircled and what the experimenter had counted from what they had actually done.

Of the total population of 111 young people, 53 percent cheated regardless of their experimental condition. However, only 43 percent (not an encouraging figure) of the control groups cheated, compared to a surprising 56 percent of the success group and 61 percent of the failure group.

Apparently, in a modern college preparatory high school such as Shelton and Hill worked in, a sizable percentage of students will cheat even though they have been assured that the task on which they are working is unrelated to school success, that the results will not be placed on their school records, but that the task is related to the socially valued trait of creativity. The percentage who cheat is markedly increased regardless of whether the student is doing better or worse than a comparison group about whose results he has been informed. This, presumably, is due to rivalry, and operates regardless of whether the student is told he is doing better or worse than the reference group. Apparently, if he is doing better, he wants to be still more superior; if he is doing worse, he at least wants to catch up.

Shelton and Hill then related scores on their anxiety test with

Table 6.3

Percentages of high school students with achievement anxiety who cheated under three conditions

Level of Anxiety	Experimental Condition			All Conditions
	Success	Failure	Control	
High	91	83	57	76
Moderate	43	69	36	50
Low	36	31	33	33
All levels	56	61	43	53

(Adapted from Shelton and Hill, 1969.)

cheating, and found that achievement anxiety correlated a substantial .45 with cheating across all conditions.

Since achievement anxiety is presumably related to worry over possible "aversive social consequences," to use Shelton and Hill's term, this correlation throws some light on the increase of incidence of cheating among both success and failure groups. The former, knowing how their peers performed, want to be so clearly in the lead that no possible doubt can be cast on their superior competence. The failure group, with potential danger of losing face looming, take dishonest means to avoid the threat.

Anxiety about social esteem, then, may be a powerful motive for using deviant methods to gain success. Shelton and Hill separated their 111 subjects into three groups: The group highest in achievement anxiety, the middle group, and the one-third lowest in anxiety. Percentages of each group in each experimental condition who cheated are summarized in Table 6.3.

While the Ns in each cell of the table are small, the trends are clear: For the high anxiety youngsters, about as many of the success group (91 percent) as of the failure groups (83 percent) cheated. It may be speculated that their insecurity is so great that almost every one of them will cheat to enhance his status (ten of the eleven did so). Failure makes them equally desperate (ten of twelve cheated): Even though they are comparing themselves only with themselves, the control group is also so strongly motivated to succeed that 57 percent (eight of fourteen) cheated.

The moderately anxious group is more compelled to "avoid disgrace" than "to seek highest status." Under failure conditions, 69 percent (nine of thirteen) cheated, but under success conditions only 43 percent (six of fourteen) cheated. In the control condition, only four of the group of twelve cheated. Thus, the strongest motivator for "average" youngsters toward deviant behavior as represented by cheating seems to be to avoid loss of public face. In this connection, but working with sixth grade boys, Hill and Kochendorfer (1969) find that, when this loss of face is related to comparison with *specific known friends* rather than an unknown general reference group, as in the Shelton and Hill group, the effect remains about the same: If the risk of detection was low, two-thirds of Hill and Kochendorfer's boys cheated (ten of fifteen). If the risk was high, only about half cheated (seven of fifteen). When there was low risk of detection, about half of Hill and Kochendorfer's sixth grade boys cheated even when they did not know how their friends had performed. This figure is not significantly different from the 43 percent of Shelton and Hill's high school students. But, when risk of detection was high for Hill and Kochendorfer's boys, incidence of cheating fell for the control boys, and only three of fifteen (20 percent) cheated.

What about relaxed, nonanxious youngsters? Does a youngster who is well adjusted in this society, at least according to the criterion of low anxiety about cheating, incorporate the Protestant ethic into his life? As can be seen from Table 6.3, this is not necessarily so. While no more low anxious youth cheat under conditions of failure than of success, one-third of them cheat under all circumstances: 33 percent in the control condition (four of twelve), 31 percent (four of thirteen) in the failure condition, and 36 percent (four of eleven) in the success condition. Thus, while anxiety intensifies dishonest behavior, within a group of presumably perfectly normal Minnesota sixth grade boys, 33 percent cheat even when they are not comparing themselves with anyone; under the same condition, 43 percent of Shelton and Hill's presumably equally normal total population of high school youth cheated, and one-third of even the least anxious cheated.

The Hill and Kochendorfer and Shelton and Hill studies leave some questions about cheating: Even though it is sharply in contradiction to "honest behavior," is it deviant in the sense of signifying *anomie*, or alienation? More data are needed to answer this question. Only the cheating youth themselves can say whether their cheating signifies contempt for and alienation from the system (some of Tallman's results suggest that this may be the case). Cheating may mean that the values of the system are held so dear that many American youth will do almost anything to achieve them, or appear to measure up to them.

While the evidence from Tallman and Hill and Kochendorfer is clear (their subjects cheat more or less only as a last resort), a dismaying number of youth have also been seen to cheat when there is no perceptible external gain involved. This, presumably, is a result of having internalized the values of the culture: One can have self-respect only if one presents a favorable set of personal performance results to the public, and for Hill and Kochendorfer and Shelton and Hill's control groups this "public" was *only hypothetical.*

These results give one pause to think: For many (between one-third and one-half), is the American ethic to *look* good or to *be* good? Is it *Keep the Faith, Baby*, or is it *Save the Face, Baby*?

SUMMARY

The characteristics of the human organism deeply influence the behavior of individuals; but, regardless of the nature of their physical make-up, the structure of the environments in which individuals live also direct their behavior in fundamental ways. This chapter has been devoted to exploring the influence of the community (the people who interact and make it like it is) on adolescent behavior.

Central to this chapter is the legitimate–illegitimate opportunities hypothesis as developed by Durkheim (1897, translated 1951), Cloward and Ohlin (1960), and Merton (1961). The central hypothesis is that, if a community does not provide its members with legitimate means of reaching the goals it has taught them to strive for, they are likely to become anomic, or alienated. A frequent result of alienation is deviant and often openly delinquent behavior. Availability of legitimate opportunities is thought to be more important in determining deviant behavior than is availability of illegitimate opportunities: Adolescents will become delinquent, or will cheat, only when legitimate ways of realizing their goals are denied to them. Failure to provide legitimate opportunities to reach socially inculcated, lofty goals is conceived to be profoundly frustrating.

Rather than make an exhaustive survey of the literature, the author has chosen to review four studies in considerable detail. He has adduced additional research literature when relevant.

The hypothesis is well supported by the literature: Middle-class youth, in general, are more inclined to perceive their environments as including adequate legitimate opportunities, but lower-class youth are less optimistic in their reported perceptions. Black youth, realistically, are less optimistic than white youth. Gang members and institutionalized delinquents are the most pessimistic of all, and Afro-American gang members more so than white gang members.

There are no important sex differences in perception of or adjustment to legitimate and illegitimate opportunities, when this topic has been studied for both sexes. However, the Black population reports far more *anomie* than the white population. While Afro-Americans seem to be more optimistic than indexes of actual opportunity justify, a high percentage of the white community reports rather profound alienation.

When deviant behavior does occur (cheating has been most studied), it seems to be only as a last resort. Two very different samples, one of sixth grade boys, one of junior college students, have been found to cheat only when all legitimate opportunities to reach their goals have been exhausted.

United States society seems to include within it—perhaps to have produced—a dismaying number of members who will cheat even without any apparent external justification for doing so. This percentage of cheaters ranges, in three different studies, from 33 percent of a group of sixth grade boys to 43 percent of a group of high school students in college preparatory classes.

Cheating seems to occur more frequently when the cheater knows how others have performed on the task he is attempting. He apparently cheats either to enhance his superiority or to catch up. For most, anxiety about one's achievement, or fear of unpleasant social consequences, seems to be related to cheating, with the more anxious individual being most likely to cheat.

7

Intelligence and Intellectual Growth

INTRODUCTION

Perhaps the proudest achievements within the science of psychology concern theory, research, and practice related to learning and intelligence. In recent years, theories and research about cognitive behavior have also flourished after many years of neglect. The principles of learning, all too briefly sketched in Chapter 1, underlie almost all the developmental processes and interactions that have been discussed in this book. It should be obvious to the reader, and it has often been pointed out, that intelligence and cognitive, problem solving behavior are central to school and community functioning, to socialization, to moral development and identification, and to vocational adjustment. These topics are treated in the following chapters of this volume; this chapter and Chapter 8 provide the foundations. Cognition and intelligence may be equally closely linked to sexual behavior, emotional differentiation and adjustment, and the formation and function of the self concept.

The intimate interrelation of intelligence and cognitive behavior with all other aspects of development is strongly stressed in this and the following chapter in an attempt to begin correctly by not thinking of intelligence and cognition as isolated entities and processes. For practical reasons, however, particular aspects of behavior and development will be singled out for treatment, but these aspects are by no means isolated from the total process. Teachers must focus more on learning behavior than on emotional development, but any teacher who has spent a few days in a classroom knows that a youngster's classroom learning is inseparably linked to his health and physical well-being, his interests, his motivation, his social congruence with the group, and his personal adjustment. The interactive nature of intelligent and cognitive behavior will be a theme throughout this chapter in the coverage of the growth, development, and function of intelligence. However, in Chapter 8 the area of cognitive function will be discussed specifically, for there exist different philosophical approaches to intelligence and cognition.

In reading Chapters 7 and 8, it is helpful to keep in mind a distinction commonly made between "intelligence" and "cognitive behavior." Usage gives the term *intelligence* the connotation of a *product*: something that is finished, *is* rather than *is becoming*, is represented by a quotient (for example, the IQ) rather than being conceptualized as on-going behavior.

Cognition, cognitive development, or cognitive behavior are terms that carry with them more a connotation of *process*. Perceiving, learning, reasoning, problem solving, remembering—these are all illustrations of cognitive processes. An intelligence test (an assessment of the product) is only a measurement of a number of cognitive processes, such as memory span, reasoning with words or numbers, solving jigsaw-type puzzles, or giving the meaning of words.

Thus, intelligence and cognition are inextricably linked to each other. While necessary for purposes of discussion, it is hoped that the concentration on intelligence in Chapter 8 and on cognitive processes and their determinants in Chapter 9 will not obscure the interdependence of intelligence and cognitive behavior and development.

DEFINITIONS OF INTELLIGENCE

Many volumes have been written about intelligence, and attempts to define it are legion. If one was to imagine a continuum defining intelligence, at one extreme end would be the notion that "Intelligence is what intelligence tests measure," while toward the other end of the continuum would be a definition such as "Intelligence is the ability to do abstract thinking" (where "abstract thinking" is not clearly defined). From this polar understanding of intelligence, it is perhaps easy to see why it is the subject of intense controversy.

Many argue against the concept of a single or unitary intelligence. The case has been put for a number of types of intelligence (for example, Ferguson, 1954, 1956; Thorndike, et al., 1926). Others believe that intelligence is made up of a number of pure or primary factors, each relatively independent of the other (Guilford, 1967; Thurstone and Thurstone, 1950). The Thurstones have developed tests for children, adolescents, and adults that purport to measure a number of primary factors, such as ability to deal with spatial concepts, number ability, word fluency, and vocabulary. Guilford (1967), whose *Structure of Intellect* will be discussed in more detail later, also espouses a factorial theory of intelligence.

Spearman (1927) was a pioneer in the field of intelligence theory and assessment. He held that there was a general or g factor that relates to all intelligent, sentient behavior. Additionally, there were many special or s factors, some of which are rather closely related to g (number ability, for example), while others are practically independent (for example, music or motor ability). Wechsler (for example, 1944), one of the leading practical test construction men, has developed his tests so as to measure performance and verbal intelligence. The former is presumably quite free of the effects of language, while the latter stresses vocabulary, verbal reasoning, similarities, and comprehension. Cattell (1941) and Horn (1968) also believe that intelligence is dual, and think that their constructs of fluid and crystallized intelligence satisfactorily handle both the notions of general intelligence (g) and factorial intelligence as conceptualized by Guilford. Cattell's and Horn's *crystallized intelligence* represents the effect of acculturation on human ability. *Fluid intelligence* is thought to indicate a pattern of neural-physiological and incidental learning influences.

Theories of Intelligence

In the 1950s, theory of intelligence and assessment strategies seemed to have reached their asymptote. Ferguson (1954) wrote at that time.

> At present no systematic theory, capable of generating fruitful hypotheses about behavior, lies behind the study of human ability. Current approaches are largely empirical.... The concept of intelligence ... is no longer a useful scientific concept except as subsuming some defined set of clearly distinguishable abilities. (p. 95)

Ferguson's Overlearned Skills Theory Following this negative pronouncement, Ferguson goes on to develop a theory of intelligence that the author finds plausible and compatible with his own learning bias. As will be seen, it also fits well with some of the most promising current developments in the field. Ferguson's theory is more a learning than a genetic, and more a process than a structural, theory. It seems to have been prompted at least indirectly by Hebb (1949). Ferguson believes that intellectual ability as currently measured consists of correlated types of overlearning. Overlearning, in interaction with an individual's biological heritage, results in different asymptotic levels of the separate abilities that, when grouped, are called intelligence. In other words, no matter how much an individual tries, he will become no more proficient in performing intellectual tasks. Conversely, regardless of how seldom these tasks are practiced, they will lose little or nothing in efficiency. Ferguson would say that a score from an intelligence test is useful in predicting success in school simply because the overlearned skills represented by an IQ transfer substantially to the types of learning an individual must master in school.

Ferguson believes that those abilities essential for adjusting satisfactorily to a given culture increase regularly with age up to perhaps age 17 or older. Those abilities that are not necessary in adapting to a culture increase more slowly. Indeed, they may not grow at all, or only to a very low level. By such reasoning, he accounts for the differences in measured intelligence between people who live in different countries, in rural rather than urban areas, in institutions rather than homes, and in circumstances of cultural disadvantagement or isolation rather than cultural advantagement or rich intercommunication. Differences in tested intelligence scores between the different socioeconomic classes can be accounted for in a similar way.

For example, evidence suggests that children growing up in culturally isolated rural areas such as the mountains of eastern Tennessee show a progressive *decrease* in intelligence as measured by standard intelligence tests (Wheeler, 1942). Older brothers and sisters obtain substantially lower IQs than younger brothers and sisters. Ferguson would explain this by saying that the skills measured by a standard United States test of intelligence are simply not very important in adapting to life in the Tennessee mountains. Hence, such skills decline with age, and IQs[1] consequently drop. McCandless (1967) has reviewed cultural influences on intelligence in some detail. But, since the maximum effects of cultural determination have already been partially exerted (for better or worse) by the time of adolescence, there is no need to provide a similar detailed analysis here.

It is worthwhile to present one illustrative study, however. Havighurst and Hilkevitch (1944) studied two groups of Indian children. One group of ninety-two Hopi youngsters lived quite remote from the core United States white culture. Another somewhat less remote group was made up of twenty-nine Shiprock Navaho children. The Hopi children scored substantially higher on a performance (nonverbal) intelligence test than the white Minnesota children on whom it was standardized (115 for the Hopis compared with a normative IQ of 100 for white children). The Navaho youngsters averaged only 96 IQ. Conjecture, following Ferguson's point of view, leads one to consider the elaborate tribal organization and ritual, the high artistic level, and the well-developed architectural abilities of the Hopi. Additionally, the Hopi are farmers and depend completely on an environment so hostile that survival demands that it be studied in exquisite and painstaking skill. These aspects of Hopi life suggest that very high level performance ability fits well into the necessities of their culture. The Navaho are artistically and architecturally less proficient than the Hopi and are herders rather than farmers. Thus the skills that go into a performance intelligence test may not need to be so highly developed as among the Hopi. The white Minnesota children who made up the standardization sample, living as they do in comfortable, nondemanding environments, may likewise have less need for high level performance abilities.

Ferguson's statement applies well to this speculative account of

---

[1] IQ is a measurement obtained by dividing mental age by chronological age and multiplying by 100. Other, more complex, and often more suitable measures of obtained IQ equivalents are also employed, but they correlate closely with this traditional definition.

Hopi–Navaho–white differences in performance intelligence: "Presumably children reared in different environments, which demand different types of learning at different ages, develop different patterns of ability" (1954, p. 99). Ferguson also hypothesizes that different abilities may be required at different stages of learning a task. This will result in different asymptotes for different types of intelligence test items. "An individual might possess the ability to improve rapidly in the early stages of learning, but might lack the abilities necessary to obtain high proficiency at the stage of high habituation or overlearning" (1954, p. 102). One might illustrate by saying that almost everyone can learn the elements of playing the piano, but few will be good enough to become concert pianists. This notion of changing abilities with skill development receives support from the research literature (for example, Fleishman and Hempel, 1954, 1955). In one study of young men, Fleishman and Hempel found that in the early stages of learning a visual–motor task, the rate of learning depended most strongly on spatial and verbal abilities. Those who could best manipulate spatial concepts and those who were superior in verbal ability picked up the first steps of the task most rapidly. However, eventual mastery to the superior finished performance level depended more on speed of reaction time and the rate at which the individual moved. Ritchie, Aeschliman, and Pierce (1950) worked with rats as subjects. They found that the first stages of learning a maze depended strongly on the animals' visual discrimination ability, while perfecting the maze performance was a function of the animals' ability to use motor and kinesthetic cues.

Bayley (1955), who has conducted longitudinal studies of the development of intelligence in United States children, regards intelligence much as does Ferguson. She states:

> I see no reason why we should continue to think of intelligence as an integrated (or simple) entity or capacity which grows throughout childhood by steady accretions. . . . Intelligence appears to me, rather, to be a dynamic succession of developing functions, with the more advanced or complex functions in the hierarchy depending on the prior maturing of earlier simpler ones (given, of course, normal conditions of care). (p. 807)

In one sense, Ferguson's approach is unitary in that it consists of overlearning. On the other hand, this overlearning is applied to many different types of skill that may be subsumed under the heading of intelligence, most broadly construed as problem solving. Bayley implies a hierarchy of simpler skills that peak, perhaps as something like Spearman's g. The g, too, ultimately consists of skill at solving problems.

Guilford's Structure of Intellect Guilford (1967) also thinks of intelligence as problem solving ability, but rejects the hierarchical and g theories. He conceives of intelligence as consisting of many factors—to be precise, 120 factorial cells. In simplified terms, a factor is a commonality among a set of correlations. (This concept was discussed in Chapter 2.) It is the name for the common element that links a number of components together (in this case, performance on intelligence test items of different types). Guilford's *Structure of Intellect* is conceptualized as a rectan-

Figure 7.1

OPERATIONS
Cognition
Memory
Divergent Production
Convergent Production
Evaluation

PRODUCTS
Units
Classes
Relations
Systems
Transformations
Implications

CONTENTS
Figural
Symbolic
Semantic
Behavioral

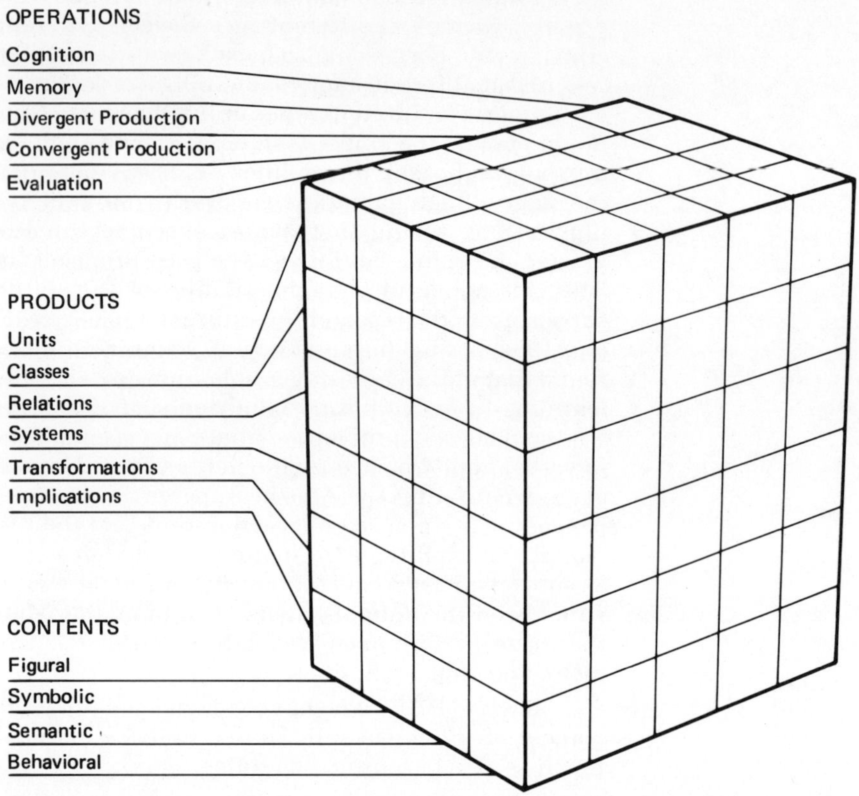

Guilford's model of the structure of intellect. (From J. P. Guilford "Intelligence," American Psychologist, 21, 1966, 20–26. Copyright 1966 by the American Psychological Association and reprinted by permission.)

gular cube. Guilford's model is shown in Figure 7.1. On its face in "layers" from top to bottom are six *products*. Cutting back at right angles from the face in "slices" or "layers" are *contents*, four in number. Intersecting these in vertical slices from the front to the back of the cube and parallel to the face are five *operations*.

What one sees in manifest human behavior is thus some combination of the *content* and the *product* (the forward face of Guilford's schematic cube). One must infer the *operation* that has produced such overt behavior. The meaning of these two statements will become clear as the three components of Guilford's *Structure of Intellect* (SI) are defined and illustrated.

A. Guilford's "products": From the simplest to the most complex, Guilford's six products (the horizontal "layers" from top to bottom of the face of his cube) are:

1. Units. Units are basic, and thus appear at the top. A unit can be an integer, such as the number 1. It can be a musical note.
2. Classes. According to Guilford, classes are next in order of complexity. A class is a more complex conception than a unit. The musical scale is a

broader concept than a single note. The number system is broader than any single number or combination of numbers.

3. Relations. To Guilford (p. 64) a relation is a connection between two things having its own character, like prepositional phrases beginning with "belonging to" or "higher than."

4. Systems. The next complex among the products is system. An outline or a mathematical equation is a system.

5. Transformations. "Changes, revision, redefinitions, or modifications, by which any product of information in one state goes over into another state" (p. 64) are transformations. Participles (verbs in noun form) are chosen by Guilford to illustrate transformations, as in the case of "reversing" or "coloring."

6. Implication. The most complex (the highest order) of the products is implication, by which Guilford means "something expected, anticipated, or predicted from given information" (p. 64): One thing suggests another. The term association is relevant to implication. An implication is less specifiable and verbalizable than a relation. In an implication, one thing, it is suggested, *may* derive from another. Guilford's usage is quite like that of regular speech.

B. Guilford's "contents": There are four types of content:

1. Figural: This first content refers to conceptions of space.

2. Symbolic. Here the referent is to number or to letter tests (p. 61).

3. Semantic. Semantics refers to meaning, and this type of content is usually measured by verbal or word tests.

4. Behavioral. Guilford (p. 61) says this category was arrived at on purely logical grounds, while the first three categories came from previous findings about test construction. Behavioral content refers to gathering and formulating information about the behavior of people. Thorndike's notion of social intelligence also influenced Guilford in setting up this category. Guilford's illustrative test unit for behavioral content consists in selecting from a set of four pictures representing common human gestures the one picture that most closely matches the stem item in meaning.

C. Guilford's "operations": Guilford postulates five operations.

1. Cognition. This first operation is recognizing, knowing, or discovering the basis of what one knows. Recognition would seem to belong here, also.

2. Memory. The second operation is memory, without which none of the other facets of the SI can work.

3. Divergent production. This operation implies fluency, flexibility, and elaboration. The emergence of originals also belongs to this operation, implying creativity.

4. Convergent production. The fourth operation refers to logical induction or deduction, usually from possession of a relatively complete set of facts and according to a formal logical procedure. Convergent production "must satisfy a unique specification or set of specifications" (p. 62).

5. Evaluation. Evaluation involves judgment (placing a value upon, or allocating a place thereunto).

Now one can look logically at how Guilford's contents and products combine into behavior from which the operations can be inferred: If a six sided figure is presented to a seventh grader, and he is asked to name it, he says it is a hexagon. One infers, first, that the operation of cognition has taken place (he knows what it is), and, further, that memory is involved, since he must at one time have learned it and summoned memory to recognize and name it. Conversely, he may look at it, seem momentarily alert and insightful, then stumble and say he does not know. One infers that he has recognized it but his rapidly changing expression says that memory has failed him and he has forgotten the name.

Guilford is steadily building tests to tap the various factorial cells, but has no single set of tests like the Thurstones' Primary Mental Abilities Scales. He believes that different kinds of information come into experience at different times, and that ability to handle them progresses at different rates, a position similar to Bayley's. Guilford points out that figural and behavioral information are present almost from birth, while symbolic and semantic information come much later. The brain, he believes, develops different ways of processing information and its products, as well as different mechanisms for the five types of operation.

Both the environment and body, or soma, feed into the SI. Bodily information may be motivational and emotional, as well as purely informational. Both the brain and sensory receptors provide input. Filtering and screening occur, varying from age to age, individual to individual, and, within an individual, from time to time or situation to situation. Some sorts of input are shut off, others facilitated. Attention is closely related to the concept of filtering. The human organism is always evaluating, checking, and self-correcting. Such checking is not the final stage of problem solving, but occurs throughout the process. Being aware of a problem, identifying it, and structuring it, Guilford believes, are cognitive operations that call for memory and evaluation of cognized information. In the process of problem solving, the individual is often motivated to seek new information, both from memory and direct new experience. Guilford also thinks that the factorial structure of intellect may be complex from birth. Piaget's formulation of the sensorimotor stage of development during the first two years seems to be in agreement with such a position.

Crystallized and Fluid Intelligence Horn (1968) attempts to carry Cattell's (1941) ideas of a crystallized and a fluid intelligence still further. The basic process underlying both types of intelligence is *anlage* function, the "very elementary capacities in perception, retention, and expression, as these govern intellectual performance" (p. 243). A reasonably pure test of *anlage* function is memory for digits, where the tester reads a series of digits at the rate of one second each. At the end of the reading, the subject repeats them aloud. The upper limit of such an *anlage* function item is about nine digits forward. *Anlage* function is elementary, yet must be present in some substantial amount to support higher order functions such as Guilford's evaluation or convergent thinking or even transformations and systems. Crystallized intelligence is that which is involved in mastery of the common elements of the culture. "The major educational institutions of a society (including the home and its substitutes) are directed at instilling this intelligence in the persons (i.e., the young) who are expected to maintain the culture. The anlage capacities of individuals are thus harnessed, as it were, by the dominant culture for the purpose of maintaining and extending the 'intelligence of the culture'" (pp. 246-247). This process builds from a base of simple experiences and concepts. When experiences are limited so these are not developed (as, for example, when a disadvantaged child is not given the experiences necessary to translate the three dimensional object to the two dimensional picture—a type of learning that is automatic in the home experiences of middle-class children), then later development of crystallized intelligence is retarded. Crystallized intelligence, in other words, develops from experiences that have been arranged for the child, literally from his birth.

Fluid intelligence, on the other hand, develops relatively (but not entirely) independently from the arrangements others make for one. Almost all children learn eventually to conserve (this topic will be discussed in more detail in Chapter 8). An example of conservation is that children come to know and be able to verbalize the principle that five pennies spaced in a long line are not more pennies than when bunched in a short row (conservation of number). Word fluency, attention span, and figure-ground differentiation all play a part in fluid intelligence. Such intelligence is relatively independent of acculturation.

Models of Intellectual Development Gagné (1968a) classifies theories about human behavioral development, of which intellectual development is only a special case, into three types of models. Like Ferguson's (1954, 1956), Gagné's own preference is for a learning model. In the first model discussed by Gagné, which is a rather traditional child development model, certain organized patterns of growth must occur before learning can be usefully incorporated into development. Some influential current curriculum theorists (for example, Kohlberg, 1968) use such an argument to question the usefulness of compensatory education programs in promoting intellectual development. They say that only when an organism is in a special state of readiness can functions derived from experience be plugged in. Implicitly, they seem to believe that stages of readiness are maturational [that is, fall into Horn's (1968) category of "experiences not arranged for one by others"]. Efforts to modify experience such as reported by Bloom (1969) and Skeels (1966) that are discussed later suggest that the rigid developmental model of intellectual growth is unduly pessimistic.

The second model, interactionist in principle, is most conspicuously represented by Piaget (1950, 1951, 1952). Piaget and his followers give the child's learning as he interacts with his environment a role in their theory of intelligence, but learning is only moderately contributive and, implicitly, even then, only learning such as Horn's "unarranged learning" is effective. The developmental stages of intellectual growth postulated by Piaget are taken up in Chapter 8 under the heading of cognitive growth.

Gagné's third model is the traditional associationist model, which in its simplest form is based on connections or associations. Such a straightforward "simple or multiple connections" model is dismissed by Gagné as "weak and virtually empty" (1968a, p. 181).

Gagné calls his own model *cumulative learning.* "The child progresses from one point to the next in his development, not because he acquires one or a dozen new associations, but because he learns an ordered set of capabilities which build upon each other in progressive fashion through the processes of differentiation, recall, and transfer of learning" (p. 181). This definition employs a sophisticated definition of readiness that is also espoused by Bruner (for example, 1965), which may be paraphrased as follows: A child or an adolescent is ready to move on to a new skill when he has mastered all the tasks that are necessary for learning the new skill.

The notion of transfer of training implicit in such a definition of readiness is basic to Gagné's model of intellectual development, as it is to Ferguson's theory of socially adaptive overlearned "traits." Gagné (1968b) also postulates two types of learning strategy, one based on learned verbalizations and the other on intellectual skills. The former seems akin to Cattell's and Horn's crystallized intelligence, although certainly the operation of crystallized intelligence requires intellectual skill. Horn's *anlage* functions would seem to be intimately involved in Gagné's intellectual skills. Furthermore, the higher the level of intellectual skill, presumably the greater the facility in transferring learning and thus the greater the intellectual power.

To summarize, there are many theories of intelligence that range from the old but practical conception of g (Spearman's) to such sophisticated factor theories as Guilford's. One can not escape the conclusion that there is no single entity that may be called intelligence; nor can one escape the conclusion that learning or acculturation opportunities enter strongly into intellectual growth, power, and efficiency; nor can one escape the conclusion that certain basic, very directly neurophysiological abilities such as the *anlage* functions underlie intelligence and may set its upper limits.

For practical purposes, the author must return to the position he has taken earlier (McCandless, 1967) that intelligence is that set of operations by which an individual solves problems. The most useful measure of intelligence is the one that most closely resembles the problem task about which one wishes to make a prediction. Interest in the assessment of intelligence is to predict who will be able to solve which problems and master what tasks. To predict an adolescent's probable success or failure in a Ph.D. program in physics, a different measure of intelligence is employed from predicting his success as a key-punch operator.

APPROACHES TO MEASUREMENT

This topic has already been approached in the discussion of Guilford's *Structure of Intellect* and Cattell's theories about crystallized and fluid intelligence. While most present day intelligence tests are strongly influenced by theories of intelligence, and while the chances are good that the best prediction of problem solving behavior will eventually be made by means of tests designed according to theory, intelligence tests originated from practical necessity.

Binet, who is commonly but not entirely accurately given the credit for fathering intelligence testing, was assigned a very practical problem to solve: Why are so many young French children failing school? This led to the broader question of predicting which children would succeed and which children would fail in school. As Schweiker (1968) puts it:

> First grade teachers told Binet that most children had opportunity to learn many things before starting school. Those children who had learned many of those things, later learned well in school. Binet made a test of many of those things-which-most-children-had-opportunity-to-learn, and found that the test gave a fair prediction of success in school. Binet's test—and useful subsequent IQ testing—was dependent upon:
> 1. Item content:
>   a. Whether similar to material and processes to be learned in school.
>   b. Whether background material useful for learning in school.
> 2. How much opportunity a child had had to learn the item content.
> 3. How much was learned, when the child did have the opportunity. (p. 718)

Schweiker believes that if one keeps his eye on such functions of intelligence testing, confusion about intelligence will diminish and that the often mischievously used terms intelligence and mental ability will either disappear from the arguments, or be sensibly anchored to behavioral realities and learning opportunities. The case is probably not quite so simple, but an approach like this (and like Ferguson's) seems useful and realistic.

Types of Intelligence Tests

There are many different types of intelligence tests and many different versions of each type. The *Sixth Mental Measurement Yearbook* (Buros, 1965) includes reviews of 130 different intelligence tests or instruments similar to intelligence tests. Such tests are most simply classified according to the age group for which they are suitable and their type. The tests range from tests that must be given individually (as for infants and preschool children) to group tests designed such that only the most superior adult can pass all items. A perfect score is indeed a rarity for such tests. There are tests of so-called verbal intelligence, such as verbal reasoning analogies: "*Good* is to *bad* as *love* is to . . .," and tests of vocabulary. There are also performance tests that deal with spatial relations, memory span, visual motor abilities, and so on. Performance tests do not involve the use of words to make a response, although most subjects appear to guide their behavior by thoughts expressed to themselves by words. Examples of such tests are: solving paper mazes by drawing a trace through them with a pencil; fitting together individual pieces to make more complex forms; replacing missing pieces into a picture from which they have been cut; or selecting from a series the section that will complete a pictured pattern from which a section has been blanked out. There are tests and individual items within tests that tap speed: the faster the individual works, the higher his score; power (problems range from very simple to extremely difficult, but no time limit or a very long one is set); and breadth (such as range of vocabulary or information). The most commonly tested abilities are grouped as Wechsler groups them, into verbal and performance tests. Additionally, tests of number facility (Q for quantitative) are widely used with older children, adolescents, and adults.

Intelligence Testing for Adolescents

The most common reason for giving an adolescent an intelligence test is to predict how well he will do in school. Tests also may be administered for screening purposes (to keep him out of something he can not master or to put him into something that it is believed will challenge him to capacity). Guidance toward college is a type of screening, and college admission officers make much use of intelligence test results in admitting or declining students. Placement in a technical or college preparatory secondary school is often entirely and usually importantly influenced by intelligence test results.

An intelligence test is also frequently given when an adolescent presents a problem of some sort. If he tests low, all too frequently his difficulties are attributed entirely to a low IQ and little further attention is paid to him. It happens fairly often that a youngster will test low on a group intelligence test but high on an individual test. Other things being equal, group tests probably predict school success better than individual tests. They have more factors in common with the school situation in that they are a work sample taken in a group situation, usually timed, and thus more like the standard school working and examination situation than the more personalized and leisured individual intelligence test. Anxious children and youth tend not to do as well in group as in individual testing situations. For obvious reasons, young people with reading problems will perform poorly on a typical verbal reasoning test. Calm, efficient young people who read well probably achieve about equally on group and individual tests. A common school aim is to help those with high potential but low achievement. Herein lies one value of individual intelligence tests: If a young person scores 20 points higher on an individual than on a group test, but his school performance fits better with his group test score, the inference can be made that he "has the capacity" to do better schoolwork. Remedial measures may involve additional coaching, remedial diagnosis and treatment, counseling, home consultation, or all of these.

Special Considerations in Using Intelligence Tests

Many of those who are concerned with educating the disadvantaged (who typically obtain low IQs on conventional intelligence tests) are skeptical about intelligence tests. Results from tests have often been misused or inadequately used. The usual intelligence (IQ) test is a measure of both previous opportunity to learn and of ability to learn something new in a given setting. To a considerable degree, intelligence tests measure "social acculturation," referred to earlier in the chapter. But included in many tests are items that may be thought of as learning samples, which may be both more accurate in predicting a given type of achievement and fairer to disadvantaged children and youth whose opportunities to learn standard middle-class acculturation have been limited and have varied widely from home to home. Schweiker (1968) describes Cronbach's Semantic Test of Intelligence (STI), where the type of learning required is associating symbols with pictured verbal concepts. Such a test, Schweiker believes, "is directly related to the school task of learning to read. You might even say that the STI is a single lesson of learning to read a foreign language by the look-say (recognize-think) method" (p. 719). Schweiker goes on to say that "Practically all higher SES [socioeconomic status] children have ample opportunity to learn the material in the IQ test, so how well they have learned it is closely related to how well they do on a learning sample test. The lower SES children vary widely in their opportunities to learn the material in an IQ test, so their IQ scores are more related to their opportunities to learn than to their scores on a learning sample test" (pp. 719-720). Schweiker seems to want to drop conventional intelligence tests in favor of learning sample tests, a point of view that is perhaps not too different from the ultimate aims of Guilford and the Thurstones. However, the latter two believe that work sample tests represent factors of intelligence rather than simple learning.

On the practical side, adequate batteries of work sample tests do not yet exist and standard intelligence tests, wisely employed, add much to the guidance potential for young people. Thus, whether or not they are the best instrument to employ for the purposes, they will be around for a long time. One of the adults' tasks at present is to learn how to use them wisely and appropriately. An appropriate use is certainly *not* to put down disadvantaged youth.

The most experienced test users often seem to forget that the best of tests, given under ideal circumstances and to conventionally acculturated middle-class youth, can make only a partial prediction of how well a young person will do in school. In the search for precision and exactness, adults often forget that IQs do not remain constant for individual children: A high tester in fifth grade may test average or even below in eighth grade, and vice versa.

Some who oppose intelligence tests say that any good teacher knows how bright her children are without going through complex testing machinations. Alexander (1953) decided to test this point of view. As subjects, he used 978 public school pupils in grades three through eight, and their thirty-five teachers. Fifty percent of the teachers had completed 120 semester hours of college training, and their median teaching experience was twelve years. The study was conducted in about the middle of the second semester of the school year, so that each teacher had had ample opportunity to come to know the children. Alexander asked each teacher to list the five students in her class who in her opinion were the most intelligent, and the five who were the least intelligent. The teachers were then asked to list the five pupils who were working closest to their capacity and the five who were performing furthest below their capacity in the major academic subjects. All pupils were then given intelligence and standardized academic tests.

Alexander found that the teachers were accurate in picking the highest and the lowest IQ students in only a few more than half the cases (57 and 58 percent, respectively). They picked only about one-fourth of the highest and lowest achievers in relation to their capacity. The tendency of the teachers was to rank as "achieving up to capacity" those youngsters who stood toward the top of their class, disregarding factors of age, and to operate in the same fashion in picking the low achievers. Even allowing for the fact that they judged in relation to their own classes, they were accurate in judging the high achievers only about two-fifths of the time and the low achievers only about one-third of the time. In view of the fact that marks indicating absolute success or failure are widely assigned by teachers and accepted as true indexes of performance and ability by both children and their parents, such findings as Alexander's suggest that a majority of children are being graded according to some factor other than their true academic achievement, and that they receive psychologically very important judgments of brightness or dullness from their teachers that are often widely different from their objective ability. The very bright, high achieving young person, under such circumstances, will probably be graded lower than the older child who, although achieving up to capacity, is doing *relatively* less well.

Pegnato and Birch (1959) provide further evidence of teachers' inexactitude in selecting gifted children. Teachers were asked to nominate children of above 136 Binet IQ. "Significantly, the teachers missed . . . more than half of the gifted . . . while 31.4% of those named by them as gifted were of average intelligence on the Stanford-Binet" (p. 180). Since gifted children are the nation's future treasure, this degree of imprecision in locating them is dangerous.

This discussion of using intelligence tests needs some treatment of the topic of anxiety as it relates to test taking. The relation between the two is reasonably close, and is important. Two relevant studies have been selected for brief summary and discussion.

Anxiety and IQ Scores Yamamoto and Davis (1966) were interested in the interactions between the types of instruction they gave to their subjects before a test was taken, the subjects' scores on the Task Anxiety Scale for Children (see Hill and Sarason, 1966), and the children's and young people's tendency to be dependent on adults. They worked with 480 students from fourth, seventh, tenth, and twelfth grades in a large suburban Midwestern school. The Kuhlmann-Anderson group test of intelligence was employed as an aptitude measure. The tests were administered with different sets of instructions. The type of instruction seemed to make little difference in the results (whether instructions were for an intelligence test, an achievement test, a routine class test, or the instructions given in the Kuhlmann-Anderson manual). The most significant results from the Yamamoto and Davis study indicate that the more anxious subjects for all four types of instruction, at every grade, and for both sexes, scored lower in intelligence than the less anxious children. The average difference of 8.0 points favored the less anxious children. The difference was highest for the oldest subjects, twelfth grade students who were told they were taking an intelligence test. Here the difference of 16.4 IQ points favored the less anxious young people. One may conjecture that anticipations that their results might affect high school graduation and college entrance raised the anxiety level and drastically reduced the performance of those who were most anxious.

Hill and Sarason (1966) report similar results for younger children from first through fifth grades. Their more anxious children score lower not only in intelligence, but also in tests of proficiency in the regular school subjects. As in the Yamamoto and Davis study, the older Hill and

Table 7.1

Correlations between predictor variables and college grades

Predictor Variable	Semester of College	
	1	8
High school rank	.51	.28
English	.40	.20
Mathematics	.40	.15
Social Science	.36	.17
Natural Science	.36	.16
Composite	.47	.21

(Adapted from Humphreys, 1968.)

Sarason's children were, the greater the interference by anxiety. This held true both for achievement and for ability tests.

In short, undue anxiety interferes with all sorts of school, life, and intellectually related functions. These range from freedom to ask questions and seek information to question *answering* as represented by intelligence and achievement tests.

Predictions from Intelligence Plus Motivation Holtzman and Brown (1968) and Khan (1969) demonstrate that many other factors need to be considered in genuinely efficient use of intelligence tests. For example, Khan finds that measures of motivation in addition to intelligence add much more precision to predicting boys' than girls' school achievement. Both Khan (who worked with Florida children) and Holtzman and Brown (whose subjects came from a number of areas in the United States) find that measures of motivation added to measures of intelligence greatly improve the prediction of academic achievement for both boys and girls.

We will see in Chapters 9 and 10 that intelligence tests are not very useful in predicting achievement for disadvantaged youth. The reasons for this inefficiency have been plausibly explained above (particularly by Schweiker and the related discussion). Finally, it should be repeated that even the best of intelligence tests given to middle-class youth under ideal conditions seldom account for as much as half of the total variance that goes into succeeding in school.

Intelligence and Educational Growth Humphreys (1968) provides sobering data about trying to predict college success throughout the eight conventional semesters to graduation at the University of Illinois. He used as his predictors rank in high school graduating class and the sub- and composite scores of the American College Testing Program. Table 7.1 is adapted from Humphreys, and vividly illustrates the declining precision of prediction of college achievement from the first semester of the freshman year to the last semester of the senior year. Humphreys' correlations are corrected for restriction of range of talent between the predictors and the criteria (p. 377).

There is a steady decline in efficiency for the predictor with each succeeding college semester. According to Humphreys, the composite score from the academic ability (intelligence, loosely speaking) test and each of its components shows similar patterns although at a somewhat *lower* level of common variance. "The data suggest that people are changing and that 'aptitude for college work' is far from stable" (p. 377).

From Table 7.1, it is obvious that high school rank is the best predictor of college graduation; but even it accounts for less than 8 percent of the variance. The composite score, so frequently employed for admitting students to college programs, accounts for only a little more than 4 percent of the variance. This suggests that one might almost as well admit students by lottery!

It is worthwhile to quote Humphreys at some length:

> In place of these all or none assumptions about ability and motivation, a radically different interpretation should be attempted. The first supposition will be that intelligence is not fixed, that there is no measurable or inferable (from measurements) innate capacity, and that gain in intellectual functioning continues indefinitely with adequate stimulation in a healthy organism. By the same token loss occurs without adequate stimulation. The second supposition will be that intellectual functioning, either on psychological tests or in the classroom, depends on a very broad, cumulative, well-learned repertoire of skills, knowledge, modes of performance, etc. Furthermore, this repertoire increases with age and experience . . . the amount of change which is of interest here is a function of age and experience. . . . There is also an economic argument to suggest changes in probation and failing regulations. Once the student has invested a semester in college study, and once the college has invested in the student by admitting him, housing him, and teaching him, if he can attain graduation standards on or near schedule, the social gain is maximized, and the expense minimized, by retaining him. This approach, incidentally, should not be termed "coddling," and it need not deteriorate into coddling if graduation standards are maintained (pp. 378-379).

Although Humphreys' research was done with college students, its implications for education, probation, grade retention, and so on, seem equally appropriate for high schools.

Test Scores and Guidance No indictment of test scores is provided by Flook and Saggar (1968). Rather, they suggest that test scores are very useful when efficiently employed. Flook and Saggar worked with sixty first year students in engineering at the University of St. Andrews, Scotland. The experimental group was carefully matched with controls, and its members were given detailed knowledge about their entrance test scores, while the controls received no knowledge. The latter practice is the more common one. In the end of year examinations, the experimental group (at the .001 level of probability) performed significantly better than the control group. The authors believe that knowledge of their test scores enabled the experimental men to plan more realistically, that they improved in self-evaluation through social comparison, and that the knowledge of the test scores was the catalytic agent in their relative efficiency over the controls. Improvement (the numbers are small, so this result must be taken cautiously) was greatest for the group with low test scores.

Mental Age versus IQ as a Learning Predictor   There is some controversy in the literature about whether the mental age (MA) or the IQ[2] is the better predictor of learning efficiency. The practical significance of the MA versus IQ argument, among other things, applies to retaining children in school. If the IQ is the better predictor, one can expect young bright youngsters to do as well as and probably better than much older children with similar MAs. This argument is particularly pertinent to policy about gifted children, as will be seen later. Zigler (1967, for example) and Jensen and Rohwer (1968) have both contributed to this debate. Zigler flatly believes that MA and not IQ determines the rate of learning. Jensen and Rohwer present data that suggest that the IQ is the better predictor. In one of the studies they report, normal third graders learned both serial and paired-associate[3] tasks three to four times faster than retarded adults with the same MA level (9 years) but much lower IQs (58 compared to 105).

In another study reported by Jensen and Rohwer (1968), retarded adults were compared with disadvantaged preschoolers, kindergarten, and grades one, three, and six children on paired-associate learning. Again, the adults did less well than any of the children. Jensen and Rohwer proceed to demonstrate the confounding and thought provoking effects of social class on such predictions. They report a study in which white middle-class children were closely matched for chronological and mental ages (and thus, IQs) with a group of white disadvantaged children. The *latter* performed significantly better in paired-associate learning. This finding should be placed in the context of the earlier discussion of IQ as a joint function of opportunity to learn and learning ability. It can be plausibly assumed that the disadvantaged children had had less opportunity to pick up the middle-class acculturation that permeates conventional IQ tests. Thus, they scored poorly on items that reflect acculturation, but earned higher scores on items that tapped learning ability. The converse may have been true for the middle-class children. Thus, equal IQs between the two groups were earned for different reasons: poor acculturation among the disadvantaged, low level of learning ability among the middle class. Since the paired-associate task primarily reflects learning ability, it could have been predicted that the disadvantaged children would perform better. This finding and interpretation are sufficiently important for practical educational purposes to merit considerable attention.

Testing Conditions   The final study on uses of intelligence testing to be reported in this section is related to the circumstances of test administra-

---

[2]See footnote 1, this chapter.
[3]Serial learning is sequential learning, or learning a series; paired-associate learning is learning what things go with what other things, under controlled circumstances, as, for example, when *cat* is presented on a flash card, the number *9* is supposed to follow. Serial learning is analogous to the *look-see* or, as Schweiker (1968) puts it, *recognize-think* method of teaching reading vocabulary.

tion. Its results are somewhat reassuring to those who must administer tests in less than ideal surroundings. Stevenson, Friedrichs, and Simpson (1970) tested a total of 125 educable retarded adolescents under three conditions: group testing, individual testing, or individual testing with a supportive adult present. The young people averaged about 14¼ years of age, and their IQs were about 70. The tests consisted of paired-associate learning, discrimination learning, incidental learning (learning apparently irrelevant things at the same time the central task is being mastered), verbal memory, and anagrams (a game form of analogies). While some differences among the testing conditions and the tasks appeared, the over-all results suggest equal efficiency for such a population in each of the testing circumstances. Additionally, when compared with normal fourth graders, the retarded adolescents showed important deficiencies only in the verbal memory and anagrams tests.

Since much of the special work professional people do is concerned with retarded children, the Stevenson, Friedrichs, and Simpson data are of considerable practical importance.

GROWTH OF INTELLIGENCE Many studies have been conducted to investigate the rate of growth, the time of leveling off, and the onset and rate of decay of intelligence. Findings are often contradictory, and the conclusions given here can be disputed by data from individual studies. However, the present conclusions are reasonable.

First, the rate of intellectual development decreases with increasing age. Chapter 8 will show that adolescence brings with it changes in ways of organizing knowledge, but there is no spurt in intellectual growth at adolescence that compares with the physical growth spurt, or that seems directly to reflect the upsurge of drive at adolescence hypothesized in Chapter 1.

Figures 7.2 and 7.3 have been adapted from different sources of data to provide a schematic view of the rate of intellectual growth from about 10½ to about 20½ years (Figure 7.2), and from birth to middle age (Figure 7.3). It can be seen in Figure 7.2 that somewhat more than 40 percent of mature intellectual status has been reached by 10½ years of age, and that growth from then on is progressively slower. The data from which Figure 7.2 was originally adapted (Jones and Conrad, 1944) appear to show that additional intellectual "power" is not acquired after about 19½ years of age. There is evidence to indicate that intellectual growth continues longer for the bright, superior, and well educated and stops earlier for subjects of low intelligence (Gurvitz, 1951; H. E. Jones, 1954; Miles and Miles, 1932). Other evidence indicates that intellectual growth continues until well into maturity for both superior and average persons (Bayley, 1955, 1968; Green, 1969; Owens, 1953; and Schaie and Strother, 1968).

A curve of intellectual growth from birth to the middle years is presented in Figure 7.3. From birth to the late teens, it can be seen that the curve takes the shape of a very shallow, steeply slanted S. This means that during infancy and the early preschool years, growth is positively accelerated (faster with age). At school age, the growth curve has be-

Figure 7.2

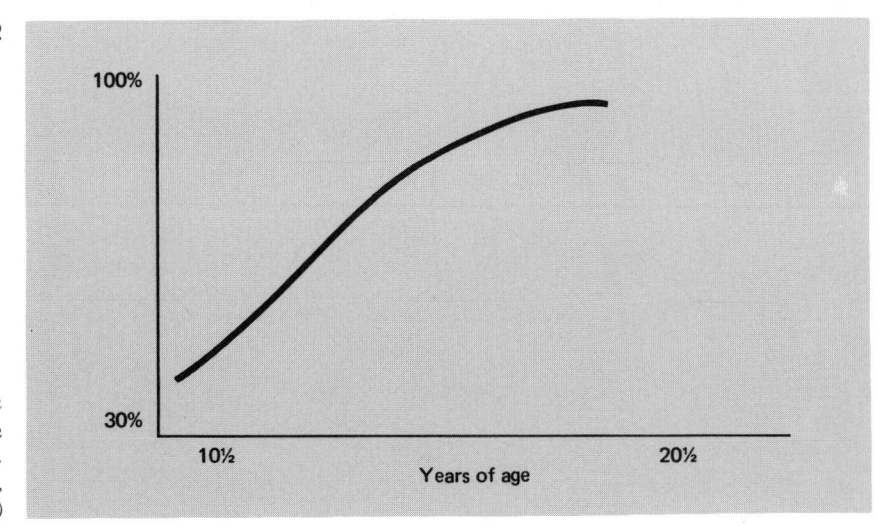

Intellectual growth from 10½ to 20½ years of age. (From McCandless, 1967.)

come negatively accelerated (slower year by year). This tendency is shown more clearly in Figure 7.2. Growth is very gradual (Figure 7.3) from the late teens onward. Zubek and Solberg's (1954) review of the literature reveals that, in most studies, it has been found that intellectual performance begins to drop at about the mid-20s. This drop is minimal until a person reaches his 40s. From this age, there is a steady decrease in efficiency for most mental functions. Tests that involve speed and, possibly, close attention or concentration seem to elicit decreasing scores earliest in life (mid-20s or earlier); scores for power tests decline later; and scores in a type of test that Zubek and Solberg call breadth tests show a negligible decline and in some cases an increase. These are tests like vocabulary and information, and probably reflect acculturation (after Cattell, 1941; and Horn, 1968). Speed tests may be more associated with physical condition, and attention and concentration may reflect Horn's *anlage* function. In short, the suggestion is plausible that ability remains stable or increases in culturally determined intelligence, but it may decline for items more closely related to neurophysiology. Horn believes this to be true, thinking that crystallized intelligence remains stable or increases with an active intellectual life, while fluid intelligence will be more likely to reveal neurological deterioration and insult, and the effects of aging.

Longitudinal Studies of Intellectual Growth

Owens (1953) readministered the same test to 127 men after an interval of from 30 to 31 years. The men had taken the first tests as college freshmen, the second as middle-aged men. The men retested by Owens did not differ in their general characteristics from the men he was unable to reach, so he infers that his retested sample represents the entire original sample. As mature men, Owens' subjects were significantly higher in total IQ than they had been as entering college freshmen (see Humphreys, 1968). Their gains were greatest for tests that presumably tap abilities called practical judgment, and tests of synonyms–antonyms, disarranged sentences, information, and analogies. Abilities to follow

Figure 7.3

A hypothetical composite age curve representing the growth of intelligence from birth to the middle years. (From McCandless, 1967.)

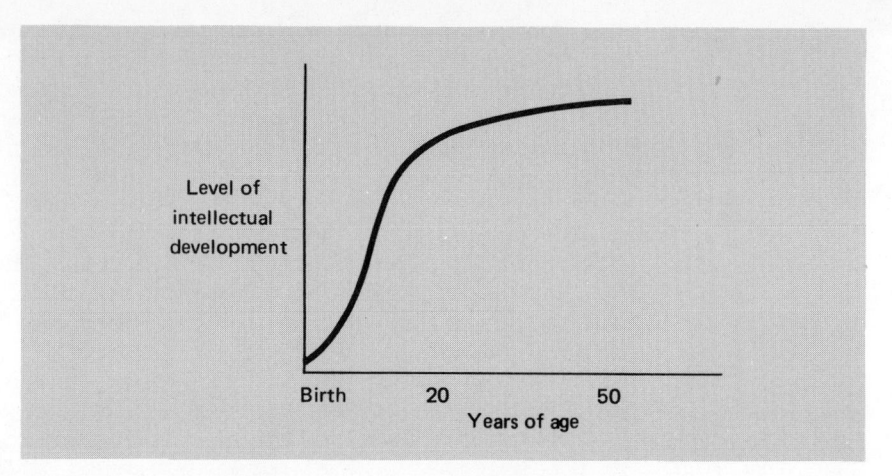

directions, handle arithmetic problems, and manage number series stayed constant or decreased slightly but not significantly. Men who were below 50 years of age gained a little more than those who were above 50. Those who had completed the most college work gained more than those with less education; general science majors showed more upward movement than agriculture or engineering majors. Those who had moved from rural to urban settings during their lives appeared to have gained more than those with other residence patterns. Gain was not related to type of job held, income, physical exercise, marital status, number of children, or number of brothers and sisters.

Bayley's 1955 report is similar. However, she finds a sex difference (1968). Subjects she had followed from infancy for thirty-six years, and who were subjects of the California Growth Studies (see Chapter 5), on the whole increased in intelligence up to age 26, but after that leveled off and remained unchanged through age 36.

> However, there are increments after 26 years in the males' scores on the verbal scale. The female scores either actually drop (in performance scores) or remain unchanged (in verbal scores) between 26 and 36 years. . . . Given the motivation, however, a larger proportion of men than women may maintain into later age higher levels of capacity in the various cognitive functions—in particular, in abstract reasoning. (p. 6)

Bayley believes that verbal facility and knowledge (this looks like Cattell's crystallized intelligence) are more likely to remain stable or to show gain than "fluid abilities" like reasoning processes, arithmetic and verbal reasoning, perhaps attention span or short term memory, and speed. These latter (with the possible exception of the reasoning tests) seem more related to Cattell's fluid intelligence.

Bayley's and Owens' are two of the few studies that follow the same subjects for a period of many years. Many of the studies that have provided data for change in intelligence have been cross-sectional in nature, and have included different age cohorts (a population that represents a certain characteristic). In such studies, a group of 15 to 18 year olds, another group of 19 to 21 year olds, and so on, have been tested. As one moves up the age scale from youth to maturity and old age, one is likely to find that the older populations represent very different earlier educations and vary in other important characteristics (such as urban-rural residential distribution) from the younger populations. Schaie and Strother (1968) believe that the cross-sectional cohort method of study has resulted in very deceptive data about intellectual change, accentuating factors of decline. They tested a stratified random sample of 500 subjects from 20 to 70 years of age. The authors stratified their sample according to such factors as sex, social status, and education, then randomly selected twenty-five men and twenty-five women each for each five year age interval from 20 to 70 years of age. The population from which Schaie and Strother drew consisted of about 18,000 members of a prepaid medical plan. The population is fairly representative of census figures for a large metropolitan area, although the lower socioeconomic levels are a bit underrepresented. All subjects were originally tested with the Primary Mental Abilities Test that has been discussed earlier, and with the Test of Behavioral Rigidity. Seven years later, the authors were able to relocate and retest 302 of the same subjects with the same instruments. The second sample quite accurately represented the first (that is, the retested subjects did not differ much from those who were not retested), except that females were somewhat overrepresented.

Schaie and Strother report their data in two ways: First, from the longitudinal gains made over seven years by each subject, they construct a hypothetical individual longitudinal developmental curve; and second, they report the age differences by age of the cross-sectional cohorts. In four of the five cases for the five primary abilities (verbal meaning, space, reasoning, and number) the curve for individual longitudinal growth remains steady, or increases longer, or falls less sharply than the curve for the cross-sectional cohort technique. In the fifth case, word fluency, the reverse is true.

Table 7.2 gives the longitudinally projected test scores for five primary mental abilities (the first five lines), a composite score made up from verbal meaning and reasoning that is considered a convenient scholastic aptitude test, three scores from Schaie's Test of Behavioral Rigidity and, in the last line of Table 7.2, the scores from an attitude test devised to measure social responsibility. A T-score is a convenient standard score, the mean is 50, and about two-thirds of a population falls within 10 points (1 S.D.) above and below the mean. The figures in Table 7.2 are taken from Schaie and Strother's graphic representation and are correct to within the nearest whole number.

It is interesting to note that for only two tests (word fluency and psychomotor speed) is peak performance reached at age 25. For other tests, such as verbal meaning, number, the composite educational aptitude, and social responsibility, peak performance is not reached until 50 years of age or later. Indeed, performance in the area of motor cognitive rigidity improves to age 60. For five scales, performance at age 70 is actually a little better than at age 25 (verbal meaning, number, the composite educational aptitude, motor cognitive rigidity, and social responsi-

Table 7.2

Course of development, longitudinal projections, of primary mental abilities and behavioral rigidity test scores from ages 25 to 70

Test	T-Score at Age 25	Highest Point of Developmental Curve Age	Highest Point of Developmental Curve T-Score	T-Score at Age 70
Verbal meaning (V)	53	55	60	56
Space (S)	56	35	57	53
Reasoning (R)	57	40	59	53
Number (N)	48	50	53	51
Word fluency (WF)	51	25	51	26
Educational aptitude (2V + R)	54	55	59	56
Motor cognitive rigidity	57	60	64	63
Personality-perceptual rigidity	55	30-50	57	50
Psychomotor speed	53	25	53	28
Social responsibility	48	50-55	56	52

(Constructed from graphic presentations by Schaie and Strother, 1968.)

bility). In only two scales does performance deteriorate drastically between ages 25 and 70 (word fluency and psychomotor speed).

Schaie and Strother (1968) conclude:

> ... a major portion of the variance attributed to age differences in past cross-sectional studies must properly be assigned to differences in ability between successive generations. Age changes over time within the individual appear to be much smaller than differences between cohorts'.... levels of functioning attained at maturity may be retained until late in life except where decrement in response strength and latency interferes. (p. 679)

Green (1969) has conducted a similar study with Puerto Rican subjects who were tested to standardize the Spanish language version of the Wechsler Adult Intelligence Scale (WAIS). Like Schaie and Strother, Green worked with stratified random groups in four cohorts, ages 25 to 29, 35 to 39, 45 to 49, and 55 to 64. His subjects were retested after five years, and his longitudinal projection is thus made from a five year test-retest interval. The full scale WAIS score rose from age 16 to age 40. Most of the decline of the performance scale quotient was due to the Digit Symbol Substitution Test, where symbols coded to numbers must be filled into blanks with a strict time limit and a bonus for speed. Thus, Green's findings within another culture and a different spoken language, with a five year rather than seven year interval between tests, are parallel to Schaie and Strother's.

Adolescents, in other words, may look forward to still further increment over their current level in most skills, and may anticipate a long and potentially useful cognitive life. Schaie and Strother and Green are exceptionally reassuring to "old dogs that wish to learn new tricks."

Gagné (1968b) provides a certain theoretical rationale for such stability or gain of intelligence, which he regards as essentially a set of intellectual skills.

> ... one can see repeated many times the general affirmation of the hypothesis that the learning of each particular category of intellectual skill depends substantially, in a positive transfer sense, on the previous learning of another particular category of intellectual skill. In brief, problem-solving draws positive transfer from prior rule learning, which is contributed to in the same sense by prior classification learning, which is in turn strongly affected by prior discrimination learning, and so on. (p. 6)

Stability of Intelligence Level

Three other studies deserve mention in this section about growth of intelligence. In the first (Bradway and Thompson, 1962), adults were tested with the Binet and WAIS when their ages ranged from 27 to 32 years of age. They had been tested with the Binet when they were of preschool or early school age twenty-five years earlier, and again in 1956 on the Binet or WAIS when they were adolescents. The average gain in IQ from adolescence to adulthood was 11 IQ points, males showed significantly more gain than females, and high IQ girls showed the least gain. Gain was greatest in items testing abstract reasoning and vocabulary (again, this seems like Cattell's crystallized intelligence, or Horn's intelligence of acculturation). The correlations between the preschool and adult tests were .59 for the adult WAIS and .64 for the adult Binet. These correlations mean that preschool intelligence accounts for between approximately 33 and 41 percent of the variance of adult intelligence. Thus, while a certain lawfulness is shown—bright preschoolers more often than not become bright adults—tremendous individual variation is more the rule than the exception. Correlations between adolescent and adult IQ averaged about .83, which suggests that the intelligent adolescent is more likely also to be the intelligent adult than is true for the intelligent preschooler. Even so, only about 70 percent of the variance of adult IQ is accounted for by adolescent IQ, suggesting that there is considerable fluctuation in rate of intellectual development from adolescence to early adulthood.

Meyer (1960) reports test–retest correlations for the five primary mental abilities over a three-and-one-half-year span. The initial tests were given to 100 boys and girls from the lower middle class as they entered the eighth grade and again at the end of the eleventh grade. He finds almost the same test–retest correlation for total primary mental abilities score from eighth to eleventh grades that Bradway and Thompson found from adolescence to adulthood. The correlation between the two tests was .82. As stated above, this indicates considerable consistency for the total population, but allows for substantial variation for given individuals. As might be expected from earlier discussions of fluency tests, the least reliable test from eighth to twelfth grades was word fluency, for which the correlation was only .43.

Finally, Kennedy (1969) has followed up his sample of Southeastern United States Afro-American children. When first tested in 1960, the children ranged in age from 5 to 14 years. On retest, in 1965, the age range was from 10 to 19. The average Binet IQ in 1960 was 79.2. In 1965 it was 79.4. Kennedy's statement that this represents "holding the line" must be qualified by another statement he makes: "The reaction of the children themselves to white and Negro examiners who were strange to the setting was also more relaxed and natural than seemed to be the case in 1960." (pp. 16–17). One is left with the question about whether a decline such as might be expected from a predominantly disadvantaged group (the one studied by Kennedy) may not have been masked by an improvement in attitude and a reduction in anxiety. There is no way to answer the question. Parenthetically, the fourth graders in Kennedy's 1965 sample averaged only slightly below grade norm on standardized achievement test scores, whereas in 1960 fourth graders had averaged about 1.3 grades below norm. But in 1965, tenth graders ranked on the average about 2.5 grades below the national norm in achievement. As Kennedy points out, this may be due to the fact that some of the older children are less intelligent and are also academically deficient, having repeated one or more grades in school (although only thirty-seven of the total sample of 312 were older than 15 years of age and thus over age for grade, and of these thirty-seven, only eleven were 17 years or older).

Scott's (1966) results with Northern United States Afro-American children come closer to the patterns revealed in the literature about intellectual decline in culturally disadvantaged surroundings. Ferguson (1954, 1956), of course, would put this a different way (see the earlier part of the chapter). Rather than culturally disadvantaged, he would say "different from the prevailing middle class." It is probably well to phrase it in that fashion so as to avoid value-laden terms. In any event, Scott worked with first through ninth grade Black boys and girls. The median family income was $4800 per year, the parents averaged ninth grade education, and all families lived in slum neighborhoods. Average IQs were lower in the successive grades.

FACTORS THAT AFFECT COGNITIVE DEVELOPMENT

The preceding section reviewed substantial evidence for reasonable IQ consistency from one age level to another, and pointed out great individual variability. It was mentioned repeatedly that some children and groups of children seem to be losers in IQ, others hold stable, and still others gain. What evidence is offered in the literature about reasons for differential intellectual growth rates?

It has been pointed out earlier that anxiety typically inhibits curiosity. Also, anxiety is negatively related to performance on both intelligence and achievement tests. It seems probable that curiosity facilitates intellectual growth (see McCandless, 1967), although the author knows of no evidence on the subject that is directly relevant to adolescents. The Datta, Schaefer, and Davis (1968) and Hathaway, Reynolds, and Monachesi (1969a and b) studies, which are extensively reviewed in Chapters 9 and 10, show results about the withdrawn and passive nature of low achieving children and high school drop-outs, many of whom are described as apathetic and isolated, and suggest that the hypothesis about a link between curiosity and accelerated intellectual growth and cognitive behavior holds as much for adolescents as for children. On the whole, it cannot be expected that adolescents' patterns of intelligence will change as much as in infancy and childhood. Indeed, patterns of intellectual configuration and growth stabilize with age.

Cognitive Style Eagle (1965) presents evidence that suggests that rates of intellectual growth may to some degree be a function of the individual's cognitive style (roughly, his methods of solving problems). Eagle selected five types of cognitive style, and investigated them among 267 eighth grade students who had been tested for intelligence when they were in the third and fourth grades. The cognitive styles he investigated were:

1. Category width: the ability to make fine discriminations.
2. Field independence: the ability to separate figure from ground.
3. Tolerance of ambiguity: the ability to tolerate unclear stimuli and to wait to make decisions until the situation is clear.
4. Semantic spontaneous flexibility: the ability to produce widely diverse ideas when given the opportunity to do so (like Guilford's divergent production).
5. Acquiescence to cognitive habit: the inability to develop performance against the interfering effects of ways of behaving that have previously been strongly reinforced.

Eagle predicted that individuals who performed well on tests in the first four of the above abilities would be IQ gainers, and that those high in the last category would be IQ losers. He emerged with no dramatic results, but some of his hypotheses were supported. His most impressive finding was that children who were very high in IQ in the third and fourth grades were either gainers or held stable in IQ up to eighth grade, while those low in third and fourth grades lost by eighth grade.

Eagle's results bring to mind two other pieces of research. The Fitzsimmons, *et al.* (1969) study will be more fully discussed in Chapters 8 and 9. In this study, the authors discovered that the patterns of eventual school failure and drop-out were already evident as early as second and third grades. Kagan *et al.* (1964) have published a series of studies of first through fourth graders. In these studies, the authors investigated how children process information and produce responses in solving problems. They emerge with the postulation of a rather enduring cognitive style. On the one hand, a child (and adolescent) may show an analytic, reflective style: He works relatively slowly and deliberately, and his responses are relatively free from error. On the other hand are impulsive children who work quickly and with many errors. Implicit but not explicit in Kagan and his coworkers' studies is the suggestion that the more the child analyzes, the less he jumps to conclusions, and thus the more likely he is to do well on tasks of an intellectual nature. For such reasons, he may gain more rapidly than the impulsive child in mental age and thus increase in IQ. It may be that Kagan's impulsive children are high drive with all the associated behaviors of strong responses that are difficult to inhibit (see Chapter 1). They may also be children who do not value intellectual goals highly. People are willing to take more chances to gain goals that possess low value than when the stakes are high. In this connection, Mischel and Metzner (1962, for example), have found that impulsivity is greater for those with lower mental ages, who are younger, and who are lower in IQ.

Schimek's (1968) results are relevant in this connection. He studied twenty-eight males who took a battery of tests at ages 14, 17, and 24 (some had also been tested at age 10). One of the tests administered was the Rorschach Inkblot Test of Personality, which was scored for what Schimek calls "intellectualization." This refers to a "cognitive way of handling one's affairs." Scoring of Rorschach responses for intellectualization is based on the degree to which a subject emphasizes clarity and accuracy in his answers, his productivity as judged by the number of responses he makes, and his tendencies as shown by his responses to maintain a distance from his own answers and to introspect about his thought processes. Intellectualization style was relatively consistent (for example, the correlation between scores earned at 10 and 17 years was .73; and between 17 and 24 years, it was .68). Intellectualization as a way of personal–social life was also significantly correlated with Wechsler-Bellevue IQ. Correlation with the total scale IQ was .57; with the verbal IQ, .52; and with the performance IQ, .31 (this last correlation is not statistically significant). Kagan and Moss (1960) report that, among their 6 to 10 year olds, those who are highly achievement motivated are more likely to gain in IQ, and that boys are more likely to gain than girls.

As one ponders the results from these different studies about cognitive styles, certain definite hypotheses emerge. For example, intellectual competence is indeed a way of life. It makes for school success, sometimes almost despite oneself. That is, many bright, creative, unconventional children and youth are in constant rebellion against the rather staid system but learn anyway because of the organizing attitudes they take toward the world. Often their learning is not reflected in grades assigned by teachers, and it may come at a terrific cost. When such youngsters do not "succeed" in school, both society and they are the losers. But as a group they manage. Those who conform succeed conspicuously within the system. The over-all approach of highly competent children and youth to their environment seems to provide them with constant rewards, and successful experiences alter the structure of their intellect; their efficiency and power of function follow an accelerating, rather than a linear or declining, curve, as expressed by an increasing IQ, greater and greater subject matter mastery, and so on. Piaget's concepts of *assimilation* and *accommodation* are related to this idea. In accommodation, structure is altered, as it were, and the alteration in structure is reflected in different and hopefully more adaptive ways of responding within the environment. Piaget's accommodation is very similar to the more traditional concept of learning, except for its more explicit connotation of structural modification. Piaget's term, assimilation, is very similar to the conventional "responding," except that it carries a more general connotation. The interaction of accommodation and assimilation is required for the individual's over-all adaptation.

Sex Differences Haan (1963) presents data for youngsters followed into adulthood. Males who gained in IQ were happier and better adjusted than those who lost,

Table 7.3

Median scores for an intelligence test among father-absent and father-present males and females for Q(uantitative), V(erbal), and T(otal) intelligence test score

	Father-Absent				Father-Present				Significance of Difference by t Test		
	Q	V	T	(N)	Q	V	T	(N)	Q	V	T
Total males	53	49	44	(97)	71	55	63	(320)	.001	.001	.001
Total females	56	65	61	(198)	67	54	66	(440)	.001	— —	— —

(Adapted from Sutton-Smith, Rosenberg, and Landy, 1968.)

and were also more masculine in their adjustment. Females who gained were less happily adjusted and more masculine in their adjustment than females who remained the same or lost. Bayley (1968) and Bradway and Thompson (1962) report that being male is more likely to be associated with IQ gains than being female. It is difficult to account for such findings. The most plausible hypothesis, the author believes, is one of cultural determination: The cultural goals of obedience, nurturance, and responsibility held for girls (see Chapters 1, 13, 14, and 15) are not such that they keep a girl reaching intellectually. Competence, as we have seen, is not highly valued for women. Boys' goals, however, are toward autonomy, independence, and initiative, and roles directed toward such ends may result in intellectual acceleration. The differential shelter from competition (and thus stimulation) between the sexes may also be important, and if it is important, there should be a difference between career women and equally well-trained and intelligent women who remain homemakers. To the author's knowledge, this difference has not been investigated.

Father Absence

Among other factors that affect intellectual development and cognitive behavior are father absence or presence. The literature is fragmentary, and such things as duration and timing of father absence and the reason for the absence are not often specified. Illustrative evidence suggests that boys with absent fathers are more likely to show feminine than masculine patterning in their test results (Carlsmith, 1964). Carlsmith worked with college men who had taken a group intelligence test that provided two scores, one of V(erbal) intelligence, the other of Q(uantitative) intelligence. The "masculine" pattern is Q equal to or higher than V; the "feminine" pattern is Q lower than V. Sutton-Smith, Rosenberg, and Landy (1968) reveal dramatic evidence of the effect of father absence. Among their sample of father-absent college students, male students whose fathers had been absent during their childhoods were lower in V, Q, and total intelligence score; and females were lower in Q (the "masculine" type of intelligence).

Selected results from Sutton-Smith, Rosenberg, and Landy's study are presented in Table 7.3.

Carlsmith's findings are clearly replicated. Not only were both Q and V scores lower for father-absent men, but the pattern for father-present men was high Q, much lower V; and there was relatively little difference between the Q and V scores for father-absent men. Total scores are much depressed for the father-absent men. Father-present females approach the masculine pattern of Q higher than V, while father-absent females are lower in average Q than V. The difference in total score between father-present and -absent females is not statistically significant, nor is their V score. Differences in all three scores strongly favor father-present men.

Additional findings from Sutton-Smith, Rosenberg, and Landy indicate that the effect of father absence on intellectual development during early and middle childhood is more serious than later father absence; that the effect is greater on boys without brothers than with brothers; that only girls are affected more than only boys; and finally, that girls with a younger brother are more affected than other girls. Curiously enough, while the timing of the father's absence made a difference, its duration did not.

Farnham-Diggory (1970) reports similar results for a small number of disadvantaged Black boys. Boys whose fathers were absent scored much lower in spatial abilities than boys of the same social class whose fathers were present.

Prejudice and Rigidity

A few other studies deserve mention in connection with rate and type of intellectual and cognitive development. Kutner and Gordon (1964) followed up a group of children among whom they had investigated the relationships of racial prejudice and cognitive development at the age of 7 years. The follow-up occurred when the subjects were 16-year-old adolescents. The results are not definite, since many children changed in degree and type of prejudice and, after nine years, many subjects could not be located, or permission to take part in the study was refused. A total of twenty-three girls and ten boys were relocated and re-evaluated. While there had been no average IQ differences between prejudiced and nonprejudiced youngsters at age 7, at age 16 the prejudiced averaged 111 IQ and those relatively free from prejudice averaged 119. The nonprejudiced achieved higher scores on a test of critical thinking. Of interest, but tangential to the present topic, is the degree of inconsistency in attitudes. Eighteen of the thirty-three subjects fell into the same prejudice classification after nine years, while fifteen of them changed (from high to low prejudice, or vice versa).

Prejudice has often been associated with rigidity of thought processes (see McCandless, 1967). To link prejudice with IQ change or level obviously requires some intervening variable. Budoff and Pagell (1968) provide such a speculative link. They worked with forty educable mentally retarded subjects between 12 and 17 years of age, as well as with two control groups, one of fourth graders of the same mental age (but younger), and the other of normal ninth graders of the same chronological age but much higher MAs and IQs. The authors' purpose was to study the relationship between rigidity and learning efficiency. Their tests of rigidity were satiation on a simple repetitive task (putting marbles in holes: the shorter the time worked, the quicker the satiation time); and ease and frequency of change from one conceptual method of sorting cards to another. Among Budoff and Pagell's retarded subjects, those who satiated most quickly and changed concepts most easily (were least rigid) profited most from instructions in how to handle a nonverbal reasoning task. The older normal IQ group proved to the most flexible, and the gainers among the retardates closely resembled them in rigidity patterns.

Background and Child Rearing

Dockrell (1966) suggests that it is not too late at adolescence to affect the nature of intellectual patterning and function. Dockrell argues that the environmental demands in a middle-class home are such that a high level of development has been reached in all areas by the time a youngster goes into secondary school. Thus, it matters little (as far as basic change in cognitive function is concerned) whether he goes to a technical industrial or to a college preparatory school. The environment in lower-class homes has not brought children to such a level of development. Thus, it can matter profoundly to them what type of secondary school they attend. Dockrell designed his study as a test of Ferguson's learning theory of intelligence. Among a population of 171 middle-class British 12 and 14 years olds, and 101 lower-class children of the same ages, Dockrell found that indeed type of school made no difference in intellectual growth for the middle-class sample. For the lower-class group, on the other hand, verbal abilities developed more rapidly in the academic school, while numerical, spatial, and nonverbal skills developed more rapidly in the technical school.

Methods of child rearing also seem to make a difference in rate and type of intellectual development. Bayley (1968) reports:

> In boys, early maternal love and acceptance correlates with slow early development but later high achievement in mental abilities. The pattern is reversed for boys with punitive, rejecting mothers. In girls, early maternal love and high scores in infancy are associated, but the influence of early maternal love diminishes after 3 years and then drops out completely." (p. 11)

Cross (1966) worked with a sample of 377 boys from junior and senior high school. He separated his sample into high conceptual level (HCL) and low conceptual level (LCL) boys. An HCL person, according to Cross, has more dimensions available to him conceptually, and can apply more than one concept to a given stimulus. He is more likely to explore situations and be creative and adaptable when faced with a changing environment. The LCL person applies overlearned methods of evaluating and responding to his world, frequently opposes change, and adheres religiously to rules and pronouncements of authority. These definitions seem to fit rigidity as defined earlier by Budoff and Pagell.

Cross used the incomplete sentences blank (which will be discussed in Chapter 15) to infer conceptual level. Eventually he found twenty-seven pairs of boys from eighth through twelfth grades, who were well matched with each other in terms of intact families, grade, and IQ. Mean age for both the HCL and LCL groups was 16 years, and mean IQ was 117 for HCL and 114 for LCL. The average socioeconomic status of the parents of the HCL boys was higher than the LCL boys, but the difference was not statistically significant at the .05 level that has been employed throughout this book.

Parents of the boys were given a questionnaire from which their authoritarianism in child rearing was judged, and were interviewed to determine the interdependence between them and their children. Scoring of interviews was satisfactorily reliable. Both fathers and mothers of HCL children manifested more interdependence between themselves than the parents of LCL boys; the mothers of the HCL boys were significantly less authoritarian than the mothers of the LCL subjects; and the tendency was the same for the fathers, but was not great enough to prove statistically significant. Scores of mothers and fathers of HCL boys were more closely related to each other ($r = .64$) than fathers and mothers of LCL boys ($r = .26$). This can be thought of as "consistency in power administration" (see Chapter 12). Whether or not the mother was instrinsically accepting of the boy did not differentiate between HCL and LCL boys; but fathers of HCL boys were rated higher in intrinsic acceptance.

Kent and Davis (1957), in a study of British children, obtain findings that are congruent enough with Cross' and fit well with the conclusion that children respond better with some interactions with their parents, benign or malign, than with no interactions at all. Demanding parents who provide a stimulating home and good opportunities to learn and who establish a firm model to which they expect their children to conform had children who averaged 124 IQ. Anxious parents were described as follows: "tend to be ambitious for their child, but in particular . . . are ceaselessly anxious lest he fall short of what they expect. . . . Their model is inconstant, although it may be emphatic. Also, they tend to be inconsistent in their use of reward and punishment; they are sometimes indulgent and sometimes intolerant. . . ." (p. 28). They have children who average 107 IQ. A group of tolerant, patient, placidly child enjoying parents who are affectionate have children who average 110 IQ. But a group of unconcerned parents, content if their child keeps out of trouble and does not make demands on them, and who are haphazard and inconsistent in their use of punishment have children who average 97 IQ. This pattern of average IQ differences is over-all significant, with the demanding parents' children being higher, the unconcerned parents' children, lower on the average than the children of the normal parents. Children of anxious parents do not differ from those of normal parents.

McCandless (1967) devotes a chapter to "Sources of Variation in Measured Intelligence" (pp. 337–373). Although the emphasis is placed on younger children, he considers influences of adoption and foster homes, studies of twins, effects of institutional living and isolation, the effects of nursery school attendance, relations with social class and child rearing, the relevant findings from the literature about subcultural mental deficiency, the role of language, and results from selected animal studies. This discussion is too lengthy to include in the present volume, and is less relevant for adolescents, who are reasonably fixed in intellectual level, than for younger children. However, McCandless concludes that the bulk of evidence suggests maximal influence of environmental learning circumstances on intellectual development. Those interested in greater detail about nature and nurture and influences on intellectual function may wish to consult this chapter, as well as the pertinent section of Chapter 8 of the present volume.

SUMMARY

The problem of defining intelligence is complex. The classical notion of general intelligence or g does not fit the over-all data about intelligent behavior accurately. Factor theories do not do justice to questions of acculturation as a determinant, but factor theories do treat acculturation combined with intellectual skills, the genesis of which is not clear. A satisfactory working definition should take Ferguson's notions of overlearned, socially adaptive skills into account, acknowledging the powerful influence of acculturation (a highly verbal "intelligence of the culture") and fluidity (which may be likened to mental adroitness). Cattell's rather neglected two-factor theory of crystallized and fluid intelligence seems plausible, theoretically justified by the data, and useful.

The most common classification of intelligence tests is according to whether they are designed for individual or group administration, the age level and degree of mental maturity for which they are designed, and whether they are performance (nonlanguage) or verbal in their item content. Group intelligence tests often include a Q (quantitative) factor, a V (verbal) factor, and a total score. Conventional intelligence tests, while they are the single best predictor of school achievement for middle-class adolescents, fall woefully short in predicting learning ability for disadvantaged youth. It may be that the "intelligence test of the future" will be a work sample test, designed very specifically for circumscribed prediction, such as for proficiency in English, or spatial relations, or mathematics. The use of work sample tests rather than intelligence tests will help avoid many of the superfluous values attached to the concept of intelligence. For middle-class, and probably all, youth, academic achievement is better predicted by combining measures of motivation and work habits with measures of intelligence than by intelligence tests alone. A measure of creativity may add somewhat to the efficiency of predicting school achievement; and some measures of achievement seem to be meaningfully and usefully related to incidental learning (that which occurs tangentially as the main task is learned).

At least one study indicates that knowledge of intelligence test and achievement test scores serves as a catalyst for academic performance. Anxiety clearly interferes with test taking performance. Thus, high anxious students (except perhaps for the very highly intelligent) are likely to score lower for both intelligence and achievement tests. The intelligence quotient (IQ)—a ratio indicating rate of growth—seems to predict learning ability better than mental age alone. Scores on learning tasks, including intelligence test type items, seem to be relatively little affected by circumstances of administering the tests, within reasonable limits.

Recent longitudinal studies of intellectual growth suggest that the traditional literature has not been correct about the time growth levels off, and its course during maturity. Newer data, both from very long and shorter (five to seven years) studies of the same individuals suggest that intelligence continues to increase long after the teens, that many of the more complex intellectual skills reach their peak as late as age 50, and that only items that depend on speed and intensity of response show the drop beginning in the mid-20s, as has so long been considered characteristic. While the prediction of adult intelligence level from adolescent status is reasonably accurate (correlations in the .80s have been reported), considerable variation may occur. There are suggestions in the literature that highly trained people and people living in demanding circumstances gain more and continue this gain longer than those with less training and who live in more intellectually sheltered circumstances. The evidence seems clear that, as United States culture is now organized, boys and men are more likely to gain in intelligence than girls and women. This may be a joint function of differential cultural expectations for the two sexes (competence is not highly valued for girls and women) and differential life experiences, women being less likely to live intellectually competitive and demanding lives.

A number of factors other than sex seem to facilitate or interfere with intellectual growth. Both males and females are negatively affected in their intellectual development by father absence, males more so than females. The earlier in childhood the paternal absence occurs, the more handicapping its effects seem to be. Reflective and intellectual life styles seem to facilitate intellectual development; rigid life styles, to interfere with it. The parent-child relationship seems to affect the child's intellectual functioning. Research has indicated that the existence of parental influence — good or bad — plays a constructive part in the child's intellectual and cognitive development.

8

Cognitive Function: Determinants, Development, Applications

INTRODUCTION

In a continuation of the discussion of intelligence and intellectual growth, in this chapter are presented recognized determinants of intelligence, processes of assessment of intelligence, and a treatment of cognitive behavior, which is, in simple form, "intelligence at work." In recent research, the fundamental issue of what determines intelligence has been revived; in this debate, colloquially known as the "nature-nurture" controversy, participants examine whether environment or heredity are responsible for intellectual development. The current level of sophistication regarding the nature-nurture controversy is such that additional factors have been introduced without which sound experimentation can not be conducted.

The distinction is stressed between what, up to this point, has been identified as "intelligence" or "intellectual growth" and cognition. Throughout Chapter 7, subtle differences between intelligence and cognition emerge, but the primary focus of that chapter is on the theories and tests and measurements—the quantitative—of the intelligence aspect of human growth and development. Chapter 8 can provide a deeper understanding of the cultural environmental and hereditary foundations that are part of the study of cognition.

Then, since intelligence and cognition are so closely woven into educational practices, the academic world's approach to adolescents who deviate from the normal intellectual distribution is discussed. In the past, schools have dealt with exceptional children in ways that varied from isolated classes to integrated teaching methods that do not differentiate either among groups with different problems or among individual children.

THE NATURE–NURTURE CONTROVERSY

A major, only mildly profitable psychological debate that often bordered on the polemic was carried on during the 1930s and 1940s about whether environment or heredity was the chief determiner of intellectual development and ultimate level. Definitions of intelligence that stressed learning and opportunity to learn, such as Ferguson's (1954, 1956) and Schweiker's (1968) treatment of the topic, seemed to put the matter more in perspective, and debates diminished and tempers cooled for a while. The recent popularity of Piaget's thought (for example, Inhelder and Piaget, 1958; Piaget, 1951, 1952) about the development of thinking and the organization of knowledge has brought the matter back to people's attention. Piaget's notions of developmental stages, little influenced by learning opportunity, have reopened the issue of whether environments can be so manipulated as to raise or lower children's levels of cognitive efficiency. As stated earlier, Kohlberg (1968), for example, raises the question about whether compensatory education can accomplish anything for disadvantaged children, and throws doubt on the whole philosophy of promoting intellectual growth through enriched experience. Practical matters, such as whether or not to support government learning enrichment programs or to conduct crash courses for remediating adolescents, make the question of nature–nurture in intellectual development of great strategic importance. In early 1969, Jensen added gasoline to the already smoldering coals with his article, "How Much Can We Boost IQ and Scholastic Achievement?" In this article, he places considerable faith in heredity, and suggests that racial differences in intelligence may be due to heredity.[1]

In any event, whether or not the nature–nurture controversy is a useful one, no author can avoid touching briefly on it. Many of its faces are presented in the following sections.

Structure versus Function

Anastasi and Foley (1948) provide a sensible way to look at the nature–nurture problem, although they suggest no answers. First, they

[1]Since this chapter went to the printer, Light and Smith have taken Jensen's assumptions but followed United States census figures, in which it is shown that Blacks are situated unfavorably socioeconomically compared to whites (Light, R. J., and Smith, P. V. Social allocation models of intelligence. *Harvard Educational Review*, 1969, 39, 490–510). Light and Smith's analysis results in the conclusion that Black-white differences in intelligence are at the very least as plausibly explained by differential educational-economic opportunities as by differential heredities.

require a definition of terms and a decision as to whether one is talking about *structure* or *function*. After that, they ask that one specifies whether he is considering *hereditary* structure and function or *environmentally* determined structure and function. About many matters, there is no dispute: Body build, a matter of genes (albeit influenced somewhat by nutrition), is clearly a matter of hereditary structure; time of sexual maturation (again, probably influenced by important but secondary matters such as nutrition) is almost certainly genetically determined, thus it can be thought of as a hereditary function. As Chapter 5 describes, hereditary structure and function interact with and alter learning opportunities so that, for boys at least, there seem to be important personal and social consequences that result from being mesomorphic and early maturing. In other words, an explanation of the advantages of early maturing for boys must be interactionist in nature, and take account of hereditary structural and functional qualities as they interact with the learning or environmental situation.

An illustration of environmentally determined structure is provided by an amputee. Such an environmental trauma is bound to affect an individual's life adjustment profoundly. An illustration of environmentally determined function is provided by verbal language. A child of French ancestry placed at birth in a Midwestern English speaking home most certainly does not inherit the French language. Strength, correlating closely as it does with body build, is a fairly good illustration of hereditary function. Being strong-jawed or big-boned, or very short, typically, are instances of hereditary structure.

Practical Urgency of the Problem

Intelligence is conceived by most people as made up of both function and structure. Practically, it is important to isolate the contributions to its variance made by heredity and environment. If heredity plays little part, then there should be no bias against adoptive placement of children born to intellectually inferior mothers and fathers. If environment is the major determinant, then there is an urgent social obligation to provide a sufficiently rich environment from birth for every child so that he may develop normal intelligence and the associated cognitive skills. If heredity is a major determinant, then one must be careful about adoptive placement of children of the retarded, and compensatory education is a relatively idle gesture (at least insofar as it is designed to improve intellectual power).

The argument about compensatory education is not an idle one for adolescents, despite the fact that as a group adolescents have partially stabilized in intelligence. Dockrell's (1966) reasoning and data indicate that the nature of his education is no trivial matter for an early adolescent, particularly if he comes from a somewhat disadvantaged background. The whole thesis of this book, that adolescence is a time of high drive and thus of great potential behavioral flexibility, applies as much to intellectual-cognitive behavior as to social, emotional, or sexual behavior.

The author's position on the nature-nurture issue is interactionist: The behaviors from which intelligence is inferred, like all behavior, are ultimately grounded in neural and physiological function. At this time, one can only conjecture about what the nature of the interrelationships between neural structure and function and complex cognitive behaviors may be. Hebb (1949) presents one of the most intriguing sets of speculation about these interrelationships. His speculations have led to much supportive research, and the present author's interactionist position has been much influenced by Hebb. Hebb, too, is an interactionist, but gives major importance to influences of learning opportunities, including amount of stimulation, on neural structure and function. Up to limits of overstimulation, Hebb and his followers believe that, on the whole, intellectual development is maximized by maximal stimulation.

Stern's (1956) analogical description of the interaction of heredity and environment is appealing:

> The genetic endowment in respect to any one trait has been compared to a rubber band and the trait itself to the length which the rubber band assumes when it is stretched by outside forces. Different people initially may have been given different lengths of unstretched endowment, but the natural forces of the environment may have stretched their expression to equal length, or led to differences in attained length sometimes corresponding to their innate differences and at other times in reverse of the relation." (p. 53)

Relevant Research It is well to look at some research bearing on the issue. In the matter of Black–white racial differences in intelligence, Jensen (1969) has come out on the side of genetic differences favoring whites. Shuey (1966), in her exhaustive treatment of "Negro intelligence testing," demonstrates a consistent inferiority of the Black to the white. Such a finding is comforting to some, discomforting to others. Tulkin (1968), whose research is discussed in more detail in the next two chapters, investigated intelligence differences among middle-class white and Black boys and girls, and lower-class white and Black boys and girls. Like the consensus of Shuey's research, he found IQ differences favoring whites in both social classes. Upon further analysis, he found that for the middle class, the inferiority of the Black children could be entirely attributed to the Black boys, and that the Black girls did not differ from the white girls. He exerted statistical controls for broken homes and crowded housing, and found that the differences among middle-class Black and white boys disappeared. But even with such statistical controls, lower-class Black children tested lower than lower-class white children. Tulkin introduces tentative, plausible, but unproved explanations of caste and prejudice to account for the residual difference.[2]

In the present context, it is sufficient to draw upon Bloom's (1969) reply, in which he summarizes the intensely serious Israeli efforts to modify general intelligence. Israel, as most readers know, has welcomed immigrants from widely different cultural backgrounds. Among them have been Oriental (mid-Eastern) Jews who have lived in circumstances of extreme poverty and hardship, cultural as well as economic. Under home rearing circumstances, their children have averaged 85 IQ. This is

---

[2]Interested readers should go to Jensen's article (Issue 1, *Harvard Educational Review*, 1969, *39*). Also, in the next issue of the *Review* other points of view, some of them sharply different, are presented.

about the same level as that found among severely disadvantaged children and youth of any race in the United States (see Kennedy, 1969). However, Israel has introduced the practice of kibbutz rearing for many children. Kibbutzim (child centers) are professionally staffed, and children stay in them all day for four years in many cases, the adult-child ratio is high, the environment is rich, and on-going interaction with parents is provided. Under such circumstances, Oriental children average 115 IQ. Thus, they match perfectly the children of European Jews who have also been kibbutz reared. But home-reared children of European Jews average about 105 IQ. United States research on effects of infant enrichment through special training both of children and of mothers, and through parent-child centers, has to date produced rather exciting though as yet unpublished results that are congruent with the Israeli data reported by Bloom.

It is obvious that results such as those Bloom reports for kibbutz-reared children fit almost perfectly with Ferguson's (1954, 1956) culture-adaptive overlearning theory of intelligence, or with Horn's (1968) conceptions of "learning resulting from arrangements made by the culture."

Interactional Effects

It is interesting and sometimes profitable to speculate about the interactions between heredity and environment. One valid seeming argument for a predominant influence of heredity is provided by the literature about the correlations in intelligence between identical twins, fraternal twins, and nontwin siblings. This literature also illustrates perfectly the dangers of inferring simple causation from correlations. To summarize the literature drastically, correlations between the IQs of identical twins reared together are typically found to be around .90 or a little higher; between nonidentical twins reared together, the correlations have typically been found to be in the mid-.70s; and between nontwin siblings, the typical correlations between sibs' IQs are around .50. It has often been assumed that the influence of environment on twins has been controlled by the fact that the pairs of children have all been reared in the same homes and are the same age. The difference in the correlation between nontwin sibs and nonidentical twins, it is reasoned, is environmentally produced, since they are genetically equally related and only the environment and matters of timing distinguish them. The difference in correlation between nonidentical and identical twins, it is reasoned, is due to heredity, since environmental and temporal factors are controlled by the fact of twinship and only heredity varies, the identicals being "mirror images" of each other genetically.

Such reasoning overlooks interactional effects: If both identicals are attractive, bright, and healthy, their environments are going to be much more similar (cultural stereotypes in perceiving and reacting, such as are discussed in Chapters 13, 14, and 15) than for nonidentical twins, who may differ greatly in appearance, and who may be of different sexes. Thus, both genetics and environment interact to produce the greater similarity of identicals to each other. This reasoning also holds for identicals reared apart. Typically, they have gone into homes that are not dissimilar from those into which they were born; and in those homes, the phenomenon of cultural stereotype will produce similar social reactions, advantages, and disadvantages in much the same way it does when they are reared together. A homely, rabbit toothed, skinny, not very bright boy is unquestionably treated much the same way in Calgary, Canada, as he is in rural Georgia. In short, the present author does not regard the twin and sibling correlational studies as anything but interesting evidence that, at best, deals with the interaction between heredity and environmental factors and goes no further ahead in determining respective variance.

Pollack (1969) offers a provocative bit of evidence bearing on the question of the interaction between heredity and environment. He believes that primitive perception such as that involved in the Mueller-Lyer illusion (wherein differential perceptions of length are likely to occur depending on whether arrows opposed in a line point in or out) depends on such factors as sensitivity to contour, intensity, and duration, and that its efficiency declines with age as the retina darkens. Such perception may be inferior from the beginning among those who are darkly pigmented. If indeed intellectual differences exist between dark- and light-skinned people, this provides a cue and one that, it seems, could be compensated for by special training early in life. Along this line, but with his impressions backed by no quantitative research evidence whatever, the author has spent much time in the homes of the dark-skinned poor in Pakistan, Jamaica, and the United States. He has been struck by the fact that these homes are typically dark (particularly where it is hot and darkness seems cooler). The combination of dark rooms and dark faces could, it seems, result in less effective learning of figure–ground relations, and might also have some bearing on attentional factors. If attention develops, as seems plausible, through interaction of very young children and their parents, both in close proximity and at a distance such as across the room, will not its learning be more difficult when both the room and the people involved are dark? To highlight the practical importance of this speculation, it is obvious that efficiency in figure–ground relations is important in almost all perceptual behavior and crucial in reading. Attention is fundamental to all cognitive processes.

There are scattered bits of evidence that are plausibly related although they do not pertain directly to the interaction between skin color and perception. Farnham-Diggory (1970) finds that in general his kindergarten and elementary school aged Afro-American subjects perform more poorly than whites on measures of cognitive skills involving spatial relations such as map-like problem solving. However, Sitkei and Meyers (1969), investigating Guilford's *Structure of Intellect* model among Black and white 4 year olds of middle and lower class, find the major Black–white difference to be in cognitive semantics, with no racial differences associated with divergent semantics, figural (spatial), and memory factors.

Both Pierce-Jones and King (1960) and Clarke (1941) worked with Black and white adolescents. Pierce-Jones and King gave four types of tasks to their subjects: making up sentences with four words supplied by the experimenter; producing a graphic synthesis of mutilated words; copying pictorial figures; and recognizing mutilated pictures. The Afro-American subjects were significantly superior for the first of these tasks;

there was no racial difference for the second; and the Black adolescents were significantly inferior on the last two tasks, the first of which is perceptual–motor, the second, figure–ground synthesis.

Clarke matched his two racial groups on Stanford-Binet IQ, then compared their performance on different types of items. The Afro-American subjects performed better on dissected sentences, memory for sentences, and vocabulary, while they did less well on picture absurdities. The last task involves attention to, contrasting elements within, and detecting incongruities in, illogical pictorial representations. It can be thought of as involving visual perception, attention, and spatial relations to a substantial degree.

Finally, when he was in Pakistan, the author was required to teach a course on individual tests and measurements. Translations of the Wechsler Adult Intelligence Scale (WAIS) into Urdu and Punjabi were made, and graduate students in the course tested more than 100 adolescents among their acquaintances. The subjects so secured ranged socioeconomically from the disadvantaged to upper-middle class, and included more males than females (about a 70 percent–30 percent ratio). The prediction was made that the resulting quotients would show a pattern of P(erformance) quotient at least equal to and probably higher than V(erbal) quotient. It was believed that the verbal items, based as they were on a United States, English speaking population, would reflect the culture strongly. Thus the Pakistani youth would be handicapped in performance. The performance items were thought to be relatively free of cultural influence and thus they would not put the Pakistani youth to a disadvantage.

Dramatically converse results were obtained. The mean performance quotients (PQ) were some 30 points lower than the mean verbal quotients (VQ). Within the entire sample, only one subject matched his VQ and PQ, and only two obtained equal quotients. Discrepancies among apparently normal youth of as many as 60 quotient points favoring the VQ were found. The tests that make up the performance scale are detecting the missing parts in a picture, making patterns from blocks (the Kohs Block Design Test), arranging objects that had been cut up jigsaw fashion, putting scrambled cartoon sections into meaningful sequence, and coding. A premium is given for speedy performance for most items. These results, informal and unacceptable from a rigorous scientific vantage point as they are, fit with the interaction hypothesis the author advanced above. A second interpretation involves learning: Manual and mechanical work is not esteemed in Pakistani society, play with toys and puzzles is not institutionalized as it is in the United States, and good Muslims are discouraged from portraying and otherwise dealing with the pictured human face and figure, a cultural carry-over from the prohibition against worshiping graven images. Thus, performance skills like those tapped by the WAIS are not learned.

The Pakistani sample did not differ significantly in VQ from the United States standardization sample. A similar cultural learning influence may be hypothesized: Demographically, the literacy rate in Pakistan is very low, and in villages, the essence of which influences even the great cities, illiteracy is often 100 percent. The tradition of the "wise old man"—the story teller—is strong, and it is through stories and verbal recounting that much of the history and nature of the culture are transmitted. Thus, it may be hypothesized, the prestige of verbal behavior is high. Informal evidence suggests that, particularly among lower class Blacks, verbal facility is equally valued. Whether in Harlem, Watts, Vine City (Atlanta), or in Trenchtown, Kingston, Jamaica, the facile talker (particularly the male) is esteemed. "Rapping" and "playing the dozens" are popular pastimes and sources of esteem.[3]

In connection with the nature–nurture question and of great practical importance, it is well to quote from Bloom (1969):

> The psychologist and the geneticist may wish to speculate about how to improve the gene pool—the educator cannot and should not. The educator must be an environmentalist—bridled or unbridled. It is through the environment that he must fashion the educational process. Learning by providing the appropriate environment. If heredity imposes limits—so be it. The educator must work with what is left, whether it be 20% of the variance or 50%. (p. 1)

To Intervene or Not? In introducing the topic of socialization in Chapter 12, the author points out the degree to which values enter into one's choice of criteria and definitions. Middle-class values operate to handicap the educational and vocational progress of disadvantaged youth. The disadvantage occurs because of a conflict in value systems, the middle class being on the whole tenser, tighter, more achievement oriented, more controlled (loosely speaking, more Apollonian, as this is discussed in more detail later); while people at the lowest end of the socioeconomic scale (the lower-lower class, or the disadvantaged) are more inclined to seek immediate gratification, control impulses less firmly, perhaps enjoy their sense more fully and, loosely speaking, are more Dionysian. Many thoughtful people have questioned whether one modal way of life is superior to another; and have asked what right those who exert power within the middle-class educational and social system have to impose its values on those who would live another way. There are different ways even of looking at identical data.

In their work dealing with differences in early experiences between advantaged and disadvantaged children, Bee, *et al.* (1969) report results as follows: From a block building task, it was inferred that disadvantaged Black children used poorer judgment in their goal aspirations; from time spent in drawing a line, that middle-class children possessed more impulse control, that disadvantaged children were uninhibited in spontaneous explorations, that middle-class children were more persistent in key tapping, and that middle-class mothers used more instruction, were less physically intrusive, and were generally more aware of the needs and qualities of their children.

Sroufe (1970) is one of those thoughtful people who question many aspects of intervention research, particularly when it is clearly based on middle-class values and apparent philosophy that "I know

---

[3]Rapping is akin to haranguing, but (at least to the author) does not include the hortatory overtones or urgency. Playing the dozens consists of verbal maneuvering between two people with the intent of the victor's forcing the vanquished to lose his cool.

better than you." In his critique of intervention studies and efforts, he reinterprets the Bee, *et al.* data as follows:

> White M[iddle] C[lass] parents can be seen to be much more subtly manipulative and controlling of their children, fostering great dependence and conformity through the use of powerful psychological reinforcers. Such subtle control, in many ways more potent than physical control, reveals its effects in the following ways in the child's behavior: (1) rigid persistence in a meaningless, boring key-tapping task merely because of instructions to do so from an adult, (2) drawing a line more slowly than L[ower] C[lass] controls, again with no internal satisfaction or external reward, but merely to conform with adult wishes, (3) compulsive imitation of an adult model, and (4) an inability to dare or aspire to greatness as manifest by an only moderate level of aspiration. (They were, however, no less curious than LC children at this young age.) (Page numbers not available.)

The Sroufe quote poses the value question of intervention exceptionally sharply. Sroufe vividly contrasts the less likable aspects of middle-class values with the more relaxed values of the disadvantaged. In a sense, the Bee *et al.* interpretation is Apollonian, and Sroufe's is Dionysian.

For reasons implied by Sroufe, the whole notion of compensatory education (prekindergartens for disadvantaged children, compensatory, remedial programs for youth) has been questioned. Are not such educational efforts simply means whereby achievement, competence-oriented, possibly uptight middle-class people are attempting to force another and not necessarily " right" way of life on disadvantaged people and their children?

The author has asked such questions, since he is deeply involved in programs of compensatory education in terms of both research and application. He has no firm answer but an explication of his thinking may serve to stimulate the thinking of others about this socially vital issue.

Briefly, it is questionable on grounds of either moral rectitude or scientific data to attempt by deliberate educational or action policy to change the social-moral way of life of other people unless others are being hurt by such a way of life. On the other hand, matters of intellectual, linguistic, and other symbolic proficiency are not limited in usefulness to any particular personal or social style of life. In a technical society, it is important to think, talk, and solve problems well whether one is the truest of Puritans or the loosest of Dionysians. It seems safe to say that no one can be harmed by possessing sharper intellectual skills, richer vocabularies, and a larger reservoir of symbolic behaviors and strategies for using them. Psychological knowledge, it seems to the author, has progressed to the stage where techniques of developing such tools for proficiency can be applied; and the evidence that their application produces gains in what we loosely call intelligence is by now quite impressive (for example, Bloom, 1969; Skeels, 1966; Skeels and Harms, 1948; and Skodak and Skeels, 1949).

Culture-Fair Intelligence Tests The nature–nurture controversy (which Bloom's quote above puts into a practical context) has stimulated equally lively controversy about culture-fair or culture-free intelligence tests. This debate is at the heart of the rejection of intelligence tests by many people. If intelligence is entirely or substantially environmentally determined and if intelligence test scores provide educational labels, expectancies, and opportunities for disadvantaged children, youth, and adults such that discrimination against them is practiced, then intelligence tests that reflect middle-class culture are exceptionally unfair and handicapping to those who have not grown up in such a culture.

Schweiker's (1968) argument (see Chapter 7) for substituting work samples for intelligence tests is sensible, but, as has been pointed out, this stage of methodological sophistication is a long way off. In the meantime, wise employment of the best instruments will be useful to many young children and youth and harmful to few if any. To date, such tests, sophisticatedly employed, provide the single best prediction of how well children will succeed in school as it is now organized. School organization, as Chapters 9 and 10 shall show, is certainly not optimal, and particularly penalizes boys and disadvantaged children and youth. An interactionist approach will include endless tinkering with the system (which works rather well from the formal point of view for most bright middle-class children and young people) so as to produce certain over-all changes that will probably help all children and youth, and to create subsystems and special procedures which will work better for all.

Conventional IQ tests predict well for middle-class youth, poorly for disadvantaged youth. Culture-fair tests have not been demonstrated to predict any better *under the present system* than conventional tests (McCandless, 1967). The recommendation, then, must be to continue using what has worked for the population for which it works, and look for other prediction and guidance methods for the substantial sections of the population for which conventional tests do not work. Holtzman and Brown's (1968) and Khan's (1969) techniques for measuring motivation and study habits are profitable seeming extensions of assessment devices. G. M. Harrington (1968) has pointed out that it is conceivable that genetic-environmental interactions may be such that educational methods suitable for advantaged children will depress the performance of disadvantaged children. If there is such a depressive effect, he says, the intensification of such an educational program can actually intensify the depression. Only research and application can answer the complex issues of providing the best possible education for all. The American ideal is a magnificent one.

COGNITIVE GROWTH IN ADOLESCENCE

Until now in this and the preceding chapter, coverage has dealt with intelligence as variously defined by intellectual theorists and test developers. Elkind (1968a) refers to such a discussion as one of "quantitative aspects of cognitive growth in adolescence" (p. 129). Cognition can be distinguished from intelligence, although not altogether clearly, by calling it, as Elkind does, "qualitative aspects of cognitive growth." If intelligence be thought of as both crystallized and fluid in nature (Cattell, 1941; Horn, 1968), then the type of intelligence discussed up to this point, Horn argues, belongs mainly in the crystallized category. To a major degree, it seems to develop as a function of and be correlated with environmental *arrangements* for children's learning (see Ferguson, 1954, 1956). Other types of cognitive function seem to arise with minimal cultural arrangement. These are the types of function Piaget (1950) and Inhelder and Piaget (1958) study, and that Elkind identifies as qualitative aspects of cognitive growth.

Traditionally, cognitive behavior includes concept formation, problem solving, thought processes, and higher learning in general. Piaget broadens it to include organization and manipulation of knowledge, which is a special case of thought processes. The author shares with many the belief that Piaget's belated recognition on the American scene has resulted in new, refreshing, and constructive attention to cognition in general and cognition among adolescents in particular.

Piagetian Thought To understand cognition among adolescents, it is necessary to review the steps through which normal adolescents have already passed. Piaget conceives of cognitive development as proceding through four stages: sensorimotor; preoperational; concrete operational; and formal operational. The sensorimotor stage pervades in infancy, lasting until about the time normal children begin structuring their world symbolically (most importantly, probably, verbally) at the age of about 2 years. Here, the infant masters his sensorium and his motor system, coordinates his reflexes and his senses, and learns to reach toward where he is looking. Elkind (1967a) has provided a handy verbal guide through the often difficult-to-understand stages of Piaget. According to Elkind, the major cognitive task during infancy is the *conquest of the object.* It is this author's belief that much of the failure to develop intellectual skills for mastering middle-class environments manifested by severely disadvantaged children and youth results from circumstances toward the end of this sensorimotor period that mitigate against full transfer from the sensorimotor stage to later symbolically and particularly verbally dominated stages.

The preoperational period lasts approximately from age 2 to age 6 years. Here, language mushrooms, symbolic play emerges, obvious modeling and imitation take place constantly (although imitation has occurred earlier), and children begin to report dreams. The child has magical notions of causation; his experiences, including his dreams, are real to him; the word is the thing, and vice versa. Elkind's label for the major preoperational task is the *conquest of the symbol.*

The stage of concrete operations lasts from age 7 to age 11 years. Here, Elkind says, the major cognitive task is *mastering classes, relations, and quantities.* But the child regards his logic as irrevocable. He is likely to be dogmatic, to alter the data to fit his logic, and to be singularly rigid, as can be seen among the younger children in Adelson, Green, and O'Neil's (1969) discussion of adolescence and the concept of the law (see Chapter 14). On the other hand, the all important notion of conservation is mastered. Conservation gives the environment its lawfulness and predictability. There are many conservations: of number, volume, weight, and displacement, for example. As has been mentioned, the very young child will believe that five or ten pennies strung out in a long line are more than five or ten pennies bunched closely together; and that, when equal volumes are used, there is more liquid in a filled tall thin glass than in partly filled short wide glass. Conservation involves being able to covary dimensions conceptually. In the realm of concrete objects, young children learn through experience to do this quite effectively.

Adolescents and Formal Operations Most normal adolescents have reached and are beginning to consolidate the final stage of formal operations. Elkind calls this *the conquest of thought*. Adelson, Green, and O'Neil provide illustrations of maturing formal operations between the ages of 11 and 18 years. The type of development represented by Piaget's stages seems normally to occur without deliberate environmental arrangement. Thus, they should be more a function of mental than chronological age. This was the case in the Adelson, Green, and O'Neil study. At each of the four age levels studied, $10^{9}/_{10}$, $12^{3}/_{5}$, $14^{7}/_{10}$, and $17^{7}/_{10}$ years, youngsters from two intelligence levels served as subjects. Two-thirds at each age tested between 95 and 110 IQ, while one-third tested 125 IQ or above. There were no differences between the bright and average youngsters, nor were there differences between boys and girls. Adelson and O'Neil (1966) earlier reported findings similar to those reported above, but in the earlier study they were dealing with development of thought about the community rather than, more abstractly, about law.

As Elkind illustrates adolescents and their progressive mastery of thought, he reports from his own research that not until age 11 or 12 do children spontaneously begin to introduce concepts of belief, intelligence, and faith into their discussions of their own religious faith. He believes that the egocentrism of adolescents comes about because, while for the first time the adolescent can both think about his own thought *and* the thought of others, he does not differentiate between the objects he is thinking about and those that others are thinking about. Since he is preoccupied with himself (this is accountable for by his own need to handle his high drives, as discussed in Chapter 1 – a type of tunnel vision), he assumes that others are likewise thinking about him. He lacks objectivity. This, Elkind believes, may be one of the reasons he is so often intensely self-conscious.

Elkind (1967a) concludes his discussion of adolescent egocentrism by saying:

> After the appearance of formal operational thought, no new mental systems develop and the mental structures of adolescence must serve for the rest of the life span. The egocentrism of early adolescence nonetheless tends to diminish by the age of 15 or 16, the age at which formal operations become firmly established.... On the cognitive plane (adolescence) is overcome by the gradual differentiation between his own preoccupations and the thoughts of others; while on the plane of affectivity, it is overcome by a gradual integration of the feelings of others with his own emotions. (p. 1032)

Adolescents also come to be able to think formally, both in the sense of mathematical and algebraic thought, and in terms of logic and philosophy. Adolescents can reason not only about things (as in concrete operations) but about ideas and about their own thoughts and the thoughts of others. Their perception of abstract ideals and their newfound critical ability to detect the departure of reality from the ideal, plus their egocentrism that makes them think their own thoughts are new and unique, all combine to produce the intolerance so often seen among adolescents. For similar reasons, they are easily "betrayed." Their drive is so high and their needs so great that, as has been said, they often develop crushes. But the object of their crushes can not live up to their ideal, and the revelation of clay feet is often crushing to the adolescent.

Deliberate formulation of hypotheses and testing them against fact and experience seems also to be a phenomenon that emerges fully for the first time after 11 or 12 years of age. Generalizations come to include both positive and negative instances. Combinations and permutations (such as all the possible combinations of the letters a, b, c, and d in serial order into single letter units, double letter units, triple letter units, and the final four letter unit for a total of sixteen) are spontaneously possible for the first time when a child moves to the stage of formal operations. As Adelson, Green, and O'Neil have said, adolescents are both more flexible and more realistic in formal thought than younger children. Double meanings and plays on words come for the first time to be appreciated. With the new reproductive drive, the emergence of the *double entendre* is the adolescent's joy (and often his teachers' and parents' despair). It may be speculated that adolescents are as entranced with their newfound ability to introspect as 15 months olds are with their newfound ability to walk.

It is tempting to speculate that the new reproductive drive and the other intensifications of socially mediated drives precipitated by it motivate adolescents' transition into the formal operations stage. As far as the author knows, the only fact to support such a speculation is the approximate correlation in time of pubescence and entry into the stage of formal operations. While girls reach puberty earlier than boys, but the sexes do not differ in time of reaching the formal operations stage, the difference in intensity of the new drive may be such that boys are compelled developmentally earlier. But, as has been stressed repeatedly, one can not and must not think of correlation or temporal correspondence as causation.

Their introspectionism and their capacity to formulate the ideal and detect deviations from it may be among the reasons Katz and Zigler (1967), whose research is summarized in Chapter 15, find increasing discrepancies with both older age and higher intelligence between self and ideal self concepts.

It is almost certain that no one emerges cleanly from one stage of thought to another. Regressions are possible, and may even bridge more than one stage. Sophisticated adults may resort to magic in the absence of any known explanatory data about a phenomenon.

The Piagetian literature has by now become enormous. Piaget's epistemology has held up remarkably well in that children seem on the whole to move in an orderly fashion through the stages of thought he describes. His own research methods have often been criticized but, even under rigorous scrutiny, his descriptions are generally valid and exceptionally stimulating both to research efforts and to expansions of theory. Piagetian curricula are being tried out at many educational levels and informal reports suggest that they are promising. It seems possible (this research has been conducted with children younger than adolescents) to provide well-specified teaching techniques based on readiness[4] that will advance the age at which children progress to a later stage of thought earlier than Piaget would have predicted, but the sequence of the stages seems to have been rather well vindicated. Few if any studies have revealed sex differences in the Piagetian studies. Intelligence level seems to play something of a role (Adelson, Green, and O'Neil are an exception) and it may be concluded tentatively that the time of reaching a given stage of thought is an interaction between chronological age and intelligence.

The role of formal language production in defining Piaget's stages has raised some questions. Conservation, for example, is not judged to have occurred unless the principle can be clearly enunciated. As will be noted below in discussion of the Kugelmass and Breznitz (1968) study, the highest scores for moral development can not be obtained without clear enunciation of the abstract principle of intentionality and the experimental subject's justification of his reasoning. Observation suggests that many "behave" as though they understand conservation or high level morality perfectly, but questioning fails to elicit that they have verbalized their behavior or "reasoning." On the other hand, the sophisticated person who resorts to superstition or magic when confronted by situations about which he has no data can often provide an elaborate verbal rationale of his behavior. At this stage of research, one can only raise questions but it seems that there is much still to be understood about the relations of language and explanation to cognitive and moral development, and the individual's movement away from egocentricity as he grows older.

Two Research Studies

To conclude this section about Piaget, two studies will be summarized briefly. In the first, Kugelmass and Breznitz (1968) worked with 1014 Israeli children in a range of families from lower- to upper-middle class, and from ages 11 to 17. All children in each of the five schools were tested at the same time to prevent communication among subjects. Each subject was presented with twelve variations of a transgression, and the transgressions were designed to differ systematically in intentionality and results. There were three possible levels of intentionality: planning, lack of caution, and insanity; and four levels of results: death, a wound, a possible hurt, and nothing. Each subject was required to indicate on a 4-point scale the degree of blame to be assigned to the transgressor. A mature response was scored if, throughout the twelve items, a higher score was never given to results of an act than to intentions that lay behind it. In the second part of the test, the subjects ranked the twelve transgressions. They received the highest possible score if ranking corresponded to degree of intentionality, not blame. In other portions of the study, questions were asked about the subjects' criteria for judging a

---

[4]Readiness is possession of all the skills requisite to move to the next stage.

transgressor in a situation where someone was hurt; subjects were asked to give the most important two questions to ask the transgressor in such a situation; and then to explain the reasons for answering as they did.

Kugelmass and Breznitz also tried out their test with a sample of highly selected university students, averaging 22 7/10 years in age. Their mean score was 3.29, which Kugelmass and Breznitz believe represents the realistic maximum. For their younger experimental subjects, difference in score was very slight between the ages of 11 and 14. Eleven year olds' scores averaged about 1.4, 12 year olds' about 1.5, 13 year olds' about 1.6, and 14 year olds' about 1.7.[5] From 14 years of age on, the curve graphing the average scores rises linearly and steeply to age 16. Fifteen year olds average about 2.2, 16 year olds about 2.7. The curve decelerates somewhat to 17 years, when the average is about 2.9. Kugelmass and Breznitz suggest that after 17 years, cognitive-moral growth is very slow. To estimate intelligence, the authors administered a twenty-five word vocabulary test to their subjects. Correlations between vocabulary and movement from stage to stage of maturity are positive but low (the range is from a correlation of .17 to a correlation of .28). Sex differences are not reported.

In the second study selected for purposes of illustration, Rockway (1970) worked with thirty-two boys from each of grades six, nine, and twelve. All boys attended a middle-class suburban school in New York state. Their average ages were 12 1/5, 14 9/10, and 18 1/10 years at the respective grade levels; they averaged 120 IQ, but the oldest group was significantly more intelligent than the two younger groups. Rockway made two predictions: (1) the hypothetico-deductiveness of the social judgment process increases with age throughout adolescence; and (2) the egocentricity of the social judgment process decreases with age throughout adolescence.

Rockway asked all subjects to complete a programmed case history. At each of twelve choice points, the subject must decide which of several behavioral descriptions is the true or real information about the case. "Right" choices deal with the actual case, "wrong" choices with behavior of another case. After each response, the subject was given the correct information. The boys who took part in the study said they believed the case was an actual person who attended their school. Scoring was quite reliable. It was based on a score of 0 if no answer was given, one if the answer was self-contradictory, whimsical, or obviously illogical. A maximum of 4 points was given "where multiple logical antecedents produce a single consequent (e.g. 'he did well in prep school because he was bright and also because there aren't many people there and he didn't like people')" (page number not available).

Rockway analyzed his data so as to control for differences in intelligence between his age groups (he used analysis of covariance). The adjusted averages resulting from covariance were mean scores of 22.2 for the sixth graders, 33.3 for the ninth graders, and 31.8 for the twelfth

---

[5]These approximations are given because the authors present their data in graphic rather than table form.

graders. The trend toward more hypothetico-deductive thinking with age was significant at less than the .01 level. Egocentricity decreased from sixth to ninth grades, but did not change from ninth to twelfth grades. Egocentricity had been scored according to self-references in answers. Only 37.5 percent of the sixth graders produced any egocentric responses, only 8.6 percent of the ninth graders did, and 18.7 percent of the twelfth graders did.

These studies illustrate a number of points that have arisen in earlier more general discussion of the qualitative aspects of cognitive development. The Kugelmass and Breznitz study is also relevant to moral development. Kugelmass and Breznitz show the transition from a rigid, external locus of morality, founded entirely on the specific results of a transgression and typical of the morality of the level of concrete operations to a person-centered, internalized criterion of morality based on the thoughts (intentions) of other persons as projected from the subject himself.

In Rockway, we see illustrated the capacity to put oneself in another's place, manipulate environmental, situational, and interpersonal relations in the abstract, and emerge logically with conclusions that realistically fit life circumstances.

EDUCATIONAL PRACTICES AND INTELLECTUAL LEVEL

What are the responsibilities and what special provisions exist concerning the education of adolescents at one or the other extreme of the intellectual distribution? A thoughtful observer is likely to conclude that American public schools on the whole do a rather good job of special education (training children who are partially sighted or blind, partially hearing or deaf, cerebral palsied and orthopedically handicapped, or with rheumatic hearts). Rapid progress is now being made for children and youth with specific learning disabilities (who do not learn despite normal intelligence and no gross neurological defects). The techniques of special education for low grade mentally retarded children and youth have recently been much improved by training methods derived from Skinner's notions of operant conditioning with their implications for behavior shaping. Serious questions have been raised about special classes for the educable mentally retarded (the higher grades of mental retardation). There seems no doubt but that smaller classes and teachers better trained in diagnostic techniques and treatment of individual differences often accomplish wonders with retarded children. But Dunn (1968) points out that the results have not been commensurate with the time, expense, and expertness of staff. It may well be that the social stereotypes about retardation and segregation into special classes more than offset the special efforts made on behalf of high grade retarded children and youth. In this connection Dockrell's (1966) findings should be mentioned again. This study was concerned with differential patterns of cognitive development depending on placement in a technical or academic school, with the latter being associated with relatively great growth in verbal ability.

As has been suggested, schools do quite well in providing children and youth in the average-to-bright ranges with good formal educations, in the sense that they read, write, and compute reasonably well. The case is not so good, as has been pointed out repeatedly, for the disadvantaged or for the gifted.

The Intellectually Gifted

Intensive studies of the characteristics of bright and dull children and youth have been conducted. As a group, the bright are taller, handsomer, stronger, healthier, show fewer behavior problems, are less likely to have cavities in their teeth, and do better work in school. They are also more self-critical (Katz and Zigler, 1967), and less conforming (Lucito, 1964). Their good qualities may have been somewhat overstressed in the literature, as basic data came from Terman's *Genetic Studies of Genius* (1925). Terman first recruited subjects for his study by asking teachers for nominations. As has been pointed out, the teachers were not particularly accurate (although well above chance in accuracy), and it seems almost certain that their nominations were considerably influenced by the halo effect: Other things being equal, handsome, well-mannered, well-adjusted children would be selected, who were also good students and who were possibly among the older children in a class. This teacher-nominated group was then winnowed by intelligence test screening. The resulting group may have had some of the characteristics described above "built in by means of halo." On the other hand, the low positive correlation among socially valued traits (and its converse) is so well established as a statistical rule of thumb as to permit of no serious argument. There is no question from the voluminous literature that children toward the lower end of the intellectual scale do less well in school, are less popular, less healthy, and so on. But both the very intelligent and the dull achieve below expectancy in American schools.

For example, Ketcham (1957) reports about a group of forty gifted boys as they progressed from 6 to 12 years of age and from the first to the seventh grades. At age 7, for example, their mental age average was $9\frac{1}{4}$ years, but their educational achievement age was only $7\frac{1}{6}$ years. The same figures for Ketcham's forty-two gifted girls were $9\frac{1}{4}$ years and $7\frac{1}{6}$ years (essentially identical). At 12 years of age, the boys averaged $17\frac{11}{12}$ years in mental age and $15\frac{2}{3}$ years in educational achievement age. The girls averaged $17\frac{5}{12}$ years in mental age (note the less rapid mental growth on the part of the girls, in line with tendencies that have been pointed out earlier in the chapter), and 15 years in educational age. Achievement quotients for the two sexes (educational achievement age divided by mental age) are identical, however (.87 for boys, .86 for girls). We expect some regression to the mean, but even so, these quotients are low. This again points up the fact that when academic achievement is determined by objective measures, there is generally no demonstrable difference in academic achievement between the sexes. Youngsters of both sexes were relatively most accelerated in reading and lagged furthest behind in arithmetic and mathematics.

Paradoxically, this tendency to underachieve also characterizes students of all ages at the opposite end of the intellectual spectrum. However, the dynamics are probably very different: The bright may be victims of underexpectation, understimulation, as well as boredom and uninvolvement; while the slow learners may suffer from frustration, defeat, overexpectation (or, ironically – see Beez, 1968 – underexpectation). It is also possible, as G. M. Harrington (1968) has suggested, that disadvantaged and other slow learning children learn by different methods, thus demanding a drastic overhaul of teaching and learning methods and of curriculum.

Acceleration, Segregation, and Enrichment Historically and currently, United States schools have employed the following techniques with gifted children and youth: They are accelerated, admitted early to school (a special form of acceleration), segregated, or given an enriched curriculum (as in honors courses). It has been widely argued that acceleration is bad for a child: Pushed ahead, he will be with children of similar mental age but will be behind in physical maturity and social development. To some extent and in extreme cases, this is true. But discreet acceleration of children normal or advanced in physical size and intellectual maturity seems actually to be beneficial, or at least no harm from it has been demonstrated. Among Terman's gifted children (Terman and Oden, 1947) at adulthood, those who had been accelerated a year or two were most successful and seemed to suffer no social emotional handicaps. Massive studies conducted by Hobson (1956) in Massachusetts, and Klausmeier, Goodwin, and Ronda (for example, 1968) in Wisconsin suggest that early school admission (Hobson) and grade jumping (Klausmeier, Goodwin, and Ronda) are associated with many positive status characteristics and no negative ones. A possible exception is that accelerated and early-school-admitted boys are underrepresented in contact sports (basketball, football).

Worchester (1959) sums up the situation:

> It is interesting that, although acceleration has undoubtedly been used far more than any other method of providing for the rapid learner, and although there has been more research as to the outcomes of acceleration than there has been for any other method, and although almost all the research has shown results favorable to acceleration with hardly any study showing negative values, still a large proportion of teachers and administrators will have little or none of it. (p. 1)

Worchester comments further that acceleration is "a sort of daylight saving. We get the chores of the world done early in the day so that there may be more opportunity for the real joys of living a little later" (p. 3), and estimates that "if we got the top 3 percent of our gifted into their life work a year earlier, the country would have the advantage of some million years' additional use of its best brains, and it could probably find use for them. Only good effects, in general, have been found for up to two years of acceleration" (p. 4). The case cannot be argued more effectively. It is difficult to understand the reluctance of school people to follow out the implications of research. It may be that selective overemphasis on social development at the cost of competence is partly responsible; and that the heavy representation among school administrators of physical education men may also be implicated. The average coach may not be interested in bright but young and thus physically immature boys in junior and senior high school: They do not win football or basketball games.

Segregation has also been tried, but there are now very few classes for the gifted. They are thought to be undemocratic, although no compulsions now exist about segregating musically gifted young people into the band or glee club, athletically talented young males into the basketball or football squad, academically mediocre students into technical and vocational schools or, at least until recently, retarded children and youth into special classes (again, see Dunn, 1968). It may be that while Americans admire competence up to a point, too much competence is suspect.

Enrichment, while excellent in the ideal sense, is often impractical in either elementary or secondary schools. The school does not have the materials, the teachers do not have the time. What often passes for enrichment (and even for honors courses) consists only in assignment of more of the same thing. Grading practices in a grade conscious society often militate against honors students. The Procrustean recipe of the normal curve is applied to them so that when enrolled in a regular class, they could easily receive all As according to the normal curve, but in their segregated or honors classes, they are graded against each other, with predetermined proportions of grades A through F, again according to a normal curve. However, for the honors group, the curve is skewed impossibly upward relative to the general school population.

In justice to United States public education, it should be added that attitudes toward training the gifted are becoming more flexible, major methods of furthering their progress are being explored in depth or are being developed, state and local level consultants for the gifted are being employed, special summer programs are being conducted, and so on.

Perspective on Giftedness One last research reference highlights the crucial role of high level intellectual competence, even when measured by conventional intelligence tests with all their limitations. Kwall and Lackner (1966) studied the effects of ability, popularity, and parent–child relations on school achievement. Ability was much the most important variable. Even so, when it was coupled with teacher and peer ratings of high leadership it was more closely linked to achievement than when considered alone. High ability children of well-educated mothers also did better than high ability children of less well-educated mothers. Mothers mediate the culture, in other words.

It is well to end this section with a mention of the criteria of giftedness. The discussion above has centered on children with very high IQs (in the upper 5 percent or so of the population) as measured by conventional, single score intelligence tests. But if one changes measurement techniques and employs, for example, tests like Thurstone's Primary Mental Abilities Tests, using all seven of his factors, some 50 percent of the population is gifted by being in the highest 10 percent of the population for at least one or more of the intelligence factors (Bloom, 1969). Bloom speculates that, if more factors were added, 100 percent of the population could be defined as gifted in at least some aspect of cognitive function.

There are also many other than purely intellectual aspects of giftedness, little understood but of vital social importance: motor skills, creative artistry, refinement of tasting, to mention only a few. Such gifts should be detected and fostered for the good of both society and the individuals who possess them.

Other Exceptional Children and Youth

As stated earlier in this section, the evidence about special classes for high grade mentally retarded children is such (for example, Dunn, 1968) that no firm conclusions can be made about what is the best thing to do educationally for such children. McCandless (1967) documents that the situation for such children in regular classes is very bad. But Dunn presents convincing evidence that, while they may be happier and more expertly attended to within a homogeneous group, the over-all criterion of educating them for maximum competence is not being well met. French (1960), for example, concludes that both high and low ability high school students achieve better in high ability classes. The situation concerning education for the disadvantaged is in ferment, as will be discussed in more detail in Chapters 9 and 10. The problems are both urgent and legion, many dedicated and able professional workers are desperately trying to improve things at all levels, the federal government is investing great sums of money, and the situation, while cloudy, is hopeful. All are agreed that traditional methods do not work well.

The movement is away from institutions for the education of the blind, deaf, and severely retarded, but this movement, too, has a mixture of implications. Conclusions will have to await the results of further research. For example, the advantages of maintaining a severely retarded child in a home with normal children must be carefully weighed: The child is probably better off, but what is the cost to parents and siblings? Similar arguments pertain to the deaf and blind, and there are no easy answers. Fortunately, much energy coupled with increasingly sophisticated research and evaluation efforts are being applied to all areas of exceptionality.

Creative Children and Youth

Much research literature and educational advocacy about the creative children have accumulated in the past several years. Guilford (1967) seems to equate giftedness with divergent thinking (see the definitional section earlier in this chapter). Golann (1963) defines creativity as "that process which results in a novel work that is accepted as tenable or useful or satisfying by a group at some point in time" (p. 551). His definition (taken from Stein) is similar to Guilford's, but adds to Guilford's criterion of simple originality or divergence the notion of social usefulness or enjoyment). Getzels and Jackson (1962) have studied gifted adolescents intensively. Torrance (for example, 1962, 1965) has worked with a wide age range of subjects, and Wallach and Kogan (1965) have contributed to the literature about young children.

Problems with the Criterion   Cronbach (1968) addresses himself particularly to the Wallach and Kogan study, and cautions about making too much of a thing about creativity. In his reanalysis of Wallach and Kogan's extensive data, Cronbach concludes that most of their results can be accounted for by two factors, the first of which he calls A and likens to achievement. It closely resembles what these two chapters have described as crystallized intelligence (after Cattell and Horn). As such, it can be seen that it is closely related to the whole discussion of conventional, or structural, intelligence. Cronbach labels the second factor F (he tries to avoid evaluative labels, quite properly), and likens it to fluency or flexibility: "appropriate enough in referring to tasks that call for diverse responses to a single stimulus. . . . The high-F child is one who produces many associative responses, including unusual ones, when encouraged to do so in a game-like setting" (p. 493). In terms of Apollonian and Dionysian life styles, A or crystallized intelligence seems more related to the Appollonian than the Dionysian way of life, while F or "looseness" seems more Dionysian in quality. A also seems to resemble Kagan's reflective cognitive style, F his impulsive style.

Golann's (1963) workmanlike review of the literature up to that date should be consulted by the reader deeply interested in the topic. Guilford has been the pioneer in designing tasks to measure creativity, and many of the research workers in the field employ his techniques or adaptations of them. Typical tests of creativity are these: stating defects in common implements or institutions; producing words that include a specified letter or a combination of letters—while working against a time limit; giving synonyms for stimulus words; naming objects that possess specified attributes; listing as many uses as possible for a common object in a specified time; elaborating shapes, making complex objects from one or two simple shapes, giving remote or very unusual responses to words (this last is Mednick's, 1962, technique). Creativity tests are usually divided into verbal and nonverbal, and emphasis is placed on frequency of unusual responses rather than conventional quality. Novelty of a response is statistically defined: The more unusual the response, the more creative it is judged to be (hence, the term divergent thinking). As has been said, one criticism of work in the field concerns its failure to recognize social desirability. Nor are the different creative subtests, particularly motor and verbal tasks, closely related to each other. Intelligence, as Cronbach points out, accounts for much of the variance in many of the creativity tests. What few studies there have been of validity have not turned out too well. For example, Klausmeier, Harris, and Ethnathios (1962) find almost no relation between tested creativity and teachers' judgments of creativity among the students who took the creativity tests.

Representative Research and Implications With such cautions and synthesizing threads kept in mind, a look at representative literature about creativity or Cronbach's conservative F is appropriate.

One of the most ambitious and influential studies of creativity was conducted by Getzels and Jackson (1962). They used a very atypical school from which to select their subjects, and have been roundly criticized for doing so. Their data typically consist of comparing adolescents from the highest 20 percent of their population in creativity but the lowest 80 percent in conventionally measured IQ, with those in the highest 20 percent of measured IQ but the lowest 80 percent in creativity scores. Representative findings are that IQ ceases to be an effective correlate of performance after IQ levels of between 120 and 130, with creativity, originality, diligence, and motivation accounting for superior achievement from that level on up the IQ scale. The suggestion is that their findings may reflect the situation in their school but not in more conventional schools. Cicerelli (1965) checks their findings with sixth graders, and fails to uncover an interaction effect like Getzels and Jackson report for their older subjects. Cicerelli's data indicate that creativity has little effect on achievement, and what effect there is is additive, not interactive, at all levels. Nor does Torrance (1962, 1965) replicate Getzels and Jackson. Additionally, Hasan and Butcher (1966) attempted to replicate the Getzels and Jackson study among Scottish adolescents in the second year of their secondary education. Hasan and Butcher found that their divergent thinking tests correlated higher with verbal reasoning quotients than with each other. As in Cicerelli's results, when there was a relationship between creativity and intelligence, it was not interactive but supplementary in nature. Thus, youngsters high in verbal reasoning quotient *and* creativity were the highest in English achievement, although not in arithmetic. Teachers also gave "highest desirability as students" ratings to students with high verbal reasoning quotients and to those with both high verbal reasoning quotients and high creativity scores. When creativity was considered apart from its relationship with intelligence, high creative youth were lower in both English and arithmetic achievement, a finding that goes along with the comparison of creativity with Dionysian life style and Cronbach's notion of *F*.

One of the most imaginative and potentially useful studies of creativity was conducted by Laughlin, Doherty, and Dunn (1968), who worked with 348 male and 348 female high school students. All students were tested for intelligence and creativity, the latter by Mednick's (1962) Remote Associates Test. All were given a concept learning test, which was scored in two ways, once for *intentional* and once for *incidental* learning. The task consisted of ten sets of six words per set. Four of the words were high associative value, all designed to elicit a common response. The example the authors give is *globe*, *wheel*, *spool*, and *baseball*. The words illustrate the concept, *round*. Additionally, two words with different association value were included. In the illustrative instance provided by Laughlin, Doherty, and Dunn, the words were *sauerkraut* and *vinegar*, exemplars of the concept *sour*. Intentional learning consisted of instructions to learn the four words that go together. Incidental learning was measured by degree of recall of the other two words in each set.

The findings that are most relevant to creativity concern relations between intelligence–creativity and sex differences: The higher the level of both intelligence and creativity, the better both incidental and intentional learning. Males performed better than females on both intentional and incidental learning. Laughlin, Doherty, and Dunn conclude, after rather complex statistical analysis, that "creativity is a more sensitive predictor than intelligence for [incidental learning], and intelligence a more sensitive predictor than creativity for [intentional learning]" (p.

401). Laughlin (1967) earlier obtained similar results with a population of college students.

These findings are of substantial practical importance. As has been seen earlier, it is well to be purposive and task oriented, but it is well also to be sufficiently flexible and even distractible that other important environmental stimuli are perceived and acted on in addition to those directly related to the goal. It was hypothesized in Chapter 1 that adolescents' exceptionally high drive makes them so self-preoccupied and intent on their own goals that such incidental learnings as are related to social sensitivity, for example, do not occur. Elkind (1967a) comes to similar conclusions, reasoning along Piagetian lines. If creativity (as measured by Laughlin and his colleagues) is related to such incidental learning, then it is a valuable attribute. Some compromise between being able to attend to incidental cues but not being distracted and immobilized by them, seems a useful human condition. As with the Apollonian and the Dionysian life styles, a happy medium may well be the goal toward which to strive.

Levy (1968) suggests that, rather than being a trait, originality (creativity) is a role defined behavior. Through a combination of instructions and reinforcement for unusual responses, he was able substantially to increase the number of "original" responses among a group of volunteer college students. His results are of considerable practical importance for training and classroom practice. Perhaps he suggests a way we may move toward the happy medium.

SUMMARY

In this chapter, an interactionist point of view was taken about the newly rekindled nature–nurture controversy. The author acknowledges that heredity must be important in determining intellectual development but argues that learning opportunities play a more significant role. Evidence from Israeli kibbutzim, where intensive intervention programs have been implemented for disadvantaged children, and from longitudinal studies of United States children from intellectually inferior parentage suggests that environment may make the difference between IQ averages of perhaps as low as 80 or 85 to as high as 115. The practical significance of a difference of this size is obvious. While "social engineering" designed to alter any other than socially pathological (harmful to other) life styles and value systems may be questioned, the evidence seems such as to justify intervention at any age level so as to improve intellectual, verbal, and other symbolic skills. Studies conducted with British children show that type of secondary schooling can be influential in changing adolescents' intellectual functioning, and most particularly when the adolescents concerned are disadvantaged. While there is no spurt in intellectual growth at adolescence corresponding to the physical growth spurt and the rapid rise in total drive level, the very personal–social–behavioral flexibility that has been postulated as the hallmark of adolescence should apply also to potential environmental effects on intelligent, school, and other competence-related behavior.

While a spurt in intellectual growth does not occur at adolescence, adolescence does bring with it marked changes in the quality of thinking and intellectual behavior. Piaget's level of *formal operations* seems to appear for the first time at adolescence. The stage may be labeled the *conquest of thought*. Elkind's convenient verbal labels for Piaget's stages of intellectual and cognitive development were adopted: adolescence is the period for *conquest of thought*; the ages between about 7 and 11 years, the period of *mastering classes, relations, and quantities*; the period from about 2 to 6 years of age as one of *conquest of the symbol*; and infancy as the time for *conquest of the object*.

Educational practices as a function of intellectual level and type of intelligence were discussed in the last part of the chapter. The gifted seem to be rather neglected, although they perhaps constitute society's single most valuable resource. When they are accorded special treatment, acceleration, segregation into special classes or honors programs, and enrichment are the procedures most usually followed. The field of education of the gifted is in considerable ferment at present. Ferment is even more characteristic of philosophies and practices of educating the disadvantaged and the educable mentally retarded. There is general agreement that present practices are not successful, and widespread experimentation, formal and informal, is being carried on. The ferment is believed to be healthy if confusing.

The final topic in the chapter was creativity. Criticisms of the concept were discussed and it was concluded that perhaps a better term than creativity was flexibility. Traditional notions of intelligence were likened to the Apollonian way of conducting one's intellectual affairs, while that which is measured by the newer efforts to assess creativity or flexibility were likened to a Dionysian style.

9

Youth and the Schools

INTRODUCTION

In Chapters 7 and 8, the ground was laid for describing the function of America's most ambitious institution for the young, the schools. The paramount traditional function of schools is to take a youngster with a given level of intellect and basic if untrained capacities for inquiry and problem solving and to challenge and exploit the intellect, to provide "mental furniture" for it, and to hone and synchronize the cognitive processes so that, at age 16 or later, a youth can go forth into society, earn a living, keep out of trouble, contribute to the society in which he lives and, over all, enjoy and appreciate the process.

Chapter 6 dealt with youth and the community in a broad, informal sense, with the focus on how the community provides legitimate and illegitimate opportunities for adolescents. In this and the next chapter, the emphasis is narrowed. Chapters 9 and 10 are mainly concerned with the two major formal institutions designed to provide legitimate opportunities for young people: the school and the church. (Chapter 10 will cover, among other things, church influences on youth.

Every community in the United States has developed at least one institution to open the wide world of opportunity to children and young people: the school. The prevailing American ethos seems to be that, after the family has brought the child to 5 or 6 years of age, he is taken to the door of the schoolhouse and turned over almost totally to the school system. The family asks the school[1] to make him a good citizen, in addition to teaching him to read, write, and cope with the numbers system. It asks that he also be made a well-socialized human being. It wants the school to carry much of the load of moral development, although it expects that some of this burden will be carried by the church of the family's choice. It expects the school to see to it that more and more recreation is provided as a child progresses to the upper grades, until by high school the school is the forum of the child's recreational as well as his intellectual life. A great majority of parents want the school to provide *safe* and sound sex education. Parents expect from the school vocational training of their youngsters, as well as transmitting the culture to them and, hopefully, instilling in them a high enough level of skills that they can live efficiently within society and possibly even add something worthwhile to it.

The turning over of children to schools by families is not voluntary but mandatory. By law, children in the United States must begin school in the kindergarten or first grade when they are about 5 or 6 years old. In most communities and states, children must remain in school full time until they reach age 16. About one-fourth of the nation—some 50,-000,000 children and adolescents—are principally occupied in going to school. Next to their families and coequal with their communities, the principal arena of life for children and young adolescents is the school. Here the young person tests himself against his peers. Here he faces a more objective and often less kindly set of judges than his parents. Here he practices the skills that will enable him to earn a living, live in a cooperative society, make friends, and win a mate.

Because the chapters are closely interlinked, both Chapters 9 and 10 are summarized following Chapter 10.

THE FUNCTIONS OF A SCHOOL

At the most general level, schools are expected to and certainly should perform two functions. These functions are *maintenance–actualization*, and *skills training–cultural transmission*.

Under maintenance–actualization, the school should provide a child with a happy, challenging, and self-fulfilling environment. No person should be worse off from a psychological, social, and emotional point of view because he attends school, and almost all should be better

---

[1] The same caution must be made about using the word school as an "animate abstraction" as was made about the use of "community" and "society" in Chapter 6. Schools are systems made up of people who hold their jobs by the courtesy of the citizens of a community, and who are also citizens of the community, often very influential ones. A school is *not* an abstraction, it does not have a superordinate life of its own; it is simply a group of trained people working together in a rather formalized structure to educate the young while themselves following their chosen way of professional life.

off. If a child enters school richly endowed, he should leave it more richly endowed. If he enters school from a background of cultural, emotional, and financial poverty, the school should have helped him go a long way toward overcoming this background by the time he goes out on his own.

Skills training–cultural transmission includes the conventional functions of the school: to provide the child with skill in and knowledge about reading, writing, math, science, social studies, art, music, health, and so on.

There are many problems in melding these two functions. Lively and sometimes violent disagreement exists among school people themselves, between school-related people and interested laymen and theorists, among politicians and parents, and among parents, teachers, administrators, and the students themselves.

The Maintenance – Actualization Function

About 98 percent of babies are born without any type of genetic defect (Valenti, 1968). In addition to genetic defects, birth injuries, later unavoidable accidents, and disease condemn another small percentage to blighted lives. But the *social mortality rate* approaches 25 percent! One can only conclude that society and not genetics, accidents, and disease bears the responsibility for distorting the later lives of most children, youth, and adults who fail.

No thoroughly convincing evidence exists to indicate that there is any innate or genetic reason for children born normal to grow up mentally retarded, severely neurotic, psychotic, sexually deviate, illiterate, suicidal, or socially crippled in other ways. Physically and neurologically normal babies, properly reared, seem to carry within them the potential for intellectual growth sufficient to graduate from high school with an *earned* diploma and adequate personal adjustment.

School drop-out rate comprises one simple statistic of probable failure in today's society. The high school drop-out rate is about 33 percent nationally (Schreiber, 1968), and is far higher in many isolated places. Among some discriminated-against segments of our society, the average educational leval – even of those who do struggle through to high school graduation – is only about eighth or ninth grade. One can not live effectively in today's technical society with only a junior high school level of competence.

The conclusion from such figures is clear and devastating: A very large number of American homes and a very large proportion of American schools fail to maintain and actualize their children adequately. The organism, normal at birth, is socially and educationally blighted somewhere along its course of development, most likely sometime before the end of the third grade of school (for example, Fitzsimmons, *et al.*, 1969).

Compensations With its surge of new drives and motives, the adolescent period is one during which much compensation can be provided for young people whose earlier life circumstances have crippled them severely. Three representative, classic studies (Bijou, Ainsworth, and Stockey, 1943; Curran, 1955; and Kephart and Ainsworth, 1938) demonstrate that rehabilitation of young people who are retarded intellectually and/or emotionally and behaviorally can be accomplished for between 70 and 85 percent of the cases who receive a massive compensatory training program between about 13 and 16 years of age, on the average.

In the earliest of these studies of children paroled from an institution for retarded, delinquent children and youth, Kephart and Ainsworth (1938) found that nearly three-fourths of the boys in their sample had become law abiding, self-supporting citizens, and had remained so for a period of from five to ten years after their return to the community. This was true despite the fact that the era of the study was also that of the social confusion and despair of the Great Depression, and despite the fact that a population of this type is one of the least promising of the various problem subgroups in society. Most of the youngsters studied by Kephart and Ainsworth had attended inner city Detroit schools for some seven to eight years before being committed by the courts to the Wayne County Training School, usually for combined reasons of mental retardation and criminality, but all were officially certified to be mentally retarded. They came from homes of great disorder, confusion, and deprivation. The majority were from discriminated-against minority groups: Afro-American youngsters whose parents had come North; Polish-American boys and girls whose parents or grandparents had migrated from the Old World; Appalachian youth whose parents had come North from the mountains to work in the factories; and Italian- and Sicilian-American adolescents whose parents or grandparents, like those of the Polish-American boys, had come to the New World for a better life, but who all too often had not found it.

These youngsters averaged about 65 IQ when admitted to the Wayne County Training School, most were physiologically and neurologically normal, they were committed at an average age of about 13 years, and they stayed, on the average, for about three years. When they entered, their educational age was generally less than second grade level; and their behavioral records were on the whole horrendous. Yet, after an average of three years of rather expensive and luxurious-seeming compensatory, 24-hour-a-day, total life education, 75 percent of them went back to their communities and made it. Without such intervention, the norms suggest that no more than perhaps 10 percent could have done so.

Bijou, Ainsworth, and Stockey (1943) carried out a similar study of girls from similar backgrounds and with similar histories of delinquency (although with a much higher rate of sex delinquency), and found that 70 percent of the girls also succeeded after parole. This percentage is even more remarkable than the figure for the boys, since girls seem more vulnerable than boys to life circumstances, and less the determiners of their own fates: For example, to a very large degree, the success of a woman is judged and determined by the man she marries. Obviously, these girls were not prime matrimonial prospects in any conventional sense.

Curran (1955), reporting on the postinstitutional careers of disturbed and delinquent boys, finds a striking 85 percent of them successful after return to the community. For boys like those on whom he reports, the predicted rehabilitation rate is only about 20 to 30 percent.

In short, even with severely disadvantaged and blighted youth, sophisticated, expensive effort can produce striking returns. But the initial expense seems to be a superb long term investment.

Positive Noncontingent Reinforcement The maintenance–actualization task of the school is to help the child toward happiness, self-acceptance, realistic self-esteem and pride in himself, and the techniques to take fullest advantage of his potential—indeed, perhaps to increase it. In another context (McCandless, 1967), the author has referred to the mechanics of the maintenance–actualization function as "reducing as many irrelevant frustrations as possible." In effect, such frustration reduction may help to reduce total drive from a level that interferes with efficient function to a more manageable level (see Chapter 1). Technically, maintenance–actualization seems to be best accomplished in a setting where the child receives consistent noncontingent, preponderantly positive, reinforcement. Translated to nontechnical terms, this means that he is accepted as a worthwhile human being; that while he may be punished for what he *does*, he is not punished for what he *is*; that he is liked rather than disliked by his teachers and other caretakers; that confidence in him and his potential is manifested even though he may often flounder; that the authorities do not stand in the way of his legitimate attempts to achieve his own goals, even though these may not always seem to be school-related; and that what he has to say in all seriousness is judged to be worth listening to.

It is obvious that in the United States noncontingent reinforcement and irrelevant frustration vary sharply by social class and skin color. A white middle-class child is typically born into a friendly, accepting world that automatically reaches out to provide him with the advantages that are his birthright: a *maximum of built-in positive noncontingent reinforcement* and a minimum of irrelevant frustration. In sharp contrast, the "birthright" of an Afro-American, American Indian, or Hispaño child is a maximum of irrelevant frustration because of what he is, not because of what he does or does not do, and a maximum of *negative noncontingent reinforcement*. Among the types of negative reinforcement are discriminations because of his parents, his color, his poverty, his language and, often, his religion. Furthermore, advantaged parents stress positive, accepting methods of child rearing, while disadvantaged parents are more likely to be authoritarian, negative, and physically punishing (for example, see Bowerman and Elder, 1964; Horrocks, 1969). Thus are the ways of the larger world translated almost from birth by the child's intimate family.

As Grier and Cobbs (1968) point out, the central function of the family is to provide positive noncontingent reinforcement and freedom from irrelevant frustration. Those who are poor, the "wrong" color, and uneducated can not give even this minimum of protection to their children; nor can spouses provide it for each other.

Coopersmith (1967) found that parents who provide general, positive noncontingent reinforcement produce children with high self-esteem; and that high self-esteem children, at least as fifth and sixth graders, are more successful than low self-esteem children. As will be discussed later, there is little the school can do that will damage children from homes that give them competence and high self-esteem; there is much the school can do, on the one hand, to damage children from less fortunate homes still further, but, on the other hand, to compensate them for what they do not receive in their homes and the larger community. The three studies cited above demonstrate this potential for compensatory maintenance–actualization. Cautions about compensatory education were documented in Chapter 8, however. Where the explicit or implicit goal is to superimpose the value system of the "power elite" on a less powerful coculture, compensatory education becomes suspect.

Actualization and Behavior Control The schools' current efforts at maintenance–actualization represent a mixed bag of efforts, results, and community response. As has been pointed out in earlier chapters, many programs of physical education in junior and senior high schools would be laughable if they were not so unfortunate in their implications for the youth exposed to them. Yet, community reaction to a winning basketball or football team verges on ecstasy; and a coach or an athletic director who has a good physical fitness program for *all* youth in his school but whose team is a loser may have his contract terminated.

Home economics is well accepted by the community but is not often well fitted to girls who come from very poor homes, and almost never reaches boys. Drivers' training is regarded as a frill by many communities and boards of education, but it is successful enough that insurance companies (by no means charitable institutions) offer rate benefits to young people who have passed drivers' training courses. At this time, sex education—certainly a maintenance–actualization program—is both coming into its own and is under serious and in some places violent attack. It is regarded in most communities with a mixture of hope and apprehension. However, it may safely be predicted that a third grade teacher who gives sex education at the level of sophistication already attained by most of her pupils would be fired out of hand; and that in most schools a teacher who grapples openly and honestly with the day-in-and-day-out sexual problems faced by youth from sixth or seventh grade on would likely be discharged with censure. Some of the popular media present the picture of sex education, the schools, and the various forces in the community quite well (see, for instance, *Look* magazine, September 9, 1969). In the absence of clear data such intelligent lay surveys are quite helpful.

Many traditional educators, boards of education, and parents concern themselves preponderantly with the problem of order and discipline in the classroom, school building, and school environs. About half the reference forms that come to the author for young men and women being considered for teaching positions prominently include and often begin with probing questions about the candidate's ability to maintain discipline. No one argues that learning can occur in a group situation unless there is a reasonably smooth and efficient classroom organization. But the atmosphere need not be martial or prison-like, and the noise level can well be higher than that of a research library. Indeed, Slater (1968), in her study of seventh grade boys and girls, found that noise level made no difference in students' efficiency in performing a short, written task demanding concentration. Neither boys nor girls were affected by noise, although the boys worked somewhat faster and with more mistakes under noise conditions (but not at a statistically significant level).

Many classrooms that might be called *negative maintainers* (actually, they might as well be called interest and motivation destroyers) exist because the teachers or principals justify the military camp atmosphere on the basis of its being a well-disciplined class. By the same token, the often rather noisy, informal, and spontaneous class filled with enthusiastic learners is sometimes decried as one that coddles children and youth. Ideally, a set of classroom rules must be sensible, firm, and established by open joint agreement between a teacher and the class members. Considerable individual student freedom is both enjoyable and useful but, when an individual's freedom jeopardizes the class goals, as it often does, then the individual must be controlled. When a class and a teacher are working well together, most instances of potential disruption are handled almost automatically by class-teacher teamwork. There will always be times, however, when a teacher must take firm and immediate steps; and there are almost certainly bound to be occasions when a student will be asked to leave his group for a time until he is ready to behave within the allowable limits. Isolation has been found to work well with young children, but the technique has not often been tried with adolescents.

The best and only legitimate criterion for limits on student behavior is a documented answer to the question, "Does the behavior interfere with the learning goals of the class?" The author has been surprised at how many classroom rules can fall by the wayside when this criterion is imposed. Since enforcement of each rule requires considerable teacher and class time and energy, it follows that the fewer the rules, the more time and energy available for the basic goals of a class, and the less friction among class members and between class members and the teacher. What rules there are should be lucid and consistent. Nothing breeds confusion and dissent more effectively than ambiguous and inconsistently followed rules.

The Training— Acculturation Function

The traditional functions of education—training and acculturation—have been most emphasized in school organization and teacher education. If the school does not succeed in imparting the culture to its students and helping them acquire the skills to function in society, it fails not only in its training function but also in its maintenance-actualization function. Most well-educated and competent people are reasonably *happy*. But can a semiliterate or an illiterate person without marketable skills be happy in this society? It is doubtful he can.

The training-acculturation and maintenance-actualization functions of schools *can* be independent. Research exists suggesting that bored, uninterested, and discontented students *do* or at least *can* learn (for example, Jackson and Lahaderne, 1967; Lahaderne, 1968). But it is not known how much *more* they would learn if they were involved and happy. All evidence from psychological research suggests but does not fully prove that they would learn much more, and that many who seem to learn nothing would learn well if they were involved (Jensen, 1968). The conclusion can be made quite firmly that maintenance-actualization and training-acculturation are and should be *interdependent:* Maintenance and actualization are most effectively achieved when training and acculturation are efficient and effective, and vice versa.

While maintenance-actualization seems to depend on a general atmosphere of acceptance, or positive noncontingent reinforcement, training-acculturation seems to be most effectively managed by contingent reinforcement administered within the specific arena of training (or teaching[2]). A *general* pattern of effective contingent reinforcement is provided by social values, but it needs to be especially tailored to be effective for all children. For reinforcement to change a person's behavior, or to motivate him, it must tie in very specifically to his own motivational system, which is, in turn, established by his personal history. Considerable research has been done concerning differential reinforcement patterns using children of different social classes as subjects, with ages ranging from nursery school through high school (for example, Douvan, 1956; Ostfeld and Katz, 1969). Results of these studies suggest that the children of the poor, when compared with advantaged children, respond more to tangible than intangible rewards; to praise of themselves "as people" than to stress on whether or not they have done a good job; and to severe verbal threat and punishment rather than mild threat and punishment. The pattern is reversed for advantaged children.

The general social pattern for United States culture is to give praise, approval, or some other positive thing for a job well done, or for trying hard to do it well, and reproof, disapproval, rejection, blame, or other punishment for doing it poorly, or for not trying hard.

Motivational Strategies For students in groups, current research suggests three reinforcement strategies: (1) By observation and manipulation, a teacher looks for what works best for most of the young people in a class. Disadvantaged children, as has been suggested, will work harder for tangible goals and personal approval, while advantaged children can be better motivated through intangible, long range goals and approval of the adequacy of their product. Boys may work harder if their reward consists of granting them independence in some suitable undertaking, while girls may work harder for a closer relationship with the teacher.

(2) These group patterns will not work for some individual children. It then behooves the teacher to observe and explore to find out what is particularly important to a given child, and then to employ it to motivate him to acquire the skill or learning that is the objective of the class or of the curriculum. One acutely shy and academically inefficient and uninvolved eighth grade boy with whom the author once had dealings was immobilized when the attractive young woman teacher spoke to him or touched him; but he responded when she caught his eye but did not signal to any other member of the class that he and she were looking at each other. A program of planned eye contact served effectively to moti-

[2]Many people object to the word training when used in an educational context.

vate him and keep him working and he improved in self-assurance as he began to experience some success with his academic tasks, at the same time becoming assured that he would not be singled out for verbal attention or physical contact. This teacher did much touching and patting of her students, an effective technique with some but not others. By the end of the year, the student in question was doing adequately academically and had progressed socially to the extent that he sometimes talked briefly with this and other teachers, although only when he was alone with them.

Functions of the Class as a Group The classroom is much more than an interaction of a child with a teacher. It is well to look at how the group can be employed to motivate and to facilitate both functions of training–acculturation and maintenance–actualization. In some classes, often in neighborhoods where few or no children can reasonably expect to go to college, being a good student is unfashionable. In other classes, any mark of approbation given by a teacher to a student singles him out for teasing or open aggression by his classmates. This seems to be particularly true for boys. The class, in other words, can actually work against as well as for the teacher. In the former type of class, teacher behavior construed by the teacher as a positively reinforcing contingent reward may in actuality be exactly the opposite: It will bring to the receiver of the reward the derogation and hostility of his peers. In such classes students are thus likely to *avoid* the learning that is the teacher's goal.

The possibility of conflicting goals held by a teacher on the one hand and the class on the other is very real. Such conflict often occurs (1) in disadvantaged neighborhoods, where family and community mores outrage (or shock, or are disapproved of by) teachers, (2) in extremely and particularly in coldly and punitively maintained authoritarian classrooms, and (3) between teachers and boys, where the teacher demands conformity and obeisance and normal boys want independence, initiative, and respect.

When conflicting goals do occur, it is likely that teachers and students will work at cross purposes, which will interfere with learning efficiency. The teacher rewards one thing, the class another; the teacher punishes one thing, while the class rewards the very behavior that is punished. Among adolescents, the approval of the peer group is much more likely to be meaningful and valuable, while the over-all academic goals of the teacher are more likely to be worthwhile to students in later life. The net result of the conflict is that all parties lose.

The frequency of such unconstructive situations appears to be the best argument for democratic class and school organization, where ground rules are plotted in advance after full discussion and understanding of expectations and needs of all concerned administrators, teachers, parents, the community, and students. When a democratic classroom exists, it is often likely that teachers and administrators will argue leniency for "culprits" rather than strong discipline. By eliminating such conflicts, the teacher is dissolving the adversary situation, and youth can be given a responsible sense of participation in the classroom activities.

The group serves different functions for different members. Bass (1967) distinguishes among three functions a group may serve for its members. Presumably, each member has a consistent pattern for what a group means to him, although it seems likely that different groups can serve different purposes for members; and the same person may employ a group to serve his needs as they vary from one time to another. In groups, Bass says: ". . . the social situation involves a group task (the aims, purposes, and goals of the group and the means for their achievement). This task may be the focus of attention for some individuals, the group may be the center of attention for others, and personal concerns may be the focus for still others" (p. 260).

When the group member is less concerned about the needs of others than about his own needs, when the intrinsic satisfaction of work is secondary to extrinsic reward, then the value of the group to the individual consists of *self-orientation.* Bass says the group can be construed as both the cast and the audience before which the self-oriented youngster can aggress or dominate, gain esteem and status, or air his personal difficulties.

Interaction orientation characterizes group members who use their group as a setting for sharing things with others, gaining a feeling of belonging, forming friendships, and building strong interpersonal relationships. Bass has built a scale to indicate which function groups characteristically perform for individuals. Those high in interaction orientation, he says, typically prefer to have fun with friends, to have helpful friends, to work cooperatively, to make more friends, and to be an easy-to-talk-to leader. People high in self-orientation want to be respected leaders, to take it easy, to receive personal praise, to have loyal friends, and to be recognized for their efforts.

Still another type of group member may be characterized by *task orientation.* A member inclined in this direction is likely to persist at assignments, to work to overcome barriers to the group's goals, and to concentrate on solving its problems. On Bass' inventory, a task-oriented group member prefers to be thought wise, to work at a hobby, to have the feeling of doing a job well, to possess bright and interesting friends, and to be thought a leader who gets things done.

Bass' classification can be helpful to group leaders, whether teachers or club organizers. Important variations of contingent motivation can be devised to meet the needs of group members who hold different goals for the group and their membership in it. The self-oriented member may be motivated by the chance to be the class star in a public function, the interaction-oriented member may work hardest to earn the class free time for "buddy interactions," while the task-oriented member may be most motivated, for example, by being put in charge of arranging various class functions.

Punishment and Reward Over-all classroom control seems best to be gained by accentuating the positive and ignoring, rather than punishing, the negative. In this manner, behaviors that disrupt the class or interfere with either an individual's or the class' goals seem simply to become extinguished because of lack of reinforcement. This pattern of classroom management is derived in a general way from Skinner (for example, 1953, 1954, 1958). The author and his colleagues (Hodges, McCandless, and Spicker, 1969) have applied it to classroom management of younger children with what they believe to be great success. When he works informally, the author uses this technique in group management of adolescents, and he believes it is highly successful.

The general rationale for this positive reinforcement pattern comes from experimental psychology, where researchers believe it modifies and consolidates behavior, but it does not *inhibit* other potentially positive "spontaneous" behavior the subject may exhibit. When such additional positive behavior occurs, it too can be reinforced and consolidated. While punishment may very effectively stop the behavior punished for the time being, it also seems to inhibit other spontaneous behavior, much of which may be desirable and constructive. And if positive behavior does not appear, it can not be reinforced and thus strengthened. Thus, a classroom climate that stresses positive reinforcement, letting nonreinforcement take care of undesirable behavior, broadens the spectrum of positive child behaviors that can be elicited and consolidated. But for a class with a central focus of punishment all behavior is decelerated, thus denying the group members the chance to learn constructive things in addition to the specific task on which the teacher is concentrating. These additional behaviors are very likely to include *learning to be interested* in what is being taught and general intellectual curiosity and zest for learning.

HOW SUCCESSFUL ARE SCHOOLS?

A few survey figures suggest that United States schools by no means accomplish all that their supporting communities expect them to.

The Sizer report (1967) on the fifteen largest cities declares that 31 percent of the children who completed ninth grade in these big cities failed to receive a high school diploma. Six percent of the children who start the fifth grade in these cities never even enter the tenth grade. In one representative city among the fifteen, the rate of unemployment for male drop-outs is 15 percent higher than for the high school graduates. In another, 48 percent of the boys between 16 and 21 years of age *with* high school diplomas were unemployed. While admitting that the fact is difficult to document statistically, Sizer believes it is clear that the great majority of high school drop-outs and a large proportion of high school graduates are unemployable except for unskilled occupations. Both the number and proportion of those employed in such unattractive occupations are steadily diminishing in this technological society.

Nationally, only two-thirds of the United States population complete high school (Ginzberg, 1968). In parts of the United States, this figure shrinks to less than 50 percent (for example, in the rural South). Such figures suggest school failure in training-acculturation.

The Detroit Board of Education spends up to one-and-one-half million dollars a year replacing schools' broken windows. This signifies a singular lack of love for their alma maters by a very large number of urban boys and girls.

The Dodd Subcommittee on Juvenile Delinquency reported in 1966 that at any given time, exclusive of delinquents whose acts are not reported to any agency, there are nearly two million young males currently or recently delinquent who have also experienced single or multiple juvenile court appearances. The figure for girls is 500,000.

FBI crime statistics (suspect by many social scientists) routinely report year after year increases in the incidence of juvenile crimes that are greater than the increase in the actual percentage of juveniles. For example, the report by J. Edgar Hoover in 1967 noted a 7 percent increase in juvenile crime over the previous year. Such delinquency figures suggest school and community failure in maintenance-actualization.

At the time of writing, the student protests and rebellions that have at times immobilized such very different institutions as Cornell and Columbia universities and San Francisco State College are moving down into the high schools and junior high schools in such disparate locations as Boston, Chicago, New York, and even Jeffersonville, Georgia. There are often very legitimate reasons for the students' behavior, as following sections of the chapter will make clear. There is, of course, serious question as to whether violence is best designed to correct the causes of the disaffection. Polls suggest a real backlash: 70 percent of the sampled adult population supports the actions of the Chicago police at the time of the Democratic Convention in 1968, and sentiment against violent student protest is extreme. Support of what was apparently brutal and repressive action in Chicago (see the Walker Report to the President's Commission on Causes and Prevention of Violence, winter of 1968) can be all too easily mobilized into severe and self-defeating—indeed destructive—repression of the young.

On the more positive side, figures about the cash value of education testify that schooling is successful in that it "pays off." A compilation by the Georgia Educational Improvement Council, representative of other such compilations, indicates that, with projections based on figures for the year 1964, a person with an elementary education can expect to earn only about $205,000 in his lifetime, while a college graduate can be predicted to earn more than twice that amount; that a high school diploma "is worth" $273,000, while a college education pays off to about $500,000. A college graduate can expect to earn about $140,000 more than a high school graduate, even though he starts work four years later on the average. These figures have increased and will presumably continue to increase by 3 to 6 percent annually, owing to the combination of an expanding economy and inflation.

Hathaway, Reynolds, and Monachesi (1969a and b) provide extensive data about 1000 male and 812 female high school drop-outs. The sample of boys comprised one portion of a statewide study of adolescent behavior and personality that was begun in Minnesota in 1953 when the boys were ninth graders in the Minnesota schools. Follow-up data were gathered for them and 1000 control boys between 1962 and 1966, when both groups averaged about 28 years of age. The controls were graduates of the same high schools attended by the drop-outs, picked on a random basis.

The authors provide a one sentence statement of the most striking finding of their study: "To a large degree, the dropout of the 1950s is the

Table 9.1

Correlations for boys and girls between a group intelligence test and teachers' marks in four basic subject matter classes

School Subject	Boys	Girls
English	.56	.76
Social Studies	.48	.82
Science	.65	.75
Mathematics	.39	.68

(Adapted from Olson, *et al.*, 1968.)

The picture for the correlations between intelligence and teacher grades is about the same as for intelligence and scores on standardized achievement tests. However, teachers' grades are typically lower for boys; and the correlation between intelligence and teachers' grades is lower for boys than for girls. It may be ventured that teachers both view boys more harshly and estimate their achievement less accurately (for example, Arnold, 1968). Boys may also be less interested in saving face than girls. When they do not know (or care) they may be quite open about it, while girls will pretend (see Joe Dillinger and Mary Epworth, in Chapter 2). Teachers may thus underestimate boys' efforts and interests, but overestimate them for girls.

Olson, Miller, Hale, and Stevenson (1968) provide typical evidence about this point. They calculated the correlations for forty-six girls and fifty-one boys from three middle-class seventh grade classrooms in Minneapolis. The intelligence test they used was the Verbal Lorge-Thorndike, a widely used group intelligence test. Table 9.1 has been adapted from their study.

In every instance, relations between teachers' marks and boys' grades were lower than for girls. Indeed, the lowest correlation for girls (between mathematics grades and intelligence) was higher than the highest correlation for boys (between science grades and intelligence). The conclusion must be either that factors other than intelligence enter more heavily into teachers' grade assignments for boys or that the determinants for learning for boys are more complex than for girls. Much evidence exists to support the former conclusion. (The correlations between intelligence and standardized tests' assessments of achievement are about the same for boys and girls, and, as will be seen later, teachers are more punitive toward boys. Boys, of course, probably elicit more punitiveness because of their high initiativeness and assertiveness, which do not fit well with schools' emphasis on order and quiet.)

Attitudes toward School

Insofar as the matter has been studied, attitudes toward school seem to have little relation for either boys or girls to how well they achieve or to how attentive they are. However, the degree to which they are attentive is a good predictor both of how well they achieve in school and of how intelligent they are.

that the ideal of universal free education held by Americans is good. An examination of the defects of the system should not conspire against the ideal but rather move people toward action which will achieve the ideal. Knowledge exists whereby really good schools can be created. One of the most serious problems of today is society's failure to apply it.

FACTORS CONTRIBUTING TO SCHOOL SUCCESS

The Coleman Report (Coleman, *et al.* 1966), the most ambitious although not the least controversial report of the educational opportunity open to children and youth and the degree to which they profit from it, suggests that home background is by far the most important predictor of who will profit from school. Evidence suggests that this finding is not entirely simple and straightforward: Families living in "good neighborhoods" expect, demand, and receive schools that are at least moderately successful in fulfilling their training function; while the less affluent family, which expects and indeed demands much the same from its schools, is grievously short changed. Considerable evidence also exists that the children of the poor are treated differently in the classroom than the children of the comparatively affluent middle class.

Intelligence

It is well to set some of the general and theoretical material from Chapters 7 and 8 into the more applied context of this chapter. Generally, the correlation between intelligence and academic achievement as measured by some external test (standardized rather than teacher constructed and graded) ranges from about .50 to about .70 or .75. There is little difference in these correlations between girls and boys. The achievement of disadvantaged children is less well predicted by standard intelligence tests than that of advantaged children.

Results from Day (1968) illustrate the typical relationships between intelligence and achievement. He worked with seventh and eighth grade Canadian students, and correlated their IQ scores as measured by the Dominion Group Test of Learning Capacity (Intermediate) with their marks on end-of-term examinations. He does not report sex differences for these correlations.

For academic subjects, Day finds the following correlations, from high to low: intelligence with English literature, .67; with English (language), .64; with history, .61; with mathematics, .53; with science, .53; and with geography, .41.

Meyer and Bendig (1961) conducted a longitudinal study of the relations between the Primary Mental Abilities Test (PMA) and over-all school achievement. They report their results separately for boys and girls, and find the predictions somewhat more accurate for boys than for girls. For example, the verbal subtest (which correlates highest with school achievement for the Meyer and Bendig sample) correlates .70 with a high school achievement test among eighth grade boys, and .74 among the same boys later when they are in eleventh grade. The correlation for eighth grade girls is .56, and for the same girls in eleventh grade it is .45. For the children as a group, the results are directly in line with Day's results (.58 for youngsters in the eighth grade, .52 when they moved into eleventh grade).

slightly skilled or unskilled laborer of the 1960s." They go on to say, "Even if a bright boy drops out of school, the data show that he is much less likely than his bright schoolmate who graduates to get later training of any kind and that he is much more likely to subsequently fall into the ranks of the semi-skilled, slightly skilled, day laborer, and unemployed. In view of the nationwide search for talent, this finding is important: boys of high ability *are* being lost" (p. 377). In this study, 14 percent of the drop-outs were at or above the 64th percentile in intelligence test scores—in short, were in the top 36 percent of the national population intellectually.

Of the male high school drop-outs studied by Hathaway, Reynolds, and Monachesi, 72 percent were working at semiskilled, slightly skilled, or day labor jobs, or were unemployed. Of the controls who were graduated from high school, 42 percent fell into these categories.

There was little later career difference between early (tenth grade and before) and late (after tenth grade) drop-outs, although more of the former came from farm families. Drop-outs came more frequently than would be expected on the basis of chance from large families and were the first or last child of such families. Some personality differences between drop-outs and controls appeared, with the former more likely to be withdrawn, odd, or rebellious. The drop-outs' career patterns showed downward social mobility (they did less well occupationally than their fathers had done). The drop-outs fathered more children than the controls, and included a higher proportion of men with records of criminal activity. All these differences persisted even when the factor of intelligence was controlled statistically. As one example, 37 percent of the drop-outs with high intelligence had committed crimes ranging from misdemeanors to crimes resulting in prison sentences. This was true of only 9 percent of the high school graduates.

The picture for girl drop-outs (Hathaway, Reynolds, and Monachesi, 1969b) is much the same but, characteristically, less dramatic. The authors summarize by saying: "Dropout for girls seems less catastrophic than it does for boys" (p. 383).

As American society now operates, a high school diploma is clearly a valuable commodity. However, if the drop-out rate is reduced at the expense of the *quality* of education, a high school diploma will rapidly lose its value. Current employment practices suggest that this may be the case.

> Diploma devaluation already exists in the job world as evidenced by the fact that the educational attainment of the unemployed is increasing more rapidly than that of the employed.... The net effect of reducing dropout rates is to add more graduates to the army of unemployed rather than to guarantee jobs for those young people who have to be persuaded to graduate. (Tannenbaum, 1968, p. 1)

Nor do high school diplomas mean the same things to all members of the society. According to Tannenbaum, 25 percent of unemployed Black males 18 years old and over had high school diplomas in 1964 compared with 32 percent of the employed—a difference of only 7 percent. In contrast, 57 percent of employed white males of the same ages had high school diplomas, while only 38 percent of unemployed white males were high school graduates. The value of a high school diploma, thus, seems to interact with one's skin color.

It becomes evident as one thinks of the youth he knows and as he reads about the matter (for example, Schreiber, 1968; Tannenbaum, 1968), that dropping out of high school is only one symptom among many among adolescents. Simply keeping a youth in school will not correct his other ills. This point is well supported by Hathaway, Reynolds, and Monachesi's (1969a) descriptions of the personality and family background characteristics of high school drop-outs compared with youth who had been graduated.

Thus, while the rate of high school academic mortality is cause for alarm, putting all youth through high school will not solve all problems. As one attempts to evaluate the success of the American secondary school, it is clear that the picture is far from rosy. Yet, this country does have one of the highest percentages of citizenry who can read, write, and deal with numbers. This near universal literacy has provided the invaluable condition of better communication across social classes than is true in most nations. Although this is a desirable goal, the educational situation is *very* far from ideal.

It is well to consider how the school as a major social system fits into the conceptual framework of a psychology of adolescence. The question raised here provides a perspective for the more detailed review of literature later in this chapter.

Are schools successful with adolescents in the important task of understanding and socializing the sex drive? Many schools today attempt to do an honest job of giving sex education, although few probably succeed. The fault lies as much with society at large as it does with the school. Even such sex education as is now given is under vigorous attack, and the future of sound sex education is unknown. Indirectly, schools provide young people with a special society within which they can experiment with dating, observe how their peers are adjusting in this and other social areas, profit from successful models, presumably learn what not to do from unsuccessful models, and conduct considerable social sexual experimentation. To summarize, junior and senior high schools provide the arena in which growth toward a sound psychosexual adjustment *can* occur, but the assistance that is given to adolescents is more likely to be indirect than direct. The peer group is probably more useful than the teachers and counselors.

Junior and senior high schools *do* provide a setting in which most adolescents can make the change from childhood to adulthood less painfully and perhaps more efficiently than they could if they were thrown on their own into the open society. As has been discussed, advantaged young people adjust better to schools than disadvantaged youth, and girls better than boys within all social classes. However, at least among the middle class, the benefits, as judged by the possession of academic skills and mastery of the culture, are not greatly different for boys and girls.

Much of the evidence presented later in this chapter about the effect of schools on adolescents is depressing. The author believes strongly

Table 9.2

Correlations for boys and girls between attentiveness, subject matter, academic achievement, and group intelligence test scores

Subject	Boys	Girls
Reading	.46	.39
Arithmetic	.53	.39
Language	.48	.37
Kuhlmann-Anderson Intelligence Test	.48	.44

(Adapted from Lahaderne, 1968.)

Lahaderne (1968), for instance, obtained essentially no relationships between two measures of pupils' attitudes toward their schools, their schoolwork, and their teachers, and their standing on standardized academic achievement tests. This was true for both boys and girls. Nor did Lahaderne obtain any relationships between attitudes toward school, schoolwork, and teachers, and the degree to which either boys or girls were attentive.

However, she did find rather strong relationships—stronger for boys than for girls—between attentiveness and achievement as measured by the Stanford Achievement Test. Lahaderne's findings are summarized in Table 9.2.

Lahaderne's subjects were sixth graders; thus, most of the boys were presumably prepubescent, and many of the girls were pubescent. There is no particular reason to believe that the results would differ for older subjects. Morsh (1956), for example, studied a group of young men in an Air Force school, and found a correlation of $-.58$ between his measure of *inattention* and school achievement. This figure, as might be expected, is a little higher for the older youth than for Lahaderne's prepubescent boys.

Lahaderne's subjects were working-class white children. In an effort to explain her rather surprising findings that attitudes toward school are not related to achievement, she describes the composite of the four classrooms in which she conducted her research. Her description is strikingly similar to one the author might have written from his own observations about classrooms for older youngsters. It is so graphic that it must be quoted rather than paraphrased:

> Perhaps the constraints imposed on pupils to be attentive were so strong that attitudes could not influence behavior. Consider, for example, the following restrictions. Pupils could not leave the classroom, or for that matter, get up from their desks without permission. They could not chatter with their neighbors. They had to be recognized before speaking up in class. Their actions at any given moment had to be within the sphere prescribed by the teacher. Moreover, one of the teacher's major functions was to preserve the classroom order. She called on the reluctant, snapped the daydreamer back to attention, reprimanded the cutup, and often reminded the pupils of the designated focus of attention. In short, pupils were coaxed and

compelled to adhere to a code of conduct that supported the order of the classroom. Thus, regardless of how he felt about school, the disgruntled pupil had little chance to do anything about it in the classroom. (pp. 323-324)

As seen earlier, one out of three United States pupils eventually *does* do something about the school situation: He drops out before he graduates from high school. Furthermore, the average male drop-out gives up a year or two earlier than the average female, or at least finishes one or two fewer grades.

One can guess that, among Lahaderne's subjects, the bright children were bored, while the slower children were bewildered. These two conditions would produce a zero correlation between school attitudes and achievement.

In an atmosphere such as Lahaderne describes, it is not surprising that teachers are remarkably inaccurate in judging whether or not their pupils like school, schoolwork, or their teachers. Jackson and Lahaderne (1967) also worked with sixth graders. They found that teachers' judgments of pupils' attitudes (two measures each, reported separately for boys and girls) correlated only from .25 to .28 with the pupils' actual attitudes. This is only a little better than the teachers could have done by chance. There is no reason to think that teachers are more accurate about older youngsters' attitudes. They are likely to be even less accurate, since in a platoon system they are responsible for more classes, and see each youngster for a shorter period during the school day.

Parenthetically, Jackson and Lahaderne's teachers were also surprisingly inaccurate in their estimates of their pupils' performance either on intelligence tests or standardized tests of subject matter achievement. Their estimates of girls' IQs correlated only .39 with girls' IQs as measured by the Kuhlmann-Anderson Group Intelligence Test, and a slightly higher .44 for boys' IQ. Their estimates of girls' achievement correlated from .31 to .37 with girls' actual achievement, and .45 to .51 for boys' actual achievement, in reading, language, and arithmetic. It is interesting that these teachers were more accurate for boys than for girls. Perhaps the fact that teachers as a group discipline boys more often than girls forces them to observe the boys more closely, and thus to judge them more accurately. Or, as suggested, boys' greater openness permits more accurate judgment. The differences in accuracy between boys and girls, however, while they are sizable, are not of great practical significance.

If schools are like Lahaderne describes them, it is scarcely surprising that Flanders, Morrison, and Brode (1968), in a study of thirty Midwestern sixth grade classes, find that children consistently become more negative in their attitudes toward school as the school year moves from fall to spring. These authors do not report sex differences in change, unfortunately; but the declines in morale are as great for advantaged as for disadvantaged, for bright as for less bright, and for high grade getters as for low grade getters. In another study of junior high school students, N. A. Flanders (1963)—again not surprisingly—obtained similar results.

Teacher behavior made a distinct difference in the morale of Flanders, Morrison, and Brode's sixth graders. In the fall, youngsters in the classes of teachers classified as high-praise scored 183.9 in morale, while those in the low-teacher-praise classes scored only 143.9. (The higher the score, the higher the morale. Maximum score, although this figure is not given, seems to be 295.) Even though they started lower, the low-teacher-praise group of pupils also dropped somewhat more than the students of the high-praise teachers.

Style of Personal Control

Flanders, Morrison, and Brode administered still another test to their sixth graders: a measure of internal and external control. Children and youth who score high in internal control perceive themselves as masters of their own fate and as relatively self-sufficient and independent of the whims of others; while children with high external scores take a cynical view of their own power to influence their personal destinies. It can be predicted that high internal children will perceive school as something that, despite its rigors, is designed to help them become even more effectively masters of their own fate. For such reasons their morale, regardless of how they are treated, will be higher and will decline less because of their classroom experiences. This prediction was supported precisely by Flanders, Morrison, and Brode's results: high internal children had higher morale than high external children, whether they were with high- or low-praise teachers, and lost less in either type of class as the school year went on. Both they and the external children had higher morale with high-praise teachers. However, there was no statistically significant difference in the amount of change of the internal and external children between high- and low-praise classrooms. Both types of children lost more in morale when taught by low-praise teachers.

In short, it seems from the evidence surveyed here that young people's success in school depends less on the school than it does on what the youngsters bring to school with them (intelligence, ability to attend, perhaps degree to which they have developed inner control systems).

Leader Behavior, Group Management, and Learning

From laboratories but seldom from real life classrooms, much evidence is gathered that suggests that teacher behavior and group management *can* make an enormous amount of difference in students' learning efficiency. The suggestions made earlier in this chapter about the manipulation of contingent motivation come from laboratory data where differences in learning have been secured through differences in management. While Flanders, Morrison, and Brode did not study differences in learning outcome as a function of high and low teacher praise, it is likely that there were such differences.

Clark and Walberg (1968) conducted the one relatively normal classroom situation study known to the author. They studied the effects of rewards. Their subjects, disadvantaged 10- to 13-year-old Black youngsters in remedial reading classes, ten to fifteen to a class, were divided into an experimental and control set of groups under the leadership of five different teachers. After a baseline of teacher behavior had been established, experimental teachers were asked to step up their administration of rewards (praise), and be sure that each child received some praise. Control teachers were simply asked to keep up the good work. The experimental and control children recorded each reward they received by a tally made with a special pencil. The teachers checked the accuracy of the children's reports. Clark and Walberg do not say how many pupils were boys and how many girls, but all had been selected as potential drop-outs. The IQs of both the control and experimental groups were in the low 90s, low normal.

At the end of the three week experimental period, the experimental children—those given massive praise—had improved significantly more on a standardized test of reading achievement than the control group.

Other more general studies of compensatory education and remedial education, as well as the data that are emerging from studies of programmed learning, suggest innovations in classroom and pupil management that may greatly improve both classroom learning and morale.

Domino (1968), for example, has published an interesting study of college students. He was reliably able to distinguish college classes which stressed conformity (for example, formal lecture–paper–examination classes) from those that stressed student independence, such as seminars and classes where self-study was the organizing theme. Domino's study of older students is summarized here because it would be difficult to find any representative junior or senior high schools where such different classifications of class conduct exist.

Domino used the California Psychological Inventory as his motivational measure. He was able to assign his college juniors scores for need for achievement through being independent (Ai) and scores for need for achievement by being conforming (Ac). As one might predict, total college performance was highest for those liberal arts college students who strove for achievement in whatever situation they found themselves, whether it demanded from them conformity, as in the conventional classes, or independence, as in the self-study types of class. High Ac–Ai youngsters were successful regardless of the class setting.

There was no over-all grade point difference between the two contrasting groups of high Ac-low Ai and low Ac-high Ai; but the former group did better in structured, conforming classes, and the latter in independent types of classes. The poorest performers of all, as might be expected, were students low in both Ac and Ai.

This study provides an interesting illustration of the effect of different contingencies applied to students with different need systems: The high Ac–Ai students manage well regardless of the contingency pattern; the high Ac–low Ai manage better when the contingencies are arranged in a formal setting; the low Ac–high Ai work better when they are left reasonably free to administer their own contingencies; and neither type of contingency manipulation works well for the low Ac-low Ai young people.

Tyler and Brown (1968) provide another interesting manipulation of contingent and noncontingent reinforcement with a population of fifteen court-committed delinquent boys, aged 13 to 15 years. All youngsters lived in the same cottage in a state training school. Five nights a week, their television was turned to a national newscast. The boys were not required to watch, but had to remain quiet so that those who wished to watch and listen could do so. Each evening, teachers wrote a set of questions about the newscast. The boys took these tests the next day in school. Under noncontingent reinforcement, the boys were paid a set number of tokens upon returning to their cottage, regardless of how well they had performed on the test. In the condition of contingent reinforcement, they received tokens in proportion to their score on the day's quiz. The tokens could be traded for canteen items, such as gum and candy, or for privileges in the cottage. The boys' average scores had been studied for 20 school days before the experiment began (the baseline). Half the group experienced contingent reinforcement for the first 17 days of the experiment proper and noncontingent reinforcement for the last 12 days. The pattern was reversed for the second group of boys. Under noncontingent reinforcement, a boy received 21 cents per day regardless of his performance; under contingent reinforcement, he was rewarded for his performance as judged against how well he had done on the average during the 20 school days that preceded the experiment: For example, if a boy "had been averaging 6 items correct, and had been earning approximately 20¢ a day in tokens, he would be given about 15¢ for 6 items correct, 20¢ for 7, 25¢ for 8, 27¢ for 9 and 30¢ for 10 correct. The goal was to let each S earn his previous average 'income' with a slight improvement in performance and even more with greater improvements" (p. 165). Twelve of the fifteen boys did better under contingent reinforcement, and only three did worse. This ratio would be expected to occur by chance fewer than once in 100 times.

Assuming that Tyler and Brown's boys followed the usual pattern of relatively disadvantaged home backgrounds that is found for institutionalized delinquents, the results seem also to support the principle of inducing learning in disadvantaged youngsters through tangible rewards.

THE SCHOOL AS A SOCIAL SYSTEM

Anthropologists and psychologists (for example, Barry, Bacon, and Child, 1957; and Datta, Schaefer, and Davis, 1968) describe cultural organizations as masculine or feminine in nature. For adult males in most cultures, the most highly valued individual characteristics are independence, autonomy, and initiative; and most cultures work hard to develop these characteristics in boys and young men. For women, highest esteem is likely to be given to traits of responsibility, nurturance, conformity, and, in this culture, obedience. Women who hold a strong respect for the conservative traditions of the culture (chastity, religiosity, for example) are culturally more esteemed than women who do not; and rebellious women are usually less kindly viewed than are rebellious men. Women who strive toward professionalism, independence, and high level expertness may pay considerable price in personal conflict (for example, Constantinople, 1969; Haan, 1963). These sex differences in goals and thus in reward contingencies that will be effective were more fully discussed in Chapter 1 within the broad conceptual framework of adolescence.

Traditionally, United States culture has been masculine in its emphasis: It has been a frontier culture, preoccupied with conquering deserts, forests, plains, the bowels of the earth for minerals, and the skies and outer space for transportation, science, and military superiority. Cowboys and Indians are still included in the games of every American boy, and a surprising amount of wistfulness for these old days is shown by adult television programming. But the frontiers are gone, the wild Apache has become a psychosocially disadvantaged minority group, and the culture is overwhelmingly urban, technological, and, perforce, cooperative rather than ruggedly individualistic.

However, the male roots of the culture go deep. Such masculine qualities as initiative, fearlessness, independence, and autonomy are desperately needed in helping to solve the problems of the great cities, racism, poverty, education for both the masses and the elite, and alienation of the youth. Each of these problems involves people. Thus, their solution depends on such feminine qualities as nurturance, an interest in human relations, compassion and forbearance, and tireless assumption of responsibility. The culture has a long way to go before it can blend these male and female qualities into its organization and operation. It may be that the schools—particularly the public schools—have an even longer way to go.

The schools are feminine organizations, and are remarkably authoritarian in organization and operation (reread Lahaderne's statement, an eloquent exposition of this point, on pp. 275, 276). Creative, original, and questioning children of either sex, and neither *little* boys nor *big* boys who are *all male* in their orientation and behavior fit into the system at all well. It has been stated earlier that schools succeed fairly well with middle-class children as a group. This statement should be further qualified: Schools succeed well with middle-class children who are reasonably bright and generally conforming. However, impressive evidence (for example, Combs and Cooley, 1968; Getzels and Jackson, 1960, 1962; Golann, 1963; Torrance, 1962) exists to show that, while such children may be made to toe the line academically, schools fail to develop creativity in children and, indeed, may discourage and extinguish it.

In the Combs and Cooley (1968) study, for example, while male drop-outs from high school received less desirable scores and rankings than high school graduates on a number of intellectual, academic, and personal factors, they ranked significantly higher in leadership and impulsivity. (Impulsivity, while hard to live with, may be related to creativity.) Ironically, Combs and Cooley's male high school drop-outs at age 19 were earning more and had been earning it longer than those comparable members of their sample who had been graduated from high school but had not gone to college. However, even at that, they were not earning enough to support a family with any margin of comfort (they averaged $3650 in contrast to the high-school-graduate-but-no-college boys' average of $3500).

Schools and Creativity

Creativity was discussed and critically evaluated as a construct in Chapter 7. In its practical manifestations, it is often inconvenient to its possessor and to the system. A creative youth is likely to be a nonconformer, a questioner, and an arriver at embarrassing conclusions. He often becomes labeled as an oddball and a troublemaker. The author recently had occasion to counsel and console a moderately wise and sophisticated friend of his. The man's 14-year-old daughter had transferred to a large and, by conventional standards, very good, upper-middle-class college preparatory suburban high school. Her previous schooling had been in carefully selected private schools. Before his visit to the author's office, the friend had been called three times in the span of about two weeks to the principal's office. Each call had been because of the daughter's disciplinary infractions. For none of these infractions could the friend or his wife find any justifiable reason really to condemn or even criticize their daughter.

The principal of the school had been educated to the doctoral level in one of the better known colleges of education. His comments on the occasion of Mr. – –'s third visit occasioned the latter's visit to the author's office. "Mr. – –," the principal had said, "Your daughter is a delight to have in school. She is spontaneous and an original thinker. She asks good questions in class, and speaks right up. She is all heart and warmth and bounce. If I had a school full of youngsters like her, my job would be pure pleasure. But," and here he paused for a long time, "if you don't get that girl in line I'll have to suspend her!"

Mr. – – was able to handle the situation with a mixture of wry amusement and mild despair. With the help of him and his like-minded wife, his daughter will undoubtedly be one of those who, by formal standards, succeeds. But she will not like high school![3]

Another family had moved their 16-year-old son from a reasonably easygoing school, in terms of discipline, to one that prided itself on the order, neatness, and well-barbered quality of its student body. The boy, who had never before encountered serious trouble in school, was in conflict with the authorities almost from the first day he reported for classes. The parents struggled with his despondency and his denunciation of the system of which he was an unwilling part through the fall term of school, but to no avail. The boy's conduct marks were bad, and his grades were far lower than they had ever been before. However, things improved dramatically after the beginning of the second term of school and the boy, while not happy, seemed resigned, his conduct marks were better, and his academic marks were back up to where they had typically been in the past.

The parents queried him as to the reason for this improvement, getting nowhere until at last he said with some annoyance, "Mrs. Rogers told me how to do it." Mrs. Rogers was the lady who worked in the house. The boy would expand no more on his explanation and, after some time, the parents were pushed to asking Mrs. Rogers themselves, preceding their question by expressing rather effusive gratitude to her for helping their son. She responded straightforwardly, "I just taught him how the good colored get along in the South." She herself was a Black immigrant to the North.

These anecdotes, coupled with the earlier quote from Lahaderne, depressingly illustrate the composite picture the author has formed of secondary schools, not only in the United States but also in foreign countries. He is not surprised at the high rate of high school drop-outs nor is he surprised that, included among them, there are many youth high in leadership, creativity, and intelligence. Nor is he surprised that the

---

[3] It is relevant to add here that anecdotes often serve to document situations to which scientific descriptions have not yet been applied, and that they may even document them better.

system itself is under attack, though, unfortunately, more from without than within. It is not unlikely that the days of the regimented secondary school, particularly in the urban ghettoes, are on their way out. The author hopes that some orderly transition to a more creative system, rather than anarchy, will occur, but has no confident prophecy. At this time anarchy seems more likely in the North, and it is not unlikely that the South will be close behind.

Society and School Drop-outs

The nation is currently much preoccupied with the problem of youth who drop out of school before they receive a high school diploma, and with youth who receive high school diplomas having moved little beyond the point of illiteracy. As Schreiber's edited volume, *The Profile of the School Dropout* (1968) and the Hathaway, Reynolds, and Monachesi Studies (1969a and b) testify, the prospects for such drop-outs are indeed dim. The Combs and Cooley (1968) data are the only ones the author knows where drop-outs in any sense compare favorably with those who finish high school.

The United States makes a pathetically minimal effort to do anything about young people who drop out of high school. While in no sense should America copy the British 11+ or 12+ system (the British have now abandoned it), there are aspects of it that may be profitable to study and even to emulate, or at least to experiment with.

Under the 11+ or 12+ system, children were "streamed" at about ages 11 or 12. Children who did well on the state examinations administered at that time were sent on to schools that prepared them for college, while those who did poorly went into vocational schools. Unfair as the system was to many, many children, it carried with it certain compensations that are not present in the United States. In Britain or Australia, for example, youth could drop out of school at about age 15 and still maintain a degree of face and honor. Good opportunities were provided for them to continue their educations, both practical and liberal. Apprenticeships were available that gave them status as well as an opportunity to learn and practice skills while being paid. They enjoyed a degree of autonomy and personal dignity denied to youth of the same age in the United States, whether in or out of school. Under such circumstances, it was possible for early termination of formal full time school to lead to modest but clear and worthwhile goals.

The modification of the 11+ system that has been introduced in the United States—the technical high school—is usually a second-rate institution. Youngsters feel dishonored when they are channeled into it. Morale in the technical high schools is atrocious, and the vandalism, truancy, and other infractions of discipline are higher at tech schools than they are at college preparatory schools in the same neighborhoods.

Statistically erroneous though it may be, Americans believe that possessing a high school diploma is one minimal criterion for being in the mainstream of life. The impact of being out of the mainstream of American life is likely to result in feelings of alienation. The effects of such feelings were documented in Chapter 8.

The Louis Harris Poll, as reported in the Atlanta *Constitution*,[4]

[4]December 16, 1968.

asked whether its sample believed such statements as the following: What I think doesn't count very much; People running the country don't really care what happens to people like me; Few people really understand how it is to live like I live; Important things that happen don't affect my life; I feel left out of things going on around me.

Those who endorse such statements obviously have important feelings of alienation. One of the items, "People running the country don't really care what happens to people like me," was endorsed by 19 percent of the sample who had finished college (a surprisingly high figure) but by 52 percent of whites with only an elementary school education. Sixty-two percent of poor Blacks (with incomes under $3000) thought the statement was true. Of those who voted for George Wallace in the 1968 election, 58 percent agreed with it. The relevant thing here is that most technical school students feel that they *are* out of the mainstream.

It may be that a good technical high school with high morale students is impossible in this increasingly automated and constantly changing society. Almost overnight, a once respected and lucrative trade may pass out of existence. And, in the stable trades, the equipment necessary to provide proper training to students is likely to be so expensive that few schools can afford to install equipment of the necessary quality or to keep it modern once it is installed. On the whole, industry seems to handle the training of its skilled labor force more efficiently and cheaply than public schools do and possibly can ever do. It may well be more efficient for schools to concentrate on producing good twelfth grade "generalists"—young people who *truly* know how to read, write, and handle numbers in complex and sophisticated ways, who know some history and sociology and natural science and psychology—and let industry take them from there, training them to fit its highly specialized needs.

Almost no schools give good training in the service occupations; perhaps they should not. American youth and adults generally regard the service occupations (cooks, barbers, housekeepers) dimly; but they are almost the only modest-skill occupations for which the market is steadily expanding. This expansion is due to the specialized tastes of the affluent society and to the fact that leisure time enables society to take advantage of these special services.

Nevertheless, survey after survey reveals that almost all United States parents want their children to go on to college, unrealistic though this desire often is. Youth mirror their elders' ambitions for them. This mirroring is one of the reasons for low technical school morale. Yet even the very good college preparatory schools typically follow curricula that are remarkably sterile, and that are focused almost exclusively on passing a set of examinations set up by a state or a testing service as a hurdle that must be surmounted before one can hope to be admitted to college. These examinations produce a state of near panic even among the population of relatively gifted professors' children whom the author knows most intimately, and seem likely to be a major source of youth's feelings of personal alienation. The goals these examinations express are rejected today as irrelevant or even malignant by many thoughtful people of all ages.

10

School and Church Influences on Youth

INTRODUCTION

It is necessary to turn from broad theoretical and practical issues of youth and the school to more specific interactions of youth with schools and churches. Youth can be classified in many ways. One of the most useful classifications, as has been seen, is by sex. Another useful and often deceptively simple classification is by social class. Interacting in complex ways with social class, a discussion, to be meaningful within the contemporary American scene, must include matters of race. This is a third classification.

It is to these classifications as they vary in their interrelations with schools and churches that this chapter is devoted.

Church, which is voluntary, not mandatory, is the second formal institution in the community designed to guide youth toward legitimate opportunities. American parents vary much more among themselves in what they expect their churches to do for their children than in what they expect their schools to accomplish. For many children and young people, the relationship with the church is very circumscribed. Contact with it is likely to be limited to Sunday or the Sabbath day, typically with a formal service in the morning, and, for adolescents, church-sponsored and thus spiritually acceptable youth activities, the principal thrust of which is social-recreational, in the evening. Many Americans have no direct contact with churches.

Modern church leaders deplore such circumscription, and many denominations devote major efforts to broader and more meaningful relationships with youth.

SCHOOLS, BOYS, AND GIRLS

The issue of the authoritarian and feminine organization of the school as a system was explored in Chapter 9. While the evidence is spotty and exceptions (sometimes entire large city systems, sometimes individual schools) occur, observation as well as more formal evidence suggest that the typical United States school and more inclusive school system are quite authoritarian and feminine in their orientation. It follows logically that girls will do better within them than boys. It can also be predicted that the relatively conforming, obedient, responsible, and conservative middle class will do better than the working class and the children of the very poor, even with intellectual and background factors controlled for.

Evidence fits the predictions. More boys than girls drop out of school before high school graduation, and drop out earlier. At least in the lower middle and lower socioeconomic strata, girls obtain an average of one to two more years of education than boys (for instance, see Garner and Sperry, 1968; and Hodges, McCandless, and Spicker, 1969).

Pressures on Boys to Leave School

There are three major reasons for boys' greater eagerness to leave school. First, the drive is greater for boys than for girls to get out on their own and prove themselves. Second, the restless energy that appropriately accompanies their culturally determined traits of independence, autonomy, and initiative is likely to be abrasive within the orderly, quiet, and autocratic framework of the school. Third, the schools, being feminine institutions, are nurturant, and adolescent boys do not want to be nurtured.

Push for Autonomy and Self-sufficiency Boys are more driven by autonomy and independence needs than girls (see Chapter 1). The goals of teenagers are not for security in their middle age but for cars and money in their pockets and excitement and the wherewithal to live *now*, not later. The average teenage male thinks he can get a job, and with his job he can achieve his pressing immediate goals of status, independence, possessions, and sexual gratification. He drops out of school as early as the law allows so he can get a job and seek his goals. Opportunities are likely to be more available to him than to girls of the same social class and age. Many such boys, of course, do not find jobs, particularly youngsters from disadvantaged minority groups, where as many as 50 percent of Black male youth in some of the urban and very depressed rural areas are chronically without work.

But partial reinforcement is an effective motivator. Many youth find jobs at any age and with any level of training. Almost every boy occasionally finds a temporary job that he hopes will turn into a permanent one. So, even though not all youth are rewarded with paying work, and most poorly educated youth have only intermittent jobs, enough work is available that they do not lose hope. Even for the unemployed, at least in the cities, the streets and the excitement of hustling may offer more rewards and fewer or at least more endurable frustrations than were offered by the schools.

A period of time on the street convinces many a young man or woman that he should return to school. But by that time, he has reached a psychological and chronological point of no return. Perhaps also there is a spouse and child or children to take care of. After a certain age, the average young person thinks that he is too old for high school, and the system lends support to his belief. Secondary schools, as they are set up, simply do not know what to do with fully mature young men in their late teens or early 20s, with young married women; whether or not they are pregnant or are mothers, or with illegitimately pregnant girls.

For most male drop-outs, the jobs they obtain provide the foundation for an appearance of autonomy: the down payment on a car, enough money to date and run around, cash to pay for certain necessities. During temporary bachelorhood, this state of affairs provides a pleasant contrast to their singularly disadvantaged existence in the feminine world of the school. However, biology and tradition typically take over, marriage occurs, and the boy and his wife are faced with the grim realities of stretching an inadequate budget—with poor prospects—so as to cover their own needs and those of their typically unplanned and numerous progeny. To recapitulate, Hodges, McCandless, and Spicker (1969) worked with a sample of extremely disadvantaged Appalachian 5 year olds and their families. The average father was 34½ years of age at the time of the study, had married at 21 a 17-year-old wife who was 30 at the time of the study. This marriage in the subsequent thirteen years had produced an average of five living children. Many of the wives' first marriages to boys of their own age had broken up and the next time they had married a man somewhat older. Although the wives in this group had married on the average almost five years earlier than their husbands, they had completed eight-and-one-half grades of school. This is about one grade more than the husbands. The true picture for *all* the husbands is probably worse even than this grim picture, since many of the men in the sample were missing. When it was possible to check, the data for the missing men were found to be even more dismal than for those who were in the home at the time of the study. These figures represent only those who were in the homes.

Special Problems of Afro-American Youth Sad as the picture is for disadvantaged American youth as a whole, it is even grimmer, as has been stated, for Afro-American youth. About 400,000 Black youth reach age 18 annually. Almost two-thirds of them have dropped out of high school by this age, or, projecting from the past, will drop out soon. Of the one-third who remain through the twelfth grade, performance on standardized achievement tests stands only a little higher than the nationwide average for those youth who have completed eighth grade. Only one-tenth of Black students who graduate from high school average as well as the nation's typical high school graduates.

Thus, American schools are giving Afro-American youth even less than what might be called a "modest blue-collar" education. This is one of the many facts that lies behind the series of summer ghetto outbreaks—the Watts and the Detroits—and lies behind the steady and growing alienation of Black youth, not only from the white society but from their Black elders. Separatism springs naturally where the power structure has given nothing or far too little. Certainly, American society must soon come to terms with its failure to educate Black youth properly.[1]

If anything, the discrepancy between academic achievement of Afro-American boys and girls is greater than that between white boys and girls (see, for example, Tulkin, 1968). To place his work in the applied setting of the schools (as discussed in Chapter 7), Tulkin finds that an apparent inferiority in intelligence of middle-class Black late elementary school children to white children of the same social class is due to the lower IQs of the Black boys in his sample. When Tulkin makes statistical corrections for the Black boys for the number of broken homes and the crowdedness index in the homes, the difference in intelligence between Black boys and girls and Black and white middle-class subjects as a group disappears. These statistical controls do not cancel the intellectual inferiority of the Black lower-class children who may, according to Tulkin and many others, live in an "underclass" of discrimination and hopelessness, perhaps including early childhood malnutrition, that simply "blunts the human spirit." Evidence about the great academic discrepancy between Afro-American males and females can be gained by counting the sex distribution in high school classes and colleges, and is reported in such research as Datta, Schaefer, and Davis (1968) and Lamb, Ziller, and Maloney (1965).

Black boys may suffer even more than white boys in either segregated or nonsegregated schools. The author believes that predominantly Afro-American schools, those in the over-90-percent-Black category and with a preponderance of Black teachers, are even more authoritarian and feminine in their orientation than predominantly white schools. This is a subjective judgment based on his own school observation, and observations and judgments of his colleagues and friends. Authoritarianism is, after all, based on suspicion. Black people certainly have more reason to be suspicious than white people. Furthermore, power is so scarce a commodity for an Afro-American that he is likely to guard what he has doubly zealously. No one likes to relinquish power (see Silberman, 1964; and this volume, Chapters 11, 12, and 13). Assuming this observation to be correct, the aggressive young Afro-American male is bound to be severely frustrated. One prominent Black social worker, speaking informally, said that the only place an intelligent, aggressive young Black male can gain a real education is in prison. She cites Eldridge Cleaver and Malcolm X as illustrations.

[1] "Coming to terms" with this problem is long overdue in America. Perhaps this failure is a reason for the growing militancy of Black America, and the search for a "Black" identity, as evidenced by the growth of Black Studies departments in many colleges and universities.

The first factor that seems logically responsible for boys doing less well in school than girls and more frequently leaving without high school diplomas is, then, the positive pull of "life on the outside," with all its freedom and all-too-illusory promises of goodies, autonomy, and independence.

Boys in Conflict with Schools The second factor responsible for boys' disaffection with schools is intertwined with the first, which is that boys' higher autonomy needs do not fit well with the authoritarian nature of the school itself. Thus, not only do young males yearn for the outside but they are propelled toward it by the very operation of the system of the school. Boys are more frequently in conflict in school, are more often deeply frustrated in expressing their independence and manhood, and are more often suspended and expelled. Thus, the interaction between the lure from the outside and the conflict and frustration on the inside often send them out into the world before graduation.

There are certain advantages given to adolescents, which accrue mainly to the middle class. Erikson (1963) speaks of a psychosocial moratorium that society, including high school and possibly college, provides for adolescents. There is a cushion, as it were, that guards children from fracturing because of a too sudden transition from the dependence and succor of childhood to the harsh realities of independent adult life. Society allows youth a number of provisional tries: If these tries are disastrous, the adolescent is not usually held irrevocably responsible. Society forgives him and lets him try again.

Ausubel (1954) speaks of the functions of the school as including the chance for an adolescent to acquire primary status, which is being important in his own right, free from and independent of his parents. Ausubel thinks that school provides the arena in which youth develop greater personal and volitional independence.

Such things are true enough for middle-class, advantaged youth. But do they hold for disadvantaged youth, and perhaps particularly for disadvantaged male youth? Do they hold for the girl who becomes illegitimately pregnant (perhaps the greatest single risk factor any girl encounters)? The author submits that neither society nor its creation, the schools, provides the psychosocial moratorium that youth seem to need; nor are disadvantaged youth given much opportunity to acquire primary status in any legitimate way or to constructively explore their personal and volitional independence. It seems quite probable that the disadvantaged Afro-American or American Indian or Hispaño male is flagrantly cheated.

Nurturance in Schools The third pressure on boys to leave school is also related to why girls do better in school than boys: schools are feminine institutions *dedicated to nurturing and molding the young.* Boys do not want to be nurtured or, if they must be, it has to be done very subtly. In elementary school, except in a few states where men can earn high enough salaries to attract them, a male teacher is a rarity, and the ultimate power—the school principal—is often a woman. Data gathered from his graduate classes by the author over many years indicate that men who move up to positions of power in the public schools are highly socially mobile. Typically, they have come from humble homes, and are headed for or have already reached a higher social class.

Informal observation and some data (see McArthur, 1955) indicate that highly socially mobile men have been pushed along by their mothers. Indeed, McArthur believes it is part of the middle-class ethic for mothers (typically with fathers' full concurrence) to urge their sons to do better than their fathers did. Such men are likely to identify with the obedient, conforming, and conservative ethos of the feminine school organization and, indeed, to perpetuate it. Also, if a man has risen to a respectable height from a humble beginning, he is not likely to jeopardize his position by being too innovative, daring, and independent. Thus, even though many junior and senior high school teachers, most principals, and almost all school superintendents are male, their investment in the safe, obedient, nurturant, and conforming aspects of the system is great.

Perhaps such men have had to do battle against their strong mothers for the autonomy they have. Thus they are jealous of the power they have earned and are fearful lest it be taken away. This may be why they not only acquiesce with but create the authoritarian system that is the public school. Communities, as has been said, support their endeavors in this direction—indeed may demand that they do as they do.

In short, schools are a woman's world. Plentiful evidence exists, much of which has been discussed earlier, that lower-class males are particularly energetic in asserting their masculinity. Their notion of what is masculine—toughness, shrewdness, vigorous sexuality, aggression—is ill-suited to the authoritarian, feminine orientation of schools. Obviously, such youth can not be allowed to act totally masculine, but neither can they be flatly repressed, for they would vigorously rebel if they were.

The investment of enormous power in a woman (much power is given to teachers of both sexes) threatens lower-class male youth. This is true, although in different ways, for an Appalachian, a South European, a Hispaño, or an Afro-American boy (see, for example, Gans, 1962; Pettigrew, 1964). In the white, South European, and Hispaño lower social classes, women are clearly second in the power hierarchy, men clearly first. Moving from a home where the male is boss to the school where the male is disadvantaged can be a severe threat to such boys.

The Afro-American boy, if Glazer and Moynihan (1963), Pettigrew (1964), and Riese (1962) are correct, is doubly threatened. He comes from a cosociety that deviates from the national pattern in being matriarchal, or at least matrifocal. He is doubly insecure, since he is both dark skinned and disadvantaged in his essential maleness. Thus, the feminine world of the school may be well nigh intolerable to him.

Punitive Handling of Boys   Datta, Schaefer, and Davis (1968), Jackson and Lahaderne (1966), and Sears and Feldman (1966) document the disadvantages boys work under in schools as currently organized. Boys are more frequently scolded, reprimanded, shamed, commanded, and otherwise disciplined. They are less frequently praised and rewarded.

Jackson and Lahaderne, for example, observed four representative classrooms. In the first, 50 percent of the class were boys, yet boys received 89.5 percent of the prohibitory teacher–pupil interactions; in the second classroom, 59 percent of the class were male, but boys received 85.5 percent of the prohibitions. In the third class, boys made up 45 percent of the class but received 70 percent of the prohibitions; and in the fourth class, while they again made up only 45 percent of the class, the boys received a little more than 90 percent of the prohibitions.

Under the system as it is now set up, teachers perhaps have no opportunity to behave toward boys in any other way. Boys, by the rules of the system (which curiously run directly counter in intent to what adult society demands of males) are simply naughtier than girls. There can be no escaping the conclusion that a system is dead wrong which trains boys in exactly the opposite way to that which society demands of them when they are grown! The school, in this instance, is cheating the society.

It has already been pointed out that the disadvantaged young Black male, already beaten down enough by society, is apparently the most discriminated against of all in school, the setting that should instead do the most for him. Datta, Schaefer, and David (1968) say of him, as he is represented in their sample of seventh graders, that he "appears to have resigned from the educational process and is seen as poorly adjusted, unruly, and uninvolved, behaving in ways generally considered to be associated with educational failure and classroom management difficulty" (p. 99). This statement represents the authors' conclusions from their study of teachers' perceptions of students in their classes.

There is at least one important piece of evidence (Davis and Slobodian, 1967) that not all teachers discriminate against boys, at least in early elementary school and during the all important experience of reading instruction. Of the ten first grade teachers involved in this study all were women. They ranged in age from 23 to 38 years, with the median age being 27½ years. All held at least the baccalaureate degree. They had taught from two to nine and one-half years, with a median teaching experience of four years. Nine of the ten were married, and each had children of her own. The classes themselves "were chosen from the first-grade sections in a large public school system in the Detroit, Michigan, suburban area" (p. 262). The presumption is that the pupils were white, and middle- and upper-middle class. All the teachers had previous experience in first grade teaching, and all had volunteered to take part in the study.[2]

Data from children's interviews indicated that the children *thought* (in terms of the total number of nominations of pupils who were criticized, but not in terms of total number of individual boys or girls nominated) that boys were more often handled punitively than girls. However, direct observations of teacher–pupil interactions revealed no differential treatment between the sexes. There were no sex

---

[2] As has been pointed out previously, a characteristic of volunteers is that they tend more than a random sample to be involved and in agreement with the purpose of a study. Even with the best intentions, the research worker's goals are almost always transmitted to participants. Volunteer participants are more susceptible.

differences in reading achievement as tested in the spring of the first grade year, although differences in favor of girls are typically found.

The Davis and Slobodian study suggests that, at least in first grade in the presumably white and advantaged suburbs, with relatively young, married, tenured, well-prepared and experienced women teachers who volunteered for the study, there need be no disciplinary differential during reading instruction between boys and girls; and that, when there is none, there are no differences in reading progress between the sexes.

In short, if the Skinnerian model (reinforce the positive, and let the negative die out because of lack of reinforcement) were adopted, the chances are that equality of treatment and thus of achievement between the sexes can be reached. Davis and Slobodian ought to have given information about how closely their first grade teachers followed the Skinnerian model. That it is not simple for teachers (or pupils) is indicated by Clark and Walberg (1968). In discussing their dramatic positive results secured when potential school drop-outs were given massive positive reinforcement during remedial classes, they say:

> Although the idea that reinforcement enhances learning has long been known in the field of psychology, it seemed revolutionary to the teachers and children in this experiment. It is not enough apparently, simply to instruct student teachers or regular teachers to use rewards to control behavior. The use of a reward tally card which focused the attention of the teacher and the child on the rewards seemed much more convincing. (p. 309)

It seems sensible to suggest that boys' high spirits, initiative, and drive for autonomy and independence may be recruited to motivate them toward academic excellence. If they are involved through the use of positive incentives, it can be predicted that they will stop battling the system. The prevailing interaction of the school with such male motives seems to be negative: The school seems to stamp out the very things the boys need to succeed in out-of-school life. In attempting to control, or repress, these sometimes disturbing male reaction patterns, it seems that all too often school management subverts its own broader goals.

Teachers' Expectancies for Boys and Girls

It is well to look again at the Datta, Schaefer, and Davis (1968) results. It will be recalled that analyses were made separately for "other"—presumably white—and Afro-American seventh grade boys and girls. The results of this study generally indicate that regardless of scholastic aptitude or race, teachers describe boys when compared with girls as more likely to be hyperactive, asocial, verbally and physically aggressive, and tense. Girls, on the other hand, are more likely to be seen as friendly, methodical, perservering, task oriented, and well adjusted.

Evidence abounds that the expectancies of powerful figures become incorporated into students' self-perceptions and behavior, and, of course, that the students will then behave in line with the expectancies (the self-fulfilling prophecy). Teachers are powerful people in the world of pupils. Payne and Farquhar (1962), among others, document this. Working with high school juniors they find that exceptionally high achieving boys think they present the following type of picture of themselves to teachers: that they are ambitious and eager to learn the subject matter required to get good grades; that the teacher regards them as conforming to socially acceptable classroom behavior; that the teacher thinks they want to dig deeply into the subject matter and master it. They also think their teachers see them as alert and sensitive to the teachers' biases, and as integrating cues about these biases into their class activity. In other words, they believe they have convinced the teachers that they are hard working, conventional, establishment youngsters. The low achievers (those who get poor grades from teachers relative to their aptitude) view their teachers' attitudes toward them as being toward the opposite end of the pole.

High achieving girls believe teachers see them as prompt, orderly, efficient, and intelligent. Unlike the high achieving boys, high achieving girls believe the teachers see them as nonconformist, competitive, independent, and different. From these results, the girls apparently think they are viewed as rather masculine in their behavior; the high achieving boys think teachers see all the feminine virtues in them.

It almost seems that the school organization works at cross purposes with the culture for *both* sexes!

Ringness' (1967) study of 261 eighth grade boys also adds some light on the question of perceptions. Ringness split his sample into high, average, and low achievers. Almost all Ringness' boys in all three groups believed that teachers regard the ideal or model pupil as a conformer. Most of the boys identify well with teachers, and "at this point in their lives they are generally willing to accept the conformity role, and care how they are regarded by their teachers." (p. 99)

Ringness' high achievers were the most conforming; his low achievers tended not to conform so much and to identify less with teachers than with the peer group. The core ethic of the peer group was academic mediocrity. Ringness, in conclusion, says:

> The image of the teacher needs revision. He is viewed as demanding conforming behavior, but is not seen as fostering intellectual development or liveliness. Schools are seen as places to prepare for future vocations, but are seen by relatively few as places to develop talents, pursue interest, or to improve social adjustment.... It is apparent that the stereotype of school tasks as being necessary evils seems still to exist. Social reinforcements such as teacher praise and blame, grades and marks, and other typical reinforcements provided by the school are not as effective with low achievers as could be wished.... Efforts to make the curriculum more meaningful to boys like those in these samples may also bear fruit. (pp. 101-102)

School Is a Useful Experience

The utilitarian value of schooling expressed by Ringness' eighth grade males also characterizes Johnstone and Rosenberg's (1968) advantaged 16-year-old males and most of the 16-year-old girls in their sample. The study included between 90 and 95 percent of the white 16 year olds who lived in Webster Groves, Missouri. Almost all of them were attending public or parochial schools in Webster Groves or nearby St. Louis. Webster Groves is a privileged suburb, long well-reputed for the quality of its schools.

Seventy-two percent of the Webster Groves 16 year olds reported that their parents "very strongly" urged them to go on to college; and only 11 percent indicated that their parents would leave the decision up to them. There was no real disagreement over this issue between the adolescents and their parents: 81 percent of the adolescent sample indicated that they would be disappointed if they did not get to go to college, and only 3 percent said they did not want to go.

The majority of both boys and girls expressed a utilitarian view of a college education. One of the "very important" reasons for attending college was to prepare oneself for a job with a really good salary, and 85 percent of the boys and 65 percent of the girls endorsed this reason. Intellectual interest fared less well. Only 61 percent of the boys thought that it was very important to learn more about subjects that really interested them. The girls were a bit more idealistic: 75 percent of them endorsed this reason as very important. To be stimulated by new ideas was endorsed by only 44 percent of the boys but 73 percent of the girls; to develop one's personality and become a more interesting person received the vote of only 59 percent of the boys, but 83 percent of the girls. The thought of meeting new and interesting people also appealed to 59 percent of the boys, but 85 percent of the girls. A minority of the boys (34 percent) expressed any interest in being prepared to make a real contribution to mankind; but 54 percent of the girls found this notion to be appealing.

In short, suburbia, as exemplified by Webster Groves, is not breeding idealistic boys, although girls more frequently profess such concerns. Perhaps they can afford to, planning as they do on marriage, home, and motherhood (the second face of the double code, as described in Chapter 1).

SEXUALITY AND THE SCHOOL SYSTEM

The topic of sexuality between caretakers, such as teachers, and charges, such as pupils, is a sensitive one. Honesty demands that it be touched on, even though no evidence about it exists other than the occasional true story concerning sexual liaisons, some heterosexual, some homosexual, between high school or college teachers and their students.

Relations between teachers and pupils of necessity take on a new dimension following pubescence. Prepubescents, in the eyes of United States' society, are essentially asexual. The very definition of pubescence, on the other hand, is sexual. Life might be simpler if it were not so, but the world of the postpubescent—male or female—is surcharged with sexuality.

The open sexuality of many disadvantaged young people and the many evidences of an equal concern about and involvement with sex on the part of advantaged adolescents that constantly break through the organizational surface are bound to complicate the relations of teachers and pupils. Because of their place in the public eye, if for no other reason, teachers as a group are rather conservative in their sex lives. The crushes on their teachers for which adolescents are notorious must put considerable strain on normally sexed teachers, whether their pattern of sexual outlet is conventional or unconventional. There is no evidence to suggest that teachers' sexual *adjustments* are distributed any differently between "normal" and "abnormal" than any other United States' group, even though it is obvious that as a group they are better *behaved* than most other large groups of the population.

The upsurge in vigilance—the heightened attempts to tighten controls—that occurs in junior high school may be one symptom of the new sexuality of the students in the system. In ways that are probably not acknowledged by most teachers, their charges now have a new appeal or hold a new threat as sex objects or sexual competitors. This appeal/threat is probably not openly recognized by many teachers, or at least is not admitted.

The topic of differences in sexual tension between teachers and pupils as a function of ethnicity is even more sensitive than the more general topic of sexuality. In this society, for example, the myth of the prowess of the Black male is pervasive. Many Black youth do their best, for reasons of their own, to live up to it. This is particularly true of disadvantaged Afro-American boys and the girls among whom they accomplish their conquests.

In moments of frankness, women teachers in disadvantaged predominantly Black schools have discussed with the author their concern about the sexuality of their male students. Their middle-class husbands and boy friends are often more concerned than the women teachers themselves; and a sometimes serious recruitment problem is posed for schools in disadvantaged areas in general and Black disadvantaged areas in particular by this aspect of teacher–student relations.

The problem of pupil sexuality is, of course, most acute for the teacher who has homosexual leanings. Unless his suppressive mechanisms are exceptionally strong, it is probably better for this person to stay away from the field of educating adolescents. The temptations may simply be too strong, and the consequences of surrendering to them too severe both for students and for the teacher himself. It is not narrowly moralistic to say again that, while the society can not demand that teachers be well adjusted sexually, it must demand that they be well behaved, at least as far as their students are concerned.

SCHOOLS, THE ADVANTAGED, AND THE DISADVANTAGED

In 1961 the author published a summary of the effects of schools on boys and girls from different social classes. This summary was updated, but for elementary schools only, in 1967 (McCandless, 1961, 1967). In summary, schools succeed relatively well with upper- and middle-class youngsters. After all, schools are built for them, staffed by middle-class people, and modeled after middle-class people. The coculture that dictates the authoritarian, feminine structure and function of United States schools is the WASP middle-class core culture.

This core culture has many virtues, and its central values are logical if a democratic and capitalist society is to work. The aspects of it that are self-defeating rather than self-actualizing are more those of the lower-middle class than the middle- or upper-middle class. It is the *petit bourgeoisie* rigidity, pettiness, tensions, and intolerance of the WASP middle-class culture that are deplored, not its stress on honesty, thrift, loyalty, a fair deal for all, a society of laws rather than men, and so on.

At this time, the middle-class WASP core culture is thought by many, with good reason, to have fallen behind the times: to be, for example, property- rather than person-conscious, and to have lost humane perspective. In terms of its enlightened self-interest (which is a perfectly good motive for either an individual or a society), no society can function permanently when its organization fails to meet the needs of any large segment of its population. At best, as has been suggested throughout the preceding sections of this and the preceding chapter, the WASP-oriented public schools and very likely the entire society can well stand some shaking up and revitalizing.

Despite respectable beginnings through compensatory education, school desegregation, and poverty programs, the situation of disadvantaged children in American schools does not seem to be any better than it was when the author wrote his earlier summaries. Some of the distressing data have been given earlier in this chapter, and need not be repeated.

As a general rule, both disadvantaged and creative children receive lower grades than are predicted either from their aptitude scores or their relative representation in a class. For disadvantaged youngsters, this is particularly true when a school draws from a wide socioeconomic range. When a school population is quite homogeneous, the tendency is not so marked. The probable reasons for this are: teachers expect disadvantaged children to do less well; the students know this; they incorporate the expectations into their own self concepts and motive systems, and therefore actually do less well (note again Beez, 1968; Payne and Farquhar, 1962; Rosenthal and Jacobson, 1968).

School-Related Characteristics of the Disadvantaged

Again, it is necessary to bring to bear in an applied context some of the thinking and data that were discussed in broader perspective in Chapters 7 and 8. Disadvantaged children of any age do not bring to school the variety of well-digested school-related experiences that advantaged children do. Gans (1962), among others, has demonstrated the acute provinciality of many children of the poor. Typically, they have seldom left the rural or urban slum area where they were born. This may be particularly true for Afro-American children, who feel even more conspicuous than white-skinned poor children. Such children and young people have not read, have not been to zoos, have not visited museums.

Other skills, such as listening discrimination, often fail to develop during early childhood in many of the crowded, noisy homes of the very poor. It is not that such children are understimulated; rather, they may be overstimulated, but the stimulation may lack the systematic patterning that is essential if the foundation is to be laid for effective schoolwork. In these homes attention span is poor, and attention is essential for learning. Lahaderne's (1968) data about attention, which she finds related significantly to both intelligence and achievement, were cited in Chapter 9. Grim, Kohlberg, and White (1968) present findings suggesting that attention may be central even to such matters as moral development (high attention children are more resistant to temptations to cheat).

Disadvantaged children and youth have not been talked to by their caretakers in the attention demanding and information conveying nuances that characterize verbal interactions in advantaged families.

Bernstein (1960, for example), among others, has documented the fact that disadvantaged parents use restrictive rather than expansive language with their children. Restrictive language is direct, often exclamatory, lacks embroidery, subheadings, explanations, and other complexities of meaning. "Stop it!" "Do what I said!" "Shut up!" "Go on!" If the child questions why, the most complex explanation he often gets is "Because I told you so."

Expansive language forces the receiver to look beyond the immediate and concrete. It is more likely than restrictive, concrete language to lead to questions and efforts to answer them and thus to the sorts of problem solving and learning to learn sets that are useful in both school and broader life learning.

The work on the language of the disadvantaged has almost all been done by middle-class people, however. It may be that research workers impose a set of rules that disguises or keeps them from seeing much of the complexity that actually exists. To the degree that the problems and goals of disadvantaged people differ from the problems and goals of middle-class people, to that degree will their type and use of language differ. Sroufe (1970) sharply criticizes the assumptions and methods that characterize much research conducted with disadvantaged, particularly Black disadvantaged, people by middle-class, usually white, research workers. He wrote in response to the Bee, *et al.* (1969) article, discussed in the next paragraph. The implications of his criticisms were discussed rather fully in Chapter 7, and should be kept in mind here.

Bee, *et al.* (1969) demonstrate the failure of disadvantaged parents to teach their children effectively, when compared to the teaching techniques of middle-class parents. The disability of the parents who took part in this study was a function of their social class, not of their race. Disadvantaged mothers were less likely to allow their children to find things out for themselves, were more likely to show their children specific solutions without explanations that would logically lead to more general application of principles, and otherwise seemed to fail to provide foundations for solving problems of the sort that a child meets in school.

As a result of all these things, disadvantaged children often learn while very young to use and respond only to simple declarative sentences or commands. Their language is short on terms for expressing subtleties and complexities of meaning. Nor does such a child possess a language through which he can receive or convey subtle emotional messages. He is thus formally handicapped as he works to learn to read, or tries to gain vicarious experiences from listening to stories, the experiences of others, school lectures, and so on. His inability to pinpoint emotional nuances may interfere with informal relations such as friendship and courtship, or with self-understanding. It is not unlikely that one needs a rich language to gain self-understanding or high level moral development. On the other hand, the expressive language of disadvantaged children may be very free. Such children may be richer in gestures, freer kinesthetically, and more spontaneous in art work (see Miller and Swanson, 1960, for example).

Language quotients are an expression of the sort of verbal intelligence that is demanded by most schoolwork. The language quotient of the average disadvantaged child or youth is 10 to 15 score points lower than his general IQ. Thus, young disadvantaged children enter school perhaps a year behind their more privileged classmates in verbal learning ability. In addition to being behind in ability to manipulate language, they are deficient in the work skills necessary to catch up. Speaking a foreign language is not confined to children of foreign birth or parentage, for many disadvantaged Afro-American children literally speak a language different from formal English. To treat them as though they can either listen to or express themselves in conventional white middle-class (and particularly Northern) English is futile. Black ghetto language, very rich in and of itself, may have arisen from bringing colloquial, rurally accented Southern talk to the cities, and then consolidating such a special language by the ingrown and limited exposure received in a Black ghetto. In any event, much of the talking and reading that go on in the early days of school are absolutely incomprehensible to a large share of disadvantaged children. Teachers might as well be talking to them in Urdu. A destructive downward spiral is set up on the first day of school.

Disadvantaged children, in spite of certain adult exceptions, as in boxing, lag behind advantaged children in both gross and fine motor skills, but particularly the latter. These skills are essential for writing, painting, and arts and crafts. Such skills must be present for sewing, tool and dye making, typing, shorthand, accounting, and most other skills that form a part of vocationally useful behavior.

Disadvantaged children and youth lack many other attributes that make for good adjustment in school. They have lived in a world of poverty where, if something is not grabbed at once, it is gone. If one has grown up in a family of five or seven or nine children on a marginal or submarginal budget, good manners are a disadvantage at mealtime: food must be eaten quickly to be eaten at all. This background is likely to work against the habit of delaying gratification that is essential for both academic success and conventional moral behavior.

It takes a lot of believing in the future for a boy to put up with what he must go through in his classes in order to reach that future and master it. Disadvantaged children's and young people's histories, typically, have not been such as to give them much trust in anything—past, present, and particularly future. The "pie in the sky" has been snatched away too often for them to be willing to do much work for it. Experience has taught them they had better get theirs here and now.

Many such children have been ill-trained to handle frustration. Altogether too many have learned from their busy and harried mothers and their teachers that the best life stance is to "Be quiet and be good." Datta, Schaefer, and Davis (1968) describe their subsample of low IQ (presumably disadvantaged) children as "task oriented, low in verbal aggression, compliant, cooperative, and considerate . . . [and] . . . lower in self-esteem, and as more tense and fatigued" (p. 98). Many have pointed out that apathy and incuriosity are almost a hallmark of acutely disadvantaged youngsters.

On the other hand, such children have often seen their parents act out their frustrations angrily; and the children may have learned to handle frustration the same way, by cursing, breaking, and hitting. Such a pattern may not show up until the child becomes big enough and strong enough to get away with it; and its emergence is likely to cause great trouble for both such aggressive youngsters and the authorities in schools and the community (see Datta, Schaefer, and Davis' description of their most disadvantaged group of Afro-American seventh grade subjects that was quoted earlier in this chapter). Since boys are both more frustrated and physically more able to get away with it, one would expect them to show more such behavior in school and the community than girls. Data bear out the expectation.

Teacher Attitudes toward the Advantaged and the Disadvantaged

Yee (1968) reports a depressing set of results from a study he conducted with a large number of teachers and their classes. About half (102) of the teachers taught in middle-class (advantaged) neighborhoods, while the other half (110) taught in disadvantaged neighborhoods. The classes (from a total of fifty schools in the San Francisco and central Texas areas of the United States) ranged from fourth through seventh grades. Thus, a majority of the subjects were preadolescent, but enough were adolescent to make the results of the study relevant.

Yee's most striking finding is that *teacher attitudes predominate over disadvantaged children*, while there is a *much more mutual influence relationship between teachers and advantaged children*. On the whole, the teachers of disadvantaged children held much more negative attitudes toward teaching and toward their students than the teachers of advantaged children. They "possess traditionalistic and inflexibly negative attitudes toward child control" while the teachers of the advantaged "show a more permissive, positive, and flexible attitude" (p. 278).

For disadvantaged children during the school year, "interaction became more teacher dominated, pupils became more conforming, and classroom climate grew colder. School became less appealing" (p. 280) and ". . . teachers' less positive attitudes of warmth, permissiveness, and favorability toward pupils tended to make pupils' attitudes toward their teacher become more unfavorable" (p. 281). For advantaged children, on the other hand "the teachers' more positive attitudes made less difference, that is, had less effect on pupils' attitudes" (p. 281).

This last finding is significant: Disadvantaged children and youth have few positive models (at least as judged by the middle- and upper-middle-class power elite) available to them, compared with those who are advantaged. Thus, their teachers are in a position to influence them more, for better *or* for worse. That this influence should be malign is tragic indeed.

Many argue that one of the problems in schools for disadvantaged children is that inexperienced teachers are assigned to them. However, it is interesting that Yee finds that the influence of the seasoned teacher is more malign than that of the newcomer to the field. The longer Yee's teachers of the disadvantaged had taught, the more negative they became. "The more negative attitudes of this study's teachers with 9+ years' experience working with LC pupils and their incongruent attitude relationships with LC pupils raise serious questions concerning such teachers' placement with LC pupils and value as teachers in general." He goes on to say that, despite all the training in the world, "such preparation may be for naught unless school administrators develop pedagogical and employment policies that recognize the affective needs of disadvantaged pupils as well as their cognitive needs. The practical significance of these findings and interpretations is that the teacher's attitudes of warmth and permissiveness are even more important to LC children than to MC children" (p. 281). A downward spiral of mutually disadvantageous socialization between teachers and pupils is produced and (according to Yee) progresses depressingly over the years.

It may be that school administrators assign less able teachers to disadvantaged areas. Observation suggests that such practices are not uncommon, and if the idea is correct, such practices probably play a considerable part in Yee's findings.

Constructive Strategies for Disadvantaged Youth

The vicious circle or downward spiral—the combination of poor skills, maladaptive behavior, and bitter teachers—does not *have* to characterize disadvantaged children. Clark and Walberg's (1968) research about the effect of massive reward on pupil learning has already been cited. Rohwer, Lynch, Levin, and Suzuki (1968) demonstrate with first, third, and sixth graders that disadvantaged children, when put into a laboratory learning situation where each is treated according to his learning pattern, learn as well as advantaged children.

Douvan has reported an experiment (1956) that suggests methods of "getting to" disadvantaged young people. With appropriate reward, they show as much behavior shift as advantaged youngsters.

In Douvan's study, middle- and lower-class high school seniors were tested to determine their achievement motivation. Douvan used two conditions: (1) The subjects were told that they were expected to do as well as other adolescents, and were asked to do as well as they could; (2) They were offered a cash prize. After a contrived failure in the experimental situation in which she put them, their achievement motive—their wish to succeed—was measured. Under the first condition, "intellectual or achievement appeal," the two social classes showed a sharp difference in motivation, the middle-class youngsters scoring significantly higher (a rating of 7.6 on the average to 4.9 for the lower-class subjects).

But, when Douvan shifted her reward to one that was concrete and had immediate use, the differences between middle- and lower-class children vanished. The middle-class children scored even a little (but not significantly) higher—8.1; and the lower-class children jumped to 8.3.

Any discussion of social class must include the consideration of whether or not its officially catalogued members *really* think they belong to that class. Some middle-class youngsters are uncomfortable with their "class" mates, and may be thought of as downwardly mobile. Others wish to move upward in social class, and should be considered to be upwardly mobile. One suspects that the personal rather than the statistical label will be more important in determining behavior. This was true of a third sample that Douvan studied: youngsters who were officially lower social class, as judged from their fathers' occupations, but who thought of themselves as middle class. True to their own labels, they behaved like middle- rather than lower-class children under both of Douvan's experimental manipulations.

It is easy to use official labels to categorize and often stigmatize children. There is no such thing as "a typical middle- or lower-class child." In dealing with groups, a label is useful *in order to reduce the range of one's best guesses* to know how the group in general is likely to react. But individuals must be judged independently of the group.

The Antecedents of Curiosity

Curiosity is one of the strongest motivators for learning. But the ways in which lower-class children have been reared are likely to blunt their curiosity about intellectual matters, hence retard learning. It is likely that they are as curious about things they think are available to them (that is, how to make money, how to secure sexual gratification, how to gain prestige in their particular set) as children are in any other class.

Lower-class children, for understandable reasons, are likely to be more anxious than middle-class children. Two studies of preadolescents suggest that, in addition, children high in anxiety are low in curiosity (Mendel, 1965; Penney, 1965).

Curiosity must be learned. It feeds on stimulation. Frances Horowitz (1968)[3] has patterned stimulus change such that if a baby stops fixating on an object another is substituted at the end of 2 seconds. She has noted infant fixation times for infants from 3 to 14 weeks old of as long as 19 minutes, with 5 minutes not being at all unusual for a fixation. Such concentration on the part of an infant has not previously been thought possible. The relations between attention, intelligence, and moral development have also been discussed previously.

Denenberg (1964) and Glanzer (1958), in reviews of research done with animals, suggest that curiosity—and indeed, all emotional reactivity—depends on early stimulation. An organism learns to demand what is fed into it. If nothing is fed in, it demands little of its environment. If much is fed in, it demands more and more. Human beings possess a potential for endless self-correction: They can organize and feed back reinterpretations of what has been given them. In this reactive skill lies the human being's capacity for self-improvement.

As a group, disadvantaged children and youth seem to demand little of their environments, and are relatively ineffective in using what teaching is given to them, at least in reaching the goals prescribed by the middle class. There is, however, suggestive evidence that, given a world without sensible rules—not unlike the world in which many such children live—they can adapt their behavior more quickly than more systematic middle-class children so as to secure the maximum benefit from the particular "absurd" situation (for example, see Epworth, 1968); and that, when advantaged children are thrown into an unpredictable setting, they lose their systematic, logical approaches to new learning (Bresnahan and Blum, 1970).

Self-improvement demands a rich supply of tools with which to think, plus the ability to delay action in order to reflect and plan. Disad-

---

[3]In personal communication.

vantaged young people are relatively short on symbols with which to think; and their understandable reluctance to delay gratification makes them unlikely to reflect.

Reflection, in this extroverted society, is likely to be confused with daydreaming, and thus to be discouraged. Children are encouraged to keep busy, and reflection may even be considered a bit pathological. However, if one is to plan ahead or to create originals, reflection, or daydreaming, is essential. Few Americans seem to realize this, but Lewin (1935) makes a most convincing case for fantasy as a necessary precursor for long range planning. Lewin was far ahead of his time in many ways: In the absence of data other than his acute personal observations, he illustrates graphically how authoritarianism and the grim, necessarily reality-based existence of the poor militate against fantasy. Without some fantasy, it seems unlikely that men can dream realistically, and without dreams, both the individual man and society would lead futile existences.

Authoritarianism and Social Class

The authoritarianism of the poor may have little to do with their personality needs, in the sense that authoritarian theorists believe. It may simply be that the disadvantaged are authoritarian because they do not have the language and the time to allow them to be democratic in their interactions with each other and with their children. If one stops to think about it, explanation is the heart of democracy. With few exceptions, one can not explain things without an adequate vocabulary. The poor have meager vocabularies as well as meager budgets. The poor usually have many children, too. Explaining things to a child, as one must do to be democratic, takes not only many words but much time. Thus, the interactions of disadvantaged parents and their offspring of all ages may be authoritarian not because of inner personality needs, but because the parents have neither the words nor the time to be democratic.

While democratic training seems to work best in the long run, it is also often slower than autocratic child handling methods. A slap may get the job done much more parsimoniously than an explanation. In crisis situations, adults are seldom democratic in their behavior: They rap out orders (or blows) if they are the bosses, and conform like sheep if they are the followers. Many a politician or a general has whipped up an emergency in order to impose a dictatorship.

Thoughtful leaders who see the present high tension level between the races as posing the danger of a "law and order" crisis during which the Black man will again be "put in his place" have historical precedents on which to anchor their fears. In this same vein, perhaps the authoritarianism in secondary schools is a protective device to overcome the threat posed to the authorities by their students, who are adult but not yet predictably controlled in size, strength, and sexuality.

Extracurricular Activities and Social Class

Part of "normal, happy youth" is participation in the social life — the extracurricular activities — of the school. Extracurricular life poses serious problems for disadvantaged youth. For a youngster to take part in an extracurricular activity, he must be accepted by both the sponsor and the other participants. Also, extracurricular activities eat into after school free time when disadvantaged youth, if they can find jobs, need to work. If a youngster is too young to drive, or if he does not have a car, special effort and expense are required for him to get home from school after the school bus has gone.

The activities themselves usually require extra money for special clothes or costumes or tutoring in music, dancing, or dramatics. The popular and prestigious youth take over the activities with, perhaps, the single exception of boys' athletics, where the disadvantaged boy can find an opportunity to shine. If he is also fairly bright, he may be hooked on academics by way of athletics. Even this opportunity is rarely open to disadvantaged girls, among whom athletics possesses little appeal and carries little prestige (see McCandless and Ali, 1966).

Popularity and social class are not strongly related from about the ninth grade on, although there is a low relationship (the disadvantaged are least popular, particularly with the opposite sex) which is of statistical significance but no great practical importance (see Horowitz, 1967). The reason for the low relationship is probably that most disadvantaged youth who remain in school much beyond the legal age for mandatory school attendance are themselves upwardly mobile. Consequently, they have adopted the values and behavior of the middle-class school system, personnel, and students. They are thus comfortable with others like themselves, and are little discriminated against.

Study after study (for example, Waheed, 1964) demonstrates a close link between taking part in extracurricular activities, persistence in school, and plans to continue schooling at the college level. It can not be argued that the relationship is causal, but successful participation in extracurricular activities certainly increases the morale of students (see Wicker, 1968; Willems, 1967).

Wicker obtained data from high school juniors (eleventh grade students) enrolled in small high schools that served communities of less than 1200 population. His high school juniors from large high schools attended high school in a community of 22,000. He found that reports of experiences of self-confidence, working hard, being concerned about the success of an activity, and working closely with others were more characteristic of students of small than large high schools (72 percent of the students of small high schools were high level participants, while only 42 percent of students of large high schools were). Morale boosting experiences were directly related to intensive participation in extracurricular activities. In both large and small schools, such participation was most easily obtained in undermanned activities (those that had high manpower needs in relation to supply). This state of affairs is obviously more typical of small than large high schools.

Willems' (1967) study is similar but, additionally, he found that marginal eleventh grade students—those considered to be high drop-out risks—were much more involved in extracurricular activities in small than in large high schools. In fact, in small high schools, they felt as strong a sense of obligation for nonclass activities as average students. In sharp contrast, the typical marginal student in large schools reported little if any such sense of obligation. The ratio of students to activity tells much of the story: For large high schools, Willems found this to be between 3.33 and 4.20 from sampling done in 1965 and 1961, but only .43 for 1965 and .47 for 1961 in his small high schools.

It is much easier for a student in a small high school to find a niche for himself, for less aggressiveness and self-assurance are required. Certainly, the ratio reported by Willems would be much higher—many more than 4.20 students per available activity—in the very large high schools in urban areas. Perhaps this is one factor in the discouraging picture presented in the Sizer (1967) report on schools in the fifteen largest American cities.

In extracurricular activities, students are likely to find a spontaneity and opportunity for personal initiative and contribution that seems typically to be lacking in their classrooms. Regrettably, extracurricular activities, artificial as they often seem to the observer, may be closer to real life than classes. Certainly, participation in extracurricular activities constitutes a promising pull toward remaining in school and, perhaps, to continuing school. Disadvantaged children are almost certainly even more likely to be excluded from activities than from meaningful participation in classes. The minority group youngster in any integrated school stands the best chance of all of being excluded. Someone should study the participation opportunity and rate of, for example, disadvantaged Afro-American high school males in an integrated school: What do they do at the dances, for the plays, in debate? The only place for them is typically athletics and, all too often, they are not eligible even to compete for the team because of scholastic ineptitude.

TOWARD MORE POSITIVE INTERACTIONS BETWEEN YOUTH AND SOCIAL INSTITUTIONS

A great deal of the data, conclusions, and even much of the philosophizing in this chapter and Chapter 8 are depressing and negative in direction. Yet almost no one wavers in the belief in universal education. Even though many of them are caught up unhappily, ineffectively, or even viciously in the worse aspects of the system, there are few school people who do not believe in education passionately and who do not earnestly desire to produce the best possible schools, for the good of students as a group and as individuals. They want good schools for their own personal welfare, because they will be happier and more fulfilled if they can work in a setting that they believe is operating efficiently and constructively. They want good schools because they know that good schools are essential for the best working of a democratic society.

School people's hopes, dreams, and beliefs are shared by the overwhelming majority of the school's clientele, whether school board members, community leaders, parents, or students. The desire for the best possible education for all in the United States characterizes all socioeconomic levels, all geographic areas, and all races.

In the following pages an attempt is made to abstract from the data and discussions of Chapter 8 and the present chapter a set of principles for improving the quality of the interaction of youth with schools. The principles fit churches, which are discussed at the end of the present chapter, as well as they do schools, and also apply in most cases to families. These principles have been derived from too many sources for them to be adequately documented; full data to support them are all too often lacking; and personal and thus idiosyncratic experience has shaped many of them. All of them fit well enough within the general conceptual framework for learning and change that was developed in Chapter 1. In some of this section, brief statements that have been made in conjunction with earlier discussions of research in this chapter and in Chapter 8 are repeated. It is worthwhile to cover these areas again to enable this "principles section" to be relatively self-contained, and to fit isolated pieces of research into broader contexts.

Relevance and Programming   For students to learn and for teachers to function efficiently, a curriculum must possess two characteristics: it must be *relevant* and it must be *efficiently programmed*. As students mature, relevance becomes increasingly important, formal programming less so (efficient students learn to do their own programming). This is not to say that good programming is ever anything but vital.

Relevance   Relevance, upon analysis, can be understood to mean three things in modern society: (1) Something is relevant if an individual sees it as being important to his life and well-being. (2) Something is relevant if it is seen to bear on issues that are currently plaguing society. (3) When a student sees something as relevant, he is motivated to learn about it. Semantically, points 1 and 2 may be thought of as the heads, point 3 as the tails, side of the same coin. The meanings of relevance pertain to teachers' views as well as to students'.

A sense of or a belief in relevance is difficult to achieve in the first, laborious, factual stages of mastery of a subject. Only relatively mature, rather insightful and forward looking students are able to supply their own built-in relevance for the things they study in school. Very young children may have no direct, personal sense of relevance whatsoever, and, in such cases, relevance must be mediated through the teacher and a trust in the system. Relevance comes indirectly, because the student believes that what is held in mind for him is indeed for his own greatest good. Many youth have lost such trust, or are wavering in it, and have found themselves alienated from an important mainstream of American life.

Many academic undertakings, perhaps for a majority of youth, are relevant at least in their beginnings mainly because of the personal relationship between teachers and students. Relevance is induced when this relationship is important, rewarding, and full of trust. In this connection, the full discussion of power and socialization in Chapters 11, 12, and 13 is pertinent. Where appropriate, parts of that discussion are introduced here.

Young people will learn almost anything that is relevant to them. They will also learn it easily and remarkably cheerfully. Curricula should be programmed so as to capitalize on this reinforcing aspect of relevance. If young people can be made to see that learning something will be good for them here and now, or predictably good for them in the not-too-distant future, they *will* learn it. If something bad for them can be made to disappear, or if something painful can be avoided, they *will* learn how to make it so.

It then follows that an important part of curriculum planning at both group and individual levels is to find out what youth—collectively and singly—like and value, and what they dislike and reject. The tool for learning this is the insight, interest, and concern of the individual teacher, for which there is no substitute. To some degree, insightfulness about such a search for reward contingencies among students can be developed, but interest and concern seem more to be innate human qualities, which undoubtedly mark "the born teacher."

The best technique for "programming" an individual or a group is to keep running notes on what works and what does not work. A good teacher repeats things that work, and drops things that do not, from his repertoire. Unsystematic observation and mental notes are not enough. Some part of each teaching day should be set aside for thinking over the episodes of the day and setting them down in individualized folders, at least until the group and each individual are quite well known. Unfortunately, for many overworked teachers, the teaching day is not long enough to practice this ideal, and their teaching is less effective than it might otherwise be.

This philosophy and procedure is effective in reducing teacher anxiety. Most conscientious, traditionally trained teachers are quite anxious about their failures to understand children and youth. This anxiety has been induced in them during their training and in their professional and lay reading by (among others) dynamically oriented psychologists and psychiatrists (for example, many from the psychoanalytic school of thought, or from the motivational learning orientations). Teachers believe they should understand the "whole child," that they should be able to get at the roots of behavior, and all other such developmentally oriented and excessively difficult undertakings that are probably more appropriately, efficiently, and safely done in face to face counseling and small therapeutic settings.

Relieved to some degree from guilt and anxiety about tasks that they neither are trained for nor have the time to do, teachers should be freer to teach effectively. This is, after all, their principal function. It seems clear that a well taught and efficiently learning young person becomes steadily more competent, and better personal adjustment, improved self concepts, and greater happiness ordinarily accompany enhanced competence. Thus, a really good teacher makes a very direct contribution to the mental health of his students.

For most children and for many young people, relevance must be induced via the *person* of the teacher. This is achieved if the teacher develops power with his students. Power can be benign, or more or less neutral and impersonal, or it can be malign (punitive, hurtful, rigidly authoritarian). Benign power vested in warm, democratic teachers seems the most efficient type of power by which to induce curriculum relevance. (Data bearing on this conclusion have been cited earlier, and more will be given in Chapters 11, 12, and 13.) In an emotionally warm democratic setting, youth feel free to manifest a wide variety of behavior—positive, neutral, and negative. Thus, the teacher and the peer group can reinforce positive behavior and work together to extinguish the interfering and negative behavior. On the other hand, punishment and punitive restrictiveness inhibit *all* behavior, both that which is being punished and other potentially useful, adaptive behavior.

Under a benign democracy, youth's anxiety is reduced. Since adolescence is a time of overdrive, where there is so much drive that efficient function is often impeded, reduction of anxiety usually promotes more efficient learning of complex material. Finally, as has been said, in a reasonably warm democratic setting, it is likely that the "generation gap" will be minimized, that teachers and students will drop their adversary relation to each other, and that they will share mutual goals and thus be able to move more harmoniously, rapidly, and efficiently toward these goals together.

A teacher who makes himself a relevant power factor is also likely to achieve the following characteristics for his teaching style and his class organization. Over all, the points listed below comprise a good working definition of the positive noncontingent reinforcement that was discussed in more abstract terms in Chapter 8.

1. The class will have a general climate of nonsugary warmth.
2. The class will be operated with scrupulous fairness (for example, essay examinations will be graded by code number, not by name).
3. The teacher will be concerned and will demonstrate his concern for the welfare of each member of the class. This will not be a fussy, overprotective concern, but a lively interest. It will include the broader but not the intensely personal aspects of young people's out of school lives and families, and will be focused on things that are directly relevant to school and later out of school careers.
4. Rules will be clear, will be set in advance of when they are invoked, and will be arrived at by joint teacher-student negotiation (or clearly and understandably imposed from above, such as rules about truancy).
5. The criterion for establishing a rule will be that it is necessary to facilitate the learning process. There is no other sensible criterion, although a teacher who has made himself relevant in the sense of the present discussion can get by with an occasional idiosyncratic rule: "Don't do it because it drives me crazy!" The idiosyncratic nature of the rule should be made clear, however. Any pretext that it is "for the good of the learning process" or "in the best interests of the group" will be immediately spotted as false by the students.

A class of adolescents is best handled in a friendly, not saccharine, business-like, task-oriented fashion. The students know that school is business and they are quite willing to accept it as such. Of course, both the students and their teachers would like it to be as pleasant a business as possible.

Knowing when to laugh rather than to storm or cry is an invaluable teacher trait. Unfortunately, no guidelines for developing such knowledge can be offered. Either people seem to have a socially adroit sense of humor or they do not. Those who possess it are usually better teachers and they are certainly happier teachers (and parents). Day in and day out interactions with adolescents inevitably include occasions when helpless laughter is the only workable substitute for real rage, or for tears that approach grief. Tears are unlikely to accomplish much with adolescents, and giving way to genuine anger has dangerous side effects (including the risk of modeling and retaliation by the students). However, even though anger is usually self-defeating—students know they have really *got to* the angry teacher—it is a sincere emotion and has its place. Acting in anger is likely to be maladaptive, as it is an overwhelming drive, and behavior motivated by it is often senseless and compounds rather than solves the problem that caused it. However, bottled-up, reflected on to see if it had legitimate cause and, if it did, used deliberately (semirole played) when a situation arises later, anger can be useful. It should be employed sparingly and with extreme caution.

There seems no question (from research data to be reported in more detail in Chapters 11, 12, and 13) that learning is faster and more efficient when positive reinforcement greatly exceeds negative reinforcement (punishment) in frequency. As has been said, the easiest and most effective way to do away with behaviors that are not liked within an individual or a group is to ignore them, while, at the same time, rewarding constructive behaviors that may be substituted for them.

Almost all the reinforcements for adolescents must be intangible: teacher praise, popularity, teacher approval, teacher concern, signs that the teacher likes one. These reinforcements seem to be even more important for disadvantaged than for advantaged youth.

Programming   The "most relevant" teacher in the world, operating in a classroom that is optimally noncontingent positively reinforcing in nature can not teach well unless the curriculum is correctly programmed. But programming is technical in nature: What aspects of what subjects come first, and how are they presented? When and how often are visual aids introduced? What should be the relative proportions of discussion, independent research, and lecture from the teacher? What are the respective merits of the didactic and the discovery systems?

These are matters of concern in educational psychology books or in methods courses related to specific subject matter areas, such as languages, sciences, and the arts. This being a general adolescent psychology book, space is not available to discuss programming in any detail. It is sufficient to say that effective programming is essential for efficient learning, but guidance in programming must be obtained elsewhere for those who are interested.

The Adversary Relationship[4]   While there is not a state of war between the young and their elders, their relations sometimes closely resemble it. There are, however, chronic and probably unavoidable tensions between the young and their teachers and parents. These tensions may be minimized by taking such steps as those advocated in the discussions of *relevance* and *noncontingent positive reinforcement* in this text; good curriculum programming further reduces friction (or keeps the class sufficiently efficient and interested that friction is minimized). But even at best, the young have many needs and interests that teachers and parents can not always meet and must

---

[4]The discussion in this section is derived from R. K. White's (1968, 1969) thinking about the causes of war.

sometimes thwart. Thus, some of the steps White (1968, 1969) advocates in the interests of international peace or that have occurred to the author as a consequence of White's thinking pertain very plausibly to relations between the young and their caretakers.

First, when it becomes clear that the young and their elders have assumed adversary positions, it is well to pause and for both sides to take a long, hard, mutual, and, preferably, documented look at their common ground. For example, a high school senior class in political science wanted to be dismissed from school to hear a charismatic candidate for national public office. The instructor feared that their motives were frivolous but resisted his reflex to say "No." The students were sure that he would say "No," because saying "Yes" would interrupt the school routine. A thoughtful survey of common ground suggested that few of the students had ever heard or seen a candidate for national office in the flesh, nor had the instructor. The candidate had both substance and charisma, so there were formal as well as informal things to learn, both by students and by instructor. The students and the instructor realized that the class preceding and following the candidate's speech would be interfered with, and both sides agreed to negotiate with the two teachers concerned to make up the time and to prevent the other teachers from thinking that the political science instructor was infringing on their rights. Both students and instructor regretted that some important instruction needed for the political science course, but for which there was not time in the crowded term, would have to be scanted if time was taken off to go to hear the national candidate for office.

The upshot was a vote of about two to one in favor of going to hear the candidate. There was 100 percent attendance at the candidate's speech, and a clear improvement of already good relations between class and instructor.

When an analysis of common ground is carefully and calmly made, both sides are usually surprised to find out how much they are in agreement, and the issues of disagreement become much clearer and thus open to negotiation.

Second, it is important for the adversaries to conduct an analysis of the common ground. Adversaries often overestimate the good will and agreement that exist toward them among members of the other side. The political science teacher in the illustration above is likely to infer that his students had more interest in his subject and more appreciation of his role as "servant of the school system" than actually exist among his students. The students are likely to overestimate their teacher's confidence in them as responsible young adults capable of planning their own out of school conduct. A naïve analysis of common ground can lead to bruised feelings, disillusionment, and acceleration of conflict. A tinge of resigned cynicism about the degree to which one is understood is useful in most human relations, particularly those with caretaker-youth interactions.

Third, it is sometimes useful to employ a technique tested by social psychologists (see White, 1969, for details). Before the sides enter into debate (conflict), ground rules provide that side 1 must state clearly, in detail, and to the satisfaction of side 2 all the issues side 2 advocates. The converse is also true. Only when both sides are satisfied can debate begin. By that time, conflict is often unnecessary. This procedure is remarkably thought provoking, and the intellectual effort involved is very useful in calming emotions. The technique is also a good exercise in attention, analysis, and articulation of principles and issues, and logical thinking in general.

Fourth, there may be self-fulfilling (sometimes paranoid) perceptions of ill will held by each side about the other. A middle-class teacher faced with a class of strapping disadvantaged youth may believe sincerely that they are "out to get" him. The students in turn (often on the basis of past experience) may confidently believe that the instructor is "out to get" them. Mutual paranoia is common between races, different social classes, and, of course, between nations. Acting on mutual assumptions of ill will may precipitate a situation where the gloomiest expectations of both sides are speedily confirmed.

When there are hostile, suspicious, paranoid-tinged expectations, it works well to assume deliberately a role of believing in the best in human nature. The role may have to be abandoned later, but its frequent success is due to the nature of the self-fulfilling prophesy. It is not an idle guess that good things happen to those who expect them. The fact that this optimistic stance is to some degree a role, not sheer naïvete, prevents anyone from being seriously hurt when it proves to be inappropriate, as it sometimes does (for example, some situations involving groups or individuals are simply realistically bad and are bound to disintegrate). Role playing, with some degree of sincerity, will not psychologically crush someone when things work out badly.

The fifth and final point about adversary relations concerns the concept of territoriality. Animal ecologists have demonstrated the widespread existence of a "territorial drive" among subhuman species, and many psychologists attribute it also to man. Youth and their caretakers often come into conflict about territoriality: the (usually) well meaning mother who reads her children's mail or diaries; the teacher or parent who inquires too insistently into the private life (psychological territory) of the youth in his care. There is much generational conflict over the "right" to guide youth that is a common assumption of parents and teachers; likewise, youth's "right" to self-determination is a matter about which particularly male youth feel strongly. In turn, parents and teachers possess certain psychological territories: they are more experienced, better trained, and ordinarily more discreet, and they deserve to have these qualities respected.

Territorial problems like privacy and rights to action are amenable to each of the procedures and considerations advanced in discussing the first four points in this section.

THE CHURCH AND YOUTH Social scientists have documented the influence of the church on young people even less well than the influence of school on youth. There are several plausible reasons. For one thing, religion is a sensitive area, whereas schools belong to everyone. Everyone is an expert on education, in the sense that he has attended a school and is probably helping to pay for schools through his taxes. Also, everyone has to go to school, but no one has to go to church. In a certain sense, the influence of schools can be investigated without stepping very hard on important people's toes. Schools are neutral, or at least objective territory.

Churches, literally and figuratively, are sacred. Parents go to the church of their choice, and it is their decision whether or not their children attend church. Thus, an investigation of the church and youth may be judged an invasion of privacy. Nor does one check up on feelings about God. Americans may not act like it, but about 96 percent of them believe in God. Investigating beliefs, particularly those that concern a man's immortal soul, is touchy business.

Church records are typically not very well kept, so it is difficult to determine facts, even such basic ones as rate of attendance. The average family devotes little time per week to church, so a minister or priest or rabbi or church school teacher is reluctant to release church time for research purposes.

Most churchmen and other church workers known to the author, either in their inner hearts and often much more accessibly, entertain doubts about the effectiveness of their programs, even though they believe devoutly in them. Stark and Glock (1968), to be discussed more fully later, support the author's impressions with data. A man or woman devoting his life to the church does not want it proved that he is wasting his time. Hence, relatively few of those responsible for the work of church are eager to have their endeavors subjected to the cold light of data gathering and analysis.

It may even be that there is a fundamental conflict between things of the spirit and the subject matter and methods of science. Certainly, the church and science have long been uncomfortable with each other (as in the cases of Galileo and Darwin). It may also be that social scientists do not take a keen interest in the church. It occupies little of the average person's time and, while almost everyone gives lip service to it, observation suggests that it has remarkably little influence on the daily lives of its members.

Stark and Glock (1968), eminently respectable sociologists, are among the scientists who have looked searchingly at the church. Their findings are not cheering to the church. Among other things, they conclude that *"the current religious revolution is being accompanied by a general decline in commitment to religion."* (p. 7)

Among Christians (with whom Stark and Glock concern themselves in their research) *orthodoxy* consists of such behaviors as prayer and private worship; emphasis on religious experience and knowledge; and the belief that only Christians can be saved. Public worship and regular attendance are also stressed. Among *ethicalists*, however, importance is placed on behavior and attitudes, such as loving thy neighbor, doing unto others as one would have done to him, and doing good to others.

For Protestants, there is actually a slight *negative* correlation between orthodoxy and ethicalism, only 42 percent of the highly orthodox being high in ethicalism, while 47 percent of the least orthodox are high ethicalists. On the other hand, the orthodox support the church and the unorthodox do not. Stark and Glock report that 44 percent of highly orthodox Protestants pay $7.50 or more per week for the support of their church, while only 17 percent of the low orthodox contribute that much. Catholics show the same trend, but not as dramatically.

It is understandable, then, why the churches remain orthodox. In American society and almost everywhere else, money is an exceptionally important form of power (see Chapters 11, 12, and 13). If the orthodox provide the power, then they will shape the church. It can also be predicted that the ethicalists are relatively disenchanted with their churches. Being disenchanted, they will be low attenders. Stark and Glock's data support this prediction among Protestants, but their data for Catholics are not clear. The best financial contributors as well as the best attenders, among both Protestants and Roman Catholics, "are those of unwavering orthodoxy, who reject the religious importance of loving their neighbors or doing good for others" (p. 12). For such reasons, the efforts of liberal clergymen to move their congregations toward "deeds, not words," seem foredoomed to failure. The orthodox not only support the church and its clergy but they interact with and communicate with them more fully, and thus are in the best position to exert their power.

It is thus not surprising that the relatively few studies in depth of religious commitment as related to other social attitudes have turned up little evidence favorable to church attendance and commitment. Among the tenets of the major Christian, Jewish, and Muslim faiths is a firm basis of good will toward one's fellow man. If church membership is taken seriously—*ethically*—then the more devout the person, the less prejudiced he should be.

Two studies give perspective about this issue. In the older of the two, O'Reilly and O'Reilly (1954), quite the opposite is revealed. The authors devised a measure of religious devoutness—"the extent to which the subjects (Ss) agreed with the Catholic Church on certain social, moral, and religious questions" (p. 378). They also measured anti-Semitism and prejudice against Black people. Their subjects, 92 men and 120 women, were seminary and university students. There was a modest and statistically significant tendency for the most devout to be both anti-Negro and anti-Jew. For example, of those who favored segregation of the races in the parish, 76.5 percent scored in the upper half of the devoutness scale. Of those lowest in devoutness, 74.5 percent *opposed* parish segregation. The fit with Stark and Glock's findings is precise.

Allport and Ross (1967) report findings that are not quite as discouraging to sincere church members. They review the research literature dating from 1946 and, as a whole, agree that church attenders and affiliates, when compared with nonattenders and nonaffiliates, are more tolerant not only of ethnic minorities but of such diverse groups as criminals, those in need of psychiatric help, atheists, socialists, communists, delinquents, homosexuals, and prostitutes; and that church attenders are somewhat less humanitarian. Allport and Ross conclude that "on the average religious people show more intolerance in general." (p. 432)

However, they believe that most research has failed to distinguish between people who hold *extrinsic* and *intrinsic* affiliations to religion. Those who are extrinsically religious, Allport and Ross believe, *use* religion for their own purposes. For such people, church is instrumental and utilitarian. In it they find things like "security and solace, sociability and distraction, status and self-justification." But intrinsic people *live* their religion: They internalize it and live it fully (p. 434). The likeness to internal and external locus of control as discussed in the preceding chapters is striking.

Allport and Ross developed a test to measure extrinsic and intrinsic orientations to the church and religion. They then performed studies to determine how the scale related to prejudice of different types. They found consistently higher prejudice scores for extrinsic than intrinsic religious types. A third, *indiscriminately proreligious* type was most prejudiced of all. Allport and Ross' somewhat hopeful conclusion is that genuinely intrinsically religious people internalize not only the total creed of their religion, but also its values of humility, compassion, and love of neighbor. For such people "there is no place for rejection, contempt, or condescension toward one's fellow man" (p. 441).

In short, if churches can make genuinely religious people out of their members, then the basic values of the church may be put into practice. No one can quarrel with such a conclusion, although one must ask how this is done.

It has been mentioned that the author has a large collection of autobiographies given to him by students who averaged about 24 years of age at the time they prepared them, who were at the beginning of their professional lives, and most of whom were in one of the welfare or helping professions. For this group, the formal or spiritual aspect of the church, which is its central reason for being, has made little impact. Among the effects of church attendance, they most frequently mention the guilt induced by the teachings about their adolescent sex behavior. (The sample includes an overrepresentation of conservative, Midwestern Protestants).

However, many among this sample said positive things about the extracurricular side of their church, that is, its youth groups, with their preponderantly social emphasis. Many of the sample had found a home away from home and a social life not provided by the school. Church-related social activity contributed not so much to their spiritual welfare as to their feelings of social adequacy, their sense of being accepted as worthwhile people, and their competence as social human beings. This is no small benefit. Repeatedly, they mention warmly that the church group took them as they were; that competition for status within the group was not so deadly as at school; and that within their church groups, they were considered to be worthwhile and even superior persons. A church *should* give this to a person, since he is valuable because of himself and his spirit, regardless of his social class or skin color.

By giving young people a chance to participate intensively, church youth groups may have afforded them some of the benefits of extracurricular activities documented in the Willems and Wicker studies of small and large high schools that were mentioned above.

Church participation seems to be less frequent among the disadvantaged than among the advantaged, although church plays an important role in the lives of many disadvantaged rural people, Black and white. In the Hodges, McCandless, Spicker (1969) sample of Appalachian fathers of acutely disadvantaged status, for example, fewer than 50 percent claimed even so much as an affiliation with a church; and 30 percent of their predictably more conforming wives volunteer the information that they have no commitment to any church. These figures are all the more striking, since they were gathered in the Bible Belt of rural and semirural Indiana, where church is a way of life.

Of those in this sample who do belong to church, half the men and about two-thirds of the women belong to Fundamentalist or Primitive Protestant churches. The figures provide one more illustration of the social isolation that characterizes the extreme underclass in American society. This isolation may not be so great for some disadvantaged groups. For example, Hill and Larson (1966, 1967) find the church to be a real source of community strength and action in the poor Black inner city area they studied.

However, it is doubtful if the church touches the young and violent and/or alienated, whether they are Black or white. There are many indications, undocumented by solid evidence as far as the author knows, that the young Black activist leaders reject the church contemptuously. At the time of the Detroit riots, Dan Watts, editor of the *Liberator*, is quoted by the *Detroit News*[5] as saying, "Pork-chop preachers. In Detroit, they dealt with some old Baptist preacher. But when the trouble started the minister was the last to know and the first one under the bed." The ministers are considered to be out of touch with the poor people in their areas, particularly the young and disadvantaged. On the other hand, the name of the Reverend Martin Luther King, Jr., stands as big as ever, long after his death; in a different way, Malcolm X, a loved and respected maker of history, was a minister; and many of the more prominent leaders of the poor, Black and white, are church leaders.

Churches, Boys, Girls, and Social Class

Like the school, the church is a feminine organization. It stands for obedience, responsibility, conservatism, and reliability. Among Christians, God is the Father, but it is the *Mother* church. Consequently, it can be predicted that girls and women will affiliate more with and be more influenced by it than men and boys. Its leaders are "men of the cloth," but it is expected that they be gentle and rather feminine. The current image of Christ, perhaps quite erroneously, is one of a gentle, meek, and mild Being. American men, stereotypically, are uneasy with churchmen, while women traditionally dote on them.

Little is firmly known about differential effects of the church on male and female adolescents. The present treatment is consequently more hypothesis than fact.

The "elite" church is largely a middle-class organization. To be religious demands that one be rather verbal, since, in its essence, religion is symbolic. Religion asks for renunciation of things of the flesh and demands postponement of immediate gratification for the sake of future reward. The three major monotheistic religions (Christianity, Islam, and Judaism) regard sex as wicked. All three condemn aggression. But sex

[5]July 28, 1967.

and aggression are sometimes the principal means of expression available to the disadvantaged. In one sense, the church demands curiosity — seeking the light — ; in another, it discourages it — "Trust in God and do as He says." Such appeals seem aimed at the introspective, conforming, verbal middle-class people.

To be a good church member, one needs most of the same qualities he needs to be a good student in elementary and secondary school. Disadvantaged young people *must* attend school, at least until they are old enough to drop out. But they can choose not to attend church. Overwhelmingly, they choose simply to leave the institution alone. They feel isolated within the church, in many cases; and they do not possess the qualities highly esteemed in church members. Many churches, perhaps most notably the respectable Protestant denominations, seem almost to have abandoned the disadvantaged. At this time, however, considerable effort is being made to reverse this trend, although many, many "respectable" churches have moved or are considering moving out of the inner cities. The city slums now mainly contain churches that minister to disadvantaged minorities. These include the Catholic Church. There are also many Fundamentalist sects and storefront churches whose congregations are largely or entirely made up of disadvantaged people. Stark and Glock's analysis of the Protestant churches does not suggest that the present state of affairs is likely to change greatly.

In summary, the church and its influence on American life have not been well studied. It is reasonably easy to define a church (although the courts have had their problems with Mohammed Ali and the Black Muslims), but it is hard to judge or measure the influence of any given church. Even the church people themselves are in the midst of developing conflicts. Catholicism, heretofore a rock of central orthodoxy, has been seriously disturbed about birth control and doctrinal issues in recent years. Judaism ranges from liberal (reformed) to conservative (orthodox). The Protestants number among them radical "left wingers" as well as lunatic "right wing fringers."

The impact of church on a given youth certainly varies according to the church he attends. Since churches as well as individuals are wonderfully discrete and various, there can be no single influence of the church on youth. In some parts of the nation, churches have stood strongly against racism and separatism, while in the Deep South they have been major vehicles for perpetuating and institutionalizing these beliefs.

Factors, such as disparity between the tenets of churches and the behavior of its "best members," the church's conservatism and orthodoxy, the all too often pallid religious education programs, the catering to the old and the established middle class, suggest that the church and most youth are far apart, and that they are not likely to be reconciled soon. Failure seems likely to be greater among boys than girls, and among disadvantaged than middle-class youth.

SUMMARY

The United States supports mandatory schooling from 5, 6, or 7 years of age to about 16 years of age for all its children. The schools are the country's major investment in its attempt to provide legitimate opportunities for its children and youth. While belief in the system is strong, criticism is vigorous. There are many indications that the schools are not functioning as well as they could or should. Chief among such evidence is the 33 percent national high school drop-out rate.

The first major function of the school is *maintenance-actualization*: developing the whole child or youth; reducing irrelevant frustrations; presenting positive noncontingent reinforcements so that a child is accepted for what he is rather than because of his family, his skill at athletics, or the color of his skin. The second function is *training-acculturation*: imparting to youth the knowledge of the culture, and helping them gain skills to function within it and contribute to it. Success in training-acculturation, although open to improvement, has been greater than success in maintenance-actualization.

Evidence suggests that school success is determined more by the home and community from which a child or young person comes than by his school, although it is clear that this need not be the case. Many instances can be cited where both day and residential schools have helped children and young people compensate for horrendous personal, home, and community deficits. It seems that schools as now operated stress discipline and control, often at the expense of fairness to boys when compared to girls, and at the expense of fairness to disadvantaged children when compared to advantaged children.

Morale of school children seems to decline as a school year wears on; teachers generally treat boys more punitively than girls, and disadvantaged children more punitively than advantaged children; and, or so the available evidence indicates, poor Black boys most rejectingly and punitively of any subgroup that has been studied. Since disadvantaged children on the average have fewer positive models than advantaged children, teachers seem to have more influence on them. Unfortunately, this does not seem to be typically benign. Experienced teachers seem to be more negative than inexperienced teachers.

Teachers have compiled a poor record of judging students' interest in and liking for school; nor are they accurate judges of aptitude or even achievement. When principles from learning laboratories have been put into practice, they have worked well in motivating children to learn, regardless of social class, ethnicity, or sex. When equally treated, for example, boys seem to learn as well as girls, and to receive comparable grades, although usually boys attain lower grades than girls. However, boys do not typically obtain poorer scores than girls on standardized achievement tests.

Boys may do less well in school than girls because of their high autonomy needs. They are pulled toward the wider world because of its challenge, while, at the same time, their masculine traits of autonomy, independence seeking, and initiative often put them into conflict with the nurturant, feminine, and authoritarian atmosphere of the school. Their higher activity level and liking for excitement also seem to contribute to their difficulty. Conflicts, often derived from their own families or their cocultures, are singularly acute for disadvantaged boys placed under the control of women teachers. Boredom and the need for excitement to offset it may also compound the difficulties of low, relatively nonverbal, school underachievers or low achievers.

While it is seldom discussed, the sexual maturity of adolescents undoubtedly complicates teacher-pupil relations. Since sex is more insistent for boys, and since more teachers are women, this may constitute another differential disadvantage for boys. The problem may be particularly relevant for Afro-American boys as a group, particularly when disadvantaged, although the question has not been realistically studied. An attempt to control the sexual behavior of its charges may be related to the authoritarianism of secondary and junior high schools.

Disadvantaged children enter school lacking many personal, social and work skills necessary for school success. But since the organization and staffing of schools is middle class, consequently such children often emerge at 16 or earlier into the community from their school experience no better able to cope with life than when they entered school. Again, children from discriminated minority groups, particularly Afro-American, American Indian, and Hispano youngsters, seem to suffer most and, among them, the males more than the females.

Disadvantaged youth seem to experience even less success extracurricularly than they do in regular school. Athletics represents an exception available to a few unusually gifted disadvantaged boys.

While the summary of data about junior and senior high schools seems pessimistic, Americans of all ages, races, and walks of life hold fast to the splendid dream of a public, free education for all. Suggestions for modifying the system so as more closely to approach the dream without in any way harming the schools were advanced. The principles come from reasonably well-established psychological theory and in most cases are buttressed by data. Relevance is the quality of being important in and to an individual's life and well-being, as well as important for issues that currently plague society. Students are strongly motivated to learn that which is relevant. However, for many students, the relevance or positive reward value residing in the subject of study must be induced by the teacher, and for teachers to induce relevance, data suggest that a warm but not saccharine democratic classroom organization is optimal. Such an atmosphere may be provided when teachers can predict what interests their students. The democratic classroom reduces anxiety among students and teachers, thus reducing drive to more manageable proportions; it reduces teacher (or parent) conflict and thus provides a team relation for moving toward common goals; it permits a wider range of student behavior toward which to apply behavior modification.

The teacher who achieves this type of relevance will likely supply general positive noncontingent reinforcement to all students through matter of fact warmth, fairness, and simple or noninterfering concern about the welfare and progress of students. Rules will be fair, set in advance, and established by mutual negotiation of teacher (or any other caretaker) and adolescents. The only useful rules in a classroom are those that facilitate the learning experience. The ratio of positive to negative reinforcement should be very large. Extinction of undesirable behaviors by ignoring (nonreinforcement) is the ideal technique, although punishment must sometimes be administered by caretakers or by the group, preferably according to democratic consensus.

The best classroom atmosphere in the world, however, will not result in efficient learning if there is not adequate programming of subject matter. Expertness in such programming is not the function of the present book, since it is highly technical and belongs more in the province of educational psychology.

Despite all precautions, there remains the likelihood of some strain and even conflict between youth and their caretakers. Possible steps to prevent open conflict and deepen understanding and mutuality are: (1) seeking out the common agreed upon ground between the two sides; (2) accurately estimating the agreement and sympathy that exist between the two sides (there seem to be two extremes in this matter, one of paranoid suspicion, the other of naïve assumption that everyone appreciates one's own point of view); (3) entering debate only after each side has stated the other side's issues to the satisfaction of both; (4) avoiding self-fulfilling hostile prophecies when both sides are merely being wary, not hostile; (5) clearly delineating the legitimate territorial rights of both sides, and respecting them.

Little formal research information exists about the influence of the church on youth. What evidence there is suggests that the church may be very valuable for social development as youth participate in youth groups, but that the over-all value of church to youth or adults depends on their orientation to religion. The goals of the church seem to be realized when religion is seen by its participants as *intrinsic* to them—that is, when they live it—but perhaps even maladjustive when it is *extrinsic* —when they use the church purely for such purposes as security and self-justification. The amount as well as the quality of impact currently being made on youth by the church remains an open question.

11

Adolescents and Work

INTRODUCTION

Most adolescents of the ages on which this book is principally focused live in three worlds: home and family, the peer group, and school and/or work. For some like Nedra, whose story is given below, these worlds overlap extensively and agreeably. For others like Carrie, whose story follows Nedra's, they are partially independent, but when they touch there is conflict. For Doug, who comes next, they are independent but quite compatible; while Lonnie at 19 lives a man's life.

The brief biographies of these young people illustrate the large number of purposes work serves for adolescents, and also bring to life the more abstract principle that in technological, predominantly urban United States society, work is to a considerable degree a way of life. Thus, discussions and theories of vocational choice and vocational development are also discussions of real life, including dimensions of cognitive development, socialization, personality, and self concept.

WORK PATTERNS OF FOUR YOUNG PEOPLE

As these four young people are described, it becomes clear that the meaning of work differs greatly according to the sex of the working youth, the social class to which he belongs, and, as in Lonnie's case, his skin color. The complex pressures toward working are also illustrated: the desire of the adolescent (he wants or needs money, he wants to be independent of his family, he works because his friends work); and parents' pressures to work, either because the family needs the money, or will not give the adolescent the money he needs for recreation; or because the family believes that work "develops character."

Nedra: A Middle-Class Girl

Nedra works because most of her friends work, because she can use the money both for luxuries and to apply toward college in the future, and because her parents think it is good for their children to work.

She lives in a town of 10,000 in central Michigan, and will be graduated from high school at the end of her current school year. She is a solid B student. There are five children in the family. She is the middle child and second daughter. The family, although not rich, lives comfortably in a large, pleasant older house in a good but not the best part of town. The oldest child, a girl, goes to college in a town not far away, and does not live at home. A brother, who is a year older than Nedra, is also a high school senior, having lost a year of school due to illness. Another sister is two years younger and is two years behind Nedra in school, and there is a little brother in second grade. The parents are concerned but not deeply worried over their next year's prospect of three children in college.

Nedra's father owns the best shoe store in town. Her mother works in it on weekends, helps to keep the books, sends out bill, and handles paperwork concerned with orders.

The parents hold the philosophy that they would rather have the children at home than on the road to Grand Rapids—the nearest large city, some miles away via a heavily traveled, high accident rate highway. Thus, the big comfortable house is always full of youngsters of all ages, from the baby brother's after school friends to college friends of both sexes whom the older sister brings home on weekends.

Nedra works after school and on weekends in a drug store, a popular teenage hangout. It is owned by one of her parents' closest friends, and is located on the same block as the shoe store. Nedra's father in earlier years had given the drug store proprietor's son a job in his shoe store, so the families have established a mutual interest relationship. In the drug store, Nedra has much concourse with young people who are her buddies during school. However, she does not waste time with them. Besides them, she is exposed to clientele of all ages and social classes, as well as to the different ethnic groups that live in the town. She waits on all of them with courtesy, good manners, and a real desire to please that characterizes almost all her behavior.

The parents are interested in her work, partly because they want to know what all their children are doing and how they like it; and partly (being human) because they want to know how their friend's business is going. By appropriate illustrations, of teenagers who have worked in their own store, they attempt to set a model for Nedra's on-the-job performance. Her work experience is almost entirely positive, and exceptionally well blended into her home, school, and peer life. Occasionally she is pushed for time; and she believes her grades might be somewhat better if she did not have to work. The money she earns goes for special clothes and treats, and the modest sum she lays away for college makes her feel mature and self-sufficient. The fact that many customers treat her like an adult saleslady seems to have given her extra maturity. Her knowledge of budgeting and her ability to plan time have almost certainly been helped by her job. The fact that she is a good worker and that her employer feeds back this information to her parents gives her added prestige in their eyes, and they accord her an almost adult status in the home.

Carrie: A Poor White

Carrie is an urban tenement dweller. Like Nedra, she is a senior in high school, but is on both academic and behavior probation. Her grades are borderline, she smokes in the rest rooms, she is in frequent conflict with her teachers, particularly the women, and she is often truant.

Like Nedra, she is the middle child of five, but the family is fatherless. The father disappeared from the family when Carrie was 10 and has not been heard from since.

The family manages, meagerly but respectably, from the mother's and childrens' earnings. The mother is a strong, dour, religious woman who takes great pride in the fact that she has never had to go on relief. She works very hard as a hotel maid. The oldest boy is 20, has spent six months in a juvenile home, was married by necessity, and became a father shortly after his 17th birthday. His wife deserted him and the infant, and his 3-year-old son is the seventh member of the family. An old widow from the floor below looks after the child during the days. Currently, the brother is not in trouble of any serious kind, and works regularly in a filling station, where he is making visible strides toward becoming a mechanic. He has had no formal school since "juvenile," where he finished something approximating the ninth grade.

He and his mother are in constant conflict over moral issues. He dates a great deal, and although she objects because he is not yet divorced, he makes no move toward official termination of his marriage. His off work hours partially coincide with his mother's work hours, so he often brings his girls to the apartment; when she learns about it, they commence to battle.

Carrie models herself more on her brother than on her mother and her intensely religious and moral older sister. She declared independence from her mother when she found steady, reasonably well paying work in a neighborhood restaurant. The mother and she fight over the hours she keeps, the place where she works, the out of school friends she has, the fact that she smokes and often smells of liquor, the fact that she does not always come home at night, and her school probation. The brother sides with Carrie, reinforcing Carrie's financial autonomy: "She earns her own way, and she has a right to live her own life."

Carrie pays her board and room plus a share of the expenses of the total household. She will not help with any of the duties of the household, however, except those involved with the care of the 3-year-old nephew, whom she adores. Her work in the restaurant enables her to meet many men, and she often goes out with them after work. She accepts many gifts from them, and her mother and sister accuse her of whoring, which she denies indignantly and sincerely. While she is not virgin, she sleeps only with men she likes and goes out with them for fun and excitement, not money. To some degree, she dates to punish her steady boyfriend, a young married man who will not break with his wife. She has been pregnant by him once and he paid for her abortion. He objects to her dating, but she only points out that he has neither the logical nor the legal right to interfere. They have continued in their surly, complex but affectionate relationship for nearly three years, and neither seems eager to terminate it or change it in any fundamental way.

Carrie's and Nedra's lives are not much alike. Where Nedra's three worlds complement one other, Carrie's are independent and in conflict. For Carrie, work interferes with school and vice versa, and as information about her school or work or peer life filters back into her home, it creates conflict. Nor are her school friends her work friends, as they are in Nedra's case. About the only contact between her school and work world is that she occasionally gets dates for school friends with men whom she meets at the restaurant.

Carrie, essentially, is alienated from her school peers. She finds the boys in high school gauche and immature, as well as short on funds. Her dating is entirely with older men. Her casual school girl friends are fringers like herself. She asks them for nothing and only rarely gives them anything other than an occasional dating introduction. She does not enjoy school, takes no part in extracurricular activities, and would probably not be welcomed or eligible because of her probationary status if she expressed an interest. Her only reason for staying in school is her acceptance of the norm expressed in Chapter 8: Survival in the society of today requires one to hold a high school diploma.

Except for her older brother and his preschool-aged son, her relations to her family range from neutral (with her younger brother and sister) to hostile (with her mother and older sister). While her independence from her mother's authority has never been openly acknowledged by her mother, it exists and both know it. Thus, the mother attacks when presented with evidence about Carrie's way of life; but on the other hand, the mother rather goes out of her way to keep from learning solid facts about what Carrie actually does and whom she dates. The sister, although more intrusive, is no more effective in influencing Carrie's way of doing things. As to why Carrie continues to live at home, probably it is because nothing better has turned up.

Carrie's work holds no intrinsic interest for her. She illustrates "occupational selection by drift," a fact of life for many youths, particularly the disadvantaged. She does her work moderately efficiently since she wants to hold the job because it provides her money and thus independence. The side benefits of social relations with the other waitress, the cook, the cleaning and dishwashing boys, and manager-owner are only marginal. She appreciates meeting men who will take her out and show her a good time.

Her attitude toward her work is quite typical of that held by unskilled and semiskilled workers of either sex (see Liebow, 1966; Morse and Weiss, 1968). Morse and Weiss (1968), reporting on interviews of 401 randomly selected employed men concerning the meaning work holds for them, find that the unskilled "mention money, and those in service occupations tend to give as reasons for satisfaction the fact that it is the only type of job they could get and that they like the people they work with and meet" (p. 15). This statement summarizes Carrie's motive accurately. Liebow (1966) points out that what seem to be the casual, irresponsible, even cavilier attitudes of unskilled workers to their jobs are simply mirrors of the attitudes their employers hold toward the jobs: The jobs (and the men and women who hold them) are of no more prestige and importance to the employers than they are to the workers.

Doug: Upper Middle Class

Doug, 20 and a college senior majoring in physiology, represents an almost pure case of a late adolescent socialized according to an ideal that is commonly held by the upwardly mobile middle class in United States society. Doug is a middle child with a sister three years older than he (employed as a social worker, married), and a brother three years younger, who is a college freshman. The father is a Ph.D. level industrial chemist with a current annual income of about $35,000. The mother, who had worked as an elementary teacher and school supervisor before her marriage and until her first child was born, returned for further education when all the children were in school, and now holds a supervisory position in an urban school system at a salary of $14,000 per year.

Both parents came from lower middle-class, limited income backgrounds, and it was necessary for them both to work hard to finance their educations even as early as their high school years. They hold firmly to middle-class values that stress the importance of work for its own sake, for its influence in "molding character," and for its financial returns. Even though they are prosperous, they deliberately keep from "spoiling their children."

Through a business friend, the father found Doug a summer job on the assembly line in light industry as soon as Doug was old enough to obtain working papers. Doug has held this job during each consecutive summer, working his way up in skill until he was a substitute foreman by his last summer on the job. From his earnings, he bought and has maintained a small car, paid for his clothing and recreation, and banked a solid contribution to his college education. He says of his work experience: "I am surer of myself because I know I can learn a skilled trade and work my way up in it. It has been good for me to meet the working class of people. It rubbed a lot of snobbery off me, and taught me how to get along with all kinds. I've learned what responsibility means."

Doug remains a bit of a snob, although he accommodates easily and in a natural seeming, unpatronizing way to those less well educated, intelligent, and talented than he. It has never occurred to him to mix socially with his skilled and semiskilled colleagues outside of working hours, even though he has had invitations. He has never responded to flirtatious advances made by some of the female workers, even though his male colleagues have encouraged him to do so, and have assured him that he could thus easily take care of his sexual needs.

During his junior year of high school, he decided that he needed a part time job during the school year, and also came to the conclusion that he lacked outgoing, friendly, social skills. Although his parents discouraged him from taking even part time work, fearing that his grades might suffer, he sought a job in door-to-door sales as a solution to his double problem. He obtained one independently, and was successful at it. By spring, he had polished his social skills well enough to be elected president of the senior class. He had also been offered full time employment by the company for which he worked. Doug kept this job during his senior year, fitted easily into school politics, and maintained his academic average.

After two years of college, having settled on his academic major, Doug decided that his summer factory job was no longer satisfactory, and that what he needed was something that tied in with his future career (he plans doctoral work in physiology, with an academic and research career to follow). Thus, apparently with no second thoughts, he took a job as a laboratory technician in a hospital, even though it paid much less than his industrial employment would have. His plans for the summer following his college graduation arise from his belief (not atypical of upper- and upper-middle-class people) that all men owe a certain social obligation to those who are less fortunate than they. Thus, he has obtained a tutorial, counseling position at very low pay in a summer camp program for slum preadolescent and adolescent boys, most of them from disadvantaged minority groups.

Doug's work history to date has effectively contained everything his parents (and the experts) might have prescribed: He has earned money, he has rubbed elbows with and learned to accommodate himself to different socioeconomic and ethnic groups, he knows what it is to put in "an honest day's work," he has acquired skills in dealing with the public, he has built a foundation for later skills that he will need in his professional life, and he will in all likelihood have made—by the time his summer with disadvantaged youth has come and gone—a modest social welfare contribution, with attendant benefits to himself. He will have had enough experience with different vocational life styles that he can be confident that other ways of life are not as rewarding as the one he has chosen, thus avoiding the trap that affects so many workers. Finally, he has built a firm foundation of expectancies and self-esteem for himself: He has learned that he is good and that, if he works, he is likely to succeed at almost anything he tries.

Lonnie: Poor and Black

Lonnie, 19, has already been discussed in Chapter 5. It may be recalled that he is tall, thin, poor, and Black. He is also quite near-sighted. Thus, it was posited, he was insulated from the world of illegitimate opportunities surrounding him by being physically unable to take advantage of them.

His case is not quite that simple. It was mentioned that Lonnie is "a good boy." He did not become good *entirely* because he was tall, thin, and relatively weak during adolescence, although from a sociological point of view, these factors helped. Lonnie is also a first-born child. MacDonald (1969) presents convincing evidence that first born children, regardless of their sex, are "better socialized" than later born children. This is presumably due to the chance they have for interaction without competition with their primary socializing agents, their parents. Parents may try harder with first borns, coming as they do into parenthood with high ideals and a relatively strong sense of responsibility that may be attenuated for later children.[1]

Lonnie was an only child for two years, and received good mothering and fathering from both parents until his father's death. His father was a steady worker and, even though the couple had only a marginal income, his mother was able to stay home with the children until the father was killed in an industrial accident when Lonnie was 7 years old. There was sufficient compensation that the family has always had a small buffer against actual want and has not had to go on welfare, even though their living has been very meager. After the father's death, the mother maintained an on-going and quite accurate image of him as a good, steady man and a good provider. Her second marriage was not successful, partly because of her enshrinement of her first husband. This marriage, contracted when Lonnie was 9, lasted only two years, and she has not subsequently taken any courtship interest in men, although she is an attractive woman. There are four living children from the first and two from the second marriage.

Lonnie's stepfather introduced him to the world of work, setting him up as a shoeshine boy outside the fashionable restaurant in which he worked. He served as the boy's protector. In the later evenings, after the shoeshine work slacked off, he brought Lonnie into the kitchen world of the restaurant, He and the boy continued to be friendly after the marriage with Lonnie's mother broke up and Lonnie, before he became adolescent, moved from the thankless shoeshine job to easier and more congenial work in the restaurant. He picked up role-and-regional appropriate "Yes sir," "No ma'am" skills, learned to balance trays, became sensitive to customers' needs, grew adept with a warm, polite, flashing smile, was punctual and did not loaf on the job, moved to his present cafeteria, and now, although one of the youngest men, substitutes as headwaiter on the headwaiter's day off. In the large Southern city where Lonnie lives, trays are carried by waiters in most cafeterias; the low wages of the waiters are supplemented by small tips given after the contents of the tray have been placed on the table before the customer. Regular customers soon come to know the waiters and, when they receive extra service or their needs for refills are anticipated politely, typically tip more generously.

Lonnie's amiable and hard working ways have won him the liking of the cafeteria manager, who has urged him to go on with his education. Lonnie is now taking business courses in the urban downtown college, and, as stated in Chapter 5, if given an even break, he will very likely become a middle-class, white collar worker within a few years. While he has not confided this to Lonnie, the cafeteria manager has determined to integrate his office and cashier staff and, when the time is ripe, plans to use Lonnie as his first experiment in this direction.

[1]This attenuation, if it exists, may be due to nothing more than lack of time. The novelty of child rearing also wears off after the first child.

Lonnie illustrates how community characteristics may influence job satisfaction (see Hulin, 1966). Lonnie, unlike Carrie above, sees his service occupation as satisfactory. It offers him much more than money and socialization, and he does not feel that it was the only sort of job he could get. Hulin states:

> ... a worker's feelings of satisfaction do not arise out of context. Rather, the worker evaluates his present position in the context of the alternatives open to him. If he lives in a slum, in a poor community, or in a community in which there is a great deal of unemployment, even if he has a relatively poor job, he is probably better off than any of his neighbors.

Lonnie, a poor Black slum boy, has a better job than most of his peers. While the cafeteria manager's estimable dreams have not been made known to him, it has been made clear to him that he is a good boy who may make something of himself.

At this time in his life, Lonnie's work, peer, and home worlds mesh together very differently from, but as well as they do for, Nedra. He is succeeding vocationally, and, both objectively and subjectively, seems to be on the way up in the world. He enjoys an amiable, bantering relationship with his fellow waiters, but socializes little with them. Much of his social life is spent with the headwaiter who has, in a sense, adopted him and often includes him as a guest in his home. After college classes, he mixes pleasantly but superficially with some of his classmates.

His steadiness, combined with being the eldest son in a mother-headed household, gives him authority and status at home at least equal and in some ways superior to his mother's, since he seems to be upwardly mobile and she is vocationally fixed at the unskilled level. He exerts a strong, firmly benevolent authority over his younger brothers and sisters; and his mother makes few moves without consulting him. He does not date at all, but has an informal liaison with a woman in the same apartment building whose husband works different hours from Lonnie's work and classes. This arrangement seems to be carried out with maximum satisfaction and minimum conflict for both partners. Lonnie's mother regards the relationship with an uneasy mixture of tight-lipped disapproval and resignation, and has not made an issue of it.

RESULTS OF ADOLESCENT WORK EXPERIENCES

The recounting of the work experiences of these four 18 to 20 years olds suggests the great variety of results that accrue from working. It is obvious from the discussion that for each of the four *work for pay serves as an important bridge between childhood and full adult status.*

Specifically, at least eleven different results from working are illustrated by their four different patterns of work experience.

First, each individual has gained in personal autonomy: taking responsibility for his own behavior, independently of his parents. Nedra, Doug, and Lonnie were introduced to work by their parents, a frequent, even typical circumstance for this culture. Only Carrie went out entirely on her own to find her first job, although, by the time their life experiences were set down above, both Doug and Lonnie had secured jobs independently. But their performances on their jobs, regardless of how the jobs have been obtained, have been largely free from parental supervision. Carrie's mother has never known anything of her daughter's work except its general nature. Lonnie's stepfather provided loose supervision in his earlier working days as shoeshine boy and apprentice kitchen helper, but for the past two years has played no role. Nedra's parents keep themselves informed of how she is doing, but do not interfere. Doug's parents are sometimes able to inquire about how he makes out on the job, but only when he is working for friends. His door-to-door sales job and his upcoming summer "social welfare" job are entirely outside their ken.

The "weaning process," then, is clearly illustrated by these young people, and is common for adolescents in American society.

Second, the four youths have received considerable satisfaction as well as both a *feeling of independence* and *real independence* through their earnings. However, only Lonnie and Carrie have depended on their work for full support and, even in their cases, their money has gone further because they remained at home. For three of the four, income from their jobs has made future training and vocational advancement more concrete and possible, at least psychologically. Doug, prosperous though his family is, says he is more deeply interested in his career because he has made some financial contributions toward it. Nedra, too, says she will appreciate college more because she will be paying for part of it.

Third, their jobs have supplemented their social lives, made them more independent from and broader than their high school or college social group would have permitted. To be sure, neither Lonnie nor Carrie has a wide circle of friends, and it is debatable whether the friends Carrie has made are "good for her." But, without her work, she quite literally would have no friends. Lonnie's closest friends, the headwaiter and his wife, serve almost as a part of the kinship circle, and their influence is benign. Nedra and Doug, while not intimate with the friends they have made at work, feel that they are better people for having made such friends.

This third "broadening" outcome of working leads to the fourth and fifth, closely related, outcomes. Fourth, all four youngsters have become more flexible people from their work experiences. Nedra and Doug have to some degree been shaken from their protected, middle- and upper-middle-class nests by being with the working classes, and with customers and clients of all types. Lonnie has learned economically useful middle-class ways and incorporated them adaptively into his personal repertoire. He blends fairly easily into the upward mobile group of young and not so young people going to evening classes at his urban college. He eschews the slick tight clothes of his lower-class peers, dressing casually but rather conservatively for his age and ethnic group. While this is not good in any socially absolute sense, it is adaptive for Lonnie's purposes, which by now clearly include upward social mobility. For good or ill, Carrie has learned to wear a social veneer that hides the complex, insecure and frightened, often surly "true Carrie." For her purposes, too, this is adaptive. In other words, all four youngsters have learned considerable role flexibility from their job experiences. But Carrie may have lost innocence; Lonnie, *soul*.

Fifth, as part of this role flexibility, they have learned the manners and social skills that smooth the way, often artificially, for adult living. Carrie and Lonnie, Lonnie more effectively than Carrie because he puts more heart in it, know how to give service so as to increase tips, and, in Lonnie's case, obtain advancement. For less immediately obvious reasons, Nedra and Doug, also, have learned how to please people, and to conduct themselves without appearing to be snobs.

Carrie has become adept at attracting men so as to further her ends: going out on the town to have fun, and, possibly, keeping the jealous interest of her principal boy friend.

Sixth, all four youngsters have learned to live with the remorseless routines and within the power hierarchy that accompany being an adult in this scheduled world. They have learned to be punctual, to engineer themselves so as to accomplish what must be accomplished on their work shifts, to control their tempers rather than flare up in order to keep their jobs, to fit their work styles with those of their working peers, to bend their own wills to the needs of the job and the demands of the boss. Although these adjustments are not happy by any means, within limits they are necessary. A certain degree of conformity in the interests of long range personal goals is essential for most people. Of the four young people, only Carrie is without any real life plan (although Lonnie's plans are hazy). What Doug, Lonnie, and Nedra would probably say if one asked them is that they view what they are giving up now as an investment leading to worthwhile future gains.

However, for adolescents (or adults) with no future higher feasible vocational goals, the sacrifice of individuality demanded by jobs—often all levels of jobs—may indeed be demeaning. The stereotyped "corporation man" is perhaps as likely as the garbage man to sacrifice the things that make living worthwhile in the interests of advancing in his job, or even of holding on to it.

Seventh, Doug and Lonnie, at least, are obtaining relevant training for their future careers. Doug's work in a physiology lab gives him a valuable foundation for his later career as a Ph.D. university physiologist. Lonnie's experience on the line in the cafeteria and, previously, in the kitchen of the restaurant should add substantially to the future in restaurant work ahead if all goes well for him, and if his manager's half-formed plans work out. Direct applications of Carrie's and Nedra's jobs to their later lives are less clear. This may be generally true for girls. That it is, is suggested by Douvan and Adelson's analysis of the different life goals of boys and girls (see Chapter 1).

Eighth, and for Doug only, his upcoming summer social welfare job contributes to his image of himself as a "good," altruistic member of an interlinked society. Helping the underprivileged helps him to think of himself as a good person.

Ninth, the self concept of each of these young people has been made firm and enhanced. This is true even for Carrie, whose work experience has been the least positive of the four. Each has tested himself against others in a competitive situation, where results have ranged from adequate (in Carrie's case) to excellent, in the case of the other three. Since his experiences have ranged most widely and his successes have been most dramatic, and since he is the oldest of the four, the effects are clearest for Doug, but, considering the place where he started, they have been most dramatic for Lonnie. Quite literally, Lonnie seems about to emerge from the ranks of the disadvantaged into the company of the advantaged. He may be able to pull his younger brothers and sisters with him, as well as give his mother a security in her old age that she would not likely have known otherwise.

Tenth, even as their self concepts have been firmed and enhanced, they have been broadened. This has been documented above in the discussion of points four, five, and six.

Finally, the provisional-try nature of work for adolescents is illustrated. Three of the four of these young people have enjoyed the psychosocial moratorium discussed earlier: protection by their caretakers from irrevocable commitment to adult life—including their own mistakes—that is typically provided by middle-class parents. This is very obvious in the cases of Doug and Nedra, less striking for Lonnie. But Lonnie had a protector at a time when he needed one. The stepfather found him his first job, helped him stake out his shoeshine territory, stood behind him if other more muscular boys threatened to pre-empt it, introduced him to the kitchen of a good restaurant and thus, although not with clear intent, opened a door for a vocationally more rewarding life that would probably have been impossible otherwise.[2]

Only Carrie has had no protector. True, her older brother will shield her, at least for a time, from dramatic catastrophe. But she has had to plunge from being a little girl to the rugged life of waitressing in a tough cafe. She has had no time to experiment with the feelings and emotions of adolescence. Early in her sexual exploration, she became pregnant and was subjected to the traumatic experience of an abortion. Nor does there seem to be an optimistic future to her major courtship interest—a married man who seems to have no intention of ever breaking up his marriage.

Carrie is almost certainly a more accurate representation of her social class than Lonnie. Her work is *not* rewarding. Going to work at too young an age and in harsh circumstances has very possibly plunged her into adulthood beyond her depth. Her later life, either in the context of interpersonal relations or vocational experiences, does not seem any more promising than her present fashion of getting along from day to day.

THE NONCONFORMERS

Carrie, Nedra, Doug, and Lonnie are conforming young people to the degree that they accept the middle-class core ethic of getting an education and working at a job. Even Carrie, marginal and rebellious student that she is, accepts the need for a high school diploma. Doug and Lonnie, the former with clearer plans than the latter, accept the ethic that a man works hard and thus moves up the ladder, faster and more congenially if he is well educated. Carrie does her work well enough not to get fired; the other three young people are excellent, conscientious workers.

It was made clear in Chapter 6 that conformity in educational and

[2]For every Lonnie, of course, there are probably scores of other similar boys, Black and white, who do not enjoy such a moratorium, and who go under.

vocational matters is partly a function of the legitimate opportunities that are available to young people. For example, McCandless, Persons, and Roberts (1969), exploring Cloward and Ohlin's (1960) theory that was summarized in Chapter 6, have found that even among a group of disadvantaged, legally committed 15- to 17-year-old delinquents, the amount of admitted delinquency correlates −.42 with the degree of legitimate opportunity the boys see as being available to them in their communities. For white boys, perhaps closer to the core values of the community, this correlation rises to −.58.

One type of nonconformer, then, is the youth who sees conventional doors to vocational security and advancement closed to him. Such a youth may become delinquent or (as many do) may seek escape into drifting, alcohol, and even drugs. Delinquency may follow addiction, if the addiction becomes such that the person can not support it by legal means. Such youth, almost by definition, are more frequent among the disadvantaged, and, among the disadvantaged, are almost certainly most frequent among the minority groups that are discriminated against. It is hardly surprising that there is a high delinquency rate among disadvantaged young Black males. Society on the one hand has provided no legitimate opportunities for advancement; on the other, it has provided many apparently successful delinquent and criminal models, partly because it has created ghettos that are segregated both racially and economically. Society has lost power over the young to a considerable degree, because it has provided insufficient positive rewards for youth, and because either it has failed to exercise effective punishment or its efforts at punishment are no longer feared by the youth toward whom they are directed (see Chapters 11, 12, and 13).

Delinquents Delinquency is by no means uncommon among youth who possess bountiful legitimate opportunities (for example, Roff and Sells, 1968). By the time they are 18, most boys and a substantial proportion of girls have committed at least one offense that, had it been detected or had the law followed through, would have led to formal legal punishment. Such youth, presumably, see their legitimate and *desirable* opportunities as being so far in the future as to be, in effect, unavailable. Partly because of frustration, partly from boredom, and partly because of temptation to conquer, they have committed a delinquent act, often a very serious one.

Relatively bright delinquent youngsters have escaped detection. Many others, those who come from homes with influence, have been let off once caught.

Middle-class delinquency compared with the delinquency of the disadvantaged is much more likely to be one shot, although often as serious. Delinquency among disadvantaged youth may or may not be accompanied by other signs of poor personal adjustment and, at least among boys, is *not* strongly related to whether or not a boy is liked by his peers. Persistent middle-class delinquents are more likely to be maladjusted in other ways, and are less likely to be well thought of by their peer group (Roff and Sells, 1968). The topic of delinquency is more formally discussed in Chapter 13.

Alienated Nondelinquents Less frequent than disadvantaged, alienated youth are alienated advantaged youth. Two highly publicized generations—first of beatniks, then of hippies—tuned themselves out of their milieu, and actually "dropped out" of society. Such youngsters, as a group, seem to have been middle- and upper-middle class in social origin, were (and are) bright and literate, and, with greater frequency than would be expected by chance, come from liberal and permissive homes headed by people who live rather easily and successfully by the book. These young people, on the whole, seem to be rather gentle and possessed of high ideals. Many have chosen to remain within college settings and have shown considerable activity that has often turned into violence in fighting the system that has alienated them. This battle seems to be moving from the colleges into the high schools. If the picture of high schools drawn in Chapters 8 and 9 is accurate, more and not less such rebellion may be expected.

There seems to have been little union for action between white advantaged alienated youth and alienated disadvantaged youth. The socioeconomic chasm has not been effectively bridged. For the peace of society, this is probably just as well, although, if one listens, alienated youth of any social class have much that is worthwhile to tell.

Middle-class and disadvantaged Black youth seem more to be able to unite for action programs. Black militancy is by no means confined to either the disadvantaged or the advantaged. The bond may be the mutuality of discrimination that all Black youth know, or it may be a function of urban ghettos, where middle-class Black youth are more likely to rub shoulders with truly disadvantaged young Blacks than is true for their white counterparts. Both factors probably operate. The passive dropping out of the hippy seems not to be frequent among minority group young people. Perhaps, not having drunk so deeply at the well of affluence, they choose to fight for what they do not have rather than give up those comforts with which they have not yet had the chance to become disenchanted.

Advantaged nonconformers include the drop-outs. These young people seem to have decided that the many benefits, most particularly the material benefits, of the system are not worth the cost. It is easy to see the price their middle aged parents and society's power figures have paid, and the social muddles they have produced: public responsibility and private corruption, high incidence of unhappy and broken marriages, borderline or full alcoholism, poverty and superficiality in personal–social relations, wars that a large proportion of the most intelligent and articulate citizens of the society deplore, an unfair draft system, vocational advancement through influence, discrimination by one segment of society against another, pollution of natural resources, and so on, almost indefinitely. In Chapter 7, cognitive and developmental theory was presented, and it is useful in understanding the shock and rage of the young about the often glaring faults of even the best society.

It seems fair to say that the drop-outs have decided that there is little that they as individuals can do, and that in the face of overwhelming odds against their efforts, or even their "happy" survival, it may be best simply to retreat. Theirs seems to be a hedonistic adjustment, understandable, often personally rewarding, and socially nonconstructive. It is also fair to say that such young people as individuals and groups do little if any harm to society, and that on the whole they are more sinned against than sinning.

Other alienated young people, more of them college than high school age, partially drop out of the system but fight it. Many Students for a Democratic Society, many "yippies," many belonging to some of the Black militant groups have chosen such a path. Since violent action breeds counteraction, their revolutionary efforts may provoke a strong and potentially dangerous shift to the right, whose adherents seek to maintain their version of the status quo. Some alienated young people say that society is so corrupt that their only hope is to destroy it and then rebuild it. Their elders find them short in ideas about such rebuilding, and are concerned, even fearful, about the social repression they incite. On the other hand, liberals, with their endemic fear of confrontation, have left many festering social sores still to be tended. If indeed man is more naked ape than fallen angel, perhaps revolution or near revolution is required to save him.

More appealing to most Americans are the realistically somewhat disenchanted but still optimistic youth (again, concentrated among the college ages) who seek by spirited protest and vigorous but nonviolent action to change the system while remaining a functioning part of it. One hopes, wistfully and anxiously, that their elders as well as their peers will have the sense to listen to them, that society will exert its power over them wisely and keep them as a vital, growing part of it, and that their leadership in constructive change will benefit not only them but all society. A majority of reasonably well-educated, thoughtful young people from all the major groups in American society seem to cluster around this midpoint of reform-minded common sense.

Delinquent youth and youth who have dropped out may be thought of as vocational drifters. The great majority of nondelinquent disadvantaged youth, perhaps almost all of those who follow lines of work that demand no skills, also illustrate vocational drift. Revolutionary (as opposed to radical and liberal) youth often let vocational training slip by as they pursue their vigorous, even violent, social aims, although some combine both activities. Most of the radicals and liberals accept the necessity for vocational planning, and envision conventional work careers for themselves, although many plan to continue vigorous *avocational* social action.

THE MEANING OF WORK

The lives of Nedra, Carrie, Doug, and Lonnie have shown what types of meaning work may have for different young people of somewhat different ages, different sexes, different socioeconomic classes, and different skin colors. It is now well to explore the more general meaning of work in this culture.

United States culture is capitalistic, competitive, preponderantly Christian (at least in name), republican, heavily urban and suburban, and strongly oriented toward technology, efficiency, management and government, and professionalism. The prestige of occupations (see Chapter 8) reflects the culture: The six high occupational status slots are held by U.S. Supreme Court Justice, physician, nuclear physicist, scientist in general, government scientist, and state governor. The six low ranks, from the lowest, are occupied by shoeshiner, streetsweeper, garbage collector, sharecropper, soda fountain clerk, and clothes presser in a laundry (Hodge, Siegel, and Rossi, 1968).

In a culture like this, with no formal inherited aristocracy and a strong pioneer tradition, which gives more than lip service to folk sayings such as "The devil finds work for idle hands to do," and in which the adjective "shiftless" is a fighting word, people should expect work to possess a value far over and above that of earning money by which to live.

Work Leads to Adulthood

For the adult, the world of work is the arena in which he displays his competence. For the child, the world of school is such an arena. Adolescents—most particularly male adolescents—fall somewhere between children and adults in this respect. The meanings of work to the four adolescents discussed earlier in this chapter were a complex blend of utilitarian, social, and personal values.

Morse and Weiss (1968) interviewed a random sample of 401 American men about their work. Unique to these men's working lives—not available to them elsewhere—was the fact that "Working gives them a feeling of being tied into the larger society, of having something to do, of having a purpose in life." (p. 8)

When asked the question, "If by some chance you inherited enough money to live comfortably without working, do you think you would work anyway or not?" an overwhelming majority of 80 percent answered that they would indeed continue to work (p. 8).

Morse and Weiss report that two-thirds of the men give positive reasons for wanting to continue working, such as to keep occupied and interested, to keep healthy, because work is good for one, and because they enjoyed their work. But a distressing one-third give only negative reasons, which illustrate the lack of inner resources for which Americans are so often criticized by others. Such men would "feel lost" if they did not work, "go crazy with idleness," and "not know what to do" with their time. These negative answers, Morse and Weiss believe, suggest that many work to ward off the dangers of loneliness and isolation (p. 9). Fourteen percent of Morse and Weiss' total sample expressed fears that they would be lost or go crazy if they did not work. Thus, these authors conclude that work is an important and even crucial positive element in the emotional lives of many, since it is the means by which they are anchored to the society. For many, it is the only meaningful anchor they have.

If work is so indispensable an earmark of adulthood, it follows logically that adolescents are eager to enter the work world. As seen in Chapter 9, boys are likely to be particularly eager, as work offers them a chance to gain the autonomy and independence from school and parental authority that they so sorely need and urgently desire.

Under the right conditions—and these vary enormously—work provides a useful bridge between the world of school and world of full time vocation. Researchers have only begun to explore the relations between the work or vocational world and the school or educational world. Generally a sharp, unnecessary, and artificial distinction is drawn between them, with the result being a loss to both.

During the years he worked at the Wayne County Training School, the author visited with many boys who had left the school on parole, had taken jobs in industry or service, and had returned to the campus for a friendly visit. When these boys had gone on parole, they had been functional illiterates (reading at perhaps a third grade level). When they returned a year or so later to visit, most of them were reading at the sixth or seventh grade level, well enough to follow a newspaper reasonably well. Whenever he could, the author asked most of them how it happened that they had learned to read in so short a time. (The average boy entered the Training School at age 13 after eight or nine years in the Detroit public or parochial schools, and stayed at the Training School for three years. The average IQ of parolees was about 80, officially "dull normal.")

The standard answer, repeated by each boy, was: "I never realized it was so important to read until I went to work." Boys had suffered embarrassment because they could not read their union contracts, could not read the instructions for assembling machinery or delivering goods, could not follow directions that had been left for them in the form of notes, and so on. Thus embarrassed—threatened both by the exposure of illiteracy with an accompanying loss of status and by the job handicaps—the boys had simply sat down and learned to read *on their own*. Few had resorted to tutors. This, of course, suggests that they had learned *something* during their years of school, otherwise self-tutelage would not have worked.

The complaint that school is unreal and irrelevant to the world of work can be alleviated if work experiences are tied to school. The mechanics of this plan should not be too difficult to work out: Half-day school, perhaps one semester a year, coupled with half-day work, may well serve to point out the very real connection between a good education and vocational competence. Relevant motivation will thus be fed into the interaction of the boy or girl and school, and increased competence will be entered into the relationship of the boy or girl with his work. Such linkage may be particularly important for underachieving and disadvantaged youth; but the interrelation may be equally useful to the "elite," of whom Doug is an example.

Colleges and universities where this pairing is exercised have been successful. It may be significant that, at the time of writing, no dramatic unrest has been reported from any such campus to the author's knowledge. Early exposure to work is also often a real incentive to pursue the career. An unpublished study of teacher education (F. Wilhelms, 1964) suggests that the most effective factor in enlisting teachers and keeping them in the field is exposure very early in their training to the actual teaching experience.

Rewards from Work   Additional findings of the Morse and Weiss study suggest that the need for work for work's sake more often characterizes men at higher than lower occupational levels. This is by no means surprising. But even of those at the lowest levels of job prestige—unskilled workers—50 percent would want to continue working even if they inherited enough money to live comfortably the rest of their lives. For them, as has been mentioned earlier, the satisfactions of work are often social (about one-third of all men in the interview sample stressed social aspects of their jobs as the most rewarding component. This was particularly true of the service occupations).

There is, of course, a sharp difference in style between white and blue collar jobs. The former typically stress verbal and conceptual skills; the latter physical skills (or simply brute labor). The white collar jobs involve interactions with people, blue collar jobs are more likely mainly to involve interactions with tools and things. The service occupations may also involve high level technical skills, but usually also include much interpersonal occupation.

In line with these occupational characteristics, Morse and Weiss find that workers emphasize as their sources of enjoyment a sense of accomplishment coming from a job well done, and the interest they take in their jobs. Working-class men are more likely to stress that they need some directed activity to fill their time. For the middle class, jobs provide purpose, stimulation, and challenge. For the working class, jobs provide activity. Morse and Weiss also find that for farmers and middle-class occupations, particularly professions, jobs are much more important than they are to working-class men.

While most men (80 percent) say they like their jobs, their reasons vary widely. Money seems especially important to managers, while the content of the job is the important thing to professional men. Sales people likewise stress the content of the job itself. Craftsmen and tradesmen like the kind of work they do, but the unskilled stress the money they earn. Service people like the people they work with and meet, but are likely to mention that the job is the only sort they could get (this was mentioned earlier in connection with Carrie's work).

Data for women similar to the Morse and Weiss report for men do not exist in the same complete form. The working picture for women is complicated by their more complex reasons for working. Some women work simply to fill the time between graduating or dropping out from high school, or college, and marriage. If they can be self-supporting and save money toward their future during this period, so much the better. Girls and women, like boys and men, may work to be autonomous and independent, and these motives are as strong for many females as for males. Wives work to add savings until their first baby comes, or to buy furniture, or to be ahead on the down payment for a home. In times of financial duress, wives may go to work to help out. Many women with older children, like Doug's mother, become bored and restless and resume earlier careers for a mixture of motives, the predominant ones probably differing little from those found for men in similar occupations. Many women work simply because they must: Their husbands' incomes simply do not meet the family's minimum needs; or there is no husband for one reason or another. A relatively small proportion of women are true career women. Some who have never married fall into this role not entirely by their own choice. Others stick at their jobs through thick and thin, interrupting their work only for relatively short maternity leaves.

This is more true for professional than nonprofessional women, and is particularly characteristic of Afro-American women (Goldstein, 1967).

THEORIES ABOUT CAREER DEVELOPMENT

Zytowski (1968) has assembled a wide variety of research and theoretical papers concerning theories of the meaning of work and the determinants of choice and success in work. It is interesting but not entirely encouraging to read through the pages of his book. If, as seems to be the case, work is so important to at least 80 percent of American men that they would continue to work even if they had an income sufficient to meet all their needs, then why have research workers devoted relatively so little time and attention to factors of vocational selection, job morale, the fits of jobs to boys and men, girls and women, the meaning of work to workers, and ways to make men and women happier on their jobs? In a society so "magnificently technological" as this, why has the human factor been relatively neglected?

No clear answer to these questions emerges.

Trent and Medsker (1968) present data that dramatically if depressingly underscore this puzzlement. Their book (*Beyond High School: A Psychosociological Study of 10,000 High School Graduates*) should be required reading for all concerned with counseling in junior and senior high schools. The book is, of course, far too long, complex, and packed with data to review here, but it is most worth reading.

Evidence is overwhelming that most high school students leave high school with inadequate background to help them move toward any sort of objective that they have thought through and developed on their own. They are the students—and many of them are very able indeed—who become the victims of vocational drift.

The conclusion is inescapable that theories of vocational development and selection fit, and even then not too well, principally those students who are attending college and for whom college graduation is a realistic possibility. This group includes perhaps 10 percent of American youth, and this may be a generous estimate.

Osipow (1968), whose *Theories of Career Development* should be read by those interested in pursuing in more depth the topics taken up in this chapter, summarizes the criticisms of career development theory. First, he believes, "The theories appear to be much too broad in scope and generally too skimpy in detail. What vocational psychology needs at the present time is a collection of miniature theories, each dealing with circumscribed, explicit segments of vocational behavior, to be woven into a broad theory after the smaller theories have been shaped by empirical findings" (p. 247).

Second, Osipow questions the assumption that everyone wants to work. Although Morse and Weiss' data, cited earlier, suggest that almost all men do, the growing emphasis on "being," particularly among the intelligent and well-educated young, suggests that this may not always be the case.

Third, Osipow notes that "Few special explanations or concepts have been devised to deal with the special problems of the career development of women" (p. 247). As has been noted, there are simply too many women who work or want to work for their needs to be neglected.

Osipow opts for a developmental theory of vocational behavior and career development, in which a growth pattern not unlike that described in Chapter 7 for cognitive development occurs. However, he grants that in a developmental theory, the role of social forces and accidental factors is likely to be neglected.

Even though current theories are incomplete, it is well to look briefly at selected examples of vocational theory. In psychoanalytic theory, an earnest effort is made to relate personality development and type to vocational behavior.

Psychoanalytic Theories

Neff (1968) draws implications from psychoanalytic theory about the meaning of work. Psychoanalysis stresses the fact that working efficiently and reasonably contentedly is one aspect of good adjustment. Working represents conformity to the reality rather than the pleasure principle. Within such theory, it seems likely, it will be reasoned that one will be happiest in the career that fits his personality structure and his dynamically determined needs. For example, girls who may have been (at least by their perceptions) deprived of enough love when they were growing up may, in an abstract, compensating or sublimating or displacing fashion (the mechanism is by no means clear), want to give others the love they believed they were denied. Thus they may go into teaching because of a special interest in young children, or into nursing. This may also give them what they think they missed (albeit not consciously, perhaps): abundant love from their charges. Little boys frightened of their own aggressive impulses as children, but with such impulses still present in a hydraulic sort of way, may channel them off in socially acceptable—even constructive—ways as surgeons. The very young child who received great rewards for successfully staying clean and dry may develop a strong predilection for neatness and order, and happily translate such habits into a successful career as a certified public accountant or an art critic or electronics engineer.

As a group, however, psychoanalytic theorists have not often devoted their attention to selection of a vocation and adjustment to it. In an indirect way, psychoanalytic theory may have been useful to one's thinking about the world of work. In such theory notions of need fulfillment are stressed, and few will argue but that a person's needs should be considered in his choice of a vocation, and that a very large part of his satisfaction with his work and thus of his life may depend on the degree to which his work satisfies his major motives.

Erikson (1963), who conceives of the life of man as consisting of eight stages or psychosocial crises, devotes one stage to the psychosocial crisis of learning to work realistically and taking enjoyment from one's industry. His fourth stage of man is *learning industry as opposed to inferiority*. This stage begins, Erikson thinks, when the primitive instincts of childhood have been partially mastered—at 6 or 7 years of age—and extends on into adolescence. Constantinople (1969) finds that a substantial proportion of sampled college men and women are still struggling with this stage of psychosocial development, and that they make considerable progress in resolving it—particularly the men in her sample—during their college years.

One needs only to introspect briefly to realize that this particular psychosocial crisis is perhaps never totally resolved: How many individuals put off what at an intellectual level they *know* must be done, until the time grows so late that they do it sloppily? Many. How many consistently do the "chores" of life first so that they may relax later and at the optimally appropriate time? Probably few. However, with the high premium placed on work in American life, the opposite approach also has its representatives: the man who neglects his wife and children for his job; the woman who values a clean and orderly house to such a degree that she sets up an atmosphere in which her husband is uncomfortable. Many secondary school students are so hag-ridden with pressures to make grades so they can get into the "right school" that they lead only half-lives. Every college and professional school includes overachievers who have no time to stop and savor the essential immediate pleasures of living.

Erikson believes this stage of man is best resolved by the choice of industry over inferiority. Thus, he stresses the joy that well-adjusted people should take in a job well done. He believes that well brought up children who have passed through the earlier crises in their personal–social development rather effortlessly take pleasure in the tasks of preadolescence and adolescence: learning to read and handle numbers, to think abstractly and logically, to handle tools to build something or ingredients to make a cake. Enjoyment of such mastery in school, he believes (by implication), is then translated into an appropriate pleasure in one's vocation.

R. W. White (1959) has also made a significant although indirect contribution to the theory of vocational choice and adjustment. He posits, in addition to the other more typically named drives that motivate man, a drive for *effectance*. In infancy and early childhood, this is manifested in the joys children so obviously take in learning to control their bodies, in building with blocks, in working with clay, in riding tricycles and bicycles. This same pleasure in effectance should characterize schoolwork and, later, formal jobs.

For such neoanalysts as White and Erikson, then, an appropriate pleasure in work is one important part of being a well-adjusted human being. This is a sensible concept in American culture.

Social Development Theories

Roe (1956, 1968, for example) combines psychoanalytic theory with learning theory to predict that the nature of childhood experiences is the most important occupational determinant. To her, the most meaningful dimensions of early childhood experiences concern parental treatment. First, what are the types of emotional concentration in the parent–child relationship? Roe believes these range from overprotectiveness on the one hand to overdemandingness on the other.

The second dimension ranges from warm acceptance to avoidance of the child. Avoidance may be of two types, emotional rejection (which is not necessarily accompanied by neglect) and neglect. The third dimension that Roe believes is important as an occupational determinant is whether or not the child is accepted. The central factor in acceptance is warmth, which may range from *casual* to loving acceptance.

In the basic sense, Roe believes that patterns of early childhood experience either turn people on as far as other people are concerned, or turn them off. The individual who is strongly pro-people is likely to be happiest in a people-oriented occupation, such as service, business contact, general cultural work, or arts and entertainment. Those who are not people oriented are likely to be happier in technology, outdoor lines of work, or science. Her eighth category of occupations—organizations—includes many people who are pro-other people.

Roe's position is plausible but, like analytic theory, is exceptionally broad. For many reasons, her predictions are difficult to test. Among the major difficulties is that reporting on the atmosphere of one's home is subject to all sorts of error, as was discussed in Chapter 2. Thus, when the theory has been tested as, for example, Green and Parker (1965), Powell (1960), and Switzer, *et al.* (1962) have done, it has not fared particularly well. It may be far simpler to determine reasons for vocational choice and adjustment in the here and now, without worrying about how the person was reared, and simply by asking the relevant questions. It is self-evident that one who does not like people will not do well in service or sales or, if he hides his true self and *does* succeed, will do so only at a severe personal cost. One who is as gregarious as a starling obviously is not going to be very content as a forest ranger. One who cannot endure emergencies or stand the sight of blood has no business being a physician. The woman who dislikes children should not go into teaching, at least not of young children. A research or cashier's job is no place for one who dislikes and is nervous about numbers.

DETERMINANTS OF VOCATIONAL CHOICE

It is evident from the foregoing selection of theories that vocational choice is so complicated that no single theory can account for it satisfactorily, as Osipow comments. Vocational choice is often unrelated to one's volition. A large number of boys, for example, choose their fathers' occupations (Jenson and Kirchner, 1955). Modeling and power theory undoubtedly account for some of this, but simple availability and expediency also play an important part. If a boy will inherit his father's farm, it is easier for him to be a farmer than an accountant. He will also probably please his father and mother. He does not need to be fanatical about the agricultural way of life to make his choice to farm.

If one's father is in the building trades, there is usually an apprentice's place open for him, and gaining an apprenticeship is a big part of the battle.

If the father is uneducated and unskilled, the odds are great that his son will not have available to him any other way of earning a living. If one's father is uneducated, unskilled, and Black, upward mobility is even more restricted.

Blau, *et al.* (1968) have treated occupational choice with a realistic eye to the complexity of the situation, and their schematization is worth discussing in some detail. The five authors represent different areas of study, thus bring a multidisciplinary point of view to bear on this topic.

Native Endowment

A basic determinant, *for the individual*, is his native endowment. Chapter 5 showed how such factors as physique and time of maturation can affect the course of one's life. Had Wilt "The Stilt" Chamberlain been 5 feet 6 inches rather than 7 feet 1 inch tall, it is unlikely that he would have reached the international eminence in basketball that he has attained. Few women become jockeys.

The Social Structure The individual operates within the social structure of his country. The United States, in theory, is an open society and any occupational level is open to any boy or girl. Since the American origins were in pioneering and farming, physical labor carries with it no disgrace (except that *having* to earn one's living that way is poorly regarded, at least by the middle class), and many individuals take up farming or gardening as a hobby. But in developing countries, probably particularly those with colonial histories, working with one's hands is a sign of low status. The aspiration of every village boy, for example, is to be a clerk – a civil servant. Thus, the society is clogged with clerks, accountants, lawyers, and other would-be government functionaries. Much of the unrest among the youth in the developing nations is due to the lack of jobs (as there would be in more technological societies) for the administrative man. These young people have struggled for their educations, then find there are no jobs. A major study was conducted, for example, by the government of Pakistan in the 1960s in an effort, first to find out why Pakistani youth disliked manual work so heartily; and second, how they could be induced to do it. The economic health of the nation quite clearly depended on inducing a greater proportion of its youth to take up employment as farmers, skilled tradesmen, mechanics, and so on.

The resources, topography, and climate of a country or area obviously affect the vocations of people living there. There are few mining engineers in the Bronx, few fishermen in the Sahara, and so on. New Jersey needs more industrial foremen than New Mexico does, both relatively and absolutely.

In a depressed economy, there are fewer legitimate, more illegitimate, opportunities open to youth (see Chapter 6). The implications for vocational choice are obvious.

Personal Factors At the next level of specificity in determining occupational choice come the various factors that Blau and his colleagues group under personality development. These are the obvious factors of education and educability, type of socialization (conforming, nonconforming, for example), available financial resources, and family influences.

Social Trends Paralleling personal factors, but viewed from the perspective of social determination, are historical trends within the society. In 1960, the future was wide open for computer people. In 1969, a young man and particularly a young Black man with an advanced degree in African studies apparently had a brilliant career open to him. He would hardly have known how to go about finding a position in 1959. A half-century ago, the financial lot of miners of anthracite coal was among the best in the skilled trades. Today, it seems to be a dead end. Technological change, then, closes and opens doors. The most dramatic and socially and economically distressing vocational factor of this time is the point that has been repeatedly stressed in the preceding pages: Except for the service occupations, with the relatively modest demands on skill made by many of them, *the doors are inexorably closing for unskilled and semiskilled workers*. Agricultural technology has changed United States society to the point where only 7 percent of the population now live on farms (and an only slightly larger percentage is involved in agricultural work – the production of foodstuff), while at the turn of the century about half the population lived on farms. Estimates of the number of Black agricultural workers, for the most part ill educated and unskilled, who have come into the cities from the farms since World War II ranges as high as 8,000,000. Their incorporation into the urban culture of United States society is one of the most dramatic problems that exist today. Only slightly less rosy is the lot of perhaps an equal or a larger but less visible number of "poor whites" who have made the same migration during the same period.

Personal and Social Organization

At the next level of specificity preceding actual vocational choice and entry come personal sociopsychological attributes and socioeconomic organization. The individual brings to bear on the problem of vocational selection and entry not only his general level of knowledge (what the over-all job situation is like, what the historical trends are, where the future points) but his abilities and educational level. For the well educated and bright, there are many more choices than for the ill educated and dull. One's social position and relations are important. The higher his social status, the more influential his relatives, the wider the range of his opportunities. The WASP boy or girl is singularly advantaged, the Afro-American boy or girl singularly disadvantaged. Discrimination against Jews and Catholics is not so blatant, but it operates to close many doors to them.

Youths and adults bring with them many different orientations toward work life: The youngster who is willing to do anything as long as he sees a chance of its leading somewhere is more likely to be sooner placed in a job and to move up in it more rapidly than the one who sees it only as a means of getting by (recall Doug, for example). Of course, as Liebow (1966) has pointed out, many jobs are ill regarded by those who hold them. Many jobs, too, lead absolutely nowhere: Where is a Black youth who dropped out of high school in the tenth grade going by means of the dishwashing job he obtains? Where is Carrie going in the waitress job she has obtained? But Doug seems to be able to turn almost any type of job into grist for his mill. However, his other social and psychological attributes are very different from Carrie's. Lonnie, no world beater as a scholar, seems to be moving ahead.

Socioeconomic factors that parallel the person's sociopsychological attributes include such things as occupational distribution and rate of labor turnover: There is, today, little place for the city boy who wants to farm. The prestige building trades are typically filled by sons who follow their fathers. The cost of medical school is such that most doctors come from upper-middle-class families, and it seems that not as many boys and girls are admitted to medical schools as are needed fully to satisfy the United States' need for physicians. Until very recently, there was no place for a fashion model unless he or she was white. Black or Oriental actors were in short demand. People of the Jewish faith are usually not found among the ranks of college deans or presidents, or bank presidents. A beginning is only being made to open up equally the federal government to employment for all races, religions, colors, and creeds. Even so, an avowed atheist (for example) may have difficulty finding government employment, although the crime and treason rate among atheists is demonstrably low. During the time "baby boom" youth were pouring into college, any young man or woman with an advanced degree could find a college job almost literally by nodding his head. In the late 1960s and 1970s, with the cost of education rocketing and the crest of the baby boom subsiding, many bright young Ph.D.'s are hard put to it to find positions that satisfy either their desires or needs. In a time of recession, jobs of all sorts, and particularly lower echelon jobs, decrease in number. Adolescents, like Blacks, are typically the last hired and the first fired.

Immediate Vocational Choice Determinants Blau and his colleagues (1968) then move to a classification of the immediate determinants of occupational choice and entry. For the person concerned, these are his occupational information, his technical qualifications, his social role characteristics, and his reward value hierarchy.

Occupational Information and Qualification For the first, *occupational information*, the more a generally capable individual knows about occupations, their requirements, and his objective (and subjective) qualifications for them, the more freedom of movement he has in his vocational choice. Considering the present state of the art, providing such information is perhaps the most valuable function that guidance counselors can perform.

Concerning *technical qualifications*, it is obvious that a youth who is already trained for a slot will be more likely to obtain the job than one who is not trained. However, for many occupations, the necessary specific training can be gained on the job quite speedily and often on part and even full pay. Thus, as good a foundation a young person at the beginning of his vocational life can have is a sound, general education. The *generalist* can be trained to go in all sorts of specific directions; the *specialist* may find it more difficult to take the broad view or find the long range. Of course high level special skills are essential in a technological society: One cares much less about whether a mechanic knows Shakespeare than about his skill at diagnosing the current ailment of one's automobile; nor does one want a wide range generalist performing a kidney transplant.

Social Role Characteristics *Social role characteristics* also play an important part in determining occupational choice and entry. It is more prestigious—thus "desirable"—to be a physician, a scientist, or a Supreme Court Justice than to be a shoeshine boy or a business man. Teaching seems to be increasing in prestige; business and industry, declining. (Bankers, for example, declined 14 ranks within a total of 90 ranks between 1947 and 1963—Hodge, Siegel, and Rossi, 1968; while nuclear physicists went up 14.5 ranks during the same period. Public school instructors increased 6.5 ranks.)

An individual's notion of his own social role and his self concept is likely to influence his occupational choice in a very immediate sense. If he sees himself as dynamic and outgoing, he may go in the direction of sales; if shy, withdrawn, but a strong silent man, in the direction of forest ranger or, if at ease with children and not adults, into early childhood work.

Reward Value Hierarchies   Finally, the *reward value hierarchy* of the individual is important. If it is social prestige he wants, his choice may be an occupation with, for example, low pay as opposed to a less prestigious job with higher pay. If social interaction is important, he will choose a line of work where there is much interpersonal contact. If security is paramount, one line of work will be chosen, whereas if adventure and variety are high in the person's reward system, another field may be selected.

Objective Opportunity   Parallel to these immediate personal determinants, Blau and his colleagues list four principal social determinants. First, of course, is formal opportunity or demand. No one, or almost no one, wants a harness maker today, while every college wants an African Studies Ph.D., preferably Black, as has been mentioned.

Functional Requirements   Second, and equally obvious, are the *functional requirements* for the job. A vacancy for a computer man or woman can not be filled by one who does not know a data card; a girl who has had only beauty parlor experience will not qualify as a dental hygienist. For some jobs (despite laws to the contrary), only men are suitable, for others—generally for more subtle reasons—only women.

Nonfunctional Requirements   Third, and often subterranean, are the *nonfunctional requirements* for the job. These include such things as skin color, attractiveness–unattractiveness, age (there is a not well-founded reluctance to hire both older and very young workers that puts a real and often completely unfair hardship on both older and very young people), religion, "refinement," and a host of other variables, tangible and intangible. Prejudice against those too young and with no experience is very frequent, and often presents a real obstacle to youth. The advantages of good looks and good physique in reducing frustration were included in the conceptual framework of Chapter 1 and more specifically developed in Chapter 5. Being WASP, handsome or pretty, and with a good body assures one of many noncontingent positive reinforcements (quite unearned) in American society.

As a bemusing but not necessarily amusing phenomenon of these times, the current popularity of work with the disadvantaged is worth mentioning. This embraces the two points listed immediately above. Today, it is fashionable for well-adjusted, well-intended, well-brought-up, and well-educated youth to want to work with the disadvantaged, particularly with children and youth, and even more especially with

Black children. In one urban Head Start program the author knows there were 10,000 applications for summer positions from exceptionally well-qualified girls, most of whom were white (most of the Head Start pupils were Black), less than 100 from males, and none from Black males. Since a large proportion of the Head Start youngsters were fatherless and Afro-American, the need for summer teachers was greatest in precisely the category where the supply was least.

The Payoff The fourth and final immediate social determiner listed by Blau and his colleagues is the *amount and type of rewards* offered by the position. It is not necessarily the best paying job that attracts the most desirable applicants, although money is exceptionally important in this culture. Professional and social prestige have been mentioned. Opportunity for freedom, for advancement, for security, for a routine, and for the opportunity to work with others like oneself enter into the types and amounts of reward that appeal to different people. The location of the job, the availability of a college so as to continue education at night, whether or not the schools are good, and the climate are other examples of the reward aspect of a position that has much to do with the immediate decision of a person actually to take a job.

Preferences and Expectations Regarding personal reward, all the personal–social factors mentioned previously feed into whether an individual offers himself to a particular type of vocation and a special job. He comes to the vocation with a clear preference hierarchy but also with an expectancy hierarchy. What he *expects* is usually associated with what he *prefers*, but the overlap is by no means complete. If the position, however, falls too far below what he not only prefers, but also expects, he will look elsewhere and keep on looking until he is certain that he must alter his expectancies drastically. He may move to an entirely different occupation.

For many and perhaps most young people, occupational choice is not an all or nothing thing. The various direct and indirect determinants that have been summarized above may lead one to a preferred option. When this is found to be not available, the individual makes a strategic retreat, reassesses himself and the social factors, and often comes up with another alternative. It has been said that there is no *one* right husband or wife, that any one of several would have done as well. The same is probably true for jobs. One young man first had his mind and heart set on a career in psychiatry. He found that he had little taste for the science courses necessary in premed, and the family budget would not support him all the way through medical school and psychiatric residency. He changed to a psychology major, thinking that clinical psychology would be an acceptable alternative career. He took part time work as a salesman, and found that he rather liked it and did well at it. As a junior in college, it became evident that he probably would not accumulate high enough grades to be admitted to graduate school, at least with a stipend such that he could afford to continue his education to the doctorate. Wistfully, but not despairingly, he changed his plans, kept his psychology major but loaded his course of study with business courses, and is now doing well in sales with a profitable prospective future ahead of him. He thinks he may have been happiest as a psychiatrist or clinical psychologist, but he is realistically quite content with his current and probably continuing role in life.

Job Standards and Estimates Paralleling the personal preference and expectancy hierarchy are the *ideal* standards set by the employer, and the *realistic estimates* he must make when he actually fills his position with a live human body. Every employer knows precisely what he wants for every position he fills: someone who is personable, hard working, honest, loyal, dedicated, ambitious but not so ambitious as to want to take over, courteous, neat, and so on. Realistically, he knows that in some five cases out of six (to be optimistic) he must settle for someone who falls rather short of this ideal. Only for really good jobs, and where there are extensive resources to satisfy the applicant's preference hierarchy, and where there is a broad range of prospective talent for the position, is an employer likely to obtain *the man* for *the job*. Only exceptionally competent men and women are likely to find themselves faced with the happy alternative of *exactly the right job for them*. Such a marriage of job and man is likely to be a happy one indeed for all concerned.

Summary of Job Choice Such, then, are the personal and social determinants of occupational choice and entry. The process arises from the social structure of the society in which the individual lives. This, combined with an individual's native endowment, affects the development of his personality as it unfolds and is shaped by his special and particular environment. An individual acquires a set of complex sociopsychological attributes and these, coupled with the immediate determinants (including opportunities) within his environment when he reaches the right age, set him toward a series of choices his society provides for him. What they are — what is possible — interacting with what he wants and what he expects, leads to an occupational choice or choices and, eventually and for most, to an occupational entry.

THEORIES OF VOCATIONAL BEHAVIOR

Implicit in all that has been said in this chapter is the assumption that work is a way of life, although, as Osipow (1968) says, this assumption should be questioned. But, the nature of their work is *the* indicator of status for most working men or women. Her husband's status is the surest indicator of a wife's status. One's status in society is the major index of the power he exerts (for better or for worse). Status is clearly but not perfectly correlated with competence. Competence, self-reflected by those with whom one interacts, shapes one's self concept, and, as shown, self concept is the core of one's happiness (or his unhappiness).

The point is well worth repeating that, in United States society, competence is a necessary although certainly not a sufficient condition for personal happiness. As has been said, the world is full of competent and powerful people who are not happy.

If one's work, then, is so crucial to his life, there should be comprehensive and well thought out theories of vocational development, choice, and performance. The reason that none exist (see the earlier discussion of Osipow) is that vocational development, choice, entry, and performance are as complex as life itself and it is almost certain that a satisfactory theory of vocations will not be worked out much before a satisfactory theory of human life is formulated. Since human beings are unbelievably complex, and since psychology is a relatively new and groping science, it will be a long, long time before there is a taut and comprehensive theory of vocations; and it is quite unlikely that any single theory will fit all people, or even that it will fit most people. Osipow's advocacy of specific, miniature theories is sensible.

Super (1953), one of the deans of vocational research and counseling, has listed twelve factors that must be accounted for in a theory of vocational behavior. His intent in the paper, which is discussed here, is to broaden the approach to occupational choice offered by Ginzberg, an economist, and his associates (1951). Although Super's theory is subject to each of the criticisms leveled by Osipow, it is worthwhile to summarize it briefly.

Scope of a Vocational Theory

According to Super, an adequate vocational theory must account for the following problem areas:

1. Individual differences. The variety and multiplicity of individual differences was made evident by the four youth discussed earlier in this chapter.
2. Multipotentiality. This point is obvious, and was discussed earlier. However, it may not be either obvious or palatable to the girl who must find an alternative career when she discovers she has no place on the stage, or for the boy who wanted to be a doctor but realizes that he must somehow content himself with being a lab technician. Nor is this point comforting to the disadvantaged young male or female who finds that his career choices must be made from an unappetizing selection of unskilled jobs.
3. Different occupational ability patterns. Those who specialize in fitting the right person to the right job have gone a long way in developing vocational guidance and selection tests, although they are by no means perfect tools at this stage of their development.
4. Identification and the role of models. The theoretical and research material presented later in Chapters 11, 12, and 13 on identification and modeling is relevant for vocational choice and performance. The world is full of people who entered vocations because of fathers, mothers, effective teachers, ministers, counselors, and admired peers.
5. All the stages of vocational behavior: its earliest development, clear choice, vocational entry, and later vocational development, whether this be successful or unsuccessful. The beginning of a career is a bit like adolescence: It is a time of finding one's own identity—of rehearsing for mature roles. Then comes the long period either of climb or of adjusting to the fact that one is not going to move ahead very far. Then comes stability and, inevitably, decline. Super includes all these considerations under the heading of "Continuity of Adjustment."
6. Different life stages. These are simply self-evident convenient groupings very like those discussed in topic 5 above.

7. Career patterns. Examples of different patterns are provided by the following: the athlete who, depending on his speciality, peaks in his early 20s and is likely to go downhill thereafter; the man who goes early into the military can retire young and enter a second career if he wishes; a politician or a judge who may reach his greatest status and influence in his old age; a teacher who must under most current regulations face mandatory retirement at 65, 68, or 70 years of age (this is also a standard pattern in corporate business); the self-employed man or woman who may work until he dies.

8. Guided development. Counselors are exceptionally useful, and since personal–social adjustment plays a key role in work success, personal counseling can help youth vocationally.

9. Complex interactive process between an individual and the opportunities his environment offers. Pakistan, for example, has many times more woman doctors per capita than the United States because of the Muslim tradition of separation of women from men who are not spouses or close relatives. Thus, few Pakistani women are willing to go to male doctors for infant delivery or health problems.

10. Dynamics of career patterns. Why do some succeed, others fail, and some peak early, then stabilize or decline, while others bloom late?

11. Degree of satisfaction one obtains from his work. Super (1953) espouses the "theory that vocational adjustment is the process of implementing a self concept, and that the degree of satisfaction attained is proportionate to the degree to which the self concept has been implemented" (p. 189).

12. Work as a way of life. For one to be truly happy in a culture such as this, he must like both the work he is doing and the associations that go with it.

Ten Propositions about Vocational Development

Super advances ten propositions that, he believes, can lead to a theory of vocational development:

1. People differ. The crucial variables are abilities, interests, and personalities.

2. There is no single occupation that is the one and only occupation for a given person.

3. Each occupation has at its core a set of requirements – skills, social habits, personality attributes, demands on verbal fluency – that favor some who enter it, and work against others.

4. Constantly changing adjustments are required from the time a vocation is chosen and entered through to the time one leaves vocational life. Some, for example, are great builders but poor maintainers. They have the drive to start something new, but lack the attributes necessary to keep it running once the newness has gone. Others lack initiative, but are skilled at keeping the machine running.

5. The vocational life stages may be thought of as "growth, exploration, establishment, maintenance, and decline."

6. The nature of one's career pattern is a complex interaction between what he is born with (including his social class), and his opportunities.

7. Vocational development is guided, partly by others, both those who

teach and those who counsel; and partly by the individual's own constant checking and rechecking himself against the realities of his life and vocational situation.

8. The self concept influences choice but is in turn affected by feedback after the choice is made. The complexities of the development of the self concept are treated in Chapter 15.

9. Vocational adjustment is a function of a complex series of compromises between individual and social factors. These compromises are often made consciously and intellectually, may be facilitated in counseling, can be worked out in rational ways and through fantasy, and may be quick or very slow.

10. "Work satisfactions and life satisfactions depend upon the extent to which the individual finds adequate outlets for his abilities, interests, personality traits, and values; they depend upon his establishment in a type of work, a work situation, and a way of life in which he can play the kind of role which his growth and exploratory experiences have led him to consider congenial and appropriate." (p. 190)

SUMMARY

The world of most adolescents consists of their homes and families, their peer groups, and some combination of school and work. The complex interactions of these worlds were documented for four adolescents: Nedra, a middle-class Midwestern girl; Carrie, a poor white girl from an Eastern seaboard city; Doug, a metropolitan, upper-class boy; and Lonnie, a poor Black youth from a deep South city.

From these four case histories, the following results of adolescent work experience were abstracted: (1) development of autonomy; (2) both feelings and the reality of independence; (3) broadened social lives; (4) increased role flexibility; (5) practice in social skills, or proficiency in roles; (6) adjustment to adult inevitabilities; (7) relevant training for future careers; (8) adding a dimension of altruism to the self concept; (9) firming and enhancing the self concept; (10) broadening the self concept; and (11) effects of the social moratorium.

The four young people discussed were conformers. Other young people, concentrated among but not confined to the disadvantaged, experience only vocational drift or move into delinquency, which in turn is usually a form of vocational drift. Nonconformers among advantaged groups may be the "life drop-outs," the revolutionaries, or the radical to moderate reformers. Radical and moderate reformers usually fit into accepted vocational patterns.

Work means much more to the average worker than simply a job and a paycheck. It is a way of life, providing status, need fulfillment or frustration, and power. However, this assumption is now being questioned. The estimate of competence fed back to the individual by his work experience shapes his self concept importantly. Most men say they would choose to work even though they had enough money that work was unnecessary. Their motives for continuing to work range from active self-fulfilling job employment to fear of what they would do with their time if they were not working. However, work motivations for women are more complex than for men, although many work simply because they need to. The work motivations and satisfactions of girls and women who work because they want to are probably very similar to those for boys and men, but information and theory about women and vocations are meager. A primary index of status for wives is the nature of their husbands' occupations.

Vocational guidance, selection, and adjustment are not founded on completely developed theories, although psychoanalytic, social learning, self concept, developmental, and testing and measurement theories have been advanced. The need for research in the area is acute. Most theories that have been developed seem designed for college youth. Current theories are too broad, yet skimpy. Miniature theories that can be buttressed by data should be developed. A majority of those with high school education or less seem unprepared to generate an intelligent plan for their vocational lives.

In guiding a youth toward vocational entry, whether this be done by official or informal counseling, or whether it be self-guidance, the following factors should be considered:

Native endowment, the physical and social structure of the society, vocational trends (for example, technology changes so rapidly that narrow trade specialization is not likely to be adaptive for any long period of time), full provision of vocational information, the social role characteristics of the job and their fit with the personality of the job seeker, objective opportunities, and functional and nonfunctional requirements of the job. Among nonfunctional requirements are, regrettably, often such things as race, sometimes sex, age, appearance, and so on.

The area of vocational choice finally should be carefully analyzed to see whether the job chosen will satisfy the personal needs of the individual, now and in the future. These needs include such disparate things as amount of salary, prestige, opportunity for interaction with people, work with young children, flexibility or inflexibility of duties, and so on.

Finally, the scope of a vocational theory was discussed. Requirements of an adequate theory range from accounting for individual differences through to mapping the dynamics of career progress for individuals and for different vocations.

12

Social and Emotional Development

INTRODUCTION

Personality, emotional adjustment, intellectual power, and cognition develop in a social setting. The genetic and congenital attributes of an individual interact in complex ways with his learning opportunities to make him what he is. For example, a strong, early maturing body may dramatically alter a youth's learning opportunities; a constitutionally very active, high energy child will have a very different life if born to middle aged, tired, and sedentary parents than if he comes into a home headed by young, high energy, open-ended mother and father.

Previous chapters have considered the adolescent's physical make-up and his sexuality—the personal forces he brings to life—and have stressed the social organizations of community, school, and church as they set limits for and shape his behavior. In the present chapter and those which follow, the author attempts to come to grips with the more personal process of how the adolescent adjusts to his life setting and comes to be as he is and will become.

Ideally, he will learn to be moderately comfortable with himself and at the same time a constructive contributor to society.

DIMENSIONS OF SOCIALIZATION

"Socialization" is a descriptive term covering both *process* and *product*. As an author attempts to define it and give it dimensions, he invariably reveals his own values, since the outcome, or product, of socialization is judged in terms of values. Socialization is developmentally relativistic as well. Good socialization as a product may mean one thing among the Apaches, another among the Arabs, and quite another among the American WASP middle class. The word is a poor fit with the requirements for rigorous definition set by science.

Since no substitute term is available, the dimensions of socialization are its best definition. The following definition is of *outcome*, or *product*. *Process* is here considered to follow the laws of learning.

Descriptively, socialization is the class name for everything an adolescent does that concerns other people, directly or indirectly. By his emotional development, one can refer to whether he does these things happily or unhappily, aggressively or amiably, actively or passively. These are "traits." But in turn the same characteristics are inferred from behavior, so that traits, too, are judged in a social context.

If a boy or girl is delinquent, he is considered ill socialized. If he is withdrawn or unpopular, the same judgment is made. If a youth associates only with girls or only with boys, one wonders about his socialization in the conventional sense of "fitting the norms," as well as in the emotional adjustment sense. There is a modest correlation between normative (conventional) behavior and emotional adjustment. Thus, the list of behavior and attributes included as products, outcomes, or results under the heading of socialization is as broad as the possible range of social-personal relations and characteristics.

The value components of socialization are clear: Too much competitiveness, and a youth is labeled "driven"; too little, and he is "passive." Along with his regular social behaviors, as has been inferred, an adolescent should be comfortable with himself—should be reasonably self-accepting. But if he goes too far in this direction, he may be "smug." Moving from socialization and emotional adjustment to character, one speaks almost exclusively in social value terms: honesty, modesty, good character. A gang member, entirely comfortable with himself and happy, is not considered by outsiders to possess good character.

It is immediately clear that cultural and developmental relativism operates importantly in evaluating the status of socialization and emotional development. The explicit open competitiveness with other girls and boys that an American girl shows in a coeducational school would be bad taste for a well-reared girl in a conventional middle-class Japanese family (although things are changing there too). The open heterosexual behavior in the South Seas described by Margaret Mead (1939) would put a United States boy or girl into juvenile court if it came to light. An Afro-American boy from Boston will undoubtedly find himself in serious difficulty when he behaves perfectly naturally, for him, while visiting relatives in Alabama. If a group of ninth grade boys acted with the angry and open physical aggression common among 3-year-old males, their school principal would probably call the police. If a middle-class girl employed the unlaundered public vocabulary of a disadvantaged male, she might well be considered emotionally disturbed. And so it goes.

In other words, there is no absolute, irrevocable definition of socialization, good or bad—or, for that matter, of emotional adjustment. To make an evaluative definition for any youth, one must at the very least consider the following dimensions:

1. The generally accepted ways of behaving within the *effective* culture (school, community, and, loosely, nation); and the limits beyond which behavior is not permitted.
2. The sex of the adolescent.
3. Chronological, mental, and physical age. Society holds different expectations of an 18 year old than of a 13 year old; of a youth with 150 IQ than one with a 75 IQ; of an early maturing boy or girl than of a late bloomer.
4. Socioeconomic class, at least along the broad dimensions of advantaged and disadvantaged.

At this period in the national social development of the United States, it may be that a fifth dimension, race, should be considered. But until more evidence is forthcoming, the author believes that economic, political, and educational factors—and not race—are the important determiners of behavior. Such factors *do* operate differentially for different races. However, when they are controlled, racial differences partially or totally disappear (see Tulkin, 1968). Tulkin's research is concerned with intelligence, Eppes and McCandless' with imitation and locus of control.

Tulkin's study has already been discussed (see Chapter 9). Eppes and McCandless[1] worked with seventh grade boys and girls in Atlanta. They found no differences in external–internal types of personal control (see Chapters 9 and 10) or degree of identification with teachers, including determinants of identification, between their disadvantaged Black and white seventh graders; but both groups varied sharply along these dimensions from a population of advantaged white seventh graders.

If a youngster's socialization is to proceed most constructively, it is essential that he develop at least a moderately positive self concept.[2] It is difficult to live efficiently if one does not esteem himself realistically, if one is not able to accept himself within some reasonable limit of "wanting to be better than he is," and if one is not at least somewhat optimistic some of the time.

To the degree that society militates against such wholesome self concept development for any group of children, then the characteristics of that group, whether religious, racial, or other, play a central role in determining its members' socialization. For some groups, as has been said, society (in a rough, power-elite, consensual way) provides myriad irrelevant frustrations and a climate of systematic, negative noncontin-

[1] Research in progress.
[2] The self concept is treated in detail in Chapter 15. However, it will be necessary to present some of the material in the context of this discussion.

gent reinforcement. For other groups, such as the WASP middle class, the opposite is true.

An approving sort of general acceptance—the broadest kind of noncontingent reinforcement—seems to be essential for positive self-esteem to develop. Coopersmith (1967) presents striking evidence in favor of this often recommended child development practice. He finds acceptance most often manifested in concern for and interest in the developing person.

Certainly, when an adolescent believes that "To be Black is to be bad," then counter measures must be taken to further his development so he may be both more socially effective and personally satisfied. It is worth repeating again, since the problem is agonizingly urgent, that incredible hurdles have been set up to interfere with the socialization of the approximately twenty-and-one-half million Afro-American citizens. Children, youth, and adults from Hispaño, Indian, and Appalachian cocultures face similar hurdles, and need attention as badly as Black Americans.

Such other minority cocultures as Chinese- and Japanese-Americans seem on the whole to manage about as well as the core culture. Jews are a religious grouping; but "Jew" as used by the laity carries with it ethnic connotations. Regardless, when judged by statistical socioeconomic criteria, Jews perhaps fare better than the average person in the core culture. Members of other distinctly different religious groups, such as Catholics, Mormons, Unitarians, and Seventh Day Adventists may, under special circumstances, face problems in their social interactions with the core culture. Most members of such groups, however, believe their religious commonality and social cohesiveness provide advantages that more than compensate for the disadvantages. Their parents' uniqueness, however, often presents at least temporary problems for adolescents.

Racial differences in socialization in contemporary United States are meaningful as they interact with social class and political (power) variables. It is also necessary to consider race and often religion as important socialization modifiers, although they might not be if there were an ideal democratic society.

Apollonian and Dionysian Social Expression and Conformity

The well-socialized adolescent is one who, in his current life within his effective culture, is better than average in the major areas of social behavior as valued by that culture. If he lags in one area, for his over-all average to be high, he must develop some type of constructive compensation in another.

His behavior will typically include having some good friends, occasionally assuming a role of leadership, being able to follow when the occasion is appropriate, adjusting to school and/or his job, being appropriately sex typed *and* identified (these terms will be defined later), and living without undue discomfort within his family. His contribution to the social setting should be somewhat positive (not merely neutral, certainly not negative).

This definition raises questions about the Apollonian or Judeo-Christian aspect of American culture as it comes into conflict with the "nature of man," as expressed in a Dionysian type of adjustment; and as these relate to socially conforming behavior. Still today, although there are signs of change, conformity usually means "acting like a middle-class WASP."

The Apollonian mode of adjustment has been mentioned earlier. To review, in extreme form, it refers to a life style that is all cool intellect with a high degree of personal control over emotions. It includes the ideals of the Protestant ethic, as this has been discussed earlier: a government of law, not men; planning ahead and delaying immediate gratification; work is valued for work's sake; honesty is a paramount virtue; achievement is highly valued, and so on.

The background of the Apollonian life style is "uptightness," tension, worry, intolerance of nonconformity, materialism, and many other vices of which the WASP middle class is accused, with some justice.

In its "worst" aspects, Dionysian adjustment is considered by many to characterize the way of life of the disadvantaged—the "happy" poor. Disadvantaged youth have commonly been found to be more physically aggressive, more seekers after excitement for its own sake, more openly sexual in behavior, less planful and more impulsive in action, and relatively unambitious about achievement for achievement's sake (see, for example, Datta, Schaefer, and Davis, 1968; McKee and Leader, 1955; Miller and Swanson, 1960; Silberman, 1964; and Tulkin, 1968).

But many also believe that disadvantaged people, particularly children and youth, find more fun in life, experience their sensations more fully, are free in the use of their bodies, and enter spontaneously, and perhaps more genuinely, and with more honest emotion into their interpersonal relations.

Both Apollonian and Dionysian philosophies (or socialization outcomes), if the best is taken from each, possess great virtue. It may be that the two traditions can not be melded within American society. At present, as embodied in society's official sanctions and the goals of the typical school, middle-class, narrow Apollonian virtues are paramount; Dionysian practices are suspect. Fusion between the looseness and relaxation of a hypothetical disadvantaged but Dionysian or Hellenic adolescent and the achieving spirit of his advantaged peer should make an ideal mix, combining virtues of the Protestant ethic with getting genuine fun from life.

There is no known recipe for producing this blend, although evidence begins to accumulate that it can be achieved. Coopersmith's (1967) high self-esteem subjects, for example, are emotionally quite free, but (as fifth and sixth graders) very successful by conventional social standards. The same appears to be true of their mothers, who also served as subjects in his study. Coppersmith's recipe for success, a portion of which has been given above, is: nearly total acceptance, firm and clearly defined limits leniently enforced, respect and latitude for individual action within the clear limits and, last but not least, good models for behavior.

The second question raised by the definition of good socialization status is tied to the first: What of the happy and personally comfortable adolescents who are law breakers? They may be self-accepting, may live well within the norms of their *effective* coculture, may be popular, exert constructive leadership in their subgroup and within the rules of their society, be able to follow well. They may be adequately and appropriately masculine or feminine and live peacefully enough with their families. They may even achieve fairly well in school, but may *still be officially delinquent.*

Some evidence exists to answer this question. Such children, if and when their allegiance is shifted from the delinquent group to which they belong, make good candidates for healthy nondelinquent socialization. This has worked in practice, and there is some research evidence to indicate that it is true. Certainly, if there is to be an orderly society, allegiance to delinquent parts of the society must be broken down and, if possible, the allegiance of the whole delinquent portion (for example, a gang) must be shifted. Interesting progress has been made in working with gangs, which are at the same time very vital and very destructive, so as to turn their high energy and morale to work *for* rather than *against* society. But it is difficult work.

Shore, Massimo, and Ricks (1965) provide an interesting study of rehabilitation work with individual boys. Their subjects were twenty 15- to 17-year-old institutionalized delinquents. Their treatment was academically oriented therapy: Ostensibly, the boys attended in order to remedy deficient school skills; but they were "tutored" in a free and therapeutically oriented setting. The authors found that as the boys' academic skills improved, their self concepts improved. As their self concepts improved, their attitudes to authority became more benign; and as their attitudes improved, their behavior became more acceptable. Thus does competence breed good social adjustment.

Apart from the personally comfortable delinquent, what about the child, adolescent, or adult who is personally extremely uncomfortable *in a sick society?* Many alienated youth are acutely emotionally uncomfortable, yet many of them are exceptionally able individuals who have developed to and function at the highest level of moral judgment (for example, Haan, Smith, and Block, 1968). Those who lead society in the direction of an ultimate good seem seldom to be happy, conforming people. For example, many great religious leaders, including those persecuted during their lifetimes but later sainted (literally or figuratively), seem to have been classified *when they lived* as neurotic eccentrics. A good society must be flexible enough to look, listen, live and let live, and follow, when the evidence that the way is for the greatest common welfare is good enough to deserve such action. Politics, government, education, and all of men's occupations also breed such men and women. However, they are rare at any time.

Nor must it be forgotten that the price of freedom is constant alertness for the protection of freedom for oneself and others: A vigilant person must never relent of asking embarrassing questions and demanding answers. It is not easy but it is a necessary way of life.

Sociometric Techniques The simplest and best way to measure socialization is by means of sociometric techniques, where each member of a group is asked to nominate his three or five best friends. In their choices, people of all ages seem to arrive at a happy, workable blend of Apollonian and Dionysian qualities as their good friends. Those best liked as intimates are usually reasonably competent, flexibly conforming, and judiciously relaxed and warm. On the other hand, for reasons such as those already given, people exceptionally well socialized by the sociometric criterion may not fall into the vanguard of leadership. However, as a rough technique subject to all the qualifications given later, sociometry provides a useful approximation of good socialization.

Among prepubescent children, friendship choices are usually made from among the list of like-sexed classmates. Two sets of choices should be secured from adolescents, first from among those of their own sex and second from those of the opposite sex. It is also useful to ask the same questions about the three to five of the same and opposite sex youngsters who are *least* preferred.

These measures, taken together, give a clear and remarkably stable picture of an adolescent's standing in his group and of the structure of the group itself. For example, a boy who is chosen as a best friend by five boys, but as a least preferred person by five other boys, in the class is likely to possess strong, even aggressive leadership qualities and considerable personal strength and vitality. His standing as strongly liked or disliked raises questions about his social abrasiveness. The group leader should ask, "Do I have a class full of warring cliques?" A high school senior who receives no votes from either sex or a youngster who secures only reject nominations deserve the attention of those who want to help each young person make the best progress he can in socialization.

Most youngsters who are chosen by one or two others in the group are adequately socialized according to the standards of that group. The standards of the group, contrary to the pessimistic predictions of many, are usually the same as the core standards of the community of reference. A delinquent group, of course, will prove an exception to this generalization, although its popular members will be partial conformers to its standards.

Isolates, youngsters rejected by almost everyone, and sometimes extreme stars (those chosen by almost everyone) are often found on further investigation to have socialization problems. No clear-cut cause-and-effect relationship can be demonstrated: Each such group status may be due to socialization and personality problems; or the problems may result from the status in the group; or the two may interact.

Some leaders have deep personal problems. People will sometimes sacrifice almost anything else for popularity and leadership roles (see Bass' 1967 analysis of the different purposes groups may serve for different individuals). When the quest for popularity and/or leadership is extreme, the individual's socialization should be suspect. Intense striving is often seen in high schools and colleges: The BMOC (big man on campus) syndrome strikes a thoughtful observer as a little sick.

A simple measure of popularity will not satisfy all the criteria for socialization or even for adequate functioning in the group. Society is built both on intimacy (easy friendship and acceptance) and competence (constructive contribution). A well-socialized adolescent should have both the capacity for liking and being liked and the competencies that make him a useful member of the group. It is thus well to employ an additional sociometric technique designed to tap preferences for workmates in constructive, on-going activities: With whom do you like best (or least) to work on homework assignments? Whom would you most (or least) prefer to have on your committee if you were in charge of arrangements for the school dance? These are work preference and rejection questions. A youngster who is both well liked and esteemed as a partner in conducting the business of the group is likely to be well socialized across the board. One who is chosen for neither role is likely to be in trouble. One who is liked but disregarded as a constructive citizen is likely to find trouble ahead for himself in the serious business of life; and the one who is valued only for his mathematics or class organization skills may find himself leading a lonely life.

Finally, it is often useful and sometimes necessary to obtain working or research definitions of socialization within special areas. The "buddy rating" or "guess who" technique is a useful device: Who starts the roughhousing? When things bog down, who can be counted on to help see them through? Who pushes others around when he (or she) thinks he can get away with it? Who stands up for the underdog in the group? Information gained in answer to such questions is valuable in group guidance, and the members of a class can sort each other out on such dimensions more accurately than the most sensitive teacher.

Young people can be categorized statistically by sociometric techniques, and such categorization appears to be remarkably stable over time in the same group, and from group to group (see, for example, Jennings, 1943, who worked with delinquent adolescent girls; or G. G. Thompson, 1960, who provides a detailed review of the sociometric literature). But sociometrics are more than statistical categorizations. Studied in detail, they tell who likes whom. The expression is rather valid, in that it reflects not merely preference but actual association. Thus, if a sociometric says that Mary, Jill, and Toni each considers the other two as her *very* best friends, and if they mention no one else, then one may be quite certain that they form a closely knit group. If they, in turn, are chosen by no one else in their group, one then thinks of them as a rather isolated three-person clique. But if they are chosen by many others, one must think of them as vital persons, very likely acting as one, in their influence on the group. Consideration of their *type* of leadership as elicited by observation or the "guess who" and the prestige sociometric techniques is then in order; and important implications for group management may result from such analysis.

There seems to be considerable agreement among independent judges concerning sociometric status. Bowles and Wright (1969), for example, studied sixth grade boys in three different classes—a population of forty-eight. The Personality Integration Reputation Test (PIRT), a sociometric, buddy rating instrument that the authors believe measures "effectiveness stimulus value" was administered in each class. The teachers of the classes also rated the boys for the same qualities. The correlation between the teachers' ratings and their pupils' nominations was a very respectable .77. In this case, the judgments of the teachers proved to be about as accurate as the boys' nominations in predicting differences between personally integrated groups and control groups.

Sociometric techniques must be used in a context of the best and tightest professional ethics, and are useful *only* when employed by teachers or counselors who enjoy young people's trust. The junior and senior high school student is not dull. If he has the slightest suspicion that his answers will be used lightly or in any way other than for his and the group's best interest, he will respond frivolously, misleadingly, or not at all. Nor can he be blamed for this. No youngster should be required to provide such information, nor should he even be subjected to pressure to do so. It is well, even essential, for parents to know that such techniques are being employed with their children; and for their children to be excused from answering if the parents have reservations.

In short, the right to privacy and the highest level of professional ethics in the employment of personal data should be guaranteed to every student (or anyone else). Confidentiality of results must be guaranteed and stringently safeguarded.

Adolescents are likely to be more reluctant than younger children to take part in sociometric measures. They have often been disillusioned, and the common caution, "Don't trust anyone over 30," probably has been instilled in them by the treatment they receive. But most will be glad to participate if they understand how the information is to be used, if the professional ethics of the administrators and users of the material are high and the students know it, and if staff have behaved toward them in a trustworthy manner. These things are equally true for parents.

Some group caretakers, such as group leaders, school principals, and teachers hold strong reservations about eliciting "reject" choices from children and young people. They believe it crystallizes unfavorable sentiment by making it articulate. The author believes such reservations are groundless: Children and adolescents know full well whom they like and dislike; and saying so is not going to make the slightest difference in either their attitudes or behavior. Even the most negative feelings can be dealt with more constructively if they are clearly recognized (although not necessarily publicly expressed).

The social and working relationships within a group of up to sixty are firmly laid down within a few weeks after the formation of the group, although some "soft sell" youngsters may be penalized if sociometric measures are taken too early in the school (or group) year. An index of socialization well-being should never be accepted without looking carefully at the individual who receives it: Highly creative young people with great potential for continued high level socialization may be penalized by sociometrics. So may youngsters who are much more intelligent than anyone else in the group, or the youth who holds tightly to his parents' standards when these deviate from the core culture.

Generally, when caution is exercised, sociometrics are useful as rough working measures for judging socialization.

Socialization and Personal Characteristics

The principal factor in socialization is undoubtedly learning, but many relatively unchangeable characteristics of a given youngster make the socialization process easier or harder for him (that is, he experiences difficulty in achieving a comfortable and effective status). Horowitz

(1967) demonstrates that it is difficult to predict from any formally determined characteristic what boy or girl will be popular or unpopular; and that different factors enter into the two—that is, the things that determine popularity do not, if reversed, insure unpopularity. His population consisted of 1437 males and 1505 females from eight high schools of the 1353 that make up the sample for Project TALENT. He reports, for example, that by taking the best combination of his fourteen predictors, the highest correlation with popularity obtainable is .39 (boys' popularity with girls). It will be remembered that a correlation of this size accounts for only about 15 percent of the total variance of popularity.

The best single predictor of popularity for boys, either among other boys or among girls, is "sports information." Even this correlation is only .22 for their popularity among boys and .27 for popularity with girls. The reason for the relationship, to speculate about Horowitz' results, is probably that in American culture, high masculine boys are sports-minded and thus have a good fund of sports information. In an adolescent society (and in this society in general), high masculinity in a boy is esteemed not only by other males but by girls as well. Curiously, sports *interest* among boys is less related than sports information to their popularity with either other boys or girls. For boys, sports interest correlates .18 with popularity among boys; and .17 among girls.

Tenuous though the determiners of popularity for boys are, they are even more tenuous for girls. However, for both sexes, conventional academic achievement predicts popularity at a low but statistically significant level. At equally low levels, those who score low in conventional academic skills are likely to be high in reject votes. As was mentioned in the preceding chapter, socioeconomic status is positively related to popularity (the higher the social class of one's father, the more popular. However, Horowitz' correlations range only from .11 for the popularity of boys with other boys to .19 for girls' popularity among boys). Boys' social class has nothing to do with their rejection by either sex; and the relationships for girls are very low between social class and rejection. They are only −.08 (barely significant statistically for this large sample) for girls' rejections score among girls, and −.12 for girls' rejection by boys. As mentioned in Chapter 11, youngsters who stay on in high school are usually those who have accepted middle-class values and are thus psychologically middle class even though they may be formally lower class. This fact will lower correlations between social class and popularity in later high school years, since the determiners of popularity in American high schools are almost certainly middle-class characteristics. Lower-class youth without such characteristics (perhaps well socialized by their standards) will likely have dropped out of school early.

Intelligence Intellectual level is rather well determined by the time a youngster becomes pubescent. It can be predicted that its relationships with popularity are at about the same level that Horowitz found for academic competence: low but positive. There seems to be a cutting score at both extremes. If a youngster is low enough in IQ that "it shows," he is likely to be rejected. Similarly, if he is so high that he simply does not talk the language of others in his group, he is likely to be rejected.

McCandless and Ali (1966) present results for relationships between popularity and intelligence for three very different samples of middle- and upper-middle-class ninth grade girls: For a group of girls in a coeducational university school, the correlation was .39; for a group of girls in a Catholic day school (no boys enrolled), the correlation was essentially zero (.04); but for a group of native Pakistani girls in an all girls' school in Lahore, West Pakistan, the correlation was an interesting .56 (interesting, in that a correlation of this size accounts for almost a third of the variance enough to be of practical significance as well as statistical significance).

The McCandless and Ali results are useful in reminding one that it is not safe to approach any group with a rigid set of preconceptions, but rather with a set of questions: Why is intelligence (as measured) of no importance in predicting popularity among a sample of Catholic girls such as those studied, while it is a major predictor of popularity for a group of Pakistani girls?

It is probable that in a college preparatory school, intelligence predicts social acceptance to some useful degree, as in the university school sample above; while in an inner city school, where being a good student betokens an unfashionable alliance with an unsympathetic power structure, intelligence (or more certainly, academic achievement) may even be a predictor of rejection.

Body Build and Time of Sexual Maturity

That body build and time of sexual maturity are important factors in affecting the socialization process has been fully documented in early chapters of this volume. To review: Early physical maturity and mesomorphic body build (the muscular, broad-shouldered, narrow-hipped build of the athlete) seem to facilitate a conforming type of socialization for middle-class boys, and may retard it for disadvantaged boys in the sense that they make it easier for such boys to master their environment by delinquency. Effects are less clear for girls, although "a good build" obviously aids a girl in reaching acceptance among boys and, within limits, among girls. However, the very attractive girl is more likely to be assiduously wooed, and may thus be moved to sexual indiscretions (see Chapter 5 for the histories of Marilee and Cheri).

Activity Level and Modes of Reception and Expression

The role that an individual's activity level plays in socialization was discussed earlier. Activity affects both the process and thus the product in socialization. To recapitulate, opportunities as well as frustrations differ greatly for individuals of different activity and energy levels. Not all adolescents are constantly on the go; others have low energy and seem perpetually tired, perhaps as a function of their rapid endocrine changes and growth, perhaps as a function of the psychological energy they must devote to adjusting to their new roles. A high energy level adolescent is bound to be more frustrated by the sedentary life of classes than his lethargic counterpart.

However, by adolescence, an individual has learned to manage his activity and energy level in one way or another. The addition of a new drive does not so much change his over-all pattern but rather presents new complications for adjusting it. The relative freedom from parental supervision that most adolescents gain, their acquisition of a means to travel about, the upsurge of extracurricular activities or free time to spend on the street all help to channel off restlessness for many. Others seem to alleviate their problems by fantasy. Those who can not fantasize join the horde of young people seeking excitement and kicks.

Similarly, for those to whom the world makes most sense when it is registered visually—or aurally, or kinesthetically—adolescence merely presents a certain number of new adjustments in which older characteristic ways of receiving and expressing are adapted. If the old ways have been efficient, the increase in drive at adolescence is likely to make them more efficient. If the old ways have been maladaptive, they are likely to become more dramatically so at adolescence. In other words, although adolescence brings with it a new drive and new problems, the adolescent brings to it all his earlier learned ways of adjusting, good or bad. Development is a continuous process during which the old constantly affects the shape and function of the present and the future.

CULTURAL IMPACTS ON SOCIALIZATION

On the one hand, individual differences related to congenital and constitutional factors affect each individual's socialization differently. On the other hand, all people are affected by the culture in which they live, since by definition a culture holds common values and provides common learning opportunities. Thus, there should be behavior characteristics that, on the whole, distinguish boys from girls within a given culture (many of these have been discussed), and in which members of one culture differ from those of another culture.

Within the limits of available methods, cross-cultural studies offer interesting suggestions of how socialization proceeds. Three cross-sectional studies have been arbitrarily selected for summary. Previous reference has been made to the first, which concerns male–female behavior differences and relates them to child rearing practices.

Barry, Bacon, and Child (1957) consulted anthropologists' accounts of child rearing for 110 different cultures. For intensive analysis, they selected five different training emphases. Such emphases constitute process; their outcomes, product, or status:

1. Nurturance: the behavior related to, and development of, the desire and expectation of looking after and helping others.
2. Responsibility: assuming the burden of regular duties, being dependable.
3. Obedience: conforming to wishes and rules set by elders.
4. Achievement: valuing doing and accomplishing things.
5. Self-reliance: depending on oneself to get things done.

The records available to Barry, Bacon, and Child varied in completeness. In only thirty-one accounts were they able to determine satisfactorily the practices in child rearing designed to foster or discourage achievement; but adequate data about responsibility training were available for eight-four cultures.

Sex differences were very clear for four of the five traits listed above. The majority of the cultures stressed nurturance and responsibility much more for girls than boys; while achievement and self-reliance were much more stressed for boys. Obedience training could be estimated for sixty-nine cultures. A majority of these stressed obedience equally for boys and girls, but 35 percent stressed it more for girls and only 3 percent put more emphasis on boys' being obedient.

In United States culture, strong emphasis is placed on differential training of boys and girls along the lines found by Barry, Bacon, and Child. Girls are encouraged to be nurturant, responsible, and obedient; boys, achievement oriented and self-reliant. Douvan and Adelson (1966) portray these differences vividly in their study of a cross-section of American children in their early and mid-teens, suggesting that the socialization product is clearly related to the dimensions of the process. Implications of these sex differences for adjustment in school were developed in detail in the preceding chapter.

The second study selected for review in this section was concerned with conformity. Berry (1967) made a direct measurement of conformity among carefully selected samples of Baffin Island Eskimos and the Temne people of Sierra Leone; then compared the results from these groups with subjects from an industrialized society, the Scots. He measured conformity in a way that is often used: A group of confederates makes a false but consensual report about their judgment of the length of a line. The innocent subject, who has already made his estimate, is asked to make another judgment. The degree to which he shifts his judgment in the direction of his falsely reporting peers is considered to be a measure of his tendency to conform to group pressures.

Most people know, from reading, television, and the movies, that the Eskimo must rely to an extreme degree on his own judgment and ingenuity. Berry documented this tendency from previous anthropological evidence, and predicted that his Eskimo subjects would be ruggedly independent and would resist group pressure to conform in his experimental task.

The Temne live on rice, and harvest only a single crop per year, which must be meted out to all members of the group in carefully planned and regular daily units until the time of the next harvest. Thus, the welfare of each individual is very directly related to the welfare of the group. This fact is so clearly recognized that lack of conformity to the rules of Temne society is strongly punished. The Eskimo and Temne cultures are similar in only one fundamental area: Both are subsistence cultures. There is never more than just enough food to go around.

Berry's predictions were strongly supported by his data: The average traditional Temne changed his estimate of length of line 9 units in the direction of the false group consensus, while the old line (un-Westernized) Eskimo shifted only 2.8 units. Berry also located more Westernized groups of Temne and Eskimo, and found the same patterns still holding. He points out that this signifies to the staying power of cultural norms, even when the old ways are changing.

Berry's sample of rural and urban Scots showed them to be more individualistic than the Temne, but more conforming than the Eskimo. As might be expected from the stereotype of the ruggedly individualistic Scot, they were closer to the Eskimo than to the Temne, although still significantly more conforming than the Eskimo.

In the third study of cultural impact on socialization, Berkowitz and Friedman (1967) experimented with helping behavior. Their subjects were 345 13- to 16-year-old Midwestern white boys. They divided their boys into two groups. The fathers of one group were classed as entrepreneurs. An entrepreneur was a father who owned a business (self-employed laborers were not included), or was a salesman or professional person working either for himself or in partnership. In other words, these fathers had to look out for themselves, had to be hustlers, had to plan for their own retirement, and had to compete vigorously with others in the same field.

The other group of fathers was characterized as bureaucratic. These fathers worked for someone else, usually in a multilevel organization. Such employment may include government, schools and universities, public health clinics, big business under remote or corporate management, and so on. While Berkowitz and Friedman's design is satisfactory and their findings clear, their study includes the flaw — possibly important — that the bureaucratic fathers were on the average somewhat higher in occupational prestige than were the entrepreneurial fathers.

The authors' design is elaborate and ingenious. Each boy was seen singly and told he was to take part in a study of his supervisory ability. He would have to supervise his hypothetical employee by writing notes (actually, no such person was present). Special awards would go to those who were particularly effective supervisors. Pairings were constructed so that the boys were variously led to believe they were working with boys of similar and different family and social class patterns from their own. In some cases, the "employee" was exceptionally helpful to his "supervisor," while in others he "acted" like a veritable dunderhead and prevented his supervisor from obtaining a satisfactory rating.

Each boy was then put into another situation where it was his turn to be the "employee" or helper. The boys were led to believe that this nonexistent supervisor was or was not the boy they had earlier worked with, or was the same or different from him in social class and paternal occupation type (depending on the experimental group of assignment).

The boys from the entrepreneurial families more than those from bureaucratic families gave help to their "partners" to the degree that they themselves had previously received help. The bureaucratic boys were more responsive to general ideals of social responsibility, and did not give as much expression to their specific attitudes toward their working partner — "supervisor" — as the entrepreneurial boys did. Middle-class boys from both groups were prejudiced against working-class boys, but the bureaucratic boys did their duty anyway, while the entrepreneurial boys slacked off when they thought they were helping working-class boys.

In short, both types of boys showed prejudice toward those whom they regarded as of inferior status, but the bureaucratic boys translated their attitudes less into behavior. The entrepreneurial boys seem to follow the principle of, "You scratch my back and I'll scratch yours," while the bureaucratic boys seem to operate more according to "This is the right thing to do, and I'll do it." It may be that the hustling entrepreneurial fathers pass on to their sons something like this, "It's a hard world and you'd better look out for yourself first."

SOCIALIZATION AND THEORIES OF LEARNING

The author subscribes to social learning theory as a promising method of accounting for and predicting human behavior. As has been said, socialization, particularly as it refers to product, is not a good scientific term and its dimensions are so broad that no elegant and precise socialization learning models can be constructed. Thus, learning principles must be applied to socialization by analogue (explaining something by comparing it point by point with something else). Analogues may contribute to science, and are often useful in suggesting research strategies, but they are not science. Nonetheless, as they are made public and become specific, and as they are interrelated with each other, they may contribute to new knowledge and possibly eventually even become science. But if they are glibly advanced and taken for explanations, then reasoning by analogue may hinder scientific progress.

The foundation of socialization as process is discussed in this section by analogue from classical and instrumental or operant conditioning. The basic definitions of conditioning are included in any good introductory psychology book; and reviewed simply but in more detail in many sources (for example, Marx, 1969; Mednick, 1964). In terms of the analogic nature of this section, these types of conditioning are thought of as "families."

The classical conditioning family refers to that class of socialization learning that happens automatically to a person. It is most frequent, probably most profound, and perhaps most widely generalized and resistant to later change during infancy and very early childhood before the human organism can apply appropriate labels and classifications. Devices like labels help to interrupt automatic, unreasoning learning. Conspicuous examples of classical conditioning become less frequent after early childhood. However, deep emotional and physical experiences produce powerful emotional responses that tie to stimuli associated with the experience quite in line with the classical conditioning analogue. Early or disastrous sexual experiences are often accompanied by emotions that lead to reactions that interfere with later effective sexual behavior. A serious auto accident may lead to enduring anxiety and fear reactions when the victim is riding in a car later. However, the ability to think things through and label them is likely to make such effects less profound and lasting when they occur after speech has become efficient; or than when painful or emotional events occur in a clearly understood setting. Since early sexual behavior is likely to be accompanied by strong pleasant *and* unpleasant emotions and, at least for girls, by painful physical sensations, classical conditioning is particularly likely to occur in connection with sexual behavior. This is particularly true, since few young people really understand sex very well.

The older a child becomes, the less likely he is to demonstrate classical conditioning in a laboratory setting. Perhaps in the interests of his own autonomy, he seems to resist *showing* that he has been classically conditioned. However, when involuntary responses such as the eye blink are used to demonstrate classical conditioning, it can easily be demonstrated at any age. New data[3] suggest that such conditioning strongly affects such things as blood pressure, perspiration, brain waves, and other physical functions that have earlier been thought to resist modification through learning. For reviews and evaluations of this interesting literature, see Katkin and Murray (1968) and the reply of Crider, Schwartz, and Shnidman (1969).

By the instrumental conditioned response family, the author refers to more or less voluntary behavior for helping the individual reach goals and solve problems. Once language is well established, most such behavior either is or can be cognized and thus is open to awareness and analysis. An instrumental conditioned response typically possesses little or no resemblance to the unconditioned response that will be made to the evoking (unconditioned) stimulus. For the present analogical purposes, responses that belong to the instrumental family are considered to be goal-directed. The goals of much behavior are obvious (for example, students are polite to teachers so as to keep out of trouble and help get good grades). Other behaviors require more subtle analysis before their goals become clear. A late maturing boy's clowning in class obviously gets him into trouble, interferes with his and others' learning, and is likely to lower his grades. But if one looks more deeply, perhaps one may find that he clowns to gain much needed attention (being noticed, even negatively, is better than being ignored). Such behavior may help him with his self-label of being aggressively masculine. It is often the only sort of assertive masculine behavior he can get away with.

There are other points of view about the determinants and the course of socialization. Which position an author takes is largely a matter of his preference at the present stage of knowledge. This author believes that a learning point of view handles the phenomena more efficiently than other theories.

Freud's alternative theories provide another, widely held way of viewing socialization. He says that socialization represents a transition from the pleasure to the reality principle, a statement that is more descriptive than explanatory. When one operates according to the pleasure principle, immediate gratification of primary, biological, and ego needs is sought without thought of the consequences. In contrast, the reality principle demands that one shift his behavior to fit the realities of the total life situation: obtaining maximum basic personal satisfaction while still living within the permissible limits of the family or effective society. The reality principle is planful rather than impulsive. It posits that many immediate gratifications must be foregone for larger future gratifications and that, in the long run and more often, pleasures of the senses are better served by and thus often subordinated at any given time to the rules of social intercourse and planning for the future.

Essentially, under the reality principle, an individual substitutes love, affection, and pleasant social intercourse for many immediate, direct personal satisfactions. Traditional Freudians often overlook the crucial part played by cognition—intellect, the ego—in the process of moving from the pleasure to the reality principle. Traditional Freudian theory stresses drive and libido at the expense of intelligence and ego.

[3]Neal Miller has done pioneering work in this field.

The distinction between the Apollonian principles that some believe govern the middle class, and the Dionysian principles, aspects of which are believed to typify the disadvantaged social classes, roughly parallels the distinction between reality and pleasure principles.

To continue to sketch in a learning theory of socialization, the author believes that very young infants learn through classical conditioning that results when biological drives are satisfied by primary or unconditioned rewards. The biological drives most influential in early socialization, to review material presented in Chapter 1, are those whose satisfaction demands social interaction between a helpless infant and his caretaker. Logically, the most important of such needs are hunger, elimination (also closely linked to cleanliness, modesty, and sexual training), probably aggression, dependency, and curiosity, as well as sex. By adolescence, patterns of handling each of these drives except sex are well established, and much learning about sex has already occurred.

Dependency and Imitation–Modeling in Socialization

Within the conceptual framework that the author finds useful for viewing adolescence, dependency is thought of as a drive. One is dependent on others, in a broad sense, if he modifies his behavior in order to keep their good will rather than simply because he fears the consequences of deviant behavior. Others *in general are positive reinforcers.* Dependency as a drive should be distinguished from dependency as behavior. As *behavior,* dependency may be either the clinging, open assurance seeking behavior that is subsumed under emotional dependency or the implicit or explicit seeking from others what one needs in order to accomplish a task. The latter type of dependency behavior may be thought of as instrumental dependency (see Heathers, 1955; and McCandless, 1967, for fuller treatment of this distinction).

Imitation means doing what someone else does. Gewirtz and Stingle (1968) regard imitation as a broad response category. All socialized people, they think, have acquired generalized predispositions to imitate. It is probable that one is more likely to imitate those whom he likes than those he does not like, but there are many exceptions. Specific and generalized imitations are discussed later in this chapter, and Gewirtz and Stingle's position is presented.

Modeling is an approximate synonym for imitation, but is generally used in a broader sense: In imitation, one *does* like someone else; in modeling, one tries to *become* like someone else. Modeling may or may not include direct imitation.

Dependency as a drive very likely has biological roots. If there were no one to care for the infant, he would die. In the normal course of events, infants (presumably first through classical and later through instrumental learning) associate caretaking adults with primary satisfactions such as food and comfort. These must be provided if the infant is to survive. The caretaker—and people in general—come to have reinforcing properties because they have become associated with the infant's primary gratification. They are powerful and enduring secondary reinforcers. Their association has been so frequent and over so long a period, at least for a well-reared infant, that an older child or adolescent can go for very long periods with no real satisfactions from others, yet still like people and change his behavior so as to please them. Socialized dependency when thus defined becomes a "trait" in the sense that Ferguson's "overlearned cognitive habits" become "intelligence" (see Chapter 7 for the summary of Ferguson's theory).

As was stated above, dependency, in the present context of adolescent psychology, simply means that one cares enough for others (they possess reinforcing properties for him) that he will modify his behavior to please them. Not all modification occurs because of loving dependency on others, however; much occurs because the modeler — the person whose behavior is changed — fears the model or authority.

The process of socialization is endlessly complicated by the human being's enormous capacity for symbolic development. Remarkably little attention has been paid to the relations between symbolic, cognitive, intellectual development and socialization.

The bases for socialization seem to be compounded from having learned that people are important and, ideally, well disposed (or the contrary, dangerous so that behavior must be shaped in defense). On such bases, the socialization process occurs so as to please or appease others, and thus to secure one's own ends directly or indirectly. A second process in socialization is very likely conscious and unconscious imitation of other people's behavior. This is based partly on having learned that there are rewards for both specific and generalized imitation; and partly on a "need" for imitation that has been learned because imitation has so often been rewarded (again, this brings Ferguson to mind). On this basis, one may be predicted to work for or modify his behavior so as to secure positive social interaction, whether or not it comes from someone who is highly regarded. There is, in other words, a *social drive*: Rewarding social interaction satisfies it; absence of such interaction intensifies it; negative social interaction frustrates it.

Gewirtz (1969) ascribes to such an interaction need hypothesis. In one of his studies, performed with elementary school boys, he finds that after a period of relative social deprivation (low ratio of praise from the experimenter, a person who was neutral to them) boys work harder and learn the experimental task better than other boys whose immediately previous experience has been with an experimenter who gave generous and frequent reward.

McArthur and Zigler (1970), on the other hand, subscribe to the idea that simple deprivation of positive social interaction is not a major determinant in shaping behavior. The important factor is whether or not the learner likes the person with whom he interacts. In other words, dependency is based on liking others. In the absence of such liking, imitation will be less probable. Employing second grade boys as subjects, and a male and female experimenter, McArthur and Zigler led one group of boys to view a woman experimenter as most unpleasant, while another group was taught that she was benign and kindly. This was done by means of films. In the unpleasant film, she was shown being disagreeable with a group of second grade boys, climaxing her general nastiness by drinking the soft drink and eating the cookies that had originally been designed for the group.

Three days after viewing the film, all boys were taken individually into a room where the male experimenter asked them to draw pictures for a period of 10 minutes while "waiting for the lady." For half of them, he gave frequent praise (every 30 seconds); for the other half, praise was given only twice during the 10 minutes. The woman experimenter then took over, and set the boys to putting marbles into a marble board, a most unchallenging task, since the only requirement was to put green marbles on the right, yellow ones on the left.

Regardless of whether they had had frequent or infrequent praise preceding the marble task (high and low social satiation), the boys who had seen the film showing the experimenter as a "nice lady" worked significantly longer and a bit faster (but not significantly) than the boys who had seen her at her nastiest.

While both these studies employ preadolescent subjects, they deal with general principles of reinforcement that may plausibly be thought to operate regardless of the maturity of the subject. While the evidence is by no means all in, the present author's judgment is that the emotional feeling held for a person (dependency) is more important in how one modifies his behavior than is the sheer frequency of previous social interaction, although both undoubtedly operate. One will modify behavior both because of liking and because of loneliness, in other words. But the former is more likely to produce important behavior changes, at least among adolescents. The practical implications of this reinforcement role were described in Chapter 10 within the context of the school, but fit equally well here.

Socialization as Generalized Imitation

Regardless of whether one imitates and models because he is dependent ("likes others") or because he simply needs social interaction, it is now commonly accepted that imitation is a fundamental process in becoming a social human being. The literature about imitation and modeling is now both very large and very influential. Bandura is a leader in developing a theory of imitation (see, for example, Bandura and Walters, 1959, 1963; and Bandura, Grusec, and Menlove, 1967a and b). Gewirtz and Stingle (1968) consider both Bandura's work and the work of others in the field; and they embrace Skinnerian theory in a general, often analogical way. Their treatment is recent enough, inclusive enough, and important enough to deserve considerable discussion in a psychology of adolescence.

Briefly, Gewirtz and Stingle, like a growing number of others, believe that imitation is the foundation for socialization. They present "a simple instrumental learning model, with imitation representing one type of acquired stimulus control over responses" (p. 375). Behavior is imitative if it fits the cues provided by the model's behavior but not if it is set off by the same stimulus that initiated the model's behavior. Behaving like a model because one is required to is also excluded from imitation proper. This exclusion thus confines direct imitation to behavior emanating from reinforcing or pleasant rather than punitive people as models, and to positive but not negative reinforcement. Reverse imitation and modeling, under this theory, result from dislike and fear.

The author believes that direct or identification modeling can also occur because of fear (negative reinforcement). Discussion of such modeling and of "identification with the aggressor" is presented in the next two chapters.

In Gewirtz and Stingle's terms, the modeler (or subject) learns, consciously or unconsciously, to manage occurrences in his environment (stimulus control) by behaving like the model. However, *in the model's case*, it was the stimulus itself that set the behavior off; while the modeler has as his stimulus only the model's behavior. If the behavior works for him in handling the stimulus as it did for the model, then he is likely to repeat it, whether or not the model is present. Additionally, modelers are likely to receive positive reinforcement for modeling behavior, even when the modeling behavior has no immediate goal (for example, "You walk just like your dad," received from people who like both the dad and the modeler, is likely to cause a boy to consolidate his style of walking, and may strengthen his masculine self concept).

While modeling is likely to occur upon all sorts of models, American family structure is such that it will typically be focused on members of the family, particularly parents and older siblings.

Gewirtz and Stingle reject copying as imitative behavior. The present author prefers to include it. Working with children, he has observed what he calls "purposeful onlooking." A child engaging in purposeful onlooking watches intently and seems mentally to be rehearsing what his model is doing. Often, after a period of such onlooking, sometimes days or even weeks, the child will suddenly venture forth into a situation he has not previously entered and perform successfully in it. This behavior is by no means confined to young children. The author has practiced it himself. He has sometimes succeeded in emulating others' handling of situations that he thought they handled more effectively than he was accustomed to. Practiced, such deliberate copying can become as much a part of one's social stance as more "unconscious" imitation can.

However, Gewirtz and Stingle are probably correct when they argue that modelers are often not aware of what they are doing. However, they may model by chance, or be physically assisted, or directly trained. Modelers rapidly move from discrete imitation to classes of imitation, and develop a pattern of generalized imitation that may include thoughts and attitudes as well as more overt behavior. To repeat, modeled behavior is consolidated if it works. Life patterns are such that imitation is more often rewarded than punished.

Reinforcement is likely to be triple: Since imitation is the sincerest form of flattery, the model is likely to reward the modeler for behaving like him whether or not this is done consciously. Second, the behavior imitated is as likely to work for the modeler as it did for the model, and thus be incorporated into his style of behaving and thinking for the same reasons it was originally consolidated for the model. Finally, as has been said, others are likely to reward the modeler, particularly if his modeling is of the socially approved sort that it usually is when a boy behaves like his father or a girl like her mother.

Classes of imitation are soon set up, based on the common goal for many responses that may be quite different from one another. For example, a girl usually has much opportunity to watch her mother interact with tradespeople. The goal of such interaction, of course, is to obtain as much good quality goods as efficiently and cheaply as possible. The mother is mildly flirtatious with the butcher, rather patronizing to the clerk who sells shoes, "one of the girls" with the woman in dresses, offhand and business-like when buying family toiletries. All these responses fit into a class of "relating with salespeople." If the mother is effective and her shopping usually goes well, the girl is likely to build for herself a complex set of imitative responses for her shopping. An advantaged girl's set of responses is likely to be reasonably good humored, self-assured, and thus effective, as she is usually well received by salespeople. A disadvantaged girl may build a class of responses that is maladaptively servile, uncomplaining, or, perhaps, aggressive and suspicious, reflecting her own history of often unpleasant interactions in stores, where she may have been ignored, snubbed, or possibly cheated.

Reverse imitation often occurs, but it is true imitation nonetheless. A boy who is embarrassed by his father's flirtatious ways with waitresses may reverse model and adopt a cool and distant stance with those who serve him at the table. Or the boy who dislikes much about his father, an engineer, may reverse model by choosing art or comparative literature as his college major; or reject professional life entirely, drop out of high school, or refuse college. Upward mobility may conceivably be motivated by parental rejection, as well as by imitating and adopting the standards of the parents who want the child to be more successful and better educated than they have been.

A general stance of "learning to imitate" is almost certainly picked up by socialized people. When the models are good, this is advantageous. On the other hand, imitation of "bad" models can interfere seriously with socialization. Parents, often with justification, bewail the influence of their children's peers on them. Bandura, Grusec, and Menlove (1967a) have shown experimentally that the presence of a peer model with low standards for his own performance profoundly interferes with children's modeling on an adult who holds much higher standards for himself. If the climate within a classroom is one where the standard of excellence for academic achievement stops at mediocrity, as claimed by Ringness (1967), then modeling on their peers can only interfere with school progress. Certainly, the peer group possesses much power and certainly peers model mutually on each other.

On the whole, however, a general set of adjusting by imitation, whether conscious or unconscious, is essential in the socialization process. Its necessity is acknowledged in the culture by folksayings such as, "When in Rome, do as the Romans do," "You are known by the company you keep," and the widely employed criterion of guilt by association. The watchful eye kept on teachers by the community is still another example, although this censorship of educators' personal lives is disappearing, at least in urban areas.

In general, when the model is rewarded for his behavior, the modeler assumes that it is also permissible and even desirable for him to imitate. Herein lies one of the dangers of violence as depicted in films and television. Youngsters confined to ghetto areas, and often suburbs, for that matter, often have before them the example of men and women who are well esteemed, but whose success and prestige have come via shady channels. The poor boy without two nickels to scrape together in his pocket may well model after the hustler, who seems always to be well dressed, to have a car, and to be in possession of money. This is frequently the mechanism by which a youth begins to exploit the illegitimate opportunities open to him in his community, as discussed in Chapter 6.

STAGE THEORIES OF SOCIALIZATION

Stage theories, as has been mentioned, are saltatory: An individual is thought to move from one clear descriptive level of development to another. Stage theories have the virtue of convenience and neatness, but are typically descriptive rather than explanatory. Their neatness and appearance of permanence may retard scientific inquiry and particularly inquiry into change—an individual's behavior as he moves from one level or stage to another. Stage theories, strictly speaking, are not developmental in nature, since development demands an assumption of continuity and process change. Such theories often fail to help one obtain an understanding of adolescence, since change is central to adolescent psychology.

But since much knowledge of socialization is still at the descriptive level, it is appropriate to discuss at least one stage theory. Erikson's (1956, 1963) neopsychoanalytic theory has been chosen for several reasons: He pays much attention to adolescents; he is aware of and has been influenced by modern social learning research; and he has practiced psychoanalysis with people widely different in age and social class. This distinguishes him from many therapists, whose work is likely to have been confined to upper-middle and upper-class people.

Erikson believes that socialization passes through eight phases as an individual progresses from infancy to old age and death. These he calls the "eight stages of man." He thinks of each as a psychosocial crisis that must be resolved before one can move effectively onward to the next stage. In a sense, his theory is pyramidal and hierarchical. Stage 1, for example, is *trust versus mistrust*, is resolved during infancy, and is the base on which all later stages of adjustment and socialization rest.

Erikson anchors his theory much less than Freud on instinct and the organs of the body. His major variables are social forces as they impinge on the human organism at different periods in biological and physical maturity.

He describes each stage in a bipolar manner: The adjective or phrase that describes one end of the distribution characterizes good socialization in the sense of product or status (as in "trust," above), while the other end describes ineffective or malign socialization (as in "mistrust"). Presumably a population is normally distributed from one to the other end of the continuum. Few members of the population will be at either end of the continuum. More members fall toward the middle, and, although these members may vacillate from time to time and person to person in the degree to which they trust, there will be the central tendency to be trusting or cynical.

Erikson's Theory   Erikson's eight stages of man are:

Stage 1: Trust versus Mistrust   This basic tendency of a person to be optimistic and trusting as opposed to cynical and mistrusting is thought by Erikson to develop during the first year or two of life. It seems to depend on almost total acceptance by the infant—the positive noncontingent reinforcement that has been discussed before. Since infants are predominantly nonsymbolic, classical conditioning is probably the mechanism involved in their learning of trust and mistrust.

It follows, then, that it will be difficult to retrain a mistrusting person or disillusion a trusting one, since adolescent and adult life include few opportunities (and techniques) for reconditioning an individual according to the classical paradigm. Some of the newer therapies, however, stress classical conditioning techniques, and seem to hold considerable promise. Wetzel (1966), for example, recounts the course of reconditioning a compulsive thief whose stealing seemed to be based on "total mistrust" of his world. Wolpe's (1968) book is a classic in this field.

Stage 2: Autonomy versus Shame   This stage occurs between 1½ and 3 or 4 years of age. It corresponds generally to Freud's anal stages of psychosexual development. In American culture, it is the period during which children are usually toilet trained. Erikson believes that gentle handling of this process results in a child's learning self-sufficiency and pride in himself, while unwise handling produces a child who is ashamed of his behavior and afraid of the way society regards him (another illustration of the relationship of process to product). Learning during this stage is a mixture of classical instrumental conditioning; although being toilet trained is certainly an instrumental response, while trusting or mistrusting may be classical conditioned responses. Behavior shapers (like Wetzel) offer constructive suggestions about toilet training, and employ a mixture of contingent and noncontingent reinforcements.

Stage 3: Initiative versus Guilt   This is the play age which extends from about 3 years of age or a little older until the child enters formal school. During it he learns to interact with his environment with reasonable confidence that he can cope with it; or he is immobilized and withdraws. While learning during this stage may belong to both the classical and the instrumental learning families, it is likely that the latter predominates. Thus, it might be thought, maladjustment tracing to this time of a child's life may be more easily overcome later by planned remedial action than maladjustment tracing to an earlier stage.

Stage 4: Industry versus Inferiority   An adolescent who has developed normally will already have resolved stages 1, 2, and 3; and may have resolved stage 4. However, anyone who works with youth in school, on the job, or doing chores around the home knows that most adolescents still have considerable resolution of stage 4 to accomplish (see Constantinople, 1969, and her college aged subjects in Chapter 15). Well-socialized young people realistically and energetically tackle the job of learning the skills necessary to live in their society. Ill-socialized young people may retreat into underachievement in school or show similar manifestations of their perception of themselves as inferior—as even worthless.

It may be that stage 4 is set before adolescence. Some say that, at least for groups, children either "have it made" or are "foredoomed to fail" by the end of third grade. There is modest consensus that, as far as school is concerned, most normal children who are achieving up to their ability level go rather matter of factly on to accomplish what they need as long as they remain in school; while relatively few of those who are floundering at the end of third grade manage well. Fitzsimmons, *et al.* (1969) present depressing evidence that such is the case.

Since learning industry versus inferiority seems to be largely a matter of instrumental learning, it should be possible to reverse pathology surrounding this stage. Encouraging results were reported in the previous chapters. The increased flexibility, even fluidity, of adolescents due to the addition of a new drive should make remedial work concentrated at this level a good bet. However, it is all too seldom available.

Stage 5: Identity versus Identity Diffusion This stage is the principal focus of adjustment for adolescents, according to Erikson. As has been said, successful finding of one's identity can be illustrated by saying that such a person has found a stable and satisfying answer to the question, "Who am I?" In identity diffusion, such an answer can not be given. As suggested in Chapter 1, most adolescents experience at least some identity diffusion, and are likely to experiment with delinquent, rebellious, bisexual, or underachieving roles for a longer or shorter time. Many never establish a satisfactory identity.

The psychosocial moratorium has often been mentioned in earlier pages. Such a "cushion" for role playing seems to be provided for most advantaged youth. If disadvantaged adolescents stub their toes, they are committed by society, often quite literally, whereas much charity is extended to the advantaged group.

Stage 6: Intimacy versus Isolation Many adolescents begin to enter and some even resolve this psychosocial crisis. To be intimate involves giving up one's autonomy (or at least being willing to give it up): dropping defenses almost totally and revealing oneself as he is before entering into an intimate relationship with another, whether this be sexual or in friendship. Once intimacy is reached, one becomes committed to the other, and thus, in a sense, is no longer his own man. The rewards of intimate relations are indeed rich; the loneliness known by the person who can not achieve them are great.

If girls and women have weaker needs for autonomy than boys and men, it may be that it is easier for them to find intimacy. On the other hand, they may be more aware of the need for it, thus miss it more if they do not have it. Their task or achievement orientation may help males compensate for a lack of intimacy in a way that is available for fewer females, or perhaps less satisfactory to females in American culture. The different meanings of sexuality to boys and girls, at least early in their sex lives, have already been discussed: Boys, in a manner of speaking, are task oriented—they want physical satisfaction; girls are intimacy oriented—they want a warm and loving relationship.

The last two Erikson stages typically occur after adolescence.

Stage 7: Generativity versus Self-absorption Those who resolve the seventh stage—a psychosocial crisis—successfully have typically found satisfaction in their families and their work.

Stage 8: Integrity versus Despair Stage 8 is resolved in middle and old age. Successful resolution is the comforting thought that one's life, on the whole, has been a good one, while despair includes the vain cries, "If only I could live it over again," and "Where did I go wrong?"

Observations As has been pointed out, as one moves upward through Erikson's stages, primary rewards and classical conditioning play less and less part with each successive psychosocial crisis; while secondary rewards such as relations with people and instrumental learning enter in more and more. The fifth stage, which usually includes adjustment to mature sexuality, represents a reversal to some degree. Early experiences with sex often result in classical conditioning due to the emotion that accompanies them and the ignorance that surrounds them.

The author has had the chance to observe informally but intensively in two cultures, West Pakistan and the United States; and less extensively in Jamaica. In Pakistan and Jamaica, families seem to handle stages 1 and 2 better than they are handled in the United States. There is an easy acceptance of very young children and a lack of abrasiveness in providing for their needs and comfort that contrast sharply and favorably with typical United States patterns. But stages 3 and 4 seem to be more effectively guided in the United States. Stage 5, coinciding with adolescence, seems almost nonexistent in Pakistan, and is similarly foreclosed, at least for disadvantaged youth, in Jamaica. Such respectable authors as Douvan and Adelson (1966) seem to suggest that in the United States, too much is made of stage 5.

The present author sees no average difference in the effectiveness or happiness of Jamaican, Pakistani, and United States adolescents and adults. If anything, the exigencies of the two developing nations perhaps make the existence of the average West Pakistani or Jamaican less happy than his like-aged counterpart in the United States. The fairly broad sample known to the author suggests that, sexually, Pakistani seem more troubled than United States residents. Jamaicans (at least lower-class Jamaicans) may be more relaxed in the area.

Such observations plus research data lead the author to question the concept of near irreversible pyramidal and hierarchical adjustment and socialization implicit in Erikson's theory. Dislocation at any point in the eight stage structure seems to throw the whole "building" off balance. In learning theory, it is admitted that the older a person is and the more firmly entrenched his ways of behaving are, the more difficult it is for him to regroup himself. But it is also argued in learning theory that substantial change is possible at almost any time, given enough motivation and appropriate techniques. This is both an optimistic and a logical conclusion from a social learning framework, and may be why such a theory for accounting for socialization and emotional adjustment is so appealing.

SUMMARY

While socialization as a product or a description of status is at best an unsatisfactory scientific term, attempts to define it must be made. If science is to serve society, determinants of adequate (socially useful) and inadequate (personally and socially harmful) socialization processes and products must be investigated by research workers. Emotional development goes hand in hand with socialization: The social situation is the soil in which emotional development is nurtured.

Socialization as a product can be thought of as the class name for everything an adolescent does that concerns other people, directly or indirectly. Emotional development refers to whether he does these things happily or unhappily, aggressively or amiably, actively or passively. But in turn, such characteristics are inferred from behavior. Thus, emotional traits, like socialization, are judged in a social context. The list of behavior and attributes included under the topic "socialization" is as broad as the possible range of social-personal relations and characteristics.

One of the best indexes of both social and emotional adjustment is the status of a child or an adolescent with his peers, the immediate reference group of youngsters with whom he is most closely associated. Sociometric techniques designed to elicit acceptance or rejection as a friend and as an esteemed colleague in a working relationship provide a sound measure of such status, and quite usefully and reliably reflect real life behavior and social networks. They can be employed only with the consent of adolescents and their parents, and used with rigorous professional ethics.

A discussion of social and emotional development, particularly the end results but also, necessarily, the processes, must necessarily include many value terms. Socialization adequacy is culturally relativistic; and social and emotional adjustment can not be judged without taking into account the adolescent's social reference group, his age, his sex, his socioeconomic status and, often, his race.

While it is postulated here that social and emotional development are most strongly shaped by learning, still they can not be understood or predicted without fully considering such intraindividual characteristics as intelligence, body build and time of physical maturity, activity level, and modes of sensory reception and personal expression.

A major problem in United States society is to reconcile the highly personal needs for expression and gratification as represented by the Dionysian mode; and the Apollonian characteristics of personal control, consideration for the group, delay of personal gratification, need for achievement, and so on. A generous application of noncontingent reinforcement (uncritical acceptance and liking for the *person*), combined with contingent reinforcement (that which is given to consolidate or eliminate specific types of behavior), seems to be the best recipe for combining these two life styles, each of which is necessary for socialization that is both personally satisfying and socially useful.

While intraindividual differences exert an important influence on both the process and the outcome or product of social and emotional development, the general dimensions of a culture also affect them profoundly. Girls, in American culture for instance, are shaped toward nurturance, responsibility, and obedience; boys, toward achievement and self-reliance.

An imitation, generalized imitation, and modeling theory of socialization and, by implication, emotional development was developed in the chapter. Children and youth imitate because they have learned to need social interaction, and because they like (in a sense, are dependent upon) the people on whom they model. Imitation seems to become an "overlearned habit," almost like a trait. Imitation is usually positively reinforced by the model, by the fact that it typically secures for the modeler the same things it secured for the model, and because it is rewarded by other people. Gewirtz and Stingle's specific and generalized imitation theory was discussed.

In stage theories of social and emotional development, the crucial dimensions of change from one to another level are often overlooked and such theories are often deceptively simple and straightforward seeming classifications. However, they can be useful. In Erikson's eight stage theory, each stage is depicted as a psychosocial crisis. The three of his stages most important at adolescence are stage 4 (industry versus inferiority), stage 5 (identity versus identity diffusion), and stage 6 (intimacy versus isolation).

13

Sex and Moral Identification: Modeling and the Role of Power

INTRODUCTION

Four points should be clearly articulated and re-emphasized in introducing this chapter:

First, children, youth, and adults modify their behavior because the people with whom they interact are important to them. They like or love them, want to keep their good will, and do not want to disappoint or hurt them, although modeling because of fear can also occur.

Second, modelers rely on models and need to interact with them. Dependency may be extreme or mild, clear or disguised, positive or negative, emotional or instrumental. Modeling is more likely to be positive and direct when dependency is based on liking or love, more likely to be negative and reversed when based on dislike or fear. However, such behaviors as overprotection may result in unhealthy dependency, based, at least in appearance, on love.

Third, modelers clearly know that their potential models possess power that affects or can affect them.

Fourth, the model is seen to possess skills and competencies that enable him to reach goals the modeler wants to reach for himself.

Modeling is *being* like the model, and the modeler may or may not behave exactly like (imitate) the model. However, imitation (doing like the model) is one very important part of modeling.

Chapters 13 and 14 deal with different processes and products of socialization than those which were highlighted in Chapter 12. Chapter 12 clearly emphasized the dimensions of noncontingent and contingent reinforcements as processes that shaped the outcomes of socialization (usage of the terms, noncontingent and contingent reinforcement, is not rigorously Skinnerian in the present book, being more broadly descriptive in intent). Additionally, the outcomes or products of socialization were conceived of as characteristic personal behavior that fitted well or ill with society. Chapter 13 takes up the methods by which noncontingent and contingent reinforcements are administered: the types of power possessed by adult, sibling, and peer models, and the ways in which the types of power are exercised.

While the socialization products that are chiefly dealt with in this chapter have public manifestations and are subject to consensual cultural judgment, they are more slanted in their nature toward the personal rather than the public than were most of those that were discussed in Chapter 12. Sexual and moral identifications are very deep lying personal attributes or predispositions. Both of them are complex, the latter exceptionally so. Moral identification is also more cognitively *determined* and *demonstrated* than sexual identification. Both, however, in the theoretical framework that is adopted here, develop from models, through imitation, and as a result of contingent and noncontingent reinforcement. It should be re-emphasized that, among human beings, *self-*reinforcement is often as effective as *external* reinforcement, particularly among inner-directed people. Self-reinforcement, of course, undoubtedly develops in its turn from patterns of extrinsic reinforcement that were exerted early in children's lives.

Chapters 13 and 14, being so closely interwoven, are summarized together following Chapter 14.

POWER The prime mover behind imitation and modeling seems logically to be power. In an operational sense, possession of reinforcing potential is the definition of power. It is realistic although not fashionable to talk of power in human relations. One rather likes to think of this society as equalitarian, where power rests with laws not men; where behavior is influenced by reason and not influence; and where each man may proceed according to his own rights as long as he does not transgress unduly on the rights of others.

Nonetheless, as observation and research show, power is a major variable in human relations, regardless of the nature of the society in which it is exerted. Since power is a major determinant of who is imitated by a modeler, and, since modeling and imitation are foundations of socialization, which includes sex and moral identification, it is essential to discuss power in detail. The type of power possessed, the ways it is communicated, and the styles by which it is exerted are all a part of the process of socialization.

The analysis of the types of power that follows is partly adapted from Wolowitz (1965). An analysis of power must also include its different manifestations and effects in any adolescent's particular effective culture (his family, friends, school, community, and social class). Different types and styles of power are exerted and are influential as a function of a person's age and sex.

Definition of Power

A model possesses power if he has something someone else wants or fears. However, he is powerless unless the potential modeler knows he is willing and/or able to share it or dispense it. For example, the aged poor in this culture are powerless because they have nothing anyone else either wants or is afraid of. If it is clear that one will never share what he has or that he is too weak to dispense punishment, then he is powerless. Finally, unless the fact that one has power has been communicated to the potential recipient, he is powerless over him.

Newcomers to a group are likely to brag in an effort to communicate to their new acquaintances that they have power. When a youth or a copopulation (such as many Black activists) has been alienated, power to influence has been lost. The youngster or the group no longer either wants or fears the power of the would-be model or tutor. If adults can not communicate with adolescents, then adults have lost most of their effective power. The picture of secondary schools presented in Chapters 8 and 9 suggests that teachers and administrators fear that they can not communicate "lovingly" or on equal terms with students, and possibly that they have little that the students truly want; thus, they reduce their communication to dimensions of control and punishment. Society has lost all power over the desperate man who no longer cares whether he lives or dies. Fanon (1966), writing of colonialized people, believes that they have been reduced to such straits that they figuratively and perhaps literally must destroy their oppressors, the colonizers. Only thereby can they regain their own long lost manhood and womanhood. His book makes heady reading for prejudiced-against minority groups in the United States, and is recommended as an antidote against complacency among the more socially favored.

Comfort Giving

Comfort giving is the power to nurture, take care of, comfort, and extend friendship and love. A comforter can bring change in a child or an adolescent because he wants to please, and because he does not want to hurt the comforting model or to lose his love or approval. Comfort giving also induces modeling (see, as an example, the McArthur and Zigler, 1970, study reviewed briefly in the preceding chapter). Comfort giving is traditionally ascribed more to mothers than fathers and friends, although research indicates that it is by no means confined to mothers (see, for example, Droppleman and Schaefer, 1963; Moulton, *et al.*, 1966; and Mussen and Distler, 1959).

Parsons (1955) believes that mothers and fathers fill different roles for their children. Mothers, he thinks, help children with *expressive* socialization and women characteristically occupy an expressive role in society. Expressive human functions include such things as building good human relations, freedom of emotional expression, particularly the tender emotions, and admission of fallibility. The male role and the type of model provided children by their fathers is *instrumental*. Instrumentality suggests need for achievement, task orientation, and realistic coping with the inevitable realities and tangibles of life, including being able to compete adequately.

Johnson (1963) believes that mothers typically do not supply the "teaching" necessary for clear masculine and feminine sex typing: They give unconditional noncontingent reinforcement to a child for being what he is. Fathers supply the contingent reinforcement that is necessary for a boy to learn to be masculine and a girl to learn to be feminine. Fathers, Johnson thinks, bear the brunt for achievement training in their children of both sexes.

The research literature abounds with evidence for children from infancy to young adults in college that comfort giving power shapes behavior effectively. It varies according to the sex of the giver and receiver (among young children, females seem to be more effective with girls, males with boys, for example), the age of the receiver and giver, perhaps his race, and the degree to which the giver is perceived to be similar to the receiver. J. P. Flanders (1968) has reviewed the imitation literature.

Using 3-month-old infants as subjects, Wahler (1967) finds that their mothers are much more successful in eliciting smiling during a controlled experiment than strangers. Rubenstein (1967) worked with 6-month-old babies. Those babies whose mothers had been found to be very highly attentive in a positive way were much more curious and interactive with their environment than babies of moderately or low attentive mothers.

Hartup and Coates (1967) found that nursery school aged children, whose histories included a pattern of receiving much comfort (friendly behavior) from their peers, when placed in an experimental situation imitated generous peer models more than children who typically received little comfort from other members of their preschool peer group. Hartup, Glazer, and Charlesworth (1967) found that the most popular preschool children were those who gave the most comfort to other children (were friendliest).

Kindergartners (Grusec, 1966) showed more "conscientious" behavior (blamed themselves more frequently) when the experimenter handled them with nurturant techniques rather than when she gave tangible rewards and punishments. First and second graders (Parke, 1967) who had been treated nurturantly by an experimenter, then had had the nurturance interrupted, resisted temptation more strongly than children of the same age who had received continuous nurturance from the experimenter. Those children, by having nurturance withdrawn, seemed to have learned to value it highly, to wish to have it restored, and not to risk its loss. Their finding supports the Gewirtz (1969) position described in the preceding chapter. Additionally, girls were more responsive to nurturance withdrawal than boys.

MacDonald (1969) quite plausibly believes that first born children will be more thoroughly socialized than later born children because they have had the undivided attention of more adults for longer and thus, presumably, have been closer to adults. He checked his hypothesis for a population of college men and women: First borns showed evidence of more thorough conventional socialization than later borns. More of them kept their appointments with the experimenter; fewer of them expressed doubt about the honesty of the experimenter; and fewer of the first born men withdrew from a potentially painful experiment (it was predicted that courage, as a male virtue, would have been more instilled into the well-socialized first born male more deeply than into the later born; but that, since women are permitted fear in our culture, this would not be the case for the college girls. Both predictions were supported. Otherwise, there were no sex differences).

From these selected references, it seems that there is little question but that comfort giving modifies social behavior of many types across a wide age range. Much more research is needed, however, before all the parameters of its effects can be filled in.

Comfort giving varies widely according to social class, sex, and age. Disadvantaged children receive less than advantaged children both at home and, as seen in the last chapter, at school. Boys, at least after the earliest ages and perhaps even in infancy, receive less comfort giving than girls (Johnson, 1963); and older children less than younger children. The evidence is conflicting about whether mothers give more comfort to their sons than their daughters, although fathers seem to give more to their daughters than their sons (Johnson, 1963).

Physical Power   The second type of power is physical. It, too, varies by social class, sex, and age. Parents of either sex are all-powerful to very young children. As a child of either sex grows older, he soon begins to see that his mother is less powerful physically than his father. By middle to late adolescence, boys are often stronger than their fathers; and both boys and girls have usually moved beyond the stage where their mothers can count at all on physical power to discipline them. Fathers can not be certain.

To depend on physical power as the major method of child control is, then, a short term investment. There is little or nothing in the research literature that suggests that physical discipline possesses any long term advantages. Most evidence indicates the opposite. However, exerting physical power to control children is parsimonious, being quick and, unless too often employed, effective at a particular moment in time. As has been suggested earlier, exerting physical power, like other drastic punishment, is likely to inhibit *all* behavior, not just the behavior against which it is directed. Thus at any age spontaneous constructive behavior may fail to appear so it can be reinforced.

Boys are more likely than girls to be controlled by physical power or its threat, although a startling number of fathers—including middle-class fathers—beat their daughters. Boys are more likely to value physical power than girls, for it is thought to be "masculine."

Physical power is both more frequently used and probably more esteemed as a source of prestige among disadvantaged than advantaged groups. Its value appears to be particularly high among adolescent males, who see it as a certificate of a masculinity about which they are not yet psychologically certain. For many men from disadvantaged social strata, their physical strength is almost their only source of power and esteem with their children. When they lose it, or when their children catch up with or exceed them in strength, their effective power is gone.

Sexual Power   The third class of power is sexual. This source of power, its value, its employment, and its variations have been fully discussed in Chapter 4 and need not be repeated here. It should be emphasized, however, that sexual power is a potent influence on imitative and modeling behavior at adolescence; and it is about this issue that much of the generation gap conflict centers. Pulls between the standards of the peer group (rarely as loose as the older generation believes) and caretakers (parents and teachers) over this issue are intense. I. L. Reiss' (1968) data have already been cited, indicating that adolescents view their own behavior as being more liberal than their parents, less liberal than their friends; but closer to their best friends than to their parents. By 16, most boys have had a friend or an acquaintance who has fathered a baby. Such sophistication exerts powerful pressure on boys to follow suit, although few boys wish to carry the behavior to the fatherhood stage. Almost all girls of the same age have many friends with sex experience, some of it followed by unfortunate consequences. The modeling influence is more conflicted for girls: They fear the social and biological consequences at an intense personal level not known to boys; but on the other hand, the pressure to be grown up and experienced is great. Most girls who date are also under steady sexual pressure from their boy friends.

Expertness   The fourth class of power that seems important in shaping socialization is omniscience, or knowledge, or expertness.

This type of power makes as much impact on youngsters from one social class as another, although different types of expertness exert different amounts of influence within the various social classes, on the two sexes, and on young people of different ages. Middle and upper socioeconomic status people, while they may be enthusiastic about the sports and arts, are likely to place more emphasis on expertness in professions such as law, journalism, and economics (expertness interacts with prestige, or clout, as will be seen below).

Small boys as well as adolescents strongly appreciate athletic prowess. Athletes may have more status with girls also, at least in secondary schools. Young girls still seem to idolize the actress and chanteuse; older girls may admire successful hostesses or career and professional women more. The expert at his trade is more likely to be esteemed by the skilled or unskilled tradesman than by the middle-class man (another illustration of the interaction of prestige and expertness). However, on the whole, older boys and men being themselves task oriented, as they are in this culture, are likely to give considerable respect to anyone who is good at his trade, regardless of what this trade is.

As has been suggested, some types of expertness carry minimal prestige: Male ballet dancers, who hold high prestige in the Soviet Union, are often denigrated in the United States. Salesmen are said to carry with them an air of self-apology and are reputed to tell their sons, directly or mediated through their wives, not to follow in their footsteps.

Boys model on expertness that society considers appropriately masculine, girls on expertness designated as feminine. There are, of course, tremendous individual variations in this theme. A television documentary shows the ballet dancer, Edward Villella, clearly conveying to boys attending his old high school that there is nothing at all sissy about men in ballet. The boys, initially exceptionally skeptical, visibly viewed ballet as more masculine after exposure to Villella.

With increasing age and firmly established by adolescence, children's evaluations of expertness approach their parents' standards about both expertness and occupational prestige.

In this task-oriented society, expertness at one's job is likely to be the most important source of a father's or mother's power, particularly when society esteems the job. Expertness is usually associated with steady employment and advancement. The steadily employed man who improves his status is in general a more satisfactory model for his children than the man who is in and out of work. Coopersmith (1967), for example, found that high self-esteem among the boys in his sample was related to their fathers' steady employment.

Prestige The fifth and final class of power refers to status, prestige, or influence. A vivid term for prestige, taken from the argot, is "clout." Like expertness, clout is independent of social class, but takes different forms from one social class to another. The ways in which clout operates have been implicitly discussed in the preceding section on expertness, since it is artificial to separate the two. Expertness *plus* prestige are much more influential in motivating modeling than either alone. In this society being a chemist is good. Being a *good* chemist is certainly more than twice as good.

Expertness and prestige are positively correlated in their influence on modeling and imitation, although the relationship is variable. An expert embalmer does not have the prestige in middle-class society that an expert judge has. Old but inexpert and nonaffluent families have more clout, it is said, in Boston and Savannah than they have in Los Angeles or Chicago. The mobsman may have high clout in the inner city, little or none (or negative clout) in the suburbs.

Like expertness, an adult pattern of clout is well established by adolescence. Prestige patterns seem to be remarkably stable in American society. Hodge, Siegel, and Rossi (1968), for example, report a correlation of .99 between occupational prestige among adults and adolescents as measured in 1947 and again in 1963. Girls and boys appear equally susceptible to the influence of clout, although different things carry different prestige for the two sexes. For example, "a nice family" seems to hold more impact for the average girl than for the average boy. This is perhaps another illustration of the conservatism and desire to maintain the equilibrium that is said to characterize women.

Upper-class children whose parents were born aristocratic face peculiar problems in the expertness–competence–prestige area. So do the offspring of exceptionally competent prestigious but not necessarily upper-class people. Youngsters from such families may have more difficulty with socialization than those from more humble families. It is a middle-class virtue, mediated by both fathers and mothers, for sons to succeed more than fathers, and daughters to marry better than mothers. The struggle to escape from the shadows of their illustrious parents may be very difficult for children of prestige parents.

McArthur (1955), one of the few who has conducted research with upper-class groups (college students), believes that in contrast to the middle class, upper-class persons substitute "becoming a good person" for expertness and prestige, concentrate more on the present and past than on the future, discipline themselves more strictly, and are more selflessly interested in their fellow man. This seems a sensible and constructive solution to the problem of being better than one's father.

Women face a difficult problem in this task-oriented society. As they have gained equality with men, the prestige of being a housewife seems to have declined in the eyes of many. However, almost any housewife and mother quickly sets herself a notch above the spinster.

Occupational prestige is a function of the level of education required for training for the job, plus the power over the lives of others the position is judged to carry with it (as in medicine or the judiciary), plus to a considerable degree the returns in money from the job. While wealth invariably contributes to a considerable degree to clout, it is not sufficient in and of itself to confer the fullest prestige upon its possessor. However, it is a standard criterion of both expertness and prestige.

To illustrate clout, it is useful to list the highest and lowest ranking jobs (Hodge, Siegel, and Rossi, 1968, reporting 1963 data): United States Supreme Court Justice ranked first; physician second; nuclear physicist and scientist were tied for third place; and government scientist and state governor were tied for fourth rank. Within this list of six, nuclear physics had shown a dramatic increase in prestige, having moved from eighteenth in 1947 to its tie for third in 1963.

Of the ninety occupations ranked by Hodge, Siegel, and Rossi, soda fountain clerk, sharecropper (one who owns no livestock or equipment and does not manage a farm), garbage collector, streetsweeper, and shoe-shiner occupied eighty-sixth to ninetieth place in that order. They had held almost exactly that order in 1947.

Perhaps the changes in occupational prestige over this period of sixteen years tell a little about American culture. Between 1947 and 1963, according to Hodge, Siegel, and Rossi, the following occupations changed ranks upward by five or more ranks: nuclear physicist; government scientist; chemist; lawyer; instructor in public schools; public school teacher (these two for some reason were considered to be different); electrician; policeman; carpenter; and local official of a labor union. The order of the listing is from highest to lowest prestige ranking in 1963. Labor union official holds a tie rank for fifty-fourth place of ninety. In 1947 the position ranked sixty-second.

Also given below in the order of 1963 prestige are the occupations that lost five or more ranks between 1947 and 1963: diplomat in the United States foreign service; mayor of a large city; head of a department in a state government; banker; owner of a factory that employs about 100 people; artist who paints pictures that are exhibited in galleries; musician in a symphony orchestra; farm owner and operator; radio announcer; manager of a small store in a city; traveling salesman for a wholesale concern; playground director; and farmhand. The farmhand held eighty-sixth place in 1963, seventy-sixth in 1947.

The bottom prestige ranks appear to be more stable—perhaps relentless—than the top. Of the thirty bottom ranks of ninety occupations in 1963, only two had changed five or more ranks since 1947, and both of them had lost prestige. But of the top thirty, ten had changed five or more ranks since 1947, six of them having gained in prestige.

As has been said, expertness and prestige in contrast to physical power influence modeling more among older than younger children. Adults speak proudly of father's success before retirement. Contrariwise, the man with an unskilled job or who is poor at his job rapidly loses his power as his children grow older. This poses a serious problem for modeling among disadvantaged boys. The problem is particularly acute when their fathers are not only unskilled and perhaps inept, but also discriminated against. This is true for disproportionately many Afro-American, American Indian, and Hispaño youth. Middle-class Black males also suffer from discrimination, but they may gain additional prestige in their children's eyes by having succeeded in spite of "whitey." On the whole, it is probable that boys from disadvantaged minorities must make a harder struggle for healthy masculine socialization than advantaged youth such as from the WASP middle class.

Coaches are expert at something that is highly valued by American youth (sports) as instructors in public schools. They hold considerable occupational prestige (above owners of factories that employ about 100 people, building contractors, exhibiting artists, musicians in symphony orchestras, authors of novels, economists, or newspaper reporters or columnists, according to Hodge, Siegel, and Rossi). Thus, they possess great potential power as models for boys of all social classes, perhaps particularly for disadvantaged boys. The author has made it clear that he believes that at this point in history many coaches have failed to use their potential as constructively as they might. Wistfully, he wishes they were better trained in developmental psychology and felt free to do more with all youth, not just the athletic stars. Coaches have the built-in potential for being the most effective personnel in the public schools, and certainly many *individual* coaches do provide fine models for youth.

MEDIATION OF POWER IN THE MODELING PROCESS

The assumption behind the previous discussion of types of power is that imitation and modeling occur only when the modeler perceives and esteems the power of the model. What attributes and behavior of models make it most likely that modeling on them will occur?

This question has great practical importance. This entire section should be considered for its practical as well as theoretical implications. Such products of socialization as sex and moral identification, achievement motivation, impulse control, and adaptive responses to frustration depend to a substantial degree on the nature of the model, the process by which modeling is accomplished, and the setting within which it occurs.

These matters are the concern of this section. The six factors that seem most relevant are discussed below.

Predictability Power will be ineffective unless it is meted out in a manner that the model can make sense of. As has been suggested earlier (see Bresnahan and Blum, 1970; Epworth, 1968), disadvantaged youngsters' worlds have characteristically been disordered, unpredictable, and often violent. They seem to approach new situations with fewer hypotheses than advantaged youngsters, whose lives have typically been more rationally planned. In "sensible and rational" situations, such as schools, this difference works very much to the benefit of middle-class youngsters. In the frequent irrational, even absurd situations, disadvantaged children, open minded as they are, do as well or may actually have something of an edge on their more privileged peers.

Regardless, human beings attempt to organize their worlds so as to predict what is coming next. Adolescents, like children and adults, try to adapt their behavior so as to exist as comfortably and profitably as they can in any given situation. The brighter and more socially sensitive will obviously succeed better in the long run, since there is some fragment of pattern in most human affairs. There is also at least a partial key to predicting the behavior of most people if one looks hard enough, intelligently enough, and long enough. Unfortunately, this is not always true, nor are a person's efforts to be comfortable in and profit from his setting always conscious. People are often unaware of the mechanisms they use to adjust.

No matter how expert, prestigious, physically powerful, full of sexual prowess, or abundantly comfort giving a parent or any other model may be, a child or young person is much less likely to model on him if he can not predict how the model's power behaviors will be exercised, or if the modeler can not see whether or not the behaviors are successful. Human nature being what it is, the modeler often constructs his own pattern for the model's behavior through such devices as wishful thinking and (perhaps) motivated forgetting and purposeful remembering or interpretation. On the whole, however, a clearly detectable pattern in the model's behavior makes it much more likely that modeling will result. When an outcome can be predicted somewhat more than 50 percent of the time, prediction of modeling may be made with some confidence, other things being equal. Rosekrans and Hartup (1967) provide support for this point. For the young children with whom they worked, modeling was high when the outcome of the model's behavior had consistent results; but no more modeling occurred when the results were inconsistent and thus unpredictable than for control subjects for whom no model was available.

Equitability The amount of power used should be equitable and fair. Festinger and his students (1957, 1964) present some theoretical rationale and provide some research data to support this point. When power is exerted overwhelmingly, its recipient seems to feel that he has acted without personal violation — has been a mere pawn responsive to forces outside himself. Hence, he does not commit himself psychologically to the course of action he has been compelled to take. Incommensurate punishment for moderate crime may be ineffective both for such reasons as well as because it arouses resentment instead of compliance. Parents and other caretakers frequently feel guilt or shame after they administer exceptionally or unfairly severe penalties. They then recant and fall into the two-way bind of being not only unfair but inconsistent. Extreme punishment also makes martyrs out of people. Martyrs typically receive enough reward from others who are like-minded that the intent of the punishing model is more than nullified by the positive reinforcement that the punished person receives from others.

Finally, if punishment is severe enough and frequent enough, its receiver reaches the point where he no longer cares: "Nothing any worse can happen to me." This may result in alienation with the consequent loss of all power by the caretaker or authority. Open rebellion sometimes results. The harshness of penalties toward possessing marijuana seems to produce as much sympathy for those who are caught as it does abstinence from smoking among the young. Fanon (1966) addresses himself to unreasonable punishment, subsequent loss of power, and ultimate violent rebellion among colonialized, exploited, and persecuted people.

Like overwhelming punishment, extravagant reward is likely to be construed as arbitrary and unpredictable. Consequently it is ineffective. It is possible that it also causes a person to think that he is important not because of what he *is*, but of what he *does*. Such an attitude is in the long run likely to be damaging to intrinsic self-esteem.

Perceived Similarity An individual seen by the modeler as similar to himself is apparently both more attractive to him and more effective in producing imitation than one seen as different. Byrne and his colleagues (for example, Byrne and Clore, 1967; Byrne and Griffitt, 1966) and Rosekrans (1967), using both questionnaire and experimental procedures, find that similarity even in the absence of powerful drive is a strong basis for attraction, and that imitation for those seen as similar is greater than for those seen as different. Subjects for these studies have ranged in age from 9 years to college ages.

Youth also apparently model their sexual attitudes and behavior on those whom they see as most similar to them. As has been mentioned, I. L. Reiss (1968) finds that individuals place themselves intermediate between their parents' attitudes and the attitudes and standards of their friends in sex beliefs and behavior. They rate themselves as less conservative than their parents, more conservative than their friends. In Reiss' study, 89 percent of the sample reported they were closer to their best friends than their parents. Reiss also found a rather strong relationship between sexual attitudes and practices. About two-thirds of his subjects reported that they actually behaved as they believed. They were high school and college students and adults, ranging upward in age from 16 years.

Levitt and Edwards (1970) report the apparent high influence upon one's smoking of his best friends. In making the yes–no prediction about who did and did not smoke in their sample of fifth through twelfth graders, having *best* friends who smoked accounted for 36.4 percent of the variance; the fact that *most* of one's friends smoke accounted for another 7.5 percent. Smoking and not smoking among parents had almost no influence (none for fathers, only 0.7 percent of the variance accounted for by smoking mothers), and television none either as a result of the public service advertisements against smoking or from tobacco commercials.

These studies provide good grounding for the common observation and assumption of the powerful effect of an adolescent's peers on his behavior, and testify to the important modeling dimension of perceived similarity. This perception of similarity may lie at the heart of the powerful influence of their peers on most adolescents. *Adolescents are full of drive.* Thus, their problems loom to them as very acute. Peers who are seen as like them and who are also perceived as having found some workable or dramatic solution to the problems of adolescence will become powerful models indeed (for example, the cheerleader, the prestige athlete cum scholar, the hustler, and the successful delinquent).

Communication That Power Is Possessed

Mere possession of power is not enough to make it effective in producing imitation and modeling. The potential modeler must *know* that his model possesses power. Perceived similarities he can see for himself, which probably has much to do with the great power of their peer group over most adolescents who, cognitively, have become adroit at determining similarities and relations (see Chapter 8). Other types of power are not in all cases so self-evident. For a young child, the power of his caretakers is made abundantly clear from his earliest years in that they comfort him, exert physical power over him, and perhaps demonstrate their sexual power. Omniscience or expertness is also conveyed early to a child: His shoes are tied, and his questions are answered.

More sophisticated information about expertness and prestige must await the time when the child goes out into the community and begins to compare his parents, his home, his wealth, and his parents' reputations with those of his friends. By adolescence and usually much earlier he acquires full and quite accurate information about these matters. Indeed, it may be his awareness that there are other people who are better that contributes to the disillusionment about their parents so many adolescents express, and the turning to the peer group that is apparently so characteristic. Authoritarian parents and teachers typically set themselves up as all powerful and all knowing. They thus render themselves particularly vulnerable to older children's sweeping disillusionment. It is a wise parent or caretaker who prepares himself for the inevitable by admitting he is not perfect before his children or students discover it for themselves. Such a parent or a teacher is less likely to lose an adolescent completely to the influence of the peer group.

As has been suggested, physical power (which is *very* easily and clearly communicable), becomes less important in inducing modeling with age, although its potential importance when combined with expertness is great among adolescent boys. Little is firmly known about the role of sexual power. Certainly, among one's peers, and interacting with perceived similarity, it is very important at adolescence when it is communicated. The author has known young people who modeled closely on parents of both sexes who indulged in a great deal of random sexual behavior. He has known other young people who "reverse modeled" on similar parents and became almost prudish. Children of divorce seem themselves more likely to be divorced, but whether there is a cause and effect relation is not known. In certain cultures, as was mentioned in Chapter 4, fathers' *machismo* is imitated by their sons. The homosocial way of life that is thought by some to be frequent among the disadvantaged is also likely to become the way of life of their sons and daughters. If stud behavior is frequent *and obvious* among his older and same-age male compatriots, and his father too behaves in this way, the adolescent boy will be likely to follow the same pattern, as will the girl in a community where women, including her mother, take many lovers. A boy is more likely to behave homosexually in prison, in a boys' school, on a merchant marine or navy ship, or in the service than if he is circulating freely in a coeducational society. The interaction of knowledge that such behavior is open to him, his need, models, and *opportunity* account for this. Kirkendall (1961) documents the role of the example of peers in instigating intercourse with prostitutes; and the role of communication about sex by peers as an incentive to modeling was also discussed in Chapter 4.

But obviously, much more information than is now known on the influence of sexual power on modeling behavior is needed. Communication about it is apparently a central factor in its effectiveness.

Information about the influence of comfort giving behavior is little clearer. Certainly its style must change with age. The troubled 4-year-old male may want to sit on his father's or mother's lap and be hugged and kissed. By 10, he may signal his need for comfort by lying down so that his hair lightly touches his dad's knee as the latter reads the paper. Still later, he may signal his need for comfort by simply hanging around. It takes a perceptive parent to know when his older children want him to give comfort, and to know how and how much to administer if it becomes clear that it is wanted. Adolescents' need for comfort, their embarrassed or angry rejecting it if it is not offered with exactly the right set of subtle nuances or if it comes at the wrong time, their parents' shyness or effusiveness, all produce considerable tension between parents and other caretakers and adolescents of both sexes. The problem is perhaps more acute among males. Adolescents often see comforting offers as signs of their own weakness, thus reject them vigorously.

By adolescence, boys and girls may reject all comfort from their parents and teachers. They seek and may find it among their peers, which, too, often leads to parental hurt feelings, but is probably a useful, even necessary developmental stage. It is a hard lesson for parents to learn that, to hold on to their children, they must first turn them loose. If well handled, they come back, closer in many ways than ever before. The problem of communicating to adolescents that comfort is available is a difficult one, both for adults and among adolescents themselves.

To summarize, children and adolescents learn about their models' power by interacting with them, seeing power demonstrated, observing their model purposefully or incidentally, hearing about his power from the model (this is not likely to be effective if it takes the form of bragging), and learning about the model's power from others. This last method is singularly effective. To illustrate the power of communication, it should be mentioned that the elementary school aged children studied by Bandura, Grusec, and Menlove (1967a) modeled much more on the young male model when they overheard another adult praise him for his high standards of behavior than when the other adult merely thanked him for helping with the experiment. This constitutes a singular advantage for competent people and gives established middle-class people a distinct edge over disadvantaged parents. Father may be a boor in the home, but when his children hear from others that he is a wheel (or at least, a solid and respected citizen), then they are likely to look at him with at least a touch of respect and consider thoughtfully which of his behaviors it may profit them to incorporate. On the other hand, children will experience difficulty modeling on the man who is saintly at home, but for whom community feedback is negative.

Willingness to Share Power and Ability to Inflict Punishment

If one is to model, he must know the model is willing to share with him what the modeler wants. The things shared may range all the way from tangibles, such as a job or training in a technique, to affection and comfort. Perhaps that portion of their power best used by teachers is their willingness to share their skills with their charges. As seen in Chapter 9, this is the only reason why Lahaderne's (1968) subjects could conceivably profit in the classrooms she describes. Ringness' (1967) older subjects also seemed to keep going with that as their sole motivation.

However, as has been seen, much imitation occurs without direct teaching. If one sees that the model can do something the modeler wants to do, imitation is likely to occur. Girls adopt the hair styles of their feminine heroines, boys the speech or stance of their favorite television or screen hero.[1] The leaders of the peer group produce much modeling both because of their perceived similarity and their power to share with or punish others.

Defensive Identification Freud's notion of "identification with the aggressor" has received sufficient research support that it merits discussion (see, for example, Hartup and Coates, 1967; Hetherington and Frankie, 1967). The theory may be paraphrased colloquially to "If you can't lick 'em, join 'em." It is an important part of Freud's theory of appropriate sex identification among boys. The boy, fearful of the power of his father (the concept of castration threat) incorporates the father's image (attitudes, perspective, actual masculinity) so as to be like him. Thus, the son is presumably safe from his father's powerful threat. It may be that when there is no possible escape from threat, the threatened child or person takes on the characteristics of the oppressor in self-defense. This mechanism has been used to account for the behavior of prisoners in concentration camps in World War II, or the identification with the majority group that discriminates against them by minority cocultures such as the Jews and Afro-Americans.

[1]The present author, a twiddler, once set half the population of a school for delinquent adolescents to twirling keys on the ends of their key chains. He was an important source of power to the boys, and this was one of his conspicuous nervous habits.

Something like identification with the aggressor often seems to occur when children grow up in authoritarian and punishing circumstances which they can not escape. It may be an adjustment mechanism for many disadvantaged children. Such children as a group apparently receive less comfort giving, more physical punishment and verbal abuse, and are controlled in a more authoritarian way than middle-class children (see, for example, Bowerman and Elder, 1964; Droppelman and Schaefer, 1963).

Hetherington and Frankie (1967) reveal something like defensive identification in their study of 4 to 6½ year olds from a small Midwestern town, although their finding just misses significance at the .05 level. In high stress homes where there was much conflict, children imitated the dominant parent more than was true in homes with low conflict. One can speculate that conflict was a way of life in such homes, with child seeing the winner take all. In the absence of any chance to escape or to model on anyone else, modeling–identification was made on the boss. However, among Hetherington and Frankie's families, if the nondominant parent was warm and comfort giving or if the conflict was reduced, there was less imitation of the aggressively dominant parent. In other words, the warm parent, even though not the most powerful, provided an escape hatch. It may also have been that, with a lower drive level due to lower conflict, the child does not need to "seek safety in identifying with hostile power."

In circumstances like those described above, identification with the aggressor fits well enough with behavior theory as outlined by Gewirtz and Stingle (1968). However, modeling theory does not fit well with the psychoanalytic theory that all boys identify through fear with a concept of castrating fathers. Many fathers are in actuality warm, tender, and loving to their sons. Their sons in turn perceive them as warm, tender, and loving. Since such boys seem to make the most satisfactory masculine identifications, a question about adequacy of theory is clearly raised: It becomes a choice, in this case, between Freud on the one hand, and Skinner as expanded by Gewirtz and Stingle on the other.

Straightforward Punishment and Modeling It is to be hoped that few children live in environments so harsh that they are forced to identify with the aggressor. The effect of punishment is usually more straightforward and less pervasive in shaping modeling than in the hypothetical case of defensive identification. For most children and youth, it is likely that the model's power to punish is simply seen as one facet of his total power: the logical other side of the coin from his ability to give rewards. For such children or youth, punishment may merely be a clear-cut negative reinforcement telling them *not* to repeat what they just did; or change their way of doing it (see Blum and Kennedy, 1967, where combining reward and punishment, or neutral treatment and punishment, both changed dominant behavior in children more than a treatment that combined neutrality with reward).

There is considerable evidence (see Grusec, 1966; Hoffman and Saltzstein, 1967) that modeling as manifested in moral development is more likely to occur under circumstances where children and young people are handled democratically, and where psychological rather than thing-oriented techniques of control are employed. But firm data are needed to establish this for sure, and to fill in many missing links in the explanatory chain. Hoffman and Saltzstein suggest that in the absence of adequate adult models (parents in the case of this study), disadvantaged children turn to their peer group for moral modeling.

It has already been mentioned several times, but the point is important enough to deserve repetition, that punishment tends to dampen all responses (reduce activity level, prevent behavior from occurring). This is true both for the response at which it is directed and others that may be creative and constructive. Thus, to extrapolate to real life, spontaneity may be squelched; and spontaneity is the mainspring of original, creative behavior (of course, the spontaneous behavior may be either constructive or nonconstructive, but at least it is overt).

Communication and Modeling   A model who was effective enough for a young child may lose effectiveness as children grow older if communication is closed off. This is what many adults mean by saying they can not communicate with their teenage children or students: They are inferring that, because they have no effect on them, no communication occurs. All too often, communication *does* occur, but it has the wrong content. However, as adolescents begin to do most of their talking to their peers, communication between parents and teachers and young people probably does slack off. Reduced discussion reduces modeling in both directions. Parents and teachers are quite as capable of learning from young people as young people are from them. It is a common observation that second and later children have an easier time with parental controls at adolescence than firstborns because the firstborn has trained the parents.

The Puritan tradition is strong in the United States. Many parents, probably more fathers than mothers, fail to communicate their love to their children. Love, appropriately and tactfully conveyed, is a major type of comfort giving. In addition to the Puritan ethic, or perhaps because of it, Americans are shy about showing tender emotions. For men, the strong, silent stereotype militates against expressing the love they feel, for either their children, their wives, their friends, or their parents. This makes the problem of love communication even greater between fathers and sons (where the stereotype affects both) than between mothers and their children.

The Role of Affection   The evidence is strong but not absolutely clear that mutual affection constitutes the atmosphere within which the other dimensions of power operate most benignly for modeling imitation. Moulton, *et al.* (1966) present evidence that, for sons, the parent after whom the son is most likely to model is *both* dominant and loving. Moulton and his colleagues studied college men. In about 70 percent of the cases, the sons said their fathers were dominant. Among these father-dominant families, 55 percent of the fathers were high in affection, according to their sons. In the families where the mother was reported to be dominant, only 44 percent of fathers were seen as high in affection.

Bronson (1959) worked with 9- to 13-year-old boys; Mussen and

Distler (1959) studied kindergarten boys; and Mussen and Rutherford (1963) extended the Mussen and Distler study to girls. In all three cases, the findings fit well with the Moulton, *et al.* results, despite different ages, populations, and methods of study. Parenthetically, in the complex personal–social field of study, straight replication studies are rare. Thus, writers are often compelled to conclude that something is probable if a number of different studies, each often open to criticism and none directly comparable, all point in the same direction.

Ratio of Positive to Negative Reinforcement

The sixth and final mediator (mechanism for producing modeling by the application of power) is the ratio of reward to punishment. This was discussed briefly in Chapter 10. The author (McCandless, 1967, p. 424) has conjectured that power is more effective in producing imitation and modeling when the model reacts toward the model so that the reward to punishment ratio is greater than 1. However, defensive identification is a clear exception to this hypothesis. The important factor in modeling *qua* modeling seems to be the consistency or predictability of the model's behavior. The *quality* of the modeling is perhaps even more important than the fact that it occurs, however. It is thus permissible in this context to extend the ratio hypothesis speculatively to include the concepts of good and happy adjustment and creative socialization, even though these terms are hard to define scientifically. When the hypothesis is extended in this speculative way, we can predict that the modeling which occurs in a setting where the reward to punishment ratio is substantially greater than 1 will be accompanied by less anxiety, will be more flexible and adaptive, and will be accompanied more by hope of success—optimism—and less by fear of failure—pessimism. This may even be a successful recipe for securing a useful blend of Apollonian devotion to reason and a sensible social order with the Dionysian capacity for enjoying life, human relations, and one's own senses to the fullest.

Chapter 9 showed that there are data that indirectly support such a speculative extension of the ratio hypothesis. A very generous infusion of positive reinforcement greatly facilitated reading progress for Clark and Walberg's (1968) remedial reading pupils. Behavior therapy suggests that accentuating the positive and ignoring the negative consolidates good behavior and extinguishes bad behavior. On the whole, then, it seems that up to some unknown upper limit, it is better to exert power in a setting where reward greatly exceeds punishment.

Manifestation of Power versus Uninterest

It is clear from the discussion earlier in this chapter that modeling can result from both benign and positive and negative and punitive manifestations of power, although it seems clear that the end product is a happier one if power is exerted benignly and positively. It is worth introducing Coopersmith's (1967) conclusions again in this context: His high self-esteem, middle-class, late elementary school aged boys came from homes where parents manifested concern for them, where the fathers set models of competence in their jobs, where limits were clearly defined but flexibly and realistically reinforced, and where the individual rights of the boys were respected. Goals for the boys were also clear, realistic, and rather high. There seems no reason to believe that such a pattern is not equally applicable for girls, for adolescents, and for disadvantaged as well as advantaged children and youth.

Evidence is provided by two studies that at least some demonstration of power, in the form of taking an interest in an adolescent, is better than no such demonstration (uninterest). In the first study (Rosenberg, 1963), 1684 high school juniors and seniors from New York State were studied by the questionnaire method. The young people were asked to think back to their fifth and sixth grade years, and to estimate the degree of interest their mothers and fathers showed in them at that time. Three areas of interest were chosen for study: the degree to which parents were interested in relations with their friends; whether or not their parents were keenly involved with their academic progress; and whether or not their parents were responsive to them at the dinner meal. A typical question was, "During this period, did your mother know who most of your friends were?" The possible answers were: all, most, some, or none, or a fifth alternative, "I can't remember."

The findings were exceptionally clear-cut and pointed to definite advantages for the adolescents' self-perceptions among both boys and girls when parents showed a keen interest and concern, regardless of whether this was positive or negative in direction. Manifestation of interest by fathers and mothers both was important, although it was apparently necessary for the fathers to be more extreme than the mothers in their behavior for their influence to be manifested. Rosenberg performed a number of statistical operations and exerted a number of different controls upon his data (such as for tendency to confide in the mother). The results summarized above, even with controls exercised, held equally for different religious groupings such as Protestants, Catholics, and Jews; for both male and female adolescents; for children from cities, medium-sized communities, and small towns; and for parents who were strict or lenient, or who manifested fair or unfair punishment.

A summary of Rosenberg's results given in Table 13.1 sets the picture even more clearly than writing about them.

The over-all distribution within Table 13.1 is statistically significant at less than the .001 level in the direction of the prediction that high parental interest is related to high self-esteem. It is reassuring to note that the great majority of adolescents who remember report that their parents manifest considerable interest in them and their affairs, at least as the adolescents look back to their fifth and sixth grade years (more than 80 percent report that their parents were usually or always interested and involved in what they were doing, as compared with only 19 percent who reported that their parents were only sometimes, rarely, or never concerned). While Rosenberg's evidence is not entirely clear, and while it points to the importance both of the parents' feeling tone *and* their interest, interest per se seems more closely related to adolescents' self-esteem than the quality of the interest.

Heilbrun and Gillard (1966) report similar results from a study of college girls and their reports of how their mothers reared them. Girls were more responsive to social reinforcement (in general, this is a desirable tendency) if their mothers had given them considerable attention than if they had given them little or none, even if the attention took the form of rejection or overprotection.

Table 13.1 *Relationships between parental interest and self-esteem*

Self-Esteem Category	Frequency of Interest Manifested by Parents			
	Always	Usually	Sometimes	Rarely, Never
High	52%	45%	33%	33%
Medium	23%	27%	25%	16%
Low	25%	28%	42%	52%
Number of cases	698	446	173	89

(Adapted from Rosenberg, 1963.)

Cass (1952a and b) provides evidence that fits with the two research studies mentioned above. She administered a test of modeling to high school girls. She measured modeling by summing the number of interests and activities her girls shared with their mothers, who had independently responded to the same activity scale as their daughters. Cass further assumed that high modeling is an indication of high identification, an assumption that Gewirtz and Stingle would probably find legitimate. Closely modeled girls among the middle class but not the lower class were those whose mothers knew accurately what their interests and activities were. It can be assumed that such mothers were interested and concerned with their daughters. This relationship did not hold significantly for lower-class mothers, or for mothers of delinquent girls. Apparently, the interest shown by middle-class mothers is reasonably benign and positive, by lower-class mothers more punitive and critical, and by mothers of delinquent daughters most punitive and critical of all. Although the methods and populations of their studies are very different, the parallel between Cass' and Hoffman and Saltzstein's (1967) results is striking: Rather high relations between parent and child behavior for middle-class people in the morality identification area; but low and non-significant relations for lower-class people. These findings must be interpreted cautiously, but suggest that lower-class parents may be more punitive, less involved with and aware of their children, and that they constitute less prestigeful and thus influential models for their children. It may be that lower-class youngsters seek their models among their peers rather than their parents.

RELATIONSHIPS BETWEEN MODELING AND IDENTIFICATION

Bandura, Grusec, and Menlove (1967a), in a paper that has been mentioned repeatedly, studied 7- to 11-year-old boys and girls. Some of their findings have been reported (more modeling occurs when feedback is given to the children praising the high quality of the model's behavioral standards; less modeling on the high standards adult occurs when children who are lenient in giving themselves rewards are also present in the experimental situation). Bandura, Grusec, and Menlove's adult model refused to reward himself on a bowling type game unless he had done very well indeed; when other children, confederates of the experimenters, were present and also playing the game, they were quite free in giving themselves rewards for low level performances.

In this study, the subjects were said to model when they refused to reward themselves for game performances below the adult model's minimum standard for rewarding himself. This, obviously, is not direct imitation but rather is the copying (or perhaps incorporation) of the model's *rules* for acceptable behavior. Thus, it comes very close to what is meant by "conscience," and has a certain moral ring to it.

Identification, as the term is ordinarily used, is an inferred construct. It is not directly observable. Like "intelligence," it is said to exist at a low, intermediate, or high level. Most adolescent males like girls, feel erotic toward them, are easy in all aspects of masculine behavior, are glad and even proud of being male, dream male-type dreams; walk and talk in a masculine fashion; possess masculine interests; and are easy with male friends but harbor no erotic impulses toward them. Such young males have a high level of masculine identification. Reversing the gender in the preceding sentences would provide a composite picture of an adolescent girl with a strong and easy feminine identification.

If conflict is introduced — if the boy is predominantly masculine, but has to strain consciously to keep up his masculine front and, perhaps, is erotically attracted both to males and females — then his male identification is at best intermediate. Again, there is a picture of an intermediately well-sex-identified girl upon reversing the genders. When behavior and preferences are more like those of the opposite sex, then a boy or girl is inappropriately identified sexually.

Moral identification is more complex than sex role identification, perhaps because morality is more complex than sexuality. Sexuality after all, is either-or, although its interrelationships with morality are exceptionally complex (see Chapter 4). Morality is many things to many people. It is likely that cognition is much more involved in moral than in sex identification. In an effort to define moral identity more fully and satisfactorily, Kohlberg's (1964, 1967) treatment will be discussed in the next chapter.

According to Gewirtz and Stingle (1968), generalized imitation begins to merge into identification when it shades into imitation of values, and when several or many different responses are fitted into a generalized class. Gewirtz and Stingle use the example, "Mother keeps a tidy house," to illustrate the classification a girl may make as a guide for her own behavior. Whether the girl will make such a value classification part of her own values (identify with her mother about this value) depends on a host of things about her relationship with her mother and her life as a whole, most likely along the lines of the discussion in the preceding pages of this chapter.

Imitation of values, like any other imitation, can receive an infinite variety of reinforcements, including self-administered reinforcements. Since personal perceptions among sane people bear a reasonable resemblance to real life, that which is self-reinforced is usually also that which is reinforced by others who are imporant to an individual.[2]

---

[2] As a driver, I *feel* good when I slow my car and wave so as to allow another driver boxed in on a side street to enter the mainstream of traffic ahead. I may even tell myself consciously that I am a nice and considerate man. I am likely to obtain reinforcement from the driver, if our eyes meet: He will often wave or smile gratefully. I have the mildly self-righteous feeling of setting a good example for others. A minor glow invades me, and the six o'clock traffic situation seems, on the whole, more endurable. I have been objectively reinforced, and I have also administered reinforcement to myself.

So it is with moral behavior. Unlike much other generalized imitation, moral behaviors and moral identification in general depend almost exclusively on social reinforcement or long-delayed primary reinforcement. There may be a substantial immediate *disadvantage* to not cheating when it is perfectly safe to cheat. Yet the morally identified person steadfastly refuses to cheat. He controls his impulse toward the immediate reward to be gained by cheating. He may never receive any primary reward for his honesty. On the other hand, over his life span, in perhaps many important situations and at the hands of many important people, he may receive great rewards for his honesty. These rewards or the prospects for such rewards, plus the deeply ingrained habit of being honest learned in earlier life, keep the morally identified person honest according to the guidelines of his society.

In short, Gewirtz and Stingle do not believe there is a logical difference between generalized imitation and identification. Presumably, they include both sex and moral identification in this conclusion. They conclude their argument by saying that

> ... the development of identification behaviors is due to extrinsic reinforcement of the child's imitation of his parent's (or model's) behaviors. The degree to which a child is identified with a particular model is thus grossly determined by the value to the child of the reinforcers contingent upon his imitation of that person's behavior. ... Identification with the model at the level of abstract values may require finer discriminations by the child but, as we have already shown, should follow the same principles as simpler imitation. (p. 392)

To summarize, imitation and generalized imitation are usually considered to include other people's gestures, mannerisms, and methods of obtaining goals, including the goal of avoiding punishments. Upon analysis, the reinforcers can usually be seen to be relatively tangible and immediate. Identification, on the other hand, is the adoption of another person's rather abstract code of behavior and his general life stance. The way in which a person is identified directs his general life goals (to be good, to be just, to be successful) and is invoked in his manner of facing temptations and conflicts. A moral identification, if judged by immediate rewards, is often inhibitory (refrain from doing what is wrong, even though it is rewarding and pleasant) rather than facilitating. The purely materialistic facilitations afforded by moral behavior may occur only in the distant future, and sometimes they never occur.

There is considerable evidence to suggest that identification is a well-learned habit and that, if one is pushed far enough, it will break down. Case histories from concentration and prisoner-of-war camps during World War II suggest that, for most people, when primary needs are denied to the point where an individual's life is at stake, codes of honor, truthfulness, cooperation, and altruism are shed in the interest of survival. Husbands betray wives, fathers and mothers their children, and children their parents. However, history contains the names of many who were great because, under extreme duress, they *never* regressed from a very high level of moral development.

Traditional constructions of identification include the idea of internalization and incorporation. A "father image," complete with paternal codes of ethics, is in some way assimilated whole into the son, a "mother image" into the daughter. These come complete with the appropriate sex identification and a moral code modeled on the parents, and this moral code usually reflects both parents, since there is usually agreement between parents about their children's morality, although there may be great differences in their own standards for themselves. It is often said that guilt is only evidenced by a child who is identified. By guilt is meant "self-punishment in the absence of the remotest possibility of being caught." Guilt is different from shame, a less mature method of personal control: A person is ashamed when he is caught or thinks of being caught. Shame is closer to fear, guilt is closer to anxiety. Some evidence exists that links shame to thing-oriented punishments, guilt to psychologically oriented methods of control. It may be predicted that those who are inner directed—whose locus of control is internal (see Chapters 9 and 15)—are controlled by guilt and also fluctuate less as their environments change; while those with external loci of control are controlled more by shame, and vary greatly from one to another social environment (or set of reward contingencies).

A Representative Research Study The behaviorist model of identification as advanced by Gewirtz and Stingle (1968) is simpler and easier to comprehend and more open to test than the psychoanalytic model referred to immediately above. Considerably more research will be required before a decision can be made as to which is correct if, indeed, either is. The topic of sex and moral identification is socially so important that it deserves the most careful attention of theoretical and research workers. It is appropriate to give a brief summary of one such piece of research. It suggests that identification among high school students can be usefully measured by a reasonably simple questionnaire; that identification may be closely tied to "psychological closeness" or the value attached by a person to the good opinion of another person; but that temptation breaks down the moral structures imposed by identification in a number of cases.

Piliavin, Hardyck, and Vadum (1968) worked with eighty-six eleventh and twelfth grade high school males. Eighteen of them were Afro-American, the rest white. They came from a working-class community.

The subjects were divided into high and low cost groups. High cost boys were those who indicated that it would mean a great deal to them in terms of personal cost if they lost the esteem of their fathers, mothers, and teachers. This measurement was made by a test. A boy was given a high mark for cost if he answered that "Being well thought of by my father [or mother] means everything to me," a low mark if he said "Doesn't matter at all to me" (p. 229). Similar questions were asked about school and teachers.

Each boy was then put into a test situation with three other boys who were confederates of the experimenter. One of the confederates "discovered" the teacher's key (code) to the task, a paperwork assignment, another accepted the invitation to cheat, while the third declined it but said he would not tell on anyone who cheated. The difference between cheating and remaining honest was the difference between earning fifty cents with honesty and up to five dollars by cheating.

The over-all results of the study were statistically significant. One-fourth of the boys who reported they would suffer *great* cost if they disappointed their teachers, their school, and their parents cheated. However, a full 50 percent of those to whom detection *would not be particularly painful* cheated. Dependency (liking and valuing the opinions of others) can thus be seen as an important deterrent of deviant behavior.

Regardless of their statement of the personal cost to them, many more of the boys classified as delinquent cheated than those classified as nondelinquent. If one takes "self-reported criminal acts" as the criterion of delinquency, then 57 percent of the delinquent boys cheated, while only 24 percent of the nondelinquents cheated. This criterion is logical, since a boy who admits a criminal act is willing to profess publicly that he exploits the illegitimate opportunities in his environment (see Chapter 6). Since he is already "known," the cost of being further exposed is presumably not too high, either. The implications of such a finding about "public knowledge" are great, and are further explored in Chapter 15. Once a boy has chosen delinquency, cheating more frequently occurs regardless of the professed personal cost to the cheater. Among delinquents, in contrast to nondelinquents, there is no statistically significant difference in frequency of cheating between high and low cost boys.

Two of the authors' incidental findings are interesting: More than one-fourth of these public school eleventh and twelfth grade boys had already accumulated official police records, and 43 percent of them admitted having committed criminal acts. However, fewer high than low cost boys had either acquired official police records or reported that they had committed criminal acts.

Two conclusions are suggested by this study: Youngsters who are identified with and dependent on parents, teachers, and schools to the degree that they value them strongly are less likely either to cheat or to have police records than nondependent boys. However, given opportunity and peer models who cheat, cheating occurs for a sizable minority (38 percent of the total population of the study). This suggests that a distressing number of male youth possesses rather precarious moral identifications.

It is interesting to compare Piliavin, Hardyck, and Vadum's results with Shelton and Hill's (1969) findings, reported in Chapter 6. Shelton and Hill found no difference in frequency of cheating between public high school tenth and eleventh grade boys and girls. Over all, 53 percent of Shelton and Hill's population cheated. However, percentage of cheating was perhaps inflated for the two experimental groups. The fairest comparison with Piliavin, Hardyck, and Vadum's population of boys may thus be Shelton and Hill's control population of boys and girls (those who had no special pressures put on them). Forty-three percent of the Shelton and Hill control group cheated. This compares closely with the 38 percent of cheaters in the Piliavin, Hardyck, and Vadum population.

Sex Identification and Moral Identification To this point, discussion has been centered around identification with only a general distinction being made between sex and moral identification. At this time, it is necessary to distinguish clearly between the two and attempt to account for similarities and differences between them.

Appropriate sex identification has already been defined: It is being behaviorally and attitudinally similar to the appropriate cultural definition for one's sex, both consciously and unconsciously (as in dreams); and glad of it.

Moral identification is more difficult to define. However, an adaptation of Kohlberg's (1967) highest level of moral judgment provides a good definition: An individual who is well identified morally operates according to his conscience or his principles. His orientation, when necessary, goes beyond actually ordained social rules, although he is respectfully aware of them, and extends to principles of individual choice that are based on logical universality and consistency. The orientation is toward one's conscience as a guide, and to mutual trust and respect. This can be seen as a guide to both sexual and more general morality.

A thoughtful reading of this definition reveals that anyone who followed it precisely could easily find himself in great difficulty with peers, neighbors, and authorities. Thus, for practical purposes, for one who wishes to live with a reasonable degree of peace with his fellows, this highest and totally principled level of morality is modified by less mature but probably more comfortable levels of moral adjustment. As defined by Kohlberg, these involve some attention to an obedience and punishment dimension; some orientation toward gaining approval and helping others; "doing one's duty" even though it sometimes makes no sense; showing respect for authority; and sometimes tipping one's hat to the will of the majority, even though he believes it to be dead wrong. Most people live in a perpetual state of mild to severe discomfort trying to steer their morally tinged conduct on a course that reconciles all these levels: The levels often contradict each other in their demands. In real life, one has to pick his battles carefully, for there is not enough time and energy to fight them all.

A few questions illustrate the difficulties involved in choosing moral courses of action:

1. You are male, you believe the Vietnam War is morally wrong, and you are classified I-A. What do you do?
2. You are male (or female), you believe it is essential for the freedom of mankind that the Vietnam War be brought to an honorable end, and that it is the duty of every I-A man to proceed with induction and combat if necessary. Your dearly beloved brother plans to refuse induction. What do you do?
3. Your school has adopted the honor system for examinations. The choice has been made freely by unanimous vote of the students, including you. You detect your close friend cheating. No one else has seen. What do you do?

Everyone who stops to think at all is confronted by such questions. Life is such that many of them can be evaded or avoided by one or another stratagem. However, in the really difficult case, one has to commit himself publicly to behavior; and the moral behavior is often the hard, the immoral behavior the easy, choice. The path that is chosen at such times is the ultimate criterion for the depth and consistency of moral identification. This is to say: Actions speak louder than words.

Sex and Moral Identification Differences What are some of the differences between sex role and moral identification?

(1) Sex identification seems to occur much earlier than moral identification for most people. The Hampsons (1961) and Money (1961) believe that it can be foreclosed by as early as 3 or 4 years of age, although certainly a clear sex identification is not achieved for many until much later. Everyone seems to agree that mature moral identification is not reached at the very earliest until the teens.

(2) Sex identification offers two clear biological alternatives: male and female. Moral identification, as can be seen from rereading the preceding paragraphs, is infinitely more complex and demands much more cognition and self-criticism.

(3) Sex identification, whether appropriate or inappropriate, receives much immediate, intense satisfaction through an individual's sexual behavior. He can secure such satisfaction through direct and indirect sexual relations with others. He can add materially to pleasure in self-produced sexual outlet by way of accompanying fantasy. Erotic dreams are also reinforcing. On the other hand, behavior that conforms to a strict conscience and high moral identification level is often self-sacrificing in the immediate situation. Even when it is not, its rewards are likely to be indirect and long delayed.

(4) The type of sex identification one makes depends strongly on how one is reared by his parents. Responsibility is thought to rest most heavily on the parent of the same sex. Evidence for this is relatively clear for boys (see Biller and Borstelmann, 1967, and Biller, 1970, for example). The evidence is less clear for girls. At least some authors (for example, Johnson, 1963) believe that sex identification is determined by male caretakers (fathers, typically), for both sexes. Johnson follows Parsons in arguing that mothers are expressively oriented (focused on getting along with others, expressing emotions), and thus provide undifferentiated noncontingent rather than differential contingent reinforcement for sex appropriate behavior among their children of both sexes. Fathers, on the other hand, are instrumental and task- and reality-oriented. They employ contingent reinforcement, rewarding their sons for appropriate behavior and punishing them for inappropriate (feminine) behavior. Fathers tend more to emphasize rewards in reinforcing their daughters for feminine behavior, and punish them less for masculine behavior. Further evidence about differential treatment by fathers and mothers of sons and daughters, as perceived by the tenth and eleventh grade sons and daughters, is reported by Droppelman and Schaefer (1963). Their results fit well with the pattern hypothesized by Johnson.

Katz and Rotter (1969) supply evidence that supports Johnson's argument. Interpersonal trust is a fundamental dimension in one's whole way of conducting his business with the world, and is central to all his personal relationships. It is a style of life including both one's way of behaving and his level of moral development. According to Katz and Rotter "Interpersonal trust is defined as a generalized expectancy held by an individual or a group that the word, promise, or verbal or written statement of another individual or group can be relied upon" (pp. 657–658). Katz and Rotter administered Rotter's Interpersonal Trust

Scale (in 1967) to a large number of male and female introductory psychology students. From the scores, groups of high trust males, high trust females, low trust males, and low trust females were formed. One year after measuring this college student sample, the authors mailed tests to the students' mothers and fathers, timing the mailing so the students would not be at home, asking the parents to return the completed tests within three days, and instructing the parents to fill in their questionnaires independently. Sixty percent of the parents returned the completed forms. There was no statistically significant difference in the frequency of parental return for the high and low trust college groups.

Analysis of the results revealed that the fathers of the high trusting students were themselves significantly more trusting than the fathers of the low trusting students. This effect was much more marked for the father-son than for the father-daughter analysis. The authors comment that it is especially meaningful that this significant relationship between fathers and sons resulted even though the sons had taken the test about one year earlier than the fathers.

Katz and Rotter conclude:

> Fathers and mothers appear to play different roles in the development of trust of others in their children. Fathers seem to play a highly influential role vis-à-vis their sons but seem to have little effect on their daughters. Mothers, on the other hand, appear to show a weak statistical trend of lesser but equal effect on both sons and daughters. . . . Since the father is usually the major liaison agent between the family and external groups and is more involved in the training of sons than daughters, we would expect that his influence on his son would be maximal. (p. 660)

Van Mannen (1968) also reports more influence on adolescent socialization by fathers than mothers. She studied 325 children (mostly adolescents of unspecified age and predominately middle class, white, Protestant, and Midwestern) and their parents. She broke parental characteristics down into categories of effectiveness (satisfaction with role in life), affectiveness (such things as understanding and affection), and domination. She concludes:

> Father's Affective, Effective, and Dominating roles in adolescence are interpreted as being especially strategic for socialization in the adolescent phase of development. Demands being made on teen-agers in our society are thought to leave them peculiarly susceptible at this phase to the influence of the father, who represents the reality of the world outside the family and who is the internal prototype of authority. Interaction patterns of family members tend to become structured, stylized and carried over into other group situations. (p. 150)

Still further support for the important role of fathers in sex and moral identification is provided by Heilbrun and Fromme (1965). They worked with 523 University of Iowa undergraduates, and divided them into maladjusted, slightly maladjusted, and adjusted groups according to whether they had sought counseling help for personal problems (maladjusted), for vocational-educational problems (slightly maladjusted), or had sought no help at all (adjusted). (A logical assumption is that good adjustment subsumes good sex identification.) Degree of identification with and type of role model provided by the parent was established by the students' reports about their parents' characteristics and their feelings toward their parents. The over-all findings were that the adjusted males tended to identify with more masculine father models, while the adjusted females tended to identify with low feminine mothers. This latter finding is not surprising when it is considered that the research population was made up of college women who themselves may be assumed to be seeking a role in a masculine dominated world. The Heilbrun and Fromme findings also fit well with the discussion about cross-sex identification in the next chapter.

Norman (1966) also provides indirect evidence that supports Johnson's thesis about the importance of fathers in the sex and moral identification realm. Norman's subjects were very bright (above 130 IQ) sixth grade boys and girls, some of whom were high academic achievers and thus can be assumed to have modeled after their parents' goals for them; and others of whom were low achievers. The parents of the high achieving youngsters were distinguished from those of the low achievers by being less conforming and more independent (in this culture, these are masculine traits), and by closer mother–father similarity of values than was true among the husband–wife pairs that had underachieving children. This point also relates to consistency in the exercise of power.

The hypothesis that sex identification is "overdetermined" socially is also supported by data for children as early as nursery school age. Boys and girls, particularly boys, reinforce the members of their own sex in sex appropriate behaviors and interests. This is done with great vehemence and striking consistency (Fagot and Patterson, 1969). While Fagot and Patterson's evidence is not complete, it seems that inappropriately sex identified young children (girlish boys, boyish girls) are excluded from their like sex group and thus receive reinforcement for their inappropriate sex typed behavior by their enforced association with children of the opposite sex. Fagot and Patterson's subjects ranged from 37 to 46 months of age when they began their observational study of children attending two nursery schools.

Observation in elementary, junior, and senior high schools suggests that Fagot and Patterson's results apply as well at older ages.

Moral behavior is so much more subtle that no such clear-cut pattern of reinforcement, either from peers or adults, is likely to occur. However, for some morality-linked behavior that has obvious and immediate social repercussions, peer reinforcement is clear-cut. Working with moderately disadvantaged 10- to 13½-year-old boys, Lesser (1959) related different types of aggression to popularity in the group. The only type of aggression that the boys were at all willing to accept was "fighting back when picked on." Indirect aggression, such as tattling or damaging other children's property, correlated a striking $-.69$ with popularity. Lesser's boys showed only slightly more patience with aggressive outbursts, or unprovoked physical or verbal aggression. Thus do peer groups stamp out soreheads, poor losers, squealers, and tattletales, as well possibly as high creatives, academic achievers, and a number of other types with great potential for social contribution.

(5) As was implied in (2) above, moral development depends more on information, or at least upon information that is both more complex and less readily available, than does sex identification. Males and females are present in children's lives as soon as they can discriminate the difference between mothers and fathers and brothers and sisters. Inaccurate and incomplete though it may be, information about sex comes early to all normally socializing children. The differences in social roles of males and females are perceptible almost as soon as their differences in height, weight, dress, and primary and secondary sex characteristics can be detected. This is not true for moral identification. It would be interesting to know, for example, what has been the effect of information that has become easily available in recent years about Black history. Much of the material, even as published in popular magazines, was entirely unknown even to well-educated and generally well-informed mature United States citizens of all races. Have their morally related attitudes toward racism changed as a result of this information, or following such tragic and widely publicized events as the assassination of the Reverend Martin Luther King, Jr.?

The reasons for some of the five major differences between sex and moral identification listed above lie in their differential complexity, in the information about the modeling provided, in consistency and timing of reinforcement, and in directness both of behavior and of obtaining rewards. In each case, circumstances favor earlier and clearer sex role identification.

The principal and most important difference that remains unexplained is the timing and, by implication, the reversibility of the two types of identification. Why does sex identification seem to be so often complete by the preschool years (foreclosed in the case of many with inappropriate identification); while moral identification remains open? It is easier to understand the late formation of moral identification than the early establishment of sex identification.

It may be that human mothers begin differential training patterns for boys and girls as infants, although the evidence is not clear. Among lower species, suggestive maternal differences in handling for male and female infants occur almost from the infant's birth. For example, Mitchell (1968) reports that from birth to age 3 months, rhesus monkey mothers are more than three times as likely to withdraw from their male as their female infants. They show more nonspecific contact, more clasping, and more restraining of their female infants (all but the last of these differences reaches a low level of significance only—the .10 level by two-tailed tests; the last is significant at the .05 level. All, however, suggest a general pattern). Nine of the sixteen mothers of males studied by Mitchell played with their babies, while only one mother of a female infant played, and she only one time. (Rough play may be thought to train for masculinity.) Ninety episodes of playing with their male infants were observed for mothers of males. No observation of aggression toward a female infant was observed; two mothers showed aggression to male infants. Mitchell points out that it is difficult to know whether these differences are due to the nature of the infant, since the male infants seemed to be more active. Harper (1970) documents differential treatment by sex of offspring across a wide span of species (mice to man), as well as across human cultures.

The evidence for sex differences in handling human infants begins to come in, but is too unclear at this time to summarize. Harper has gathered together what there is. If such differences exist, and Harper provides some evidence that they do, they may play a part at the "automatic and primitive" classical conditioning family level in establishing sex role and sex identification very early. The external genitals of the male suggest a very different employment from the "internal" female genitalia. However, as Mead suggests (see Chapter 4), little girls have two orifices; little boys a projection *and* an orifice. The situation for the latter may thus be more confusing than for the former, although the bewilderment and often hurt shown by little girls over their "missing part" may even things out between the sexes. It is not known in any detail what the sexual significance of the anal orifice is, except for collections of case histories in which individual significance is delineated. The common vulgarisms for anal intercourse suggest that there *is* an established although disguised cultural awareness of the possibility. The boy's problem of an appendage *and* an orifice in contrast to the girl's two orifices, plus his role of initiator and inserter in courting behavior and procreation may combine to make sex identification more cognitively tinged for the male than the female. Speculatively, this may be related to Ford and Beach's (1951) hypothesis that males are more shaped by learning in the sexual area than females (see Chapter 4).

Regardless, the accessibility of male genitalia for stimulation, intentional or incidental, is greater than for females. Certainly there must be effects on the type of sexuality for males and females. Such structural differences probably acquire all sorts of emotional and reinforcement implications long before the child has any clear labels for them. In other words, sexual stimulation is much more likely than moral training to be associated with early classical conditioning that may play some unknown role in its being tied early into an identification pattern.

This suggests that obscurely moral effects like guilt and shame are likely to be attached early and by classical conditioning to the sex organs and sexual behavior. Nothing about this culture suggests that this is anything but true.

The literature concerning the generally harmful effects of father absence on sex identification, particularly among males, is striking (see, for example, Biller, 1970; Biller and Borstelmann, 1967). It is suggested by this that boys' sexual identification is very often interfered with when no male model is present during early childhood. In unhappy marriages (and much clinical but little scientific evidence exists for this statement) mothers are likely to interfere with the modeling of sons on fathers, often by rendering the father ineffective as a model. A really hostile mother, coupled with a rejecting father, may even produce reverse male modeling in her son.

Fagot and Patterson (1969) illustrate how the peer group takes over as soon as a child enters it, so that the pattern begun in the home, whether appropriate or inappropriate, is even further consolidated by the peer group. However, their evidence deals more directly with perpetuation of appropriate than inappropriate sex identification. Fagot and Patterson also delineate the model by which boys' sex identification may be preserved in the feminine world of the school, particularly the elementary school.

These hypotheses about early sex identification are tentative, since knowledge in this critical area is very incomplete. If correct, the hypotheses provide a rationale for very early sex identification. They also provide a rationale for the apparent irreversibility of sex identification.

Data, although not very good data, abound concerning the difficulty of reversing the sex identification, for example, of "bull dike" women homosexuals, or passive, effeminate male homosexuals. The reasons may be that such clear-cut inappropriate identifications have been formed very early through classical conditioning; have been reinforced intensively and often for many years; and techniques for retraining are simply not available among those who work in the mental health fields. It is also likely that many people with inappropriate sex identifications like it perfectly well the way they are. Thus they possess no interest in reversing their sexual identification. However, even for those who would like desperately to change, the process is known to be very difficult. Opinion is sharply divided as to whether, with the present human engineering skills, it is possible. Some of the techniques of operant conditioning may prove useful (see Chapters 9 and 10).

On the other hand, where all-out efforts have been made (as in the Wayne County Training School and Hawthorne—Cedar Knolls studies cited earlier), remarkable success has been shown in altering moral identification as judged by social behavior and adjustment.

It is apparent, both from casual observation and from such research as Piliavin, Hardyck, and Vadum's (1968) that reversals of identification may occur in negative as well as positive directions. Many adults have a moral lapse once in a while but on the whole they recover and continue on as "good people." It is certain that many who have had an occasional fling at the homosexual way of life in adolescence or under special circumstances go their heterosexual way contentedly and effectively ever after, or at least so Kinsey's data suggest: Far more of his sample, male or female (1948, 1953), had homosexual experiences than continued in a homosexual way of life. Actually, he found few 100 percent homosexuals.

It has been suggested earlier that, when inappropriate sexual identification exists, or at least where appropriate sexual identification is not fully settled, then adolescence is a promising time to reverse or to tip the process in the appropriate direction. It is not fitting in a book like this to take a moralistic position. It is enough to say that, since society is organized so that severe sanctions against inappropriate sex identification exist and are often harshly applied, it is clearly simpler and less hazardous for a young person to be appropriately sex identified.

It has been predicted from drive theory that the possibilities for dramatic new learning in adolescence are better than in the span of years between preschool age and pubescence (see Chapter 1). If this is generally true, then it must also be true for sex and moral identification. Counselors, parents, and others concerned with young people should thus be particularly alert to possibilities for constructive guidance and intervention. The existing middle-class code seems in some ways designed to do the opposite of what it should do in order to encourage final appropriate sex role consolidation during adolescence. On the one hand, it places severe sanctions against open heterosexual behavior, while, on the other hand, it creates a rather homosocial environment for young people. At adolescence, the sexually ambivalent young person is powerfully pushed toward final sex role identification. For him, it is a now or never sort of thing. For almost all, this push is in the direction of sex appropriate identification. All the coeducational, dating aspects of this society favor the process, and boys and girls appear to be equally motivated to attain appropriate identification. It thus seems that, if adults can help young people to be coeducationally at ease, they can help them toward appropriate sex role consolidation. Giving this help should be a major goal of the "new" sex education, which is now under such vigorous attack.

Relationships between Sex and Moral Identification

In the previous sections, differences in sex and moral identification have been pointed out. The former comes earlier, is almost certainly more resistant to change, is more anchored to immediate reinforcements, certainly in the physical and probably in the social sense, is cognitively simpler, and requires a less sophisticated level of self-criticism.

It has also been postulated that the basic processes of acquiring sex and moral identifications are the same, despite the important differences in the nature and timing of the end result. Imitation and modeling, reinforcement, and power and its dimensions are the factors that seem to determine the process for both sex and moral identification.

There is lively controversy about whether the two types of identification are independent. Many, for example, believe that all homosexuals are "sick." As sick people, they therefore can not attain mature, well-socialized moral identification. Doidge and Holtzman's (1960) research has been cited earlier, and supports such a position. On the other hand, there are those who say that, aside from the socially disapproved nature of their sexual preferences, homosexuals may be as emotionally healthy and thus morally well identified as anyone else. Chang and Block (1960) were earlier cited as providing support for this point of view.

The differences in the Doidge and Holtzman and the Chang and Block samples have been discussed: Doidge and Holtzman's subjects were young men from the military, chronologically adolescent, and functioning in a setting where homosexuality was personally and legally disgraceful. Chang and Block worked with older, well-educated males who came of their own free will to take part in the research, and who for the most part had already proved themselves competent in the community.

The issue of independence and dependency of sex and moral identification, then, can not be readily settled. Much more research is needed, for one thing; and people have shied away from doing research on either of these types of identification because the topics are complex, socially sensitive, and subject to strong social-emotional reactions that seem to rage about all behavior to which moral connotations have been attached.

It does not require a sophisticated observer to see that the problems of moral identification posed for the individual with a shaky or inappropriate sex identification are great. He is under fire from all sides. His adjustment, if known, is likely to keep him from proving his competence, since men and women are fired from many types of jobs if they are sexually different. They are also often prevented from getting desirable jobs in the first place. Homosexuals and all others who are sexually different run great risks legally. The unsettling conviction of criminality is always a possibility. The sex drive is sufficiently powerful that it is likely to lead a homosexual individual into situations where he will indeed behave in a way that is morally reprehensible, to both him and the larger society (the "heedless" behavior that so often goes with very high drive, as discussed in Chapter 1). This is why it has been suggested that homosexuals stay away from the field of work with adolescents. In a very large proportion of society, a known homosexual is granted no status as a worthwhile human being, and this global rejection of him or her as a person is almost certain to be reflected in the self concept.

Thus, it may be concluded that for existing but not inevitable social reasons, it is difficult for one with inappropriate sex identification to reach appropriate, mature, well-socialized moral identification. On the other hand, there is no logical reason why he should not; and Chang and Block, for example, suggest that there are sizable groups of homosexuals who do. Sophisticated and fair-minded observation bears out this conclusion. To add to the problems for one who is sexually different, the type of home setting that provided the learning opportunities for inappropriate sex identification in the first place, is also likely to be the sort that impedes moral identification, although this is not necessarily the case.

It seems logical that almost any level of moral identification can be reached by a person, regardless of his sex role identification. For example, an appropriately sex identified boy or girl may model exclusively on the parent of the same sex, but this parent may provide a model of low order or immature moral development even though at the same time the parent provides an adequate and appropriate sex role model. Or a youth may model exclusively on the parent of the same sex, who is both appropriately sex role identified and who functions at a high level of moral development. Such a youth could hypothetically develop into one who is inappropriately sex identified, but whose moral identification level is high. For some inappropriately sex identified people, the socialization problems they meet may retard or distort their growth toward high level moral development. For others, such social difficulties may move them in the direction of empathy for others, strong egos, and high level moral development (the "purification by fire" or "strength of character through hardship" analogies).

Thus, there is probably a correlation between appropriate sex identification and good moral identification, but there is no direct cause and effect relationship. Most mature people have known homosexuals with high levels of moral identification, but have also known people whose sexual identification seems most appropriate but whose moral identification leaves almost everything to be desired.

CONCLUSION

To conclude this chapter and, hopefully, to make a final and clear distinction between sex and moral identification without blurring the similarities: Sexual identification much more than moral identification seems to be shaped through classical conditioning, to be emotional in nature, and to be remarkably free in many of its manifestations from cognition (sometimes disconcertingly so).

Both the process of acquiring moral identification and the behaviors by which it is manifested seem to belong much more in the instrumental learning family and to be complexly and deeply interrelated with cognition. However (and herein lies much of the confusion between sex and moral identification), the fundamental motivation for moral behavior often appears to be and may always be anxiety. Freudian theories can not be lightly dismissed. Within such theories, anxiety is primitively linked to sexuality. It may be that the origins of morality—the individual's reflexive sense of right or wrong which he later translates into cognitions about morality—lie in a classically conditioned discrimination between *right* and *wrong* that may have been originally set up within a sexual context.

However, by adolescence, there is much independence between sex and moral identification even though, in American culture, sex identification and behavior are closely tied to morality.

Since Chapters 13 and 14 are continuous with each other and inextricably interlinked, both chapters are fully summarized at the end of Chapter 14.

14

Sex and Moral Identification: Development and Problems

INTRODUCTION

Questions about how sexual and moral identification develop, and what behaviors are associated with different types and degrees of identification can best be answered by research. In Chapter 13, sex identification has been treated within a culturally stereotyped dichotomy of male and female, and, within a complex technical society where roles overlap, this dichotomy is too simple. Thus, some of the more subtle and complex issues of sex role identification deserve fuller treatment than they have been given.

While the role of the peer group in influencing behavior, as peers both provide models and exert power, has been discussed in a number of places, such discussion has been rather in passing and should be more focused than it has been previously. Finally, when moral identification is faulty or when it deviates in self- or socially destructive ways (as it frequently does among adolescents) from social prescriptions, acute problems in adolescent adjustment may arise. Some of the more common problems should be treated.

It is to such questions that this chapter is addressed.

ILLUSTRATIVE RESEARCH ABOUT IDENTIFICATION

If the concepts of sex and moral identification are as important as has been suggested by the extensive treatment accorded them in this chapter, then they must possess important consequences for behavior.

Four studies, one of sex identification, one of moral identification, one of parental influence, and one of development toward mature moral identification, have been chosen for review here.

Aggression and Sex Identification

In the first, Leventhal, Shemberg, and Van Schoelandt (1968) studied the effects of sex identification on expressing aggression. Their subjects were twenty college men and twenty college women, who had been selected from among a larger group of 400 introductory psychology students on the basis of their test scores on a masculinity–femininity test. Ten young men and ten young women each were selected from the extreme masculine end of the scoring range. The ten men so selected (the MMs, for masculine males) were considered to be well identified as males, the ten women (MFs, for masculine females) as ill or inappropriately identified for their sex. From the opposite end of the scoring range another ten men and ten women were picked. This group of ten men (FMs, for feminine males) was considered to be inappropriately identified for their sex, while the ten women were considered to be appropriately and strongly identified (FFs, for feminine females).

Each subject was told that he was to assist the experimenter in running a learning study. The person doing the learning—the "experimental subject"—was the same male confederate during the entire study. The forty Ss were tested individually. It was explained to each that learning progressed more rapidly with shock: specifically, that a strong shock following a mistake usually produced faster learning. Buttons for administering shock from 1 (light shock) to 10 (heavy shock) were shown to each person. A demonstration was given him (her) to show that shocks did indeed follow button pushing, and that button 3 produced more shock than button 1. The subject was left free to "train" the confederate, who was "hooked" to the shock machine but concealed by a black screen. A signal light told the "experimenter"—the student taking the uninformed part in the study—whether the confederate responded correctly or incorrectly on each trial for a total of sixty-one trials, thirty-one of which were "errors." Thus each student "experimenter" administered thirty-one shocks that might range from 1 (weak) to 10 (strong).

In line with appropriate ethics, the purpose of the experiment was explained to all participants when it was finished. All said they "had been taken in."

To summarize, each member of four groups, two of the groups appropriately identified for their sex, two inappropriately identified for their sex, took part in a study where shock ranging from weak to strong was justified as an aid to learning and a legitimate part of a scientific study. Leventhal, Shemberg, and Van Schoelandt consider such administration of shock to be an expression of aggression, albeit in a legitimate setting and for a legitimate purpose.

Their hypothesis was that appropriately sex identified individuals, whether male or female, will be emotionally freer to proceed with an unpleasant job that entails aggression expression than will inappropriately sex identified young people.

The results supported the hypothesis: The experiment provided thirty-one scores, one for each error made by the confederate. The scores reported below are the averages for the four different identification sex groups for all thirty-one trials.

The two groups that were appropriately sex identified (MM and FF) administered average shock intensities that were significantly stronger than the two inappropriately sex identified groups (FM and MF). There were no differences between the sexes. The mean shock intensity scores were 5.76 for the MM group, 5.00 for the FF group, 2.89 for the FM group, and 3.17 for the MF group. The authors conducted an auxiliary study that strongly suggests that their results are not due to a tendency for appropriately sex identified individuals to be more socially conforming than inappropriately sex identified persons. If conformity accompanies appropriate sex role identity, then the prediction would have been that the appropriately sex identified groups would have averaged higher shock scores because of their greater desire to go along with the purposes of the experiment.

A tentative generalization from these findings is suggested: Appropriately sex identified people more than those who are inappropriately identified are able to summon their resources to go ahead to do a job, even though it may be unpleasant and threatening. According to some personality theory, conflict reduces the energy available for dealing with reality. Leventhal, Shemberg, and Van Schoelandt's study meshes well enough with this prediction.

Some question can be raised about the ethics of deceptively recruiting college students to administer shocks to "innocent subjects" such as the confederate in the Leventhal, Shemberg, and Van Schoelandt experiment. Milgram (1965) reports that refusal to take part in such studies was more common among his subjects who had attained high levels of moral development than among subjects at developmentally earlier or less mature levels of moral development. Milgram employed Kohlberg's methods of estimating level of moral judgment and development. Kohlberg's measurements will be discussed later. It should be noted that none of the groups in the Leventhal, Shemberg, and Van Schoelandt study averaged much above the middle range of the possible shock that could have been given.

Since one aim of the present book is to induce questioning attitudes about research (see Chapter 2), it is well to consider how Leventhal, Shemberg, and Van Schoelandt might have altered their procedure so as to test their hypothesis even more definitively. In essence, their study was a test of the personality theory that conflict reduces energy for coping with unpleasant reality. They seem also to have reasoned (to some degree, words are being put in their mouths) that conflict about inappropriate sex typing is frustrating and results in enough pent up hostility that the person is afraid he will lose control if he begins to express it. Thus, he will hold it in while persons free from such sex identification conflict will be free to express it when it is realistically justified. They will have no fear of loss of control. However, the method employed in the study required each subject to administer a certain level of shock each of the thirty-one times the male confederate made an error. Parenthetically, a male confederate was chosen because it has been found in other research that subjects reduce shock when they are "administering" it to a woman, an interesting cultural and "moral" twist.

The options open to the subjects, then, concerned only the *amount* of shock, *not whether or not to administer it at all.* It seems that some combination of frequency and intensity of shock administered would test the hypothesis more fully than intensity alone.

Kohlberg's Levels of Moral Judgment and Associated Characteristics

The next study to be reviewed was conducted by Haan, Smith, and Block (1968). They used the Kohlberg techniques for estimating the level of moral reasoning among college students and Peace Corps volunteers. They then related level of moral development to the young people's political–social behavior, their family backgrounds, and measures of their personality traits.

Reference has already been made to Kohlberg's analysis of moral development. Kohlberg's thought has been strongly influenced by Piaget. Briefly, Kohlberg reasons that morality develops through three levels, each of which includes two stages, for a total of six stages. Level I, according to Kohlberg (1964, 1967), is *premoral.* At this level the child is very concrete in his values. Many adults seem never to move beyond this stage. However, as was pointed out in Chapter 13, there is often a need for each person who wants to live with some equanimity in this far-from-perfect society to practice moral behavior characteristic at other than the most mature level.

At level I, moral values reside in good and bad, external happenings, and personal needs. Stage 1 of level I consists of obeying, and expecting punishment if one disobeys. Trouble is avoided, one does not question why. Responsibility is always objective, not subjective. Control is also perceived to be external.

Level I, stage 2, means that one usually satisfies his own needs and only occasionally others'. A reciprocal orientation is manifested, as with Berkowitz and Friedman's, 1967, entrepreneurial boys who were discussed in the previous chapter.

Level II is *conventional moral judgment.* Here one lives according to the good or the correct role, lives up to the expectations of others, is conventional, and does not upset things. Within level II, stage 3 consists of looking for approval, helping and pleasing others, and living unquestioningly with the will or judgment of the majority. In level II, stage 4, a law-and-order orientation is conspicuous, and is valued for its own sake.

Level III is *moral judgment by principle.* Within level II, stage 5 is characterized by respect for contracts, the will and rights of others, and a regard for the will and welfare of the majority. In stage 6, the highest, orientation according to conscience or principle is pre-eminent. The difficulties of living in this manner were pointed out in the previous chapter, when an attempt was made to show the difficulties in defining moral identification.

It is obvious from this summary that the Protestant ethic, as it has been discussed, combines moral behaviors from stage 3 upward.

As for stage theories in general, Kohlberg's assumption is that one must move through one stage before he can assume the attitudes and behavior of the next higher one. Turiel (1966) provides some evidence that this is the case, but he also found that regression from one stage to the next earlier one can occur. Turiel used Kohlberg's interview technique to determine the dominant stage of each of forty-four seventh grade boys. The boys were then separated into one control and three experimental groups. An adult role playing experimenter exposed the different experimental groups to moral concepts that were one stage below, one above, or two above their initial predominant stage. A week later the boys were reassessed. The controls, untreated, remained about the same in their scores. Modeling by an adult advanced subjects one stage, but not two, upward on the developmental scale, but there was also evidence that, instead of rejecting regression to an earlier stage, movement backward to the previous developmental stage could be achieved.

It is also obvious as one examines the behaviors that comprise Kohlberg's stages of moral development, that a higher level of cognition is required at each succeeding stage. Fodor (1970) tests this assumption indirectly. He reasons that the level of adolescents' moral development will be related to the intellectual climate of their home. Thus, the offspring of more highly educated parents will have reached higher levels of moral development than when youth come from homes of low educational level. Fodor was also interested in determining whether Afro-American youth differed from white youth in level of moral judgment.

Fodor administered Kohlberg's Interview Schedule to two groups of boys. The first group was made up of twenty-five Afro-American boys from urban areas in all parts of the country who had come together to take part in the ABC Program at Carleton College, Minnesota. These boys all came from socially disadvantaged homes, as determined by low family income. Twenty-five white boys comprised the second sample. They had been selected randomly from the Northfield, Minnesota, telephone directory. Of the total population, only one white boy refused to participate. All boys were paid five dollars to take part in the study. The two groups were well matched in IQ (the mean was 105 for the Afro-American, 106 for the white sample), and age. Ages ranged from about 14 to 17, and the average for both groups was $15^{7}/_{10}$ years. Mothers' education differed markedly, however, with the Afro-American mothers averaging $10^{9}/_{10}$ years of education, but the white mothers 13 years. Fodor gives no data about the fathers.

Fodor found, first, that there was no race difference in the level of moral judgment. Second, level of mothers' education was clearly and significantly related to the boys' level of moral development. When boys whose mothers had received high school education or more were compared with boys whose mothers did not complete high school, the mean moral judgment score of the first group was approximately 200, while the mean score of the latter group averaged 177.

An illustration that further clarifies stage 6 behavior is provided by Milgram (1965). As has been mentioned, he ran an experiment in which subjects were required to administer severe shock to people for errors in learning (a study similar to the Leventhal, Shemberg, and Van Schoelandt experiment.) In this study, 75 percent of Milgram's students with some stage 6 (*individual principles* orientation) thinking refused to continue with the experiment because of their beliefs that it was unethical; while only 13 percent of the stage 5 (conventional, or *social contract*) subjects left the study rather than do as they were instructed.

Milgram commented that most people have no language for disobedience when confronted with situations like Leventhal, Shemberg, and Van Schoelandt's, or like Milgram's own study.

This finding leads to predicting different social actions among Haan, Smith, and Block's subjects according to their level of moral judgment. As might be predicted from the previous discussion of sex differences, more women than men fall at level II in moral development: 66 percent of the men, 79 percent of the women; while more men than women fall into the extreme categories: 28 percent of the men were at the *principled* (level III) stage, 18 percent of the women. Level I (*premoral*) included very few subjects and none at stage 1. Six percent of the men but only 3 percent of the women were included at stage 2. These data represent 510 people, 253 men, 257 women. They are by no means a representative sample of young people, or even of college students. They come from San Francisco State College, University of California at Berkeley, and Peace Corps volunteers-in-training. There are no freshmen or graduate students in the sample.

On various indicators of deviation from established social norms, Haan, Smith, and Block found a general tendency for both *premoral* and *principled* subjects to be highest in radicalism and lowest in church attendance. Obviously, these things were true for very different reasons. The premoral young people seem simply to be angry, the principled to be disillusioned. More of the former, at least the men, belong to radical movements; more of the latter but none of the former belong to liberal movements.

With relation to these two extreme types and their relationships to society and authority, the authors say: The stage 6 males (results are less clear for women than for men) "are independent and critical, but also involved, giving and responsive to others" . . . while the young men at the premoral stage of moral judgment "are angry, also critical, but disjointed, uncommitted to others, and potentially narcissistic" (p. 197).

Level II (*conventional*) young people are quite at peace with traditional institutions such as schools and the church. The authors believe this insulates them from conflicting values, and leads them to look only for the best in the behavior of authority figures. They are likely to rebel only when egregiously betrayed.

Finally, as might be predicted, membership in action groups paralleled level of moral judgment to a moderate degree. Of a total of fifty-three FSM (Free Speech Movement) arrestees, for example, thirty-one were at the third or *principled* level of moral development, but only fifteen at level II (*conventional*). Peace Corps volunteers, on the other hand, came preponderantly from conventionally moral groups: Of 116, 85 were so classified, but only 25 at level III (*principled*).

The results above suggest that, while the prime movers of society are almost certainly the most highly developed morally, they may by no means be the most comfortable to live with. These findings also argue strongly for zealous defense of the right of dissenters to dissent: Without their leadership, more conventional souls would in all likelihood be in serious trouble. Haan, Smith, and Block's results also seem to call for careful differentiation between the destructive, narcissistic, purely angry young man and the radical-because-of-principle. Society can not exist without the latter, but the former (who often joins him for less worthy reasons) often defeats him because of guilt through association.

Thomas (1970) also reports the influence of family background on college students' political activities. He studied a sample of one parent and a college age child in each of sixty upper-middle-class families. All parents were visible for community political activism, but half of them were liberal, half conservative, in political action. The student offspring of the two types of parents differed strongly in radical activism, 53 percent of the liberal group working in liberal causes but only 13 percent of the conservative group having taken part in radical conservative causes. However, the over-all influence of parental example is suggested by the fact that both groups were equally active in conventional political participation. Neither group of students were rebellers: The children of the liberal parents were liberal, the offspring of conservative parents were conservative.

Thomas' findings fit with many others about liberal student political action:

> ... liberal student activists tend to come from families characterized by: affluence, fathers with high status occupations, parents of high educational attainment, and parents who hold liberal political beliefs and are themselves politically active. Further, these findings support the suggestions that liberal activists are the product of permissive child-rearing practices. (page number not available)

While parental warmth and permissiveness were associated with modeling on parents, the *example* or presence of a model seemed to be more important than the *feeling tone between parent and child*. This is one more bit of evidence favoring an imitation learning point of view over a purely emotional identification position.

Changes in Moral Development during Adolescence

The last study to be reviewed in this section was conducted by Adelson, Green, and O'Neil (1969). They carried out interviews in which the subjects were asked to imagine 1000 people moving to an uninhabited Pacific island and setting up an entirely new society from the very beginning. Interview probes dealt with making and justifying political and social decisions and reconciling opposing opinions. Such topics as the nature of political authority, crime and justice, ideology and idealism, were taken up. Subjects were 120 suburban adolescents and preadolescents: 30 each from the fifth, seventh, ninth, and twelfth grades whose average ages, in that order, were $10^{9}/_{10}$, $12^{3}/_{5}$, $14^{7}/_{10}$, and $17^{7}/_{10}$ years.

There was an equal number of boys and girls at each grade level and, at each age level, two-thirds of the subjects had group test IQs between 95 and 110 (average range), while one-third tested 125 IQ or more (superior). There were no over-all differences between boys and girls, or between the average and the superior youngsters. All subjects were white.

Adelson, Green, and O'Neil's results fit well with Kohlberg's levels of moral judgment. For example, the younger adolescents could not usually respond abstractly, and their notions of law were constraining and coercing: curbing and punishing specific acts of wickedness. Older subjects dealt more in abstractions, and spoke much more often of the law's beneficial functions.

When it was pointed out to them that a law was not effective, younger subjects tended to suggest strengthening it, while older boys and girls regarded laws more as experiments and rehearsals: If they don't work, amend and change them. Older children referred more often to common experience as a basis for law. Younger subjects thought of laws as controlling and, more specifically, restraining bad behavior. Older adolescents conceived more of law as it affects the inner man: People in a lawless society themselves become corrupt.

Rather than the quick growth of *idealism* attributed by so many authors to adolescents, Adelson, Green, and O'Neil found a startling growth in *political realism*. The younger subjects thought of law without much concern for the social needs it should serve, or for its feasibility. Older adolescents realize that law is a human product, and that men are fallible. They treat it with the same skepticism that should be applied to all human artifacts. They are by no means cynical; they are simply realistic. Much of this shift, the authors believe, is due to increased understanding, some of which has been gained because the older youngsters have been given more autonomy, have studied and thought more, and have tested society against their own experiences. They see laws as necessary for accommodating conflicting interests and values; they know that means must be balanced against ends; and that something that is good in the short run is not necessarily equally so in the long haul. These findings clearly represent the cognitive aspect of moral development as discussed in Chapter 8.

CROSS-SEX IDENTIFICATION

While the major lines of sex identification are clear in a complex industrial society, there are many ambiguities in the roles that males and females play at all ages. First, as has been mentioned (see the Bowerman and Elder, 1964, study), the American family does not typically follow the Victorian model of dominant husband and father, submissive wife and mother. Bowerman and Elder, to recapitulate, report data obtained from 20,000 white seventh to twelfth graders from intact homes in central Ohio and central North Carolina; and nearly 1600 tenth graders from Florida. With this percentage of their sample from the Southern and border states, it may be predicted that the Bowerman and Elder findings are conservative, in that the North, Northeast, and West will show an even heavier predominance of equalitarian families. The South and central Ohio, it is commonly agreed, are conservative and traditional compared with the rest of the country.

Over all, for this large sample, 45.6 percent report equalitarianism between their fathers and mothers, 34.3 percent report that the father is dominant, and 20.1 percent report mother dominance. In line with social class theory discussed earlier, middle-class youngsters are more likely to report father dominance than lower-class adolescents. The community role of fathers, in other words, may be reflected in the home, with middle-class fathers having more power and status attributed to them than lower-class fathers. Older children are more likely than younger children to see their fathers as dominant.

The modal or most frequent type of American family in a white sample, then, is equalitarian. Since in the long run it is more comfortable and often more constructive to live and adjust very much as the majority does, then it is probably well for adolescents to adopt an equalitarian stance for themselves, to employ it in their dating patterns, and eventually to incorporate it in their own marriages.

If mothers and fathers are equally dominant in a plurality of American homes, it may be predicted from the power theory that was developed earlier in the previous chapter that children of both sexes will model to some degree on both parents; and that such modeling may well prepare them best for the mainstream of American life. It was already predicted that moral modeling on both parents occurs, if for no other reason than that parents tend to agree and reflect the cultural norm about such issues. It can be also expected that parents will set as appropriate action models for their children as they can.

If masculinity is highly valued for males, femininity for females, then cross-sex modeling may well be a trickier thing than cross-sex moral modeling. But, while firm, sex roles are not entirely clear-cut. It will be a rare man who is completely *instrumental* in his approach to life. There are times when every normal man relaxes simply to love his wife and children, to express tenderness for his friends, and to luxuriate in positive personal relationships. Nor is any woman purely *expressive*. The average American woman can get out to get the job done. It is well known that, after a period of grief, most widows manage their lives and their financial and business affairs with considerable adroitness.

About one-third of married American women manage not only the home but out of it on the job. Women cab drivers abound. In times of emergency, women make good welders, bus and truck drivers. It is a rare woman who can not change a tire if she has to. Also, household chores nowadays fall on both men and women. At least in the core culture of the middle class, fathers approach their wives' adroitness in washing dishes, running the vacuum, and often diapering the baby or operating the washing machine.

Educated men are likely to enjoy art, music, and literature. Educated women appreciate science and architecture, and often follow sports with enthusiasm. Horowitz (1967), in his study of adolescent popularity that was referred to earlier, finds that interest in sports is almost as highly related to popularity for girls as for boys.

It is evident from the research that has been cited earlier in this chapter that warmth, tenderness, and clearly demonstrated love from fathers are as important in children's development as the same feelings and behaviors among mothers. Since the average woman lives some four to five years longer than her husband, and is slightly more than two years younger than he (the current median age for marriage for United States females is 20½, for males 22⅘, years), it is essential that a woman be more than expressive in her life stance. She must also be able to fulfill an instrumental role. Typically she must do this "for keeps" when she is widowed at somewhat beyond her prime. Her declining years will most surely be more comfortable if she has had preparation for an instrumental role.

In short, there is every reason within American culture why a certain amount of cross-sex identification is useful for both sexes. It enriches life, it makes it simpler, it is better for the children who model on one. A woman with some cross-sex identification is almost bound to be a more understanding and appreciative wife to her husband and mother to her sons. A husband who, within a generally secure masculine adjustment, has certain expressive type cross-sex identifications will likewise make a better husband as well as father to his children of both sexes.

Payne and Mussen (1956) provide data that support this argument, although they include only male subjects in their study. For their adolescent male sample, they assumed that boys whose scores for a personality inventory were much more like their fathers' than their mothers' scores were father identified. As they predicted, Payne and Mussen found that father-identified boys obtained higher masculine scores on a masculinity–femininity test. Such boys, like the Moulton, *et al.* (1966) boys, also reported that their fathers were rewarders rather than punishers; and that their fathers were more rewarding than their mothers. They also said their entire family constellation was happy and low in conflict.

It seems that a boy who models easily on a friendly, probably equalitarian father will be secure and nondefensive enough to differ from his father if the difference is to his advantage. He can behave in ways unlike his father's without feeling guilty and as though, in some obscure way, he has betrayed the man who sired him. Payne and Mussen's data support this prediction: There was no correlation between the masculinity of the highly identified boys and their fathers (masculinity was inferred by test scores).

As the author has said in another context (McCandless, 1967, p. 463), "a ruggedly masculine but highly adequate father can rear a son with somewhat effeminate behavior but with appropriate sex-role identification; or a rather effeminate but good father can rear a son who is ruggedly masculine in behavior as well as appropriately sex-identified."

Finally, as has been suggested, in equalitarian, warm, and low conflict homes, children should be able to cross-model and identify morally in the way that best serves their personal and social needs. Daughters can thus incorporate those of their fathers' adjustments that are clearly superior, and a son can pattern himself on his mother in a similar way. Men so identified may feel freer to express their emotions (as has been said, this is a real problem in this culture), communicate about other than the tangible world, thus possibly become more relaxed, less often victims of ulcers and hypertension, and so live both longer and more happily, or at least more relaxedly. Women so identified may feel more at ease about the efforts toward autonomy and self-sufficiency that seem to trouble so many modern girls and women.

Vogel, *et al.* (1970) address themselves indirectly to the question of cross-sex modeling in a study of college men and women. Of their sample, forty-seven young men and women had grown up in homes where the mothers never worked, while seventy-three were children in homes that were intact, but where the mothers worked for at least a time when the students were growing up. There were no significant differences between the groups for mother's current age, parental education, father's occupation, or religion, nor in their own self-perceptions. However, the children of working mothers revealed themselves to be markedly less stereotyped about men's and women's sex roles than the students whose mothers had never worked. The breakdown in stereotypes consisted of assigning to both fathers and mothers the desirable characteristics of the traditional sex roles of the opposite sex. There was no detraction from the good qualities of the appropriate stereotypic sex role. Working mothers, to illustrate, were perceived not as less warm, loving, or nurturant but as all of these plus *more competent* (competence is stereotypically conceived of as a masculine trait). The fathers in homes where the mother worked were perceived not as *less* masculine or competent but rather as warmer, freer in human relations, and more nurturant than the fathers in homes where the mother was full time homemaker. These qualities are traditional expressive feminine characteristics, according to the cultural stereotype.

Vogel, *et al.* believe that traditional sex role stereotypes are neither necessary nor appropriate in today's society, but that they reflect an unequal status of the sexes. They also serve to maintain such differential status by derogating many desirable social behaviors among women and some, but fewer, among men. "For example, assertiveness, constructive aggression and striving for achievement and excellence, all characteristics considered desirable in adults in this society, are discouraged for women; while tenderness, emotional warmth and expressiveness, equally valued in the abstract, are not encouraged for men." For their sample, Vogel, *et al.* conclude that "sons and daughters of employed mothers each perceive their own sex as sharing the positive characteristics traditionally limited to the opposite sex to a greater degree than do the children of homemaker mothers (Page numbers not available).

Hopefully, the less restrictive and more congruent definitions of sex roles held by children of working mothers will exert a like influence upon role behavior, so that the children of working mothers will feel even freer than their parents to engage in overlapping role behaviors, and so achieve in their own lives a greater degree of sex role equality. Thus, the limited effect of maternal employment upon role perceptions reported in this paper may be envisioned as one step in a chain of successive cumulative effects, which may eventually significantly modify the traditional male–female role relationships in our society" (page numbers not available).

ROLE OF THE PEER GROUP Evidence already presented in this and previous chapters illustrates the important effects of peers on each others' behavior. This influence seems to increase steadily from the time children first begin to interact with each other until adolescence. While the data are not clear, observation suggests that the influence of the peer group peaks in middle adolescence and probably declines after that, when young people marry and set up standards for their own nuclear families. However, the adult pattern of "keeping up with the Joneses" is one form of peer influence, and it is very much a part of the American way of life.

Coleman's (1961) book, *The Adolescent Society*, makes it seem as though the *only* influence on adolescents comes from their peers. He perhaps stresses the generation gap more than any other contemporary author. His research techniques—questions he chose to ask, for example, and the form in which they were asked—seem to maximize the chances for finding adolescent–adult differences. Douvan and Adelson (1966) are frankly skeptical about the existence of any important generation gap. They maintain that the tendency to choose friends who hold to the same standards as parents simply reinforces the parents' basic codes, but liberalizes them to some degree. The Reiss (1968) findings on sexual behavior and attitudes that have been cited several times fit better with the Douvan and Adelson point of view than with the Coleman thesis, although the Levitt and Edwards (1970) study of influences of peers and parents on smoking supports Coleman's position.

In any case, the evidence of conflicting influences of peers and parents and other adults is so clear that it would be unrealistic to deny the phenomenon. For example, McDill and Coleman (1965) studied parental and peer influences on plans for attending college. When their subjects were freshmen in high school, the relative influence of parents compared with peers was in the ratio of almost 5 to 1, favoring the parents. By the time the students in their sample had reached the senior year of high school, parental and peer influences were almost equal, though parents still held a slight edge.

Research literature relevant to this point was discussed in Chapter 13 under the heading of "Perceived Similarity" (page 389). The Fagot and Patterson (1969) study illustrates how peers carry the important and constructive responsibility, at least among young children, of reinforcing appropriate masculine behavior among boys whose environment is controlled by women teachers who preponderantly reinforce feminine behavior for both their boy and girl pupils.

Where parental warmth and equalitarianism are lacking, as they so often are for disadvantaged children and adolescents, the peer group may provide both the comfort and the models that youngsters need. Hoffman and Saltzstein's (1967) results may be interpreted in this fashion. Their data revealed substantial moral and conscience modeling on their parents among middle-class youngsters, but almost none among lower socioeconomic status subjects. It may be that disadvantaged children depend more on their peers than middle-class children, and thus model on them. Among elementary school children, it has been seen (Bandura, Grusec, and Menlove, 1967a) that the presence of a morally "permissive" peer may significantly reduce modeling on a rigorous and conscientious adult model. Bandura, Grusec, and Menlove (1967b) also demonstrate how children may use their peers to overcome inconvenient and embarrassing personal adjustments (fear of dogs, in this case). In this experiment, observation of fearless peers worked significantly to help other preschool aged children to overcome their fear.

Among the other findings of the Hartup and Coates (1967) study, nursery school children with histories of little friendship are more likely to model on their peers than popular children. This suggests that socially maladroit children may be more affected by peers than children who are secure about their social standing. While it is risky to generalize this finding to adolescents, the point is worth bearing in mind, and observation suggests it may be valid. The author has had occasion to work with or to know of the therapeutic endeavors on behalf of several girls who had practiced "pulling trains," as the behavior is known locally. By this is meant girls who engage in sex parties during which many boys, in each others' company, have intercourse with the girl on the same occasion. In each case, these girls were ill adjusted socially, isolated emotionally from their peers of both sexes as well as from their parents and teachers, and pathetically hungry for love and affection. It seems that group-hungry youngsters are more willing than those who are socially well integrated to undergo the hazing that precedes acceptance into many high school sororities and fraternities, or into many gangs, even though hazing often involves committing illegal and dangerous acts.

Ausubel (1954) provides a list of seven functions that the peer group provides during adolescence. Somewhat modified in view of research that has appeared since Ausubel wrote, these functions are:

1. To some degree, the peer group takes the place of the family. The family has given the youngster derived status (a reflection, good or bad, of the family's status in the community). The peer group gives or denies him primary status: status in his own right, quite independent of what or who his family is. This is invaluable training for adulthood, although not a permanent, satisfactory substitute for primary status in the larger (adult-oriented) society.
2. Successful adolescents secure a type of derived status from their peer group, in the sense of knowing that they are important to someone.
3. The peer group provides a useful anchor during a period of rapid transition. In a sense, all adolescents are in the same boat and the peer group gives them a feeling of comfort: "Other people are going through this with me. If they can make it, so can I."
4. Ausubel takes for granted a point about which there is some disagreement—that adolescents invest their peer group with the authority to set standards. In so doing, Ausubel thinks, adolescents thus affirm their own right to self-determination, since the peer group is patently no different from them.

It may be but is not certain that the standards of the peer group are more liberal on the whole than parent–caretaker standards; that adolescents move in the more liberal direction of the peer group; but it seems that, for basic life decisions, the standards of the family win out over the standards of the peer group when the two are in conflict. Observation shows many exceptions, however. Children of liberal or radical parents may be influenced toward conservatism.

5. The peer group insulates adolescents to some degree from the coercions that adults are likely to impose on young people.

6. The peer group provides much opportunity to practice by doing. Courting, discussions about jobs, extracurricular activities, hanging around are good rehearsal situations for the later chores of being adult.

The telephone provides an interesting peer group network, perhaps more so among girls than boys. With the telephone, a certain anonymity is provided (one's face does not betray one), and one is protected from immediate behavioral consequences. Thus, many young people seem to use the telephone in an almost therapeutic sense, confiding their struggles and crises into its anonymous mouthpiece.

7. The peer group, perhaps particularly for disadvantaged youngsters, provides a type of psychosocial moratorium that many parents can not give. It is a source of interim status between childhood and adulthood. For successful adolescents, it helps to reduce or mediate the total load of frustration that seems inevitable during adolescence.

COMMON PROBLEMS OF ADOLESCENT ADJUSTMENT

The present book is concerned with the psychology of normal adolescents. However, there is no way a conscientious author can avoid addressing himself at least briefly to some of the common problems that plague adolescents and with which they in turn plague adults and other adolescents. Adults in our society still bear much responsibility for the health and welfare of the young, and on the whole they take this responsibility seriously. Additionally, adults are concerned with maintaining a stable and orderly society. A young person who is in trouble is usually both unhappy *and* threatening to the established order. Thus, people are much aroused about such problems as delinquency, drugs, emotional disturbances, problems related to sexual adjustment and behavior, and disruptions of school and work achievement. The first, second, and fourth of these carry heavy overtones of morality and legal concern; and much of the literature about them is polemic.

Serious personal and social problems are usually overdetermined, since they result from many dislocations in a youngster's life, and they usually have multiple symptoms. Thus, a chronic juvenile lawbreaker is likely to come from a bad home, to be poor, to be afforded little opportunity within the broader society, to function at a low level cognitively, to be personally unhappy as well as socially disruptive, and to underachieve while he is in school as well as to be sexually disordered. It is not uncommon for him also to use drugs and to drink unwisely. In short, he is overwhelmed by drive, his legitimate channels for reducing or satisfying drive are few, and his adaptations are poor.

Thus, there can be no simple etiology in accounting for adolescents' problems, nor can there be any simple recipe for treating them when they occur. However, in real life, one often encounters adolescents with single rather than multiple problems; often such problems can be traced to relatively simple personal and/or social dislocations; and when the dislocations are put in place, the problem is ameliorated. There is merit to the cliché that every problem (or normal) adolescent is unique.

Hathaway and Monachesi (1963), addressing themselves principally to the problem of delinquency, set the problem of treating all common adolescent problems in sensible perspective:

> The sources of delinquent children are varied. The rates of delinquency are relatively comparable in all sources. The relationships between variables are so loose that elimination of no one background factor, even if it was casual, would result in a dramatic change of the total load. . . . Programs with holistic promises of radical prevention or treatment of delinquency and deviant behavior can sap strength from and delay the adoption of newer approaches emphasizing the individual personality of the child, approaches we believe to be currently most promising. (p. 100)

In the next few pages, five of the major problems of adolescents will be discussed briefly. As will be seen, even such basic information as the incidence of the problems is woefully inadequate. On the other hand, volumes have been written about each topic. The major problems appear to be delinquency, drug and alcohol usage, emotional disturbances ranging in severity from psychosis to mild disturbances of function, sexual problems, and underachievement or inappropriate achievement in school and at work.

Delinquency Considerable attention has already been paid to the problem of delinquency and its relation to the community. However, incidence figures have not been provided. Hathaway and Monachesi (1963) give as good a set of baseline data as is available in the literature. During the 1947–1948 school year, they were able to gather data about 3971 ninth graders well distributed in the schools over the state of Minnesota. Follow-up delinquency data were secured for most of the sample.

Highly trained raters classified the youngsters' conduct into five levels of delinquency. A rating of 0 refers to no delinquency; a rating of 1, to youngsters whose names appeared in police records only as having incurred traffic violations such as overtime parking or having played a tangential role in some incident where police pick-ups occurred. A rating of 2 was given for minor offenses such as property destruction, particularly when connected with play activities, drinking, speeding, and so on; this behavior, while not serious, was clearly undesirable, according to Hathaway and Monachesi. A rating of 3 was given for one serious offense such as auto theft, assault, or shoplifting. Offenses of youngsters rated 3 were clearly worse or more numerous than those classified as 2. A 4 rating was given for repeated serious offenses and is considered to represent a well-established delinquent pattern.

The accumulated frequencies of combined delinquency ratings 2, 3, and 4 (from Hathaway and Monachesi, p. 116) were 24 percent for boys at age 18 for both the Minneapolis and the statewide sample. At the same age, the accumulated percentage for girls was 8.3 for the Minneapolis and 6.2 for the statewide sample. At age 19, this percentage had risen to 28.4 for boys and 9.0 for girls (Minneapolis sample only). As early as age 15, the Minneapolis sample showed a combined frequency percentage of delinquency levels 2, 3, and 4 of 12.6 percent for boys and 3.0 percent for girls. Statewide, delinquency apparently begins later, as the same figures for the statewide sample at age 15 were 5.0 and 1.4. In terms of established delinquency only (rating of 4), the Minnesota statewide sample included 2.4 percent of boys and 0.7 percent of girls. From the figures given, it is evident that the delinquency rate for boys runs from three to four times as high as for girls.

It is well to look back in Chapters 2 and 6 to evaluate the Minneapolis and statewide Minnesota sample to estimate how well it represents figures for the United States as a whole. Hathaway and Monachesi believe their data are quite representative. On the other hand, as they say, Minnesota's natives are mostly native born and at least second generation. There are no sizable minority groups in Minnesota, and the economic position of the state is neither high nor low compared to other states. Farming slightly outweighs manufacturing as the dominant economic activity (or it did when the Hathaway and Monachesi book was written, about 1962). It is probable that, if anything, delinquency estimates made from the Hathaway and Monachesi sample are a little low.

Hathaway and Monachesi based their estimates of delinquency on police records. It is well known that much delinquency is hidden (see Empey and Erickson, 1966, who address themselves to this topic). Thus, it may be estimated that the Hathaway and Monachesi figures are underestimates both because of the nature of their Minnesota sample, and because much serious delinquency is never entered on a police blotter. This may be particularly true for delinquency among middle-class youth.

According to FBI data as reported by the American Institutes for Research in the Behavioral Sciences (1968), the significant increase of United States crime since 1960 can be largely attributed to juveniles. Arrests of those under age 18 had increased 68.5 percent since 1960 up to 1967, the last year of data included in the report, while arrests of those 18 and over had increased a little less than 1 percent. In 1967, one of two of those arrested for murder, rape, robbery, assault, burglary, larceny, and auto theft was under age 18. One of every four was under age 15, while more than 3 percent were under 11. Crimes varied by race: Six of every ten juveniles arrested for violent crimes such as murder, rape, robbery, and assault were Black; while seven of ten arrested for crimes against property such as burglary, larceny, and auto theft were white. In the suburbs, one person of every three arrested was a juvenile. The variation in type of crime by race suggests an interpretation in line with drive theory (discussed in Chapters 1 and 4) and Cloward and Ohlin's (1960) and Merton's (1961) legitimacy of opportunity hypothesis, discussed in Chapter 6. May it not be that the types of blockage Afro-Americans meet are threats to survival itself, while the blockages most common for whites concern material welfare? This is a speculative but tempting hypothesis.

Like the Hathaway and Monachesi data, the FBI figures represent only formal police contacts, do not cover hidden delinquency, and thus underreflect the true picture.

There are many types of classification of delinquency. Hathaway and Monachesi's classification according to seriousness is one technique. Another is by type of offense: a legal classification, such as petit larceny or grand larceny, or the different degrees of homicide. Cloward and Ohlin (1960) speak of organized and solitary delinquency: "collective adaptations are likely to emerge where failure is attributed to the inadequacy of existing institutional arrangements; conversely, when failure is attributed to personal deficiencies, solitary adaptations are more likely" (p. 125). For the former group, which will include criminally inclined gangs, Cloward and Ohlin's legitimacy of opportunity hypothesis as developed in Chapter 6 clearly applies. The situation is obviously more complex and/or more subtle for the latter group.

Elkind (1967a and b, 1968a and b) is particularly interested in middle-class delinquents, about whom relatively little is known. As has been said, many of them are one shot delinquents, and they also benefit more than disadvantaged delinquents from the psychosocial moratorium. Elkind's (1967b) classification of delinquency is tailored for such middle-class youngsters but applies equally across all socioeconomic levels. For one type of delinquent, he believes, delinquency is a manifestation of some long standing emotional disturbance. This group, he thinks, will respond best to psychiatric rather than legal treatment. Second, there is a large group of delinquents who become delinquent almost by accident. A prank or party gets out of hand, and suddenly a crime has been committed and the group is in the hands of the police. Hathaway and Monachesi's seriousness rating of 2 seems reserved for such young people. Elkind believes the great majority of middle-class delinquents is made up of a third type, youth who get into trouble regularly and who have a series of past charges booked against them. These would be all of Hathaway and Monachesi's "seriousness 4" group, and would include many 3s as well.

Elkind plausibly develops the point that within middle-class families there is an implied contract between parents and children. The heart of this contract is that the "parent will take responsibility for the emotional well being of his child" (Elkind, 1967b, p. 81). Children's part of the contract is to sacrifice some of their freedom to their parents: to obey rules about curfew and premarital intercourse, for example; and to be loyal to their parents' standards (this is subtly subsumed under sacrifice of freedom) as well as loyal to them personally. Elkind believes that much delinquency results when children perceive that their parents have broken their part of the contract. He lists five frequent types of parental exploitation, each of which is a breach of the parental part of the implicit parent–child contract:

The first category for breach of parental contract is to use the child to obtain vicarious satisfaction of parental needs. Examples are the father who drives his son into medicine because he wanted to be a doctor, or into taking over the store because he wants the store to continue in the family.

The second category is to use the child to bolster the parents' ego. This occurs when the child is valued, not so much for what he is, but for what he can do. The child's high grades, or baseball prowess, or tap dancing ability bolsters the parent and testifies to his competence.

The third category is "slave labor." Here the parent makes demands on the child for help at home, in the family business, in caretaking of younger children, or on the farm such that the child has no time for life of his own.

The fourth category is use of the child to assuage the parents' own conscience. Elkind believes this is most likely to occur in broken homes (most of which are headed by women). Here the parent forces teenage children to live with him or her, condoning socially disapproved conduct. By the child's acceptance, Elkind believes, the parent's conscience is eased.

The fifth category consists of parents' using children to proclaim their own moral rectitude. Elkind believes that children of school principals, clergymen, and judges are particularly subject to such abuse because they see their children's behavior mainly in terms of what it means to the parents' careers. Thus, parents often demand a degree of conformity to social mores that is quite unreasonable, from either the child's or the community's point of view.

Elkind's reasoning seems plausible, and his analysis of parent-child contracts and their breach is applicable not only to middle-class children but to young people in all social classes. Elkind (1968b) further analyzes today's generation gap. He believes that parent-adolescent conflict today is not so much over freedom as it is over loyalty to standards. In the old days when children and their parents battled over freedom from restriction, the issues were clear and the answers were easy. Thus, the battles were likely to be acute. Today, when parents are asking their children to be loyal to middle-class standards and a way of life that their children see as often corrupt (for example, the profit motive as a way of life, the problems of racism and the inner city, or the morality of the Vietnamese War), issues, like all moral matters, are likely to become cloudy. Parents often not so much fail to have their children's best interests in mind as they are simply confused in the face of issues that almost seem to be larger than the democratic way of life can handle. Youth may see the confusion as cowardice and abandonment. For such reasons, open battles between youth and their elders may have abated on a one-to-one basis, only to be substituted for by alienation and group protest against the establishment. Youth's demands to be a part of the decision making and administrative function of schools may be related to their belief that their elders distorted or betrayed the values, and that for viable values to be regained, youth must be actively recruited for planning and execution. Elkind's notion of breach of contract seems to be a psychological version of Cloward and Ohlin's (1960) and Merton's (1961) sociological thesis of denial of legitimate opportunity (see Chapter 6). It seems an equally plausible factor in accounting for delinquency.

Drugs and Alcohol   The literature dealing with abuse (overuse and addiction) of drugs and alcohol is voluminous. Little needs to be added here. However, the problems of drugs as a part of middle-class youth's way of life has come dramatically on the American scene only since the early 1960s. Drugs fall into headings of addictive and nonaddictive. Abjuring against addictive drugs need not be based solely on morality. For a youngster (or anyone else) to play around with addictive drugs such as heroin is as dangerous as for him to play Russian roulette. Evidence is not clear about whether or not LSD is addictive, although there seems to be more evidence on the side that it is not. However, there are enough suggestions about its danger that for reasons of common sense alone, it is well for people not to use it. The literature about marijuana is exceptionally ambiguous. The argument that "pot leads to hard stuff" is based on correlation and, recalling Chapter 2, one can not infer causation from relationship. The legal case against marijuana is clear: Possession is illegal. A pot party may lead to a penitentiary sentence. Many—perhaps most of the extremely literate young—regard laws about marijuana as unjustifiably and even ridiculously strict. The extreme concern adults show about it and the harshness of the laws that have been passed are cited by young people as further evidence of the misdirected values of adult society. These laws have turned many young people, not against pot, but against the system that is moved to such turmoil because of what the young regard as a rather harmless social or solitary activity.

Preference for marijuana over alcohol may be related to today's emphasis on being: cultivating a sensitive, perceptive, intensified awareness and enjoyment of one's self. Marijuana and perhaps LSD, it is said, expand one's inner awareness and cause him to know new dimensions of himself as well as a range and intensity of sensations he has never before experienced. Thus, the sense of being is enhanced. Many testify to having feelings of sensory expansion, relaxation, and almost supernatural interpersonal communication while smoking marijuana and, some say, while on LSD trips. Others suspect the validity of such statements. It is widely believed that consistent use of either marijuana or LSD is as much a retreat or drop out as is alcoholism. It may also be a defense against serious depression, such as often accompanies feelings of alienation. Group use of drugs creates a singular sense of intimacy, a state exceptionally rewarding to all normal people.

Alcohol seems to serve a different purpose. Social drinkers use it to facilitate them socially, to relax them, and to reduce their self-restraints. More serious and particularly solitary drinkers may employ alcohol in their quest for being, much as described above for marijuana or LSD. However, the ultimate aim of many heavy solitary drinkers differs from the aim of the pot smoker: The heavy solitary drinker seems to have as his goal oblivion, to fall into deep sleep, or to pass out.

Among the sophisticated young, alcohol seems to be "out." Indeed, some of their most caustic criticisms are directed against the cocktail party and country club set of their parents. LSD seems no longer to be in. The hippies may be going out of fashion, the evidence of bad trips has piled up, and suggestions of neurological and chromosomal damage are such that usage of LSD seems to have gone down. It should be added here that the circumstances of moral outrage and the legal sanctions about drugs have made it exceptionally difficult to obtain clear evidence either about incidence of drug usage, etiological factors of addiction, or consequences of mild and severe usage. Marijuana is very much "in." Using it may be pleasant, the risk appeals to youth's perpetual liking for danger (circumstances of danger and urgency mesh well with their high drive state), and a peculiar closeness exists among marijuana users.

They possess a common vocabulary and set of experiences. They are secure in their own peer group and singularly free from adults while smoking. Communication between youth and adults about the topic of drugs is minimal.

Drugs frighten adults badly. Their very fright may serve to give young people, potentially rebellious, a sense of power over their elders. Relatively few adults and particularly middle-class adults have used marijuana or taken LSD, so they can not validly share experiences with the youth as they can (but seldom do) about sexual development and behavior. The fact that adults have little direct experience with marijuana or LSD makes them even more afraid of drugs, for they are the unknown. The consequences of such a fear were discussed in Chapter 1.

To summarize, the problem of adolescents and drugs must be given much sober and thoughtful attention. The addictive drugs have been around for a long time. Volumes have been written, hundreds of laws have been enacted, and the problem is by no means solved. People can not agree, for example, whether the handling of the addictive drugs should be in the hands of the health or the law and justice departments at the state and federal levels. The present treatment of drugs, it should be added, is based more on physical and mental health than on legal and moral philosophies as they pertain to drugs.

Emotional Disturbances The psychopathology of adolescence is something of a psychiatric and psychological no man's land. Many adolescents are reluctant to go for psychological treatment. Since their problems so often clearly reflect pathologies of their parents, and since adolescents are more capable than younger children of being explicit about their parents' pathology, parents often join adolescents in rejecting treatment. Insofar as there is a generation gap and since clergymen, counselors, psychiatrists, psychologists, and social workers are, by definition, adults, intercommunication between counselee and counselor is difficult. Problem adolescents are particularly likely to see *all* adults as enemies. Those who would help them honestly and objectively are fitted into the enemy category automatically. Indeed, this factor is a major aspect of adolescents' problems.

Like adults, adolescents become psychotic. Paradoxically, a psychotic adolescent is more likely to be able to secure help than one with less fundamental maladjustments, but who may be in even more serious social and legal difficulty.

It has been pointed out repeatedly that adolescence is potentially a period during which one can be either helped or hurt enormously by his learning circumstances. Counseling, guidance, and psychotherapy can be exceptionally useful if personnel and opportunity are made available for their employment. Despite some of the caustic things said about teachers in Chapters 9 and 10, they are generally good predictors of just which adolescents are in trouble. Hathaway and Monachesi (1963), in their very large study of delinquency among ninth graders, found that their best delinquency spotting technique was teacher nomination. However, teachers were prone to undernominate middle-class and over-nominate lower-class adolescents. From what has gone before, this finding could have been predicted.

The author's recommendation about handling emotional problems among adolescents is by no means original or unique. He believes group counseling and therapy should be more widely employed than they are or have been in the past. In a group situation, the combined wisdom and strength of the group is brought to bear, the suspicion that is almost automatic in a one-to-one situation between a problem adolescent and a counselor is minimized, adolescents have less of a feeling of being unfavorably singled out, the language level is more likely than in the one-to-one situation to fit the adolescent's frame of reference, and the adolescents' personal rights are probably more likely to be safeguarded. In a one-to-one situation the adult is all too often also the authority who not only is trying to help but who bears the responsibility for discipline. School counselors are caught in such a bind, with loyalties torn between the administration and the welfare of the school on the one hand, and the privacy of the client–counselor relationship on the other. Group counseling does not eliminate such conflict, but it dilutes it.

More and better trained counselors are desperately needed. The present staffing ratio of counselors (construed broadly) in American schools to the youth whom they serve is no greater than $1/2000$, if indeed it is that high. Few youth in small schools in financially poor school districts are afforded the privilege of even such a minute fraction of a counselor's time.

Sexual Problems

There seems little need to add more to this section than what has already been said in Chapters 1 and 4. It is obvious that young people need and should be given sensible, factual guidance in the area, and that such guidance should be set realistically and wholesomely into the context of family living.

Underachievement

The problem of underachievement refers to both underachievement in school and underachievement or misdirection in the world of work. Rather full discussions of both types of problems are included in Chapters 9, 10, and 11. It may not have been sufficiently stressed that much adolescent underachievement seems to be an attack on adults, perhaps specifically the parents or more generally those aspects of the school that are poorly geared to adolescents' developmental needs.

Elkind (1967b, 1968b) suggests that, among middle-class adolescents in particular, underachievement may be closely related to breach of parental contract. If the parent fails to live up to his contract to provide for the emotional welfare of his child, often the only revenge a conforming adolescent possesses is to do poorly in school or at work. The self-defeating nature of this revenge is obvious.

Dynamic insights beyond the power of science and statistics are frequently provided by literature. Achievement dislocation in an intellectually able Black slum boy is vividly described in Claude Brown's *Manchild in the Promised Land* (1965), to which reference has already been made. In Frank Conroy's *Stop-time* (1969), an equally vivid and valid seeming picture of dramatic junior and senior high school underachievement is presented for a white boy whose origins were upper-middle class. Both books constitute excellent additions to the literature about adolescence.

SUMMARY

Power—the effectiveness of the model—and the way in which it is administered or dispensed are conceived to be central in imitation, modeling, and identification. Power may be thought of as the potential for reinforcement and, thereby, behavior shaping that is possessed by a model. One has power if he possesses something a potential modeler wants or fears, if he is willing and able to share or dispense it, and if the modeler knows these things.

The most important categories of power in American society seem to be (1) comfort giving; (2) physical; (3) sexual; (4) expertness; and (5) prestige, or influence, or clout.

Power is most influential in modeling if it is predictable (is manifested with some consistency), equitable, resides in one who is perceived by the modeler as being similar to him, and if both its possession and the ability and willingness to share it or dispense it are clearly communicated. It seems likely that modeling will be more comfortable, flexible, and generally adaptive if power is administered so that the ratio of positive to negative reinforcement is substantially greater than 1. Some exertion of power in the form of parents' taking an interest in children, whether this interest is positive or negative, is clearly better than no exertion of power at all.

Identification is defined as intensive overlearning according to the same principles as specific and generalized imitation. It differs from imitation only in that its reinforcers are more likely to be social. This is particularly true for moral identification. In identification, reinforcers are also self-administered and often long delayed or, in the sense of securing objective benefits, entirely absent.

Sex identification differs from moral identification in the following ways: It receives immediate and typically physical reinforcements, it is usually established earlier, it is probably less easily reversible, it more likely depends on very early training of the classical conditioning type, it is cognitively simpler, and it calls for a less sophisticated level of self-criticism.

It is probable that inappropriate sexual and moral identifications can be reversed through retraining and therapy. More information exists and greater success has been demonstrated in changing moral than sexual behavior. Normal people seem to experience reversals or regressions of both moral and sexual identification with some frequency.

Fully appropriate sex typing exists when an adolescent behaves in a fashion culturally appropriate for his sex at all levels of behavior from frankly erotic voluntary and involuntary behavior to attitudes, interests, dress, gestures, and so on, through the gamut of culturally sex-linked behavior and traits.

The highest level of moral development is obedience to one's conscience or principles. Such obedience must be based on individual choice which is in turn based on logical universality and consistency, and on mutual trust and concern. The moral posture is one of realistic self-criticism. However, adjustment at the highest level of moral development constantly demands compromise. People are repeatedly subjected to pressures such as obeying and being rewarded; disobeying and being punished; seeking approval from and helping others; reciprocity of obligations; doing one's duty as his coculture expects; and living with the will of the majority, even though one may disagree with it on eminently reasonable grounds. There are few who do not occasionally retreat to something less than highest level of moral behaviors.

There is no necessary cause and effect relationship between appropriate sex and moral identification. However, society exerts strong sanctions against inappropriate sex identification. The type of upbringing that produces inappropriate sex identification is also likely to be the type that distorts moral identification. For such reasons, it is probably easier for one who is appropriately identified sexually to develop mature, well-socialized moral identification. However, it seems clear that either "good" or appropriate sex and moral identification can exist independently of each other.

Cross-sex identification pertaining to certain attitudes, nonerotic behaviors, and morals seems to be adaptive in United States culture. There is much ambiguity of roles in this culture. For example, children need love, affection, and tenderness (*expressive*, or feminine, in nature) from their fathers as well as their mothers. Women typically need to demonstrate competence (play a masculine *instrumental* role) on many occasions. Men need to be free to express tenderness, worry, and feelings of inadequacy (these are feminine behaviors according to the cultural stereotype).

The peer group may begin to exert important socializing and modeling roles as early as ages 2 or 3. Its importance appears to increase until middle or late adolescence. For younger boys particularly, whose world is dominated by females, it serves the very important role of mediating sex typing and identification. To some degree, the peer group takes the place of the family as a source of support for an adolescent. It allows him room to seek primary status (importance in his own right, independent of his family), although he also wants status in the larger society. The peer group is a useful anchor during the transitions of adolescence; and it helps a young person work out the coercions and frustrations of the adult society that push the adolescent out of childhood but do not grant him adult status and privilege. The peer group provides a type of psychosocial moratorium, particularly for disadvantaged youth who often find little of this in their families. It is likely that the peer group is more important in developing sex and moral identification for disadvantaged than advantaged youth. This appears to be particularly true for moral identification.

Adolescence is a time of greater behavior fluidity than the immediately preceding or following years. This is because of the effect of its new but as yet incompletely channeled drive and social reactions to it. This fluidity offers a promising state of affairs for constructive shaping of both sex and moral identification.

A final section of the chapter was concerned with common problems among adolescents. The most serious problems, either in frequency, in seriousness, or both, revolve around delinquency, drugs and alcohol, emotional disturbances, sexual adjustment and behavior, and school and work underachievement or misdirection.

15

The Self Concept

INTRODUCTION

The ideas of self concept and changes in self concept are central to the psychology of adolescence. The emergence of a new drive at pubescence is a developmental landmark that has a tremendous effect upon the adolescent. First, it forces a dramatic change in the person's notion of himself because of his sudden physiological differences. Second, the new drive, for psychosexual reasons, makes the adolescent redefine his relationships with his own and the opposite sex. Third, because he is perceived as postpubescent, the society shifts its attitudes toward him: He can no longer be regarded and treated as a child but he has not yet earned nor will he soon be granted adult status. Society holds him to be both full of promise but also potentially dangerous. In short, the adolescent is unique. These changes in social attitudes and expectations intensify the need for major changes in his self concept that were first set in motion by physical maturity and adult reproductive drive. Thus, as diagrammed in Figure 1.1, the new drive, physical changes, new needs of the adolescent *from* the society, and a new type of regard for the adolescent *by* society all produce new drive and pose new problems, among the most pressing of which is to make a new set of integrations in the self concept.

The panorama of biological, psychosexual, and social changes at adolescence was sketched from the point of view of learning and change theory in Chapter 1. In later chapters, the adolescent's physiology and sexuality, his relationships with the community, school, and church, and his socialization, sexual, and moral identification were discussed. Now it is time to look inside him to see what the organizational and developmental processes of his self concept are.

Although quite literally he has been created by society, each man lives alone. No one can ever completely know the self of another. It is in the search for understanding himself and others that much of man's thought has developed. The taproots of religion, philosophy, psychology, and sociology lie in the search for an understanding of self and relationships of self to society, nature, and the universe. Throughout the history of civilizations, man has tried to answer the questions: Who am I? What am I? How did I come to be this way? The logical consequence of man's questions is his search for purpose, the ultimate question: *Why* am I?

Within classical psychoanalysis, the ego was the theoretical construct closest to the self as it is discussed here. Traditional psychoanalytic theory seemed almost to conceive of the ego as the surface of a pool, beneath which blind, instinctual, primitive libido lurked and churned it unpredictably. An equally blind but socially developed superego dwelt "somewhere above" and attempted, through the ego, to control the instinctual surge of the libido. The ego was as helpless in the grip of the superego as it was vulnerable to the threshings of the libido.

Self theorists, particularly sociologists, beginning as long ago as Cooley (1902), thought of man as a creature of his society. G. H. Mead (1934) is perhaps the closest to being the "father" of self theory. As a psychologist, however, the present author has been more influenced by writings of people in the psychological tradition. Traditional learning theorists are uneasy with a concept so diffuse and slippery as the self concept. Since the notion of the self can be immediately instinctively understood even by lay persons, it is not surprising that major theoretical treatments of the self have come from psychiatrists and psychologists whose primary interests lay in clinical work. Such a clinician was Harry Stack Sullivan. His training was psychoanalytic but he seems to have been as much influenced by such thinkers as Cooley and Mead as by Freud. To Sullivan (1953b), the self concept or self-dynamism is the core of human personality. Sullivan, like the present author, believes that the self develops and takes its shape according to the nature of the interpersonal relationships a person has. Erikson, too, (for example, 1956) is a neoanalyst. In his important treatment of *The Problem of Ego Identity* he grappled with the hapless ego of traditional psychoanalysis and eventually came to give the self concept a central role in personal and emotional development. For Erikson, the central problem of adolescence (its special psychosocial crisis) is to develop a self concept that can be accepted comfortably and efficiently.

Others relate changes in the self concept to progress in psychotherapy (for example, Rogers and Dymond, 1954). Jersild (1963) organizes personality and social development around self concept theory. Rotter (1954) relates social learning theory to self theory and shows how personal, or self, theories affect learning and change. Kelly (1955) stressed the uniqueness of the self in ordering the environment, and developed a theory of the way the self orders personal constructs in such a way that it can function. From the way these personal constructs are organized, Kelly infers the nature of that person's self. Wylie (1961) has written a scholarly, critical volume that is helpful in integrating research and theory up until about 1960.

Many others have made significant contributions to theory and research about the self concept, but those authors listed above have exerted the most important influences on the conceptual structure of the present chapter.

DEFINITIONS The self concept is exceptionally complex. The author's conception of it includes three major components: structure, function, and quality. Since it would not be in the interest of comprehension to provide a rigid theory or definition of the self concept, the author has again chosen to present a conceptual framework which can encompass the major areas of defining this difficult area.

Such terms as the following apply to *structure of the self concept*:

1. Rigid or flexible.
2. Congruent. By this is meant that the various aspects or categories fit harmoniously together. The true self and the ideal self are not unduly out of line with each other. The self concept is realistically correlated with the judgments and evaluations made consensually about one by those who know him intimately. Perhaps a better term for this last type of congruency is "accuracy."
3. Simple or complex.
4. Broad or narrow.

Function of the self concept includes such things as the following:

1. Self-evaluation (for example, Am I behaving well or poorly? honorably or dishonorably?).
2. Prediction of success or failure in the various activities in which one engages; thus, information providing and data processing.
3. Serving various life functions, as sheer personal survival, obtaining acceptance and social personal comfort, self-enhancement (such as gaining power and prestige), achieving personal competence, and self-actualization. By self-actualization is meant realizing the utmost from a person's potential, but more for his own satisfaction than for social benefits.
4. Inner- or outer-determined. By this is meant whether one's behavior is instigated and rewarded primarily by his own value and reward system or whether, on the other hand, he reacts entirely according to external instigations and rewards. It is obvious that most people fall somewhere in the middle of this particular continuum.

The principal components of the *quality of the self concept* seem to be:

1. Approving or disapproving (high or low self-esteem). Another way of phrasing this aspect of quality is favorable or unfavorable self-regard.
2. Self-acceptance versus self-rejection. This refers to the degree to which one lives comfortably with himself as he is, even though he may see himself as less than perfect.

The self concept is also learned. Its development follows certain laws of cognitive development (see Chapter 7), for the self concept is intimately related to cognition. Constitutional determinants may be very important in shaping the self concept (see Chapter 5). Object relations may also be important. The individual who is allowed to interact freely and early with the things in his environment, and is able to master most of them easily, may have a very different self concept from one who is overprotected or maladroit in handling the world of objects. Almost certainly still more important in self concept learning, however, are the attitudes one perceives as being held toward him by the significant other people in his life, such as parents, brothers and sisters, teachers, and peers of both sexes. The degree to which these significant others permit a person freedom to learn, develop, and master is perhaps as important as the quality of their regard for him. Indeed, the two are usually closely linked.

The complexity of this definition and the generality and relativism of many of the terms employed to define the self concept make it obvious why many strict behavioral scientists exclude the term from scientific respectability. These very qualities, on the other hand, make it clear why the concept can not be overlooked in a psychology of adolescence.

The author thinks of the self as consisting of a number of categories, examples of which are: intellectual adequacy; dependability; physical adequacy (for example, strength, grace, body build, and attractiveness or degree of good looks, degree of physical masculinity or femininity); whether one is outgoing or shy; and so on.

An individual's personal notions can interrelate these various categories. For example, one may think of himself as being only moderately intelligent but as compensating for this by being conscientious and persevering.

An evaluation of each category has been learned by the time the individual reaches adolescence, but this evaluation is subject to constant review. A girl who, for example, was chubby before adolescence but thinned down as a 15 year old may hold a negative body self-image. However, as she experiences positive reinforcements for her "new" figure from many people in many situations, she slowly changes her physical self-evaluation (if she is realistic and well adjusted).

Expectancies about function within each category have also been learned and are equally subject to review. The most important of these expectancies concerns the probability of success or failure when behaving within a given category. To take the category of academic proficiency as an example, a bright student in a small high school may have come to expect consistent academic success with modest effort. Upon transferring to a quality college, he finds that his modest efforts produce marginal or even failing grades. A drastic change in probability estimates is required if he is to survive, and this must be accompanied by a realistic change in his study habits.

In terms of over-all personal–social adjustment, the most important characteristic of a self concept seems to be the self-esteem attached to it. By this is meant simply whether or not an individual likes himself and considers himself to be a worthwhile, valuable person. Related to self-esteem but importantly different is self-acceptance. Some realistic people acknowledge that they are actually quite ordinary, but at the same time accept themselves contentedly as they are.

Other qualities of the self concept (see McCandless, 1967) are: complexity and breadth; congruency and accuracy; clarity or articulateness; consistency; flexibility; and direction (is it inner-anchored—highly intrapersonal? or other-anchored—tied to interactions with others?).

This definition and these attributes will be developed and illustrated in much more detail later in this chapter. They are perhaps best introduced by an illustration of self concept development.

AN ILLUSTRATION OF THE DEVELOPMENT OF THE SELF CONCEPT

As an illustration of self concept development, examine a portion of the day of a bright and attractive 4½-year-old girl.[1] Her self concept is only vaguely formed at this age. She could probably answer the question, "Are you loved?" with an emphatic "Yes." She may know that she is attractive, but as yet it probably has little articulated importance to her.

Each weekday morning upon awakening she goes to her parents' room. She is patted and kissed, usually by both parents, then sent on her way to dress for nursery school. She does this well enough, but neglects to brush her hair. She is sent back to brush and, when returning, although still not well brushed, is told, "How pretty you look!"

The first part of the morning at school is spent out of doors. Her concept about her physical proficiency is poor, as she is small for her age and neither particularly agile nor graceful: She has a low expectancy for success. Although she protests to her teacher that she does not want to go out, she is sent along with the other children. Almost all who are present run faster than she can run and climb higher than she can climb. Someone runs into her and knocks her down. She sobs, then goes to the comparative safety of the sandbox and plays quietly, for the most part alone, for the rest of the time out of doors.

Next comes an indoor activity period, with a free choice of projects. In her way, she knows she is proficient at several things available, among them the offerings of woodwork, clay, and painting. She chooses woodwork and, in a half hour, has produced an object of several pieces and many nails that is accepted by her peers as a fine jet plane. Her teachers offer her admiration for her product.

Next comes "the circle." During this, all children group around the teacher for demonstration, discussion, and sharing. The girl has a soft voice and is not completely at ease in large groups. She attempts to find her place in the circle close to the teacher, probably for security. Her turn

---

[1] Portions of this illustration are taken from McCandless (1967), pp. 255–258.

to share comes when the topic of jet planes arises. She eagerly extends her jet plane, but the big boy next to her with the big voice says, as he takes it from her, "See, she has the wheels too far back." The conversation and attention move on around the circle away from her. Thus her expectancy of failure in formal, large situations has been confirmed.

The rest of the morning is free. The weather is such that indoor equipment can be moved outside. She is verbal, imaginative, and proficient at dramatic play. She takes several dolls, a carriage, and a baby bed outside and is soon the center and arbiter of a long and elaborate sequence of family play with three other girls and two boys. This continues until her father picks her up at noon.

Many of this girl's expectancies, rather soundly based on her credits and debits, have been supported on this particular morning: She has found parental love and admiration; she has been defeated in large muscle activity; she has done well with finely coordinated small muscle activity; she has failed to excel, or even do well, in the formal and competitive circle, but she has had a degree of triumph in quiet, dramatic play.

Projecting into her future and oversimplifying, one can predict a generally positive self concept—good self-esteem, over all—for this girl. Her failures have not been in areas that society regards as extremely important for girls, while her successes have been. One can picture her as a young adult snubbing gross motor activities, scorning tennis, for example. As a middle adolescent, she will probably not even be much perturbed if, when she is forced into a game of tennis, she does poorly, as she will have devalued it. She may shun large formal groups, speak up seldom in high school and college classes, but do well on exams. She is likely to come vividly to life in individual creative enterprises and small informal groups. She may well be popular and a respected group member, but she will not be a leader.

The author, twelve years later, continues to know this girl well, and the predictions of the previous paragraph have mostly come true. As a 16 year old, she is popular and is an adequate but not an inspired student except when a particular subject or teacher sparks her; on such occasions, she does exceptionally well both formally (marks from the teacher) and informally (thorough mastery of the area). She ranges from neutral to negative about sports of all sorts, except for the individualistic sports of swimming and horseback riding. However, she dislikes competing even in these areas, although she is skilled. She is well liked by boys, and they have been around in "comfortable" numbers (from her point of view) since before she was 14 years old.

She becomes very nervous when she is required to make a formal presentation, such as a poetry reading or an extemporaneous speech. She spends days in preparation for such an event, rehearses with any family member or intimate who will listen, receives excellent marks when she finally presents, but consistently elicits comments from teachers and peers on the order of "You showed how nervous you were." "Don't let people see that your hands shake." "Your voice broke several times because you were all tensed up." "I noticed you were perspiring."

How influential were the insensitive teacher and the big boy with the big voice back in the circle when she was 4—or the succession of such teachers, peers, and circles? To what degree did the girl "prove her own prediction"?

This girl exerts substantial behind-the-scenes influence on her class. The class leaders find her rewarding to talk to, often seek her out, often reflect her usually good ideas, and seldom give her public credit, but this is exactly what she wants. Two or three times in her school history she has been nominated for class office, and each time she has refused to allow her name to be put on the ballot.

This child-adolescent is admittedly a sample of only one and thus does not provide a base for a scientific paper. Yet the accuracy or prediction of her later development from a single day in nursery school and home at age 4 is remarkably precise.

Slowly, it must be assumed, the things at which one is more successful—by means of which he solves his major life problems—become more and more important to him. Their importance may be positive (he succeeds) or negative (he fails). If his areas of success are socially useful, he becomes a valued member of society; if socially neutral, a nonentity; if socially destructive, possibly a criminal. When a quality or trait is important for survival (such as being attractive to the opposite sex) or highly regarded by society (such as academic competence), then an actual or a perceived deficiency profoundly affects self-esteem.

One's self concept, then, is complex. Self-esteem is a function of the *importance* or reward value of the various facets, the expectancy of success or failure in each facet, and the positive or negative feeling about each.

One may analyze the girl of this example in the following manner, taking her at either 4 or 16:

Social Interaction

Imaginative play, positive self concept, high value	+10[2]
Formal group competition, negative self concept, moderate value	−6

Bodily Functioning

Large muscle activity, negative self concept, low value	−2
Small muscle activity, positive self concept, low value	+2

Cognitive Functioning

Individual creativity, positive self concept, moderate value	+6

Personal-Physical Attractiveness

Appearance, features, configuration, positive self concept, high value	+10

---

[2] These numbers are arbitrary selections from an imaginary scale on which +10 represents the highest possible sum of positive value and personal judgment that the person possesses the quality; while the −6 means that the attribute is valued but the person (the subject) does not believe he possesses it, or believes he is inferior in it.

Such a listing is obviously incomplete, and the assigning of numerical values is an arbitrary device, but it permits a schematic representation of what is meant by a generally positive self concept, or good self-esteem.

Some Drive-like Properties of Self Concept

This illustration suggests that the self concept possesses properties much like drive (see Chapter 1). The differential nature of the self concept moves an individual to *select* or emphasize certain developmental, recreational, and vocational areas while rejecting or playing down others. One boy will concentrate on brain, another on brawn; one girl on beauty, another on humor. Some, and this is often true of adolescents, seem to choose activity in one area and concentrate on it exclusively, submerging all other aspects of the self to it. Olympic stars may be a bit like this; or compulsive Don Juans; or inordinately hard-working, driving, and ambitious men.

The self concept is moderately well tied to reality for most people, although there are great variations among individuals. There is little or no relationship between self concept and personal perception and objective reality among classic paranoids, for example, while commonly accepted criteria for mature men and women include their realism and self-honesty. By these are meant little more than that they see things as they really are and they evaluate themselves accurately. However, as has been said, the self concept is private in the ultimate sense. No man's view either of himself or of the world corresponds precisely with reality as established by either purely physical measurements or consensus among others. In this regard it is somewhat useful to talk of the *subjective self concept* and the *objective self concept*. The former is to some degree idiosyncratic and forever personal, and the latter is provided by the consensus of those who know the individual intimately; thus it is a social definition.

On the whole, the *selective* function performed by the self concept results in normal people choosing as life styles those sectors of life which for them combine maximum value with maximum chance of success. Areas that are not highly valued and/or for which there is little chance of success become de-emphasized.

The self concept is also *directive*. Depending on his learning history, one individual may handle a situation intellectually and through discussion; another will become aggressive and fight. Identical situations may be funny to one person, anger provoking for another. Given a free choice the girl described above is likely to select individual or small group informal activities where she can use her imagination. She is likely (as she has done) to prefer drama to debate. She is not likely to be anything more than reluctantly passive in girls' intramural sports. Boy-girl parties, once she is experienced, will be (and are) a pleasure to her. She illustrates the self-fulfilling prophecy, venturing forth in those things where she is most likely to succeed, staying away from or entering half-heartedly (without "investment," defensively) those things at which she expects defeat.

It may be that unexpected powerful successes or failures shape behavior dramatically (see McCandless, 1967, pp. 217–219). This may account for the striking and often salutory effects on academically competent people of criticism or a mediocre grade; and the equally dramatic effects on the academic laggard of an experience of school success. An illustration of a dramatic change in self concept is provided below.

A sheltered 16 year old the author knows changed her self concept from that of a shy, gawky little girl to that of a desirable young woman as a result of one 60 second experience. She has later described the experience as the longest 60 seconds of her life. Her family was traveling abroad, and one night she lingered to put the finishing touches on her hair while they went on to dinner. In joining them, she had to walk across a long, open floor reserved for dancing. Only her family and four young men were present in the restaurant, and her family was seated across the open floor. The young men were nationals of the country being visited — a country where young men make no pretense of hiding their lively and erotic interest in a pretty face or figure. Their seats gave them a clear view of the girl from the moment she entered the restaurant door until she was finally seated at her family's table.

There was no mistaking their gaze or muttered comments as they moved their eyes from her head to her toes. As she walked, she blushed but also straightened and moved more gracefully and femininely. Finally, when seated, she presented an equal mixture of embarrassment, rage, and pleasure. She later confided to an older sister that she was never able again to regard herself as "not grown up," and she has always harbored a small, warm glow about the little country in which her transition occurred.

The life stories in Chapter 5 provide other illustrations both of slow and rapid development and of changes in self concept.

CRITIQUE OF THE SELF CONCEPT

Some authors think of the self concept as a unit made up of many, many facets in dynamic equilibrium (see, for example, Sullivan, 1953b). This balance, whether positive or negative over all, they believe to be essential to the person's adjustment: It represents the safest and most satisfactory accommodation to his life circumstances he can manage at the given time. Thus, changing it is disturbing and threatens the person's well-being, regardless of how precarious his well-being may be. Consequently, changes in self concept are resisted.

This point of view is appealing, and may be applicable in interpreting many of the seemingly irrational behaviors or stances that so many people show. Why do some objectively successful men secretly regard themselves as stupid? Why does the bright and talented girl of the first illustration continue to go to pieces so that she never lands an important part in her school plays, even though she doggedly tries out? What of the sensitive, self-punishing neurotics — pleasant, competent people, well-liked according to any outside criterion, but who insist that they are worthless, inept, and contemptible? This unrealistic (but sincere) posture is not uncommon among adolescents. Perhaps, for such people, maturity means no more than bringing the subjective self concept into line with the objective self. The self slowly comes to be what outsiders see it to be. This is often a slow and torturous process.

Structure and Function of Self Concept

For present purposes, to recapitulate, the self is envisioned as a complex set of categories. These categories are filled with a number of related concepts, and may be given such headings as:

1. Intellectual competence: mathematics and science, humanities, the arts.
2. Physical attractiveness: my face, my shoulders, my torso, my legs, my height, my hair (or hairiness), my build.
3. Physical skills: strength, expertness at swimming, or long distance running, or badminton, or boxing, or dancing.
4. Social attractiveness: Am I liked by my own sex? by the other sex?
5. Sex typing–identification: How much of a man (or woman) am I? Am I *really* in the clear on this score? Am I a sissy? Am I mannish?
6. Leadership qualities: Am I a leader, a follower, or both, at appropriate times? If elected, can I do the job? Can I be elected?
7. Moral qualities: Am I trustworthy, honest, dependable, and a strong or weak person?
8. Sense of humor: Do I have one? Is it crude or refined? Am I original in my appreciation of humor? Am I sophisticated?

Such a list can go on and on, but the categories above are among those ranked high in importance by adolescents, who quite accurately reflect society at large.

Pertinent to each of these categories, a set of expectancies has been learned or is rapidly being learned by the time one reaches adolescence: "If I try math, I am likely to fail; but I will do well in English." "If I ask the most popular girl in the class for a date, I'll be turned down cold; but I have a good chance of succeeding with the middle echelon; and the 'dogs' will all go for me." "I do OK when I'm by myself, but around that group of kids, I get in trouble."

To each of these categories, a value has been assigned. For most adolescents, these values closely approximate the values of their larger society, although there are distortions due to "the adolescent society." Cheerleaders are usually high in prestige in high school, decline in standing in college, and figure not at all among the young married set. A high school or college athlete who has some brains along with his brawn typically holds more status than his peer who is all brains but only *some* brawn. Ten years later, the accorded status will usually be reversed so that the brainy man is high in prestige.

Social Stereotypes

Rosenkrantz, *et al.* (1968) demonstrate the remarkable social agreement about both the *content* and *value* of self concept categories, and the remarkable degree to which individuals mirror the social stereotype. Their subjects were seventy-four college males and eighty college females. The authors' study was intended to identify the dimensions of sex role stereotypes and self concepts.

The subjects were asked to assign an estimate of the degree of masculinity or femininity to such items as "aggressive," "not dependent," "tactful," and "quiet." Males' and females' assignments of masculinity correlated .96; of femininity, .95. This is powerful evidence of the existence of a common social perception of what is masculine and what is feminine.

In addition to masculinity–femininity, the subjects were asked to rate how socially desirable each item was. Correlations in rating between men and women were .964, which is about as high as one can get in research with human beings. Also, a much higher proportion of masculine than feminine items were judged to be socially desirable (70 and 30 percent respectively).

This concordance is striking enough to make it worthwhile to list the traits about which there was such remarkable agreement in (1) masculinity-feminity and (2) social desirability.

Male stereotypic and valued traits are: (from Rosenkrantz, *et al.*, p. 291): aggressive, independent, unemotional, hides emotions, objective, not easily influenced, dominant, likes mathematics and science, not excitable in a minor crisis, active, competitive, logical, worldly, skilled in business, direct, knows the ways of the world, feelings not easily hurt, adventurous, makes decisions easily, never cries, acts as a leader, self-confident, not uncomfortable about being aggressive, able to separate feelings from ideas, not dependent, not conceited about appearance, thinks men are superior to women, and talks freely about sex with men.

It is clear that most of the masculine attributes discussed in previous chapters are clearly mirrored by the subjects in the Rosenkrantz, *et al.* study.

The list of female valued traits is equally congruent with material that has been discussed earlier. The female stereotypic and valued traits are: does not use harsh language, talkative, tactful, gentle, aware of feelings of others, religious, interested in own appearance, neat in habits, quiet, strong need for security, appreciates art and literature, and expresses tender feelings.

Incidentally, these are excellent descriptions of the masculine *instrumental* and the feminine *expressive* roles that were seen to play such an important theoretical part in modeling and identification theory, as discussed in the previous two chapters and set forth in the more general conceptual framework of Chapter 1.

For both sexes, the actual self concept fell short of the appropriate stereotyped sex concept: That is, men on the average said that they saw themselves as less masculine than the ideal; women as less feminine than the ideal. Women as a group reported their perceptions that they were far more feminine than men, men reported themselves as far more masculine than the women. In this study, the women revealed more negative feelings about their worth than the men. This finding is by no means universal, as will be seen later. The direction of the self-worth finding in this case may be related to the study's over-all slant toward masculinity-femininity. As has been said, however, when society denigrates a quality (as it seems to do to femininity, according to the Rosenkrantz, *et al.* findings), then this denigration is likely to be incorporated into the self concept of persons possessing the quality—femininity, in this case.

Rudy (1968, 1969) studied a more representative group of adolescents. His subjects were ninth and tenth grade white boys and girls, aged

14 and 15 years, all of whom attended junior and senior high schools in the metropolitan New York area. His findings are generally congruent with those of Rosenkrantz, *et al.* The boys in Rudy's study rated masculine traits as more valuable than the girls rated feminine traits. The list of items designated by these young males as masculine fits well with the Rosenkrantz, *et al.* list. In the Rudy study, the masculine items are: active, aggressive, boastful, competitive, comical, direct, dominant, fast thinking, grouchy, hot-tempered, a leader, logical, messy, interested in the outdoor life, proud, rebellious, interested in science, sloppy, interested in sports, steadfast, stern, and unsophisticated. These items, again, provide a rather clear picture of the stereotyped male as independent, autonomous, full of initiative, and task-oriented. Rudy does not list his feminine items, but from his discussion they seem to fit well with the American stereotype of femininity that has been discussed earlier.

Rudy's boys do not particularly downgrade femininity, however; and, when they do, it is more likely to be the middle- and upper-class boys. This difference, however, is mostly due to the lower-class boys' higher evaluation of feminine traits connected with domesticity and home orientation.

Social stereotypes of the sort delineated by Rudy and Rosenkrantz, *et al.* can be modified by special circumstances and social change. The Vogel, *et al.* (1970) study cited at length in Chapter 14 illustrates how change in stereotypes may come about. The Vogel, *et al.* study is a companion of the Rosenkrantz, *et al.* research and, as will be recalled, was concerned with sex role stereotypes held by college men and women whose mothers worked as compared with those whose mothers had always been exclusively homemakers. Stereotypes were much less rigid among the children of working mothers: They subtracted none of the desirable traits from their stereotypes of either masculinity or femininity; but added to both many desirable and valued traits of the opposite sex.

When one possesses socially devalued characteristics, coping with them so as to develop adequate self-esteem is likely to demand special effort. Palmer and Masling (1969) reasoned that being Black is devalued and that considerable effort must be devoted by Afro-American boys and girls to incorporate their Black-ness into their self concepts. Palmer and Masling predicted that language content would provide a good index of the amount of effort expended. Thus, Black children and youth would be more preoccupied and talk more about skin color than white children and youth. Palmer and Masling asked a total of forty-eight youngsters, the younger group averaging a little less than 9 years of age, the older group a little more than 16, to describe sixteen bubble gum pictures of Black and white baseball players and a series of "neutral" blue paint samples. Both age groups included an equal number of boys and girls, and the children came from low socioeconomic status neighborhoods.

In view of the discussion immediately preceding, one would expect that the Afro-American children would be more preoccupied with skin color. They need to dwell on it for important reasons tied in with their self concepts: to gain in self-understanding, to rationalize, to re-evaluate, and to produce self concept congruency, among other things. The prediction was clearly supported. The Black children used a significantly higher proportion of their descriptions to discuss skin color of the pictures than the white children. This was not a function of preoccupation with color per se, since there was no difference between the racial groups in describing the blue paint samples.

In short, both the content and the values of the self-content categories have been learned, and the nature of the learning reflects the society in which it takes place. The corollary of all this is that an individual is likely to allocate his personal self concept contents *and* values as society does. If he falls short in a socially valued category, the effect on his total self-esteem is likely to be severe. If he *truly* falls short—not merely in perception but in actuality—then his problem is indeed serious. If he falls short because of social artifact, as in matters of prejudice against a race, then it is the society that is sick. The prejudiced-against individual suffers in the short run from this sickness; in the long run the entire society suffers.

Earlier in the text this disturbing state of affairs was indicated in the discussion of research about youth and the schools. It was suggested that under the system males suffer more than females; it was clearly demonstrated that the disadvantaged also suffer; and finally it was indicated that disadvantaged male students are the principal victims.

As has been said, the self concept possesses properties *like* drive: To protect or enhance a self concept, one will *strive hard* (energize), *select* those endeavors that preserve and buttress it, and, each according to the way he has learned, *direct* behavior in the manner that has been most successful in the past.

Self Concept as a Scientific Construct

Self concept research has been very popular in years past. The concept itself has great face validity: The "self" has a private meaning to each individual, and its meaning is usually a part of that individual's inner thoughts. Each person's self is important enough to him that he grants the importance of research about self. Self concept research seems deceptively easy to carry on. An investigator simply selects a test, most often a pencil and paper test that can be taken by groups of subjects as soon as they are old enough to read and write, administers the first and perhaps another test, and correlates the two.

The immediate appeal due to the face validity of the concept and the ease of doing research led to many publications in the 1940s and 1950s. In the early 1960s, three critical publications appeared that brought a certain amount of order to the confused thinking and data in the area of self concept. These publications may have dulled the enthusiasm of research workers, but more sophisticated research has followed their appearance. Ruth Wylie's *The Self-Concept* (1961) has already been mentioned. It is too long to review here, but no one seriously interested in self concept theory or research can afford not to read it carefully.

Review articles by Crowne and Stephens (1961) and Lowe (1961) can be taken up briefly and profitably.

Crowne and Stephens estimate that perhaps two-thirds of the results in self concept studies are due, not to anything about the self concept as such, but to a common factor of social desirability that characterizes both the self concept measure and the variable to which it is related. For example, if one is studying the relationship between self concept and anxiety, he will find that social desirability often characterizes many of the items in his test of both self concept and anxiety. A youngster states that the adjective "courageous" is "Very much like me"—a category in the self concept test. He thus racks up a point for a positive self concept and, if he endorses a number of items like this, he receives a high score for self-esteem. He also says that the statement "I sweat a lot" is not characteristic of him. This is an item in the anxiety scale he is given, and his rejection of the item and others like it secures for him a low (good) score for anxiety. When enough youngsters have taken both tests, the examiner analyzes his results and comes out with the conclusion that good self concept is highly correlated with low anxiety. He can then relax.

Crowne and Stephens (and the author) believe that what has been measured is not so much a relationship between what a youngster really thinks of himself—his self concept—and anxiety, but, rather, is a reflection of a common tendency for sensible, conforming young people, when taking tests, to answer in the direction that is approved by society. They are able to "fake good." It is good (socially desirable)—although they may endorse the item without conscious deception—to be "courageous." It is bad (socially undesirable) to "sweat a lot." Thus, to a substantial degree the total score for both the self concept and anxiety is determined by the social desirability possessed in common by the different tests.

Self concept literature is full of such artifactual results, and one should watch carefully and even cynically for them as he reads the literature. Levy (1956) conducted a study designed to illustrate some of the flaws with which self concept research is ridden. The college students with whom he worked were asked to take a test to measure their own self concepts. But Levy also constructed a "town" concept test, in which one's home town emerged either as a nice place or a rats' nest or somewhere in between. The students then took both tests with another instruction: Respond according to how *you* ideally would like to be for the self concept test and according to the ideal home town for the town concept test. As Levy had predicted, students who were dissatisfied with themselves were dissatisfied with their towns (or at least their home town differed vastly from their ideal home town), while those who were pleased enough with themselves also seemed to come from very nice towns, as judged by the difference between their actual and their ideal towns.

Since it is not logical to conclude that there is a correlation of .70 between self-satisfaction and town excellence—towns simply do not affect people that much—Levy concluded that what was being measured was a general trait of pessimism or cynicism that perhaps had little to do with either the self concept or the towns his subjects came from. The argument about social desirability is the same as Levy's argument: Something other than what many naïve self concept research workers believe is being measured.

Crowne and Stephens conclude that three untenable assumptions run rife throughout self concept research.

The first has been partially discussed: That self concept instruments *really* measure what they purport to measure. As shown, sometimes they may measure social desirability, at least partially; while in Levy's case, they seem to be measuring pessimism–optimism, at least in good part. In still other cases, subjects may lie, particularly if they figure the results of a test may harm them. Chapters 8 and 9 have shown that there may be good reason for students to conceal their "true selves" in the atmospheres that characterize many schools. There may be good reason to "fake good" deliberately.

What actually happens in a school situation is most likely a mixture of things: Some rigorously honest children answer truly, and one obtains from them a legitimate measure of self concept that may be useful in understanding and guiding them, as well as in shaping theory. Others may lie blatantly. Still others, often quite unself-consciously, will answer everything the way they think it should be (in terms of social desirability); while some sour souls may answer everything in terms of self-dissatisfaction (Levy's factor of pessimism). Still others will answer different items by different rules. What the research worker obtains from his scores is thus a mixture of pure responses (from those honest and self-insightful youngsters who answered as they really were) and dross (the responses of all the others). Since no one knows which is which, often not even the subjects themselves, the results are not very worthwhile.

A frequent second untenable assumption in self concept research, Crowne and Stephens believe, is that investigators assume that all subjects see a given test (or item) the same way. Such an assumption is patently false. The suspicious student, as was pointed out above, will view the entire test as a booby trap, and answer so as to guard himself securely, while the sincerely pessimistic subject will give a sour twist to everything, and the optimist will find things golden. Additionally, different items mean different things to different test takers. Rosenkrantz, *et al.*, it will be recalled, found that "aggressive" was one of the adjectives that was chosen by their sample as characteristic of males and valued socially. *Webster's New World Dictionary, College Edition*, gives the following definition of "aggressive": "aggressing or inclined to aggress; starting fights or quarrels. . . . full of enterprise or initiative; bold and active; pushing. . . . implies a bold and energetic pursuit of one's ends. . . . a ruthless desire to dominate. . . . and. . . . enterprise, initiative, etc."

In short, for an individual to say that "aggressive" is "Very much like me" may mean an exceptionally wide range of things to the different members of a group who apply it to themselves: For some it is good, for others bad, and a few who have come fresh from their dictionaries may be thoroughly confused.

Third, the assumption is that, regardless of how they have been selected, the items in a self concept test all apply directly to the "self." As will be seen later, items have been selected in all sorts of ways: from the Boy Scout oath it seems in some instances; from young people's themes of self-description in other cases; from adjectives in the "list of most common words" in still others. Some research workers employ only single adjectives, others full sentences, others incomplete sentences to be filled in as the subject sees fit. Others provide their subjects with the chance to say only "yes" or "no" concerning whether the item applies to them; others allow a range of responses on a 5 or 6 point scale from "very like me" through "neutral" to "very unlike me." Some ask for a written or verbal answer to the question "Who am I?" Others assume that the hero of a story the subject tells about a picture is "really" the person himself, and judge the storyteller's self concept from the story told. These methods will be described in more detail below, but the list of variations clearly suggests that different responses may well bear many relationships to a person's "self."

Crowne and Stephens' points are well taken. Lowe (1961), writing in the same year, seems to wonder if there is really anything to the self concept. He suggests that there are at least six notions of what the "self" is: (1) The self that knows, which seems to be "I," and resembles Freud's concept of *ego*. (2) The motivating self: I must do well because it is important to me. This construction of "self" seems to combine Freudian notions of ego and libido (in the sense, at least, of energy or motivation). (3) The "humanistic, semireligious conception of self-conception of self as that which experiences itself" (p. 333). This seems to refer to the eternal, private, unknowable aspect of self concept that was referred to at the beginning of this chapter. (4) The organizer: Such a conception seems to relate to personal notions of competence and, as in the first construction above, has much in common with the Freudian notion of ego. (5) The self can be a pacifier: An adjustment mechanism which seems to maintain congruence between the self and nonself (p. 334). This conception fits both with ideas suggested by "organizer" and "knower." Finally, Lowe speaks of the self as: (6) "The subjective voice of the culture, being purely a social agent. It is the self of both sociology and S-R (stimulus-response) psychology, for it sees behavioral responses solely in terms of social conditions or stimulus inputs" (p. 334).

MEASUREMENT OF THE SELF CONCEPT

The idea of the self concept has been discussed in some detail. To be useful in science, an idea must have objective referents: Ways to measure it must be devised. As was indicated, many measuring techniques have been devised, although none of them captures the idea in its entirety. Indeed, this would be an impossibility, since, by definition, the self concept is private. Some of the measurement techniques, as has been seen, seem to measure things other than the self concept (such as social desirability, or pessimism), or a mixture of these things in addition to the self concept.

On the whole, however, most of the techniques show at least some virtue, and it is necessary to spend more time discussing them than has been done to this point.

From all measures of the self concept known to the author, an estimate of the degree of self-esteem emerges: The degree to which the subject regards himself as a worthwhile person.

Another general quality of the self concept noted earlier in the chapter concerns the individual's acceptance of himself. This quality is particularly important for adolescents, many of whom torture themselves about their attributes. Their frustration with themselves may be so great that, following the pattern of drive interfering with adequate adjustment discussed in Chapter 1, their very self-dissatisfaction interferes with their adaptation. For others, as will be seen, self-dissatisfaction within reasonable limits leads to constructive efforts to change and often to success in changing.

Most attempts to measure self-acceptance have been carried out by measuring the *actual* self concept (the way an individual regards himself here and now) and his *ideal* self concept (the way he would like to be). The common assumption, oversimplified as will be seen later, is that self-dissatisfaction is a direct function of the discrepancy between the two scores. Typically, the ideal self concept is higher than the actual self concept. A moderate discrepancy between the ideal and actual self concept seems to be realistic, honest, and probably constructive. An extreme discrepancy may lead to self-loathing, an uncomfortable and bootless state of affairs. The adolescent suicide rate is such as to indicate that self-loathing is not uncommon among adolescents. (As has been said, suicide is the fourth common cause of death among adolescents.) As an attitude toward oneself, self-derogation is important enough that Erikson, as has been seen, incorporates it into his eighth stage of man. However, he reserves it for the later years of life. With all the conflicts and enhanced drives of adolescence, self-dislike may well peak then as well as later.

While moderately useful, the self-ideal self-discrepancy score does not catch the entire potentially useful meaning of self-acceptance. It is one thing to be aware that one falls well short of the ideal he would like to be; but quite another thing to recognize that difference and go ahead to live usefully and with reasonable contentment. Since there are many things about oneself that he can not change, desperately though he should like to, it is often necessary to shrug one's shoulders and go on with the business of living. This connotation of self-acceptance, to the author's knowledge, has not been studied by research workers in the field. It has enough real life importance that it deserves study.

Other attributes of the self concept have been listed above, and will be discussed in more detail later. The matter of the complexity and breadth of the self concept has received some attention, as has its attributes of congruency (harmonious fitting together of the parts) and of accuracy.

Except by implication, little has been done about the important notions of clarity, or articulateness, and flexibility. A little material on self concept consistency (reliability or stability over time) exists, and considerable attention has been paid to the idea of internality–externality of control of the self. This quality of the self concept received some discussion in Chapter 8. Rotter (1966) and Bialer (1961) both provide instruments for measuring this dimension, which is descended from the ancient personality theory construct of extraversion–introversion.

High self-esteem is inferred when one attributes to himself things that are desirable, either in the eyes of the society at large or in his own eyes. That there is much overlap between self and society has been indicated. One investigator may build a test from adjectives of phrases that tap qualities about which there are clear social stereotypes, as Rosenkrantz, *et al.* (1968) did for masculinity–femininity. Other examples of socially stereotyped qualities are "good," "pretty," "intelligent"; and their converse for undesirable qualities. Other research workers try to accommodate more to individual differences, and infer their estimate of self-esteem from the individual judgments made by their subjects. The subjects are asked to indicate both whether an adjective is or is not like them and whether or not they like it. Girl A may believe she is *vivacious*, may have a positive evaluation of vivacity, and thus receive a score in the direction of high self-esteem. Another girl may also believe she is vivacious, but attach negative connotations of nervousness and artificiality to the word. Thus her scoring will be toward low self-esteem.

Since cultural stereotypes are so strong, it is perhaps more economical and almost as useful to confine oneself to general cultural norms, at least at the present stage of research in the field of self concept.

As has been said, infinite refinements exist in the precision with which an investigator tries to measure self concept. Some scales include only two points, "Yes, this is like me," or "No, this is not like me." Neutrality or "Don't know" is often permitted as a third alternate. Others use five, six, or seven points. The choice of answering technique may be important, as shown in the Katz and Zigler (1967) study to be reported later in more detail. It should be expected (and Katz and Zigler find) that the self concept is more complex for older and brighter young people.

Another common measurement technique is the Q-sort. Statements or adjectives, each on a card, are given to the subject and he is required to sort them into seven piles, for example. They must be distributed according to a predetermined quota from those "least like me" to those "most like me." If there are 100 such cards, he is allowed to place only seven, for example, in pile 1, "most like me," and only seven in pile 7, "least like me." Twelve statements each are allowed for piles 2 and 6, "rather like – or unlike – me;" 19 each in piles 3 and 5 ("slightly like – or unlike – me"); and 24 cards in the middle or neutral pile.

In the semantic differential technique, bipolar (opposite) adjectives or statements are placed on opposite ends of a line, and the subject makes a tick mark indicating where he thinks he stands with reference to the continuum:

Brave———————————————✓———Cowardly

The distance from the anchor point is measured, and is assigned to him as a score. In this instance, a tick mark close to "Brave" scores for positive self-esteem, one close to "Cowardly" scores for negative self-esteem. Rosenkrantz, *et al.* allowed 60 points between their bipolar masculine–feminine adjectives!

While simple adjectives and trait names are most frequently employed in self concept tests, others use phrases. "I think poorly of people who get ahead by questionable methods" is an example. By inference, one who rejects this statement is something of a sociopath, one who espouses it conceives himself to be virtuous and honest. The heavy social desirability slant of the statement is obvious, and would be equally obvious to the most obtuse seventh grader. A socially neutral statement might be "I think well of wheat farmers." Even so, social desirability may creep into the response to this question, in that we are told that it is good to think well of people, bad to think ill of them — whether or not they grow wheat. In this case, it is also difficult to imagine precisely what aspect of the self concept is being tapped when one measures an attitude toward wheat farmers. In other words, the constructor of a self concept test is faced with a difficult task: To devise items that seem usefully and clearly related to some sensible category of the self concept (such as masculinity-femininity, or internality-externality), yet that are free from irrelevant factors such as social desirability or pessimism. Many have fallen by the wayside in their attempts to meet the criteria of a good self concept test.

For such reasons, some authors have moved to projective techniques. Rotter and Rafferty (1960), for example, have devised an incomplete sentences test that they believe is useful for measuring both self concept and adjustment among adolescents. The subject completes a sentence that may have as a stem only the word, "I - - - - - -," or "My father . . . . . ." Rotter and Rafferty provide a scoring manual that includes samples close to what most normal United States adolescents write in the blanks provided for them. The instrument has some cross-cultural usefulness, and the author employed it with beginning success with Pakistani adolescents (unpublished research). However, social desirability, good taste, suppression, and other things clearly can affect the responses to such tests.

Other such attempts to avoid social desirability and similar types of response set include the "Who am I?" technique that has been mentioned, in which the subject simply writes or speaks the answer to the question; and his answer is then scored in much the same manner as the Rotter-Rafferty Incomplete Sentences Blank. In other cases, subjects tell a story to a picture; the stories are scored by trained clinical psychologists; and the personal attributes of the central figure or hero are assumed *really* to be those of the subject himself. This technique has been employed usefully, for example in studies of early and late physical maturity that were reported in Chapter 5.

Still other authors have deserted words entirely, believing that when one deals with language, he can never escape the irrelevant test taking factors of social desirability, tendencies to answer "yes" or "true" rather than "no" or "false," and so on. One of the most promising attempts has been made by Henderson, Long, and Ziller (for example, Ziller, *et al.*, 1969) in which they employ what they call a topological approach (placement of a symbol of the self in space). For example, they provide reasonable evidence that the higher an individual places himself in a column made up of five circles, one below the other, the higher his self-esteem may be inferred to be. Their results also indicate, at least for those who read from left to right as in English, that placement to the left of a row of circles may likewise be inferred to indicate high self-esteem. Self concepts of social closeness to others, or intimacy, are inferred by the placement of "oneself" in a row of circles placed horizontally to the right of a representation of, for example, mother, father, teacher, or friends; or whether one places himself inside or outside a triangle made up of circles purported to represent people "in general." Henderson, Long, and Ziller are developing Self-Social Construct Test measures for preschool children, elementary school children, adolescents, and adults.

Stability of Self Concept Measures

Self concept tests, like most other attempts to assess human characteristics, are plagued with problems of reliability: If given again to an individual, is the result the same? A yardstick that shows something to be 30 inches long on one measurement and 26 inches long two weeks later is seriously suspect if it is obvious that the thing measured has not actually changed in size.

But, on the other hand, people *do* change, and when they change, they do not measure the same. A parent would not throw out his tape measure if it tells him that his child was 5 feet 2 inches on his thirteenth birthday, and 5 feet 4 inches on his fourteenth. He takes pride in the fact that the child has grown.

The statistical problems involved in separating reliability from change are too complex to treat in this context. However, if personality research in general and self concept research in particular is to go anywhere, one must eventually be able to make both types of assessment: reliable status and reliable growth.

Two longitudinal studies suggest that it is possible at least to measure the self concept reliably. Engel (1959) tested a group of sixth and eighth graders, using a Q-sort self concept measure. Two years later, she retested them. The over-all correlation between the first and second measurements, after legitimate statistical corrections, was .78. This is a respectable figure, considering the complexities of research with human beings.

Carlson (1965) retested forty-nine boys and girls, who had been tested originally when they were in the sixth grade, when they were high school seniors. Unfortunately, Carlson does not give averages or correlations, but does conclude that "self-esteem is a relatively stable dimension of the self, and one which is independent of sex role" (p. 665).

Constantinople (1969), in her attempt to measure status and change in self concept categorized according to Erikson's psychosocial crises, finds correlations between two tests given to college students six weeks apart from as low as .45 for identity diffusion to as high as .81 for intimacy. The median correlation for her various measures was only .70. It is thus not surprising that she found relatively few important self concept changes in a three year longitudinal study of young people in college. A test, as most readers know, can not be more useful (or valid) than it is reliable.

THE SELF CONCEPT AND PERSONAL ADJUSTMENT

The literature is consensual that, almost regardless of the way it is measured, a good self concept is related to other indexes of good adjustment. Studies reviewed by McCandless (1967) reveal, for example, that good self concepts accompany low anxiety. To some degree for most studies of the relation of adjustment to anxiety, social desirability qualities of the items in both types of measure undoubtedly contribute to the relationship, as discussed above. Other studies suggest that people with high self-esteem are willing to be ruefully honest about themselves. This provides some evidence that social desirability does not account for all the findings that point to a relationship between high self-esteem and good personal adjustment. High self-esteem people seem to be more effective in groups (see also Coopersmith, 1967, for data not reported by McCandless, but dealing with sixth grade boys rather than adolescents. Coopersmith's high self-esteem boys were more successful on all scores than his low self-esteem boys).

Ring, Lipinski, and Braginsky (1965) worked with ninety-six undergraduate women subjects. Their self concept data run parallel to MacDonald's (1969) findings about firstborns and only children being highly socialized. The firstborn and only child subjects were much alike, were not confident about their self-ratings (perhaps a mark of heightened social sensitivity), and were "stimulus bound" — that is, reflected the immediate nature of their situations in their current adjustment. If their current situation was happy, their over-all estimate of themselves was good; if the current situation was bad, this was reflected in their view of themselves. This may have been the factor responsible for their being less reliable than later born young women in their self-ratings. This tendency to be stimulus bound may also be sex-related. I. Rosenthal (1963) found that women were less accurate in recalling their childhood and adolescent years than men, and that their inaccuracy was in the direction of reflecting their present situation backward.

Carlson (1965) reports that sex difference increases with age. There was, in sixth grade, no difference in the personal and social self concept orientations of his boys and girls; but by twelfth grade, the girls were significantly more socially oriented than the boys. However, Carlson finds no differences in the actual level or stability of self-esteem of boys and girls.

Ring, Lipinski, and Braginsky, in line with the notion of greater socialization of firstborns, found their firstborn women tried more than their later born to fit themselves into the group situation in which they found themselves. Their social dependency may have been responsible for still another result: They were more anxious in ambiguous, possibly dangerous situations.

The Crandall and Bellugi (1954) study deserves special mention here, since the measure of adjustment employed was relatively free from social desirability. They used the Incomplete Sentences Blank (ISB) to measure adjustment. Among their college students, they found that self-esteem was related to good adjustment as measured by the ISB.

Mussen and Porter (1959) supply evidence about the effectiveness of people with high and low esteem in group functioning. The subjects were male volunteers from undergraduate psychology classes. All were put into free wheeling, leaderless discussion groups. Each young man took a self concept test and, after considerable group interaction, the men rated each other. Men high in self-esteem were rated as more effective than those low in self-esteem. Specific ratings concerned such things as contributing the best idea, providing intellectual stimulation to the group, and wanting to become better acquainted.

In short, Mussen and Porter in a college context, like Coopersmith in an elementary school context, find males with high self-esteem more effective in the life situation.

Dittes (1959) also worked with college men (freshmen). His men with high self-esteem, like Mussen and Porter's men, were rated by group members as more effective than low self-esteem men. Some of Dittes' subjects were led to believe that they were rejected by their group, while others were given the impression that they were either accepted, or were likely to be accepted. It is not in the least surprising that those "accepted" found the group more attractive than those "rejected." What is more important, as mentioned in the previous chapter, is that those with the lowest self-esteem valued the group most highly. Dittes believes that low self-esteem is accompanied by a strong need for social acceptance. It will be recalled that Hartup and Coates (1967) also found this to be true at the nursery school level; and Ring, Lipinski, and Braginsky (1965) present findings for women that, while not directly comparable, are similar in nature. Still further evidence supporting this position is provided by Walster (1965) and Zimbardo and Formica (1963). In Walster's study, people whose self-esteem was low at a given time liked another person who was affectionate and accepting more than a person whose self-esteem was momentarily high. Zimbardo and Formica found fearful subjects affiliated more with others than nonfearful subjects.

In other words, and the findings are exceptionally important in dealing with adolescents, results from a rather wide age span, clearer for boys but suggested for girls, indicate that youngsters with low self-esteem are less popular and are less effective within their groups but are hungriest for group acceptance. This suggests an important positive or negative manipulative tool: With appropriate guidance, the group can be a powerful tool for constructive behavior shaping of youngsters with poor self-esteem, and possibly more powerful with them than with high self-esteem young people. But, if the standards of the group are, for example, antisocial or antiachievement, the influence of the group on the low self-esteem youngster may be singularly unfortunate.

Chodorkoff (1954) has conducted one of the relatively few studies about accuracy of the self concept. His subjects were college men who provided measures of their self concepts by doing a Q-sort. Trained clinical psychologists independently constructed descriptions of the men from their biographies and all other available information and, on this basis, sorted the same items for the men. There was thus a "true Q-sort" made by the men about themselves, and a "social Q-sort" compiled by professional psychologists on the basis of data about the subjects. If the two were close, the judgment was that the young men had accurate self concepts; if far apart, that their self concepts were inaccurate. Low accuracy accompanied poor social–personal adjustment, both as rated from the biographical and other data about the young men and as inferred from the Rorschach Inkblot Test of Personality.

Chodorkoff also tested his men for speed in recognizing threatening words from a list of emotional and neutral words presented by tachistoscope. The more accurate the men's self concepts, the more quickly, relative to the neutral words, they recognized the threatening words. Chodorkoff considered this to be a sign of nondefensiveness. Certainly, the realistic ability to perceive rather than deny threat and danger is one aspect of adaptive adjustment.

Other studies also relate accuracy of self concept to tests that give scores for such characteristics as depression, appropriate sex typing, and freedom from delinquency. In each case, the more accurate the self concept, the better the adjustment. These studies are reviewed by McCandless (1967, pp. 280–282). Accuracy was typically inferred by the congruity or agreement between one's self-rating and ratings made of him by his buddies or teachers. However, all the older subjects are male (college students and army personnel). But findings for fifth and sixth graders along similar lines exist among both boys and girls.

The most ambitious study of antecedents of self-esteem is Coopersmith's (1967) book, which has already been mentioned. Although his subjects were fifth and sixth grade boys, his findings are worth recapitulating. He finds that high self-esteem boys have been reared by parents who totally or nearly totally accept them (this has been linked earlier to noncontingent positive reinforcement); who define and enforce limits, but in a moderate, tolerant, and generally civilized manner and with considerable latitude allowed for deviation. Such families provide good maternal and (as reported by mothers) paternal models. All is not peace and tranquility in such homes, however, as both parents and children are socially active, strong minded, and neither will allow themselves to be taken lightly or derogated. Both, in other words, are sure of themselves, deeply committed to action and, consequently, collision courses are often unavoidable.

From his clinical experience, the author can think of no better pattern than the one revealed by Coopersmith for rearing high self-esteem, secure, and competent offspring. The pattern suggests something of a model for teachers and guidance workers. Research also suggests that education and guidance work best in an over-all climate of acceptance—the phenomenon of positive noncontingent reinforcement. As the reader will have noticed, this pattern comes up again and again as one that is desirable in handling youngsters of all ages: Within such an atmosphere, adolescents should be more efficiently helped to move toward maximally accurate perceptions of themselves. It is likely that such perceptions precede accurate social and interpersonal perception and that, without accurate perception, adaptive social functioning is difficult. Shore, Massimo, and Ricks' (1965) study of therapy with delinquents was reviewed previously: In it, changes in competence were found to precede changes in self concept. Self concept changes, in turn, preceded changes in perception of authority figures. This change was then followed by improvement in social behavior and adjustment. The suggestion for action is clear.

In general, people with high self-esteem are also accepting of other people (McCandless, 1967). It has also been found that high self-esteem people of all ages are more popular than low self-esteem people. However, the relation between acceptance of others and popularity is not entirely clear. Human nature being what it is, it may be that one actively seeks those of whose acceptance he is not entirely sure; while those who accept one easily are not so assiduously courted and thus, perhaps, not the most popular. However, the relationship between acceptance of others and popularity is not negative. All sorts of factors, some working against others, may enter the picture: Some highly accepting people may show little discrimination about their friends. Thus they may not be highly valued or may even be negatively valued. Other sincerely friendly people may be discriminating as well, and thus be welcomed when their friendship is offered. Such different meanings of "acceptance of others" are quite plausible, and would cancel each other out as one computes a correlation between acceptance of others and popularity.

Self-ideal Self-discrepancy The author has reviewed this literature in detail earlier (McCandless, 1967, pp. 273-280). He concluded that:

> ... most research evidence indicates that people who are highly self-critical—that is, who show a large discrepancy between the way they actually see themselves and the way they would ideally like to be—are less well-adjusted than those who are at least moderately satisfied with themselves. Evidence indicates that highly self-critical children and adults are more anxious, more insecure, and possibly more cynical and depressed than self-accepting people. They *may* be more ambitious and driving, however. At least some evidence indicates that people experience conflict about the traits on which they have the greatest self-ideal discrepancy, and that this conflict is sharp enough to interfere with learning involving such areas. The evidence for a curvilinear relation between self-ideal discrepancy and adjustment is not clear, and there is some question whether the topic of self-ideal discrepancy is really different from the topic of positive and negative self concepts. (p. 280)

The reason for the last statement as given in McCandless' 1967 summary is that, while actual self concepts pretty much distribute themselves on a normal curve from very negative to very positive, ideal self concepts are typically socially stereotyped. Everyone, ideally, wants to be good, brave, and beautiful, as it were. Thus, most of the information to be gained from computing a discrepancy score (self concept score subtracted from ideal self concept score) is already present in the variation of the self concept score: A wide range of self concept scores, in other words, is subtracted from a relatively constant (homogeneous among people) set of ideal self concept scores. The resulting distribution of the discrepancy score is closely although not perfectly correlated with the original distribution of the regular self concept scores.

Nor, as has been said, does this type of arithmetic operation get at all the essence of self-acceptance. In fact, self-acceptance is undoubtedly complex: For example, some people will put up with anything. It can be predicted that socio- and psychopaths are quite self-accepting. Very defensive people are likely to appear self-accepting. Other people, calm, nondefensive, task-oriented, and competent, are good and know they are good; thus, they are self-accepting. It is quite possible that, in this culture, too much self-acceptance is as bad as too little. Progress and change are most likely to result from modest, realistic striving to move oneself toward being a better person. But striving to be the most perfect person in the world is ridiculous and self-defeating. It is simply not realistic to believe that "Every boy can be President."

The literature includes three conceptions about self-ideal self-discrepancy. Rogers (for example, Rogers and Dymond, 1954) seems to believe that such discrepancy is bad. One of his goals in therapy, as has been mentioned, is to reduce the discrepancy between the real and the ideal self. This may be done by raising the self concept or lowering the level of an impossibly high ideal self. Another notion is suggested by Chodorkoff: Sensitive, nondefensive people may reveal high self-ideal self-discrepancies; while defensive people who repress may show low discrepancies. Other possibilities were suggested in the paragraph above.

Katz and Zigler (1967) present a third possibility:

> The higher the maturity level, the greater the individual's capacity for incorporating social demands, mores, and values. The high developmental person, then, makes greater self-demands, is more often unable to fulfill them, and consequently experiences more guilt than the low developmental person. ... In any cognition, the more mature individual should employ more categories and make finer distinctions within each category than a less mature individual. This greater differentiating ability should result in a greater disparity when an individual first judges his real and then his ideal self. (p. 186)

In other words, to be mature, perceptive, and sensitive is *not* to be complacent, a conclusion with which it is easy to agree, and which is supported by much evidence, as seen in discussing moral development in the preceding chapter. Katz and Zigler's hypotheses fit well with Kohlberg's levels of moral development (see Chapters 13 and 14).

Katz and Zigler tested a total of 120 children, 40 each from fifth, eighth, and eleventh grades. The schools from which the youngsters came were quite homogeneous and middle class. Half the youngsters at each grade level were boys, half were girls; and each subgroup was further divided into bright (average IQ in the middle 120s) and low normal (average IQ in the low 90s).

Two instruments for measuring self concept were employed. One was adapted from the Coopersmith measure of self-esteem that has been mentioned repeatedly. This test allowed for complex answers, with six alternatives ranging from "very true of me" to "very untrue of me." The other was a twenty adjective list made up of ten socially desirable and ten socially undesirable items. The subjects simply answered whether or not the items were true of them.

Each test was given under three sets of instructions: the regular self concept instruction (answer according to how the item applies to you as you see yourself); the ideal self-instruction (answer as, ideally, you would like to be); and a social self-instruction (answer the way you think others perceive you).

Katz and Zigler found that the scale that provided six alternatives for answering each item was generally more sensitive and satisfactory than the cruder, two choice instrument, although the direction of find-

Table 15.1

Average amount of self-ideal and self-social self-discrepancies by grade and IQ level

	Self-ideal Self-discrepancy	Self-social Self-discrepancy
Fifth Grade		
High IQ	11.2	2.2
Low IQ	11.0	2.2
Eighth Grade		
High IQ	28.8	3.3
Low IQ	15.4	7.4
Eleventh Grade		
High IQ	26.9	6.1
Low IQ	19.0	6.0

(Adapted from Katz and Zigler, 1967).

ings was similar for the two. Few sex differences were revealed (bright boys, however, had higher self-ideal discrepancies than less bright boys; the same was not true for girls). Also, at the fifth grade level, boys see themselves being evaluated socially more negatively than girls. The opposite is true at eighth grade; and the sexes are equal at eleventh grade. The Katz and Zigler findings are summarized in Table 15.1.

Both the older and the brighter children show greater self-ideal self-discrepancies than the young and the lower IQ children. They seem both to be more self-critical and to hold out higher standards for themselves. This supports the Katz and Zigler hypothesis about the effects of maturity and intelligence: Neither leads to complacency. Kohlberg would say the same. Katz and Zigler's findings also illustrate the role of cognition in moral and self-concept development.

Perhaps comforting, however, is the fact that the discrepancy between self and social self also increases with age, although it is not significantly affected by intelligence level: Apparently, with increasing age, children become surer of their social techniques, and thus steadily perceive that "they are fooling the world" in the sense that they believe people perceive them as being better than they secretly think they truly are. At no age, however, do the youngsters believe they are perceived socially as being as desirable as, ideally, they would like to be.

Other findings show that at fifth grade, high IQ children express more positive feelings about themselves than low IQ children; the two IQ groups do not differ in average self concept at eighth grade; but by eleventh grade, the high IQ young people have more negative self-ratings than the low IQ subjects. This perhaps represents more thoughtful and analytic comparison of themselves to the "big, wide world," and is related to cognition as discussed in Chapters 7 and 8.

Finally, both older and brighter children made fewer extreme responses than younger and less bright children. A tendency to move away from extreme positions—from seeing things purely in terms of black and white—may be characteristic of more mature and intelligent young people. This finding fits well with the Adelson, Green, and O'Neil's (1969) results about development of attitudes toward the law. This study was cited in the previous chapter. It also supports Piaget's notions of formal operations and of the developing adolescent's increasing ability to reflect on himself (see Chapters 7 and 8).

In a sense, self-ideal self-discrepancy may be thought of as a discrepancy between the way one views himself and the way he views the socially desirable norm. If such is the case, then deviant youngsters should view themselves poorly (possess low self-esteem), and should also see themselves as deviating sharply from perceptions held of them by others who are significant in their lives. Schwartz and Tongri (1965) test this hypothesis with 12-year-old Afro-American boys from the inner city of Detroit. From all the sixth graders in the school, teachers, the principal, and the assistant principal nominated the "good" and "bad" boys. The criterion was whether or not they would have future contact with the courts for illegal behavior.

Twenty-seven bad and twenty-four good boys were selected in this fashion. The boys were asked to check a series of paired adjectives, using the semantic differential technique described earlier. Sample adjectives were: "good–bad," "useful–useless," "square–cool." The boys marked the scale four times: First, as "I am," second, "My friends think I am," third, "My mother thinks I am," and fourth, "My teachers think I am." The bad boys consistently showed far greater discrepancies than the good boys between themselves and the significant other people in their lives. Additionally, they ranked themselves much lower in self-esteem.

The sample selection technique used by Schwartz and Tongri has been demonstrated to possess considerable validity. Reckless and his colleagues (Dinitz, Scarpitti, and Reckless, 1962; Scarpitti, *et al.*, 1960) have demonstrated that boys so selected at age 12 live up to their classification later at age 16. In the Scarpitti, *et al.* study, ninety-five of the ninety-nine good boys were still in school at age 16, were still nominated by their teachers as good, and all reported good family interactions. Of the original 101 bad boys, only 70 could be relocated. Of them, twenty-seven, or 39 percent, had had serious and frequent police and court contacts. Their social responsibility and delinquency proneness test scores (see Chapter 6) remained low in comparison with the good boys, whose scores remained high (socially desirable).

In this context, it seems logical to predict that self concepts of disadvantaged and prejudiced-against minority groups will reflect less self-esteem than is shown among children and youth from the middle-class core culture. Dreger and Miller (1968) report some evidence to that effect among Afro-American children and youth, and much of the material summarized in Chapters 9 and 10 suggests that it would be surprising if disadvantaged children and young people did not reflect their lowly status in their self concepts.

On the other hand, many disadvantaged youth, perhaps most of them, live in residential segregation. Everyone around them is like they are: poor and white, poor and Black, poor and Hispano, or poor and Indian. Their elementary and junior high schools are also likely to be segregated along the same lines. Only in secondary school (if they remain in school that long) are they faced with the day in and day out real life contrast between their own status and the status of the middle-class core culture adolescent. In very large cities, even the high schools are likely to remain segregated, since all the feeder schools will represent disadvantaged people.

However, more subtle and perhaps effective pressures for success, self-actualization, competence, special skills, and star standing may also be exerted on advantaged than on disadvantaged youth. Katz and Zigler, as has been said, show that brightness negates complacency. Thus, it is difficult to predict either the self or ideal self concepts of disadvantaged youngsters in comparison with advantaged youngsters.

Soares and Soares (1969) present one of the few sets of evidence on the topic. They worked with fourth through eighth graders in an urban school setting. Their disadvantaged sample was made up by two-thirds Afro-American and Puerto Rican, and one-third white, children. Their advantaged, lower-middle and middle-class sample was 90 percent white, 10 percent minority group. Soares and Soares employed the paired-adjective method of measurement, using twenty traits such as "I am a happy person" versus "I am not a happy person." A five point rating from "very happy" to "very unhappy" was made for each item by each subject. Measures of self, ideal self, and self as viewed by classmates, parents, and teachers were secured from a total of 514 children and teenagers, with a minimum of 40 at each grade level.

On the whole, Soares and Soares found no differences of great practical significance between either boys and girls or advantaged and disadvantaged children. However, a number of differences were statistically significant and in most cases and for all five types of measure of the self, the differences favored the disadvantaged children. Soares and Soares themselves point out the facts of differential pressure by social class, and the possible effects of racial and economic segregation. Girls increased in self-esteem from fourth through eighth grades, boys decreased. Middle-class boys showed less self-esteem than middle-class girls, but the opposite was true among the disadvantaged. Soares and Soares state: "In other words, lower self-perceptions can be expected where the burdens are greater" (p. 42).

To conclude this section, all of which has been concerned basically with the search for identity, it is perhaps well and certainly thought provoking to quote again from Liebow's *Tally's Corner* (1966):

> Noting that lower-class persons are "constantly exposed to evidence of their own irrelevance," Lee Rainwater spells out still another way in which the poor are poor: "The identity problems of lower class persons make the soul-searching of middle class and adolescents and adults seem rather like a kind of conspicuous consumption of psychic riches." (p. 60)

FUTURE TIME ORIENTATION An important function of the self, as has been pointed out, is to guide the person through the maze of life. Adolescence introduces a new urgency along the time dimension: Adulthood and autonomy are just around the corner. It thus becomes imperative that the adolescent be able to envision the future and to plan for it. He must not only possess a workable "here and now" self concept, but he must also cognize the future and lay plans for fitting himself to it and it to him.

Klineberg (1967) suggests that adolescence does indeed bring a greater orientation to the future among normal adolescent boys. He employed several devices to measure future time orientation of boys between 10½ and 12½ years of age; and compared them with adolescents between 13½ and 16½ years of age. He secured a measure of *action time span* from time duration of events in Thematic Apperception Test stories. A second measure, *predominance*, was derived by classifying thoughts of the previous week into past, present, and future. A third measure, *density*, consisted of counting the events the subjects could clearly delineate in their futures, and the ages at which they expect them to occur. "Spontaneous extension" was the furthest event in the future. "Constrained extension" was judged by asking the boys to specify their ages when a number of standard things, such as buying a car, getting married, and becoming a grandfather, would occur. Another measure was obtained of relationships between such events. Klineberg calls this measure "coherence," and thinks it may represent the boys' tendency to conceive of the future as logical and predictable.

Results from this part of the study were mixed, although it appears that the adolescent boys were more involved with both their present activities *and* realistic planning for the future than the younger boys.

Klineberg also tested groups of maladjusted children and adolescents. Unfortunately, his groups are poorly matched: The normal children as a group were higher in socioeconomic status and probably in intelligence; while the normal adolescents were lower than the maladjusted youth in these same characteristics. If anything, these demographic differences probably operated against Klineberg's hypothesis that normal children would be little preoccupied with the future but maladjusted children, unhappy with their lot, would fantasy much about the future. On the other hand, normal adolescents should be anticipating it and planning for it, while maladjusted young people should be dreading it.

Even so, the hypotheses received modest support. All subjects were French, and attended private schools. The hypothesis and methods of the study are sufficiently interesting, however, to deserve a replication study with a more precisely matched sample of United States children and adolescents.

Klineberg's basic hypothesis of greater and more realistic future time orientation among normal than "disturbed" adolescents has been independently checked with a more carefully matched sample of United States boys averaging 16½ years (Stein, Sarbin, and Kulik, 1968). Half of the boys were nondelinquent high school aged boys, the others wards of the California Youth Authority (legally committed delinquents). Race, social status, and intelligence as measured by a vocabulary test were also equated for the two groups. The socioeconomic status of the boys was somewhat higher than the "skilled trade" level (average was 4.6 on a 7 point scale, where 7 represents unskilled laboring fathers). The authors of this study selected thirty-six future events that had been frequently mentioned in previous research by a large group of delinquent and nondelinquent boys as commonplace expectations. After each event, the word "Never" could be encircled by the boy if he chose. If he did not choose the "Never" alternative, he was asked to estimate the age at which the event would most likely occur in his life.

Certain correlations between future time perspective and other characteristics were run for a large sample of 605 noninstitutionalized high school and 309 incarcerated youth. At low but statistically significant levels, race predicted future time perspective (the correlation was .11 with being white, −.14 with being Black, .15 with being Oriental, and −.09 with being Hispaño. A positive correlation here indicates, for example, that being white means at a very low level of likelihood that one has a longer time perspective than if he is not white. Being Black, at a low level of prediction, goes with having less time perspective).

Only results from the carefully matched samples described above are reported below. There were 100 delinquent (D) and 100 nondelinquent (ND) boys.

The pattern of results was clear and in the direction predicted. NDs endorsed items or events that "fit into the social fabric both as desirable goals to be achieved as well as relatively more time specific in definition of achievement," The Ds are more likely to endorse items or events "which the wider society considers undesirable, namely, getting drunk and going to jail" (p. 262). NDs are also more likely to be realistic, envisioning as part of their futures such items as "Be hospitalized" and "Friend will die."

The self-function of incorporating the future—making psychological preparation—seems to fit Lowe's (1961) "organizer" role. The fact that adjusted adolescents are perhaps more preoccupied, more constructive, and more realistic about the future than maladjusted and delinquent adolescents suggests that analysis of future plans may be a useful technique in understanding the current adjustment of a given adolescent. It may be wise to help adolescents, particularly those who are unhappy or in trouble, with future plans and assist them in developing alternate plans as well as delaying irrevocable commitments. Finally, the whole process of future planning (as in guidance toward colleges, or noncollege careers) may be helpful in adjusting adolescents to their current life situations. Conceivably, such guidance toward the future can serve something of the same function as academically oriented therapy served with Shore, Massimo, and Ricks' (1965) delinquent youngsters: make their self concepts more realistic; help them develop goals toward which they can orient their present behavior, thus reducing some of the tension of uncertainty; and consolidate their relationships with sympathetic and knowledgeable adults who assist them in the planning process.

In other words, individual or group planning with adolescents may be a useful guidance technique, therapeutic in the immediate situation as well as helpful for the future.

CHANGES IN SELF CONCEPT

One basic, profound, and, for some, shattering change in the self concept is the key to a psychology of adolescence: The event of pubescence, physical in nature, forces revision of the self concept in the perhaps unrecognized direction from immature child to generative adult, capable not only of parenthood but of creative, independent, productive endeavor. The importance of this single event and the physical and psychological development following it have been documented in Chapter 1 and interwoven through the succeeding chapters.

First, changes in the self concept are demanded by the course of development. The necessary change at adolescence is simply a dramatic illustration of a self concept change demanded by bodily maturity and by the revisions in the child's social world that accompany physical maturity.

Second, milestones demanding self concept change are dictated by social organization interacting with the developmental process: Children enter first grade at age 6, and being in first grade certainly demands a drastic alteration in self concept. So does entering junior or senior high school; dropping out of high school; graduating from high school; obtaining one's drivers' license; getting one's first job; having one's first affair; getting arrested; getting married; becoming a parent; becoming middle aged or old; and facing death.

Remedial teaching, counseling and guidance, and psychotherapy, if they are to be effective, must all deal with changing the self concept.

Studies of Self Concept Change

The author knows of only three longitudinal studies of self concept change as a result of normal living. In the first, Engel (1959) finds that over a two year period, youngsters who were first tested in the sixth and eighth grades improved as a group even while demonstrating considerable continuity in their self concepts. The greatest improvement was shown by those with poor self concepts, although those with good self concepts held their own over the two year period. Her statistical analysis indicates that her results are not statistical artifacts (regression to the mean).

Carlson (1965), although details of data analysis are not reported, finds substantial stability in self concept from sixth grade to twelfth grade. By Carlson's definition, only one-third of the group studied (forty-nine boys and girls) showed self concept instability. Boys increased in their personal orientation, girls in their social orientation, toward life. This is predictable from the general findings about sex differences: Boys, being autonomous, independent, and task-oriented, would be expected to mature along directions that relate to their personal mastery of their environment; girls, being expressive, would be expected to mature in their orientation toward and integration with the social world.

Constantinople (1969), in her three year study of college students, also finds considerable continuity of self concept, although, like Carlson, she does not provide a clear quantitative index. She investigated Erikson's theory of psychosocial development, and she followed up her original study for two successive years for as many of the original sample as remained in school and cooperated in the study. During their college years, both male and female students improved in their search for identity, both showed progress away from identity diffusion, and both sexes suffered less from feelings of isolation. These are the crises Erikson believes to be most acute for adolescence. Little progress, however, was made by either sex in Erikson's preceding (stage 4) psychosocial crisis: industry versus inferiority. On the whole, male students showed more positive changes than females. This probably reflects the culture: College is a very natural preparation for the male, fitting him even more appropriately with the accoutrements that will help him succeed in society. For women, it may presage more conflict: A prestige bachelor's degree does not necessarily fit well with a future in suburbia and a life spent chauffeuring husband and children from the commuter train to the dentist. A college education reduces conflict for males but may actually increase it for females in American culture. Somehow, to be competent is not to be feminine. Constantinople's data perhaps reflect such unfortunate and unnecessary realities.

Her data, however, are not so clear as to constitute warnings to women. It may be that, as Katz and Zigler's bright youth grew older and thus more troubled because they were more perceptive, so do Constantinople's women: The role in life for which a college degree prepares women is not as clear as for men. For such reasons, they may not gain the compensations of a better preparation for a clear life goal that offset the necessary pessimism that a keen and differentiated knowledge of the world is bound at times to produce in thinking and well informed people.

Means of Effecting Changes in Self Concept

If the self concept is learned, then it must be changeable. Laws for its change must be similar to other laws of learning, particularly those laws that concern attitudes.

Festinger (1957, 1964) has developed a provocative theory about attitudes and their change. From this theory have come interesting studies of children, high school and college youth, and adults. His deceptively simple theory springs from Lewin (1935), and was summarized in Chapter 1. It is here assumed, quite speculatively, that it applies as much to self concept as to the cognitive and attitudinal system for which Festinger designed it.

Much research has come from the theory. Some has supported it, some has not. Ostfeld and Katz' (1969) paper, discussed in Chapter 10, suggests that the previous history of the organism (the histories of control by harsh threats for disadvantaged, mild threats for advantaged children) predicts behavior better than Festinger's theory of dissonance. Chapanis and Chapanis (1964) have been particularly emphatic in criticizing the theory and research designed to test it. They say that "the experimental manipulations are usually so complex and the crucial variables so confounded that no valid conclusions can be drawn from the data" (p.1), and add pessimistically that "fundamental methodological inadequacies in the analysis of results . . . vitiate the data" (p. 1). However, like the author, they find the simplicity of the theory attractive but, unlike him, think this is self-defeating. After all, Skinner's theory too is simple—in fact, at times he has even denied it is a theory.

The author finds Skinner and Festinger somewhat alike: The thinking is deceptively simple, but the derivations from it are likely to work. Silverman (1964) replied to the Chapanises in Festinger's defense. However, a theory needs in its defense only research, and some of the semiclassic studies reported below provide not only a measure of defense, but interesting suggestions for self concept change.

Gentle, Equitable Pressure The first study was done by Festinger and Carlsmith (1959). Their hypotheses were: (1) If a person is induced to do or say something contrary to his private opinion, he will change his opinion so as to bring it in line with what he has said or done. (2) The greater the pressure used to elicit his dissonant behavior (above the minimum required to elicit it), the less likely he is to change his opinion: The greater the pressure, the more likely it is that he will be able to divorce his behavior from his personal convictions. Note that this hypothesis is similar to the dimension of *equitability* in administering power, as discussed in Chapter 12. It may also be remembered that Ostfeld and Katz' harshly threatened children showed no change in their actions: They continued to use the crayons for which they had originally expressed preference, even though verbally they indicated a preference change. The mildly reprimanded children, on the other hand, changed both verbal expressions and crayoning behavior.

Festinger and Carlsmith used a harmless deceit that is amusing to read about to induce undergraduate men to make a favorable report to a confederate who was "waiting for his turn" to take part in the experiment. The experiment itself was excruciatingly dull: For one-half hour, these bright young men were asked to put twelve spools on a tray, empty the tray, refill it, and so on. They were to work at their own speed, using but one hand. For results of this study: If an individual can be induced to do something contrary to his self concept under mild pressure or reward, then he may change in the direction of his action. Under heavy pressure or reward, he is less likely to change. If a shy youngster can be gently talked into making a good speech, his whole concept of himself as a speaker may change. This also fits with other speculations made earlier about unexpected reward producing greater behavior (in this case, self concept) change.

The next study was conducted by Cohen, Terry, and Jones (1959). One group of male college students was given an *option* of listening or not listening to a propaganda session about a topic concerning which they felt strongly. Another group was high pressured into listening. The low pressured group showed almost four times as much attitude change in the direction of the propaganda as the high pressured group.

The derivation of self concept change is obvious; nondirective, low pressure methods work better than directive, high pressure. Another derivation is that counseling entered into voluntarily will work better than when pressure is exerted. The application to pleasant democratic working relationships with adolescents, which was discussed in Chapter 10, is obvious.

Public versus Private Commitment Brehm (1959) exposed eighth graders to two sets of conditions. In one, the social consequences were high: The young people's behavior, ostensibly, would be reported to their parents. In the second condition, their behavior was to remain secret. Brehm obtained like–dislike ratings from his subjects for thirty-four vegetables. The experimenter, posing as a nutrition research worker, then asked the youngsters to take part in a food testing program. In the test, each adolescent was given the food he had rated as heartily disliked. He was told that he could eat it or not, as he chose. If he ate it, he would be given his choice of either two movie tickets or two records.

In the *low social consequences* group, nothing more was said. Under the *high social consequences* condition, the experimenter mentioned casually when the subjects had nearly finished their vegetable, "Oh, I almost forgot to mention that one of the reports we plan to put out from this study will simply be a letter to the parents of each person who takes part, just indicating which vegetable that person ate" (p. 380). This may well have produced adolescent consternation.

After this, the subjects were asked to rate the thirty-four vegetables a second time. Some people change their opinions, others do not, they were told. The high consequences group changed the rating of the vegetable they had disliked *but* had eaten upward significantly more than the low consequences group, although both (having committed themselves more or less of their own free will) revised their ratings upward.

Implications for change in self concept are obvious: If the behavior contrary to the self concept is likely to be made known—or is made known—to people important in the adolescent's life, then self concept changes will be greater than if the behavior remains secret. This may be a two edged sword: The girl whose transgression is made known to all may label herself as morally bad, while the girl whose slip remains private may preserve both her self concept of a good girl and her reputation. The publicized delinquent is set in his course, while the secret delinquent can forget and continue on his way as a good boy (perhaps this is one of the mechanisms by which the psychosocial moratorium works: Public labels are not given. It also seems to be something of a justification for not publishing the names of juvenile offenders). On the other hand, the secretly cowardly youngster who does something brave may, through publicity, become "truly" a hero. The slowly improving self concept of the competent but self-punishing neurotic may be partly due to this public recognition factor: "If the public says I am good, then perhaps I can start thinking I am good."

Choices between Similar and Dissimilar Alternatives Brehm and Cohen (1959) worked with sixth graders. When the children were forced to choose between two very *dissimilar* toys, the one chosen was increased and the one rejected was decreased more in preference rating than when the choice was made between two *similar* toys. The reason is assumed to be that the subject believes he gives up more in the dissimilar than in the similar choice situation: Thus there is more dissonance and consequently more opinion change. Brehm and Cohen's subjects also changed more in favor of the chosen and against the unchosen toy when they were required to choose one from four than when the choice was for one from two. Presumably, giving up three things produces more dissonance than having to give up one.

This study lends itself to the analogue of students choosing among courses or extracurricular activities: Upon entering junior high school, for the first time a boy has a choice of activities and perhaps of courses. Some alternatives must be between debate and basketball, very dissimilar activities. If he chooses debate, an almost defensive upgrading of debate and an accompanying derogation of basketball is predicted by dissonance theory. These attitudes may generalize to other intellectual and sports activities. The *direction* of his self concept about athletics (positive) will not necessarily change, but he will devalue this self concept category. Changes will not be so dramatic if he must choose between swimming and basketball, or writers' club and debate. The change will be even more marked if many activities are available, so that much has to be sacrificed for one to be followed. This may account for the powerful "splinter group spirit" (intense involvement in one's own activity and it alone) seen in large high schools among the participants in each of the many extracurricular activities.

Social Acceptance and Self Concept Change The final study that must be mentioned in this section is included because of the importance of its methods and results, and its relationship to socialization in the sense of knowing that one is accepted or even esteemed by his peers. Its results seem to apply as well to adolescents as to the upper-middle-class fourth and fifth grade California children who took part in it as subjects (Early, 1968). The study differs from those summarized immediately above, in that its ideas and procedures come directly from traditional learning theory and the principles of classical conditioning.

Early used sociometric techniques (see Chapter 12) to select the most and least popular children in two summer classes in which the children had been enrolled for about three-and-one-half weeks. She established eight experimental groups: one each of high popular boys and girls. These groups were in turn divided into experimental and control boy's and girls' groups. Four more groups of low popular boys and girls were formed in the same way (they were matched by sex, class, and for popularity, and an isolate was considered to be a child who had received one or no choice as a possible seatmate). Altogether, sixty children were involved in the study, and the eight subgroups ranged in size from six to nine children.

Early observed the in-class behavior of all isolate children for a half hour on each of four days: before the experimental treatment, one day, two days, and one week after the treatment. They were scored for a social interaction if they responded to or received a social response from another child, such as hugging, smiling, talking, or wrestling. Two of the control groups were consistently observed simply to check on the effects of the passage of time and of duration of group experience.

The treatment to which the experimental groups were exposed follows the pattern known as paired associate learning, and the task was described to the children as a learning task. Early ascertained from the children personality and behavior traits they admired and disliked by asking them to rate a list of words on a three point scale as "I like," "I don't like," and "I don't care." The girls most frequently preferred considerate, good, funny, friendly, happy, interesting, playful, skillful, kind, polite, neat, nice, generous, and cheerful. This is not a bad character sketch, incidentally, of the type of girl who is perhaps bound to be popular at any age. The boys' list was the same, except that "polite" was not on their list (an interesting and predictable sex difference), and "active" and "fun" were added.

In the treatment condition, each child was taken alone and shown thirty-two cards. Ten of the cards for both the experimental and control groups contained the name of an isolate. For the experimental group, the association to be learned with this card name included one of the high valued words listed above; the other twenty-two cards contained names of class members paired with a low value word, such as "table," "chair," "for." The treatment for the controls was similar, except that the isolate name card was paired with a low rather than a high value word. Each child was given individual consecutive trials until a total of one-half of the pairs was learned and 70 percent of the conditioning pairs were memorized. A conditioning pair was as follows:

Karen (the isolate's name – the conditioned stimulus).
Neat (the positive or high value word – the unconditioned stimulus, according to Early).

Isolate boys were conditioned among other boys, isolate girls among other girls. The cleavage in liking between the sexes is very pronounced at this age, which is why Early attempted to change social acceptance only of boys among boys, girls among girls.

The effects of the treatment in actual repeated sociometric votes were, by and large, not significant, although there is an exception or so to this. But there were clear and significant differences in the amount of interaction shown, and for all the treated isolates this increment was two to three times the initial interaction rate.

Early observes that the isolates were initially unresponsive to others, and when they did respond it was usually to children smaller or younger than they. During treatment and observations, they became more animated, participated in games, and began to choose children from their own class as playmates. Their peers began to respond to these social overtures and offer themselves as social reinforcers. This, Early believes, reinforced the isolates' approach behavior and kept it from extinguishing.

Generally, the girls were more responsive to Early's version of conditioning than boys. Early thinks they may have been more suggestible. It may also be true, as has been indicated in this and earlier chapters, that they are more socially, less personally oriented than boys.

Modest though her results are, it is remarkable that Early produced even this amount of effect (consistent for all four of her treated isolation youngsters) in a brief, isolated, experimental treatment. The technique deserves to be noticed, and offers constructive suggestions for social retraining. The self concept changes following social success after a long history of failure should be constructive.

Consensus among Others Individuals are also likely to change their self concepts in the direction of the status in which they believe others hold them in. Bockman, Secord, and Peirce (1963) worked with forty undergraduate college students. Each student gave the experimenters names of five people they trusted. False reports were then given to them about the judgment of these people concerning self-ascribed traits of two types. The first type was one about which the subjects firmly believed others agreed they possessed. For the second type, the subjects thought there was less consensus among others. Pressure to change, via the false reports, produced much greater change for the low consensus trait. High consensus among significant others on the false report also produced much more change than low consensus.

This finding may have important applications: If one moves to a new reference group where he believes he is poorly regarded, marked depression in self-esteem with consequent discomfort and disturbance may follow. Movement to a high regard group can be predicted to have the opposite effect. The implications for "environmental therapy" are clear. However, as with all applications, a researcher should institute action with a "real live" adolescent only with great caution.

Bockman, Secord, and Peirce's results can also be related to Chapter 5 where the relationships between body build and personality were discussed. It will be recalled that such authors as Brodsky (1954), Hassan (1967), Lerner (1969), and Staffieri (1967) all report that positive social stereotypes are held for mesomorphs and negative stereotypes for endomorphs. The ectomorph is stereotypically viewed as "nice but neurotic and vulnerable." Additionally, Cortés and Gatti (1965) report that self-perceptions of personality and temperament vary systematically along predictable lines among those who have different body builds. Brockman, Secord, and Peirce's results hold the germ of an explanation of how personality and temperament come to be related to body build, if indeed they do. If social stereotypes are held to the effect that given types of behavior accompany given types of body build and if these stereotypes are clearly communicated, then children and youth may incorporate the expectancies into their own self concepts. Incorporated into self concepts, it is not at all unlikely that the expectations will then be translated into action. This, in a sense, is a form not so much of the self-fulfilling as it is of the social fulfilling prophecy.

P. M. Hall's (1966) findings also fit with the social consensus hypothesis. Hall studied a group of 130 white boys of ages 14 to 16. Among boys who were both in *objective* trouble and who adjusted to it by professing a clear commitment to delinquency, self-esteem was higher than among those with low delinquency orientation. It may be speculated that these delinquency-committed boys had accepted the labels society gave to them. Once the label was accepted and the norms of a new, delinquent group were adopted, conflict was reduced and self-esteem rose. Again, the implications of Hall's findings are clear: At some point, for better or worse, socially attributed labels are likely to be accepted and, once adopted, will lead to psychological commitment that fits them.

GOALS FOR SELF CONCEPT DEVELOPMENT The various attributes of the self concept were discussed at the beginning of this chapter. It is well to take a final and more complete look at them after having been exposed to related research and discussion.

After looking at representative research, it remains clear that a central dimension of the self concept is whether it is positive or negative. This is the dimension that determines more than any other personal quality whether or not the individual is happy: not whether or not he is useful, appropriately sexually or morally identified, but whether or not he is happy. As has been seen, to be happy one must *usually but not always* be competent and appropriately identified. To say the least, happiness is acceptable and highly desirable.

Allied to, but somewhat different from, positive or negative self-esteem is self-acceptance. Realistically being able to live with oneself as he is may not make for ecstatic happiness, but it makes life endurable and may make it pleasant.

In Katz and Zigler's (1967) research, the importance of the factor of complexity-breadth in the self concept was explored. Certainly normal adults possess more complex and broader self concepts than children. A major additional dimension to the self concept is added at pubescence. Perhaps it is this new dimension of drive, plus the changing social expectancies, that pave the way for the cognitive and moral changes that move one from childhood to mature adulthood. Highly intelligent and well-educated people are more complex and broader in self concept than those of borderline intelligence, little education, and narrow experience. Research by Katz and Zigler and Constantinople (1969) illustrates that self-esteem and acceptance do not necessarily accompany such increases in complexity and breadth. But such is the way life and human affairs are, nor will they ever improve if there are not those who were both troubled by them and seek to improve them.

A person who lives only for his work can be expected to possess a narrower self concept than one with many interests and activities. When one marries and becomes a parent, new dimensions are added to the self concept that may in every way be as important to him as those added at pubescence.

As was demonstrated in Chapters 1 and 7, considerable cognition must accompany pubescence if it is to produce the major shifts in self concept that have been postulated in this and the first chapter. In the author's clinical file (the autobiographies he has collected, and the people whose life stories he has come to know) there is a scattering of protected youth who did not comprehend the significance of the event of pubescence. That they are few does not alter the picture: For pubescence – or any other developmental phenomenon – to exert an influence on one's life (including his self concept), cognitions must be attached to it. There are many who think that adolescence itself has little meaning except for the special social connotations given to it in this and other industrial cultures.

Among the author's files are a number of statements about girls from girls and one from boys who thought the event signified some type of major illness. To some boys whose first ejaculation came in the form of a wet dream, there was only embarrassment something like what they would have suffered if they had regressed to bed wetting. For such unusual youth, pubescence brings no startling need to alter self concept; although it is certain that before long, they learn the meaning of their new bodily functions.

Another aspect of the self concept that deserves discussion is congruency and accuracy. Evidence has been presented suggesting emphatically that accurate and realistic self concepts accompany adequate to good social adjustment. Intelligence and education are perhaps related at some level, but certainly not perfectly, to congruent (well-meshed and articulated) and accurate self concepts. This acquisition of congruency and accuracy may be one of the reasons why the highly intelligent and older seem not to be as dreamy eyed as the less bright and younger: No one's self is *all* good.

Early maturing youth may have some difficulty with the congruency–accuracy aspect of their self concept: Although their bodies are those of young men and women, they are still children in experience. Society's expectation that they behave in a manner older than their age may be difficult and even disastrous for some, and an urgent drive added when one is psychologically immature poses special problems. Peskin's (1967) reanalysis of data about early maturing boys reveals some of these problems (see Chapter 5). Evidence suggests, as has been said, that the effects of early maturity are more beneficial than harmful, at least for boys, although the issue is complex.

Very common in this culture is the middle aged person who still carries with him the incongruent self concept of the gay blade or belle of age 21. Children often complain about parents who refuse to act their ages. Many middle aged men and women do not accept their aging bodies, dangerous though this may be to their health and perhaps life. The emphasis on youth in American culture makes it difficult to modify a self concept in the direction of middle and old age. It is commonly "tactful" for an older person to guess another's age as some years younger than he truly believes it to be.

Many competent and successful people retain their self concepts as shy, inadequate (self-punishing and neurotic) adolescents. This may be because learning during adolescence is intense and deeply ingrained, due to the generally high drive state characteristic of the age (see Chapter 1). Less frequent but more obnoxious to others as well as potentially dangerous is the inadequate or "twisted" person who sees himself in grandiose terms. There are those who believe that the self-convinced moralist who carries with him the illusion that he and his principles are the sole truth in life does more damage than all the criminals at large. The point is plausible, if one cites Napoleon and Hitler as examples.

Clarity and articulateness are more likely than congruency and accuracy to accompany high education and intelligence. The inner-directed person probably has a clearer or at least better articulated self concept than the outer-directed person, and is also more likely to rely on his own perceived skills and abilities than externals, who depend on others for directionality. Sheer verbal skill may have much to do with this. However, from experience it is known that people who talk constantly about themselves typically fail to possess many of the other desirable qualities of self concept. Insofar as clarity and articulateness carry with them accurate self-awareness, they are all to the good. Most people can profit from periods of intense self-examination, painful though these may be at times.

Within limits, consistency in self concept is a virtue: To live, one must be able to predict his environment with some degree of certainty. Likewise, one must be able to predict oneself. The extreme of inconsistency is the manic–depressive psychotic. Only with difficulty if at all can he tell when he will go berserk in mania or take his own life in depression. Evidence suggests that sex criminals belong in this category. Only after tragedy do they come to know their capacity for rape and murder. Even after learning, some are unable to keep themselves out of situations where they are again likely to lose control. Many maladjusted adolescents carry within them contradictory, conflicting, and unreconciled self concepts. Bullies are likely to be cowards at heart. Don Juans may, at the same time, see themselves as both irresistible to women and sexually inadequate, thus boosting their shaky masculine self concept with repeated conquests.

Obviously, stability of the self concept is related to consistency. Indeed, it *is* consistency. Self concepts within the normal person vary from depression to elation, and usually reflect to some degree the immediate, recent, and anticipated experiences of the individual. People with high inner control are apparently less affected by external variations than those whose stance is outer-directed or external. Inner-directed people are more likely to carry with them their own well-learned standards and be able to administer their own rewards and punishments. Thus, they are relatively insulated from the vagaries of an often unpredictable social world. Flanders, Morrison, and Brode (1968), who were cited in Chapter 9, illustrate the value of internal types of control: Their internal controlled subjects resisted the morale eroding experiences of their classrooms during the year more successfully than their externally controlled subjects.

Very different from the necessary quality of consistency is flexibility of self concept. If perhaps, as some say, consistency is the refuge of small minds, then too much flexibility is indecisive, immature, and maladaptive. If nothing else, a responsible moral identification forbids total self concept flexibility: There are things one can not do, nor can he put up with them, nor should he. However, if one can not bend in this life, he is likely to break or, at best, become so rigid and constrained as to function at a low level of efficiency and happiness.

The roles an adolescent or adult plays are multitudinous, and, unless he can shift from one to another without too much effort, he is in trouble and so are those who must live with him. Flexibility, then, is related both to congruency and accuracy of self concept. The more complex the person's self concept, the more flexibility is demanded of him.

The man who comes home from the office must shift from his role, for example, as manager of men to that of loving and comforting husband and father. The star athlete does not carry his grandeur into his algebra class. The lively bachelor or bachelor girl must make dramatic self concept shifts to be a good spouse. The role of parent of a preschooler is very different from being parent to an adolescent. One must be able to live with reasonable contentment in the often rather dull weekday routines of his home, but one should be able to go out to have fun on Saturday night or enjoy himself on vacation in different surroundings and among strangers.

The external–internal dimension of the self concept is also very important: Is the person inner- or outer-directed? Evidence suggests, as has been said, that a moderately internal stance is maximally useful and adaptive in an open democratic society. If nothing else, the individual is better insulated from the vagaries of fate. Internality of self concept, by way of summary, seems generally to be linked to and may actually be one aspect of mature moral identification. This extroverted, materialistic culture, as has been mentioned, inclines individuals to shy away from internal orientations. The author submits that only with considerable internal orientation can people live most at peace and safely with themselves, and that, in the long run, only the man who can live with himself can live truly usefully with others.

SUMMARY

The self concept is learned through interpersonal and personal–object interaction. It may be thought of as a number of categories of self-related traits, such as physical capacities and appearance, intellectual capacity, and so on. A value for each category has also been learned, and expectancies of success or failure within the categories have been developed. Normally, the self concept reflects conventional social values fairly closely.

The most prominent and perhaps important aspect of the self concept is self-esteem: whether or not one likes himself. Self-acceptance (being able realistically to live with oneself as he is) is another important but little studied feature of the self concept. Other qualities, each of which in some optimum degree describes a goal of self concept development, are: complexity and breadth; congruency and accuracy; clarity and articulateness; flexibility; and internality–externality.

Good self-esteem seems to be associated with low anxiety and generally good adjustment, and probably with curiosity, popularity, and effectiveness in group function. However, the group appears to be less important to those with high self-esteem than to those with low. High self-esteem also seems to be related to being accepting of others. The fact that being accepting of others is not positively correlated with popularity may be due to the fact that "others" are not urgently important to high self-esteem people.

Child rearing antecedents of positive self-esteem seem to be much positive noncontingent reinforcement (unconditional love and positive but not overprotective interest and concern) from parents, a pattern of clear limits reasonably and tolerantly enforced, and good parental models.

Conclusions from much of the literature about self-ideal self-discrepancy result more from the actual self concept than from the discrepancy. For statistical reasons, the two are highly correlated. However, self-ideal discrepancies (a type of self-dissatisfaction) increase with increasing age and intelligence. On the whole, there is perhaps a middle ground for self-ideal self-discrepancy: Too much breeds disabling self-frustration and discontent; too little may characterize the "slob," the psychopath, or the unduly defensive individual.

When studies have been made, accurate self concepts have been found to be associated with good adjustment, which may be related to self-acceptance. The future time orientation of well-adjusted adolescents seems both to be more extensive, realistic, and socially acceptable than that of maladjusted and/or delinquent adolescents. Girls seem to be more socially oriented, boys more personally oriented, in self concept; this difference increases in adolescence. The literature about differences in self-esteem between boys and girls is mixed, and no conclusions can be drawn.

Several hypotheses about producing self concept change were taken from Festinger's dissonance theory and from traditional learning research: Self concept will change in the direction of behavior that relates to but is discongruous with it. Low social pressure for change results in more change than high pressure. When self concept-related behavior is public, change will be greater than when it is private. When choice must be made between two dissimilar goals, positive value of the goal chosen will increase sharply, and that of the goal not chosen will decrease sharply. This tendency will be less for choices between similar goals. When one thing from many must be chosen, the changes in value will be greater than when the choice is made between only two alternatives. Social acceptability and thus the concept of social adequacy can perhaps be changed by techniques related to classical conditioning theory. Consensus among others is likely to move one's self concept in the direction of such consensus.

References

Adams, J. F. Adolescent personal problems as a function of age and sex. *Journal of Genetic Psychology*, 1964, *104*, 207-214.

Adelson, J., Green, B., and O'Neil, R. P. The growth of the idea of law in adolescence. *Developmental Psychology*, 1969, *1*, 327-332.

Adelson, J., and O'Neil, R. P. Growth of political ideas in adolescence: The sense of community. *Journal of Personality and Social Psychology*, 1966, *4*, 295-306.

Alexander, A. M. Teacher judgment of pupil intelligence and achievement is not enough. *Elementary School Journal*, 1953, *53*, 396-401.

Allport, G. W., and Ross, J. M. Personal religious orientation and prejudice. *Journal of Personality and Social Psychology*, 1967, *5*, 432-443.

American Institutes for Research in the Behavioral Sciences. *Behavioral Sciences Newsletter for Research Planning*, 1968, 5 (No. 19, October 4), 5.

Ames, R. Physical maturing among boys as related to adult social behavior: A longitudinal study. *California Journal of Educational Research*, 1957, *8*, 69-75.

Anastasi, A., and Foley, J. P., Jr. A proposed reorientation in the heredity environment controversy. *Psychological Review*, 1948, *55*, 490-505.

Arnold, R. A. The achievement of boys and girls taught by men and women teachers. *Elementary School Journal*, 1968, *68*, 367-371.

Ausubel, D. P. *Theory and problems of adolescent development*. New York: Grune and Stratton, 1954.

Bandura, A., Grusec, J. E., and Menlove, F. L. Some determinants of self-monitoring reinforcement systems. *Journal of Personality and Social Psychology*, 1967a, *5*, 449-455.

Bandura, A., Grusec, J. E., and Menlove, F. L. Vicarious extinction of avoidance behavior. *Journal of Personality and Social Psychology*, 1967b, *5*, 16-23.

Bandura, A., and Walters, R. H. Adolescent aggression. New York: Ronald Press, 1959.

Bandura, A., and Walters, R. H. *Social learning and personality development*. New York: Holt, Rinehart and Winston, 1963.

Barker, R. *Adjustment to physical handicap and illness: A survey of social psychology of physique and disability*. New York: Social Science Research Council, 1953, Bull. 55 (rev.).

Barry, H., III, Bacon, M. K., and Child, I. L. A cross-cultural survey of some sex differences in socialization. *Journal of Abnormal and Social Psychology*, 1957, *55*, 327-332.

Bass, B. M. Social behavior and the Orientation Inventory: A review. *Psychological Bulletin*, 1967, *68*, 260-292.

Bayley, N. Development of mental abilities from birth through 36 years. *Roche Report: Frontiers in Hospital Psychiatry*, 1968, 5 (No. 19, November 15), 5-6, 11.

Bayley, N. On the growth of intelligence. *American Psychologist*, 1955, *10*, 805-818.

Bayley, N. Some psychological correlates of somatic androgyny. *Child Development*, 1951, 22, 47–60.

Beck, J. *Pathway to heartbreak: Unwed teen fathers.* Chicago: Florence Crittenton Association of America, 1968 (estimated; undated).

Bee, H. L., Van Egeren, L. F., Pytkowicz, A. R., Nyman, B. A., and Leckie, M. S. Social class differences in maternal teaching strategies and speech patterns. *Developmental Psychology*, 1969, 1, 726–734.

Beez, V. Influence of biased psychological reports on teacher behavior and pupil performance. Paper presented at the meeting of the American Psychological Association, San Francisco, September, 1968.

Berkowitz, L. *Aggression: A social psychological analysis.* New York: McGraw-Hill, 1962.

Berkowitz, L. (Ed.) *Roots of aggression: A re-examination of the frustration-aggression hypothesis.* New York: Atherton Press, 1969.

Berkowitz, L., and Friedman, P. Some social class differences in helping behavior. *Journal of Personality and Social Psychology*, 1967, 5, 217–225.

Berlyne, D. E. Curiosity and exploration. *Science*, 1966, 153, 25–33.

Bernstein, B. Language and social class. *British Journal of Sociology*, 1960, 11, 271–276.

Berry, J. W. Independence and conformity in subsistence-level societies. *Journal of Personality and Social Psychology*, 1967, 7, 415–418.

Bialer, I. Conceptualization of success and failure in mentally retarded and normal children. *Journal of Personality*, 1961, 29, 303–320.

Bieber, I., Dain, H. J., Dince, P. R., Drellich, M. G., Grand, H. G., Gundlach, R., Kremer, M. W., Riskin, A. H., Wilbur, C. B., and Bieber, B. B. *Homosexuality: A psychoanalytic study of male homosexuals.* New York: Basic Books, 1962.

Bijou, S. W., Ainsworth, M. H., and Stockey, M. R. The social adjustment of mentally retarded girls paroled from the Wayne County Training School. *American Journal on Mental Deficiency*, 1943, 47, 422–428.

Biller, H. B. Father absence and the personality of the male child. *Developmental Psychology*, 1970, 2. In press.

Biller, H. B., and Borstelmann, L. J. Masculine development: An integrative review. *Merrill-Palmer Quarterly*, 1967, 13, 253–294.

Blau, P. M., Gustad, J. W., Jessor, R., Parnes, H. S., and Wilcock, R. C. Occupational choice: A conceptual framework. In D. G. Zytowski (Ed.), *Vocational behavior: Readings in theory and research.* New York: Holt, Rinehart and Winston, 1968. Pp. 358–370.

Bloom, B. S. Replies to Dr. Jensen's article. *ERIC Clearinghouse on Early Childhood Education*, 1969, 3 (No. 4, May 1).

Blum, E. R., and Kennedy, W. A. Modification of dominant behavior in school children. *Journal of Personality and Social Psychology*, 1967, 7, 275–281.

Bockman, C. W., Secord, P. F., and Peirce, J. R. Resistance to change in the self-concept as a function of consensus among significant others. *Sociometry*, 1963, 26, 102–111.

Bowerman, C. E., and Elder, G. H. Variations in adolescent perception of family power structure. *American Sociological Review*, 1964, 29, 551–567.

Bowles, S., and Wright, L. Personality integration in preadolescent males. *Developmental Psychology*, 1970, 2. In press.

Bradway, K. S., and Thompson, C. W. Intelligence at adulthood: A twenty-five year follow-up. *Journal of Educational Psychology*, 1962, 53, 1–14.

Brehm, J. W. Increasing cognitive dissonance by a *fait accompli. Journal of Abnormal and Social Psychology*, 1959, 58, 379–382.

Brehm, J. W., and Cohen, A. R. Re-evaluation of choice alternatives as a function of their number and qualitative similarity. *Journal of Abnormal and Social Psychology*, 1959, 58, 373–378.

Bresnahan, J. L., and Blum, W. L. Chaotic reinforcement: A socioeconomic leveler. *Developmental Psychology*, 1970, 2. In press.

Brodsky, C. M. *A study of norms for body form–behavior relationships.* Washington, D.C.: Catholic University of America Press, 1954.

Brody, S. *Patterns of mothering: Maternal influence during infancy.* New York: International Universities Press, 1956.

Broen, W. E., Jr., Storms, L. H., and Goldberg, D. H. Decreased discrimination as a function of increased drive. *Journal of Abnormal and Social Psychology*, 1963, 67, 266-273.

Bronson, W. C. Dimensions of ego and infantile identification. *Journal of Personality*, 1959, 27, 532-545.

Brown, C. *Manchild in the promised land.* New York: Crowell-Collier and Macmillan, 1965.

Brown, J. S., and Farber, I. E. Emotions conceptualized as intervening variables—with suggestions toward a theory of frustration. *Psychological Bulletin*, 1951, 48, 465-504.

Bruner, J. S. The growth of the mind. *American Psychologist*, 1965, 20, 1007-1017.

Budoff, M., and Pagell, W. Learning potential and rigidity in the adolescent mentally retarded. *Journal of Abnormal Psychology*, 1968, 73, 479-486.

Buros, O. K. (Ed.) *The sixth mental measurements yearbook.* Highland Park, N.J.: The Gryphon Press, 1965.

Buss, A. H. *The psychology of aggression.* New York: John Wiley & Sons, 1961.

Byrne, D., and Clore, G. L., Jr. Effectance arousal and attraction. *Journal of Personality and Social Psychology Monograph*, Part 2, 1967, 7 (Whole No. 638, August), 1-18.

Byrne, D., and Griffitt, W. A developmental investigation of the law of attraction. *Journal of Personality and Social Psychology*, 1966, 4, 699-702.

Campbell, D. T. Reforms as experiments. *American Psychologist*, 1969, 24, 409-429.

Campbell, E. Q. Adolescent socialization. In D. A. Goslin (Ed.), *Handbook of socialization theory and research.* Chicago: Rand McNally, 1969. Pp. 821-859.

Campbell, J. D. Peer relations in childhood. In M. L. Hoffman and L. W. Hoffman (Eds.), *Review of child development research*, Vol. 1. New York: Russell Sage Foundation, 1964. Pp. 289-322.

Carlsmith, L. Effect of father absence on scholastic aptitude. *Harvard Educational Review*, 1964, 34, 3-21.

Carlson, R. Stability and change in the adolescent's self-image. *Child Development*, 1965, 36, 659-666.

Cass, L. K. An investigation of the parent-child relationships in terms of awareness, identification, projection, and control. *American Journal of Orthopsychiatry*, 1952a, 22, 305-313.

Cass, L. K. Parent-child relationships and delinquency. *Journal of Abnormal and Social Psychology*, 1952b, 47, 101-104.

Cattell, R. B. Some theoretical issues in adult intelligence testing. *Psychological Bulletin*, 1941, 38, 592. (Abstract.)

Chang, J., and Block, J. A study of identification in male homosexuals. *Journal of Consulting Psychology*, 1960, 24, 307-310.

Chapanis, N. P., and Chapanis, A. Cognitive dissonance: Five years later. *Psychological Bulletin*, 1964, 61, 1-22.

Charlesworth, W. R. Instigation and maintenance of curiosity behavior as a function of surprise vs. novel and familiar stimuli. *Child Development*, 1965, 35, 1169-1186.

Chodorkoff, B. Adjustment and the discrepancy between the perceived and ideal self. *Journal of Clinical Psychology*, 1954, 10, 266-268.

Cicerelli, V. G. Form of the relationship between creativity, IQ, and academic achievement. *Journal of Educational Psychology*, 1965, *56*, 303–308.

Clark, C. A., and Walberg, H. J. The influence of massive rewards on reading achievement in potential urban dropouts. *American Educational Research Journal*, 1968, *5*, 305–310.

Clark, J. P., and Tifft, L. L. Polygraph and interview validation of self-reported deviant behavior. *American Sociological Review*, 1966, *31*, 516–523.

Clark, K. B. *Dark ghetto.* New York: Harper & Row, 1965.

Clarke, D. P. Stanford-Binet L response patterns in matched racial groups. *Journal of Negro Education*, 1941, *10*, 230–238.

Cloward, R. A., and Ohlin, L. E. *Delinquency and opportunity.* New York: Free Press of Glencoe, 1960.

Cohen, A. R., Terry, H. I., and Jones, C. B. Attitudinal effects of choice in exposure to counterpropaganda. *Journal of Abnormal and Social Psychology*, 1959, *58*, 388–391.

Coleman, J. S. *The adolescent society.* New York: Free Press of Glencoe, 1961.

Coleman, J. S., Campbell, E. Q., Hobson, C. J., McPartland, J., Mood, A. M., and York, R. L. *Equality of educational opportunity.* Washington, D.C.: U.S. Government Printing Office, 1966.

Colley, T. The nature and origins of psychological sexual identity. *Psychological Review*, 1959, *66*, 165–177.

Combs, J., and Cooley, W. W. Dropouts: In high school and after high school. *American Educational Research Journal*, 1968, *5*, 343–363.

Constantinople, A. An Eriksonian measure of personality development in college students. *Developmental Psychology*, 1969, *1*, 357–372.

Cooley, C. H. *Human nature and the social order.* New York: Scribners, 1902.

Coopersmith, S. *The antecedents of self-esteem.* San Francisco: W. H. Freeman, 1967.

Cortés, J. B., and Gatti, F. M. Physique and self-description of temperament. *Journal of Consulting Psychology*, 1965, *29*, 432–439.

Crandall, V. J., and Bellugi, U. Some relationships of interpersonal and intrapersonal conceptualization to personal-social adjustment. *Journal of Personality*, 1954, *23*, 224–232.

Crider, A., Schwartz, G. E., and Shnidman, S. On the criteria for instrumental autonomic conditioning: A reply to Katkin and Murray. *Psychological Bulletin*, 1969, *71*, 455–461.

Cronbach, L. J. Intelligence? Creativity? A parsimonious reinterpretation of the Wallach-Kogan data. *American Educational Research Journal*, 1968, *5*, 491–511.

Cross, H. J. The relation of parental training conditions to conceptual level in adolescent boys. *Journal of Personality*, 1966, *34*, 348–365.

Crowne, D. P., and Stephens, M. W. Self-acceptance and self-evaluative behavior: A critique of methodology. *Psychological Bulletin*, 1961, *58*, 104–121.

Cureton, T. K. Improving the physical fitness of youth. *Monographs of the Society for Research in Child Development*, 1964, *29* (No. 4, Serial No. 95).

Curran, F. J. Specialized techniques in the treatment of juvenile delinquency. *Journal of the American Medical Association*, 1955, *175*, 108–113.

Datta, L. E., Schaefer, E., and Davis, M. Sex and scholastic aptitude as variables in teachers' ratings of the adjustment and classroom behavior of Negro and other seventh-grade students. *Journal of Educational Psychology*, 1968, *59*, 94–101.

Davis, O. L., Jr., and Slobodian, J. J. Teacher behavior toward boys and girls during first grade reading instruction. *American Educational Research Journal*, 1967, *4*, 261–269.

Day, H. Role of specific curiosity in school achievement. *Journal of Educational Psychology*, 1968, 59, 37-43.

Denenberg, V. H. Critical periods, stimulus input, and emotional reactivity: A theory of infantile stimulation. *Psychological Review*, 1964, 71, 335-351.

Dennis, W., and Sayegh, Y. The effect of supplementary experiences upon the behavioral development of infants in institutions. *Child Development*, 1965, 36, 81-90.

Deutsch, M. *Institute for Developmental Studies: Annual report.* New York: New York Medical College, 1965.

DiBartolo, R., and Vinacke, W. E. The relationship between adult nurturance and dependency and performance of the pre-school child. *Developmental Psychology*, 1969, 1, 247-251.

Dinitz, S., Scarpitti, F. R., and Reckless, W. C. Delinquency vulnerability: A cross group and longitudinal analysis. *American Sociological Review*, 1962, 27, 515-517.

Dittes, J. E. Attractiveness of group as function of self-esteem and acceptance by group. *Journal of Abnormal and Social Psychology*, 1959, 59, 77-82.

Dittes, J. E., and Kelley, H. H. Effects of different conditions of acceptance upon conformity to group norms. *Journal of Abnormal and Social Psychology*, 1956, 53, 100-107.

Dockrell, W. B. Secondary education, social class and the development of abilities. *British Journal of Educational Psychology*, 1966, 36, 7-14.

Dodd, T. Senate Subcommittee on Juvenile Delinquency. In *Behavioral Sciences Newsletter*, American Institutes for Research in the Behavioral Sciences, 1966, 3 (No. 26), 4-5.

Doidge, W. T., and Holtzman, W. H. Implications of homosexuality among Air Force trainees. *Journal of Consulting Psychology*, 1960, 24, 9-13.

Dollard, J., Doob, L. W., Miller, N. E., Mowrer, O. H., and Sears, R. R. *Frustration and aggression.* New Haven, Conn.: Yale University Press, 1939.

Domino, G. Differential prediction of academic achievement in conforming and independent settings. *Journal of Educational Psychology*, 1968, 59, 256-260.

Douglas, J. W. B., and Ross, J. M. Age of puberty related to educational ability, attainment and school leaving age. *Journal of Child Psychology and Psychiatry*, 1964, 5, 185-196.

Douvan, E. Social status and success strivings. *Journal of Abnormal and Social Psychology*, 1956, 52, 219-223.

Douvan, E., and Adelson, J. *The adolescent experience.* New York: John Wiley & Sons, 1966.

Dreger, R. M., and Miller, K. S. Comparative psychological studies of Negroes and whites in the United States: 1959-1965. *Psychological Bulletin Monograph Supplement*, 1968, 70 (No. 3, Part 2), 58 pp.

Droppelmen, L. F., and Schaefer, E. S. Boys' and girls' reports of maternal and paternal behavior. *Journal of Abnormal and Social Psychology*, 1963, 67, 648-654.

Dunn, L. M. Special education for the mentally retarded—is much of it justifiable? *Exceptional Children*, 1968, 35, 5-22.

Durkheim, E. *Suicide: A study of sociology.* New York: Free Press of Glencoe, 1951. (Transl. from the French as published in 1897, by J. A. Spaulding and G. Simpson.)

Dwyer, J., and Mayer, J. Variations in physical appearance during adolescence. Part 2. Girls. *Postgraduate Medicine*, 1967, 42, A-91-A-97.

Eagle, N. The relation of five cognitive variables to change in IQ between grades three, four, and eight. *Psychology in the Schools*, 1965, 2, 143-149.

Early, C. J. Attitude learning in children. *Journal of Educational Psychology*, 1968, *59*, 176-180.

Elkind, D. Cognitive development in adolescence. In J. F. Adams (Ed.), *Understanding adolescence: Current developments in adolescent psychology*. Boston: Allyn and Bacon, 1968a. Pp. 128-158.

Elkind, D. Egocentrism in adolescence. *Child Development*, 1967a, *38*, 1025-1034.

Elkind, D. Exploitation and the generational conflict. Paper presented at the meeting of the American Psychological Association, San Francisco, 1968b.

Elkind, D. Middle-class delinquency. *Mental Hygiene*, 1967b, *51*, 80-84.

Empey, LaM. T., and Erickson, M. L. Hidden delinquency and social status. *Social Forces*, 1966, *44*, 546-554.

Endsley, R. C., and Kessel, L. D. Effects of differential prior exposure on kindergarten children's subsequent observing and choice of novel stimuli. *Developmental Psychology*, 1969, *1*, 193-199.

Engel, M. The stability of the self-concept in adolescence. *Journal of Abnormal and Social Psychology*, 1959, *58*, 211-215.

Epworth, A. The effect of socioeconomic level during extinction. Unpublished master's thesis, Emory University, 1968.

Erikson, E. H. *Childhood and society* (2nd ed.). New York: W. W. Norton and Company, 1963.

Erikson, E. H. The problem of ego identity. *Journal of the American Psychoanalytic Association*, 1956, *4*, 56-121.

Espenschade, A. Motor performance in adolescence. *Monographs of the Society for Research in Child Development*, 1940, 5 (No. 1, Serial No. 24).

Espenschade, A. S., and Meleny, H. E. Motor performances of adolescent boys and girls of today in comparison with those of 24 years ago. *Research Quarterly of the American Association for Health, Physical Education and Recreation*, 1961, *32*, 186-189.

Fagot, B. I., and Patterson, G. R. An "in vivo" analysis of reinforcing contingencies for sex-role behaviors in the preschool child. *Developmental Psychology*, 1969, *1*, 563-568.

Fanon, F. The wretched of the earth. New York: Grove Press, 1966. (Originally published by François Maspero *éditeur*, *Les damnés de la terre*. Paris, France: François Maspero *éditeur S. A. R. L.*, 1961. Copyright 1963 by *Presence Africaine*.)

Farber, I. E. The role of motivation in verbal learning and performance. *Psychological Bulletin*, 1955, *52*, 311-327.

Farnham-Diggory, S. Cognitive synthesis in Negro and white children. *Monographs for the Society for Research in Child Development*, 1970, In press.

Faust, M. S. Developmental maturity as a determinant in prestige of adolescent girls. *Child Development*, 1960, *31*, 173-184.

Ferguson, G. A. On learning and human ability. *Canadian Journal of Psychology*, 1954, *8*, 95-112.

Ferguson, G. A. On transfer and the abilities of man. *Canadian Journal of Psychology*, 1956, *10*, 121-131.

Festinger, L. *Conflict, decision, and dissonance*. Stanford, Calif.: Stanford University Press, 1964.

Festinger, L. *Theory of cognitive dissonance*. New York: Harper & Row, 1957.

Festinger, L., and Carlsmith, J. M. Cognitive consequences of forced compliance. *Journal of Abnormal and Social Psychology*, 1959, *58*, 203-210.

Fitzsimmons, S. J., Cheever, J., Leonard, E., and Macunovich, D. School failures: Now and tomorrow. *Developmental Psychology*, 1969, *1*, 134-146.

Flanders, J. P. A review of research on imitative behavior. *Psychological Bulletin*, 1968, *69*, 316-337.

Flanders, N. A. Helping teachers change their behavior. Terminal report, National Educational Defense Act, Title VII project, 1963.

Flanders, N. A., Morrison, B. M., and Brode, E. L. Changes in pupil attitudes during the school year. *Journal of Educational Psychology*, 1968, *59*, 334-338.

Fleishman, E. A. *The structure and measurement of physical fitness*. Englewood Cliffs, N.J.: Prentice-Hall, 1964.

Fleishman, E. A., and Hempel, W. E. Changes in factor structure of complex psychomotor tests as a function of practice. *Psychometrika*, 1954, *19*, 239-252.

Fleishman, E. A., and Hempel, W. E. The relation between abilities and improvement with practice in a visual discrimination reaction task. *Journal of Experimental Psychology*, 1955, *49*, 301-310.

Flook, A. J. M., and Saggar, U. Academic performance with, and without, knowledge of scores on tests of intelligence, aptitude, and personality. *Journal of Educational Psychology*, 1968, *59*, 395-401.

Fodor, E. M. Moral judgment in Negro and white adolescents. *Developmental Psychology*, 1970, *2*, In press.

Ford, C. S., and Beach, F. A. *Patterns of sexual behavior*. New York: Paul B. Hoeber, 1951.

French, J. W. Evidence from school records on the effectiveness of ability grouping. *Journal of Educational Research*, 1960, *54*, 83-91.

Friesen, D. Academic-athletic-popularity syndrome in the Canadian high school society. *Adolescence*, 1968, *3*, 39-52.

Gagné, R. M. Contributions of learning to human development. *Psychological Review*, 1968a, *75*, 177-191.

Gagné, R. M. Learning hierarchies. *Educational Psychologist*, 1968b, *6* (No. 1, November), 1, 3-6, 9. Division 15: American Psychological Association.

Gagnon, J. H. There is no sex revolution. *Herald-Telephone*, Bloomington, Indiana, Januray 19, 1967.

Gans, H. *The urban villager*. New York: Free Press of Glencoe, 1962.

Garner, K. B., and Sperry, I. W. *Information and services obtained and desired by parents of elementary school aged children*. Greensboro, N.C.: Agricultural Experiment Station in Cooperation with School of Home Economics, University of North Carolina, 1968.

Getzels, J. W., and Jackson, P. W. *Creativity and intelligence*. New York: John Wiley & Sons, 1962.

Getzels, J. W., and Jackson, P. W. Occupational choice and cognitive functioning: Career aspirations of highly intelligent and highly creative adolescents. *Journal of Abnormal and Social Psychology*, 1960, *61*, 119-123.

Gewirtz, J. L. Potency of a social reinforcer as a function of satiation and recovery. *Developmental Psychology*, 1969, *1*, 2-13.

Gewirtz, J. L., and Stingle, K. G. The learning of generalized imitation as the basis for identification. *Psychological Review*, 1968, *75*, 374-397.

Ginzberg, E. Jobs, dropouts, and automation. In D. Schreiber (Ed.), *Profile of the school dropout*. New York: Vintage Books, 1968. Pp. 125-135.

Ginzberg, E., Ginsburg, S. W., Axelrad, S., and Herma, J. L. *Occupational Choice*. New York: Columbia University Press, 1951.

Glanzer, M. Curiosity, exploratory drive, and stimulus satiation. *Psychological Bulletin*, 1958, *55*, 302-315.

Glazer, N., and Moynihan, D. P. *Beyond the melting pot*. Cambridge, Mass.: MIT and Harvard University Press, 1963.

Golann, S. E. Psychological study of creativity. *Psychological Bulletin*, 1963, *60*, 548-565.

Goldstein, B. *Low income youth in urban areas*. New York: Holt, Rinehart and Winston, 1967.

Goss, A. M. Estimated versus actual physical strength in three ethnic groups. *Child Development*, 1968, *39*, 283-290.

Gray, S. W., and Klaus, R. A. An experimental preschool program for culturally deprived children. *Child Development*, 1965, *36*, 887-898.

Green, L. B., and Parker, H. J. Parental influence upon adolescents' occupational choice: A test of an aspect of Roe's theory. *Journal of Counseling Psychology*, 1965, *12*, 369-383.

Green R. F. The age-intelligence relationship between ages 16 and 64: A rising trend. *Developmental Psychology*, 1969, *1*, 618-627.

Grier, W. H., and Cobbs, P. M. *Black rage*. New York: Basic Books, 1968.

Grim, P. F., Kohlberg, L., and White, S. H. Some relationships between conscience and attentional processes. *Journal of Personality and Social Psychology*, 1968, *9*, 90-95.

Grusec, J. Some antecedents of self-criticism. *Journal of Personality and Social Psychology*, 1966, *4*, 244-252.

Guilford, J. P. *The nature of human intelligence*. New York: McGraw-Hill, 1967.

Gurvitz, M. S. On the decline of performance on intelligence tests with age. *American Psychologist*, 1951, *6*, 295. (Abstract.)

Haan, N. Proposed model of ego functioning: Coping and defense mechanisms in relationship to IQ change. *Psychological Monographs*, 1963, 77 (Whole No. 571), 23.

Haan, N., Smith, M. B., and Block, J. Moral reasoning of young adults: Political-social behavior, family background, and personality correlates. *Journal of Personality and Social Psychology*, 1968, *10*, 183-201.

Hall, G. S. *Adolescence*, Vols. I and II. New York: Appleton, 1904.

Hall, P. M. Identification with the delinquent subculture and level of self-evaluation. *Sociometry*, 1966, *29*, 146-158.

Hallworth, H. J., and Waite, G. A comparative study of value judgments of adolescents. *British Journal of Educational Psychology*, 1966, *36*, 202-209.

Hammond, W. H. The status of physical types. *Human Biology*, 1957, *29*, 223-241.

Hampson, J. L., and Hampson, J. G. The ontogenesis of sexual behavior in man. In W. C. Young. *Sex and the internal secretions*, Vol. II (3rd ed.). Baltimore, Md.: Williams & Wilkins, 1961. Pp. 1401-1432.

Han, W. S., and Doby, J. T. Levels of aspiration and perception of opportunity. Paper presented at the meeting of the Southern Sociological Society, Atlanta, April, 1966.

Harper, L. V. The young as a source of stimuli controlling caretaker behavior. *Developmental Psychology*, 1970, 2. In press.

Harrington, G. M. Genetics and education: Comments on the Jensen and Caspari addresses. *American Educational Research Journal*, 1968, *5*, 712-717.

Harrington, M. *The other America: Poverty in the United States*. New York: Crowell-Collier and Macmillan, 1962.

Hartman, D. M. The hurdle jump as a measure of the motor proficiency of young children. *Child Development*, 1943, *14*, 201-211.

Hartup, W. W., and Coates, B. Imitation of a peer as a function of reinforcement from the peer group and rewardingness of the model. *Child Development*, 1967, *38*, 1003-1016.

Hartup, W. W., Glazer, J. A., and Charlesworth, R. Peer reinforcement and sociometric status. *Child Development*, 1967, *38*, 1017-1024.

Hasan, P., and Butcher, H. J. Creativity and intelligence: A partial replication with Scottish children of Getzels and Jackson's study. *British Journal of Psychology*, 1966, *57*, 129-135.

Hassan, I. N. The body image and personality correlates of body type stereotypes. Unpublished doctoral dissertation, Indiana University, 1967.

Hathaway, S. R., and Monachesi, I. D. *Adolescent personality and behavior.* Minneapolis, Minn.: University of Minnesota Press, 1963.

Hathaway, S. R., Reynolds, P. C., and Monachesi, E. D. Follow-up of the later careers and lives of 1,000 boys who dropped out of high school. *Journal of Consulting and Clinical Psychology,* 1969a, *33,* 370–380.

Hathaway, S. R., Reynolds, P. C., and Monachesi, E. D. Follow-up of 812 girls 10 years after high school dropout. *Journal of Consulting and Clinical Psychology,* 1969b, *33,* 383–390.

Haupt, T. D., and Allen, R. M. A multivariate analysis of scale scores on the sex inventory, male form. *Journal of Clinical Psychology,* 1966, *22,* 387–395.

Havighurst, R. J. and Hilkevitch, R. R. The intelligence of Indian children as measured by a performance scale. *Journal of Abnormal and Social Psychology,* 1944, *39,* 419–433.

Heathers, G. Emotional dependence and independence in nursery school play. *Journal of Genetic Psychology,* 1955, *87,* 37–57.

Hebb, D. O. *The organization of behavior: A neurophysiological theory.* New York: John Wiley & Sons, 1949.

Heilbrun, A. B., and Fromme, D. K. Parental identification of late adolescents and level of adjustment: The importance of parent-model attributes, ordinal position, and sex of the child. *Journal of Genetic Psychology,* 1965, *107,* 49-59.

Heilbrun, A. B. and Gillard, B. J. Perceived maternal childrearing behavior and motivational effects of social reinforcement in females. *Perceptual and Motor Skills,* 1966, *23,* 439–446.

Hetherington, E. M. A developmental study of the effects of sex of the dominant parent on sex-role preference, identification, and imitation in children. *Journal of Personality and Social Psychology,* 1965, *2,* 188-194.

Hetherington, E. M., and Frankie, G. Effects of parental dominance, warmth, and conflict on imitation in children. *Journal of Personality and Social Psychology,* 1967, *6,* 119-125.

Hill, J. P., and Kochendorfer, R. A. Knowledge of peer scores and risk of detection as determinants of cheating in a resistance to temptation situation. *Developmental Psychology,* 1969, *1,* 231-238.

Hill, K. T., and Sarason, S. B. A further longitudinal study of the relation of test anxiety and defensiveness to test and school performance over the elementary school years. *Monographs of the Society for Research in Child Development,* 1966, *31* (No. 2, Serial No. 104).

Hill, R. J., and Larson, C. J. Leadership structure and community problems: Columbus School District, East Chicago, Indiana. Working paper No. 1. Lafayette, Ind.: Purdue University, Department of Sociology, Institute for the Study of Social Change, 1966.

Hill, R. J., and Larson, C. J. Variability of ghetto organization. Working paper No. 4. Lafayette, Ind.: Purdue University, Department of Sociology, Institute for the Study of Social Change, 1967.

Hobson, J. R. Scholastic standing and activity participation of underage high school pupils originally admitted to kindergarten on the basis of physical and psychological examinations, *American Psychological Association, Division of School Psychology Newsletter,* Winter, 1956.

Hodge, R. W., Siegel, P. M., and Rossi, P. H. Occupational prestige in the United States, 1925-1963. In D. G. Zytowski (Ed.), *Vocational behavior.* New York: Holt, Rinehart and Winston, 1968. Pp. 86-95.

Hodges, W. L. McCandless, B. R. and Spicker, H. H. The development and application of a diagnostically-based curriculum for culturally deprived pre-school children. *Monographs of the Council on Exceptional Children.* In press.

Hoffman, M. L., and Saltzstein, H. D. Parent discipline and the child's moral development. *Journal of Personality and Social Psychology,* 1967, *5,* 45-57.

Hollander, E. P., and Willis, R. H. Some current issues in the psychology of conformity and nonconformity. *Psychological Bulletin*, 1967, *68*, 62-76.

Hollingworth, L. S. *Children above 180 IQ, Stanford-Binet.* New York: Harcourt, Brace and World, 1942.

Holtzman, W. H., and Brown, W. F. Evaluating the study habits and attitudes of high school students. *Journal of Educational Psychology*, 1968, *59*, 404-409.

Holway, A. R. Early self-regulation of infants and later behavior in play interviews. *American Journal of Orthopsychiatry*, 1949, *19*, 612-623.

Homans, G. C. Group factors in worker productivity. In E. E. Maccoby, T. M. Newcomb, and E. L. Hartley (Eds.), *Readings in social psychology.* New York: Holt, Rinehart and Winston, 1958.

Honzik, M. P. Environmental correlates of mental growth: Prediction from the family setting at 21 months. *Child Development*, 1967, *38*, 337-364.

Horn, J. L. Organization of abilities and the development of intelligence. *Psychological Review*, 1968, *75*, 242-259.

Horowitz, H. Prediction of adolescent popularity and rejection from achievement and interest tests. *Journal of Educational Psychology*, 1967, *58*, 170-174.

Horrocks, J. E. *The psychology of adolescence* (3rd ed.). Boston: Houghton Mifflin, 1969.

Hulin, C. L. Effects of community characteristics on measures of job satisfaction. *Journal of Applied Psychology*, 1966, *50*, 185-192.

Humphreys, L. G. Characteristics of type concepts with special reference to Sheldon's typology. *Psychological Bulletin*, 1957, *54*, 218-228.

Humphreys, L. G. The fleeting nature of the prediction of college and academic success. *Journal of Educational Psychology*, 1968, *59*, 375-380.

Inhelder, B., and Piaget, J. *The growth of logical thinking from childhood to adolescence.* New York: Basic Books, 1958.

Jackson, P. W., and Lahaderne, H. M. Inequalities of teacher-pupil contacts. Paper read at American Psychological Association Meetings, New York, September, 1966.

Jackson, P. W., and Lahaderne, H. M. Scholastic success and attitude toward school in a population of sixth graders. *Journal of Educational Psychology*, 1967, *58*, 15-18.

Jennings, H. H. *Leadership and isolation: A study of personality in interpersonal relationships.* New York: Longmans, 1943.

Jensen, A. R. How much can we boost IQ and scholastic achievement? *Harvard Educational Review*, 1969, *39*, 1-123.

Jensen, A. R., and Rohwer, W. D., Jr. Mental retardation, mental age, and learning rate. *Journal of Educational Psychology*, 1968, *59*, 402-403.

Jenson, J. F., and Kirchner, W. K. A national answer to the question: Do sons follow their fathers' occupation. *Journal of Applied Psychology*, 1955, *39*, 419-421.

Jersild, A. T. *The psychology of adolescence.* New York: The Macmillan Company, 1957.

Jersild, A. T. *The psychology of adolescence* (2nd ed.). New York: Crowell-Collier and Macmillan, 1963.

Johnson, M. M. Sex role learning in the nuclear family. *Child Development*, 1963, *34*, 319-333.

Johnstone, J. W. C., and Rosenberg, L. Sociological observations on the privileged adolescent. In J. F. Adams (Ed.), *Understanding adolescence: Current developments in adolescent psychology.* Boston: Allyn and Bacon, 1968. Pp. 318-336.

Jones, H. E. Adolescence in our society. In Anniversary Papers of the Community Service Society of New York, *The family in a democratic society*. New York: Columbia University Press, 1949a, Pp. 70-82.

Jones, H. E. The environment and mental development. In L. Carmichael (Ed.), *Manual of child psychology* (2nd ed.). New York: John Wiley & Sons, 1954. Pp. 631-696.

Jones, H. E. *Motor performance and growth*. Berkeley, Calif.: University of California Press, 1949b.

Jones, H. E., and Conrad, H. S. Mental development in adolescence. *National Society for the Study of Education, 43rd Yearbook*, Part I. 1944. Pp. 146-163.

Jones, M. C. The later careers of boys who were early- or late-maturing. *Child Development*, 1957, 28, 113-128.

Jones, M. C. Psychological correlates of somatic development. *Child Development*, 1965, 36, 899-911.

Jones, M. C., and Bayley, N. Physical maturing among boys as related to behavior. *Journal of Educational Psychology*, 1950, 41, 129-148.

Jones, M. C., and Mussen, P. H. Self-conceptions, motivations, and interpersonal attitudes of early- and late-maturing girls. *Child Development*, 1958, 29, 491-501.

Kagan, J., and Moss, H. A. The stability of passive and dependent behavior from childhood through adulthood. *Child Development*, 1960, 31, 577-591.

Kagan, J., Rosman, B. L., Day, D., Albert, J., and Philips, W. Information processing in the child: Significance of analytic and reflective attitudes. *Psychological Monographs*, 1964, 78 (No. 1, Whole No. 578).

Katkin, E. S., and Murray, E. N. Instrumental conditioning of autonomically mediated behavior: Theoretical and methodological issues. *Psychological Bulletin*, 1968, 70, 52-68.

Katz, H. A., and Rotter, J. B. Interpersonal trust scores of college students and their parents. *Child Development*, 1969, 40, 657-661.

Katz, P., and Zigler, E. Self-image disparity: A developmental approach. *Journal of Personality and Social Psychology*, 1967, 5, 186-195.

Kelly, G. A. *Psychology of personal constructs*. New York, W. W. Norton and Company, 1955.

Kennedy, W. A. A follow-up normative study of Negro intelligence and achievement. *Monographs of the Society for Research in Child Development*. 1969. 34 (No. 2, Serial No. 126).

Kent, N., and Davis, D. R. Discipline in the home and intellectual development. *British Journal of Medical Psychology*, 1957, 30, 27-33.

Kephart, N. C., and Ainsworth, M. H. A preliminary study of the community adjustment of parolees of the Wayne County Training School. *Journal of the American Association on Mental Deficiency*, 1938, 43, 161-166.

Ketcham, W. A. Growth patterns of gifted children. *Merrill-Palmer Quarterly*, 1957, 3, 188-197.

Khan, S. B. Affective correlates of academic achievement. *Journal of Educational Psychology*, 1969, 60, 216-221.

Kinsey, A. C., Pomeroy, W. B., and Martin, C. E., *Sexual behavior in the human male*. Philadelphia: W. B. Saunders Company, 1948.

Kinsey, A. C., Pomeroy, W. B., and Martin, C. E. *Sexual behavior in the human female*. Philadelphia: W. B. Saunders, 1953.

Kirkendall, L. A. *Premarital intercourse and interpersonal relationships*. New York: Julian Press, 1961.

Klausmeier, H. J., Goodwin, W., and Ronda, T. Effects of accelerating bright, older elementary pupils — a second follow-up. *Journal of Educational Psychology*, 1968, 59, 53-58.

Klausmeier, H. J., Harris, C. W., and Ethnathios, Z. Relationships between divergent thinking abilities and teacher ratings of high school students. *Journal of Educational Psychology*, 1962, 53, 72-75.

Klineberg, S. L. Changes in outlook on the future between childhood and adolescence. *Journal of Personality and Social Psychology*, 1967, 7, 185-193.

Kohlberg, L. Development of moral character and moral ideology. In M. L. Hoffman and L. W Hoffman (Eds.), *Review of child development research*, Vol. 1. New York: Russell Sage Foundation, 1964. Pp. 383-481.

Kohlberg, L. Early education: A cognitive-developmental view. *Child Development*, 1968, 39, 1013-1062.

Kohlberg, L. Moral and religious education and the public schools: A developmental view. In T. R. Sizer (Ed.), *Religion and public education*. Boston: Houghton Mifflin, 1967.

Kretschmer, E. *Korperbau and Character* (2nd rev. ed.). London: Routledge and Kegan Paul, 1925. (Transl. by W. J. H. Sprott as *Physique and character*.)

Kugelmass, S., and Breznitz, S. Intentionality in moral judgment: Adolescent development. *Child Development*, 1968, 39, 249-256.

Kutner, B., and Gordon, N. B. Cognitive functioning and prejudice: A nine-year follow-up study. *Sociometry*, 1964, 27, 66-74.

Kwall, D. S., and Lackner, F. M. Ability, sociometric and parent-child relationship variables in the prediction of elementary school achievement. Paper presented at the meeting of the American Psychological Association, New York, September, 1966.

Lahaderne, H. M. Attitudinal and intellectual correlates of attention: A study of four sixth-grade classrooms. *Journal of Educational Psychology*, 1968, 59, 320-324.

Lamb, H. E., Ziller, R. C., and Maloney, A. W. The development of self-other relationships during Project Head Start. Project No. OEO-511, 1965, University of Delaware.

Landauer, T. K., and Whiting, J. W. M. Infantile stimulation and adult stature of human males. *American Anthropologist*, 1964, 66, 1007-1028.

Landis, J. R., and Scarpitti, F. R. Perceptions regarding value orientation and legitimate opportunity: Delinquents and non-delinquents. *Social Forces*, 1965, 44, 83-91.

Laughlin, P. R. Incidental concept formation as a function of creativity and intelligence. *Journal of Personality and Social Psychology*, 1967, 5, 115-119.

Laughlin, P. R., Doherty, M. A., and Dunn, R. F. Intentional and incidental concept formation as a function of motivation, creativity, intelligence and sex. *Journal of Personality and Social Psychology*, 1968, 8, 401-409.

Lauten, D. A. H. Relationship between intelligence and motor proficiency in the intellectually gifted child. Unpublished doctoral dissertation, University of North Carolina, 1968.

Lehrman, N. (Ed.). Playboy interview: Masters and Johnson. *Playboy*, 1968, 15, (No. 5, May), 67-82, 194-202.

Leinert, G. A., and Crott, H. W. Studies on the factor structure of intelligence in children, adolescents and adults. *Vita Humana*, 1964, 7, 147-163.

Lekarczyk, D. T., and Hill, K. T. Self-esteem, test anxiety, stress, and verbal learning. *Developmental Psychology*, 1969, 1, 147-154.

Lerner, R. M. The development of stereotyped expectancies of body build-behavior relations. *Child Development*, 1969, 40, 137-141.

Lesser, G. S. The relationship between various forms of aggression and popularity among lower-class children. *Journal of Educational Psychology*, 1959, 50, 20-25.

Leventhal, D. B., Shemberg, K. M., and Van Schoelandt, S. K. Effects of sex-role adjustment upon the expression of aggression. *Journal of Personality and Social Psychology*, 1968, 8, 393-396.

Levitt, E. E., and Brady, J. P. Sexual preferences in young adult males and some correlates. *Journal of Clinical Psychology*, 1965, *21*, 347-354.

Levitt, E. E., and Edwards, J. A. A multivariate study of correlative factors in youthful cigarette smoking. *Developmental Psychology*, 1970, *2*, 5-11.

Levy, L. H. Originality as role-defined behavior. *Journal of Personality and Social Psychology*, 1968, *9*, 72-78.

Levy, L. H. The meaning and generality of perceived actual-ideal discrepancies. *Journal of Consulting Psychology*, 1956, *20*, 396-398.

Lewin, K. *A dynamic theory of personality.* New York: McGraw-Hill, 1935.

Lewin, K., Lippitt, R. and White, R. K. Patterns of aggressive behavior in experimentally created "social climates." *Journal of Social Psychology*, 1939, *10*, 271-299.

Liebow, E. *Tally's corner.* Boston: Little, Brown, 1966.

Lombroso, C. *The man of genius.* London: Scott, 1891.

Lowe, C. M. The self-concept: Fact or artifact? *Psychological Bulletin*, 1961, *58*, 325-336.

Lucito, L. J. Independence-conformity behavior as a function of intellect: Bright and dull children. *Exceptional Children*, 1964, *31*, 5-13.

MacDonald, A. P., Jr. Manifestations of differential levels of socialization by birth order. *Developmental Psychology*, 1969, *1*, 485-492.

Mallick, S. K., and McCandless, B. R. A study of catharsis of aggression, *Journal of Personality and Social Psychology*, 1966, *4*, 591-596.

Marshall, H. H. The effect of punishment on children: A review of the literature and a suggested hypothesis. *Journal of Genetic Psychology*, 1965, *106*, 23-33.

Marx, M. H. *Learning: Processes.* London: Macmillan, Collier-Macmillan, Limited, 1969.

Maslow, A. H., and Sakoda, J. M. Volunteer-error in the Kinsey study. *Journal of Abnormal and Social Psychology*, 1952, *47*, 259-262.

Masters, W. H., and Johnson, V. E. *Human sexual response.* Boston: Little, Brown, 1966. See also N. Lehrman, 1968.

McArthur, C. Personality differences between middle and upper classes. *Journal of Abnormal and Social Psychology*, 1955, *50*, 247-254.

McArthur, L. A., and Zigler, E. Level of satiation on social reinforcers and valence of the reinforcing agent as determinants of social reinforcer effectiveness. *Developmental Psychology*, 1970, *2*, In press.

McCandless, B. R. Changing relationships between dominance and social acceptability during group democratization. *American Journal of Orthopsychiatry*, 1942, *12*, 529-536.

McCandless, B. R. Childhood socialization. In D. A. Goslin (Ed.), *Handbook of socialization theory and research.* Chicago: Rand McNally, 1969. Pp. 791-819.

McCandless, B. R. *Children: Behavior and development.* New York: Holt, Rinehart and Winston, 1967.

McCandless, B. R. *Children and adolescents: Behavior and development.* New York: Holt, Rinehart and Winston, 1961.

McCandless, B. R., and Ali, F. Relations among physical skills and personal and social variables in three cultures of adolescent girls. *Journal of Educational Psychology*, 1966, *57*, 366-372.

McCandless, B. R., Bilous, C., and Bennett, H. L. The relation between peer-popularity and dependence on adults in preschool-age socialization. *Child Development*, 1961, *32*, 511-518.

McCandless, R. B., Persons, W. S. III, Roberts, A. Body build and the legitimate opportunity hypothesis in a biracial group of adolescent delinquents. Emory University, Manuscript in preparation, 1969.

McDill, E. L., and Coleman, J. Family and peer influences in college plans of high school students. *Sociology of Education*, 1965, *38*, 112-126.

McKee, J. P., and Leader, F. B. The relationship of socioeconomic status and aggression to the competitive behavior of preschool children. *Child Development*, 1955, *26*, 135-142.

Mead, G. H. *Mind, self and society: From the standpoint of a social behaviorist.* Chicago: University of Chicago Press, 1934.

Mead, M. Cultural determinants of sexual behavior. In W. C. Young (Ed.), *Sex and the internal secretions* (3rd ed.), Vol. II. Baltimore, Md.: Williams & Wilkins, 1961. Pp. 1433-1479.

Mead, M. *From the South Seas: Studies of adolescence and sex in primitive societies.* New York: William Morrow, 1939.

Mednick, S. A. *Learning.* Englewood Cliffs, N.J.: Prentice-Hall, 1964.

Mednick, S. A. The associative basis of the creative process. *Psychological Review*, 1962, *69*, 220-232.

Melton, A. W. Learning. In W. S. Monroe (Ed.), *Encyclopedia of educational research* (2nd ed.) New York: The Macmillan Company, 1950. Pp. 668-690.

Mendel, G. Children's preference for differing degree of novelty. *Child Development*, 1965, *36*, 453-465.

Meredith, H. V. Body size of contemporary groups of preschool children studied in different parts of the world. *Child Development*, 1968, *39*, 335-377.

Meredith, H. V. Comments on *The varieties of human physique. Child Development*, 1940, *11*, 301-309.

Meredith, H. V. A synopsis of puberal changes in youth. *Journal of School Health*, 1967, *37*, 171-176.

Meredith, H. V. Physical growth. *Encyclopedia Americana*, 1959, *13*, 499-502.

Merton, R. K. *Social theory and social structure.* New York: Free Press of Glencoe, 1961.

Meyer, W. J. The stability of patterns of Primary Mental Abilities Test among junior high and senior high students. *Educational and Psychological Measurement*, 1960, *20*, 795-800.

Meyer, W. J., and Bendig, A. W. A longitudinal study of the Primary Mental Abilities Test. *Journal of Educational Psychology*, 1961, *52*, 50-60.

Miles, C. C., and Miles, W. R. The correlation of intelligence scores and chronological age from early to late maturity. *American Journal of Psychology*, 1932, *44*, 44-78.

Milgram, S. Some conditions of obedience and disobedience to authority. *Human Relations*, 1965, *18*, 57-76.

Miller, D. R., and Swanson, G. E. *Inner conflict and defense.* New York: Holt, Rinehart and Winston, 1960.

Mischel, W., and Metzner, R. Preference for delayed reward as a function of age, intelligence, and length of delay interval. *Journal of Abnormal and Social Psychology*, 1962, *64*, 425-431.

Mitchell, G. D. Attachment differences in male and female infant monkeys. *Child Development*, 1968, *39*, 611-620.

Money, J. Sex hormones and other variables in human eroticism. In W. C. Young (Ed.), *Sex and internal secretions* (3rd ed.), Volume II. Baltimore, Md.: Williams & Wilkins, 1961. Pp. 1383-1400.

Moore, H. R. Geographic mobility and performance in high school: Part I. *Journal of Secondary Education*, 1966, *41*, 327-331.

More, D. M. Developmental concordance and discordance during puberty and early adolescence. *Monographs of the Society for Research in Child Development*, 1953, *18* (No. 1, Serial No. 56).

Morse, N. C., and Weiss, R. S. The function and meaning of work and the job. In D. G. Zytowski (Ed.), *Vocational behavior.* New York: Holt, Rinehart and Winston, 1968. Pp. 7-16.

Morsh, J. E. Development report—systematic observation of instructor behavior. USAF: *Personality Training Research Center Development*. 1956, No. AFPTRC TN 56-52.

Moulton, R. W., Liberty, P. G., Jr., Burnstein, E., and Altucher, N. Patterning of parental affection and disciplinary dominance as a determinant of guilt and sex-typing. *Journal of Personality and Social Psychology*, 1966, 4, 356-363.

Musgrove, F. The social needs and satisfactions of some young people. *British Journal of Educational Psychology*, 1966, 36, 137-149.

Mussen, P. H., and Bouterline-Young, H. Relationships between rate of physical maturing and personality among boys of Italian descent. *Vita Humana*, 1964, 7, 186-200.

Mussen, P. H., and Distler, L. Masculinity, identification, and father-son relationships. *Journal of Abnormal and Social Psychology*, 1959, 59, 350-356.

Mussen, P. H., and Jones, M. C. Self-conceptions, motivations, and interpersonal attitudes of late- and early-maturing boys. *Child Development*, 1957, 28, 242-256.

Mussen, P. H., and Porter, L. W. Personal motivations and self-conceptions associated with effectiveness and ineffectiveness in emergent groups. *Journal of Abnormal and Social Psychology*, 1959, 59, 23-27.

Mussen, P. H., and Rutherford, E. Parent-child relations and parental personality in relation to young children's sex-role preferences. *Child Development*, 1963, 34, 589-608.

Neff, W. S. Psychoanalytic conceptions of the meaning of work. In D. G. Zytowski (Ed.), *Vocational behavior*. New York: Holt, Rinehart and Winston, 1968, Pp. 17-27.

Nisbet, J. D., Illsley, R., Sutherland, A. E., and Douse, M. J. Puberty and test performance: A further report. *British Journal of Educational Psychology*, 1964, 34, 202-203.

Norman, R. D. The interpersonal values of parents of achieving and nonachieving children. *Journal of Psychology*, 1966, 64, 49-57.

Offer, D. *The psychological world of the teen-ager*. New York: Basic Books, 1969.

Olson, G. M., Miller, L. K., Hale, G. A., and Stevenson, H. W. Long-term correlates of children's learning and problem-solving behavior. *Journal of Educational Psychology*, 1968, 59, 227-232.

O'Reilly, C. T., and O'Reilly, E. J. Religious beliefs of Catholic college students and their attitudes toward minorities. *Journal of Abnormal and Social Psychology*, 1954, 49, 378-380.

Osipow, S. H. *Theories of career development*. New York: Appleton-Century-Crofts, 1968.

Ostfeld, B., and Katz, P. A. The effect of threat severity in children of varying socio-economic levels. *Developmental Psychology*, 1969, 1, 205-210.

Owens, W. A., Jr. Age and mental abilities: A longitudinal study. *Genetic Psychology Monographs*, 1953, 48, 3-54.

Palmer, R. J., and Masling, J. Vocabulary for skin color in Negro and white children. *Developmental Psychology*, 1969, 1, 396-401.

Parke, R. D. Nurturance, nurturance withdrawal, and resistance to deviation. *Child Development*, 1967, 38, 1101-1110.

Parnell, R. W. *Behaviour and physique*. London: Edward Arnold, 1958.

Parnell, R. W. Simplified somatotypes. *Journal of Psychosomatic Research*, 1964, 8, 311-315.

Parsons, T. Family structure and the socialization of the child. In T. Parsons and R. F. Bales (Eds.), *Family, socialization, and interaction process*. New York: Free Press of Glencoe, 1955. Pp. 35-131.

Payne, D. A., and Farquhar, W. W. The dimensions of an objective measure of academic self-concept. *Journal of Educational Psychology*, 1962, 53, 187-192.

Payne, D. E., and Mussen, H. Parent-child relations and father identification among adolescent boys. *Journal of Personality and Abnormal Psychology*, 1956, *52*, 358-362.

Pegnato, C. W., and Birch, J. W. Locating gifted children in junior high schools: A comparison of methods. *Exceptional Children*, 1959, *25*, 300-304.

Penney, R. K. Reactive curiosity and manifest anxiety in children. *Child Development*, 1965, *36*, 697-702.

Peskin, H. Pubertal onset and ego functioning. *Journal of Abnormal Psychology*, 1967, *72*, 1-15.

Peters, F. *Finistère*. New York: Farrar, Strauss and Giroux, 1951.

Pettigrew, T. F. *A profile of the Negro American*. Princeton, N.J.: D. Van Nostrand, 1964.

Piaget, J. *The child's conception of the world*. London: Routledge and Kegan Paul, 1951.

Piaget, J. *The language and thought of the child*. London: Routledge and Kegan Paul, 1952.

Piaget, J. *The psychology of intelligence*. London: Routledge and Kegan Paul, 1950.

Pierce-Jones, J., and King, F. J. Perceptual differences between Negro and white adolescents of similar symbolic brightness. *Perceptual and Motor Skills*, 1960, *11*, 191-194.

Piliavin, I. M., Hardyck, J. A., and Vadum, A. C. Constraining effects of personal costs on the transgressions of juveniles. *Journal of Personality and Social Psychology*, 1968, *10*, 227-231.

Pollack, R. H. Some implications of ontogenetic changes in perception. In D. Elkind and J. H. Flavell (Eds.), *Studies in cognitive development*. New York: Oxford University Press, 1969. Pp. 365-408.

Poppleton, P. K. Puberty, family size and the educational progress of girls. *British Journal of Educational Psychology*, 1968, *38*, 286-292.

Poppleton, P. K., and Brown, P. E. The secular trend in puberty: Has stability been achieved? *British Journal of Educational Psychology*, 1966, *36*, 77-86.

Powell, D. H. Careers and family atmospheres: An empirical test of Roe's theory. *Journal of Counseling Psychology*, 1960, *7*, 251-256.

Pytkowicz, A. R., Wagner, N., and Sarason, I. G. An experimental study of the reduction of hostility through fantasy. *Journal of Personality and Social Psychology*, 1967, *5*, 295-303.

Redl, F. *When we deal with children*. New York: Free Press of Glencoe, 1966.

Reiss, A. J., Jr. How common is police brutality? *Trans-action*, 1968, *5* (No. 8, July/August), 10-19.

Reiss, I. L. America's sex standards—how and why they're changing. *Trans-action*, 1968, *5* (March), 26-32.

Rhodes, L. Anomia, aspiration, and status. *Social Forces*, 1964, *42*, 434-441.

Riese, H. *Heal the hurt child*. Chicago: University of Chicago Press, 1962.

Ring, K., Lipinski, C. E., and Braginsky, D. The relationship of birth order to self-evaluation, anxiety reduction, and susceptibility to emotional contagion. *Psychological Monographs*, 1965, *79* (Whole No. 603).

Ringness, T. A. Identification patterns, motivation, and school achievement of bright junior high school boys. *Journal of Educational Psychology*, 1967, *58*, 93-102.

Ritchie, B. F., Aeschliman, B., and Pierce, P. Studies in spatial learning: VIII. Place performance and the acquisition of place dispositions. *Journal of Comparative and Physiological Psychology*, 1950, *50*, 150-154.

Robbins, L. C. The accuracy of parental recall of aspects of child development and child-rearing practices. *Journal of Abnormal and Social Psychology*, 1963, *68*, 261-270.

Robins, L. N. Which Negroes will die young? *Trans-action*, 1968, *5*, (No. 7, June), 15-19.

Rockway, A. M. Cognitive factors in adolescent person perception development. *Developmental Psychology*, 1970, 2, In press.

Roe, A. Early determinants of vocational choice. In D. G. Zytowski (Ed.), *Vocational behavior*. New York: Holt, Rinehart and Winston, 1968. Pp. 232-239.

Roe, A. *Psychology of occupations*. New York: John Wiley & Sons, 1956.

Roff, M., and Sells, S. B. Juvenile delinquency in relation to peer acceptance-rejection and socio-economic status. *Psychology in the Schools*, 1968, 5, 3-18.

Rogers, C. R., and Dymond, R. F. (Eds.) *Psychotherapy and personality change*. Chicago: University of Chicago Press, 1954.

Rohwer, W. D., Jr., Lynch, S., Levin, J. R., and Suzuki, N. Grade level, school strata, and learning efficiency. *Journal of Educational Psychology*, 1968, 59, 26-31.

Rosekrans, M. A. Imitation in children as a function of perceived similarity to a social model and vicarious reinforcers. *Journal of Personality and Social Psychology*, 1967, 7, 307-315.

Rosekrans, M. A., and Hartup, W. W. Imitative influences of consistent and inconsistent response consequences to a model on aggressive behavior in children. *Journal of Personality and Social Psychology*, 1967, 7, 429-434.

Rosenberg, M. Parental interest and children's self perceptions. *Sociometry*, 1963, 26, 35-49.

Rosenkrantz, P., Vogel, S., Bee, H., Broverman, I., and Broverman, D. M. Sex-role stereotypes and self-concepts in college students. *Journal of Consulting and Clinical Psychology*, 1968, 32, 287-295.

Rosenthal, I. Reliability of retrospective reports of adolescence. *Journal of Consulting Psychology*, 1963, 27, 189-198.

Rosenthal, R. *Experimenter effects in behavioral research*. New York: Appleton-Century-Crofts, 1966.

Rosenthal, R., and Jacobson, L. *Pygmalion in the classroom: Teacher expectation and pupils' intellectual development*. New York: Holt, Rinehart and Winston, 1968.

Rotter, J. B. Generalized expectancies for internal versus external control of reinforcement. *Psychological Monographs*, 1966, 80 (No. 1, Whole No. 609), 28 pp.

Rotter, J. B. A new scale for the measurement of interpersonal trust. *Journal of Personality*, 1967, 35, 651-665.

Rotter, J. B. *Social learning and clinical psychology*, Englewood Cliffs, N.J.: Prentice-Hall, 1954.

Rotter, J. B., and Rafferty, J. E. *Manual for the Rotter Incomplete Sentences Blank, College Form*. New York: Psychological Corporation, 1950.

Rubenstein, J. Maternal attentiveness and subsequent exploratory behavior in the infant. *Child Development*, 1967, 38, 1089-1100.

Rudy, A. J. Sex-role perceptions in early adolescence. *Adolescence*, 1968/1969, 3, 453-470.

Samorajczyk, J. F. Children's responsiveness to motivational suggestions during school entry. *Developmental Psychology*, 1969, 1, 211-215.

Scarpitti, F. R., Murray, E., Dinitz, S., and Reckless, W. C. The "good" boys in a high delinquency area: Four years later. *American Sociological Review*, 1960, 25, 555-558.

Schaie, K. W., and Strother, C. R. A cross-sequential study of age changes in cognitive behavior. *Psychological Bulletin*, 1968, 70, 671-680.

Schimek, J. G. Cognitive style and defenses: A longitudinal study of intellectualization and field independence. *Journal of Abnormal Psychology*, 1968, 73, 575-580.

Schonfeld, W. A. Inadequate masculine physique as a factor in personality development of adolescent boys. *Psychosomatic Medicine*, 1950, 12, 49-54.

Schreiber, D. (Ed.) *Profile of the school dropout*. New York: Vintage Books, 1968.

Schwartz, M., and Tongri, S. S. A note on self-concept as an insulator against delinquency. *American Sociological Review*, 1965, *30*, 922-926.

Schweiker, R. Discard the semantic confusion related to "intelligence." A comment of "Social class, race, and genetics: Implications for education." *American Educational Research Journal*, 1968, *5*, 717-721.

Scott, R. First to ninth grade IQ changes of northern Negro students. *Psychology in the Schools*, 1966, *3*, 159-160.

Sears, P. S. Child-rearing factors related to playing of sex-typed roles. *American Psychologist*, 1953, *8*, 431. (Abstract.)

Sears, P. S. Doll-play aggression in normal young children: Influence of sex, age, sibling status, father's absence. *Psychological Monographs*, 1951, *65* (Whole No. 323, No. 6).

Sears, P. S., and Feldman, D. H. Teachers' interactions with boys and with girls. *National Elementary Principal*, 1966, *46*, 30-35.

Sears, R. R., Maccoby, E. E., and Levin, H. *Patterns of child-rearing*. New York: Harper & Row, 1957.

Seashore, H. G. Some relationships of fine and gross motor abilities. *Research Quarterly*, 1942, *13*, 259-274.

Sheldon, W. H. *The varieties of human physique*. New York: Harper & Row, 1940.

Sheldon, W. H. *The varieties of temperament*. New York: Harper & Row, 1942.

Sheldon, W. H., Hartl, E. M., and McDermott, E. *Varieties of delinquent youth*. New York: Harper & Row, 1949.

Shelton, J., and Hill, J. P. The effects on cheating of achievement anxiety and knowledge of peer performance. *Developmental Psychology*, 1969, *1*, 449-455.

Shipman, W. G. Age of menarche and adult personality. *Archives of General Psychiatry*, 1964, *10*, 155-159.

Shore, M. F., Massimo, J. L., and Ricks, D. F. A factor analytic study of psychotherapeutic change in delinquent boys. *Journal of Clinical Psychology*, 1965, *21*, 208-212.

Short, J. F., Jr., Rivera, R., and Tennyson, R. A. Perceived opportunities, gang membership, and delinquency. *American Sociological Review*, 1965, *30*, 56-67.

Shuey, A. M. *The testing of Negro intelligence* (2nd ed.). Lynchburg, Va.: Bell, 1966.

Silberman, C. E. *Crisis in black and white*. New York: Random House, 1964.

Silverman, I. In defense of dissonance theory: Reply to Chapanis. *Psychological Bulletin*, 1964, *62*, 205-209.

Sitkei, E. G., and Meyers, C. E. Comparative structure of intellect in middle and lower class four year olds of two ethnic groups. *Developmental Psychology*, 1969, *1*, 592-604.

Sizer, T. R. *The metropolitan enigma: Inquiries into the nature of America's "urban crisis."* Washington, D. C.: U.S. Government Printing Office, 1967.

Skeels, H. M. Adult status of children with contrasting early life experiences. *Monographs of the Society for Research in Child Development*, 1966, *31* (No. 3, Serial No. 105).

Skeels, H. M., and Harms, I. E. Children with inferior social histories: Their mental development in adoptive homes. *Journal of Genetic Psychology*, 1948, *72*, 283-294.

Skinner, B. F. Reinforcement today. *American Psychologist*, 1958, *13*, 94-99.

Skinner, B. F. *Science and human behavior*. New York: The Macmillan Company, 1953.

Skinner, B. F. Science of learning and the art of teaching. *Harvard Educational Review*, 1954, *24*, 86-97.

Skodak, M., and Skeels, H. M. A final follow-up study of one hundred adopted children. *Journal of Genetic Psychology*, 1949, 75, 85-125.

Slater, B. R. Effects of noise on pupil performance. *Journal of Educational Psychology*, 1968, 59, 239-243.

Sloan, W. The Lincoln–Oseretsky Motor Development Scale. *Genetic Psychology Monographs*, 1955, 41, 183-252.

Soares, A. T., and Soares, L. M. Self-perceptions of culturally disadvantaged children. *American Educational Research Journal*, 1969, 6, 31-45.

Spearman, C. *The abilities of man.* New York: The Macmillan Company, 1927.

Spence, K. A theory of emotionally based drive (D) and its relation to performance in simple learning situations. *American Psychologist*, 1958, 13, 131-141.

Sroufe, L. A. A methodological and philosophical critique of intervention-oriented research. *Developmental Psychology*, 1970, 2. In press.

Staffieri, J. R. A study of social stereotype of body image in children. *Journal of Personality and Social Psychology*, 1967, 7, 101-103.

Stark, R., and Glock, C. Y. Will ethics be the death of Christianity? *Trans-action*, 1968, 5 (No. 7, June), 7-14.

Stein, K. B., Sarbin, T. R., and Kulik, J. A. Future time perspective: Its relation to the socialization process and the delinquent role. *Journal of Consulting and Clinical Psychology*, 1968, 32, 257-264.

Stern, C. Hereditary factors affecting adoption. In M. Schapiro (Ed.), *A study of adoption practice.* New York: Child Welfare League of America, 1956. Pp. 47-58.

Stevenson, H. W., Friedrichs, A. G., and Simpson, W. E. Learning and problem-solving by the mentally retarded under three testing conditions. *Developmental Psychology*, 1970, 2. In press.

Stolz, H. R., and Stolz, L. M. *Somatic development of adolescent boys.* New York: The Macmillan Company, 1951.

Stricker, L. J. The true deceiver. *Psychological Bulletin*, 1967, 68, 13-20.

Sugarman, A. A., and Haronian, F. Body type and sophistication of body concept. *Journal of Personality*, 1964, 32, 380-394.

Sullivan, H. S. *The collected works of Harry Stack Sullivan.* New York: W. W. Norton and Company, 1953a.

Sullivan, H. S. *The interpersonal theory of psychiatry.* New York: W. W. Norton and Company, 1953b.

Super, D. E. A theory of vocational development. *American Psychologist*, 1953, 8, 185-190.

Sutton-Smith, B., Rosenberg, G. G., and Landy, F. Father-absence effects in families of different sibling compositions. *Child Development*, 1968, 39, 1213-1221.

Switzer, D. K., Grigg, A. E., Miller, J. S., and Young, R. K. Early experiences and occupational choice: A test of Roe's hypothesis. *Journal of Counseling Psychology*, 1962, 9, 45-48.

Tallman, I. Adaptation to blocked opportunity: An experimental study. *Sociometry*, 1966, 29, 121-134.

Tannenbaum, A. J. The school dropout today. *Information Retrieval Center on the Disadvantaged Bulletin*, 1968, 4, 1-2.

Tanner, J. M. *Growth at adolescence* (2nd ed.). Oxford, England: Blackwell Scientific Publications, 1962.

Taylor, J. A. Drive theory and manifest anxiety. *Psychological Bulletin*, 1956, 53, 303-320.

Teicher, J. D., and Jacobs, J. Adolescents who attempt suicide: A preliminary finding. *American Journal of Psychiatry*, 1966, 122, 1248-1257.

Terman, L. M., et al. *Genetic studies of genius: I. Mental and physical traits of a thousand gifted children:* Stanford, Calif.: Stanford University Press, 1925.

Terman, L. M., and Oden, M. H. *Genetic studies of genius: IV. The gifted child grows up.* Stanford, Calif.: Stanford University Press, 1947.

Thomas, L. E. Family correlates of student political activism. *Developmental Psychology*, 1970, 2. In press.

Thompson, G. G. Children's groups. In P. H. Mussen (Ed.), *Handbook of research methods in child development.* New York: John Wiley & Sons, 1960. Pp. 821-853.

Thorndike, E. L., et al. *The measurement of intelligence.* New York: Bureau of Publications, Teachers College, Columbia University, 1926.

Thorndike, R. L. Review: Rosenthal, Robert, and Jacobson, Lenore. *Pygmalion in the classroom.* New York: Holt, Rinehart and Winston, 1968, *American Educational Research Journal*, 1968, 5, 708-711.

Thorne, F. C. A factorial study of sexuality in adult males. *Journal of Clinical Psychology*, 1966, 22, 378-386.

Thurstone, L. L., and Thurstone, T. G. *Primary Mental Abilities Scales: Primary, elementary, and intermediate.* Chicago: Science Research Associates, 1950.

Torrance, E. P. *Guiding creative talent.* Englewood Cliffs, N.J.: Prentice-Hall, 1962.

Torrance, E. P. *Rewarding creative behavior: Experiments in classroom activity.* Englewood Cliffs, N.J.: Prentice-Hall, 1965.

Trent, J. W., and Medsker, L. L. *Beyond high school: A psychosociological study of 10,000 high school graduates.* San Francisco, Calif.: Jossey-Bass, 1968.

Tucker, W. B., and Lessa, W. A. Man: A constitutional investigation. *Quarterly Review of Biology*, 1940, 15, 265-411.

Tulkin, S. R. Race, class, family, and school achievement. *Journal of Personality and Social Psychology*, 1968, 9, 31-37.

Turiel, E. An experimental test of the sequentiality of developmental stages in the child's moral judgments. *Journal of Personality and Social Psychology*, 1966, 3, 611-618.

Tyler, V. O., Jr., and Brown, G. D. Token reinforcement of academic performance with institutionalized delinquent boys. *Journal of Educational Psychology*, 1968, 59, 164-168.

Valenti, C. The child: His right to be normal. *Saturday Review*, 1968, 51 (No. 49), 75-78.

Van Mannen, G. C. Father role and adolescent socialization. *Adolescence*, 1968, 3, 139-152.

Vincent, C. E. Unmarried fathers and the mores: "Sexual exploiter" as an *ex post facto* label. *American Sociological Review*, 1960, 25, 40-46.

Vogel, S. R., Broverman, I. K., Broverman, D. M., Clarkson, F., and Rosenkrantz, P. S. Maternal employment and perception of sex-role stereotypes. *Developmental Psychology*, 1970, 2. In press.

Waheed, A. A study of certain environmental factors and extraclass experiences as related to college plans of high school seniors. Unpublished doctoral dissertation, Indiana University, 1964.

Wahler, R. G. Infant social attachments: A reinforcement theory. *Child Development*, 1967, 38, 1079-1088.

Walker, D. Report to the President's Commission on the Causes and Prevention of Violence, December, 1968.

Walker, R. N. Body build and behavior in young children: I. Body and nursery school teachers' ratings. *Monographs of the Society for Research in Child Development*, 1962, 27, Serial No. 84.

Wallach, M., and Kogan, N. *Modes of thinking in young children.* New York: Holt, Rinehart and Winston, 1965.

Walster, E. The effect of self-esteem on romantic liking. *Journal of Experimental Social Psychology*, 1965, 1, 184-197.

Warner, W. L., Meeker, M., and Eells, K. *Social class in America.* Chicago: Science Research Associates, 1949.

Washburn, W. C. The effects of physique and intrafamily tension on self-concept in adolescent males. *Journal of Consulting Psychology*, 1962, 26, 460-466.

Wechsler, D. *The measurement of adult intelligence.* Baltimore, Md.: Williams & Wilkins, 1944.

Wetzel, R. Use of behavioral techniques in a case of compulsive stealing. *Journal of Consulting Psychology*, 1966, 30, 367-374.

Wheeler, L. R. A comparative study of the intelligence of East Tennessee mountain children. *Journal of Educational Psychology*, 1942, 33, 321-334.

White, R. K. *Nobody wanted war.* Garden City, N.Y.: Doubleday, 1968.

White, R. K. Three not-so-obvious contributions of psychology to peace. Paper presented at the meeting of the American Psychological Association, Washington, D.C., August/September, 1969.

White, R. W. Motivation reconsidered: The concept of competence. *Psychological Review*, 1959, 66, 297-333.

White, W. F., Anderson, H. E., and Cryder, H. Allport's theory of the emerging self concept applied to secondary school students. Paper presented at the meeting of the American Psychological Association, New York, September, 1966.

Whiting, J. W. M., Landauer, T. K., and Jones, T. M. Infantile immunization and adult stature. *Child Development*, 1968, 39, 59-67.

Whitten, N. E., Jr., and Szwed, J. Negroes in the New World: Introduction. *Transaction*, 1968, 5 (July/August, No. 8), 49-56.

Wicker, A. W. Undermanning, performances, and students' subjective experiences in behavior settings of large and small high schools. *Journal of Personality and Social Psychology*, 1968, 10, 255-261.

Willems, E. P. Sense of obligation to high school activities as related to school size and marginality of student. *Child Development*, 1967, 38, 1247-1260.

Wolowitz, H. M. Attraction and aversion to power: A psychoanalytic conflict theory of homosexuality in male paranoids. *Journal of Abnormal Psychology*, 1965, 70, 360-370.

Wolpe, J. *Psychotherapy by reciprocal inhibition.* Stanford, Calif.: Stanford University Press, 1968.

Worchester, D. A. Acceleration: Good or bad? Paper presented at the meeting of the Midwestern Psychological Association, Chicago, May 1959.

Wylie, R. *The self-concept.* Lincoln, Neb.: University of Nebraska Press, 1961.

Yamamoto, K., and Davis, O. L., Jr. Test instructions, test anxiety, and dependence proneness in relation to children's performance on a test of intelligence. *Psychology in the Schools*, 1966, 3, 167-170.

Yee, A. H. Source and direction of causal influence in teacher-pupil relationships. *Journal of Educational Psychology*, 1968, 59, 275-282.

Zigler, E. F. Mental retardation, technical comment. *Science*, 1967, 157, 578.

Ziller, R. C., Hagey, J., Smith, M. D. C., and Long, B. H. Self esteem: A self-social construct. *Journal of Consulting and Clinical Psychology*, 1969, 33, 84-95.

Zimbardo, P., and Formica, R. Emotional comparison and self-esteem as determinants of affiliation. *Journal of Personality*, 1963, 31, 141-162.

Zubek, J. P., and Solberg, P. A. *Human development.* New York: McGraw-Hill, 1954.

Zytowski, D. G. (Ed.) *Vocational behavior: Readings in theory and research.* New York: Holt, Rinehart and Winston, 1968.

Index

Academic success, 173-175
Acceptance of others, self-acceptance and, 440, 471-473, 474
Accommodation, 228
Accuracy, quality of self concept, 439, 458-459, 475
Achievement, anxiety and, 198-200
   classroom structure and, 278
   training of goal of, 382
Adams, J. F., 174-175
Adelson, J., 19, 20, 31, 32-33, 34, 42, 46, 98, 116, 175, 179, 245, 246, 247, 248, 375, 419-420, 463
Adjustment, adolescent,
   areas of, 31-32, 34-35
   common problems of, 426-434
   future time orientation and, 464-466
   personal, self concept and, 456-464
   vocational choice and, 337-338
Adolescence, adjustment to change during, 31-32, 34-35
   aspects of, psychoaffectional, 97, 101, 109, 116, 119
      psychobiological, 69-70, 101, 117, 118
      psychosocial, 69-70
   behavioral adaptation, 31-32
   body build, 142-155
   career development, theories of, 336-338
   church and youth interaction, 310-315
   cognitive growth during, 244-250

Adolescence (cont.)
   common problems of adjustment during, 426-434
   conceptual framework for, 1-35
   defined, 5
   imprinting theory of sexuality, 88, 115
   industrialization as influencing, 31 n.
   loss of emotional support during, 27
   major changes during, 30-32
   motor development and physical fitness, 167-175
   parent-teacher relations during, 21-22
   physical growth norms, implications of, 74-76
   physical maturity, development and deviant time of, 128-142
   search for identity, 19, 30-32
   sex role differentiation, 101-105, 114-115
   sex-specific social goals of, 32-33, 229, 279
   sexual behavior, special problems concerning, 107-120
   sexual careers, choice of, 98-100, 116-119
   social expectations, changes in, 27, 30
   socialization, cultural impacts on, 362-365
      dimensions of, 352-362
      stage theories of, 372-376
      theories of learning and, 365-372
   theory of change applied to, 28
   trust and intimacy during, 22
   vocational choice and development, representative patterns and meaning of, 320-336

Adolescence
   vocational choice and development (cont.)
      theories of, 339-348
Adolescent development, research in, dimensions of, 38-45
      methodological problems, 45-58
      statistical and measurement considerations, 58-64
   theoretical framework, development of, 1-35
Adolescent Society, The (Coleman), 424
Adversary relationship, conflict resolution and, 308-310
Aeschliman, B., 207
Affection, modeling and, 394-395
Aggression, 17-18, 25-26
   handling of, social class differences in, 25
   sex identification and, 414-416
   Yale-Iowa learning theory explanation of, 10-11
Ahistorical-historical approach to research in adolescent development, 42-44
Aid to Family and Dependent Children (AFDC), 120
Ainsworth, M. H., 116, 261-262
Alcohol and drugs, common problem of adolescent adjustment, 430-432
Alexander, A. M., 215
Ali, F., 96, 162, 172-173, 303, 361
Alienation, Black, 192-193, 283
   nondelinquents and, 331-332, 356
Allen, R. M., 112-114
Allport, G. W., 312-313
Ambiguity, tolerance of, 227
"American Dream, The," 182-183, 189, 192
   See also Value system, middle class; Protestant ethic
American Institutes for Research in the Behavioral Sciences, 428
Ames, R., 129, 134, 135, 136, 162
Anal stage of psychosexual development, 373
Analogues, use of, 365
Anastasi, A., 236
Anatomical growth changes, 80-92
Animal behavior, studies of, differential rearing treatment by sex, 406-407
   intelligence, 207
Anlage function, 210, 211, 212, 221
Anomie (alienation or normlessness), 179, 181-182, 200
Anxiety, 17, 18-20, 26, 30
   adult-adolescent interaction and, 18-19
   body build and, 150
   cheating and achievement, 198-200
   curiosity inhibition due to, 19-20, 226
   test, 213, 215-216
Apollonian style of social expression, 97-98, 108-109, 111, 242, 243, 255, 354-356, 367
Arnold, R. A., 274
"Arranged" experiences (*see* Crystallized and fluid intelligence, theory of)
Articulateness, quality of self concept, 453, 475

Asher, William, 60 n.
Assimilation, 228
Athletic success, 172-175
Attitudes toward school, school success and, 274-277
Ausubel, D. P., 5, 29-30, 69, 70, 71, 96, 97, 101, 105, 107, 109, 121, 127, 289, 425
   theory of adolescence, 29-30
Authoritarian—*laissez faire*—democratic group management, studies of, 38, 40
Authoritarianism, intellectual growth, and child rearing, 232
   self concept, 133-134
   social class related to, 302
Autonomy, 20, 27, 32-33, 326-327, 333-336, 374-375
   physical maturity and, 132
   versus shame, learning, 373
Avoidance of pain, 22-24, 28
Awareness of limited opportunities (ALO), 186, 187, 189

Bacon, M. K., 20, 33, 116, 279, 362-363
Bandura, A., 23, 25, 121, 369, 371, 392, 397-398, 424-425
Barker, R., 28
Barry, H., III, 20, 33, 116, 279, 362-363
Bass, B. M., 268, 357
Bayley, N., 129, 131, 133, 161, 207, 220, 222, 229, 231
Beach, F. A., 101, 102, 115, 407
Bee, H. L., *et al.*, 242, 243, 297
Beez, V., 46-47, 51, 251, 296
Behavior, actualization and control of, 264-265
   effect of peer group on, 389-390
   vocational, theories of, 345-348
Bellugi, U., 457
Bendig, A. W., 273
Bennett, H. L., 25
Berkowitz, L., 17, 364-365
Berlyne, D. E., 17
Bernstein, B., 27, 297
Berry, J. W., 363
Beyond High School: A Psychosociological Study of 10,000 High School Graduates (Trent and Medsker), 336
Bialer, I., 453
Biased sample, 53, 54-55
Bieber, I., *et al.*, 102, 104, 114
Bijou, S. W., 116, 261-262
Biller, H. B., 403, 407
Bilous, C., 25
Binet, A., 212
Binet Intelligence Test (Stanford-Binet Intelligence Test), 225
Biological drive, 14-16
   reproductive (sex drive), 14-15, 16, 18, 26, 29-30, 71
Biomode, 160
Birch, J. W., 215

Black alienation, 192-193, 283
Blau, P. M., et al., 339-345
Block, J., 105, 356, 409, 416, 418-419
Bloom, B. S., 211, 238-239, 242, 243, 253
Blum, E. R., 393
Blum, W. L., 301, 388
Bockman, C. W., 472-473
Body build, 143-155
   anxiety and, 150
   classification of, 143-166
   data concerning, college male population and, 147-148
      elementary school-aged population and, 148-151
      high school male population and, 151-153
      preschool population and, 144-147
   physical maturity and, 155-167
   self concept and, 30-31, 32, 73, 149, 150-153, 440, 473
   socialization and, 361
   temperament classification of, 153-155
   time of physical maturity and, 142
Borstelmann, L. J., 403, 407
Bowerman, C. E., 7, 109, 263, 393, 420-421
Bowles, S., 358
Bouterline-Young, H., 133-134
Brace Test, use of, 168-169, 172
Bradway, K. S., 225, 229
Brady, J. P., 104-105
Braginsky, D., 457, 458
Breadth, quality of self concept, 439, 453, 474
Breast, growth changes, 85, 91
Brehm, J. W., 469-471
Bresnahan, J. L., 301, 388
Breznitz, S., 248-249, 250
British National Survey of Health and Development, 136-137
Brode, E. L., 276-277, 476
Brodsky, C. M., 147-148, 149, 473
Brody, S., 16
Broen, W. E., Jr., 12
Bronson, W. C., 394
Brown, C., 4, 60-61, 158, 433
Brown, G. D., 278-279
Brown, J. S., 17
Brown, P. E., 91-92
Brown, Rap, 26n.
Brown, W. F., 216, 244
Bruner, J. S., 211
"Buddy rating" sociometric technique, 358
Budoff, M. 230-231
Buros, O. K., 212
Buss, A. H., 17
Butcher, H. J., 256
Byrne, D., 388

California Growth Studies, 128-142, 148, 155, 161-162, 170, 220
   design of, 128
   methodological drawbacks of, 129, 136

California Psychological Inventory, 186, 278
Campbell, D. T., 52
Career choice, theories of, 337-339
Carlsmith, L., 229, 469
Carlson, R., 456, 457, 467
Cass, L. K., 397
Castration, effects of, 45
Cattell, R. B., 205, 210, 211, 212, 221, 222, 224, 225, 255
   crystallized and fluid intelligence theory, 205, 210, 221, 222, 225
Caucasoid (Caucasian), 82n.–83n.
Cerebrotonic temperament, 153
Chang, J., 105, 409
Chapanis, N. P., and Chapanis, A., 468
Charlesworth, R., 382
Charlesworth, W. R., 17
Cheating, 195-200
Child control, techniques of, 23-24
Child, I. L., 20, 33, 116, 279, 362-363
Child rearing practices, social class differences in, 263
Chodorkoff, B., 458-459, 461
Church, 310-315
Cicerelli, V. G., 256
Clarity, quality of self concept, 453, 475
Clark, C. A., 277-278, 292, 300, 395
Clark, J. P., 25, 49-50, 109
Clark, K. B., 195
Clarke, D. P., 240-241
Classical conditioning "family," 15, 365-366
Classroom management, 269, 277-279
Cleaver, Eldridge, 288
Clore, J. L., Jr., 388
"Clout" (see Power, types of, prestige)
Cloward, R. A., 181, 188, 193, 330, 428, 429, 430
Coates, B., 382, 392, 425, 458
Cobbs, P. M., 263
Coculture, definition of, 119 n.
Code duello (see Double codes)
Cognition, process-product distinction, 204
Cognitive behavior, interaction of intelligence and, 204
Cognitive development, factors influencing, 226-233
Cognitive dissonance, theory of, 28-29, 71, 76, 108
   self concept research and, 468-473
Cognitive growth, Piagetian theory of, 245-250
Cognitive style, types of, 227-228
Cohen, A. R., 469, 470-471
Coleman, J. S., 10, 161, 173-174, 175, 424
Coleman, J. S., et al., 273
Coleman report, 273
Colley, T., 160
Combs, J., 280, 282
Comfort seeking, need system, 22-24
Communication of power, modeling and, 394
Community, definition of, 178-180, 183n.
Community opportunity, criteria of, 181-182
Community and opportunity hypothesis, studies of, 182-200, 329-330

Community and opportunity hypothesis
  studies of (cont.)
    Black and white opportunity hypothesis, 193
    Landis and Scarpitti study, 188-192, 194
    Shelton and Hill study, 197-200
    Short, Rivera, and Tennyson study, 188-192, 194
    Tallman experiment, 195-197
Compensatory education, 211, 236-237, 242-243, 261-262, 264
Competence, 32-33, 34-35, 229, 356
  See also Self-governance
Complexity, quality of self concept, 439, 453, 474
Concept, definition of, 61
  poor definitions of, 49-50
Concept, self (see Self concept)
Conceptual level, high (HCL) and low (LCL), 231-232
Concrete operational stage of cognitive growth (Piaget), 245-246
Conflict resolution, adversary relationship and, 308-310
Conformity, 356, 363
Comfort giving, type of power, 381-383, 391
Congruency, quality of self concept, 439, 453, 459, 475
Conrad, H. S., 220
Conroy, Frank, 433-434
Conservation, 245-246, 248
Consistency, quality of self concept, 439, 453, 476
Constantinople, A., 279, 337, 373, 456, 467, 468, 474
Contamination, problem in research, 45-47
Control, classroom and school, 264-265, 267, 268-269, 276
  locus of, internal-external, 277, 400, 439, 441, 475, 476, 477
  school success and personal style of, 277
Cooley, C. H., 438
Cooley, W. W., 280, 282
Coopersmith, S., 263, 354, 355, 385, 395-396, 457, 458, 459
Correlation, consideration in research, 58-61
Cortés, J. B., 153-155, 161, 473
Courting behavior (U.S.), social class and, 102-103
Crandall, V. J., 457
Creativity, 254-257
  cheating and, 198
Crider, A., 366
Critical period, 72 n.
Cronbach, L. J., 214, 254-255, 256
Cross, H. J., 231-232
Cross-sectional cohort study, research design and problems of, 222-223, 224
Cross-sex identification, 420-423
Crowne, D. P., 449-452
Cultural and social stereotypes, 423, 447-449, 454, 473
Culture, socialization and, 362-365
"Culture of poverty," sociological theory of, 120

Cumulative learning, 211
Cureton, T. K., 169
Curiosity, 17, 19-20, 27, 28, 226
  antecedents of, 301-302
  anxiety-inhibited, 19-20, 226
  encouragement of, social class differences in, 27
Curran, F. J., 261-262
Curriculum planning, 305-306

Dark Ghetto (Clark), 195
Darwin, Charles, 311
Datta, L. E., 226, 279, 288, 290, 291, 292, 298, 299, 355
Davis, D. R., 232
Davis, M., 226, 279, 288, 290, 291, 292, 298, 299, 355
Davis, O. L., Jr., 215-216, 291-292
Day, H., 273
Daydreaming, 302
Deception, experimental, 196n.
Definitions, operational or experimental in research, 49-50
Delinquency, 184, 269-270
  classification of, 427, 429
  common problem of adolescent adjustment, 427-430
  socialization and, 356
  treatment of, 262
  vocational opportunity and, 330
Denenberg, V. H., 301
Dennis, W., 64-65
Dental growth changes, 81, 89-90
Dependency, 17, 20-22, 27, 32-33
  instrumental, 367-368
Deprivation, social, 368-369
Desatellization, 29-30
Deutsch, M., 27
Development, career, theories of, 336-339
  cognitive, factors influencing, 226-233
  moral, 248-249
    changes in, during adolescence, 419-420
    cognition and, 417
    levels of, 417
  self concept, goals for, 473-477
  skeletal, determination of, 129, 134
  vocational, 347-348
Developmental differences in hairiness, 82-84
DiBartolo, R., 48
Dinitz, S., 463
Dionysian style of social expression, 97-98, 108-109, 111, 242, 243, 255, 354-356, 367
Directive function of drive, 14, 101
Disadvantaged, self concept and, 463-464
Discipline (see Control)
Discrepancy between self-ideal self, 439, 453, 460-464
Discrepancy score (see Self concept, self-ideal self-discrepancy)
Distler, L., 381, 395
Dittes, J. E., 458

Divergent thinking, 254
Doby, J. T., 182-183, 189
Dockrell, W. B., 231, 237, 250
Dodd Subcommittee on Juvenile Delinquency, 269-270
Doherty, M. A., 13, 256-257
Doidge, W. T., 105, 409
Dollard, J., *et al.*, 17
Dominion Group Test of Learning Creativity, 273
Domino, G., 278
Double codes, emotional-expressive, 33-34
    sexual, 33
        new formulation of, 100
Double standard (*see* Double codes, sexual)
Douglas, J. W. B., 136-137, 140-141
Douvan, E., 19, 20, 31, 32-33, 34, 42, 46, 98, 116, 175, 179, 266, 300-301, 375, 424
Dreger, R. M., 463
Drive, biological, 14-16
    reproductive drive as, 26, 30, 71: erogenous receptors and, 88
    biological-social interaction, 15-16
    defined, 9
    directive function of, 14, 101
    energizing function of, 2, 12-13
    major functions of, 11-17
    reduction and arousal of, 9, 12-13
    selective function of, 13-14, 101
    sensitizing function of, 2, 12-13, 46, 105
    social (learned), 15-22, 368-369
        autonomy as, 20, 27, 32-33
        physical growth norms and, 74-76
    theory of, applied to adolescence, 7-11
    tunnel vision and, 2, 15, 31, 38-39, 48, 246
Dropouts, 270-271, 282-283
Droppelman, L. F., 381, 393, 403
Drugs and alcohol, common problem of adolescent adjustment, 430-432
Dunn, L. M., 250, 253, 254
Dunn, R. F., 13, 256-257
Durkheim, E., 181-182, 188, 193
Dwyer, J., 25, 148
Dymond, R. F., 439, 461
Dynamic equilibrium, 445
Dynamometer handgrip (strength test), 170-172
Dysplasia, 144

Eagle, N., 227
Early, C. J., 471-472
Ectomesomorph, 147
Ectomorph, 142, 144-166
Education, compensatory, 211, 236-237, 242-243, 261-262, 264
    physical, 161, 167, 169
    sex, 26, 96-97, 106, 115-116, 122, 264, 272, 409
    unemployment and, 269
    value of, 270
Educational achievement age, 251
Educational practices, advantaged and disadvantaged social classes and, 242-243, 262, 287-289, 295-304

Educational practices (cont.)
    constructive strategies for disadvantaged youth and, 300-301
    creative children and, 254-257
    educable mentally retarded children and, 250, 254
    intellectually gifted children and, 215, 251-254
Edwards, J. A., 389-390, 424
Eells, K., 6
Effectance, 338
Ego, concept of, 438, 452
Egocentrism, adolescent, 246
Ejaculation, first, 14-15, 135
Elder, G. H., 7, 109, 263, 393, 420-421
Elimination, need system, 24-25
Elkind, D., 244, 245, 246, 257, 429-430, 433
Emotional disturbance, common problem of adolescent adjustment, 29, 432-433
Empey, LaM. T., 193-194, 428
Endocrinology, 71, 72n.
Endomesomorph, 147
Endomorph, 142, 144-166
Endsley, R. C., 27
Energizing function of drive, 2, 12-13
Engel, M. 456, 467
Environment, intelligence and, 236-244
Eppes, J., 352
Epworth, A., 301, 388
Equitability, power mediation in modeling and, 388-389, 469
Erickson, M. L., 193-194, 428
Erikson, E. H., 22, 30, 109, 289, 337-338, 372-375, 438, 453, 456, 467-468
    theory of socialization, 373-376
Erogenous receptors, 88, 101, 102
Eroticism (male and female), sexual behavior and, 45, 114-115
Escalona, S. K., 16
Espenschade, A. S., 168-169, 172
Estrogens, 45, 71, 115
Ethnathios, Z., 255
Ethnic differences in hairiness, 82-84
Ethnic groups, definition and differentiation of, 82 n.-83 n.
Evaluation, teacher, correlation of student performance and, 274, 276
Evers, Medger, 26
Executive independence, 5, 7,
    See also Self-governance
Expertness, type of power, 384-385
Expressive role, socialization of, 381-382, 403, 421, 447
Extracurricular activity, church and, 313
    schools and, 302-304

Facial growth changes, 88
Factor analysis, statistical technique of, 112, 167
Factorial structure of intelligence, 207-210
Fagot, B. I., 405, 407-408, 424

Family, lower-class black, structure of, 110-111, 119-121
　matrifocal or matrilinear, 110-111
　mobility of, 179 n.
　self concept related to tension in, 151-153
Fanon, F., 381, 389
Fantasy rehearsal, heterosexuality and, 109, 111, 132, 162
Farber, I. E., 11, 17
Farnham-Diggory, S., 230, 240
Farquhar, W. W., 292-293, 296
Father absence, intellectual growth and, 229-230
Faust, M. S., 141
Feldman, D. H., 290-291
Ferguson, G. A., 204, 205-207, 210, 211, 212, 226, 231, 236, 239, 244, 368
Festinger, L., 28, 71, 108, 388-389, 468, 469
　cognitive dissonance, theory of, applied to adolescence, 28-29
Fitzsimmons, S. J., *et al.*, 227, 261
Flanders, J. P., 382
Flanders, N. A., 276-277, 476
Fleishman, E. A., 167, 169, 207
Flexibility, quality of self concept, 439, 453, 476
Flook, A. J. M., 218
Fodor, E. M., 417
Foley, J. P., Jr., 236
Forced choice test response technique, 151-152
Ford, C. S., 101, 102, 115, 407
Formal operational stage of cognitive growth (Piaget), 246-247
Formica, R., 458
Frankie, G., 392
Frederichs, A. G., 219
French, J. W., 254
Freud, S., 17, 124 n., 366, 372, 373, 392, 393, 438, 452
　theory of socialization, 366
Friedman, P., 364-365
Friesen, D., 161, 173-174, 175
Fromme, D. K., 404-405
Frustration, 17-18, 25-26
　handling of, disadvantaged and, 298-299
　reduction of, 263
　sexual, middle class problem of, 108-109
　social goals and, 183
Future time orientation, self concept and, 464-466

Gagné, R. M., 210-211, 225
　cumulative learning model of intelligence, 211
Gagnon, J. H., 106, 110 n.
Gans, H., 290, 296
Garner, K. B., 286
Gatti, F. M., 153-155, 161, 473
Generalization, unsound, problem in research, 55-58, 60, 64
Generation gap, discussion of, 430, 432
Generativity versus self-absorption, learning, 375
Genetic Studies of Genius (Terman), 251

Genital function, developmental trends in, 105-106
　erogenous zones and, 101
　organization of, 98-106
　styles of, 101-103, 114
Genital growth changes, 84-85, 88-89
Georgia Educational Improvement Council, 270
Getzels, J. W., 254, 255-256, 280
Gewirtz, J. L., 17, 23, 367, 368, 369-371, 382, 393, 397, 398-399, 400
Gillard, B. J., 396, 404-405
Ginzberg, E., 269
Ginzberg, E., *et al.*, 346
Glanzer, M., 301
Glazer, J. A., 382
Glazer, N., 110, 119, 290
Glock, C. Y., 311-312
Goals, conflicting, teacher-class, 267
Golaan, S. E., 254, 255, 280
Goldberg, D. H., 12
Goldstein, B., 336
Goodwin, W., 252
Gordon, N. B., 230
Goss, A. M., 89, 170-172
Gough Socialization Scale, 185-186
Gray, S. W., 27
Green, B., 245, 246, 247, 248, 419-420, 463
Green, L. B., 339
Green, R. F., 220, 224
Grier, W. H., 263
Griffitt, W. A., 388
Grim, P. F., 296
Group, functions of, 268
Growth, intellectual (*see* Intelligence, growth of)
Growth curves, diagrams of, intellectual, 220, 221, 222
　physical, 78, 86
Grusec, J. E., 369, 371, 382, 392, 393, 397-398, 424-425
"Guess who" sociometric technique, 358
Guilford, J. P., 204, 205, 207-210, 211, 212, 214, 227, 240, 254, 255
　structure of intellect, 207-210
Guilt, 400
Gurvitz, M. S., 220
Gynandromorphy, 144

Haan, N., 228-229, 279, 356, 416, 418-419
Habit, 8-11
Hairiness, 81-84, 91
Hale, G. A., 274
Hall, G. S., 37
Hall, P. M., 473
Hallworth, H. J., 33
Halo effect, 141, 250
Hammond, W. H., 143
Hampson, J. L., and Hampson, J. G., 71-72, 88, 89, 403
Han, W. S., 182-183, 189

Hardyck, J. A., 400–401, 408
Harms, I. E., 243
Haronian, F., 150
Harper, L. V., 406–407
Harrington, G. M., 244, 252
Harrington, M., 110
Harris, C. W., 255
Hartl, E. M., 74, 143
Hartman, D. M., 168
Hartup, W. W., 382, 388, 392, 425, 458
Hasan, P., 256
Hassan, I. N., 142, 147, 150, 152, 155, 161, 473
Hathaway, S. R., 226, 270–271, 272, 282, 427–428, 429
Haupt, T. D., 112–114
Havighurst, R. J., 206
Hawthorne studies of working conditions (Hawthorne effect), 50–51, 63
Heathers, G., 367
Hebb, D. O., 205, 237–238
Height, growth changes, 85–86
Heilbrun, A. B., 396, 404–405
Hempel, W. E., 207
Heredity, intelligence and, 236–244
Hermaphrodites, 72
Heterogeneous population, definition, 62
Heterosociality, 111
Hetherington, E. M., 392
Hilkevitch, R. R., 206
Hill, J. P., 41, 197–200, 401
Hill, K. T., 17, 215, 216
Hill, R. J., 195, 314
Hippies, 331–332
Hippocrates, 143, 144, 148
Hirsutism, 144
Hobson, J. R., 252
Hodge, R. W., 333, 342, 385, 386–387
Hodges, W. L., 110, 179–180, 269, 286, 287, 314
Hoffman, M. L., 108, 109, 393–394, 397, 424
Hollander, E. P., 187
Hollingworth, L. S., 76
Holtzman, W. H., 105, 216, 244, 409
Holway, A. R., 48
Homans, G. C., 50
Homogeneous population, definition, 62
Homosexuality, 21, 79, 88, 102–104, 114–115, 408, 409–410
Homosociality, 111, 112
Hoover, J. Edgar, 270
Horn, J. L., 205, 210, 211, 221, 225, 239, 244, 255
  crystallized and fluid intelligence, theory of, 205, 210, 221, 222, 225
Horowitz, F., 301
Horowitz, H., 303, 359–360, 421
Horrocks, J. E., 167, 168, 263
Hulin, C. L., 326
Human Sexual Response (Masters and Johnson), 44
Humphreys, L. G., 143, 216–218, 221
Hunger, need system, 16, 24–25

Hunt, Morton, 106

Identification, defensive, 392–393
  moral, 380, 393–394, 397, 398–399
  sex and moral, 401–402
    common problems of adolescent adjustment, 426–434
    cross-sex identification and, 420–423
    differences in, 403–409
    illustrative research in, 414–420
    mediation of power in modeling and, 387–397
    parental role in, 403, 404–405
    relationships between modeling and, 397–411
    role of peer group in, 405, 407–408, 424–426
    role of power in, 380–387
Identity, search for, 19, 30–32
  versus identity diffusion, learning, 374
Imitation, 367, 369–372, 398, 399
Imprinting theory of sexuality, 88, 115
Impulsive cognitive style, 227
Incidental learning, 12–13, 219, 256–257
Incomplete Sentences Blank Technique (ISB), 231, 455
Indiana University Institute for Sex Research, 106, 110
Industrialization, adolescence as function of, 31 n.
Industry versus inferiority, learning, 373
Inhelder, B., 244
Initiative versus guilt, learning, 373
Instrumental conditioned response "family," 367
Instrumental learning, 13–14
Instrumental role, socialization of, 382, 403, 421, 447
Integrity versus despair, learning, 375
Intellectual growth, factors influencing, 226–233
Intellectualization, cognitive style of, 228
Intelligence, animal research in, 207
  black-white differences, factors of, 238, 240–241
  crystallized and fluid, 205, 210
  cultural determination effects on, 206, 226, 231
  definitions of, 204–212
  growth of, 219–226
  level of, educational practices and, creative children and, 254–257
    disadvantaged and, 242–243, 262, 287–289, 297–298
    educable mentally retarded children and, 250, 254
    intellectually gifted children and, 215, 251–254
  measurement of, 212–219
    culture-fair or culture-free intelligence test and, 214, 241, 243–244
    special considerations in use of intelligence tests and, 214–219
  nature-nurture controversy, 236–244
  overlearning as, 205–206, 207
  popularity and, 360–361

Intelligence (cont.)
   process-product distinction, 204
   school success and, 273-274
   self concept and, 462
   sex role, 160-161
   social class and effects of, 214, 219
   stability of, 222-223, 225-226
   tests of, adolescent, 213-214
      culture-fair and culture-free, 214, 241, 243-244
      special considerations in use of, 214-219
      testing conditions of, 213-214, 219
   theories of, 205-212
      crystallized and fluid intelligence theory, 205, 210, 221, 222, 225
      cumulative learning model, 211
      environmental interaction model, 211, 218
      "g-s" factor theory, 205, 207
      overlearned skills theory, 205-207, 231
      structure of intellect, 207-210
   twins, studies of, 239-240
   verbal and quantitative, 229-230
Intelligence quotient (IQ), 51, 186, 204, 206 n., 213-216, 221, 225-233, 244
Intentional learning, 256-257
Interaction orientation, group function of, 268
Interpersonal Trust Scale, 403-404
Intimacy versus isolation, learning, 374-375
Investigator, direct influence of, problem in research, 46-47, 50-52
Israeli kibbutzim, 238-239

Jackson, P. W., 254, 255-256, 265, 276, 280, 290, 291
Jacobs, J., 29
Jacobson, L., 46, 296
Jennings, H. H., 358
Jensen, A. R., 218-219, 236, 238, 266
Jenson, J. F., 339
Jersild, A. T., 169, 170, 174, 439
Johnson, M. M., 382, 383, 403, 405
Johnson, V. E., 15, 44, 89, 102, 107
Johnstone, J. W. C., 293-294
Jones, C. B., 469
Jones, H. E., 129, 137, 140, 142, 170, 171, 220
Jones, M. C., 58, 129, 131, 133, 135, 140, 162
Jones, T. M., 85-86, 87

Kagan, J., 27, 228
Kagan J., *et al.*, 227
Katkin, E. S., 366
Katz, H. A., 247, 403-404
Katz, P. A., 58, 251, 266, 454, 461-462, 464, 468, 469, 474
Kelly, G. A., 439
Kennedy, John F., 26, 87n.
Kennedy, Robert, 26
Kennedy, W. A., 225-226, 238, 393
Kent, N., 232
Kephart, N. C., 116, 261-262

Kessel, L. D., 27
Ketcham, W. A., 251
Khan, S. B., 216, 244
King, F. J., 240
King, Martin Luther, Jr., 26, 192, 314, 406
Kinsey, A. C. 14-15, 37, 42, 44, 55, 89, 101, 102, 103, 104, 106, 107, 110, 111, 135, 146, 148, 408
Kirchner, W. K., 339
Kirkendall, L. A., 100, 116-118, 122, 391
Klaus, R. A., 27
Klausmeier, H. J., 252, 255
Klineberg, S. L., 465
Kochendorfer, R. A., 41, 197, 199-200
Kogan, N., 254
Kohlberg, L., 211, 236, 296, 398, 402, 416-417, 420
Kohs Block Design Test, 241
Kretschmer, E., 74, 143
Kugelmass, S., 248-249, 250
Kuhlmann-Anderson Group Intelligence Test, 216, 276
Kulik, J. A., 465-466
Kutner, B., 230
Kwall, D. S., 253

Lackner, F. M., 253
Ladies' Home Journal, 106
Lahaderne, H. M., 265, 275-276, 280, 281, 290, 291, 296, 392
Lamb, H. E., 288
Landauer, T. K., 85-86, 87
Landis, J. R., 182, 184-189, 195, 197
Landy, F., 229-230
Language development, disadvantaged and, 297-298
Lanten, D. A. H., 168
Larson, C. J., 195, 314
Laughlin, P. R., 13, 256-257
Leader, F. B., 11, 25, 355
Learning, classical conditioning "family," 15, 365-366
   cumulative, 211
   definition of, 8
   drive theory and, 9-14
   imitation, 367, 369-372
   incidental, 12-13, 219, 256-257
   instrumental, 13-14
   instrumental conditioned response "family" and, 367
   intentional, 256-257
   over-, 205-206, 207
   prediction of, 218-219
   serial and paired associate, 218 n.
   social, 22-35
   socialization, theories of, and, 365-372
   stimulus control and, 369, 370
   stimulus threshold and, 9, 10-11, 13, 14
   testing and evaluation of, 8
   transfer of, 205, 211
   Yale-Iowa theory of, 10-11
Lekarczyk, D. T., 17

Lerner, R. M., 473
Lessa, W. A., 143
Lesser, G. S., 11, 25, 405
Leventhal, D. B., 160, 414-415, 418
Levin, H., 15, 23, 44, 48
Levin, J. R., 300
Levitt, E. E., 104-105, 389-390, 424
Levy, L. H., 257, 450-451
Lewin, K., 28, 38, 191, 302, 468
Liberator, The, 314
Liebow, E., 323, 341, 464
Lincoln-Oseretsky Motor Development Scale, 168
Linearity index of body type classification, 144, 151
Lipinski, C. E., 457, 458
Lippitt, R., 38
Locus of control, inner-outer director personality and, 277, 400, 439, 441, 475, 476, 477
Logic, faulty, problem in research, 48-49
Lolita (Nabokov), 103
Lombroso, C., 74
Longitudinal study design, historical approach to research, 43, 50, 51, 128-129
Louis Harris Poll, 192-193
"Love"-oriented technique of child control, 23-24
Lowe, C. M., 449, 452, 466
Lower class, sexual behavior, special problems concerning, 109-112, 119-120
Lower-lower class, 6
  problem of research dealing with, 52
Lower-middle class, 6
Lucito, L. J., 251
Lynch, S., 300

Maccoby, E. E., 15, 23, 44, 48
MacDonald, A. P., Jr., 324, 383, 457
Machismo, 111, 119, 391
Maintenance-actualization, function of school, 261-265
Malcolm X, 288, 314
Male sexuality, components of, 112-114
Mallick, S. K., 11, 17, 25
Maloney, A. W., 288
Manchild in the Promised Land (Brown), 4, 60-61, 158, 433
Marijuana, use of (*see* Adjustment, adolescent, common problems of)
Marriage, anxiety concerning, 19, 26
  physical-psychoaffectional mixture within, 96-97, 135
  self-governance and, 7
Marshall, H. H., 58
Martin, C. E., 15, 89, 102, 103, 104, 110, 135
Marx, M. H., 365
Masculinity, hairiness and, 81-82, 83
Masling, J., 448
Maslow, A. H., 37
Massimo, J. L., 356, 459, 466
Masters, W. H., 15, 44, 89, 102, 107
Masturbation, 4, 15, 38-39, 107, 109
Matrifocal or matrilinear family, 110-111

Maturity, 78-79
  early, self concept and, 475
  physical, body build and: life story examples of, 155-167; time of, 142
    descriptive determination of, 136-137
    See also Skeletal age
  educational ability and, 136-137, 140-141
  female development and deviant time of, 137-142
  male development and deviant time of, 129-137
  personality development and, 128-142
  social success and, 134-135, 136-137
  sexual, 88-89, 92
    changes in timing of, 91-92
    direction of sexual behavior and, 104-105
    landmarks of (*see* Menarche; Ejaculation, first)
  self concept and, 474
Mayer, J., 25, 148
McArthur, C., 290
McArthur, L. A., 368-369, 381, 386
McCandless, B. R., 6n., 8, 11, 16, 17, 23, 25, 40, 51-52, 96, 110, 152, 162, 172-173, 179-180, 206, 212, 226, 230, 232, 244, 254, 263, 269, 286, 287, 295, 303, 314, 330, 352, 361, 367, 395, 422, 441, 444, 456, 457, 459, 460
McDermott, E., 74, 143
McDill, E. L., 424
McKee, J. P., 11, 25, 355
Mead, G. H., 438
Mead, M., 31n., 37, 72, 75, 98, 99-100, 104, 112, 114-115, 140, 352, 407
Mean, definition of, 61
Measurement concepts, general, consideration in research, 61-62
Measurement considerations in research in adolescent development (*see* Statistical and measurement considerations)
Medians, definition of, 61-62
Mednick, S. A., 8, 255, 256, 365
Medsker, L. L., 336
Meeker, M., 6
Melton, A. W., 11
Menarche, 4, 91, 92, 142
Mendel, G., 20, 301
Meleny, H. E., 172
Menlove, F. L., 369, 371, 392, 397-398, 424-425
Menopause, 100
Mental age (MA), 206 n., 218-219, 228, 251
Meredith, H. V., 70, 72 n., 74, 80, 143
Merton, R. K., 181-182, 188, 193, 428, 430
Mesoendomorph, 151, 152
Mesomorph, 142, 144-166
Methodological problems in research in adolescent development, 45-58
  concepts, poor definition of, 49-50
  contamination, 45-47
  generalization, unsound, 55-58, 60, 64
  influence of investigator, direct, on results, 46-47, 50-52
  logic, faulty, 48-49

Methodological problems (cont.)
   reconstruction through retrospection, 47-48
   sampling, problems of, 52-55
Metzner, R. 227-228
Meyer, W. J., 225, 273
Meyers, C. E., 240
Middle-class youth, special problems concerning sexual behavior of, 107-109
Middle-middle class, 6
Miles, C. C., and Miles, W. R., 220
Milgram, S., 415, 418
Miller, D. R., 297, 355
Miller, Errol, 119
Miller, K. S., 463
Miller, L. K., 274
Miller, Neal, 366n.
Mischel, W., 227-228
Mitchell, G. D., 406
Modeling, 367, 379-380
   cross-sex, 420-423
   mediation of power in, 387-397
   relationships between identification and, 397-411
   social feedback and, 390, 397
Monachesi, E. D., 226, 270-271, 272, 282, 427-428, 429
Money, J., 44-45, 114, 403
Mongoloid, 82n.–83n.
Moore, H. R., 179n.
Moral development, 248-249, 296
Moral identification, 380, 393-394, 397, 398-399
Moral judgment, levels of, associated characteristics and, 416-419
More, D. M., 137, 140, 141
Morrison, B. M., 276-277, 476
Morse, N. C., 323, 333, 334-335
Moss, H. A., 27, 228
Motivation, intelligence testing and, 216
   learning and, 266-267, 274-277, 278
Motor ability, 167-175
Moulton, R. W., *et al.*, 381, 394, 395, 422
Moynihan, D. P., 110, 119, 290
Mueller-Lyer illusion, 240
Murray, E. N., 366
Muscular, growth changes, 89, 90-91
Musgrove, F., 33
Mussen, P. H., 129, 131, 133, 140, 381, 395, 422, 457-458
Myopia, adolescent, 77

Nabokov, Vladimir, 103
Naturalistic-manipulative approach to research in adolescent development, 38-40, 44-45
Nature-nurture controversy, 236-244
Need systems, 22-28
   achievement and classroom structure, 278
Neff, W. S., 337
Negative maintainers, 265
Negroid (Negro), 82n.–83n.
Neural physical growth, pattern of, 76-77
Nisbet, J. D., *et al.*, 141

Noguchi, Y., 169
Nomothetic network, importance of, 186-187
Normal distribution, 3, 61
Norman, R. D., 405
Normative-explanatory approach to research in adolescent development, 40-42, 53, 74-76
Norms of physical growth, implications and problems of using, 41-42, 74-76
Null hypothesis, 63
Nurturance, schools and, 289-290

Obesity, 25, 86-87
Objective self concept, 444
Occupational prestige, 386-387
"Occupational selection by drift," principle of, 322-323
Oden, M. H., 51, 252
Offer, D., 31
Ohlin, L. E., 181, 188, 193, 330, 428, 429, 430
Olson, G. M., 274
O'Neil, R. P., 245, 246, 247, 248, 419-420, 463
O'Reilly, C. T., and O'Reilly, E. J., 312
Orgasm, 100, 102
   physiological consequents of, 88-89
Orientation, group functions of, 268
Oseretsky Tests of Motor Proficiency, 168
Osipow, S. H., 336-337, 339, 345, 346
Ostfeld, B., 58, 266, 468, 469
Overlearning, 205-206, 207
Owens, W. A., Jr., 220, 221-222

Pagell, W., 230-231
Pain avoidance, need system, 22-24, 28
Paired associate learning, 218n.
Palmer, R. J., 448
Paranoia, self concept and, 444
Parental consistency of reward and punishment, 23
   See also Equitability; Predictability
Parent-child contract, breach of, 429-430, 433
Parke, R. D., 382
Parker, H. J., 339
Parnell, R. W., 142, 147, 148, 151, 153
Parsons, T., 381-382, 403
Patterson, G. R., 405, 407-408, 424
Payne, D. A., 292-293, 296
Payne, D. E., 422
Pearsonian correlation coefficient, 59n.
Peer group, role of, sex and moral identification and, 405, 407-408, 424-426
Pegnato, C. W., 215
Peirce, J. R., 472-473
Penney, R. K., 19, 301
Perceived similarity, power mediation in modeling and, 389-390
Percentile score, 8n.
Performance quotient (PQ), 241
Personal adjustment, self concept and, 456-464
Personality development, body build and, 143-155
   data concerning, 147-153

Personality development
  body build and (cont.)
    temperament classification of, 153-155
    inner-outer directed, self concept and, 277, 400, 439, 441, 475, 476, 477
    physical ability and, 172-175
    physical maturity and, 128-142
Persons, W. S., III, 330
Peskin, H., 132-133, 134-135, 136, 162, 475
Peters, F., 21
Petit bourgeoisie (*see* Lower-middle class)
Pettigrew, T. F., 110, 290
Physical education, 161, 167, 169
Physical fitness, 87, 87n., 167-175
Physical growth, 62-92
  anatomical changes, 80-92
  differential effects of early maturity on, 58
  functional changes, 95-106
  implications of norms of, 74-76
  maturity, 78-79, 88-89, 91-92
  obesity, problem of, 86-87
  patterns of, 70-72, 76-78
  types of, 80-92
  weight and growth curve, 78, 86
Physical maturity, body build, life story examples of, 155-167
  descriptive determination of, 136-137
    See also Skeletal age
  development and deviant time of, 129-142
  educational ability and, 136-137, 140-141
  personality development and, 128-142
  social success and, 134-135, 136-137
  time of, 142
Physical power, 383-384, 390
Piaget, J., 178, 210, 211, 228, 236, 245, 246, 247, 248, 416
  cognitive growth, theory of, 245-250
  environmental interaction model of intelligence, 211
Pierce, P., 207
Pierce-Jones, J., 240
Pigmentation, growth changes, 90
Piliavin, I. M., 400-401, 408
Playboy way of life, 100, 108
"Playing the dozens," 242n.
Pollack, R. H., 240
Pomeroy, W. B., 15, 89, 103, 104, 110, 135
Poppleton, P. K., 91-92, 141
Popularity, determinants of, 360-361
Population, definition, 61, 66-67
  homogeneous and heterogeneous, 62
  social class(es) of, 5-7
Porter, L. W., 457-458
Possession of power, communication of, power mediation in modeling and, 390-392
Powell, D. H., 339
Power, definition of, 381
  mediation of, in modeling, 387-397
  role of, 380-387
  types of, 381-391
  uninterest versus manifestation of, 395-397

Predictability, power mediation in modeling and, 388
Prediction through correlation, consideration in research, 59-61
Prejudice,
  intellectual growth and, 230-231
  religious affiliation and, 312-313
Preoperational stage of cognitive growth (Piaget), 245
Prestige, type of power, 385-387
Primary Mental Abilities Test, 209, 223, 253, 273
Primary source, reading of, 64-67
Primary status, 289
Problem solving ability (*see* Cognitive style, types of)
Profile of the School Dropout, The (Schreiber), 282
Promiscuity, 121
Prostitution, 99, 117
Protestant ethic, 108-109, 123, 355, 417
Psychoaffectional aspects of adolescence, 97, 101, 109, 116, 118
Psychobiological aspects of adolescence, 69-70, 101, 117, 118
Psychology, vocational, 336
Psychomode, 160-161
Psychosocial aspects of adolescence, 69-70
Psychosocial moratorium, 109, 163, 289, 329, 374, 426, 429, 470
Puberty, 3-5
  See also Maturity, sexual
Punishment, 10, 23-24, 31, 389
  willingness to inflict, power mediation in modeling and, 392-395
Punitive-permissive continuum, 23
Pygmalion in the Classroom (Rosenthal and Jacobson), 46
Pytkowicz, A. R., 17

Q-sort, 454, 456, 458
Quantitative intelligence (Q), 229-230

Rafferty, J. E., 455
Random sample, 53
Rank, Otto, 121
"Rapping," 242n.
Readiness, concept of, 211, 248n.
Reckless, W. C., 463
Reconstruction through retrospection, problem in research, 47-48
Redl, F., 19
Reflective cognitive style, 227
Reinforcement, differential patterns of, 266
  modeling and ratio of positive to negative, 395
  noncontingent, 263, 266, 269, 279, 292, 307-308, 353-354, 382
  self-administered, 380, 398
Reiss, A. J., Jr., 39-40, 424
Reiss, I. L., 107, 110, 384, 389
Relevance, importance of, 305-308

Religious affiliation, extrinsic-intrinsic, prejudice and, 312-313
Remote Associates Test, 255, 256
Reproductive physical growth, pattern of, 77
Research in adolescent development,
  dimensions of, 1-2, 38-45, 53, 74-76
  methodological problems, 45-58, 60-64
  statistical and measurement considerations, 58-64
Research design, examples of, 45-46, 63-64
Response probability (*see* Yale-Iowa theory of learning)
Reward, 10, 23-24, 31
  classroom management and effects of, 269, 277-278
  modeling and, 395
Reynolds, P. C., 226, 270-271, 272, 282
Rhodes, L., 179
Ricks, D. F., 356, 459, 466
Riese, H., 290
Ring, K., 457, 458
Ringness, T. A., 293, 371, 392
Ritchie, B. F., 207
Rites de passage (see Self-governance)
Rivera, R., 188-192, 193, 195, 197
Robbins, L. C., 48
Roberts, A., 330
Rockway, A. M., 249-250
Roe, A., 338-339
Roff, M., 330
Rogers, C. R., 439, 461
Rohwer, W. D., Jr., 218-219, 300
Role flexibility, vocation and learning of, 327-328
Ronda, T., 252
Rorschach Inkblot Test of Personality, 228, 458
Rosekrans, M. A., 388, 389
Rosenberg, G. G., 229-230
Rosenberg, L., 293-294
Rosenberg, M., 396-397
Rosenkrantz, P., *et al.*, 446-447, 448, 451, 454
Rosenthal, I., 44, 48, 142, 457
Rosenthal, R., 46, 296
Ross, J. M., 136-137, 140-141, 312-313
Rossi, P. H., 333, 342, 385, 386-387
Rotter, J. B., 403-404, 439, 453, 455
Rubenstein, J., 382
Rudy, A. J., 447-448
Rutherford, E., 395
Ryan, Thomas, 65 n.

Saggar, U., 218
Sakoda, J. M., 37
Saltzstein, H. D., 108, 109, 393-394, 397, 424
Samorajczyk, J. F., 32
Sampling, 52-55
Sarason, I. G., 17
Sarason, S. B., 215, 216
Sarbin, T. R., 465-466
Satellization, 29-30
Sayegh, Y., 64-65
Scarpitti, F. R., 182, 184-189, 195, 197, 463

Scarpitti, F. R., *et al.*, 463
Schaefer, E., 226, 279, 288, 290, 291, 298, 299, 355, 381, 393, 403
Schaie, K. W., 220, 223-224
Schimek, J. G., 228
Schizophrenia, 29
Schonfeld, W. A., 72 n., 83
School, advantaged and disadvantaged social classes, treatment of, 295-304
  Black youth and, 287-289
  contextual definition of, 260 n.
  dropouts from, 270-271, 282-283
  extracurricular activities and, 302-304
  feminine organizational orientation of, male conflict with, 286-293
  functions of, 260-269
  nurturance function of, 289-290
  principles for positive interactions with youth and, 304-310
  sexuality and, 294-295
  social system, as a, 279-283
  success of, 269-273
School success, factors contributing to, 274-279
Schreiber, D., 272, 282
Schwartz, G. E., 366
Schwartz, M., 463
Schweiker, R., 212, 214, 216, 236, 244
Scott, R., 226
Sears, P. S., 25, 290-291
Sears, R. R., 15, 23, 44, 48
Seashore, H. G., 167
Secord, P. F., 472-473
Segregation, *de facto*, 185, 190
Selective function of drive, 13-14, 101
Self-acceptance, 440, 453, 474
  acceptance of others and, 439, 471-473
Self-actualization, function of self concept, 439, 464
Self concept, 437-477
  accuracy of, 439, 458-459, 475
  anxiety and, 450, 456
  authoritarianism and, 133-134
  body build and, 149, 150-153, 440, 473
    interaction with physical maturity for girls, 141-142, 161-162
  body image and, 30-31, 32, 73
  changes in, 445, 459, 466-473
  critique of, 445-452
  definitions of, 439-441
  development of, illustration of, 441-445
  drive-like properties of, 444-445
  effectiveness in groups of, 457-458, 469-473
  family tension and, 151-153
  future time orientation and, 464-466
  goals for development of, 473-477
  internal-external dimension, 277, 400, 439, 441, 475, 476, 477
  measurement of, stability of, 456
  personal adjustment and, 456-464
  physical maturity and, 131, 132, 133
  school achievement and, 440-441

Self concept (cont.)
   self-acceptance, acceptance of others and, 440, 453, 460, 471-473, 474
   self-esteem and, 443, 448-449, 457
   self-ideal self-discrepancy, 439, 453, 460-464
   sexual behavior and, 112
   social drive and, 78-80
   socialization and, 353-354, 356
   subjective and objective, 444
   vocation (work) and, 328-329
Self Concept, The (Wylie), 449
Self esteem, 355
   antecedents of, 459-460
   measurement of, 452-456
   parental interest and, 396
   self concept and, 443, 448-449, 457
Self-governance, 5-7, 29-30, 31-32
Self-ideal self discrepancy, 439, 453, 460-464
Self-orientation, group function of, 268
Self-rejection, 440
Self-Social Construct Test, 455-456
Sells, S. B., 330
Semantic differential technique, 189, 454, 463
Semantic Test of Intelligence (STI), 214
Semihistorical approach to research in adolescent development, 43-44
Sensitizing function of drive, 2, 12-13, 46, 105
Sensorimotor stage of cognitive growth (Piaget), 245
Serial learning, 218 n.
Sex characteristics, primary and secondary, 77-80
   sex hormones and, 45
Self-confidence, 133-134, 151
Sex assignments, factors involved in, 71-72
Sex differences in hairiness, 82-84
Sex drive, 14-15, 16, 18, 26, 29-30, 71
Sex education, 26, 96-97, 106, 115-116, 122, 264, 272, 409
Sex hormones (androgens and estrogens), 44-45, 71-72, 114-115
Sex role, adoption of, 160-161
   differentiation of, 101-105, 114-115
   identification with, 160-161
Sexual behavior, cultural determinants of, 98-100
   decline of, 135
   eroticism (male and female), 45, 114-115
   parental values and, 110
   promiscuity, 121
   racial-ethnic differences and, 107, 110
   religiosity and, 110
   self concept and, 112
   socialization (male) of, 106-112, 116-120
   styles of, social class differences and, 103
   time of physical maturity and, 135
Sexual careers, choice of, 98-100, 116-119
Sexual dichotomy, 70-72
Sexual identity, 30-31, 32

Sexuality, components of, 71-72, 112-114
   hairiness and, 81-82, 83
   imprinting theory of, 88, 115
   schools and, 294-295
Sexual maturity, 88-89, 92
   changes in timing of, 91-92
   direction of sexual behavior and, 104-105
   landmarks of (*see* Menarche; Ejaculation, first)
   self concept and, 474
   time of, socialization and, 361
Sexual mutilation, 99
Sexual physical growth, patterns of, 70-72
Sexual power, 384, 391
Sexual problems, common problem of adolescent adjustment, 433
Sexual revolution, criteria and data, 106-107
Shamans (*bedarche*), 99, 115
Shame, 400
Sheldon, W. H., 74, 143-144, 146, 147, 151, 153
Shelton, J., 197-200, 401
Shemberg, K. M., 160, 414-415, 418
Shipman, W. G., 141, 161
Shnidman, S., 366
Shore, M. F., 356, 459, 466
Short, J. F., Jr., 188-192, 193, 195, 197
Shuey, A. M., 238
Siegel, P. M., 333, 342, 385, 386-387
Sigma (*see* Standard deviation)
Silberman, C. E., 110, 288, 355
Silverman, I., 468
Simon, William, 110n.
Simpson, W. E., 219
Sitkei, E. G., 240
Sixth Mental Measurement Yearbook (1965), 212
Sizer, T. R., 269, 304
Sizer report, 269, 304
Skeels, H. M., 211, 243
Skeletal age, 129, 134
Skeletal growth changes, 80-81
Skills training-cultural transmission (*see* Training-acculturation, function of school)
Skinner, B. F., 250, 269, 380, 393, 468
Skinnerian reinforcement model, 268-269, 292
Skodak, M., 243
Slater, B. R., 264-265
Sloan, W., 168
Slobodian, J. J., 291-292
Smith, M. B., 356, 416, 418-419
Soares, A. T., and Soares, L. M., 464
Social action, problems of research in area of, 52
Social class, 5-7
   aggression, differences in handling of, 25
   authoritarianism and, 302
   child-rearing practices, differences in, 263
   curiosity, differences in encouragement of, 27
   disadvantaged, church membership and, 313-314
   drive and, 12-13
   extracurricular activities and, 302-304, 313
   intelligence and, 214, 219

Social class (cont.)
   lower class Black family structure, problems of, 110-111, 119-121
   popularity and, 360
   self-governance and differences in achieving, 7
   sexual behavior and, 103, 119-120
Social deprivation, 368-369
Social desirability, self concept research and, 449-450, 451, 455
Social drive (learned), 15-22, 368-369
   self concept and, 78-80
Social goals, sex-specific, 32-33, 229, 279
Social institutions, principles for positive interactions of youth and, 304-315
Socialization, birth order, 383
     differential effects of, 324-325
     self concept as related to, 457
   cultural impacts on, 362-365
   dimensions of, 352-362
   social expression, Apollonian and Dionysian, 354-356, 367
   expressive role and, 381-382, 403, 421, 447
Socialization, instrumental role and, 382, 403, 421, 447
   measurement of, 356-359
   sexual behavior and process of, 106-112, 115-123, 141-142
   stage theories of, 372-376
   theories of learning and, 367-372
Social learning, 22-35
Social mortality rate, 261
Social status, 345
   See also Social class
Social success, 134-135, 136-137
Society, contextual definition of, 183n.
Socioeconomic status (*see* Social class)
Sociometric techniques, 356-359
Siciomode, 160-161
Solberg, P. A., 221
Somatic physical growth, pattern of, 77-78
Somatophenotype, 144, 148, 153
Somatotonic temperament, 153
Somatotypic rating (*see* Body build, classification of)
Spearman, C., 205-207, 211
   "g-s" factor theory of intelligence, 205, 207
Spence, K., 79, 191
Sperry, I. W., 286
Spicker, H. H., 110, 179-180, 269, 286, 287, 314
Spiker, C. C., 38
Sroufe, L. A., 242-243, 297
Staffieri, J. R., 25, 146, 147, 148-150, 151, 155, 473
Stage theories, discussion of, 372
   Erikson's Eight Ages of Man, 373-376
   Kohlberg's Levels of Moral Judgment, 416
Standard deviation (SD), 62
Standardized tests, use of, 66
Stanford Achievement Test, 275
Stark, R., 311-312
Statistical confidence, level of, 62-64

Statistical and measurement considerations, research in adolescent development, 58-64
Stein, K. B., 254, 465-466
Stephens, M. W., 449-452
Stereotypes, 423, 446-449
Stern, C., 238
Stevenson, H. W., 219, 274
Stimulus control, 369, 370
Stimulus threshold, 9, 10-11, 13, 14
Stingle, K. G., 23, 367, 369-371, 393, 397, 398-399, 400
Stockey, M. R., 116, 261-262
Stolz, H. R., and Stolz, L. M., 96, 136
Stop-Time (Conroy), 433-434
Storms, L. H., 12
Stratified sample, 55
Stricker, L. J., 196 n.
Strother, C. R., 220, 223-224
Structure of Intellect (SI), 205, 207-210
Sugarman, A. A., 150
Suicide, 29, 453
Sullivan, H. S., 438, 445
Super, D. E., 346-348
Sutton-Smith, B., 229-230
Suzuki, N., 300
Swanson, G. E., 297, 355
Switzer, D. K., *et al.*, 339
Szwed, J., 120

Taboo behavior, 38-39
Tallman, I., 182, 195-197
Tally's Corner (Liebow), 464
Tannenbaum, A. J., 174-175, 271-272
Tanner, J. M., 72 n., 74, 82, 85, 91, 142
Task Anxiety Scale for Children (TASC), 215
Task orientation, group function, 268
Taylor, J. A., 17
Teacher attitudes, social class and, 299-300
Teicher, J. D., 29
Tennyson, R. A., 188-192, 193, 195, 197
Terman, L. M., 51, 252
Terman, L. M., *et al.*, 251
Territoriality, 310
Terry, H. I., 469
Test anxiety, 213, 215-216
Test of Behavioral Rigidity, 223
Thematic Apperception Test (TAT), 131, 133, 137, 140, 465
Theoretical framework, development of, research in adolescent development and, 1-35
Theories of Career Development (Osipow), 336-337
Therapy, environmental, 473
"Thing"-oriented technique of child control, 23-24
Thomas, L. E., 419
Thompson, C. W., 225, 229
Thompson, G. G., 358
Thorndike, E. L., *et al.*, 204, 208
Thorndike, R. L., 46

Thorne, F. C., 112–114
Thurstone, L. L., and Thurstone, T. G., 204–205, 214, 253
Tifft, L. L., 25, 49–50, 109
Toilet training, 15, 24, 373
Tomboy behavior, 100
Tongri, S. S., 463
Torrance, E. P., 254, 256, 280
Torso growth changes, 87–88
Training-acculturation, function of school, 265–269
Transfer of learning, 205, 211
Transvestism, 98–99
Trent, J. W., 336
Trust, interpersonal, 403–404
 versus mistrust, learning, 372, 373
T-score, definition of, 223
Tucker, W. B., 143
Tulkin, S. R., 120, 238, 288, 353, 355
Tunnel vision, adolescent phenomenon of, 12, 15, 31, 38–39, 48, 246
Turiel, E., 417
Tyler, V. O., Jr., 278–279

Underachievement, common problem of adolescent adjustment, 19, 251, 433–434
Unemployment, educational level and, 269
Unwed fathers, discussion of, 122–123
Upper class, 6
Upper class, problem of research dealing with, 52
Upper-lower class, 6
Upper-middle class, 6

Vadum, A. C., 400–401, 408
Valenti, C., 261
Value orientation (VO), 186, 187
Value system, middle class, 242
 See also "American Dream, The"; Protestant ethic
Van Mannen, G. C., 404
Van Schoelandt, S. K., 160, 414–415, 418
Variance, definition of, 62
Venereal disease, 15
Verbal intelligence (V), 229–230
Verbal Lorge-Thorndike intelligence test, 274
Verbal quotient (VQ), 241
Vinacke, W. E., 48
Vincent, C. E., 122–123
Viscerotonic temperament, 153
Vital capacity, 96
Vocation (work), career development, theories of, and, 336–339
 choice of, 337–345
 experience of, utility to adolescents of, 326–329
 meaning of, 332–336
 nonconformers and, 329–332
 patterns of, representative examples of, 320–326
 vocational behavior, theories of, and, 345–348
Vogel, S. R., et al., 423, 448

Wagner, N., 17
Waheed, A., 303
Wahler, R. G., 382
Waite, G., 33
Walberg, H. J., 277–278, 292, 300, 395
Walker, R. N., 144, 146–148, 155, 161
Walker Report to the President's Commission on Causes and Prevention of Violence, 270
Wallach, M., 254
Walster, E., 458
Walters, R. H., 23, 25, 121, 369
Warner, W. L., 6
Washburn, W. C., 147, 151–153, 154–155
Watts, Dan, 314
Wayne County Training School, 262, 334, 408
Wechsler, D., 205
Wechsler Adult Intelligence Scale (WAIS), 224, 225, 241
Weight, growth changes, 86–87
Weiss, R. S., 323, 333, 334–335
Wetzel, R., 373
Wheeler, L. R., 206
White, R. K., 38, 308–310
White, R. W., 338
White, S. H., 296
White Anglo-Saxon Protestant culture (WASP), definition of, 119n.
Whiting, J. W. M., 85–86, 87
Whitten, N. E., Jr., 120
"Who Am I?" technique, 455
Wicker, A. W., 303
Wilhelms, F., 334
Willems, E. P., 303–304
Willingness to share power, power mediation in modeling and, 392–395
Willis, R. H., 187
Wisdom (omniscience) as a type of power, 384–385
Wolowitz, H. M., 381
Wolpe, J., 373
Worchester, D. A., 252
Work (see Vocation)
Wright, L., 358
Wylie, R., 439, 449

X-ray indices of skeletal development, 129, 134

Yale-Iowa theory of learning, 10–11
Yamamoto, K., 215–216
Yee, A. H., 299–300

Zigler, E. F., 219, 247, 251, 368–369, 381, 454, 461–462, 464, 468, 474
Ziller, R. C., 288
Ziller, R. C., et al., 455–456
Zimbardo, P., 458
Zoolagnia, 99
Zubek, J. P., 221
Zygote, 80
Zytowski, D. G., 336

ADOLESCENTS
Behavior
and Development